TT 3164

3620

DEVON GENERAL
a fascinating story

by
Leslie Folkard
Edited by Nigel Bruce-Robertson

First published in 2007 by the Devon General Society
© Copyright 2007 - L. F. Folkard, N. Bruce-Robertson & the Devon General Society

ISBN 978-0-9555514-0-6

Design & type-setting by Chesley Hill, mainly in 11pt Gill Sans MT type, and printed by Coles Printers Limited of Warmley, Bristol. BS15 4NU. April 2007.

Front cover photograph:
A sight which epitomises summer holidays in the sixties is an open-top Leyland 'Atlantean' bus cruising along Torquay sea front on a hot summer's day when most holiday-makers were probably on the beach or messing about in boats. 930 (Sir John Hawkins) is not however on a proper open-top service (12A, 12C or 12D) but being used as a duplicate to the 12 service, running between Torquay and Paignton. *(L.F.Folkard)*

Inside front cover:
Three of the Lancias delivered in 1925 to replace the original vehicles of Fleet Cars on tours from Torquay. These were centre gangway coaches and not charabancs, and ran until 1933 after which Devon General ran the tours under their own name, later reviving the Grey Cars fleet-name, which company they took over in 1933. *(Torbay Library Services)*

Inside back cover:
At the end of the day, ten AEC Regent V double-deckers are parked up ready for the morning run out at Exeter bus station. Nearest the camera is 731 followed by 812, 816, 778, 811, 776, 786, 763, 947 and 819. *(Barry Spencer)*

Back cover photograph:
One of the last double-deckers to arrive new to Devon General in traditional livery is 544, a Bristol VR/ECW. Technically as it was a lowbridge bus, the upper ivory band was correctly omitted as on previous lowbridge buses, DL640-645. It is at Newton Road when new. *(N.Bruce-Robertson)*

This book, whilst commemorating the Silver Jubilee of the Devon General Society, founded in 1982, is also dedicated to the memory of the last General Manager of the Devon General Omnibus & Touring Company Ltd., Mr. Thomas Lawrence Cresswell Strange (1909-1993) who held the position in high esteem from 1957 to 1969.

Acknowledgements

The material in this publication has been culled from numerous sources to supplement my own lifetime's records and recollections. Documents kindly made available for my inspection included Devon General Omnibus & Touring Company Ltd., Minutes, Articles of Association, legal agreements, time-tables, fare-tables, Directors' tour handbooks, press cuttings, body and engineering records, Staff News magazines, as well as Torquay Tramways Co. Ltd., Minutes, Grey Cars Ltd., Minutes, Torquay Corporation Minutes, Devon Motor Taxation records, Exeter hackney carriage records, and the Devon General Society's 'DiGeSt' magazine. Unfortunately not all of these were available to cover the entire span of the Company's history, so particularly regarding the early years, there are some gaps which may now never be filled. Newspaper cuttings included those from the following, some of which have long ceased publication: Brixham Western Guardian, Devon & Exeter Gazette, Devon Times Guardian, Exmouth Chronicle, Exmouth Journal, Express & Echo, Herald Express, Mid-Devon Advertiser, Mid-Devon Times, Paignton News, Sidmouth Herald, Sidmouth Observer, South Devon Journal, Teignmouth Post, The Independent, Tiverton Gazette, Torquay Times & Directory, Totnes Times, Western Times, Western Times Guardian and Western Morning News.

A previous and much abridged 'History of Devon General' (Omnibus Society/PSV Circle) was published in 1966 by Ian Allan Ltd, (10/6d) for which the present author prepared the draft. PSV Circle news-sheets provided useful information as to subsequent events, while 'The Blue Triangle' (Townsin) and 'The Leyland Bus' (Jack) were useful sources of reference.

Individual enthusiasts and former Devon General staff members provided much useful information and sadly some of these passed away during the long gestation period of this book. Principal contributors were: Geoff Bruce, Ken Brown, Nigel Bruce-Robertson, Robert Crawley, Dave Drinnan, Keith Falconer, Noel Folkard, Geoff Foskett, Roger Grimley, Frank Harrison, Bill Hannaford, Malcolm Luty, Royston Morgan, Philip Platt, F. Simpson, Martin Sutton, Gerry Truran, Eddie White and Pat Young.

To all these and to any others whose name may have been inadvertently omitted, heartfelt thanks are due, and their efforts have been combined to make this publication possible.

Grateful thanks too go to Stephanie and Pauline for their long-time spent efforts in trawling through the text to check and correct my spelling and grammar, and to Simon White for technical assistance.

Any errors of fact are down to the Author and Editor.   LFF   April 2007

Photographs

Illustrations have been culled from a variety of sources; many of the original photographers have passed away over the years, nevertheless in cases where the negative still exists, every effort has been made to trace the present holder and to obtain permission for its use. Many thanks are due to those who have allowed their photographs to be included, many of which have not previously been published, though because of constraints, it has not been possible to include an illustration of, for instance, every depot or every type of vehicle operated. Credits for the illustrations appear after each caption, and many of those credited to the Devon General Society (DGS) are from negatives kindly donated by Mr. W. Cansick.

Foreword

The Devon General Society celebrates its Silver Anniversary during 2007, and to commemorate this achievement by a dedicated few, the opportunity is being taken to launch this publication which represents the culmination of many years of research by Les Folkard of Torquay, and I have been very privileged to be able to contribute towards it.

The Editor, Nigel Bruce-Robertson joined Devon General in 1963 as a Traffic Apprentice on a four-year scheme that involved working in most sections and in most areas, leaving in 1969 to take up a position with Eastern National. Following the changes to Devon General whilst under the new National Bus Company, it soon became clear that the familiar name and traditions of the old Company were soon to disappear. Discussions with fellow enthusiast Philip Platt led to the formation of the Devon General Society in 1982 with Nigel as founder Chairman and Philip as Secretary. The stated aim was:

'To perpetuate interest in the Devon General Omnibus & Touring Company Limited, and its successors, to stimulate preservation for future generations'.

The Society grew, with some 600 members joining up during the twenty-five years since 1982, and is still going strong, with new members always being welcomed. For a very reasonable annual subscription, members receive six Newsletters a year, three DiGeSt magazines a year as well as the chance to attend local meetings and often, local trips using preserved buses.

This book has hopefully attracted your interest, and if you wish to pursue this, may I invite you to contact us through the website at: www.devongeneral.org.uk or at: www.devongeneral.info
See also Section 16.

For all those who came to Devon for their holidays in the forties, fifties and sixties, and those Doctors, Dentists, members of the Clergy and other professionals who spent their summer vacation from University as bus conductors, I know the book will bring back many memories.

Thank you to everyone who has either worked for Devon General or been instrumental in any way in keeping alive the memory of that Company and its fine reputation that was a part of the life of so many people.

Nigel Bruce-Robertson
Editor,
Founder Chairman of the Devon General Society

April 2007

Contents

DEVON GENERAL
a fascinating story

Section 1. The beginning of Devon General (1919 - 1922)

1919   The Devon General Omnibus & Touring Co. Ltd., was incorporated on 22nd May with an authorised capital of £4,000. The Directors were Messrs. Charles Mill (commercial traveller), John Stuart Mill (motor engineer), Ernest David Bullock (accountant), Harry Clark (ironmonger) and Thomas Timberley (fruit grower). The first three named lived at Forest Hill, London SE23. whilst the other two came from Littlehampton in West Sussex. The Registered office was initially at number 2, Kilmorie Road, London SE23, that being the home of the Mill family.

Apart from carrying on the business of omnibus, motor car and cab proprietors and carriers, the Company's memorandum of association empowered it, inter alia, to manufacture, repair, and deal in all kinds of motor vehicles and parts as well as to generate heat, light and power!

Mr. John Stuart Mill (who was related to the 19th century economist of the same name) was the driving force, becoming General Manager and Managing Director. He had, since February, been in negotiation with the Devon County Council and other various highway authorities concerned, and by May of that same year, had obtained three buses and the permission to run them from Exeter to Torquay via Dawlish and Teignmouth, and another route via Chudleigh. Before the services could actually commence however the Company had the expense of trimming overhanging trees along the 50 miles of route, and this task was ever present. Services then began in July, operating from New North Road, Exeter to Newton Abbot and Torquay via Chudleigh, which they referred to as route 1, and via Teignmouth, which became route 2 and took some 2 hours and 35 minutes to complete with a fare of 4/6d.

The first three buses were open-top AEC 'YC' type double-deckers with bodies built by Hora and had begun their life with London General as 'B' type buses, but being too short for the longer 'YC' chassis they were converted and positioned rearward, the original drivers' bench seat becoming passenger accommodation. An additional pew-type seat was fitted in front of this for the driver and two passengers with the roof canopy extended forward and a windscreen fitted. This canopy was then strengthened with front and side screening around to form a parcel and luggage compartment which was able to carry 8cwt. The buses were numbered 1, 2 and 3 and carried names of 'Sir Francis Drake', 'Sir Walter Raleigh' and 'Sir John Hawkins' after famous West Country 'sea-dogs'. All were usually garaged in a yard at the rear of Gold's Garage in Paris Street, Exeter, (now the site of the swimming baths in Heavitree Road). One often spent the night in the yard of the Bradley Hotel in Newton Abbot (now the Jolly Farmer) but all three buses were required to cover the services and were reputed to have been very reliable. The livery they carried was similar to that of the London General which was red with white relief, brown wheels and black chassis frames.

Concurrently with the bus operation, Devon General built up a service for the collection and delivery of parcels and goods, the lighter items being carried on luggage racks within the buses whilst heavier goods were conveyed by an ex-War Department Wolseley lorry acquired for the purpose. An agent was appointed in each town and village and goods were collected from the agent by bus or lorry, being delivered by the receiving agent at the destination, usually the same day.

The Company had only been operating for a couple of months when it became apparent that there was scope for expansion with additional routes, along with a public demand for charabancs to operate coastal and moorland tours. Accordingly, the capital of the Company was increased and orders were placed with AEC Ltd., for 4 new chassis, two of which were to be fitted with 35-seat single-deck bus bodies again by Hora, whereas the other two were to have 28-seat charabanc bodies to be built by the Exeter firm of Dowell.

Meanwhile, the Torquay Tramways Company Ltd., was becoming concerned at the prospect of motor bus competition within its area, and announced its own proposals to operate motor bus services between Torquay, Newton Abbot, Teignmouth, Dawlish and Exeter, for which it intended to order no less than ten new buses.

1920   The two single-deck buses on order were delivered and entered service in January. Two ex-army lorries, which had been fitted with bench seats for carrying passengers, were acquired from London General and re-registered locally in March. The two charabancs began working in April, and a Federal lorry was purchased in July, which could be converted to a charabanc for private hire and tour work at weekends. Finally, an AEC 'B' type double-decker was purchased from London General towards the end of the year and it too was re-registered locally in the March of the following year. With these additional vehicles, further new routes were introduced, and from Easter Monday, services commenced between Newton Abbot and Buckfastleigh, and between Torquay and Shaldon.

On 17th April, Mr. J. S. Mill wrote to Exmouth Urban District Council stating that the Company would shortly be opening up a service of omnibuses and asking if the council would be good enough to cause any overhanging trees on the routes to be pruned up to a height of fifteen feet in order to avoid any possible injury to passengers. The local authority asked their surveyor to attend to the matter, and later issued licences for 2 motor-buses, each to carry 30 passengers, to ply for hire in the district. Drivers' licences were issued to Thomas Spear and Robert Bennett, both themselves of Exeter. From 24th May, the Company extended their services to run between Exeter, Exmouth and Budleigh Salterton. The routes in July were:

1, Exeter-Chudleigh-Newton Abbot-Torquay (two return journeys daily, worked from Exeter)
2, Exeter-Dawlish-Teignmouth-Newton Abbot-Torquay (two return journeys a day with an
    additional Newton Abbot-Torquay journey each morning, and Torquay-Newton Abbot each
    evening, common to routes 1 and 2)
3/3A, Newton Abbot-Ashburton-Buckfastleigh (three return journeys on Wednesdays and
    Saturdays only, one of which worked through from Newton Abbot to Chudleigh and
    back. Connections were made at Newton Abbot for Exeter (service 3) and for Torquay
    by service 3A)
4, Torquay-Maidencombe-Shaldon (one daily return trip in the afternoon worked by the
    bus that had come from Exeter on the 2)
5, Exeter-Clyst St. Mary-Woodbury-Exmouth-Budleigh Salterton (three daily return trips that could be worked with one vehicle. Originally one of the trips was Exeter-Exmouth and return only. An extra run was often made to pick up passengers left behind on what should have been the last run of the day)

The complete basic service could be worked by five vehicles; however the Company only possessed five saloons so the charabancs and lorry-buses were pressed into service on numerous occasions, particularly on the Exmouth route. With such a small fleet, it was essential to maintain them all in good order and all were oiled and greased each day and checked mechanically twice a week.

On 29th September, the Company completed purchase from the Exeter Co-operative & Industrial Society, land for the construction of a garage and workshop. The site lay on the south side of Blackboy Road, Exeter and had an area of 3,505sq. ft. It was bounded on the south and west by Silver Lane and on the east by Belmont Pleasure Ground. It had formerly been occupied by buildings known as 99, and 100, Blackboy Road.

A through Exmouth-Woodbury-Exeter-Crediton service started on 16th December following the acquisition of the 'B' type double-decker.

The Company's 1920 literature listed its depots as at J. Douglas & Son, 7, Victoria Parade, Torquay and at Thorn's Commercial Hotel, Station Parade, Exmouth. In actual fact these were just booking, parcels and enquiry offices. The Exeter address was shown as Paris Street and facilities advertised were 'Regular passenger services and holiday tours in glorious Devon by luxury chars-a-banc, express goods and parcels to all parts of Devon, and delivery vans and lorries for hire at reasonable rates'.

1921
An office and waiting room were opened in February at 15, Exeter Road, Exmouth, with a garage to hold five single-deck vehicles around the corner in New Street. One bus was left overnight outside the Rolle Arms in East Budleigh for the first trip from Budleigh Salterton to Exmouth the next day. The principal stopping place in Exmouth was Rolle Street, but buses called at 15, Exeter Road (where a large wooden clock-face was used to show the time of the next bus) to pick up passengers and parcels. The Company's affairs were conducted from the Exmouth office from February until July.

By February the Company was also using a rented garage at Kingsteignton and no longer left a bus at the Bradley Hotel overnight. The garage and adjoining house and land were situated on the north side of Newton Road, near the fountain, and had previously formed part of Oakford Farm. A 99-year lease was formalised on 31st December 1921 with the owner, the Rt. Hon. William Hugh, Lord Clifford of Chudleigh.

In May, the Devon General Omnibus & Touring Co. Ltd., was reconstituted as a public Company, and the capital was increased to £40,000 authorised (£20,070 issued). Mr. Walter Flexman French became Chairman with Mr. E. D. Bullock as General Manager & Secretary, Mr. M. E. Fergusson was Traffic Manager and Mr. W. J. Holmes of Margate (a retired publican) a Director. It will be seen therefore that the Mills were no longer on the Board. (Mr. French was also a Director of Maidstone & District Motor Services as well as of United Services Transport of London).

Three more AEC single-deck buses were put into service during May, and in July, six Daimlers (three single-deck buses and three charabancs) plus a parcels van were registered, all in Exeter rather than in Devon as previously. The Wolseley lorry was sold in October.

An early 1920/2 view. This is AEC 'YC' saloon bus No:5 (T 7752) at Woodbury, on the Exeter to Exmouth service.   (DGO&TC)

AEC 'YC' No:15 (FJ 1698) first registered in 1921, on the Exeter to Torquay service, probably at Chudleigh.   (L.F.Folkard collection)

The new garage and premises at Blackboy Road, Exeter were formally opened on 1st July, and was established as the registered office. From the same date, a booking office was rented at 13, Northernhay Place ('London Inn Square') and seats could be booked in advance or for return travel on the same day. The departure point for services remained close by, in New North Road. The Company appointed its first Inspector in July, Mr. W. H. Tucker who was based in Exeter and who purchased an F & S two-stroke motorcycle (TA 733) for £30 and used it to cover the entire system, apparently clocking up between 1,400 and 1,800 miles a month.

As tramway services had been reduced because of a fuel shortage, Devon General ran an evening bus service between Alphington Village and Pinhoe Road over the route of one of the tram routes from 23rd June until about 11th July with the authority of Exeter City Council.

The Exmouth services were revised and increased during June. Exeter to Exmouth and Budleigh Salterton journeys became worked via Topsham, while Exmouth to Crediton via Clyst St. Mary became service number 8. Further changes took place and in November, the 8 was Crediton to Exeter only, and the 5 ran either via Clyst St. Mary or Topsham. With the additions to the fleet, the Company was able to start two new services, and on 31st July, route 9 from Exeter to Sidmouth was introduced. The first bus left Exeter at about 10.30am on the Sunday morning and its first passenger was a Mr. R. J. Davey who recalled boarding the bus at Clyst St. Mary, paying his return fare of 2/6d and riding on woven cane seats. The Sidmouth Motor Company also started a similar service and there was keen competition on this popular route. Passengers would often ride on the front mudguard or on the rear ladder! On Fridays, Devon General provided an extra short working as far as Newton Poppleford, and in October, the Exmouth to Budleigh Salterton service was extended to that point as route 6 (though later to become 10).

The other new service was the 4. This began on 17th August between Exeter, Ottery St. Mary and Honiton and which survived some early competition from the Devon Motor Transport Company Ltd. By this time, the original services 3 and 4 had ceased due to the services being run by the Torquay Tramways Company's own buses. Short workings of the 2 between Torquay and Teignmouth were at the time referred to as 3.

That August, weekly mileage totaled 10,641 with the nineteen buses and charabancs, carrying 26,683 passengers between them. By November however, only 14 buses were needed and these ran 7,810 miles and carried 11,018 passengers. Exeter to Teignmouth bore the heaviest traffic in summer and the lightest in winter.

Tiverton Council at the time, strongly opposed attempts by Devon General to introduce a service there and instead favoured the applications by their local operator, Croscols. They took the view that Croscols service was adequate and that it was undesirable to have competing buses in their narrow streets. The Ministry of Transport upheld each Devon General appeal so on 15th May the company commenced a circular Exeter-Tiverton-Cullompton-Exeter service, numbering it 6. However, Tiverton Council again refused to grant licences so it was suspended from 2nd June. The section of route between Exeter and Cullompton continued in operation as service 7.

More new daily direct services were announced, Exeter to Bovey Tracey and Exeter to Ashburton but never actually started. Towards the end of the year some of the Crediton workings were extended to Sandford on Mondays, Wednesdays and Fridays, and to Shobrooke on Tuesdays, Thursdays and Saturdays, the latter being short-lived.

A timetable booklet was advertised but was not numbered (number 1 being actually marked as such in 1923), as it was usual for timetables to be published as handbills. An agency office was opened at 55, Fleet Street, Torquay that was about a quarter of a mile from the terminus at the Mallock clock on the Strand. Previously the agency had been on the harbour-side at 7, Victoria Parade.

Devon General joined various trade organisations - the London & Provincial Omnibus Owners Association, the Exeter Trade Association and the Commercial Motor Users Association. Accounts for this year showed a profit of just £135.

1922
No more routes were introduced or vehicles obtained during the early part of the year, intense competition with other operators resulting in Devon General running at a loss. On 4th May the premises at Exeter and Exmouth were mortgaged, along with the lease of the Kingsteignton garage, for £10,000.

The National Omnibus & Transport Company Ltd., of 206, Brompton Road, London SW3 purchased £3,000 worth of shares in April, and on 8th May, came to an agreement regarding the eastern boundary of operations and this was to remain in force for ten years. The boundary was actually formed by roads from Minehead to Sidmouth via Bampton, Tiverton, Cullompton, Honiton and Ottery St. Mary. In addition, Devon General was to operate the road from Honiton to Axminster, the route onwards from that point to Charmouth being jointly operated with the National. Each party however had the right to run private parties or charabancs wherever they thought fit but could not station vehicles in each others 'territory'.

An amendment in June put Honiton to Axminster in the National area but either party could work it. National was similarly empowered to work Honiton to Sidmouth in the Devon General area. Such territorial agreements were to become a feature of bus operation in the area for quite a while.

Meantime in May, talks were being held between the Directors of Devon General and the Torquay Tramways Company regarding a takeover by the latter, and agreement was reached on 22nd June whereby the Tramways would purchase at least 90% of Devon General's issued capital (which amounted to £31,635 in £1 ordinary shares) on or before 1st July. In accordance with the terms of the agreement, a Board meeting of Devon General was held on 12th July at which the transfer of shares was passed and new certificates were issued to the purchaser or their nominees. All the existing Directors resigned and agreed not to be concerned directly or indirectly with motor-bus operation in the area lying between a line drawn from Minehead to Sidmouth and one drawn from Plymouth to Bideford. Mr. E. D. Bullock, the General Manager and Secretary also resigned only to become joint Manager of the Devon Motor Transport Company at Okehampton. New Directors were elected pro tem, Mr. L. D. H. Jacobs, and Mr. E. A. Bond and Mr. C. Tuson. The mortgage on the premises was to be repaid within six months and the new Board was to be responsible for all outgoings apportioned from 1st June. Assets transferred were the freehold garages at Exeter and Exmouth, the leasehold garage at Kingsteignton, 19 buses all described as single-deck (of which five were in fact charabancs), one Federal lorry, one parcels van, all stock, fixed plant and machinery and the various licences and contracts.

Daimler 'Y' charabanc number 23 is in Torquay Tramways livery and carrying registration T 8192 which was originally on the AEC bus that was destroyed in the June 1921 explosion at Torquay depot.

(R. Grimley)

Section 2. Torquay Tramways Company - Bus undertaking (1907 - 1934)

Tram services commenced operating in Torquay on 4th April 1907, at first under the auspices of the Dolter Electric Traction Ltd. The Torquay Tramways Company Ltd., (a member of the National Electric Construction Co. Ltd., Group) was founded on 10th December 1907 with the purpose of taking over and operating the tramways in Torquay from the Dolter Company, for a consideration of £60,000. Six hundred debentures of £100 each, mortgaged all of the undertaking of the Company and its assets for the time being both present and future (including uncalled capital) by a Trust Deed dated 8th December 1908, and the transfer of the Dolter Company's assets was completed on 25th March 1909.

The tram depot was at St. Marychurch in the district also known as Plainmoor, and power was supplied by Torquay Corporation from their generating station situated at Beacon Quay.

By 1911 the trams enjoyed a virtual monopoly of public services in Torquay, as well as on the route to Paignton which opened on 17th July of that year, following conversion of the rest of the system from Dolter surface-contact to overhead collection, certified complete on the 23rd March 1911.

The provision of a bus service was first considered in 1914, and three Daimler single-deck buses were ordered on 15th July for delivery on 14th September 1914. However, war was declared and the order was cancelled, the buses being requisitioned by the Government. Faced in 1919, with the prospect of the newly-formed Devon General Company running bus services in its area, the Tramways Company sought and obtained powers to run its own buses between Torquay, Newton Abbot, Teignmouth and Dawlish. It was unsuccessful in obtaining powers to run to Exeter.

The Directors at their meeting on 2nd July 1919 approved the decision made by the Chairman and Mr. Cownie (Managing Director) in consultation with the Manager, Mr. Nisbett, to order ten motor buses. These were to be AEC 'YC' type 45hp chassis actually ordered on 25th July 1919 and registrations booked for them by Devon County Council were T 8188 to T 8206 - even numbers only (the missing odd numbers were being allocated to motor cycles!) Soon after, one bus of the order was cancelled, so T 8206 was never issued. Brush of Loughborough built the bodies which had 32-seat, front-entrance, six-windows per side, top-light saloon and windscreen consisting of no less than seven small panes. They carried fleet numbers 1-9 but not in the order of registrations. Three buses were available to commence a limited service on 6th May 1920, and they opened a route between Torre Station (tram terminus) and Newton Abbot (Commercial Hotel). Drivers on the opening day were W. A. Hannaford, W. G. H. Hodge, and C. C. Beer with conductors S. Youlden, C. Brooks and L. Brooks. The event went totally unrecorded in the local press, in marked contrast to the coverage afforded to the opening of the tramways in 1907.

Devon General had nine AEC 'YC' buses with Brush body that came from Torquay Tramways in 1922. 65 (T 8198) is seen alongside tram 23 of its former owning Company on Torquay Strand in the mid 1920s. (L.F.Folkard collection)

The remaining six buses of the order were in service from 20th May 1920 and the route was extended along the tramway from Torre Station to the Strand. Two additional routes were opened, Newton Abbot-Teignmouth-Dawlish and Torquay (Strand)-Watcombe-Maidencombe-Shaldon. The nine buses, eight drivers and eight conductors were licensed by Torquay Council without inspection of the vehicles or interviewing the men. It was resolved on 10th February 1921 that all future applicants were to appear before the Hackney Carriage Committee for interview, and buses were to be examined by the Hackney Carriage Inspector before licensing.

Plans were approved on 27th September 1920 for an extension at the side of the tram depot at St. Marychurch, in the road which later became known as Westhill Avenue. The extension was built on a 60' x 300' plot, at the time owned by the Corporation, and was completed during 1921. The contract for its construction was with the National Electric Construction Ltd., at a cost of between nine and ten thousand pounds.

From the commencement of services, the terminus at Newton Abbot had been at the Commercial Hotel in Queen Street, but following complaints, it was moved around the corner to Kingsteignton Road, near a point known as the Drum Clock, where Queen Street, Courtenay Street and Kingsteignton Road all met.

The Company was able to introduce services from Paignton Station to Brixham Quay during 1921, for which three vehicles were licensed, as well as from Torquay to Buckfastleigh via Newton Abbot and Ashburton. Approval for services from Newton Abbot to Totnes via Ipplepen, and from Paignton to Newton Abbot via Totnes, Buckfastleigh and Ashburton was not forthcoming from the Paignton and Totnes Authorities.

A further three Daimler 'Y' type charabancs (10-12) were delivered in April 1921 for excursions and private hire, and also for use on stage services in summer, when the conductor had to clamber along the foot-board to collect fares. They were followed in the same month by six AEC 'K' 46-seat open-top double-deckers (13-18) identical to those being built for London General at the same time, and these were at first mainly used on the Torquay to Newton Abbot service. Six more Daimler 'Y' charabancs (19-24) came in June and July 1921.

The depot at St. Marychurch, Torquay was seriously damaged on 3rd June 1921 when a barrel of petrol exploded causing a fire which also destroyed saloon bus number 3 and badly damaged a brand new charabanc plus four other buses and two trams. Much of the cladding was blown off the depot, but fortunately the incident took place in the lunch-hour and there were no fatalities although one employee was seriously injured, and two others, together with a policeman, were treated for burns. A tram was passing at the time and its conductor was blown off his platform by the explosion. The fire-engine was summoned but broke down on the way, at Ellacombe Green! Fortunately too, the Company was fully insured and arrangements were put in hand for repairs and replacements. The Century Insurance Company settled the claim of £6,945 and £100 was claimed and received from the Commercial Union Insurance Company for loss of profits whilst damaged tramcars were being repaired. There later followed a claim from motor-man Mr. S. Cornhill who was seriously injured while removing tramcars from the depot and considered unable to work again.

Devon General was by this time feeling the weight of competition from the better equipped Tramways Company, and their services between Newton Abbot and Buckfastleigh, as well as their once-a-day return trip between Torquay & Shaldon had both ceased operation by the summer of 1921.

The Tramways Company arranged in July for a garage to be built at the saw mills in The Avenue at Newton Abbot with a five-year lease at £100 per annum being taken out on the premises from 12th December with a Mr. A. Kirby. Four vehicles were then based there under the supervision of Inspector Bishop.

The freehold of the land on which the St. Marychurch depot was built, was purchased from Torquay Council on 11th April 1922 for a consideration of just £200.

A proposed service from Torquay to Paignton via Newton Abbot and Totnes did not materialise until 1923, by then under Devon General auspices, and aspirations which the Tramways Company held earlier in the direction of Bovey Tracey likewise did not achieve fruition until that year too.

The Company set its sights on providing services in East Devon, and in May 1922 made application to run services in the Sidmouth area - however the outcome was overtaken by events.

Talks were being held in the same month between Mr. W. B. Cownie, Managing Director of Torquay Tramways Ltd., and Mr. W. Flexman French, Chairman of Devon General, and it was agreed on 22nd June 1922 that the Tramways Company would purchase at least 90% of Devon General's issued share capital of £31,635 in £1 ordinary shares, and this was duly effected on 12th July 1922. Signatories on behalf of the Tramways Company were Messrs. Cownie and Bernheim, as Directors, and Mr. L. D. H. Jacobs as Secretary.

Meanwhile, during May 1922, another four Daimler 'Y' charabancs (25-28) and eight Daimler 'Y' buses (29-36) had been delivered, the buses having single-deck, 32-seat front entrance bodies by Strachan & Brown who also built a new 39-seat body for the explosion damaged number 3 chassis. It had to be re-registered however as its original number (T 8192) had by then been re-used on charabanc 23.

Decorated for the 1923 visit of the Royal Navy fleet to Torbay, is Daimler 'Y' No:32, another ex-Torquay Tramways bus that kept its original number at first under Devon General. The picture was taken at Blackboy Road garage, Exeter. (K.J.Brown collection)

The Devon General Omnibus & Touring Company Limited still existed, but now under the control of Torquay Tramways. The Devon General Board was re-constituted to comprise Messrs H. T. Barnett (Chairman), W. B. Cownie (Managing Director), H. J. Nisbett (Manager of Torquay Tramways), B. W. Stedham (local businessman), and A. L. Radford. The Company Secretary was Mr. E. A. Bond and the registered office of both companies became 62/63, Queen Street, Cannon Street, London EC4 which also happened to be the headquarters of the National Electric Construction Co. Ltd., of whose group both companies were a part.

An Extraordinary General Meeting of Devon General on 17th July 1922 passed the following resolutions, which were confirmed by another meeting on 1st August:

1.   To divide the issued capital of £31,635 into ten thousand ordinary shares of £1 each, and Twenty one thousand, six hundred and thirty five preference shares of £1 each.
2.   The existing un-issued shares (8,365 of £1 each) to be designated as preference shares.
3.   The capital of the Company to be increased to £110,000 by creation of seventy thousand new preference shares of £1.

The Torquay Tramways Company resolved that all their bus operations would in future be carried on under the Devon General name, and under the terms of a Deed dated 28th August 1922, the bus undertaking was transferred to the Devon General Omnibus & Touring Company Limited, with retrospective effect from 1st June 1922 for a consideration of £65,365 in preference shares. This had been calculated as at 31st May 1922 to be:

Garage, excluding land	£11,366. 11s. 8d.
Motor buses and charabancs	£45,285. 19s. 11d.
Electric Light installation	£ 168. 13s. 9d.
Plant and tools	£ 1,012. 15s. 11d.
Stock	£ 3,107. 17s. 1d.
Goodwill	£ 4,337. 0s. 0d.
Staff uniforms	£ 86. 1s. 8d.

Of the vehicles from the former Torquay Tramways bus fleet, the six AEC 'K' double-deckers went back to AEC Ltd., in 1926 in part exchange for new vehicles, the old ones being immediately transferred to the London General Omnibus Company which ran them until 1930/31. Most of the remaining ex- Tramways vehicles were withdrawn during the period 1929 to 1931 although some were rebuilt or re-bodied as charabuses, a named coined for centre-gangway charabancs.

Devon General buses continued to use the St. Marychurch depot until September 1931, when all the vehicles and equipment were moved to a new depot at Newton Road. The remaining tram depot and offices remained in use until final closure of the tram system in 1934. Twelve trams were then sold to Plymouth Corporation and the other thirty were scrapped on site.

At an Extraordinary General Meeting on 19th April 1934, the Torquay Tramways Company passed a resolution of voluntary winding-up, and appointed Messrs. Barnett and Bond as liquidators. All the debentures had been repaid on 31st December 1933, and a memorandum of satisfaction filed on 6th July 1934. The liquidators jointly with Devon General, agreed terms on 13th July 1934 for sale of the bus depot, tram depot and offices back to the Borough of Torquay, along with the Tramway houses (42-52 St. Margaret's Avenue, built in 1925), and the Babbacombe Cliff Railway (opened in 1926), all for a global sum of £10,000. The transaction was completed on 13th March 1935. The Cliff Railway remains in operation to this day, and the six houses are still referred to locally as the 'Tramway' houses. The former depots and offices were used as the Central Depot for the Torbay Borough Engineer's departmental vehicles until 1992 when they were vacated and demolished a year later. Social housing now occupies the site and given the name 'Tramways' with a short length of rail in setts together with a somewhat inaccurate commemorative plaque!

The Torquay Tramways bus fleet was in a livery of maroon with cream rocker panels, window surrounds and main panels, all elaborately lined out. However, the rocker panels and window surrounds on the 1922 vehicles were orange rather than cream. The entire bus fleet wore a white roof, whilst the charabancs were in all-grey.

Fleet Numbers were carried on the bonnet (in rings on some) and on the rear of the vehicles in tramway style shadowed numerals.

The Fleet Name - 'Torquay Tramways Co. Ltd' was carried in tramway style shadowed lettering on the rocker panel of the buses, with a garter emblem on the waist panel. The charabancs carried the garter emblem only on the side panels.

After reconstitution as Devon General, the buses were gradually repainted red with cream waistband and window surrounds with black beading. The fleet-name became DEVON GENERAL on the side panels and advertisements were applied liberally. The charabanc livery was changed to all-over green but soon reverted to red or maroon, with the fleet-name inscribed across the back, the 'Devon' being in a curve above the 'General'. Fleet numbers were usually on small cast plates on the bonnet, though some vehicles had larger painted numbers.

Some statistics of the Tramway undertaking may be of interest at this point:

Bus Miles run:			Passengers carried:
1920	115,567	from 6th May	458,237
1921	312,620		1,374,905
1922	132,673	to 31st May	464,073

Section 3. Amalgamation and Growth (1922-1928)

1922   Mr. Daniel Campbell was appointed General Manager from 28th August, and a freehold house, 1, Morley Road, Exeter was purchased by the Company on 8th November for his occupation.

Mr. W. H. Geere who had been with the National Electric Construction Co. Ltd., since 1906, was appointed Chief Clerk, and his name will crop up on a number of occasions over a very long period of the Company's history.

The combined fleet consisted of 55 passenger vehicles, plus a lorry that could be used as a charabanc, and a van. Two of the buses that carried adapted lorry bodies, together with the lorry-cum-charabanc and an ex-London General 'B' type bus were disposed of in October. They were replaced by two Daimler 'Y' type 32-seat buses and two small Daimler 'CB' type which had 20 seats (some reversible) with two tables. The 32-seaters could be converted to 40 by the use of adjustable seats in the gangway, with leather straps as backrests. All four had bodies by Strachan & Brown.

Three nearly-new Daimler buses from the Torquay Tramways fleet, along with one charabanc, three AEC single-deck and three AEC double-deck buses, were licensed to work in Exeter and East Devon, which enabled new services to be opened and to provide much needed relief to the small and hard pressed Devon General fleet at Exeter. Others followed over the years, and the Tramways Co. bus fleet was gradually repainted into Devon General livery, the last one to retain its old colours being charabanc No:21, which remained grey until 1925, during which year it worked summer extras on the new service to Babbacombe, being nicknamed 'The Battleship'.

The Kingsteignton staff posed in front of the depot, about 1923. Inside the garage is an AEC 'YC' (T 8196) and two AEC 'K's. The smart man in the middle row is Inspector E. S. (Teddy) Rawle, but the lack of any uniform (other than caps) on the others is remarkable!

(DGS collection)

The lease of the depot at Newton Abbot was relinquished in 1922, and the four buses transferred to Kingsteignton, where Devon General already leased (and later purchased) a garage from Lord Clifford.

The former Tramways Company bus routes became numbered as follows in the Devon General scheme:

11,   Torquay-Newton Abbot-Ashburton-Buckfastleigh
12,   Paignton-Brixham
13,   Torquay-Watcombe-Maidencombe-Shaldon
14,   Torquay-Kingskerswell-Newton Abbot

The Newton Abbot-Teignmouth-Dawlish service was assimilated into Devon General route 2.

A depot was established at Sidmouth in the summer of 1922. Vehicles were based at premises in Mill Street rented from Martin's Lavender Garage. This was later replaced or supplemented by a garage at Newton Poppleford in Station Road rented from W. Potter (later 'Oak Tree Garage') where petrol pumps were installed and the roof was raised to house six buses. The Exmouth-Budleigh Salterton-Newton Poppleford service (10) was extended daily into Sidmouth, and a Sidmouth to Sidbury service was introduced as an extension to route 9 from Exeter. A new service 3 was introduced between Exeter and Silverton, and service 4 was extended from Honiton to Axminster. In order that a bus could leave for Exeter at a reasonably early hour, one bus was kept overnight at the end of the long routes to Axminster and Cullompton.

On a fine summer's day on the Exeter-Exmouth service, extra buses were run, and one conductor might have to collect the fares on four or five buses in turn, jumping off when he had completed one, and waiting at the roadside for the next one to come along.

An ambitious competitor, the Devon Motor Company, set up in Exmouth and offered routes to Sidmouth, Withycombe, Orcombe Point and Budleigh Salterton, but it lacked financial status and the services were unreliable and short-lived.

Sterner competition started on 31st July 1922, when Croscols Ltd., of Tiverton commenced services on the Exmouth road; the 'Exmouth Journal' relates that "Devon General driver F. Rowden of Exmouth was summonsed for allegedly driving to the danger of the public, by attempting to overtake a Croscols bus driven by E. Plume of Tiverton, who complained that the Devon General bus had obstructed him all the way from Topsham". (To put the matter in perspective, the speed limit at that time was a mere 12mph). That November, the Clerk to the Exmouth Urban District Council wrote to both companies requesting them to maintain the approved timetables. It was alleged that Devon General had twice altered their timetables so as to run just ahead of the opposition.

The long-running dispute with Tiverton Borough Council, to which town Devon General had been obliged to suspend their service from 2nd June 1921, was resolved in September when the Ministry of Transport suggested that the Council should exercise control over timetables, and to this they agreed. Licences were granted to Devon General to operate one 40-seat and one 32-seat single-deck bus and two 46-seat double-deckers on a Tiverton to Exeter service, whereupon route 3 (Exeter-Silverton) was duly extended to Tiverton from 5th October, one or two buses being kept overnight at Tiverton. Croscols Ltd., immediately started complaining of unfair competition!

On the Paignton-Brixham road, Devon General was running to a fixed timetable, but numerous other firms' charabancs were plying for hire indiscriminately on the route. Paignton Urban District Council would not at the time insist that they too should run to a timetable and were reluctant to grant Devon General any licences at all. It was not until 1924 that some measure of control was exercised on the route.

It was not the policy of Devon General to carry local passengers over tram routes worked by its associate, The Torquay Tramways Co. Ltd., but due to overcrowding on the trams at the time, instructions were given to bus drivers that they could pick up passengers for Torquay Strand at Torre Station.

Devon General buses of the period carried a lot of advertising material. A Mr. Joseph Abrahams was the contractor for three double-deck and twelve single-deck buses, and Messrs. Griffiths and Millington for the rest. They were concerned to find that the ex-Tramways 'K' type double-deckers were little used in the winter months. New contracts were drawn up, to be effective from 1st January 1923, the contractors paying the bus Company 75% of the advertising revenue, subject to a minimum. The agreements specified the portions of the buses on which the contractors were entitled to place adverts (in essence, those used by the London General Omnibus Co. Ltd.,) including such places as the interior roof panels, the backs of seats, and the platform step. All exterior adverts were to be of enameled iron or zinc plate, and interior adverts were to be of etched glass or transparencies, with cards to be used for the roof panels. The double-deckers could carry no less than 52 advertisements each, while single-deck buses of the Strachan & Brown 32/40-seat type could carry 39. These were specified as follows:-

Double-deckers: Top Deck: Sides (2) 12'6" x 1'9½", Platform step (1) 2'6" x 9", top deck front
(2) 1'9" x 2'9", top deck seat back-plates (8) 1'6" x 2¾", rear seat back-plate (1) 2' 0¾" x 1'
8¾", rear lamp panel (1) 2' 0" x 2' 6"
Lower deck: Roof cards (14) 1'2" x 1'8", top-light windows (8) 2'4"x4½",
Side windows (8) 1'8" x 6", front window (1) 1'6 x 6", back window (1) 11" x 6", space over fare-
Board (1) 1'10½" x 6", staircase plates (3) shaped to suit, under staircase offside (1) 1' 8" x 2' 6".
Total 52

Single-deckers: Exterior roof boards (2) 10" deep, transparencies on side windows (12) 1'8" x 6", roof panels (8) 1'4" x 2'0", transparencies (8) on bulkhead and rear windows, various sizes; shaped panels (9) on bulkheads and rear, various sizes.   Total 39

1923

On 1st February, the recently-formed Company published its first complete timetable, a 64-page booklet price 1d. Among the conditions of carriage it is interesting to note that bicycles were carried for 1/- if accompanied, or 2/- if unaccompanied; perambulators would only be carried at the owner's risk, on the roof of the bus if the wheels were dismantled (of the perambulators!). The solid tyred buses were extolled as giving the greatest degree of comfort without the risk of puncture!

A new route operating by 1st February was 15, Sidmouth-Honiton-Axminster (ThSaO), on which a change of vehicle to that on route 4 was necessary at Ottery St. Mary. This service was renumbered 20 on 31st March and 18 on 19th May. Two more new services were introduced from 31st March:

15,   Torquay-Newton Abbot-Totnes-Paignton
16,   Torquay (Chelston)-Strand-Meadfoot (Hesketh Crescent)

The former could be made into a circular tour by taking the tram between Torquay and Paignton. Hendra of Totnes competed over much of the route. The Chelston service was in competition with that of the Torquay-Chelston Car Co. Ltd., which had run a steam bus until 1922. The Devon General service ran from Chelston (St. Matthews Church) via St Matthews Road, Ashfield Road, Sherwell Hill, Mallock Road, Mill Lane, Belgrave Road, Lucius Street, Tor Hill Road, Union Street, Fleet Street, Strand, Torwood Street and Meadfoot Road to Hesketh Crescent, from which Meadfoot Beach was only a short walk. One bus, usually an ex-tramways AEC 'YC' provided an hourly service, at first weekdays only, but Sunday services commencing at 1.45pm were operated from May.

Timetable No:4, dated 19th May, introduced a number of new routes and extensions. 4 and 18 were extended from Axminster to Lyme Regis for the summer, by agreement with National, on condition that the service became no more frequent.

6 was a new route, Exeter-Crockernwell-Okehampton which was shown as a through service from Exmouth until 24th September. One bus stayed overnight at Okehampton from July. Devon Motor Transport Ltd., (DMT) already operated between Exeter and Okehampton.

13A was a new summer-only service which also ran in 1924 and 1925 between Torquay and Shaldon, but was routed via Meadfoot Beach, New Marine Drive, Wellswood and St. Marychurch thus giving a prettier run than the 13, and avoiding Torquay town centre. 13A was worked by charabancs and did not operate in inclement weather.

17 was a new Torquay-Newton Abbot-Bovey Tracey service. From 24th September most of its journeys were extended to Chudleigh to give Bovey a connection into the Exeter service 1. Messrs Howe & Turner ('Speedwell') were already running a Newton Abbot to Bovey Tracey service prior to Devon General.

From 24th September, service 15 was split into two routes:

15,   Torquay-Newton Abbot-Totnes
15A,   Totnes-Paignton

The Totnes terminus for both was originally at The Seven Stars, but in October the Company was given permission to terminate at the top end of the town at a point known as 'The Rotherfold'.

There was no lack of competition on some of the Company's routes; the Sidmouth Motor Co. for instance operated a rival service to Exeter, and it is related that they were in the habit of standing one of their taxis on the only bus stand in the centre of Sidmouth so that Devon General could not use it. The local Devon General Inspector, however, soon got wise to this and would detail an off-duty employee to hire the taxi and claim back the fare on petty cash! Another counter measure, practiced in Exeter, was the 'Devon General Sandwich', which would trap the competitor between two DG buses. A mutual running agreement was secured during the year between Devon General and the Sidmouth Motor Co. which brought order to the situation.

Eight vehicles were bought in 1923, all Daimler 'Y' type on reconditioned chassis. Four had Strachan and Brown bus body

(32-seat or 40-seat), and one had a second-hand charabanc body that had come from a vehicle belonging to Down of Kingsteignton, who had recently ceased operation. Solid tyres were still standard, but a set of giant pneumatic tyres was ordered for experimental use on one of the 20-seat Daimler CB buses.

During the 1921-1922 period, it had been common practice to exchange bodies so that appropriate vehicles were available to work the services, but not all these exchanges are recorded. The fleet, which in 1922 was in a rather neglected state, was brought up to standard, incurring considerable expenditure for the new Company. The work was carried out in Blackboy Road depot at Exeter, where extensions to the garage and workshops had been completed on 1st February. One of the recurring troubles was that chassis cross-members on the Daimler 'Y' type were prone to fracture where the gearbox was attached. Solid tyres were fitted and removed with a press, the hydraulic compressor for which had to be pumped by hand. The older vehicles still had acetylene headlights and oil sidelights, and a programme was put in hand during the year for conversion to electric lighting. Interiors were lit by just one acetylene lamp. Drivers had to carry their own tool kit, and minor repairs were carried out at the roadside. Conductors were liable to have to ride on the front mudguard and 'tickle' the carburettor to assist the vehicle up steep hills!

The freehold of the garage, with adjoining house and land, at Kingsteignton, which had previously been leased from Lord Clifford, was purchased by the Company during April. In the same month, a tenancy of part of Roundham Garage, near Paignton Harbour, was agreed with Messrs. F. Noble, W. Langbridge and W. Tucker (t/a 'Comfy Cars'). Devon General was at that time running a 40-minute interval service on the Paignton to Brixham route, and at intermediate times in fine weather, two charabancs joined the two buses already on the service.

A minor amendment in the territorial agreement with National was made when the 'border' between Tiverton and Cullompton was pushed east so as to include Halberton and Willand in the Devon General area, thus furthering the Company's ambitions. Mr. Campbell, the General Manager, recorded that it was a pleasure to meet the National Company's representatives and the attitude they adopted, which was something quite new in the Devon area!

Timetable No:6, dated July/August 1923, was a fascinating document and contained a description of the special features of each route. These are reproduced verbatim, though statements made regarding some of the 'beauty spots' are somewhat questionable! Journey times and fares have been added.

SERVICE 1. EXETER-TORQUAY (2 hrs 10 mins; 3/- single, 5/- return)
The direct route between Exeter and Torquay, via Chudleigh, Haldon Moor and Newton Abbot, through beautiful wood and moorland scenery. From the top of the moor a wonderful panoramic view of Exeter is to be obtained. During the summer months picnic parties cannot do better than to go to the top of Haldon Moor for a day's enjoyment. Passengers travelling from Exeter and intermediate stages change at Newton Abbot for Buckfastleigh. See service 11.

SERVICE 2. EXETER-TORQUAY (2 hrs 40 mins; 3/6d single, 5/6d return)
This service runs via Kenton, Starcross, Dawlish, Teignmouth and Newton Abbot. A beautiful trip, embracing sea, wood, hill, dale. Passengers travelling from Exeter and intermediate stages change at Newton Abbot for Buckfastleigh. See service 11.

SERVICE 3. EXETER-TIVERTON (1¼ hrs; 1/8d single, 2/9d return)
A charming trip along the Exe valley. This route is part of the journey to Minehead, which has aptly been described as the 'Cream of Devon Tours'.

SERVICE 4. EXETER-LYME REGIS (3 hrs; 4/- single, 6/- return)
Passengers travelling by this route will enjoy all the pleasures of rural Devon. The Church at Ottery St. Mary alone is well worth a visit. The next town of importance is Honiton, which is noted for its lace-making industry. We now journey on to Axminster, which was once famed for its carpets, but this industry is now extinct. After leaving Honiton, the journey to Axminster and Lyme Regis is one long stretch of beautiful country.

SERVICE 5. EXETER-EXMOUTH
(1hr, 10 mins; via Topsham, 1 hr, 5 mins via Clyst St. Mary; 1/3d Single, 2/3d return)
Intending passengers from Exeter can reach the sea in 70 minutes, travelling via Clyst St. Mary and Woodbury, returning via Topsham or vice versa. Also, connections from here to Budleigh Salterton, Newton Poppleford and Sidmouth. (See service 10)

SERVICE 6. EXETER-OKEHAMPTON (1 hr, 50 mins; 3/- single, 5/- return)
This service gives passengers a splendid opportunity of spending a day on the moor, where the two highest tors of

Dartmoor (Yes Tor, 2,028 ft., and High Willhays, 2,039 ft.) can be seen. Passengers can alight on the line of route for Whiddon Down and Drewsteignton. The country round about the latter place teems with ancient relics, amongst which is a cromlech, the only one standing in Devonshire.

SERVICE 7. EXETER-CULLOMPTON (1 hr 10 mins; 1/6d single, 2/- return)

Another delightful journey through rural Devon, passing Poltimore Park, which is well stocked with deer and contains a miniature lake. Bradninch, now a small village, was formerly a town of great antiquity, and considerable importance, sending two members to Parliament. After leaving Bradninch, from the top of Bradninch Hill a splendid view of the surrounding country can be obtained.

SERVICE 8. EXETER-CREDITON (45 mins; 10d single, 1/4d return)

Two journeys a day extended to Sandford. Crediton is situated on the main Barnstaple road. In days gone by it was particularly noted for the excellence of its woolen goods. The journey, which takes one through the quaint old-fashioned village of Newton St. Cyres, is one of the pleasantest in Devonshire.

SERVICE 9. EXETER-SIDMOUTH/SIDMOUTH-SIDBURY (1¼ hrs; 1/9d single, 3/- return)

The journey from Exeter to Sidmouth is one of the most popular of our services, and embraces hill, woodland and bracken country, and is well patronised both by visitors and residents. Those desirous of lengthening their journey can return to Exeter via Budleigh Salterton, Exmouth and Woodbury. See services 5 and 10.

SERVICE 10. EXMOUTH-SIDMOUTH (1 hr 25 mins; 1/9d single, 3/- return)

A charming coastal trip, passing through Littleham, Budleigh Salterton, with its excellent beach and bracing air, and Newton Poppleford. See service 9 for direct service Sidmouth to Exeter, and service 5 for direct service Exmouth to Exeter via Woodbury.

SERVICE 11. TORQUAY-ASHBURTON-BUCKFASTLEIGH (1hr 40mins; 2/4d single, 3/9d return)

Buckfastleigh is noted for its Abbey, which all residents and visitors should make a point of visiting. Those who enjoy the pleasures of a moorland walk should alight at Ashburton. This is in itself a moorland trip.

SERVICE 12. PAIGNTON-BRIXHAM (30 mins; 6d single, 1/- return)

A splendid view of Torbay and the sea is to be obtained by this route. The journey between Paignton and Brixham passes Churston Golf Links. Before leaving Brixham, visitors should make a point of visiting Berry Head.

SERVICES 13 and 13A. TORQUAY-LABRADOR-SHALDON

(13 - 40 mins; 1/2d single, 2/3d return, 13A - 54 mins; 1/6d single, 2/6d return)

Passengers travelling by this route will obtain a magnificent view of rugged coastal scenery. Labrador is well termed the 'Garden of Dreams'. Passengers will have a choice of travelling from the Strand via Castle Circus, or along the coast, passing Meadfoot Beach, Marine Drive, Kents Cavern, Ansteys Cove, Babbacombe, St. Marychurch and Labrador. Passengers can reach Teignmouth by crossing the bridge from Shaldon in 10 minutes. Return tickets are issued, available to return from Teignmouth via Kingsteignton, Newton Abbot, and vice versa, on any of the Company's vehicles.

SERVICE 14. NEWTON ABBOT-TORQUAY (35 mins; 10d single, 1/3d return)

The business route between the above places, which lands passengers in the centre of both towns. Alight at Kingskerswell and Milber for the Downs.

SERVICE 15. TORQUAY-NEWTON ABBOT-TOTNES-PAIGNTON (2 hrs; 2/6d single, 4/- return)

Passengers travelling by this route can obtain a charming circular tour, which is completed by electric car along the sea front from Paignton to Torquay. The quaint old town of Totnes is alone well worth a visit, and passengers can break their journey here and enjoy a pleasant trip on the River Dart as far as Dartmouth, if required, and be back in ample time to catch one of the Company's vehicles home again.

SERVICE 16. TORQUAY-CHELSTON (27 mins; 7d single, 1/- return)

This service not only gives residents in the district easy access to central Torquay, but also, during the summer months, gives residents and visitors alike an opportunity of reaching Meadfoot Beach. This charming spot has been somewhat neglected in the past owing to the lack of means of transport.

This service gives residents and visitors an opportunity of a trip into the country, who have not the time available for a long trip. The return journey can be completed in less than 2½ hours. Bovey Tracey is aptly called the 'Gateway of the Moor'. Those desiring a longer stay should visit the famous Haytor Vale and the Rocks which are within walking distance of Bovey Tracey.

SERVICE 18. SIDMOUTH-OTTERY ST. MARY-HONITON-AXMINSTER and LYME REGIS
(Sidmouth - Ottery St. Mary - 30 mins; 1/- single, 1/6d return)
See service 4

There were timetabled short workings as follows:

Service 2   between Torquay and Teignmouth or Dawlish
Service 4   between Exeter and Honiton
Service 7   between Exeter and Broadclyst
Service 10 between Exmouth and Budleigh Salterton
Service 11 between Torquay and Ashburton, Newton Abbot and Buckfastleigh
Service 13 between Torquay and Watcombe
Service 15 between Totnes and Paignton
Service 17 between Newton Abbot and Bovey Tracey.

Some journeys on most routes were run by charabancs, and the Company reserved the right to suspend these in inclement weather. They worked from Torquay, Exeter, Exmouth and Sidmouth, and at this time only worked over the stage routes. Buses were advertised for private hire, 20-, 32- and 40-seaters were available. On very few routes did any buses run before 9.00am, indicating that, at the time, services were aimed at shoppers and tourists rather than workpeople.

The same timetable described seaside resorts accessible by Devon General services, as follows:

BABBACOMBE is a delightful watering place situated on the coast of Babbacombe Bay. A short distance to the south-east is Kents Cavern, which should be explored by all visitors, as many interesting relics are to be found here, including fossils and skeletons of animals now extinct in Great Britain. Ansteys Cove, half a mile away from here, is another delightful and charming spot. Passengers should alight from our services at the Strand, Torquay, and take an electric car to Babbacombe.

BRIXHAM is a market and seaport town, and an extensive fishing station. The principal street extends for more than a mile in a rambling manner from the south side of Brixham Quay. The harbour is well protected by the bold high promontory of Berry Head. Brixham is noted in history as the place where William of Orange landed, and a landmark protected by iron railings is still in existence to commemorate this event.

BUDLEIGH SALTERTON has risen during the last century from a collection of fishing huts to a fashionable watering place. It is built along the bottom and sides of a picturesque valley. A stream of water flows through the town, and is crossed by several bridges, which tends to give the town a novel appearance. The cliffs rise from 100 to 250 feet, and are occasionally broken by romantic caves. A magnificent view, embracing Peak Hill, Salcombe Hill, Berry Head, the Valley of the Exe and Woodbury Common, is obtained from the cliffs.

DAWLISH has risen from a small fishing village to a town of considerable importance. It is a good resort for sea bathers, as a firm stretch of sand makes the sea readily accessible. The old village is some little way inland, but the modern town is built on either side of a beautiful grass plot.

EXMOUTH is situated on high ground which descends sharply to the River Exe, and commands an attractive view of the surrounding country, which is well wooded. It is the oldest sea bathing town in Devonshire, and has exceptionally fine sands and promenade. The Danes landed here in 1001 and destroyed the town, but it again flourished and gained considerable importance as a port during the reign of King John. In the reign of King Edward II it supplied ships to the Royal Navy for his expedition to Calais.

LYME REGIS, which lies between rocky hills, divided by the Lym, was made a Municipal Borough and Parish by King Edward I. It was besieged in the Civil War. Here it was that the Duke of Monmouth landed before Sedgemoor in 1685. The Church of St. Michael the Archangel, standing near the edge of precipitous cliffs, has extensive Norman remains. The surrounding scenery is remarkably fine, being very bold and rugged. It commands an extensive sea view, with richly diversified landscapes.

Landslips have occurred at various times, causing much picturesque scenery. Lyme Regis is a favourite watering place, being well sheltered from winds, and is especially suited to the nervous temperaments.

PAIGNTON, on the shores of Torbay midway between Torquay and Brixham, is a well patronised watering place. It has a large expanse of sand, Promenade, and Pier. The surrounding country is covered with orchards, and the villages are celebrated for their cider.

SHALDON, picturesquely situated on the south bank of the River Teign, one mile south from Teignmouth, is well worth a visit. The journey to and from Torquay by road, passing through Maidencombe and Labrador (with its beautiful tea gardens), is probably one of the finest in Devonshire.

SIDMOUTH is a fashionable watering place very pleasantly situated at the lower end of a beautiful vale, which is sheltered on the east, west and north by ranges of hills. The south commands an extensive view of the sea and Western Bay. From the top of Salcombe Hill a fine view of Hopes Nose and Berry Head and the surrounding country is to be obtained.

TEIGNMOUTH a seaport of considerable antiquity, sent members to the Council of the West in the reign of Edward I. It is situated on the north bank of the River Teign, and commands an extensive view of the sea. The town, although irregularly built with narrow streets, contains many good shops. There are also several fine terraces and many good residences. Den or Dene is a grass plot along the sea front over half a mile long. The front is sheltered from the east wind by a high bank. Teignmouth is connected with Shaldon by bridge and ferry.

TORQUAY is a fashionable watering place, delightfully situated at the north end of Torbay, and is known as the English Riviera. It is sheltered both east and west by lofty hills, and is open only to the south sea breezes, which makes it a desirable residence for invalids. The residential quarter is built in tiers, with delightful villas and terraces, approached by winding paths. The houses are built of limestone, of which the cliffs are formed, and this gives the whole a very picturesque appearance.

Leyland 'G7' TA 3098 of the Torquay-Chelston Car Company which became No:98 in the Devon General fleet in 1927, outside Torquay Town Hall in 1923. The driver is Bill Cole who continued to serve Devon General and Grey Cars for many years.
(L.F.Folkard collection)

Passenger's luggage was charged at 2d per package over 14lbs; folding push- chairs were carried for 2d for any distance on any one route. Small dogs (only) were carried for 2d, provided they were kept on a leash and did not cause annoyance. 'Parcels' and 'Luggage' were very loose descriptions, covering such items as bicycles, crates of rabbits, tins of cream, sacks of potatoes, boxes of fish, baskets of eggs, etc. All items carried on the roof had to be checked at each stage in case they had been swept off by over-hanging branches along the route!

The charges for the conveyance of parcels were somewhat complicated, but basically the scale was as follows:

2lbs	4d.	65lbs	1/6d.
4lbs	6d.	70lbs	1/9d.
14lbs	9d.	84lbs	2/-
28lbs	1/-	98lbs	2/3d.
42lbs	1/3d.	112lbs	2/6d.

An extra charge of 10% was made for any distance over 25 miles. Books of pre-paid stamps were available to traders at 10% discount. Returned empties were carried at 50% off the usual rates, provided that the full packages had been carried by the Company, subject to a minimum charge of 3d and no fractions of 1d.

1924
The timetable booklet took on a distinctive look from the 1st January issue (No:8), the cover of the 80-page volume being graced with a handsome etching of Exeter Cathedral, in black and gold on a dark red background. 1924 was an eventful year, in which Devon General really began to expand.

In February they made application to Tiverton Urban District Council to extend the Exeter-Tiverton service to Halberton, but this was refused on the grounds that Croscols Ltd., and National (the latter only just licensed) provided an adequate service. The matter was still being contested when, on 22nd March, Devon General purchased the business and six vehicles of Croscols Ltd. This firm traded from 8a, Fore Street, Tiverton and had connections with Colwills Ltd., of Ilfracombe. Mr. Claude Crosland Taylor of Crosville Motor Services Ltd., at Chester had at one time been a Director of all three companies, hence the name Croscols, which had been founded in 1920 under the management of Capt. H. J. Youlton, who was also a Cheshire man. Their first service from Tiverton to Cullompton via Halberton and Willand started in February 1921. From Easter they ran excursions and on 5th April opened a Tuesday only Tiverton-Bampton-Dulverton route. A Friday only Tiverton to Exeter service commenced on 6th May and became daily from 30th May. From the same date, Uffculme and Sampford Peverell were also served.

Route numbers were introduced in May:

1,   Tiverton-Cullompton
1A,   Tiverton-Uffculme (later extended to Hemyock)
2,   Tiverton-Exeter
3,   Tiverton-Dulverton.
1/1A ran either via Tiverton Junction or via Sampford Peverell and Waterloo Cross.

Incorporation as a limited Company took place on 5th July 1921, and by that September the business of F. G. Eastmond of Tiverton was acquired. Mr. Eastmond became a Director of Croscols Ltd., and rented his garage in Chapel Street to them, and later to Devon General.

From 3rd October 1921, service 4, Uffculme-Cullompton-Bradninch-Silverton-Exeter (later via Pinhoe) was introduced and from 31st July 1922, Croscols was in direct competition with Devon General on the Exmouth road, introducing services 5, Exeter-Topsham-Exmouth, and 6, Exeter-Woodbury-Exmouth, extended to Budleigh Salterton from 11th September 1922.

It would seem that Croscols could no longer operate viably once Devon General was eventually empowered to operate to Tiverton from October 1922, and the larger Company bought them out in March 1924. The Croscols Board at the time comprised Messrs. Home, C. Smith, F. G. Eastmond, and Capt. H. J. Youlton who by that time had moved to Penarth.

The six vehicles bought from Croscols comprised two 26-seat Daimlers registered in Cheshire, two 20-seat Daimler CBs, one 14-seat Fiat charabanc and one 19-seat Napier charabanc; the latter had originated with Eastmond, and never ran for Devon General, its chassis being resold during 1924. Vehicles operated earlier by Croscols had included two more Daimlers and an Austin, as well as various cars and lorries. Their livery was grey, with a large fleet-name and number on the sides in red, in the same style as Crosville and Colwills. Some of their second-hand vehicles kept their previous colours.

Three Croscols drivers continued to serve Devon General until well into the 1960s; driver Frost, who was based at Cullompton, was always on the route to Exeter right up to his retirement. Driver Garland recalled carrying a live calf on the bus from Lamb Inn to Tiverton, after the farmer had shown him a letter of authority signed by the Manager. On arrival at Tiverton, the inside of the bus was in a bit of a mess, and the fact that the Manager thought he had authorised the carriage of a dead calf does not make the episode any more savoury! The same driver also recalled an occasion when he drew up in Exeter behind a bus bearing the same registration as the one he was driving!

The ex-Croscols services were assimilated into the Devon General route structure. Exeter-Cullompton-Willand-Halberton-Tiverton-Exeter for a time being operated as a circular. Service 3, was extended from Tiverton to Halberton and Sampford Peverell; Tiverton-Uffculme became 21 and Cullompton-Uffculme became 7A. From 22nd September, 7A and 21 were merged as 18, Tiverton-Halberton-Willand-Cullompton. The previous 18 disappeared as such, being replaced by 10A, Ottery St. Mary-Sidmouth, which initially made two return trips, on Sundays only. Devon General did not include in their timetable for the time being, the former Croscols services to Dulverton or to Hemyock.

Eight more thoroughly reconditioned Daimler 'Y' chassis were ordered for delivery during 1924. These, and the very similar AEC 'YCs' formed the bulk of the fleet, and during 1924/5 they were fitted with a 'Strachan patent springing device', a sprung sub-frame mounted between body and chassis. Of the eight vehicles obtained in 1924, four had Strachan & Brown 40-seat bus bodies, two had charabanc bodies, and at least one and probably both of the other two were charabuses. They ran as buses in winter and charabancs in summer. One AEC chassis was purchased for spares.

Following a meeting which had taken place in November 1923 between Newton Abbot Urban District Council, Devon General, and four other operators, a bus shelter was erected in the Market Square (on which Devon General took a lease), the road was strengthened and the terminus was moved there from near the 'Drum Clock' during 1924. On request from the Council, Devon General erected timetable boards in Market Square, Railway Station, Oak Tree, and St. Leonard's Tower in Newton Abbot.

There were complaints that both Devon General and Speedwell were running to Bovey Tracey at the same time, and Devon General was obliged to retard their timings by 20 minutes. Gaytons of Ashburton were, in December, competing unfairly with both Devon General and Babington, by running between Newton Abbot and Ashburton without any timetable.

Many country folk were quick to take advantage of the bus services into Newton Abbot and for several months after a new country route started, its passengers could be picked out at a glance. Many had not been outside their own parishes before, and their dress and manners remained positively Victorian, which disappeared after a few visits to town.

During 1924, as a result of a letter from the County Coroner, the Licensing Authorities required vehicles to be fitted with a mirror and speedometer, and passengers were no longer to be seated on the right hand side of the driver. Licences would not be granted to left-hand drive vehicles although this did not affect Devon General.

The advertising contractor, Mr. Abrahams, was having difficulty in getting his money from some of the advertisers and one repudiated his contract on the grounds that he had not seen bus No:14 on the road at all during 1923. This was one of the ex-Torquay Tramways Co. AEC 'K' double-deckers based at Exeter, and it appears to have been laid up unlicensed behind the depot all year.

On 8th June, agreement was reached with the Devon Motor Transport Ltd., (DMT) which defined respective areas of operation. The DMT had been incorporated on 3rd December 1919 and began operating on 1st January 1920, under the enterprising direction of Commander F. T. Hare, originally providing goods as well as passenger services. It abandoned the freight side but extended its bus operations particularly around Plymouth with considerable success, before selling out to National on 1st January 1928.

As a result of the 1924 agreement, DMT ceased working east of Okehampton and withdrew their services 5, Okehampton-Exeter, 9, Moretonhampstead-Exeter, and 11, Okehampton-Newton Abbot; they had already ceased competing with Devon General between Exeter and Honiton after July 1921 and between Exeter and Crediton in June 1922. DMT had unsuccessfully applied to run services from Paignton to Torquay, Paignton to Brixham, Paignton to Totnes, Totnes to Newton Abbot, and Brixham to Kingswear. Thirteen DMT vehicles had been licensed to operate from Exeter, based at a garage in Haven Road. The former DMT services were combined with Devon General's own, and a new service which appeared from 7th June as a result, was 19, Exeter-Dunsford-Moretonhampstead-Chagford. The Okehampton-Newton Abbot service had only been operated by DMT on Wednesdays, making one return trip from Okehampton for Newton Abbot Market.

Devon General is believed to have continued these journeys, but did not put them into the timetable until 1927. DMT gave notice to vacate their garage at Moretonhampstead, the White Hart Garage in Station Road, by 29th September, but Devon General was able to stable one bus there up to that date. After that, Stevens Garage at Chagford was rented and the crew had to cycle out there each day.

Torquay Tramways had six AEC 'K' type, new in 1921. TA 1004 is working a Sunday School special during 1921/2.

(L.F.Folkard collection)

Services between Moretonhampstead and Chagford were also provided by the Great Western Railway's 'road motors', and between Exeter and Chagford via Crockernwell by the Southern Railway's only bus service. The latter was withdrawn from 20th September 1924 and it was then operated by independents.

A clause in the DMT agreement related to liveries; DMT was to have the exclusive right to green, and Devon General to red. Thus some Devon General charabancs which had been green were repainted red or maroon. A further territorial agreement was secured in July, this being with the Hardy Central Garage Co. Ltd., of Barnstaple, which at the time was the principal bus operator in North Devon. No route alterations were involved.

Agreement was reached with Exeter City Council in August that Devon General could operate their smaller buses on certain services wholly within the city, though competition with the trams was precluded. The following such routes commenced from 22nd September:

Exeter city local service 1,
Exe Bridge-St. David's Station-North Street-South Street-Barracks.
Exeter city local service 2.,
New North Road-Union Road-Mount Pleasant-Whipton-Pinhoe-Poltimore-Broadclyst .

The workings on service 2 beyond Whipton were in fact outside the boundary and also appeared in the timetable for service 7 (Cullompton). A seven-year lease on a waiting room in New North Road, Exeter was taken out in October, the premises being rented from a Mr. H. Bradbeer.

From the summer of 1924, Paignton Urban District Council restricted Devon General to licences for two vehicles on the Paignton-Brixham route, with six independent operators being granted a licence for one vehicle each: Messrs. W. H. Dalton, G. W. Heath, S. Cooper, W. Tucker, G. H. Marks and Soul & Sanders. The Paignton terminus was at Victoria Park and the

Brixham terminus at The Quay. Devon General ran a service that summer between Brixham and Kingswear, but it was then discontinued until 1927.

The extension of service 17 between Bovey Tracey and Chudleigh was also discontinued by the end of the year; a service 20, Bovey-Chudleigh-Exeter had appeared in the timetable from 1st January 1924, but this was purely a 'connectional' service using routes 17 and 1 with a change at Chudleigh, though the timetable did not specify this. Services 15 and 15A reverted to one route, 15, Torquay-Newton Abbot-Totnes-Paignton, with the Totnes timing point at the Plains. Earlier in the year, they had lain over at The Rotherfold and at The Lamb, both these points being at the top end of the town in Totnes.

A frequent local service, at first timetabled 19, but soon renumbered 1A, was introduced from 1st January between Newton Abbot and Kingsteignton, and this was normally worked by one of the ex-Torquay Tramways 'K' type double-deckers. The service had previously been provided by 'independents' Messrs. W. F. Perkins & A. S. Laramy of Kingsteignton ('Blue Bus'), and by Messrs. M. Down and C. Boucher of Kingsteignton ('Forget-me-not') who ceased operation about this time. The last bus from Newton Abbot on Saturdays waited for the end of the performance at the Imperial Picture Palace.

The Honiton-Axminster section of service 4 was curtailed to run on Tuesdays, Thursdays, and Saturdays only, and the bus stayed overnight in Honiton instead of at Axminster.

As from 1st December, the tours business of Fleet Cars Ltd., Torquay was acquired, with four Dennis vehicles and one Lancia charabanc. The firm had been founded in 1919 and operated from an office at 3, Fleet Street, hence the name Fleet Cars. This address then became Devon General's booking and parcels office in Torquay in place of 55, Fleet Street. Fleet Cars Ltd., retained its identity as a separate company, and Devon General operated their tours from Torquay and Paignton under that name until 1st November 1933.

In November 1924, Devon General was also looking into the possibility of buying out Grey Cars Ltd., and their associated company, the South Devon Garage and Motor Touring Co. Ltd. The Managing Director was authorised to offer up to £22,500 to purchase the entire share capital, but the offer was turned down. Grey Cars was the major tours operator in Torquay.

Elected to the Devon General Board of Directors during 1924 were Messrs. Home, C. Smith (formerly of Croscols Ltd.) on 26th March, and F .E. Stanley (a Director of the Torquay Tramways Co. Ltd., and the NECC Ltd.) on 5th November.

A Lancia 'Tetraiota' charabanc of 1924/5 in 'all weather' state. Erecting the canvas roof was a laborious task for the driver, and so the vehicles normally ran with the roof folded back..
(R.Grimley collection)

1925

was notable for the introduction of five local bus services in Torquay, and also for the licensing battles between Devon General, Torquay and Paignton councils and other operators.

Devon General made applications to the Torquay Borough Council and Paignton Urban District Council to run buses between the two towns, although this was a busy tram route. Other operators were also desirous of running on it, and G. B. Ashcroft of Paignton had in fact been fined in May 1924 for running an unlicensed service with a Lancia charabanc.

The saga had begun in January 1924 when Torquay Council granted licences to E. O. Babington (Torquay-Buckfastleigh), Torquay-Chelston Car Co. (Chelston-Watcombe) and Devon General (10 routes). They refused to grant licences to Messrs. G. H. Marks (Devon Touring Co.), G. B. Ashcroft or H. J. Sansom for a Torquay-Paignton service, nor to W. J. Howe of Kingsteignton or C. A. Gayton of Ashburton for Haytor-Torquay services. Both Ashcroft and Marks appealed but the Minister of Transport refused their appeal.

The Torquay and District Motor Coach Owners Association was alarmed and asked the Council not to grant Torquay Tramways and Devon General a monopoly of traffic on routes covered by their buses and trams. Mr. Ashcroft also approached the Paignton Council over Torquay's refusal to grant him licences. Seemingly as a result, Paignton Council created difficulty with Devon General's applications, particularly on the Paignton-Totnes road (on which the GWR had run since 1905) and granted licences to Messrs. Ashcroft, Marks and Ellis for a Torquay service.
A joint meeting of both licensing authorities on 5th February 1925 resulted in licences being granted to Devon General to run half of a Paignton-Torquay service, with Messrs. G. B. Ashcroft and G. H. Marks to share the other half. Licences would only be granted to vehicles with saloon bodies on pneumatic tyres, and fares were to be at least 50% more than those charged on the trams. Between 3.00pm and 5.00pm, buses were obliged to approach Paignton via Seaway Road and Marine Drive instead of via Torquay Road.

This became Devon General's Torquay local service No:5 (No:3 from 28th September). The Torquay terminus was at Abbey Place, and Ashcroft soon found difficulty in maintaining his share of the service due to having insufficient suitable vehicles to be able to run to the agreed timetable.

The Tramways Company meanwhile was obtaining large bogie cars for the Paignton service, each seating 76. Two had been licensed on 10th October 1924 and two more followed on 8th May 1925. A further two similar cars were bought new in 1928.

In March 1925, both Devon General and G. B. Ashcroft applied to run a service between Torquay (Strand) and Babbacombe. It was agreed that each would provide one vehicle, with the route to be decided by a sub-committee of Torquay Council. This was determined as starting not at the Strand but in Torbay Road (Recreation Ground), close to Torquay Station, and running via Lucius Street, Castle Circus and Bronshill Road to Babbacombe Church. Devon General commenced operating in May as local service No:2, but there was a delay before Ashcroft began. He apparently only appeared on the service when he did not have a full excursion trip load, and withdrew from it in September, when Devon General was allowed to put on a second bus.

Another local service inaugurated in Torquay was No:4, which ran to Warren Road, a hilly area near the town centre. This was linked to a Chelston service and made five trips a day, but was not a success and was withdrawn from 28th September.

Yet another Torquay local service (No:3) was introduced in June and ran from Torquay (Strand) to Watcombe and Maidencombe (most journeys not proceeding beyond Watcombe in inclement weather). This was essentially a short working of service 13, and was in addition to the summer 13A. It only ran until 27th September but reappeared permanently in another guise the following year.

Devon General introduced its first new pneumatic-tyred vehicles in 1925, being ten Dennis 40/45hp saloons, specifically for the services to Paignton, Brixham, Totnes, Buckfastleigh and Newton Abbot. They had front-entrance body by Hall Lewis, with four saloon windows each side. Four seated 26 and the remainder 28, (soon increased to 32).

Torquay Corporation refused to renew hackney carriage licences for thirty of the older vehicles until a satisfactory emergency door had been fitted. The necessary work was put in hand.

Service 12 from Brixham to Paignton was, from 9th April, extended to Torquay, and from 27th June, with the delivery of the Dennis buses, route 15 to Totnes also included Buckfastleigh and Ashburton, and a new route 16 was introduced, the resultant services being:

15,   Torquay-Paignton-Totnes-Buckfastleigh-Ashburton-Newton Abbot-Torquay
16,   Torquay-Paignton-Totnes-Newton Abbot

The existing service 16, Torquay (Chelston)-Strand-Hesketh Crescent had become Torquay local service No:1.

The Buckfastleigh-Newton Abbot-Torquay portion of the 15 was also shown under the timetable for service 11, and from 28th September, 15 became Torquay-Paignton-Totnes-Buckfastleigh-Ashburton, with the service between the latter two points still overlapped by the 11 table. A further service, 2A ran between Buckfastleigh, Newton Abbot and Teignmouth three times a day from 27th June to 27th September but was then discontinued. 2A had previously denoted short workings between Newton Abbot, Teignmouth and Dawlish.

From the 1st January timetable, Exeter local service No:1 ran from Spicer Road to St. David's Station, via St. Leonard's Road and High Street, and was again altered from 9th April to run from Bedford Circus to Topsham Road, via Barnfield Road, Denmark Road, Spicer Road and St. Leonard's Road.
A new service from Exeter was the 20, which ran via Chudleigh to Bovey Tracey, and in summer (weather permitting) on to Haytor Rocks. This first appeared in the June timetable.

Following an inspection by the Managing Director in May, Primrose Garage in Orient Road, Paignton was purchased to accommodate the coaches of Fleet Cars Ltd., Devon General's newly acquired subsidiary company. The garage had previously been occupied by Primrose Cars, a charabanc firm which had got into difficulties and ceased trading. Occupation of Roundham Garage in Paignton was given up on extension of the Brixham service to Torquay, and at about the same time, accommodation for up to five buses was rented at Prout's Garage, in Churston.

A loan was made to Devon General in July for the purchase of four saloon bus bodies. Two replacement bodies (Thompson small charabus type) had been ordered in December 1924.

From 1st October, the Company advertised monthly tickets valid for a daily return journey on any route or combination of routes, at a discount of 25% on the ordinary return fares, and three or six-monthly tickets at 33% discount.

On 19th November, the Company resolved that, in view of future Capital requirements, its Authorised Capital be increased from £110,000 to £130,000 by the creation of 20,000 additional ordinary shares of £1 each. Half of these were allotted to Torquay Tramways Co. Ltd.

The death occurred on 14th November of Mr. A. L. Radford, one of the Directors, and Mr. R. H. Campion (Manager of the Torquay Tramways from March 1926) was elected to take his place.

No vehicles were disposed of during the year, at the end of which the Devon General fleet consisted of 61 buses and 31 charabancs, plus 15 Fleet Cars coaches. The five original Fleet Cars charabancs were transferred into the Devon General fleet, having been replaced by new stock.

1926

On 1st January 1926, Devon General's subsidiary company, Fleet Cars Ltd., bought the touring business of W. P. Tucker (t/a Comfy Cars), Paignton, together with his fleet of five Lancia charabancs, and a Buick open tourer. Comfy Cars continued running under their own name during the 1926 and 1927 seasons.

A mutual running agreement was entered into on 1st July with Ashcroft's Motors Ltd., who had extended their Torquay-Paignton journeys to St. Michael's Road. Devon General did not follow suit with their share of the service; the extension was not a success and Ashcroft soon withdrew it.

A further running agreement was secured with W. Dagworthy of Sidmouth, who was very active on the Sidmouth-Sidbury road.

Extensions were made to Exeter (Blackboy Road) garage during 1926, and new workshops were erected, the contractors being Messrs. Soper & Ayres. Extensions were also made to Paignton (Orient Road) garage, and two new pits were constructed at Torquay (Westhill Avenue). A lease of a booking and parcels office at 4, The Triangle, Dartmouth Road, Paignton was taken out for five years from 20th May with a Mr. and Mrs. W. G. Couldrey.

The only route alterations of note during the year were in the Tiverton and Cullompton hinterland, and in Torquay where a battle for the Watcombe area had developed with the Torquay-Chelston Car Co. Ltd.

Service 18, which had linked Tiverton with Cullompton, was withdrawn from 1st January; one return journey on the 7 was extended from Cullompton to Willand (only) as '7A' on Tuesdays, Fridays and Saturdays, but these only lasted until 31st

March. From 18th June, the Cullompton-Willand-Tiverton link was restored by an extension of route 7, but this too was short-lived and the 7 reverted to Exeter-Hele Cross-Bradninch-Cullompton only, from 20th September. The service number 18 was used for a short time for Tiverton-Halberton-Sampford Peverell workings, but these were timetabled under the 3 also, and after 20th September, the number 18 was not allocated to any service for the time being. From the same date, the Halberton-Sampford Peverell road was closed for a few weeks and the buses terminated at Halberton. Local trains of the Great Western Railway covered this area pretty well.

At Torquay, the Torquay-Chelston Car Co. Ltd., had bought a new and superior Leyland 'Lion' bus, and was running it on new services between Chelston, Torquay and Watcombe. Devon General countered with two new services in the summer of 1926:

13A,   Torquay (Strand)-Castle Circus-Hele Corner-Watcombe Potteries, and
4,   Chelston-Castle Circus-Hele Corner-Watcombe Potteries

The previous 13A which had run in the summers of 1923/4/5 was discontinued. Before the end of the year, another local service (5) had been introduced which ran from Torquay (Castle Circus) via St. Marychurch Road, Fore Street and Park Road to Watcombe (Lummaton Cross).
The 13A and the local 4 were merged to become 4, Strand-Castle Circus-Hele Corner-Watcombe Potteries, which was a short working along the 13 route.
The Chelston area was served by local route 1, whose other end had in the summer of 1926, been extended from Hesketh Crescent to Meadfoot Beach (during fine weather only). This extension was henceforth made each summer.

Ten operators, each with only one vehicle, were sharing the service between Paignton and Brixham by 1st January; Messrs. J. Geddes, B. J. Rutter, J. Mills, F. Slatter, and D. Prout had been added to the list of those licensed in 1924, while W. P. Tucker had been deleted (from the list). He had sold his Fleet cars Company but Paignton Council would not transfer the licence for his Brixham service to them - the matter went to appeal, but to no avail. Alternate journeys on Devon General's Torquay-Brixham service 12 were, from 20th September, extended to Higher Brixham.

New vehicles purchased in 1926 were six AEC 506 single-deckers, with front-entrance 32-seat body by Hall Lewis. These had five saloon windows per side, each of which consisted of two panes, one sliding horizontally. A rear emergency door was provided, which was set into the middle of the oval rear window. Fleet numbers were 73 to 78, and they were licensed in July and August and replaced the six AEC 'K' type double-deckers which went in part-exchange and found their way to the London General Omnibus Co. Ltd., which already had a large number of identical vehicles.

A notable event was the re-bodying of two of the 1919/20 AEC chassis with new double-deck open-top body. Renumbered 71 and 72, they took over some of the duties of the 'K' type, one working from Kingsteignton on the local route to Newton Abbot (with occasional forays to Teignmouth) and the other worked from Torquay on the Newton Abbot service. They were not licensed to work at the Exeter end of the system, and in fact no double-deckers ran again from Exeter until 1928. The chassis were given reconditioned engine and pneumatic tyres, and a start was made similarly equipping some of the other solid-tyred vehicles.

One ex-Comfy Cars Lancia charabanc was transferred to the Devon General fleet, and a chassis obtained second-hand from Whitton of Cullompton was given one of two new single-deck bodies obtained as replacements. An Arrol-Johnson car bought in 1922 was scrapped.

A new feature which had appeared in the timetable booklets from 18th June 1926 was that comprehensive fare tables were shown for each route. Previously, only the fares from the termini had been included. 1926 was the last year in which illustrations of a selection of the places served appeared in the timetables.

At the end of the year, 94 vehicles were in stock plus 21 Fleet Cars and Comfy Cars.

1927   Devon General bought out two more of its competitors during this year; the first, on 3rd January, was the old-established Torquay-Chelston Car Co. Ltd., of Daison Garage, Teignmouth Road, Torquay. Two green Leyland buses and a quantity of spares were acquired from them. The Company had been formed as the Torquay-Chelston Steam Car Co. Ltd., on 28th March 1911 under the chairmanship of Mr. G. Williams, who together with co-Director Mr. F. Williams were also Directors of Williams & Cox Ltd., furnishing and household stores of 12, The Strand, Torquay. They took over the premises (43-5 Market Street, Torquay) of the former Torquay Road Car Co. Ltd., together with three Clarkson steam buses which were unserviceable.

A new steam bus was ordered, a Clarkson IV, registered T 2086, and this was delivered and tested in July 1911. A second bus was assembled from the remains of those inherited, and this was licensed on 15th August 1911, being registered T 2087. The buses were painted green, and lettered 'Chelston-Town Hall-St. Marychurch'. The route ran from Watcombe Potteries to Chelston (Walnut Road) via Teignmouth Road, Castle Circus, Tor Church Road, Mill Lane, Rosery Road, Walnut Road and terminated at its junction with Old Mill Road. An hourly service was provided at first, requiring both buses, but the 'old bus' T 2087 was ordered off the road in November 1916 following the Hackney Carriage Inspector's report. A former 'National' steam bus (F 8518) was bought in 1919 and re-bodied as a single-decker, replacing T 2086 but taking its registration. The steam bus ran until 1922, when it was replaced by Leyland motor bus TA 3098.

A new garage was acquired in Teignmouth Road, Torquay (opposite Daison Cottages) and the Market Street premises were transferred to Williams & Cox Ltd. At the same time, the Company title was changed to the Torquay-Chelston Car Co. Ltd. From 31st March 1923, it faced increasing competition from Devon General, which introduced its own hourly service running from Chelston via Castle Circus and the Strand to Meadfoot.

The Torquay-Chelston Company purchased an additional vehicle in May 1926; this was TT 8164, a Leyland 'Lion' PLSC, which was a more advanced model than anything Devon General had at the time. It was put into service on new routes from Watcombe to the Strand via Castle Circus, and from the Strand to Chelston via Abbey Road. At the same time, an extension from Watcombe to Barton was approved by the Council, and the Company was permitted to extend its Watcombe route to Maidencombe on Sundays. Devon General had operated its own Chelston-Castle Circus-Watcombe route in competition, from the summer of 1926.

On 20th May, the second competitor to be bought out was Ernest Oscar Babington, of Ashburton Motor Works, East Street, Ashburton ('Blue Saloon Motor Bus Service'), who had commenced operating in April 1920. By 1922 he was working services from Buckfastleigh and Ashburton into Torquay, as well as occasional ones to Totnes, Brent, and Plymouth, and in September 1925 he took over the Bovey Tracey to Newton Abbot route of Turner ('Speedwell') of Kingsteignton, together with three vehicles, and extended it to Torquay. He originally had a weekly service from Ashburton via Widecombe to Newton Abbot, but replaced it with a Wednesday and Saturday run between Liverton and Newton Abbot.

A Lancia saloon bus of Babington, Ashburton, two of which passed to Devon General in 1927. They were faster and more comfortable than the DG buses of the time, and provided serious competition on the Ashburton service. (K. Simpson)

Devon General did not perpetuate any of his services other than those on which they were already running themselves. Babington's fleet consisted of some unusual vehicles. Devon General took over eleven, made up of two Fiat charabancs, two

Lancia saloons, three Berliet saloons, two Maxwell charabancs, and two Albion saloons. His vehicles were of small capacity, but the 'Pullman Saloons' were considered to be faster and more comfortable than the Devon General vehicles of the day. The ten Dennis buses had been introduced in 1925 partly to counter their challenge. Only five ex-Babington vehicles were used to any extent by Devon General, the two Albions becoming fleet numbers 69 and 70, two Lancias 105 and 106, and one Berliet 107.

In February 1927 Devon General purchased land at Dropping Wells, just outside Ashburton, with plans to build a garage for four vehicles there, and from 27th February had leased premises in West Street from James Fogden for use as a parcels office, waiting room and inspectors' flat. With the purchase of Babington's business came a freehold house and garage at the rear of 34/36, West Street. The garage would hold four or five buses, and this became Devon General's depot as from 25th May. Mr. Babington remained in the motor engineering business, trading from his East Street premises, and retained one vehicle for a school contract which he held until it was taken over by C. A. Gayton at the end of 1932. Mr. Babington meantime had also acted as the Devon General parcels agent, but he was precluded by agreement from operating stage or charabanc services.

A new service 18 was introduced from 4th June, Exeter-Chudleigh-Ashburton-Buckfastleigh. Connections were advertised (but not guaranteed) between Devon General services and the DMT service from Buckfastleigh to Plymouth. Service 18 ran only until September, when it too was replaced by a revised 20, running from Exeter-Chudleigh-Bovey Tracey-Ashburton. The most significant route alterations resulted from linking Bovey Tracey and Moretonhampstead by daily buses along the tortuous, narrow and steeply graded road between the two places. Service 17, Torquay-Newton Abbot-Bovey Tracey, was extended to Moretonhampstead and Chagford (the extended journeys being referred to as 17A in the fare table), and a new summer-only charabanc service 14A ran from Newton Abbot via Bovey Tracey and Moretonhampstead to Princetown. Some journeys on 19 from Exeter ran to Princetown instead of to Chagford, and connections were made at Princetown with DMT buses to Plymouth. The timetable infers that one Devon General vehicle was kept at Princetown overnight for the summer of 1927 only. Another charabanc service which ran for that summer only, was route 14, Newton Abbot-Bovey Tracey-Haytor Rocks. The existing 14, the busy Torquay-Newton Abbot service became known as 11A.

A new service which had first appeared in the 1st January timetable was 21, Cullompton-Honiton (WSaSuO). Route 4 was extended from Honiton to Axminster and on to Charmouth, daily for the summer of 1927, and both these journeys and the 10A (Ottery St. Mary-Sidmouth on Sundays only) were also shown as extensions of the 21 from Honiton in the timetable. Buses were left overnight at Axminster and at Ottery St. Mary, but no longer at Honiton. The Axminster-Charmouth section finished at the end of the summer.

Exeter local service 2 had, by 4th June, been re-routed to run from New North Road to Old Tiverton Road via Union Road. This was worked by an extension of service 8, and two daily journeys between Crediton and Sandford at the other end of this route, were discontinued. Pinhoe and Broadclyst which had previously been served by local route 2, continued to be served by short workings of the 7. Four 'Market Day Special' services were timetabled from 10th October, each making one return journey a week:

Moretonhampstead-Chagford-Whiddon Down-Crockernwell-Exeter (Fridays)
Cullompton-Plymtree-Clyst Hydon-Exeter (Fridays)
Chagford-Moretonhampstead-Bovey Tracey-Newton Abbot (Wednesdays)
Moretonhampstead-Chagford-Okehampton (Saturdays)

The Wednesday and Saturday services had run un-publicised since 1924 when their predecessor's services had been acquired from DMT Ltd. No route numbers were at first allocated. Market day short workings between Sticklepath and Okehampton had run on route 6 since 1924.
In September, Devon General withdrew service 15, Torquay-Paignton-Totnes-Buckfastleigh-Ashburton. Both Paignton and Totnes Councils appeared to favour other operators (particularly Hendra whose operations they appeared to have no desire to regulate) and would not grant licences to Devon General. Service 16 had been altered to run from Torquay via Newton Abbot to Totnes by 4th June, but following the withdrawal of the 15 in September, was extended through Paignton and back to Torquay to form a complete circle. The circular fare from any point was 2/6d.

Several daily short workings on service 10 between Exmouth and Budleigh Salterton were extended to Otterton Cross and Otterton Village (for Ladram Bay) to counter the new service introduced on 16th April by Hart's of Budleigh Salterton. Hart's bus thus often had an 'escort' in the shape of one of Devon General's second-hand Lancias. The Company had been unwilling to divert via Otterton prior to the introduction of Hart's service.

An extension of the 12, Torquay-Paignton-Brixham service to Kingswear was made from 4th June, and operation of Brixham-Kingswear was shared with J. Geddes ('Burton Cars') of Brixham, whose successors shared the service until 1989. Arrangements were made with the Great Western Railway for turning the buses on railway property at Kingswear.

Following the takeover of the Torquay-Chelston Car Co. Ltd., the Chelston routes were revised so that a half-hourly service (local 4) ran from Chelston via Walnut Road and Rosery Road (the former Chelston Car Co. route) and another service (local 4A) ran from Chelston via Ashfield Road and Sherwell Hill. The two came together at Old Mill Road and ran via Mill Lane, Belgrave Road and Lucius Street to Castle Circus. From here, 4A ran direct to Watcombe via Lymington Road and Teignmouth Road, while 4 ran down Union Street and Fleet Street to the Strand, then came back up Union Street to Castle Circus and on to Watcombe, thus giving a quarter-hourly service to the latter point, the terminus being at Watcombe Potteries. Local service 1 was amended, to run from Castle Circus to the Strand and Hesketh Crescent/Meadfoot Beach. From September, a new local 4B made four daily journeys between Castle Circus and Barton Village via Teignmouth Road.

Torquay Borough Council was by this time taking more interest in the bus services, and requested Devon General to stop only at the following points in the main street between Strand and Torre Station: Fleet Street (W. H. Smith & Son), GPO, Conservative Club, Castle Circus and Knights Corner. Notice boards were erected on lamp posts to indicate the stopping points of the various services, and the Company was permitted to erect timetable boards, provided that they did not exceed 2'6" x 1'6". The company was also requested to look into the possibility of exhibiting fare-tables in the buses, but this is something that did not come into being.

1927 was the last year in which some journeys in the timetable were specifically shown as being worked by charabancs in summer, although every effort was made to operate the charabancs as advertised, this could not be guaranteed on Saturdays. There were daily timetabled charabanc journeys from Exeter to Torquay, Charmouth, Sidmouth, Haytor Rocks, Princetown, and Buckfast Abbey. From Torquay, charabanc services ran to Exeter, Teignmouth, Dawlish, Chudleigh, Shaldon and Totnes, while from Newton Abbot, daily services to Totnes, Haytor Rocks and Princetown were offered and from Exmouth, the service to Sidmouth was by charabanc.

Starting in July, regular weather bulletins were posted for the convenience of passengers. at New North Road and Blackboy Road offices in Exeter, giving details of the weather, at 10.15am and 2.15pm at Sidmouth, Budleigh Salterton, Exmouth, Tiverton, Chagford, Teignmouth, Torquay, Paignton and Buckfastleigh.

The January 1927 issue was the last timetable which described 'Special Features en-route', and the services which had appeared since the 1923 timetable were described thus:

SERVICE 19. EXETER-MORETONHAMPSTEAD-CHAGFORD (2 hrs 5 mins; 2/9d single, 4/3d return). This service passes through some of the most beautiful scenery in Devon. Before coming into Dunsford, the road descends into part of the valley of the Teign, of which a lovely view can be obtained from Steps Bridge and up the long ascent that follows. From Doccombe there is a gradual descent into Moretonhampstead and on the journey down, the moorland can be seen stretching away for miles. Moretonhampstead is an ancient town, and it and the surrounding district boasts many places of interest and incomparable scenery, such as the Teign Gorge at Fingle Bridge. The journey is then continued to Chagford.

SERVICE 20. EXETER-BOVEY TRACEY-HAYTOR.
This route follows the same road as described in service 1 as far as Chudleigh Station and then branches off through Chudleigh Knighton, and past a moorland scene to Bovey Tracey. This is an ancient town with a fine church, which tradition says was built as a penance by one of the de Tracys', who took a leading part in the assassination of Thomas a'Becket. The town lies very near some of the beauty spots of Dartmoor, and has earned the title of 'The Gateway of the Moor'. The famous Haytor Rock, where the Company operates a regular service throughout the summer months, is three miles distant.

New vehicles delivered to Devon General were thirteen more of the massive AEC '506' type with Hall Lewis body which had been introduced in the previous year. Five (79-83) were licensed in January, originally 28-seat but later 32. Eight more were ordered in August from ADC Ltd., four (90-93) for delivery in October and four (94-97) for delivery early in the new year, in part exchange for 'Y' type vehicles. 90-97 were always 32-seat, and some of these new vehicles replaced 1925 Dennis buses on the Torquay-Brixham service. The latter were then used on the augmented service to Moretonhampstead and beyond.

Six existing AEC 'YC' and Daimler 'Y' chassis were rebuilt by ADC Ltd., with new engine, pneumatic tyred wheels and fitted with new body by Hall Lewis, the resulting vehicles being numbered 84-89. These were 'charabuses', that is to say centre-gangway charabancs, some at least with removable hard tops that could run as buses in winter being indistinguishable from ordinary buses, and as open charabancs in summer. One was pictured in the timetable booklet.

Three more former Comfy Cars charabancs were transferred from Fleet Cars Ltd., into the Devon General fleet and were numbered 102-104; one was later converted to a parcels van.

During 1927/8 it was the practice to refuel buses at Torquay (Strand) from a hand pumped tank mounted on a van. This was in order to save buses from having to return to St. Marychurch depot for refuelling during the day, and was also carried out at Torquay Station, Watcombe Potteries, and Barton (Lummaton Cross) termini. The old and decrepit van used for this purpose was painted black and white and always reeked of petrol; it carried a 'visit Buckfast Abbey' advert on the back, and its regular driver was one 'Wally' Cooper.

A certain amount of re-numbering was carried out within the fleet during 1926/7. The ex-Torquay Tramways AEC 'YC' buses became 60-68, and the majority of the charabancs were regrouped in the 1-18 series, some being rebuilt with centre gangway. The Daimler 'Y' buses with Strachan & Brown bodywork became 19-36, and the ten Dennis buses of 1925 were 50-59, with 'oddments' being numbered in the intermediate group. Second-hand Lancia charabancs were numbered from 100.

Miscellaneous purchases during the year were:

34 sets of pneumatic tyres for conversion of most of the remaining solid-tyred fleet,
19 new engines,
one Wolseley car, and two pedal cycles.

Among vehicles withdrawn were the four little Daimler CB buses and a lot of non-standard vehicles that had been acquired second-hand, as well as the first of the old AEC 'YC' and Daimler 'Y' vehicles. Some were part-exchanged for new stock and some converted to vans. 96 vehicles were in the fleet at 31st December, plus a few more withdrawn but still on hand.

With the raising of the speed limit from 12mph to 20mph, the Company made plans to extend its services in the following year with new and faster vehicles.

It was in December 1927 that Devon was hit by the worst storms since 1891. Devon General managed to keep most of its services running except to Chagford and Moretonhampstead. In this its first winter of operation, a heavy snowfall at Hillhead rendered the Brixham to Kingswear route impassable for a day or two. As a result, buses laid over at Higher Brixham, and remained there until the due return time. The crews were dismayed to find that the Company did not pay them for this 'laid-over' time. On raising the matter, they were told that 'the snow was not the Company's fault!' - such were labour relations at the time!

It was in the late 1920s that some employees formed their own dance band and they played at staff functions, soon to be in demand for 'outside' events. The Company at one stage objected to them calling themselves the Devon General Dance Band, so they became 'The Southern Syncopating Sextet'. The syncopators included Messrs. R. Gillard, R. Brown, P. Hodge, J. Morcom, E. White and P. Perkins.

1928
was a year of great progress, with the introduction of several lengthy 'limited stop' services jointly with the 'National', for which a number of really modern Leyland vehicles was added to the fleet. The year started quietly enough, with the entry into service of the final four ADC '506s' on order (94-97) and the consequent replacement of four old 'Y' type which went in part exchange.

A new Exmouth area service in the 1st January timetable was 5A, Halsdon Cross-Exmouth-Littleham-Budleigh Salterton. This was purely a short working of services 5 and 10, but from 23rd June was extended a short distance to terminate at Halsdon Avenue.

Another touring business was bought out by Fleet Cars Ltd., on 30th April; this was from G. G. Gullick (t/a 'Heather Tours') of Paignton, together with two one year old Lancia charabancs. They ran for a few weeks at artificially low fares to draw custom away from the opposition, but the Torquay licensing authority would not agree to transfer Gullick's stand on Victoria Parade to Fleet Cars, so the two charabancs were transferred to the Devon General fleet as numbers 108 and 109, and ran on tours and private hire from Exeter.

Services in the Moretonhampstead area were greatly expanded as from Whit Sunday, 26th May. A garage was rented at Colwill Mews in Court Street, Moretonhampstead and five vehicles were kept there, though vehicles were no longer stabled overnight at Chagford or Princetown.

Extra crews were recruited from Exeter and Kingsteignton, and operations were in the charge of Inspectors Rawle, Westlake and Tucker. Inspector Rawle rode one of the Company's motorcycles when on duty, and had a habit of dropping the bike into a hedge and leaping out to stop a bus at the same time. Once, after checking a few buses, he had forgotten where he had left it, and had to ask passing drivers whether they had seen his bike anywhere!

Some employees formed their own dance band in the late 1920s, playing at staff functions and outside events. The Company did not like its name being used, so they called themselves 'The Southern Syncopating Sextet'. On the drums is P. Hodge, and extreme right is conductor/booking clerk Eddie White. (L.F.Folkard collection)

Some of the drivers and conductors taken on at this time stayed with the Company at the same depot until they retired in the 1960s. Three daily journeys on route 17 were extended from Chagford to Okehampton. The summer service from Newton Abbot to Princetown was re-introduced, but as 17A instead of 14A, making two return journeys on weekdays and three on Sundays. These journeys were also incorporated into the 19 to show an Exeter-Princetown service (change at Moretonhampstead), and a new service 18 appeared in the timetable, Okehampton-Moretonhampstead-Princetown, which was created purely by using the 17 and 17A and changing at Moreton. The market day bus from Moretonhampstead to Exeter was re-routed via Drewsteignton instead of Whiddon Down, and a return journey was made on Tuesday as well as Friday. The market day services from Chagford and Moretonhampstead to Okehampton and to Newton Abbot disappeared from the timetable for the time being as they were covered by the extended service 17.

Route 20 from Exeter ceased to run to Ashburton, and resumed its normal summer course to Haytor and from 11th August, was extended to Widecombe-in-the-Moor, down the notorious hill.

A new daily service 22, Honiton-Ottery St. Mary-Sidmouth, replaced the Sundays only 10A, though it consisted mainly of journeys made by the 4 and 21 services.

A new group of Newton Abbot local services appeared in the 23rd June timetable:

1A,	Newton Abbot-Kingsteignton
1B,	Newton Abbot-Kingsteignton-Sandygate (former 2A)
2A,	Newton Abbot-Torquay (former 11A).

Additional journeys between Newton Abbot and Teignmouth were incorporated into the main service 2. The Torquay to Plymouth service terminated in Lymington Road, Torquay adjacent to the Upton Vale Baptist Church. It was soon moved further down the road following representations from the Church.

A new municipal car park opened at Lymington Road in 1928 on filled ground behind the Town Hall. Devon General at first kept a few vehicles there as traffic spares at a cost of 1/- per vehicle per day. The car park was used as a terminus for the long distance coach services that had started to appear, and a waiting room (incorporating cloakroom and toilets) and a corrugated-roof vehicle shelter (open at the sides) were provided. This was then established as the terminal point for the joint service to Plymouth.

Eighteen pre-war 'Regals' were re-bodied by Weymann in 1948/50 with similar bodies to those supplied new some years previously. SR479 is seen climbing Widecombe Hill, although not in 1928, with the village and church in the background. The last example was sold in 1955, many going to Jamaica.   *(Herald Express Newspapers)*

The 14th July timetable introduced a variant of service 7; this was 7A, Exeter-Cullompton-Uffculme-Culmstock. The route between Exeter and Cullompton kept to the main road via Merry Harriers and did not divert via Bradninch.

In July and August, three more new 'Devon National' joint limited stop services were introduced:

Exeter-Tiverton-Dulverton-Minehead
Torquay-Exeter-Bridport-Dorchester-Weymouth
Torquay-Exeter-Cullompton-Wellington-Taunton

Another limited stop service was introduced at the same time, worked solely by Devon General:

Exeter-Woodbury-Yettington-East Budleigh-Otterton Village.

Six normal-control Leyland 'Lioness' 26-seat front-entrance coaches were added to the fleet to operate these services; numbered 118-123, their Hall Lewis body incorporated a small roof-rack and ladder, and there was a nearside emergency door towards the rear. They also had drop windows with glass louvres. Unusually, a foot-board ran the length of the vehicle. A new 'limited stop' livery of dark brown with a broad cream waistband made its appearance on this batch of vehicles and they had a front destination box. Side destination boards were originally carried on the roof racks, but were soon done away with.

Up until 1928, local services at Torquay, Newton Abbot and Exeter had route numbers which duplicated those in the 'country' section of the timetable, and most of the new limited stop services at first had no route number. A new route number structure took effect from 1st October, and whereas the previous highest number had been 22, they then ranged up to 46. A full list of routes as shown in timetable No:35 (October 1928) is appended. Many further changes took place over the next few years.

New country routes introduced at that time were a Tuesdays, Thursdays and Saturdays service, 26, from Tiverton to Willand Moor, which by connection with other routes also provided services to Culmstock and to Taunton. From 1st November, the Culmstock service was extended to Hemyock. An Exeter-Honiton-Kentisbeare arrangement was included in the timetable, but was made up of journeys on 4 and 21, changing at Honiton. A number of services were thus created in the 1920s and 1930s, and another 1928 introduction was Sandypark-Dunsford-Exeter, by courtesy of the 16 and 19.

A few minor changes took place to the Torquay local services from 1st January. Some journeys on the 5 (Castle Circus-Lummaton Cross) were designated 5A and these ran via Teignmouth Road instead of St. Marychurch. Service 1 from 23rd June became Strand-Hesketh Crescent-Meadfoot Beach, and from the same date, short workings on the 2 between Castle Circus and Babbacombe were designated 2A. From 11th August, a new local service was introduced: 4C, Castle Circus-Hele Village, via Lymington Road, Teignmouth Road and Hele Road.

A notable innovation from 23rd June was a 'limited stop' service between Exeter, Newton Abbot and Torquay direct, taking 1hr 20 mins as against 1hr 45 minutes by service 1, or 2hrs 20 mins by the 2. At first un-numbered, it became 1A by 14th July and ran every two hours.

Two lengthy routes commenced on 2nd July, jointly operated with the National Omnibus & Transport Co. Ltd., and described as 'Devon National Amalgamated Services'. Also at first un-numbered, they were:

Exeter-Chudleigh-Ashburton-Ivybridge-Plymouth (Sherwell Arcade)
Exeter-Crediton-Barnstaple-Ilfracombe

The Plymouth service made four return trips each weekday, and there were three (soon reduced to two) return workings to Ilfracombe (two on each service on Sundays). Fares were 10/- return to Ilfracombe and 7/6d to Plymouth. Luggage up to 28lbs per passenger was carried free.

From 23rd June, Ashcroft's had been granted a licence to run a 'limited stop' service between Torquay and Plymouth, provided that local passengers were not carried between Torquay and Paignton. In response to this, Devon General applied on behalf of themselves and National, to jointly work a similar service. Their timetable was required to maintain at least half an hour's difference between their starting times and those of Ashcroft (who had by then obtained four modern Leyland 'Lions'). The service appeared in the Devon General timetable from 14th July as 16A, and from the same date, 16 was cut back to operate Torquay-Newton Abbot-Totnes only, where connection was made, albeit rather loosely with the 16A.

In 1928, Devon General started taking delivery of new Leyland buses of the Lion, Tiger and Titan types, and these had by 1934, replaced virtually all older vehicles. No:115 (UO 7470) is seen when quite new, on the Torquay to Exeter limited stop service.
(L.F.Folkard collection)

To work the above major new services, Devon General purchased eight Leyland 'Lion' PLSC type buses (110-117), their first new vehicles to have the 'half-cab' arrangement that was to become almost universal in the fleet for the next thirty years. They had Hall Lewis 32-seat dual-entrance body in a slightly modified livery of red up to waist level, and cream above. The front destination was on a roller blind showing ultimate destination only, and route boards were carried on the sides at roof level. They had full-drop windows with glass louvres. Four of the buses were initially based at Torquay and four at Exeter. Only the most proven and experienced drivers were entrusted to work the limited stop services.

Up until 1928, and maybe for a little longer, drivers had been paired with a regular conductor, an arrangement which had mixed blessings. At the other end of the vehicle scale, nine early Daimler 'Ys' were given centre-gangway charabanc bodies built (or most probably re-built) by the Company.

The Exeter-Otterton limited stop service was, at the end of the summer, demoted to a normal service, running on Tuesdays, Fridays, Saturdays and Sundays, and from 1st November was further curtailed to run on Fridays and Saturdays only. From the same date, the Halsdon Avenue to Exmouth service ceased, while a new Torquay local service 35 ran from Lawes Bridge to Hesketh Crescent via Hele Village, Castle Circus, and Strand. This replaced the short route 30 and also one leg of the 34.

Exeter Corporation had meanwhile promoted a Bill seeking to operate its own bus services. Devon General submitted a petition against this, but without success.

At Torquay, estimates for the building of offices at St. Marychurch depot were invited, and that submitted by Wilkins & Sons was accepted. A 30cwt floor crane was purchased in November for use at that depot.

The booking and parcels office at 4, The Triangle, Dartmouth Road, Paignton was sub-let for the remainder of the lease, and in its place, premises at Waterloo House, 10A, Torquay Road, Paignton were rented. Towards the end of the year, an office was opened in Ford Street, Moretonhampstead.

On 5th November, Chief Clerk Mr. W. Geere was appointed Assistant Manager at Exeter. The Assistant Manager at Torquay was Mr. Anderson. His office was in a converted railway carriage at the depot, and among his duties was interviewing job applicants. He always wore a trilby hat, and it was a well known fact that, if the hat was on the back of his head, the applicant did not have an easy interview! One instance concerned a young fitter who was sent to the Strand to bring back a certain bus for attention, and who came back with the wrong one. He was sent home to ponder on his future, later returning to continue with the Company until retirement!

The fleet at the end of 1928 comprised 111 buses and coaches, not including Fleet Cars Ltd.

Services, as revised from 1st October 1928:

1,	Exeter-Chudleigh-Newton Abbot-Torquay
2,	Exeter-Dawlish-Teignmouth-Newton Abbot-Torquay
3,	Exeter-Silverton-Tiverton-Halberton-Sampford Peverell
4,	Exeter-Ottery St. Mary-Honiton-Axminster
5,	Exeter-Exmouth-Budleigh Salterton
6,	Exeter-Crockernwell-Okehampton
6A,	Okehampton-Sticklepath short working (NSu) from 1st November
7,	Exeter-Bradninch-Cullompton
8,	Exeter-Newton St. Cyres-Crediton
9,	Exeter-Newton Poppleford-Sidmouth-Sidbury
10,	Exmouth-Budleigh Salterton-Sidmouth
11,	Torquay-Newton Abbot-Ashburton-Buckfastleigh
12,	Torquay-Paignton-Brixham-Kingswear
13,	Torquay-Maidencombe-Shaldon
14,	Newton Abbot-Moretonhampstead-Princetown (ex-17A. Princetown section summer only)
15,	Torquay-Newton Abbot-Totnes (ex-16)
16,	Torquay-Newton Abbot-Bovey Tracey-Moretonhampstead-Chagford-Okehampton (ex-17)
17,	Torquay-Newton Abbot-Bovey Tracey
18,	Torquay-Newton Abbot-Bovey Tracey-Moretonhampstead-Chagford
19,	Exeter-Moretonhampstead-Chagford
20,	Exeter-Chudleigh-Bovey Tracey-Haytor-Widecombe (Bovey-Widecombe Summer only)

21,	Cullompton-Honiton-Sidmouth (TuThSaSuO) (MSaO from 1st Nov)
22,	Axminster-Honiton-Ottery St. Mary-Sidmouth
22A,	Sidmouth-Ottery St. Mary-Whimple-Exeter
23,	Exeter-Moretonhampstead-Princetown (ex-19) (Summer only)
24,	Exeter-Topsham-Woodbury-Otterton (ex-LS) (TuFSaSuO)
25,	Exmouth-Budleigh Salterton (ex-5A)
26,	Tiverton-Halberton-Culmstock (TuThSaO) (extended to Hemyock from 1st Nov)
26A,	Tiverton-Willand Moor-Wellington-Taunton (TuThSaO)
26B,	Tiverton-Halberton
27,	Exeter-Merry Harriers-Cullompton-Uffculme-Culmstock(ex-7A)(ext to Hemyock 1st Nov)
28,	Cullompton-Clyst Hydon-Exeter (ex-Market) (FO)
28A,	Exeter-Honiton-Kentisbeare (WSaO)
29,	Moretonhampstead-Drewsteignton-Crockernwell-Exeter (ex-Market) (TuFSaO)
29A,	Sandypark-Dunsford-Exeter (weekdays)
30,	Torquay Strand-Hesketh Crescent-Meadfoot Beach (ex-Torquay1) (Meadfoot Summer only)
31A,	Torquay Station-Castle Circus-Babbacombe (ex-Torquay 2)
31B,	Torquay Castle Circus-Babbacombe (ex-Torquay 2A)
32,	Torquay-Preston-Paignton (ex-Torquay 3)
33,	Chelston-Castle Circus-Strand-Castle Circus-Watcombe (ex-Torquay 4)
33,	Watcombe-Castle Circus-Chelston (ex-Torquay 4A)
33,	Castle Circus-Barton Village (ex-Torquay 4B)
34,	Castle Circus-St. Marychurch-Lummaton Cross (ex-Torquay 5)
34,	Castle Circus-Hele Village (ex-Torquay 4C) (Operated until 31st October)
35,	Lawes Bridge-Hele Village-Castle Circus-Strand-Hesketh Crescent (from 1st November)
36,	Torquay-Newton Abbot (ex Newton Abbot 2A)
37,	Newton Abbot-Kingsteignton (ex-Newton Abbot 1A)
37A,	Newton Abbot-Kingsteignton-Sandygate (ex-Newton Abbot 1B)
38,	Bedford Circus-Topsham Road corner (ex-Exeter 1) (Weekdays)
39,	New North Road-Old Tiverton Road (ex-Exeter 2)
40,	Torquay-Totnes-Plymouth (LS, ex-16A)
41,	Torquay-Exeter-Cullompton-Taunton (LS) (TuThSaO)
42,	Torquay-Exeter-Axminster-Weymouth (LS)
43,	Torquay-Newton Abbot-Exeter (LS, ex-1A)
44,	Exeter-Chudleigh-Plymouth
45,	Exeter-Crediton-Barnstaple-Ilfracombe (LS) (TuThFSaO) (Summer only)
46,	Exeter-Tiverton-Bampton-Minehead (LS) (TuThFSaSuO)

Notes:

LS   Limited Stop

Section 4. Modernisation and development with the Railways (1929-1933)

1929   The main line railway companies were consolidating their bus interests under the terms of the Great Western Railway (Road Transport) Act 1928, and the Southern Railway (Road Transport) Act 1928, and on 1st July 1929 agreement was reached with them that the Great Western would purchase a 30% holding in Devon General, and the Southern a 20% holding. The Devon General Company also undertook to procure that the Torquay Tramways Co. Ltd., would sell 9,000 £1 ordinary shares in Devon General to the GWR and 6,000 similar shares to the Southern Railway. Special resolutions at Extraordinary General Meetings held on 21st October and 6th November passed and confirmed that the composition of the Board of Directors was to be increased to ten, of which three were to be nominated by the GWR and two by the SR. Of the existing seven Directors, Messrs. Home. C. Smith and R. H. Campion resigned. The new Board comprised:

Mr. H. T. Barnett (Chairman), Mr. W. B. Cownie (Managing Director), Mr. J. (later Sir James) Milne, Francis Bingham - Lord Mildmay of Flete, Mr. R. H. Nicholls of the Great Western Railway, Col. G. S. Szlumper and Mr. D. S. McBright of the Southern Railway, and three original Directors, Messrs. H. J. Nisbett, F. E. Stanley, and B. W. Stedham. The Company's registered office from 1st July 1929 was at Salisbury Square House, London EC4.

Devon General agreed not to put on any new services that would directly compete with train services of the two railways, and the Great Western agreed, when called upon by Devon General, to use its best endeavours to transfer to the Company, any bus or charabanc services worked by the GWR and/or Western National that lay within the Devon General area, other than the Paignton to Totnes service. The former GWR services at Bovey Tracey and Moretonhampstead, well within Devon General territory, had passed to Western National on the formation of that Company earlier in the year, and agreement was reached on 28th August that operation of these services should be by Devon General on behalf of Western National, from a date to be determined. However, Western National continued to work the services until the end of September 1934, those concerned being;

WN.121,   Moretonhampstead Station - Chagford
122,   Bovey Tracey - Haytor - Widecombe
123,   Bovey Tracey - Becky Falls - Manaton.

At the same time, a general demarcation line was agreed between the two companies, following which Western National ceased working between Newton Abbot and Totnes direct, apart from one Sunday journey.

The Great Western Railway had, by agreement dated 18th December 1928, acquired the business of Ashcroft at Paignton, and was proposing to transfer it retrospectively to the new Western National Omnibus Co. Ltd., from 1st January 1929. This company was however precluded by agreement from working a Torquay-Paignton service, and on 25th July it was finally agreed that Devon General would take over two ex-Ashcroft vehicles and contribute to the amount of goodwill paid by the GWR to Ashcroft. The two vehicles selected were Leyland 'Lion' PLSCs, and were given numbers 142 and 143 in the Devon General fleet.

The elimination of Ashcroft's services had not meant the end of competition on the Torquay to Plymouth route, as H. B. Buses Ltd., of Plymouth had in May purchased the business of Hendra ('Totnesia') of Totnes, and coupled the H. B. Plymouth to Totnes service with Hendra's Totnes to Paignton route and run through to Torquay in competition with the 'Devon National' joint service. After a period of fierce rivalry, terms were agreed admitting H. B. Buses Ltd., as a partner in the joint service from 31st July, and their six return journeys a day were incorporated into the re-cast joint timetable. H. B. Buses had been founded by Messrs. Hopper and Berryman, but in March 1929 the limited company had been formed to take over their operations, among the Directors being Mr. C. Mumford of the Plymouth coach-building firm. Most of their fleet was of AEC manufacture with Mumford body, and the smart blue livery later carried the name Southern General. They sold out to Western National in 1931, when Devon General completed an agreement to buy out a half-share of the Southern General workings on the Torquay to Plymouth service.

An unnerving incident occurred on that route early one Monday morning; Devon General driver Jerry Crispin was driving a Western National bus on a change-over turn when, rounding a bend going down Longcombe Hill between Paignton and Totnes, he was confronted by an elephant in the middle of the road, standing on its hind legs and trumpeting loudly! Its keeper managed to get it off the road with no harm done.

Ernest Jackson & Sons Ltd., cough sweet manufacturers of Crediton, provided their staff with an outing to Weymouth in July 1929. The vehicle used was a very much rebuilt AEC 'YC' dating originally from 1920/21, but re-bodied as a charabus in 1927.

(L.F.Folkard collection)

In February of 1929, the Great Western Railway had been granted licences to operate three services in the Torquay area with 14-seat buses:

Torquay Station-Babbacombe Downs (Roughwood) via Lawes Bridge and St. Marychurch
Babbacombe Downs (Roughwood)-Newton Abbot Station, via St. Marychurch and Lawes Bridge
Babbacombe Downs (Roughwood)-Newton Abbot Station via Barton and Milber

The GWR disposed of its bus interests locally at about the same time, and there is no evidence that any of these services ever operated. Devon General worked on the first named route during 1938 and 1939, but only between Torquay Station and St. Marychurch, as service 72.

During the winter of 1928/9, Exeter City Council resolved to terminate the Agreement made in 1924 which allowed Devon General to work certain bus services wholly within the city, and three months notice of termination was given. Thus it came about that on 31st March 1929, Devon General ceased operation of services 38 (Bedford Circus-St. Leonards) and 39 (New North Road to Old Tiverton Road via Pennsylvania Road), and these were incorporated into the first three services to be operated by the city's own motor-buses from 1st April 1929.

From 30th March, the Exeter-Hemyock service 27 was diverted at Culmstock and extended to terminate at Taunton. 26, 26A and 26B were merged to become 26, Tiverton-Halberton-Willand-Culmstock-Taunton and from the same date 41, Torquay-Exeter-Taunton ceased, as did the service between Culmstock and Hemyock. The 26 ceased from 1st May, but fare-tables showed a table 26A, Paignton-Torquay-Newton Abbot-Teignmouth-Exeter-Cullompton-Taunton!

Services between Wellington and Taunton ceased from 15th June; the Devon/Somerset border area was Western National territory anyway and was also well served by the Great Western Railway. Only two vehicles were then based at Tiverton, and three new Limited Stop services were introduced:

38, Torquay-Exeter-Sidmouth-Seaton-Lyme Regis-Charmouth from 15th June, on the understanding with (Southern) National that passengers for Charmouth were not picked up after leaving Seaton and vice versa. This service was cut back to Seaton from 23rd September.

39, Exeter-Woodbury-Budleigh Salterton was introduced from 1st May and extended to Otterton from 23rd September.

41, Exeter-Topsham-Exmouth-Littleham was also introduced from 1st May and extended to Otterton from 23rd September. The 24, Exeter-Otterton, had ceased on 1st January.

Changes to the Torquay local services had taken place by 1st January: the Lummaton Cross service was linked to Barton via the Hele Village service to form one route to Barton - out via Hele Village and back via Lummaton Cross and vice versa. This also incorporated the Chelston journeys that had previously run to Watcombe. The service to Watcombe was altered to run from Castle Circus via St. Marychurch. The resulting services were:

33, Strand-Chelston-Castle Circus-Barton-Strand (circular)
34, Castle Circus-St. Marychurch-Watcombe.

A new service introduced from 1st August was 47, Torquay-Paignton-Stoke Gabriel, requiring a change at Paignton. This was often worked by the ex-Chelston Co. Leyland 'Lion' No:99. Ashcroft had run to Stoke Gabriel during 1926-8, and H. S. Fleet and his successor C. B. Foxworthy ran 'The Dart' bus over this route until bought out by Western National in 1952. Devon General exchanged the Stoke Gabriel route with Western National in 1937 for Paignton-Greenway.

Four journeys a day on service 8, Exeter-Crediton, were extended from 1st January to serve Sandford once more.
New services combining timetables of existing routes were:

39A, (later 24A) Sidmouth - Newton Poppleford
39B, (later 24B) Exeter - Clyst St. Mary

These were introduced from 30th March, the service numbers becoming 24A and 24B from 1st May. The two numbers were exchanged from 23rd September.

28, (Cullompton-Clyst Hydon-Exeter) was renumbered 21A from 15th June and was un-numbered from 23rd September.
28A, (Exeter-Honiton-Kentisbeare) ceased from 15th June.

An Exeter-Exmouth-Budleigh Salterton service briefly appeared as 26. From 15th June a through Exeter-Newton Abbot-Totnes timetable was given service number 28 and this was renumbered 15A from 23rd September, when 28 was given to an Exeter-Newton Abbot-Bovey Tracey timetable, which in turn only lasted for a few months. Short workings from Exeter to Countess Wear and Topsham were designated 41A by 1st July. The above mentioned workings (from 24A onwards) had all disappeared from the timetable by July 1930.

The 5 time-table was extended to show an Exeter-Exmouth-Budleigh Salterton-Sidmouth service from 30th March to 15th June only, when it reverted to Exeter-Exmouth-Budleigh Salterton only. It was extended to East Budleigh from 23rd September, and from the same date, 21 was split into 21, Cullompton-Honiton and 21A, Sidmouth-Sidbury-Honiton.

A new market day bus service, 29B, made one return journey a week on Wednesdays between Drewsteignton, Newton Abbot, and Torquay. 29 was terminated at Chagford instead of Moretonhampstead.

In May, the Company purchased a site at Lower Woolbrook, 1½ miles from Sidmouth, for construction of a garage for ten buses, and tenders were invited. The steelwork contract was awarded to Walker Bros. of Walsall, and the building contract to G. A. Northcote of Sidmouth.

An agreement was also made in May for garage accommodation to be rented at Axminster from Packham & Co. of Station Garage for the stabling of the bus left there overnight.

Having become surplus to operating requirements, the land that had been purchased at Dropping Wells near Ashburton was sold to Mrs. Babington, who later opened a filling station on the site.

Office accommodation at Westhill Avenue depot (St. Marychurch) Torquay was completed. Workmen's return tickets were introduced from 1st January on certain journeys from Torquay to Newton Abbot, Chudleigh, Brixham, Bovey Tracey, and Kingsteignton, and between Exeter and Crediton.

The following coach tours were offered from Exeter for the 1929 season:

Two-Day Tours

1   Lands End

Extended-Day Tours

2   Bodmin Moor and Newquay
3   Weymouth
4   Looe and Polperro
5   Lyme Regis and Bournemouth
6   Mevagissey and Tamar Valley
7   Bude, Boscastle and Tintagel
8   Lynton, Lynmouth and Ilfracombe
9   Polruan and Fowey

Day Tours

10	Dartmoor and Torquay
11	Dunkery Beacon and Porlock Weir
12	Cheddar and Weston-super-Mare
13	River Dart and Torquay
14	Plymouth (Moorland and coastal)
15	Salcombe and Brixham
16	Weymouth and Lulworth Cove
17	Dunster and Minehead
18	Princetown and Dartmeet
19	Slapton Sands and Dartmouth
20	Princetown and Plymouth
21	Doone Valley and Minehead
22	Weymouth and Lyme Regis
23	Ilfracombe and Barnstaple
24	Doone Valley and Lynmouth
25	Bude and Clovelly
26	Clovelly and Westward Ho!
27	Lynton and Lynmouth
28	Cheddar Gorge and Caves
29	Slapton Sands and Bigbury-on-Sea

Afternoon Tours

30	Tarr Steps (Exmoor)
31	Grimspound Hut Circles
32	Lyme Regis and Sidmouth
33	Ladram Bay
34	Becky falls and Haytor Rocks
35	Brixham and Berry Head
36	Beer and Seaton
37	Haytor Rocks and Widecombe
38	Widecombe and Haytor Rocks
39	Charmouth and West Bay
40	Lydford Gorge and Okehampton
41	Wellington Monument
42	Fingle Gorge and Bridge
43	Princetown and Dartmeet
44	Buckfast Abbey

Many of these tours would not have been possible before the raising of the speed limit in 1927. Only a small selection was run on any day, and the more popular ones were made into scheduled services from 1930.

The year 1929 saw further modernisation of the fleet, and new Leyland buses of four types were purchased, including the first new double-deckers since 1921. Early in the year, an ADC '426' demonstrator was on loan - it was a 32-seat saloon, registered MT 1257.

Of the new intake, four (124-127) were Leyland 'Lion' PLSC type, similar to 110-117, while four (128-131) were Leyland 'Lion' LT1 type, with Hall Lewis 31-seat double-entrance bodies very similar to those on the PLSCs.

Six (132-137) were Leyland Tiger 'TS2s' (as were 144 and 145 which came later) a forward-drive, half-cab type for the express services intended for passengers travelling 20 miles or more. Bodies were again by Hall Lewis, with 26-seats (30 on 144/5), front entrance with emergency door on the nearside at the rear, and, as on 'Lionesses' (118-123), a foot-board running the whole length of the vehicle on each side, and a small luggage rack at the rear, on the roof. They were finished in the dark brown livery with cream waistband which had been adopted for the 'limited stop' services. The rear of the vehicle was lettered 'Limited Stop' in place of the fleet name. The following extract from the 'Torbay Herald & Express' dated 6th April 1929 gives a first-hand description of their reporter's impressions: "When I stepped into the Leyland 'Tiger' I was at once struck by the sumptuous style in which the coach was fitted and furnished. The floor is covered with inlaid linoleum

Grey Cars 'Lancias' about to set out from Marine Square, Torquay on a Co-op Society outing in the summer of 1929.

(K.J.Brown collection)

and is as clean as the proverbial new pin. The passengers loll into one of the capacious seats. These are covered with moquette of rich subdued colouring. The seats are of the armchair pattern, giving ample room for each individual, and built for comfort, generously padded and well sprung. From this desirable vantage one cannot fail to note the meticulous care with which the well-being of the passengers has been considered. Curtains to match the general colour scheme adorn the clear windows, and nickel-plated fittings glisten with silvery sheen. Neatly designed nickel ash trays are fitted to each seat, thus ensuring the absence of litter on the floor. Cute little mirrors are fixed here and there - a boon to lady passengers. Running along the top of the windows is a rack for luggage, a boon to every passenger. Balloon tyres are fitted and there is an absence of jolt. Change of gear when ascending hills is accomplished by the driver with such consummate ease and smoothness that there is not the slightest trace of jerk or grinding sound...". This passage was reproduced in the Company's timetable for the next couple of years.

Delivered concurrently with the 'Tigers' were the Company's first four covered-top double-deckers (138-141) which had Hall Lewis 48-seat bodywork of the 'lowbridge' type, with sunken offside gangway on the top deck. 141 was exhibited at the Commercial Motor Show. Two worked on the Torquay to Newton Abbot service, and the other two on Exeter to Crediton.

Many of the old AEC 'YC' and Daimler 'Y' vehicles were withdrawn during 1929, and the fleet at the year end totalled 119 vehicles (excluding Fleet Cars).

The 1921 Ford van was replaced by a new Morris, and a noteworthy purchase in July was four Lancia engines and running units from the newly formed Western National Company. These emanated from four of Ashcroft's former vehicles which had come into Western National ownership via the Great Western Railway.

1930
An Extraordinary General Meeting held on 26th March passed a resolution to increase the capital of the Company from £130,000 to £170,000 by the creation of a further 40,000 ordinary shares of £1 each.

The Southern Railway disposed of its contracts with private bus operators during 1930 in favour of its newly associated omnibus companies, and Devon General thus took over the operation of town and station services at Sidmouth and Budleigh Salterton. That at Sidmouth had been run by the Sidmouth Motor Co. and before that by John Lake's horse bus. The local carrier at Budleigh Salterton from 1923 had been Albert Searle & Sons, who conveyed passengers "anywhere in comparative comfort within a reasonable distance - for sixpence". Searle had three Fords - a bus, a lorry, and a car, and his operation of the service had become somewhat erratic before the Railway finally decided to terminate his contract as from 30th June.

Devon General purchased two 12-seat Morris Commercial station buses (178 and 179) for use on these services. 178 went into service on 1st July at Budleigh Salterton and 179 in September at Sidmouth. No set routes were timetabled, buses being run at times and to destinations dictated by service requirements. Parties of six or more could hire the bus at a fixed fare of five shillings, otherwise the fares charged depended on the amount of luggage carried. The Sidmouth bus ran between station, town, and hotels, and slightly further afield to Bickwell Valley or to Salcombe Hill. Its sister at Budleigh Salterton ran between station, town and hotels, and as required within limits bounded by Lane End, Golf Road, Kersbrook, Penny Park, Knowle, Lansdowne, Exmouth Road, and Golf Links.

A parcels agency was taken over from Mrs. Searle and operated by Devon General on behalf of the Southern Railway. A 30cwt van was purchased for this purpose, and Devon General also secured a contract with the Postmaster General for the conveyance of mail between the station and GPO at Budleigh Salterton.
The association with the railways also brought about a scheme for interavailability of tickets. On designated services, holders of day-return tickets on Devon General could return by rail for a small extra supplement, and rail ticket holders could return by bus at no extra cost.

Until 1930, buses running between Torquay and Paignton charged a fare 50% higher than the fares charged on the trams, but this ceased in October and the bus fare was reduced to 3d. The Tramways Company had been enjoying the same protection as many other tram-owning municipalities while motor-bus services spread in the early 1920s, but because Devon General was, by 1930, the only bus Company running a local service over its associated tram Company's routes, the protection was no longer deemed appropriate.

In April, a large 3½ acre site at Newton Road, Torquay was purchased for the erection of a new central overhaul and repair depot and garage to replace that at Westhill Avenue. The vendor was Mr. B. Stedham, one of the Devon General Directors. Tenders were submitted in November and contracts were awarded to the Lambhill Iron Works of Glasgow for the steelwork and to P. Wilkins & Sons of Torquay for the building construction, completion of which was required in 26 weeks.

The garage at New Street, Exmouth was proving inadequate, with vehicles being washed in the street, and some having to park in the station yard, for which a fee was paid to the Southern Railway. The railway company offered Devon General a lease on land in Imperial Road, next door to the station, for construction of a new garage, and this was accepted from 29th September for a period of 42 years. The steelwork contract was awarded in December to J. Partridge & Co. Ltd.

Meantime the new depot had been opened at Woolbrook, on the outskirts of Sidmouth. It had a capacity of ten vehicles, and replaced accommodation that had previously been rented at Newton Poppleford. There was a booking and enquiry office at Woolbrook and a parcels office at Radway in Sidmouth.

Extensions to Kingsteignton depot that had been commenced in 1929 were also completed this year.

Buses were again based in Paignton from 1930, and up to five garaged overnight at the Orient Road depot of Fleet Cars (adjacent to the Preston tram depot). The rented accommodation at Prout's Garage, Churston was then relinquished.

At Newton Abbot Market Square, a booking and parcels office was rented from Mr. A. J. Parkin and the parcels office in West Street, Ashburton was closed.

No:1 in a row of six kiosks at Lymington Road Car Park, Torquay, was rented from the local Council from June, and was for many years the office of Traffic Regulator (later Inspector) H. Jackson, who controlled the services in the Castle Circus area of Torquay. After his retirement, Inspector P. Hutchings became the incumbent of kiosk number 1.

Devon General was in litigation during 1930 over an alleged nuisance caused to residents in St. Marychurch Road, Torquay by buses using the depot at Westhill Avenue. A writ was served on the Company, and to dispose of the matter they bought a house 'Dungarvan' from a Miss E. H. Slocombe. The house was situated at the junction of Westhill Avenue and St. Marychurch Road, and was almost opposite the entrance to the tram side of the depot. It was No:20 in St. Marychurch Road, being renumbered 112 after the war. Devon General re-sold it in 1933, and it was demolished in 1982 along with adjacent property to make way for a supermarket.

Several new limited-stop services were introduced on 8th June. These were also known as 'scheduled tours' and in general, made one trip out from Exeter in the morning and back in the evening, summer only, on certain days of the week. A few intermediate stops were made to pick-up and set-down, and return tickets were valid for 15 days. The following such services operated:

37	Exeter-Okehampton-Bude	TuThSaSu
38	Exeter-Winkleigh-Clovelly	MWFSa
39	Exeter-Tiverton-Lynton	MWFSa
40	Exeter-Cheddar-Wells	TuThSu
41A	Exeter-Dunkery Beacon & Exmoor	MTh
41B	Exeter-Devils Punchbowl & Tarr Steps	TuF
41C	Exeter-Doone Valley	WSaSu
42	Exeter-Dartmeet-Princetown	Daily
43	Exeter-Sidmouth-Lyme Regis	MWF
44	Exeter-Charmouth-West Bay	TuThSa
50	Exeter-Crediton-Ilfracombe	Daily
51	Exeter-Totnes-River Dart	Daily

Service 50 replaced the Devon National joint service 45 which had run during the previous two summers. The River Dart service, which also ran from Torquay as an un-numbered adjunct to the 12, operated according to tides. The bus from Torquay or Exeter would take passengers to Totnes Quay where they would embark on to one of the River Dart Steamboat Company Ltd., fleet of paddle steamers (Totnes Castle, Kingswear Castle, Dartmouth Castle or Compton Castle) or one of their motor cruisers. The river trip to Kingswear took about two hours, and return was made by train from Kingswear to either Torquay or Exeter. The tour could also be effected in reverse, and starting at Totnes gave more dramatic views of the river. Each of the above services had a page to itself in the timetable with a brief description of the journey and the places served. The Dartmoor and Exmoor tours were worked by 18-seat Lancia charabancs.

Before the end of the season, 41A, B and C were combined as 41, Exeter to Doone Valley (Circular) which ran daily in the height of the season. 44 was not a success and was soon discontinued. In order to accommodate the above services, some existing routes were renumbered.

Newton Abbot local services 37/37A became 36/36A and the three local services introduced from 1st April were numbered as follows:

37B	Newton Abbot-Highweek-Mile End	36C	from 8th June
37C	Newton Abbot-Decoy	36B	from 8th June
37D	Newton Abbot-Ogwell-Denbury	36D	from 8th June

The existing 38 and 43 were combined and extended to Lyme Regis to give a new service 46, Torquay-Exeter-Sidmouth-Seaton-Lyme Regis. and other changes were:

36,	(Torquay-Newton Abbot) was renumbered 28
39,	(Exeter-Woodbury-Budleigh Salterton-Otterton) renumbered 26
40,	(Torquay-Totnes-Plymouth) renumbered 45
41,	(Exeter-Exmouth-Littleham) ceased
42,	was cut back to run Exeter-Dorchester-Weymouth and renumbered 47
44,	(Exeter-Plymouth) renumbered 49
46,	(Exeter-Minehead) renumbered 53 and operated daily
47,	(Torquay-Stoke Gabriel) renumbered 54

A short-lived new service was the limited-stop 48, Exeter-Honiton-Chard. Its three daily journeys were, in September, diverted at Honiton to serve Seaton instead of Chard, and the Honiton-Seaton leg was duplicated in the timetable by an extension of the 21 service.

An ambitious new limited stop service started in September. This was 52, Torquay-Exeter-Dorchester-Bournemouth, which ran in competition with Elliott Bros. 'Royal Blue' service and Leyland 'Tigers' 136 and 137 were regularly used on it. The service had first been mooted in February 1929, at which time National raised no objection, subject to it not competing with their local services, and reserving the right to participate in joint operation. Three return trips a day were made.

Another new service, 55, ran over existing routes from Honiton to Exmouth via Sidmouth and Budleigh Salterton. Before the end of the year it was amended to Exmouth-Budleigh Salterton-Sidmouth-Seaton-Lyme Regis, and in its place, the 10 was extended from Sidmouth via Sidbury to Honiton. In the same area, a new market day bus (4A) ran on Saturdays between Honiton and Talaton, and some workings on the 4 were operated via Marsh Green and West Hill.

A new service at Exmouth started in July which ran from the railway station to Orcombe Point - outwards via Strand, Victoria Road and Esplanade, and back either the same way or via Esplanade, Horton Road, Victoria Road and Imperial Road. It was originally an un-numbered adjunct to the 5 time-table, but ran half-hourly whereas the 5 was hourly. It was basically a summer-only service, but five through journeys a day were run from Exeter via Clyst St. Mary in the winter as well, for a cheap day return fare of 1/9d from Exeter. Local operators Miller, Abbott and Harris all shared the workings between Exmouth Station and Orcombe Point. An illuminated sign was provided at the railway station to direct passengers to the buses, and Exmouth Council required Devon General to depart alternately with one of the other operators on arrival of a train, which caused operational problems. Normal fares were 4d single, 8d return by Devon General, but only 6d return by an 'independent'. Devon General participation had been initiated by the Southern Railway, who wished to see railway passengers continue to the sea-front on buses in which they held an interest. The three independents had resisted the move, and the Council had at first refused to licence Devon General on this service. An amicable agreement was reached at the subsequent Ministry of Transport inquiry, but further trouble arose at times when the independents seemed reluctant to run their share of the service.

During the summer of 1930, services 3 and 7 had been extended from Exeter to Exmouth via Topsham and Exton, but these extensions were withdrawn at the end of the summer. 7 and 8 were re-routed as:

7,   Exeter-Crediton-Sandford
8,   Broadclyst-Pinhoe-Exeter-Newton St. Cyres-Crediton

Of the remaining Exmouth services, 5 ran from Exeter via Topsham and Woodbury, and a new 5A from Exeter via Clyst St. Mary and Exton.

The Torquay local services were recast during the year. The former 32 between Torquay and Paignton simply became part of the 12 service, and services 30 through to 35 were re-organised as follows:

30,   Torquay Station-Castle Circus-Babbacombe
31,   Cadewell Lane-Lawes Bridge-Hele Village-Castle Circus-Strand-Hesketh Crescent
         (diverted during the year to run between Hele Village and Castle Circus via Westhill)
31A,   Hele Village-Castle Circus-Strand
32,   Strand-Castle Circus-Chelston
33,   Strand-Castle Circus-Barton
34,   Chelston-Castle Circus-Barton
35,   Castle Circus-St. Marychurch-Watcombe Potteries-Watcombe Beach

The Company was unsuccessful (for the time being) in obtaining a licence to run to the Shiphay district of Torquay, as was a Mr. J. Day. Their applications were turned down because the state of the roads at the time was considered unsatisfactory. However, improvements to part of Shiphay Lane were made in time for the Company to be able to operate a special service to the Bath & West Show which was held on the Shiphay Estate during June.

Service alterations of a minor nature which took place during the year were as follows:

The summer-only route 14 became Newton Abbot-Haytor-Widecombe, while 14A became Newton Abbot-Moretonhampstead-Princetown and was only achieved by using vehicles off services 16 and 23 with a change at Moretonhampstead.

6A and 15A were discontinued as such, and the journeys between Torquay and Chagford of service 18 were all incorporated into the 16 service. Market day service 29A became Moretonhampstead- Chagford-South Zeal-Okehampton (Saturdays only) and 29B became Drewsteignton-Newton Abbot (on Wednesdays). 22 ceased and 22A was renumbered 22 (Exeter-Ottery St. Mary-Tipton St. John-Sidmouth).

A new service over existing routes was 24, Exmouth-Lympstone-Woodbury, while 24A and 24B ceased as separate tables. 27 was extended over the 1 and 15 routes so as to provide a through Uffculme-Cullompton-Exeter-Chudleigh-Newton Abbot-Totnes service. The un-numbered Fridays-only Cullompton-Plymtree-Exeter was given service number 27A.

The increase in both fleet and services was causing terminus problems, the trouble being particularly acute in Exeter around the Theatre Royal stop in New North Road. Following negotiations with the local authority, a site created by the demolition of a lot of old buildings was rented in Paul Street from the Council as from 21st May and a bus station was established on it, which was ready for use by Christmas 1930. An existing building was adapted to provide waiting rooms, enquiry, left luggage and parcels offices. The City Council retained the cleared site at the lower end of Paul Street for use as a coach station.

As from 25th December, the following routes were recorded into and out of Exeter:

Services to:
Dawlish, Chudleigh, Newton Abbot, Torquay, Totnes, Plymouth, Bovey Tracey, Widecombe, Moretonhampstead, Chagford, Princetown, Okehampton, Bude and intermediate points, left via Bartholomew Streets (East and West), Fore Street, and Exe Bridge. Stopping places were at Bartholomew Street West (corner of Fore Street) and Exe Bridge. Services to Crediton, Tiverton, Minehead, Lynton, Clovelly, Exmoor, Ilfracombe, and intermediately, left via Queen Street and Buller Memorial with stops at Queen St (Southern Railway Station) and Buller Memorial.
Services to:
Topsham, Exmouth, Budleigh Salterton (via Woodbury Common) and Otterton Village left via North Street, South Street, and Holloway Street, with stops at the top of South Street and the corner of Magdalen Street.
Services to:
Ottery St. Mary, Honiton, Axminster, Chard, Sidmouth, Seaton, Lyme Regis and Weymouth left via North Street, South Street and Magdalen Street with stops at the top of South Street and the corner of Magdalen Street.
Services to:
Broadclyst, Cullompton, Uffculme, Wells and Cheddar left via Queen Street, High Street and Sidwell Street. Stops were at Queen Street (Market) and High Street (Post Office).
Services to:
Exmouth and beyond, via Clyst St. Mary, left via Queen Street, High Street and Paris Street, with stops at Queen Street (Market), and High Street (Post Office).

Vehicles would stop at any other reasonable points beyond the stops shown above. Intending passengers were exhorted to stand at the nearside of the road and give the driver ample warning. No passenger would be both picked up and set down at points within the city boundary.

Morris Commercial station bus 179 (DV 6853) is one of two bought to replace local carriers' buses on the Sidmouth and Budleigh Salterton services in 1930. 179 was the Sidmouth bus. (L.F.Folkard collection)

With the exception of the two Morris Commercial station buses, all vehicles new in 1930 were of Leyland manufacture. The first, which entered service in March and April, were fourteen Leyland 'Lion' LT1s, of which 146-151 had front-entrance body, and 152-159 almost identical, but with dual-entrance body. These LT1s and the very similar LT2 type which followed, eventually totalled 48 vehicles and were the mainstay of many routes until the end of 1936 when replaced by LT7 'Lions'. Next came ten 'Tiger' sun-saloon coaches (160-169) for the augmented 'Limited Stop' services. Described as the 'Rolls

Royce of the coaching world', the first six were of type TS2 and the remainder were the slightly shorter wheelbase TS3 model, seating 30 or 31. They were in the distinctive 'limited-stop' livery of dark brown with cream waistband, whereas the buses were turned out in red up to waist level and cream above. 160-169 had automatically opening roof, but were otherwise very similar to the 1929 'Tigers'. They entered service in April and May 1930. These 'sun-saloons' were registered and advertised as 'Sunloon Coaches', but hardly surprisingly this name did not find popular favour, and its use was quietly dropped after a couple of seasons.

The 'Tigers' were closely followed in May and June by six LT2 'Lions' (170-175) with dual-entrance bus body, and two (176-177) with front-entrance sun-saloon coach body for 'limited stop' services. All the foregoing had bodywork built by Hall Lewis.

During the summer of 1930, a 32-seat Daimler demonstration vehicle, registered locally as DV 5055, was on loan, but the Company was evidently not impressed, as no order resulted.

Towards the end of the year, delivery commenced of another twenty LT2 'Lions' similar to 170-175, which started a new numbering series from 1 upwards. However, only two entered service during 1930, but 1 to 13 were regarded as part of the Company's stock at the end of the year, even though some had not by then, even been bodied! Body builders were Park Royal, successors to Hall Lewis, that firm having failed financially.

The new vehicles were not without their problems, whereas the old AEC and Daimler types were prone to boil when going up hills, such as at Dawlish on route 2, (the driver having to fetch water). The new Leyland 'Lion' brakes would sometimes catch fire coming down the hills! Both old and new vehicles had to be started by crank handle, and four to six drivers on one handle trying to start an unwilling engine was a common sight in the mornings. A newly overhauled Daimler 'Y', with tight bearings, was particularly to be avoided!

The General Manager proposed a scheme to replace all old-type vehicles remaining in the fleet, with modern 'coaches' in 1931, and was given approval to spend up to £35,000.

The remaining AEC 'YC' and Daimler 'Y' types were nearly all withdrawn from service during 1930, just the two double-deckers and a few of the charabancs seeing a further season's use in 1931. Withdrawal of the 1925 Dennis saloons also commenced in 1930. Most of them needed major repairs, and the Company preferred to spend the money on new vehicles, so a further four Leyland 'Lion' LT2 buses were ordered. 139 vehicles were in stock at the end of the year.

A complete bus would sell for £70 or £80 at the time, or a body only for £10. A number of old chassis went to a dealer in London, who rebuilt them as lorries, and a firm called Punchard bought a number of old bodies and converted them to static caravans for use at Dawlish Warren and elsewhere. Eighteen are believed to have gone to the Landscove Holiday Camp at Brixham.

DEVON GENERAL OMNIBUS & TOURING CO. LTD.,
Salisbury Square House, Salisbury Square, London, EC4
Licences granted upon introduction of Road Service Licences in 1931

Ref. No:	Route
H	
418	Torquay Chudleigh
419	Exeter-Teignmouth-Newton Abbot-Torquay
420	Exeter-Tiverton-Sampford Peverell
421	Exeter-Ottery-Honiton-Dalwood-Seaton
422	Exeter-Ottery-Honiton-Kilmington-Axminster
423	Honiton-Fairmile-Talaton
424	Exeter-Topsham-Woodbury-Exmouth-Budleigh Salterton
425	Exeter-Clyst St. George-Exton-Exmouth-Orcombe Point
426	Exeter-Okehampton
427	Exeter-Sandford
428	Broadclyst-Exeter-Newton St. Cyres-Crediton
429	Sidmouth-Sidbury
430	Exmouth-Honiton
431	Torquay-Buckfastleigh
432	Torquay-Kingswear
433	Torquay-Shaldon
434	Newton Abbot-Widecombe
435	Torquay-Totnes
436	Torquay-Okehampton
437	Torquay-Bovey Tracey

438	Torquay-Stoke Gabriel
439	Exeter-Chagford
440	Exeter-Widecombe
441	Cullompton-Sidmouth
442	Cullompton-Seaton
443	Ottery St. Mary-Sidmouth
444	Exeter-Princetown
445	Exmouth-Budleigh Salterton
446	Exmouth-Otterton Village
447	Uffculme-Totnes
448	Cullompton-Exeter
449	Torquay-A38-Newton Abbot
450	Exeter-Moretonhampstead
451	Drewsteignton-Newton Abbot
452	Torquay Station-Babbacombe (replaced by H 1192)
453	Cadewell Lane-Meadfoot Beach
454	Strand-Chelston
455	Strand-Barton
456	Chelston-Barton
457	Torquay, Castle Circus-Watcombe
458	Highweek-Decoy-Sandygate
459	Newton Abbot-Denbury
460	Okehampton-Princetown
461	Sidmouth Station-Hotels
462	Budleigh Salterton Station-Hotels
463	Torquay-Plymouth
464	Torquay-Lyme Regis
465	Exeter-Plymouth
466	Exeter-Minehead
467	Exmouth-Lyme Regis
468	Torquay-Paignton (via) Totnes
469	Exmouth Station-Orcombe Point
470	Tiverton-Bolham Halt, County Show
471	Exeter-Bude
472	Exeter-Clovelly
473	Exeter-Lynton
474	Exeter-Cheddar
475	Circular, Exeter over Exmoor
476	Exeter-Ilfracombe
477	Torquay-Bournemouth (application withdrawn)
1191	Exeter-Panorama Tea Gardens, Stoke Hill
1192	see 452, which it replaced
1213	Tours from Exeter
1366	Tours from Exmouth
1367	Tours from Tiverton

FLEET CARS LTD.

1823	Tours from Paignton
1960	Tours from Torquay

All licences were for stage services, unless otherwise stated.

1931   The 1930 Road Traffic Act, which brought about control of route and vehicle licensing on a national basis, took effect in February. Timetables then became a lot more stable, and the basic 1931 structure was recognisable right up to 1975, when Western National renumbered the routes.

Public Service Vehicle licensing was carried out independently of Road Fund licensing, and each vehicle henceforth needed a PSV licence. At first, they carried oval white enamel plates on the rear of the vehicle, on which was a crown and a licence number beginning with the letter 'H', denoting Western Traffic Area. Drivers and conductors were also licensed on a national basis, and wore round licence badges lettered 'HH' followed by their number. Previously these licensing functions had been carried out by Local Authorities, not always on a uniform basis. The oval plates on the rear of the vehicles were done away with after 1938 - a PSV licence disc in the cab then sufficing.

Ten AEC 'Regals' were acquired in 1931 for use on the limited stop services inaugurated in 1928. 189 (DV 9337) is on the Exeter to Minehead service in the mid 1930s.   *(Roy Marshall)*

Devon General bought out the eight independent operators who had been running on the Paignton to Brixham service on 31st March 1931, being:

D. Prout, Churston   (Prout Cars - previously Jolly Roger Cars)
J. Mills, Brixham   (Blue Ensign Cars)
J. Geddes, Brixham   (Burton Cars)
J. Low, Paignton   (Dennis Cars)
S. Cooper, Paignton   (Dandy Cars)
Soul & Sanders (Paignton) Ltd., (Redcliffe Cars)
W. H. Dalton, Paignton   (Waverley Cars)
F. Slatter, Paignton   (Slavic Cars)

No vehicles were taken over by Devon General. J. Low became a Devon General driver, Geddes continued to run on the Brixham to Kingswear service, Dalton, Slatter and Cooper joined forces as 'Waverley Tours', while Prout continued to run his garage business. Various other operators had participated in the Paignton-Brixham service during the 1920s, and most possessed only one vehicle.

The new garage and workshops at Newton Road, Torquay were constructed during 1931 and brought into use from 24th September. It was designed to accommodate 140 vehicles, with docking facilities, engineering, body, and paint shops. (Offices along the front of the building did not come into full use until 1933). The depot at Westhill Avenue, Torquay (next door to the tram depot) was vacated in September.

The contract for building the new garage at Exmouth was placed with Messrs. Abels, and it too was ready for occupation in September. The old garage at New Street and the office at 15, Exeter Road, Exmouth were vacated on 24th September and sold to C. Picketts, a fish merchant, on 2nd December 1931.

Not as originally built, but a later picture showing the left and right office additions. The lack of trees along the roadside and on the railway embankment affords a fine view that the passage of time made impossible to repeat. (DGO&TC)

The Newton Road workshops in action. (DGO&TC)

Mr. R. T. Hill, previously with Enterprise & Silver Dawn Motors Ltd., of Scunthorpe, was appointed Traffic Manager, for the Torquay area.

A site at Moretonhampstead for parking of buses and construction of a garage for 10-12 vehicles was purchased from Mr. F. East on 20th May. It was situated in Court Street, on the opposite side of the road to the parking ground used hitherto. The tender of Hugh Mills & Son, Newton Abbot was accepted for the construction of the garage and completion was sought in 11 weeks. It never had its full complement of vehicles based there, but was used for undercover storage of coaches during the war years. In its early years, no duties were worked on Sundays.

From 12th August, a garage for one (later two) double-deck buses was rented from Messrs. Searle & Trewin in Mill Street, Crediton and these two buses worked on the Crediton to Exeter service.

Additional premises rented by the Company in 1931 were an office in Station Road, Budleigh Salterton and a mess-room in Bearnes Lane, Newton Abbot.

A new advertising agreement was signed with Griffiths & Millington Ltd.

The Company's first wayside bus shelters were built in 1931. There was a large shelter with inspector's office at Torquay (Strand) of wooden construction, with windows at the ends and a tiled roof. It was painted red and black. Smaller wooden shelters (painted green) were erected at Old Mill Road (Chelston) and at Milber, while at Lawes Bridge, Torquay, a plot of land was rented from Waycotts, a local house agent, on a 21-year lease. A wooden shelter was built there which always carried a large enamel 'Waycotts' advertisement, the ground rent paid to Waycotts being the same as that which Devon General charged them for the advertising right!

A system of queuing for passengers waiting to board buses was introduced in May at Castle Circus, and was later extended to the Strand and other busy stops. Prior to this there had been a free-for-all, the problem being particularly acute at Teignmouth on summer evenings with passengers waiting to return to Newton Abbot.

Shelter styles 1 - The large, mainly wooden, shelter at Torquay Strand which dated from 1931. It also incorporated an Inspectors' office, and survived until around 1970. *(DGO&TC)*

DEVON GENERAL

Shelter styles 2 - The wooden shelter at Milber, on the outskirts of Newton Abbot, with the houses of local yellow brick in Addison Road high on the bank at the rear. The shelter was painted dark green and carried a bus side Devon General fleet-name across the front. It dated from 1931 and had been in use up to contemporary times, being replaced by a more modern steel and glass unit. The concrete base survives to identify its exact location.   *(Wilson Gould)*

Most of the share capital of Devon General's parent company, the National Electric Construction Co. Ltd., (NECC) was acquired by the British Electric Traction Co. Ltd., (BET) in 1931, though the NEC Company continued to exist.

In November, it was resolved that long-service badges should be awarded to employees with five years service, and that 'a badge of distinction' should be awarded after ten years. The design was left in the hands of the General Manager.

A Leyland lorry, known as 'the covered wagon', which had been converted from ex-Chelston Car Co. bus No:98, had been doing a daily run between Torquay and Exeter with driver L. J. Potter, conveying stores and parcels. However, by June 1931 it sometimes came back from Exeter carrying as few as two small parcels, so it was decided to put the parcel traffic back on to the buses of route 2 as from July. At the same time, the maximum permitted weight of a parcel was reduced from 112lb to 56lb, though charges remained at the 1923 scale.

New vehicles purchased in 1931 were ten AEC 'Regal' limited-stop saloons (180-189) which had Park Royal bodywork incorporating a roof rack and an illuminated fleet-name above the front destination box. They had a front entrance with nearside emergency door, and the cream waistband was broader than previously. They had a single rear window with a sharply curved roof dome and lower panels that curved inwards correspondingly.

The remaining seven of the Leyland 'Lion' LT2s left over from 1930 were delivered (14-20), followed immediately by the four additional ones (21-24) that had been ordered in preference to overhauling the 1925 buses.

Later in the year came six LT3 type 'Lions' (25-30) in part exchange for the AEC and Daimler (1927 rebuild) charabuses (84-89). These 'Lions' differed by having the emergency door set in the centre of the back of the vehicle, with a small window on each side of it, setting the style for single-deckers of the 1932-5 period. Their front destination box was less angular than on previous deliveries, being shaped into the front roof dome, and they had deeper side panels.

A large number of Leyland 'Lions' of progressive types were bought in the early 1930s, and No:31 (OD 832) was the first of the type LT5 in 1931 (whereas the remainder came in 1932) with Park Royal body, taken at Exmouth.   *(L.F.Folkard collection)*

Finally, there was the prototype LT5 'Lion' (31) whose body was similar to 25-30 but the chassis could be distinguished by its fully-floating rear axle which had a larger hub than hitherto. All of the 1931 deliveries had been built by Park Royal.

The remaining AEC 'YC' and Daimler 'Y' charabancs were withdrawn in 1931 and the fleet assumed a fairly standardised character, few vehicles being more than five years old. The last of the old open-top double-deckers ran its final trips between Newton Abbot and Kingsteignton on a 20 minutes service for ten hours with driver H. Woodward. On the very last run there were no less than 123 passengers aboard! Veteran buses either had some great mysterious attraction or else there was a good film on in Newton Abbot!

Rolling stock authorised for 1932 envisaged at least 30 new vehicles, 20 to replace obsolete stock and ten for expansion, with some new coaches for Fleet Cars as well. Expenditure of £35,000 - £40,000 was sanctioned, but this programme was modified somewhat, as things turned out.

The principal route alteration during the year was the discontinuation from 21st September of the Torquay-Bournemouth service 52. The Traffic Commissioners had refused to grant a licence, and the Company decided not to appeal.

The summer only limited-stop service 42 (Exeter-Dartmeet-Princetown) was discontinued as such but remained operable under the licences for tours from Exeter, Exmouth and Tiverton which had been granted. (Tours from Torquay and Paignton were licensed to Fleet Cars). A new summer only 42 was introduced, Okehampton to Princetown via Chagford and Beetor Cross. Surprisingly, Moretonhampstead was avoided.

The timetable showed some journeys on service 10 (Exmouth-Sidmouth-Honiton) was extended from Sidmouth alternately to Beer and Seaton instead of Honiton.

The Stoke Gabriel service (54) was renumbered 18 from 7th June.

1932 The purchase of Grey Cars Ltd., from the Timpson family, together with A. Timpson & Sons' own local tours and private hire business in Torquay was considered in January, and agreement was reached between the parties on 1st March, following which Devon General purchased the assets of Grey Cars Ltd., and continued to run it as a separate company. Included in the purchase was the South Devon Motor Co. Ltd., (whose only assets were shares in Grey Cars Ltd.), and thus the fleet of 36 Grey Cars and their garage at Torwood Street, Torquay came under Devon General control. The agreement provided that, on completion, A. Timpson & Sons Ltd., would sign a deed of covenant under which they would undertake not to compete with Grey Cars for a period of five years, and that their own thirteen coaches in the area would then become the property of Grey Cars Ltd. This deed was duly signed in June. Mr. Mudge, previously Manager of Fleet Cars, became Traffic Manager of Fleet Cars and Grey Cars.

The Fleet Cars garage at Orient Road, Paignton was closed on 1st March 1932; their 21 Lancia coaches joined the Devon General buses at Newton Road depot, and parked in the corner of the garage at the Lawes Bridge end. This arrangement lasted for less than a year, as in 1933 they shared Torwood Street garage with their former rivals, the Grey Cars.

It was resolved on 6th December that the capital of Devon General would be increased by £130,000 to £300,000. This was to be financed by the issue of 60,000 - £1 preference shares, the railways to take up 50% of these and the Torquay Tramways Co. Ltd., to take up 50% of any shares not taken up by the public. Thirty-thousand ordinary shares would be issued at par to ordinary shareholders, and an additional 20,000 ordinary shares would be issued as a bonus by capitalisation of reserves, leaving £20,000 capital available for future issues.

The registered office of the Company had in April, moved from Salisbury Square House, London EC4 to 88 Kingsway, London WC2, and the first meeting of the Directors took place there on 20th April. The question of land purchase for a new depot at Exeter was given consideration. The Southern Railway had a piece of land available for sale near Paul Street, and it was left for Mr. Cownie, the Managing Director, to consider whether the Company should acquire it, or alternatively pursue the acquisition of a house and land in Haven Road. As things turned out, neither course was pursued. Mr. Cownie died suddenly on 4th December, and his place on the Board was filled by Mr. Sidney E. Garcke, a Director of British Electric Traction Ltd., who also became Managing Director of Devon General. Mr. D. Campbell, the General Manager, had purchased a villa on the Honiton Road in Exeter, so the Company sold his former residence at 1, Morley Road to a Mr. R. J. Hall.

Negotiations were started on 28th November regarding the possible acquisition of Milton's Services of Crediton, together with one Dennis 'Lancet' bus, however, it was to be a few more years before a deal was finalised.

The Company wished to extend service 13, Torquay to Shaldon, into Teignmouth across the new Shaldon Bridge. An agreement regarding tolls was reached with the Shaldon Bridge Company and signed on 20th December, following which the route was extended over the bridge and via Bitton Park Road, to terminate at Teignmouth (Triangle).

The Torquay to Plymouth bus service had run into a problem with Plymouth Corporation, which sought an agreement whereby they would take 50% of the fares of local passengers picked up within the city. A special meeting of the Devon General Directors resolved to complete the agreement, and it was further agreed between the parties and the Traffic Commissioners that Devon General could refuse to pick up local passengers on journeys outward from Plymouth. At Paignton, an attempt by W. A. Rogers (t/a The Paignton Bus Co.) to run a town circular service was successfully opposed by Devon General, who themselves introduced a new Paignton Circular service 44, Paignton Station-Maidenway Road-Upper Manor Road-Sea Front-Station (in both directions) to serve residential development in the hilly Maidenway Road area.

From 1st January, service 30 was extended from Torquay Station to Paignton Station. Torquay local service 31 was extended from Cadewell Lane along that road to Shiphay Village, where it terminated at Water Lane. Unlike Hele Village (qv), Shiphay was then really just a village, with narrow lanes and high hedges. The area became totally built-up just before and just after World War II.

31A had disappeared from the 1932 timetable, but reappeared in 1934. Service 5A from Exeter through Exmouth was diverted to Littleham instead of Orcombe Point, from 19th September. The latter was then served only in summer, by the joint route from Exmouth Station. The Exmouth-Lyme Regis service 55 was renumbered into the vacant 52.

The summer only 42, Okehampton-Princetown was re-routed via Moretonhampstead where a change of vehicle became necessary. In fact the journey was achieved by means of selected workings on the 16 and 23 routes.

Some journeys, generally alternate ones on services 1, 2, 11, 15, 16 and 17, were terminated at Newton Abbot (Market Square) instead of all running through to Torquay, connections being provided by a strengthened service on the 28.

DEVON GENERAL

Three AEC 'Regent' lowbridge type double-deckers were bought in 1932, and after a couple of years on the Torquay to Newton Abbot route, they became familiar on route 7 between Exeter and Crediton. (J.F.Higham)

Three AEC 'Regents' (190-192) with petrol engine and lowbridge-type Brush body were put to work on the 28. They sported a new livery of red lower panels with maroon (or possibly black) waistbands and cream top deck, window surrounds and roof. They were among the first vehicles in the fleet to carry die-stamped registration number plates, as previously most had been painted on.

Other additions to the fleet were three Leyland 'Cubs' (100-102) with 20-seat 'all-weather' body which had a canvas roof folded back between the front and rear roof dome. They were used on services over Dartmoor and Exmoor which were restricted to small vehicles.

Thirteen Leyland 'Lion' LT5s (32-44) having front-entrance bus body with rather wide doorway, replaced 1926/7 AEC and ADC buses on normal services, and these were followed by 45-52, rather similar vehicles but 'sun-saloons' with opening roof. These latter replaced a miscellany of vehicles which had been used on tours from Exeter and Exmouth, and carried another livery variation - red below waist level, with black waistband and roof, and cream window surrounds.

All the single-deck vehicles obtained in 1932 were built by Weymann of Addlestone, Surrey, the start of a long association with this firm.

Only a few vehicles were disposed of during 1932 and these included the two open-top double-deckers (71/ 72) and three of the 1926/7 AEC '506s' (77, 78 and 83).

At the end of the year, the fleet strength - not including Grey Cars or Fleet Cars stood at 160 vehicles.

Crews at this time were still not issued with full uniforms, but were just given brown dustcoats for summer and dark blue greatcoats for winter use, plus a uniform cap, with white top for use in summer. Some drivers wore breeches and gaiters, but in any event black shoes had to be worn. Any driver wearing brown shoes or a coloured shirt would be sent home, with a day's suspension and loss of pay. Rates of pay applicable at the time were:

Traffic staff

Drivers - Commencing rate-1/2d. per hour, experienced-1/2½d. per hour, 1/3d. per hour after five years service.

Conductors - Commencing rate 10d. per hour, 11d. per hour after six months service, 1/- per hour after twelve months service.

Traffic Inspectors - £3-15s-0d. per week.

Area Traffic Inspectors - £4-5s-0d. per week, £5-0s-0d. per week at important centres.

Clerical staff

£2-0s-0d. to £4-10s-0d. per week, according to service and ability.

Indoor Staff

Washers and cleaners 10d. per hour, 11d. per hour after six months service.

Semi-skilled labour - 1/- to 1/2d. per hour.

Special employment - 1/6d to 1/7d per hour.

1933

Since 1929, there had been much acrimonious discussion as to the future of the Torquay trams, and in 1930 the Tramways Company with the agreement of Torquay Borough Council had promoted a Parliamentary Bill to authorise the substitution of the trams by trolleybuses. The Council wished to defer their right of purchase of the undertaking until 1935 so that the expense of removing the tram track would fall on the Company.

The Bill came before a Select Committee of the House of Lords and was opposed by Devon County and Paignton Urban District Councils on points of detail only. The main opposition came from the newly-formed Torquay Citizens League, on the grounds that the Council's right of purchase of the tramway undertaking was being deferred without consulting the ratepayers. The League succeeded in influencing the Labour Party to oppose the Bill, and it was duly rejected. There was a feeling that the Parliamentary speakers against the Bill had little or no knowledge of the issues involved, and the rejection was nothing less than a thinly-veiled means of scoring a point off the then Torquay Member of Parliament, Commander Charles Williams, who at the time was the arch-obstructionist of the opposition party.

Be that as it may, the route network as envisaged would soon have become hopelessly inadequate in the light of development. The issue was revived in 1933 when the Torquay Tramways Co. Ltd., sought to promote another Parliamentary Bill to substitute trolleybuses. Western National objected to new routes proposed in the sea-front and St. Michael's areas of Paignton.

In March, Torquay Council conducted a postcard poll, and of 22,490 cards sent to households, 14,588 were returned - 64% poll. There was a large majority against trolleybuses, the votes being 2,988 for, and 11,196 against.

On the second question, as to whether the Council should purchase the tramways and continue their operation, the voting was 4,214 in favour and 9,935 against, with Western National and the railways strongly opposing. The Torquay Tramways Co. Ltd., then abandoned their attempt to obtain trolleybus powers, and instead, obtained Parliamentary powers to substitute motor-buses for its tram services, and thereafter to abandon the tramways. It was considered desirable that the substitute bus services should be merged with those of Devon General. Agreement in principle on these issues was obtained in July between the bus and tram companies and Torquay and Paignton Councils. One condition was the winding-up not only of the Torquay Tramways Co. Ltd., but also of Fleet Cars Ltd., and Grey Cars Ltd., so that all Devon General's services would be operated directly by the same company.

The Devon General Board meeting on 28th August approved the scheme under which the Company would operate the tram services with their buses, and a letter was sent to each of the Tramway Company's shareholders. It was agreed that the Torquay Tramways Co. Ltd., would sell the goodwill of its business to the Devon General Omnibus & Touring Co. Ltd., including the right to operate substitute bus services. Devon General would pay the Tramways Company £95,581 with which to pay off all debentures outstanding at 1st October 1933, and as further consideration to pay to the Tramways Company or its liquidator the sum of £75,000.

Completion of the transaction was to take place immediately the substitute motor-bus services commenced, Devon General to provide all necessary rolling stock, personnel and equipment with which to operate the services in accordance with the Tramway Company's obligations.

Devon General was to endeavour to employ such of the Tramways Company personnel as it might require. A condition was that the National Electric Construction Co. Ltd., would purchase the stocks, shares and securities of the Torquay Tramways Co. Ltd., and assume the obligations of the Tramways Co. as guarantors of 150,000 preference shares of £1 each in Devon General, and also on condition that Devon General obtained, before 31st March 1934, the necessary licences for the substitute bus services.

Twenty-four double-deck buses with AEC 'Regent' CI engine and 52-seat bodywork by Short Bros. were ordered to work the tram services.

Meanwhile, the General Manager Mr. D. Campbell was in poor health, and it was resolved by the Board on 12th July to appoint a new General Manager, with Mr. Campbell being retained in an advisory position until 1937. The job was offered to Mr. R. G. Porte, then Chief Engineer of Southdown Motor Services Ltd. He accepted, taking up duties on 1st October. He immediately had three major developments to oversee: the transfer of the Company's offices from Exeter to Torquay, the replacement of the Torquay tram services, and the absorption of the subsidiary companies 'Fleet Cars Ltd.,' and 'Grey Cars Ltd.'

On the Board, Mr. R. H. Nicholls resigned on 30th June and in his place the Great Western Railway nominated Mr. C. R. Dashwood (their Chief Accountant), who was appointed on 12th July.

In December, a further increase in Authorised Capital to £350,000 was sought, and an Extraordinary General Meeting called which passed the necessary resolution.

On 1st November, Devon General bought out its own subsidiary companies of Grey Cars Ltd., for £61,000 and Fleet Cars Ltd., for £820. The deal brought 70 coaches and charabancs into the Devon General fleet, 49 from Grey Cars and 21 from Fleet Cars. 32 vehicles were unfit for further service, all Lancias, but the remaining 38, consisting of eighteen AEC 'Mercurys', ten AEC 'Rangers' and ten Lancia coaches, continued to run tours from Torquay, Newton Abbot and Paignton. The previous fleet-names and liveries were retained, and the coaches were renumbered 301-333 (Grey Cars) and 334-338 (Fleet Cars) in the Devon General fleet.

The two-level garage at Torwood Street, Torquay, built in 1930 at the time when A. Timpson & Sons controlled Grey Cars Ltd., became Devon General property as did a small garage in Bridge Road, Torquay. Rented premises assigned from Fleet Cars Ltd., were the booking offices at 3, Fleet Street, Torquay and at 'Ruby Hutch', Belgrave Road, Torquay. Offices assigned from Grey Cars Ltd., were at 3, and 9, Vaughan Parade, Torquay; 3, Palk Street, Torquay; Chillingworth, Belgrave Road, Torquay; 3, and 20, Torbay Road, Paignton; 14, East Street, Newton Abbot, and a house 'Grasmere', in Lymington Road, Torquay. An office at 22, Portland Road, Babbacombe and a garage and premises at Sherwood, Belgrave Road, Torquay were surrendered in December.

The Paignton circular service 44 was, from 1st April, re-routed to run Paignton Station-Colley End Road-Blatchcombe Road-Maidenway Road (North and South)-Colley End Road-Paignton Station and vice versa, and from May was combined as the 18 to form a Stoke Gabriel-Paignton-Maidenway Road service. The Torquay to Paignton section of the 18, which was only a connection into the 12, was no longer timetabled.
Two new services started in May:

44,   Newton Abbot-Hennock (WSaO) and
51A,   Torquay (Strand)-Torbay Hospital (WSaSuO).

The former was primarily a market day route serving a village on the edge of Dartmoor, high above the Teign valley, and the latter service was mainly for the benefit of hospital visitors. The bus left Newton Road at Lawes Bridge, and proceeded up the private drive of the hospital to terminate on the forecourt.

The 'Limited Stop' services were henceforward referred to in the timetables as Express services.
Problems were being encountered at Budleigh Salterton, where there was public disquiet about the volume of bus traffic passing through the town. The Urban District Council objected to licence renewals, and the Traffic Commissioners placed restrictions and conditions on the operators. As from 1st May, vehicles from Exmouth were obliged to turn left at the bottom of West Hill into Station Road, thence into Upper Stoneborough Lane, and back into town via Fore Street Hill, New Road, Marine Parade, Fore Street, High Street, and West Hill. Main stopping places were designated as Public Hall (vehicles from Exmouth) or Rolle Hotel (vehicles to Exmouth), with the result that vehicles terminating at Budleigh Salterton had to run about 1½ miles empty between those two points in order to start their return journey.

New vehicles ordered and delivered in the early part of the year were eighteen more Leyland 'Lion' LT5 single-deckers (53-70) with Weymann body, of which eight (63-70) were 'Sun Saloons' though of a slightly different pattern from the previous year's delivery. The rest were normal service buses.

A diesel-engined demonstration bus ran between Torquay and Newton Abbot in October, and towards the end of the year, the first of the double-deckers that had been ordered for tramway replacement were delivered. They started driver-training after overhanging trees had been suitably trimmed, for which purpose Devon General used, and later bought, the Tramways Co's AEC 'B' tower wagon, for which they paid £5.0s.0d.

The AEC 'Regent' double-deckers were numbered 200-223, and introduced a simplified livery of red with cream waistband below the windows of each deck, with a black moulding between the two colours. Fleet numbers continued to appear in white on the dumb-irons at the front of the chassis, but the cast number-plate on the bonnet was done away with, and in its place the fleet-number was painted in small red numerals on the lower waistband by the passenger entrance, and just aft of the driver's door on the offside. The rest of the bus fleet received this livery on repainting, and it remained standard until the war years, although the style of lettering and numbering was changed in 1938/9.

Vehicles sold early in 1933 comprised eight AEC and ADC 506 single-deckers (73, 76, 79, 80, 82, 91, 96 and 97) and the two Albions (69 and 70) that had come from Babington in 1927. In November, the disposal of the remaining eight AEC and ADC 506s was approved (74, 75, 81, 90 and 92-95) together with the three Leyland 'Lion' PLSCs that had been obtained second-hand (99, 142 and 143). At the end of the year, the fleet total stood at 236 vehicles, which included 32 Lancias from Fleet Cars and Grey Cars which were out of use and destined to be sold early in 1934.

The Company's offices moved from Blackboy Road, Exeter to Newton Road, Torquay in October - the move being accomplished in a single weekend. Several members of clerical staff were relocated, and the Company gave them some assistance with regard to removal expenses. A staff canteen and recreation room was built alongside the depot at Newton Road. A social and benevolent club was based here (at one time known as the Devon General Provident and Recreation Club), and a wide variety of sporting and recreational activities was organised. Football and table tennis were especially popular and there was an annual football match against the City of Oxford Motor Services for the Cownie Cup. Teams were entered in local leagues, the table tennis teams were all named after various types of bus (DG Lions, Tigers, Regals, Regents, etc). Branches were formed at Exeter, Newton Abbot, Exmouth and Sidmouth. All were keen entrants in local carnivals, often having the use of a surplus bus or service vehicle as the base for a float. Every Christmas there would be a series of Dinner Dances, with a couple of busloads of Exeter staff coming down to join in Torquay functions and vice versa.

A quarterly magazine (inaugurated in 1932) was produced by the staff and subsidised by the Company. Entitled 'Magazine of Movement and Mirth - The Official Record of our Deeds and Misdeeds', its production team was Messrs. R. T. Hill, H. F. Wyatt, and N.W. Folkard with local correspondents. During 1933 it was noticed that each of the subjects of a 'Who's Who' published in three consecutive issues, all died shortly afterwards. This fact, together with some 'aggro' from a Fleet Cars driver who did not like being featured in its pages, caused the joint editors to decide to cease publication. A Staff News magazine resumed publication in 1947, and from 1950 until Western National took over and replaced it with its own house magazine, the editorship of the 'Staff News' was in the capable hands of Mr. W. Ham.

DEVON GENERAL OMNIBUS AND TOURING CO. LTD.

NEWTON ROAD TORQUAY

ASSOCIATED WITH:—
THE BRITISH ELECTRIC TRACTION CO. LTD.
AND
BRITISH RAILWAYS

TELEPHONE: TORQUAY 63226

REGISTERED OFFICE: 88 KINGSWAY LONDON W.C.2

YOUR REF...................................

OUR REF ....

....194......

Section 5. Grey Cars Ltd., and their predecessors, (1911-1933)

Several firms in Torquay had long operated moorland and coastal tours with horse-drawn charabancs, and in April 1911 the old-established firm of Grist purchased a 22-seat Commer charabanc. It was joined that July by a similar vehicle, and they operated not from Grist's stables in Hesketh Road but from a garage forming part of 3/5, Market Street (leased from the Torquay Market Co. Ltd.,) which had earlier been occupied by the vehicles of George Senior, one of the motor bus operators who ceased running when the Torquay trams were extended to Paignton.

In March 1913, Mr. R. H. Grist, together with local businessmen W. R. Cutchey (as Manager), Thos. Crossman, W. P. Harding, and W. Farrant Gilley, plus Mr. J. Page from the Isle of Man, formed a Company known as the South Devon Garage and Motor Touring Co. Ltd., and acquired the motor tours business, vehicles and premises of Grist. They purchased two more charabancs, a 24-seat Commer and a 30-seat Dennis, which soon became known as the 'Grey Torpedo Cars' because of their colour and shape. Like the earlier charabancs, they had panelled sides, with a door each side to each row of seats. This style of body remained in vogue until the middle 1920s, though the offside doors were not used after 1919 and became panelled over. All four charabancs were inspected and licensed by Torbay Council on 15th May 1913.

Ten AEC 'Rangers' delivered new to A. Timpson & Sons in 1931 became directly owned by Devon General in November 1933, and continued to operate in the Grey Cars livery. Another ten were bought during the 1930s. One of the first series is captured outside the Grey Cars booking office in Vaughan Parade, Torquay before the street became one-way in 1934.
(The late N. W. Folkard)

Premises at 3, Vaughan Parade on Torquay harbour-side were rented from Mrs. E. Hull from 25th March 1913, and this became the Company headquarters and starting point for tours. It was for a time known as 'Torpedo House', as was the booking office rented at 12, Torbay Road, Paignton. Apart from Market Street, a small garage was rented at Sherwood, Belgrave Road, in an area of good-class family hotels.

Two more 24-seat Commer charabancs were bought later in 1913, and they were joined in 1914 by a 28-seat Dennis. War was declared on 4th August 1914, and under an order made that October, some of the fleet was commandeered by the War Office. Nevertheless in June 1915 a 14-seat Daimler was added to the fleet. The company also undertook haulage, and some charabancs had an interchangeable lorry body. A number of small open touring cars was also operated, and in addition, the company operated a bus service between Paignton and Brixham in 1915/6 and 1920/1.

The licensed fleet in May 1916 consisted of six charabancs, with five drivers and three conductors. In August of that year a Government Order prohibited the use of petrol by charabancs and private cars, and tours did not resume until this was rescinded early in 1919.

The premises 4, Vaughan Parade (next to 'Torpedo House') were leased from Mrs. A. M. Macartney from 25th December 1917; ownership of both 3 and 4 was later acquired by the Borough of Torbay. No:3 Palk Street (at the rear of 3, Vaughan Parade) was leased from Mrs. E. Hull from 5th March 1919.

The fleet was re-stocked with vehicles of AEC (5), Daimler (2), and Dennis (1) manufacture, and during a railway strike, Grey Cars ran a service to Exeter, Bristol and London. The Company purchased Walnut Mews, Chelston on 20th December 1919 from Mr. R. H. Grist (one of the Directors) and at about the same time, a garage at the rear of Bath Terrace, Bridge Road, was purchased.

The service between Paignton (Torpedo House) and Brixham (Bolton Cross) resumed in 1920 with twelve trips each weekday, the tours programme included special excursions to Ilfracombe for 25/- (depart at 8.00am, back at 10.00pm), Clovelly at the same fare and times, and Lyme Regis stopping at Exeter and Sidmouth, for 21/-. The latter was an 8.30am to 9.30pm run. Tours ran in the winter as required, and there were popular evening runs daily, departing at 7.15pm for a fare of 2/6d. Each charabanc was manned by a driver and a courier.

Every morning departure made a stop at Lawes Bridge, where local photographer Mr. Pyne was in attendance and took a picture of the charabanc with its passengers, prints being available on return. This procedure had started in 1913 and lasted until about 1928 by which time the novelty value had worn off, so vast numbers of such pictures were taken and many prints survive today, with a lot of the original plate-glass negatives being in good hands. Unfortunately the photographer always took the vehicle exactly side-on, so usually managed to chop off the front, making positive vehicle identification impossible in most cases. Fleet numbers were carried from 1919, but their use had ceased by 1923.

Early in 1920, premises at 59/61, Market Street were acquired, part of which was eminently suitable for a charabanc garage. A Company known as Grey Cars Ltd., was incorporated on 17th May, with a share capital of £25,000 in £1 cumulative preference shares, and £35,000 in £1 ordinary shares. On the 18th June they announced that they had acquired the whole of the issued capital of the South Devon Garage and Motor Touring Co. Ltd., and invited applications for an issue of 26,500 shares, subscriptions closing on 30th June 1920. The Directors were those of the South Devon Garage and Motor Touring Co. Ltd., with the addition of Mr. S. H. Easterbrook, a local solicitor, and the objects were to continue trading with both companies under the same management and:

1   to increase the number of vehicles
2   to provide adequate garage and repair equipment
3   to provide garage accommodation and repair equipment for private cars
4   to provide car showrooms for the sale of private cars

Assets were listed as the fleet, new in 1919, and premises at:

61, Market Street	3, Palk Street
3/5, Market Street	Sherwood Garage, Belgrave Road
Royal Public Hall, 59, Market Street	Walnut Mews, Walnut Road
3/4, Vaughan Parade	Garage, rear of Bath Terrace, Bridge Road
12, Torbay Road, Paignton	

The new Company was certified as entitled to commence business on 28th August 1920, the Managing Director and General Manager being Mr. W. R. Cutchey. From that date, the motor car garage, sales and services were concentrated at 3, Market Street (later numbered 5) under the title 'South Devon Garages' and the charabancs of Grey Cars Ltd., became garaged at No:59, formerly a public hall and reached through an archway between the adjoining properties. By 1923, No:61 had been disposed of, and became a feed and grain merchants, and the cottages over the stables known as 'Walnut Mews' were also sold about this time, being tenanted until 1926, after which they were used in connection with a garage which was built adjoining the site.

Eleven more charabancs were bought during 1920/1, five being Daimlers, three AECs, and three Leylands. Fleet-name 'The Grey Cars' was adopted (all mention of Torpedos being quietly dropped) and this appeared on the side of the vehicles from 1921, with the lettering in white on a blue band, superimposed on a red globe, similar at first sight to the Martini advert!

The legal ownership of the fleet passed to Grey Cars Ltd., prior to the 1921 season.

Daimler charabanc No:9 was fitted with pneumatic tyres in 1921, with twin tyres on the rear axle in place of the single giants popular at the time. The rest of the Daimlers and the Leylands were so equipped in 1922. This of course gave a much smoother ride though there was no appreciable effect on petrol consumption, which was 6.75 miles per gallon on the Daimlers and 5.5 miles per gallon on the AECs and Leylands. At the end of 1921, the fleet consisted of six Daimlers, five AECs, three Leylands and one Dennis, four of the 1919/20 vehicles having been sold.

A garage and yard at Chillingworth, Belgrave Road was leased from 25th December 1921 from Mrs. M. and Miss. F. Pike.

A large variety of tours was operated from Torquay, ranging from half-day to three-day, with Dartmoor being the most popular day tour destination. The three-day tours went to Bournemouth and the New Forest, to North Devon and Bude, and to Penzance and Lands End. The Company planned an eight-day tour to Mid-Wales for 1922, but as far as is known, this never ran.

Grey Cars Ltd., rejected a take-over offer from Devon General in 1924, and in April 1925 themselves acquired the business and nine Lancia charabancs of A. Haigh ('White Heather') of Babbacombe, successor to G. G. Gullick who had been in the business since 1920. His office at 22, Portland Road, which occupied a corner site near the Downs, became the Babbacombe booking office for Grey Cars.

During the middle years of the 1920s, the fleet was gradually re-equipped with fifteen new Lancia charabancs, a popular make at the time, and one which was well suited to the Devon hills. All of the 1919-1921 fleet had been thus replaced by 1926. Grey Cars was the first firm in the country to operate the 'Pentaiota' model introduced in 1925, which could achieve 40mph even though the speed limit at the time was still just 12mph. In their later days, some drivers reckoned on a half-hour running time from the outskirts of Exeter to Torquay - an average of 45mph! The raising of the speed limit in 1927 enabled a greatly expanded tours programme to be offered, and an attractive illustrated guide book was produced.

Due to severe congestion caused by charabancs in the Strand and Fleet Street areas of Torquay in 1926, the local Council allocated stands, and Grey Cars was allocated eight spaces at Marine Square (opposite the Pavilion). In September 1927, Grey Cars Ltd., acquired the licences and one Lancia charabanc of W. J. Brockman of Erin Hall, Torquay. He was proprietor of a number of local hotels, including Roslin Hall, on the site of which the modern day Riviera Centre now stands, and had operated the charabanc since October 1922.

Six new 'Super Lancias' replaced six of the second-hand vehicles in 1928; they were 'all-weather' coaches, having fixed side-screens with drop windows, and an unusual seating arrangement having rows of four with side gangways.

To appreciate the next part of the history, it should be borne in mind that the old-established business of A. Timpson & Sons Ltd., of Hastings and Rushey Green, Catford, London SE6, appeared on the scene in 1928, and set about obtaining a foothold in Torquay, buying up two local tours businesses that had fallen on hard times. One of these was E. Green ('Cosy Cars') whose licences were transferred on 21st November 1928 with three charabancs, of which two were unserviceable, but what was more important was their stand in the prime position opposite the Pavilion which after some discussion, Torquay Council agreed to transfer. Timpson's then took a lease on an office nearby at 9, Vaughan Parade which was rented from the Council as from 25th December 1928.

The second business to be acquired was that of F. E. Hall ('Court Cars') together with four charabancs (one an 8-seater), their stand on the harbour side at Victoria Parade, and a small garage and office adjoining the Metropole Hotel in Belgrave Road. Hall's vehicles were in generally poor condition, and probably no more than two ever ran for Timpson's. To replace the unserviceable vehicles, Timpson's transferred two 18-seat Albions to Torquay in February 1929, and two Lancias from Hastings in April, followed by another in June. They leased a booking office at 3, Torbay Road, Paignton from 25th December 1929; this was owned by W. H. Hawke, and had previously been occupied by Reliance Cars.

A. Timpson & Sons Ltd., together with Keith & Boyle (London) Ltd., proprietors of Orange Luxury Coaches, made a working agreement for joint operation of a Torquay to London service (among others) commencing on 17th May 1929. It was announced that "The services of the largest London coaching houses will provide for a combined programme of coach services between London and all the coastal resorts from Yarmouth in the east to Torquay in the west." Included were the operator's existing services and some new ones, including those to Torquay. In July it was announced that Shamrock & Rambler of Bournemouth would also be involved but there is no further reference to them. In September it was agreed that the combined services would cease from the end of that month, when the two companies would operate separately.

Timpson's proposed to continue the daily service right through the winter, and published a leaflet giving the times of their services from 1st October 1929; however the winter service did not survive for very long.

In May 1929, it had been reported in the local press that a firm known as the London and Southern Counties Motor Services had gained control of Grey Cars Ltd., together with a number of other firms in the south and south-west. The report also stated that they had bought "an old City & South London tube station at Seymour Street, near Euston Station, for development as a coach station". (Seymour Street was later renamed Eversholt Street).

Not the least consideration in the acquisition of other operators' businesses was the licences and stands that went with the businesses, although the local Authority would not always agree to their transfer. Grey Cars Ltd., acquired the coach business of the Newton Abbot firm of A. C. Bulpin & Son ('Pride of the Moor') in June 1929, together with one Dennis coach and one Reo charabanc; the booking office at 14, East Street, Newton Abbot was leased by Mr. Bulpin to the South Devon Garage & Motor Touring Co. Ltd., from 24th June, but it was not possible to transfer the Hackney Carriage licences for the coaches until the Newton Abbot UDC met again in September. Drivers Allbrighton and Peach transferred to Grey Cars.

In September 1929 Grey Cars Ltd., was also granted the licences of the Hampton Motor Co. Ltd., of St. Marychurch, Torquay, which had traded as Hampton Cars but had gone into voluntary liquidation in November 1928. Grey Cars purchased their fleet of four charabancs.

Early in 1930, the Company Grey Cars Ltd., was reconstituted under the name of the South Devon Motor Co. Ltd; the stage was then set for Timpson's major acquisition, for on 6th February 1930 they gained control of the South Devon Garage & Motor Touring Co. Ltd., and of the South Devon Motor Co. Ltd.
The six Timpson family Directors of both companies were registered as Alexander (Snr), Alexander (Jnr), Samuel Henry, Douglas Arthur, Walter Leonard, and William Alfred, the last-named being Company Secretary. All were additionally Directors of A. Timpson & Sons Ltd., which continued to run coaches locally in its own right. At an Extraordinary General Meeting of the South Devon Garage & Motor Touring Co. Ltd., held at 175, Rushey Green, Catford on 25th March 1930, a resolution was passed that the name of this Company be changed to The Grey Cars Ltd. This was certified by the Registrar of Joint Stock Companies on 7th April 1930.

In May 1930, Timpson's took the tenancy of a booking kiosk at Torquay Town Hall car park for use in connection with the London service. Grey Cars Ltd., had applied for a licence to participate in the service, but drew objections. However, Timpson's had successfully applied for a licence in their own name, and simply hired vehicles from Grey Cars Ltd., as required, to assist with the service. Bulpin's old office at Newton Abbot also became an agency for the London service.

1930 was the last season in which Grey Cars tours started from the stands opposite the Pavilion. Timpson's had a large new garage built in Torwood Street ready for operation in 1931. It was on two levels, the entrance to the lower floor being at the rear in Torwood Gardens Road. This was somewhat constricted by reason of the large number of steel upright pillars, but had re-fuelling facilities and inspection pits. The top floor was unencumbered, and after an initial period as a garage for private cars, became the starting point for Grey Cars tours, though the facilities for passengers were virtually nil. They had to enter the garage by the same door as the coaches, and there was only a small waiting room, a small office, drivers room, and toilets. On the lower floor there was a mess-room and a glass fronted lean-to type room used for the production of advertising boards, posters and notices. The garage at 59, Market Street was sold, and by 1933 was occupied by the GPO for garaging its vehicles. The leased premises at 3/5, Market Street became occupied by a firm of motor agents known as South Devon Garages Ltd.

From 1930-2, the 'Silent Guide' system was tried; the principle of this was, instead of drivers announcing points of interest on route, passengers were invited to buy a 3d. booklet describing the tour, and the driver would turn a numbered indicator at the front of the coach to denote the page which referred to each point of interest. This did not prove too popular, particularly with drivers who had been brought up to 'tell the tale', and was soon dropped by Grey Cars, though Greenslades of Exeter used the Silent Guide for many more years. Grey Cars drivers' uniforms of the period were dark grey dust coats with high peaked caps reminiscent of those worn by German officers.

Early in 1930, Timpson's drafted some new AEC 'Mercury' coaches into the area and, from November, five were licensed to Grey Cars Ltd. Six more came in the following year, together with seven of the more powerful AEC 'Ranger type, all of which had bodies by Harrington. Timpson's themselves licensed seven 'Mercurys' and three 'Rangers' in Torquay. These were all normal-control coaches, with full-height sides, doors front and rear, half-drop windows with louvres, and fully retracting canvas wind-back roof. Some were used on Timpsons service to London in June and July 1931 (for which Grey Cars Ltd., became agents) as also were some of the Grey Cars 'Super Lancias' of 1928.

Negotiations took place early in 1932 which resulted in Devon General purchasing the assets and goodwill of Grey Cars Ltd., and of the South Devon Motor Co Ltd., from Timpsons. Completion was on 1st March 1932, and for the time being Grey Cars Ltd., continued to function as a separate Company. The new Board consisted of Messrs. W. B. Cownie, R. H.

GC 4843 and 4844 were two of the AEC 'Mercury' coaches acquired from Grey Cars Ltd., of Torquay in 1932, and in this view they are seen together at Widecombe.   *(East Pennine Transport Group)*

Nicholls, H. A. Short, F. E. Stanley, D. Campbell (Manager) and W. Denis Thomas (the local solicitor who had been very involved with coach companies since 1919). The Directors of South Devon Motor Co Ltd., were the first four of the above-named. Thus Fleet Cars and Grey Cars, who for so long had been in opposition to each other, found themselves working in co-operation as subsidiaries of the same parent company.

Under the terms of the 1930 Road Traffic Act, Grey Cars Ltd., held a licence to operate 36 vehicles on Excursions & Tours from Torquay, whilst Timpsons held licences for 13 vehicles on E & T from Paignton, Brixham and Newton Abbot.

The assets of Grey Cars Ltd., were the 36 coaches, the freehold garage at Torwood Street; a dwelling house 'Grasmere' in Lymington Road, Torquay; rented offices at 20, (formerly 12) Torbay Road, Paignton; 3/4, Vaughan Parade, Torquay and 3, Palk Street, Torquay; 22, Portland Road, Babbacombe; 14, East Street, Newton Abbot and a small rented garage at 'Chillingworth', Belgrave Road, Torquay.

The only assets of the South Devon Motor Co. Ltd., were shares in Grey Cars Ltd. Following completion, and in accordance with the terms of the agreement, A. Timpson & Sons Ltd., covenanted in June 1932 not to run local tours in the area for at least five years, and transferred all their assets in the area to Grey Cars Ltd. These consisted of thirteen coaches; rented offices at 9, Vaughan Parade, Torquay; 3, Torbay Road, Paignton; a small rented garage and office at the Metropole Hotel, Belgrave Road and a freehold garage at Bridge Road, Torquay which had earlier been owned by Grey Cars Ltd. The tours licences for the thirteen coaches were amended so that four were licensed to run from Newton Abbot and nine from Paignton.

Timpsons continued to run their long-distance coach service from London to Torquay daily in the summer, worked by AEC 'Regal' coaches from their London depot; this service terminated in the Lymington Road car park (behind Torquay Town Hall). The coach, in later years at least, refuelled and parked at Devon General's Newton Road depot.

Mr. W. B. Cownie, the Managing Director, died on 4th December 1932 and both Mr. R. H. Nicholls and Mr. D. Campbell resigned their Directorships on 19th October 1933; Mr. S. E. Garcke came on to the Board in place of Mr. Nicholls.

It was on 11th April 1933 that the Great Western Railway introduced its air service from Cardiff to Plymouth. This called at Haldon aerodrome, near Teignmouth, and a connection into Teignmouth and Torquay was provided by Grey Cars. The regular driver on this duty was F. C. Tall, who had been one of the original pre-first-world-war drivers. He and the majority of drivers by this time were only taken on seasonally. Two return flights a day were operated at first, but from 22nd May 1933 the service was extended to Birmingham and reduced to one flight a day each way, a six-seater Westland Wessex being hired from Imperial Airways. Grey Cars were only involved for the 1933 season up to the end of September. For the following year the service was provided by Railway Air Services Ltd., and coach connections to Teignmouth and Torquay ceased.

For the 1933 season, Fleet Cars coaches were garaged at Torwood Street along with Grey Cars, and the two firms were run as one operation. Considerable rationalisation was possible, and the older coaches of both firms, kept on the bottom floor, were seldom used, and some never ran again. It is recalled that, in a spare hour, one tidy-minded driver parked them all in numerical order!

On 1st November 1933, the assets of Grey Cars Ltd., together with those of Fleet Cars Ltd., were transferred to the Devon General Omnibus & Touring Co. Ltd., who thus became the direct owners of Torwood Street garage and the fleet of 28 AECs and 21 Lancias from Grey Cars, as well as 21 Lancias from Fleet Cars. Grey Cars Ltd., and Fleet Cars Ltd., were then wound up, as was the South Devon Motor Co. Ltd., which still existed on paper.

The story from here belongs to Devon General, but suffice it now to say that the Grey Cars livery and fleet-name were retained until 1936, then dropped, but re-introduced in 1945. After that, tours were run from Exeter, Exmouth and Tiverton as well as from Torquay, Paignton and Newton Abbot, and Grey Cars continued to grace the roads of the West Country until 1971, when Devon General's coaching operations became the responsibility of Greenslades Tours Ltd., at Exeter.

The name and livery of Grey Cars made a surprise and most welcome re-appearance in March 1987 when a group of four drivers acquired the Torquay area coach tour and hire business which had from 1983 been in the hands of Devon General Ltd., following various re-organisations. The four new Directors were Messrs. G. Foskett, D. Pratt, J. Facey and A. J. C. Durham. Six coaches were leased from Devon General Ltd., which continued to maintain them under agreement. However, due to lack of capital for fleet expansion, and the impending closure of the Devon General facilities at Torquay, the Company was sold to Nightingales Tours Ltd., who had also purchased the Greenslades Tours business from Devon General.

The two companies, Grey Cars Ltd., and Greenslades Tours Ltd., continued to trade independently, Grey Cars Ltd., being based in a compound on the Brunel Industrial Estate at Newton Abbot, with the operational headquarters at Belgrave Road, Torquay, while Greenslades Tours Ltd., were based at a garage on the Pinhoe Trading Estate, just outside Exeter.

Early in 1990, Nightingales Tours Ltd., sold their subsidiary Grey Cars Ltd., and a little later in the year sold off Greenslades Tours Ltd. Both companies were sold to Mr. Nigel Bruce-Robertson of Bristol, who became sole proprietor and who had, in the 1960s worked for Devon General and Grey Cars early in his career. He continued to trade the companies as separate entities, though with strong ties, and as the Grey Cars fleet was re-stocked, livery was altered to off-white and light grey with maroon relief - the fleet name appearing in script style in maroon. Considerable rationalisation in the Greenslades operation took place. Unfortunately the operations proved to be unviable, and both Grey Cars and Greenslades ceased trading in November 1990, the leased fleet reverting to Nightingales.

A rescue operation was mounted by Millman's, an old-established family firm based at Buckfastleigh, who had a large fleet including some very modern coaches, and they recommenced operation of Grey Cars in December 1990. For the first time, a double-decker bore the Grey Cars insignia; this was on a Bristol VR used on school contract work and a dedicated bus service to and from a local supermarket. Operation of Greenslades Tours was similarly revived under the auspices of Hookway's Tours of Meeth, near Okehampton.

Following the increase of the speed limit from 12mph to 30mph in 1927, the tours programme was also considerably increased and the following was then offered:

Day (and extended day) Tours
1.   Lydford Gorge via Princetown and Tavistock
2.   Princetown and Plymouth
3.   Salcombe, Slapton Sands and Dartmouth
4.   Princetown, Dartmeet and Holne Chase
5.   Exmouth and Budleigh Salterton

6.	Plymouth and Bigbury Bay
7.	Fingle Gorge via Teign Valley and Chagford
8.	Tintagel and Boscastle via Tavistock and Launceston
9.	Ilfracombe via Exeter and Barnstaple
10.	Minehead, Exe Valley and Exmoor
11.	Lynton and Lynmouth
12.	Clovelly and Westward Ho!
13.	Looe and Polperro
14.	Cheddar Gorge, Glastonbury and Wells
15.	Newquay
16.	Lands End and Penzance (two day tour)
16a.	Bournemouth

Afternoon Tours
17.	Buckland Beacon and Ashburton
18.	Haldon Moor, Dawlish and Teignmouth
18a.	Exeter, via Great Haldon and Teignmouth
19.	Haytor and the Moorland
20.	Widecombe-in-the-Moor and Becky Falls
21.	Widecombe-in-the-Moor and Buckland Woods
22.	Lustleigh Cleave, via Chudleigh Rocks
22a.	Lustleigh and Teign Valleys
23.	Becky Falls and Haytor Rocks
24.	Slapton Sands and Dartmouth
25.	The River Dart (by charabanc and steamer)
26.	Buckfast Abbey

Morning and Evening Runs
27.	Coombe Cellars, on the River Teign
28.	Berry Head, via Brixham
29.	Milber Downs and Cockington
30.	Berry Pomeroy Castle and Totnes
31.	Dartmouth Ferry, via Churston
32.	Sightseeing Drive in and around Torquay
32a.	Sightseeing Drive, including Kents Cavern
33.	Compton Castle and Marldon
34.	Stoke Gabriel
35.	Dittisham Ferry
36.	Coombe Cellars and Labrador
37.	Milber Downs
38.	Brixham, via Churston
39.	Staverton
40.	Haldon Moor and Teignmouth
41.	Bradley Woods

No tours ran on Sunday mornings. By 1930, tours 6, 17, 29, 32a and 36 to 41 no longer appeared on the programme, though some were still operated as evening runs which were simply described as 'to selected places of interest'. New tours by 1930 were:

All-day tours
| 12a. | Clovelly and Bude |
| 23a. | Circular tour of Dartmoor with River Dart |

Afternoon tours
4a.	Princetown, Dartmeet and Holne Chase
7a.	Fingle Gorge, via Lustleigh Valley and Teign Valley
17a.	Buckland Beacon and Holne Chase

The programme was revised in 1931 and the Company produced a route book for its drivers with rules and regulations laying down the routes, timings and mileages of its tours and 'feeder routes' (ie. pick-up coaches). The tours with route numbers as then described, were:

1.	Lands End and Penzance (two day tour)	285 miles
2.	Cheddar, Wells and Glastonbury	188 miles
3.	Lynton & Minehead	174 miles
4.	Falmouth & Fowey	200 miles
5.	Newquay	176 miles
6.	Bournemouth	210 miles
7.	Clovelly & Westward Ho!	152 miles
7a.	Clovelly & Bude	161 miles
8.	Lynton & Lynmouth	162 miles
9.	Bude, Boscastle & Tintagel	155 miles
10.	Ilfracombe	159 miles
11.	Minehead & Exmoor	135 miles
12.	Weymouth & Lyme Regis	170 miles
13.	Looe & Polperro	128 miles
14.	Lydford Gorge	90 miles
15.	Princetown & Plymouth	85 miles
16.	Princetown & Dartmeet morning/afternoon	65 miles
16a.	Princetown & Dartmeet afternoon/evening	65 miles
17.	Salcombe & Slapton Sands	65 miles
18.	Fingle Gorge & Chagford	60 miles
18a.	Fingle Gorge	55 miles
19.	Exmouth & Budleigh Salterton	70 miles
20.	Widecombe & Becky Falls	40 miles
21.	Widecombe & Buckland Woods	40 miles
22.	Slapton Sands & Dartmouth	50 miles
23.	Lustleigh Valley & Teign Valley via Steps Bridge	45 miles
24.	Buckland Beacon & Holne Chase	42 miles
25.	Becky Falls & Haytor	39 miles
26.	River Dart via Totnes	32 miles
26a.	River Dart via Kingswear	32 miles
27.	Exeter & Haldon	48 miles
28.	Haldon Moor, Dawlish & Teignmouth	38 miles
29.	Haytor Rock	33 miles
30.	Lustleigh Cleave	34 miles
31.	Buckfast Abbey	34 miles
32.	Mystery Tour (route to be chosen) from:	
	Staverton & Totnes	30 miles
	Coombe Cellars via Haldon	30 miles
	Brixham & Kingswear (for Dartmouth ferry)	28 miles
	Lustleigh	33 miles
	Chudleigh Rocks	30 miles
	Stoke Gabriel & Compton Castle	26 miles
33.	Coombe Cellars	18 miles
34.	Coombe Cellars & Milber Downs	20 miles
35.	Berry Head via Brixham	20 miles
36.	Berry Pomeroy Castle & Totnes	19 miles
37.	Sightseeing Drive	14 miles
	(coaches over 20 seats could not proceed via Marine Drive)	
38.	Stoke Gabriel	16 miles
39.	Dittisham Ferry	16 miles
40.	Dartmouth Ferry via Brixham	25 miles

New tours introduced for the 1932 season were:

Whole day tours (afternoons on Sundays):
Belstone Tor, Spinsters Rock and Bradmere Pool, Bigbury-on-sea and Dartmouth

Afternoon tour:	**Morning tours:**
Belvedere Tower, Teign Valley & Haldon Moor	Shaldon Brixham

Section 6. Fleet Cars Ltd., (1919-1933)

Fleet Cars Ltd., was founded in 1919 Capt. C. Norman Hutt, of 21, Walnut Road, Torquay. It was at first known as the 'ex-Service Co.' as manager and staff were ex-HM Forces. The charabancs, originally in a primrose colour, were referred to as 'Capt. Hutt's Yellow Perils!'

The registered office was at Bank Chambers, Torquay, which was the address of local solicitor Mr. W. Denis Thomas, who was a Director of Fleet Cars and also of Teign Cars (Teignmouth) and Devon Cars (Paignton and Dartmouth) all of whom had the same registered office.

Licences were granted for the operation of two 28-seat Dennis charabancs, and tours commenced on 21st July 1919, each of the vehicles working a day tour and an evening run. The starting point was an office under the former New Zealand Club off the Strand, the address being 3, Fleet Street, hence the name Fleet Cars. This was the Company's main trading office throughout its existence, the premises being rented from G. B. Oaks. Part of the offices was sub-leased to C. E. Riding (Accountant) from 18th June 1920 to 9th April 1931.

Licences for six more charabancs were granted in December 1919, but not all of these were taken up. Four 28-seat Dennis vehicles were operated for the 1920-2 seasons, and could alternatively be fitted with lorry bodies if required. One charabanc was badly damaged in an accident on 25th August 1920 (driver E. Head) when it was in collision with a Plymouth Co-op steam lorry on the Plymouth to Yelverton Road near Crownhill; the lorry had allegedly come out of a side road without stopping. The charabanc sustained nearside damage, but there were no serious injuries, and the vehicle was returned to service following repair.

A new 18-seat Lancia charabanc was purchased in May 1923; livery was by then dark maroon all over.

Agreement was reached during November 1924 that the Devon General Omnibus & Touring Co. Ltd., would purchase the whole of the assets and the goodwill of the Company. A Board meeting was held on 1st December at which the Directors, Messrs. J. Page Moore, C. J. Dimond, F. Dobson, R. Lorimer and W. Denis Thomas all resigned, with Messrs. H. T. Barnett and W. B. Cownie of the Devon General Board elected in their place, to be joined by the re-elected Mr. W. Denis Thomas.

All Devon General's touring interests in the Torquay and Paignton area subsequently ran under the name of Fleet Cars Ltd. The five charabancs, by then fitted with pneumatic tyres, were given fleet numbers 76-80, and a number of Devon General drivers transferred to the touring company. A fleet of ten Lancia coaches was ordered for delivery in 1925 and these were closely followed by five more. The original five charabancs were then transferred to the Devon General fleet.

Preston Garage in Orient Road, Paignton was purchased by Devon General in May 1925 to house the Fleet Cars vehicles, and it was extended in 1926. It was close to the Preston tram depot, and had previously housed A. K. Gully's Primrose Cars, which had ceased trading after getting into financial difficulties.

One new coach was purchased in 1926, and five new 'Super Lancias' of a more powerful design were introduced in 1927. These were 'all weather' coaches, having fixed side screens with a retractable canvas roof.

Devon General advertised the Fleet Cars in their timetable as having a modern and up-to-date fleet - all cars alike, four-wheel brakes, adjustable transparent side-screens, armchair seats, rugs, etc. All cars had centre gangways at a time when most other operators locally were still running charabancs, but in reality they were not really all alike - however this was well before the days of the Trades Descriptions Act!

It was a sore point with the Fleet Cars staff that the Torquay trams, run by a company connected with Fleet Cars and Devon General, advertised the Grey Cars which at that time were Fleet Cars principal rivals. Despite representations, the trams continued to advertise the opposition coaches, though Fleet Cars adverts did get put on to local buses.

Routine maintenance of the fleet was carried out at Orient Road, but for major work, the coaches were sent to Devon General which carried out the work at its St. Marychurch depot.

Devon General also administered the wages of the staff - drivers received from £3. 0s. 0d. to £3.10s. 0d. per week, and supplied most of the summer drivers from among selected busmen. Drivers W. G. H. Hodge and W. Hannaford were on Fleet Cars all the year round, three more coming on at Easter, and the rest were from June to September. Coaches were licensed on the same basis, which still held good, well into the post-war years on Devon General's touring side, which by then was run under the Grey Cars name. The General Manager, in common with Devon General, was Mr. D. Campbell but the everyday running of Fleet Cars was in the hands of a Traffic Manager, Mr. Mudge. The Managing Director, again common to Devon General, was Mr. W. B. Cownie.

Coach driving in those days was something of a 'glamour' profession, and several of the drivers had their regular followers - ladies who would find out which tours their favourites were due to work, and then book seat number one (next to the driver) for several days ahead! Bookings were taken up to about a week in advance, a seating plan being maintained for each coach for each trip - sometimes three in one day. It was thus an advantage for each coach to be of the same layout. As well as the booking clerks, the 'tout' was an important member of the staff - immaculate in long white dustcoat and uniform cap, he would stand outside the office and engage passers-by in polite conversation, extolling the virtues of the tours and encouraging them to travel (having regard to which tours were lightly booked!).

There was quite a number of coach operators in the Strand and Fleet Street areas of Torquay in the 1920s, each with offices, touts, and a row of pictorial boards outside their own office to advertise the tours currently on offer.

Fleet Cars Ltd., published their first guide book in 1926, price 3d. which contained an illustrated description of all tours.

Tours operated by Fleet Cars Ltd., in 1927 were as follows:

Extended Tours:

Tintagel and Boscastle	(MWF)	Fare	15/-
Lynton and Lynmouth	(MWF)		15/-
Looe and Polperro	(MTThSa)		12/6d.
Ilfracombe and Bray Valley	(TuF)		15/-
Clovelly & Westward Ho!	(TuSu)		15/-
2-day tour to Penzance & Lands End	(W)		35/-
Cheddar Gorge, Glastonbury & Wells	(W)		20/-
Bournemouth	(Th)		17/6d.
Newquay	(Th)		18/6d.
Minehead & Exmoor	(Th)		12/6d.
Lyme Regis & Sidmouth	(Th)		12/6d.
Clovelly & Bude	(F)		15/-

Most of these tours were of 12 hours duration, 9.00am to 9.00pm. Fares in most cases went up by 1/- in 1928. It would not have been possible to run such an ambitious programme prior to 1927 with the speed limit at 12mph. Shorter tours operated by Fleet Cars were:

Day Tours: (10.00am to 6.00pm approx.)
Teign and Lustleigh Valleys
Grimspound Hut Circles
Drewsteignton & Fingle Gorge
Dartmoor & Holne Chase
Dunkery Beacon
Princetown & Dartmeet
Slapton Sands & Bigbury
Belstone Tor
Salcombe & Slapton Sands
Princetown & Plymouth
Becky Falls & Lydford Gorge

Morning and Evening runs:
Dittisham Ferry
Teign Valley & Moretonhampstead
Torquay Sightseeing
Stoke Gabriel & Paignton
Milber Downs & Babbacombe
Compton Castle & Marldon
Shaldon & Coombe Cellars

(Morning and Evening runs)
Denbury Green & Abbotskerswell
Labrador & Shaldon
Berry Head & Goodrington
Berry Pomeroy & Torbay
Bishopsteignton & Little Haldon
Totnes & Paignton
Teignmouth & Shaldon
Stover Park & Bickington
Chudleigh Rocks & Stover Park
Lustleigh Cleave

Afternoon runs:
Haytor & Widecombe
Haytor Rocks
Becky Falls & Haytor Rocks
Dartmouth
Buckfast Abbey & Totnes
Slapton Sands & Dartmouth
River Dart (charabanc and steamer)
Belvedere Tower
Buckland Beacon & Woods
Widecombe-in-the-Moor

New or special tours could, before 1930, be put on without formality, and one rather off-beat excursion was Haytor Rocks to see the eclipse of the sun which was due to take place at 6.30am, and the staff booked on at 4.30am and sent out five full coaches. They all had a magnificent view of the eclipse from Haytor, but those who stayed at home and watched it from the higher parts of Torquay saw it just as well! That took place on 29th June 1927.

Foreman at Orient Road was Mr. Ernie Knowles, who also drove one of the coaches. He was a Londoner, and had been a driver and conductor on the Torquay trams from 1908, leaving the Company for a while but returning to drive their buses. He transferred to Fleet Cars on their acquisition by Devon General.

On 1st January 1926, the business of Comfy Cars, Paignton was bought out, together with their fleet of five Lancia charabancs and a Buick touring car from Mr. W. P. Tucker who had previously run Comfy Cars in partnership with Mr. W. Langbridge. The lease of a booking office at 1, Torbay Road, Paignton was also transferred, but their garage at Polsham Road did not become the property of Fleet Cars. Among the equipment transferred, was one top cover for a Lancia charabanc. The Comfy Cars livery was white and black, and they continued to run with their old name and livery during 1926 and 1927. One of the Lancias was transferred into the Devon General fleet in 1926, and three more in 1927 following delivery of new vehicles to Fleet Cars. The other Lancia and the 8-seater Buick were repainted into Fleet Cars livery. The latter was used as a general purpose vehicle; apart from tours, its duties included transporting the General Manager, and surveying the routes of new tours. It ran for a few seasons with Fleet Cars, its regular drivers being Messrs. Whatman and Slocombe.

Comfy Cars had, in 1924/5, participated in the Paignton-Brixham service along with Devon General and ten small operators, but the 1926 application from Fleet Cars Ltd., as the new proprietors of Comfy Cars, was turned down by Paignton UDC An appeal against this decision was heard at Paignton Town Hall on 2nd November 1926, but the original decision was upheld. Comfy Cars had also participated in a service to Plymouth, but this licence and one Lancia were transferred to Hendra of Totnes.

Apart from Fleet Street and Torbay Road (the ex-Comfy Cars office), Fleet Cars had booking offices at Reddenhill Road Post Office, Babbacombe (rented from W. J. Coysh from February 1926); the Devon General office at 4, The Triangle, Dartmouth Road, Paignton (from May 1926 until October 1928 when it moved to 10a, Torquay Road) and 'Ruby Hutch', Belgrave Road, Torquay (rented from Messrs. Lamboll & Ingham, the proprietors of Ruby Cars, from March 1927). Pick-up coaches served all these points, and brought booked passengers to join their tours at Fleet Street, except in cases where the route of the tour took it past the booking office.

In the early days, many hotels and boarding houses had books of tickets for sale to their guests, and coaches would pick up and set down at the door, as required. With a number of coach firms all doing this, the situation soon got out of hand, and the local Councils made regulations prohibiting picking-up and setting-down except at recognised booking offices.

Following problems with congestion caused by coaches in the Strand and the lower part of Fleet Street, Torquay Borough Council, under its Motor Coach Regulations of the 18th August 1926, allocated 36 spaces to local operators for standing coaches in the Strand area. Fleet Cars were allotted eight spaces in Higher Terrace, which lay behind their Fleet Street office, albeit at a higher level.

Oil consumption by the Lancias gave cause for concern in 1927/8, new pistons being fitted to no avail. Finally, two fitters were sent from Italy with new un-machined pistons. These were of cast iron and were first hammered into the bores, and then being withdrawn, rings fitted and re-assembled. This cured the problem of excessive oil consumption.

On 30th April 1928, Fleet Cars Ltd., bought out one of their competitors, G. G. Gullick (t/a 'Heather Tours') of Paignton, the deal bringing with it two one-year old Lancia charabancs and the lease of a single-storey lock-up booking office at 5c, Fleet Street, Torquay, almost next door to Fleet Cars. This office was immediately re-let by Fleet Cars to Mr. H. B. Jaffa from 6th June for use as a novelty shop under the title of 'New Inventions Depot'.

Fleet Cars ran the two charabancs for the early part of the 1928 season at artificially low fares, and in their old livery in a move to draw trade from the opposition, but Torquay Council would not agree to transfer the Heather Tours stands at Victoria Parade to Fleet Cars, so in July the two charabancs were transferred to the Devon General fleet. Heather Tours also had a booking office at Parkside, Paignton but this was not transferred to Fleet Cars.

During 1929, 1930 and 1931, Fleet cars continued very much as before. A shop forming part of their
Belgrave Road premises was, from 24th March 1930, leased to W. H. Bathe who sold films and photographic equipment.

The fleet which consisted mainly of 1925 Lancias, was ageing somewhat; the portable celluloid side-screens had become cracked and discoloured, and the canvas roofs were proving to be an embarrassment. To erect the roof, side sticks had to be inserted into sockets on the side of the coaches and the roof canvas pulled over them. This was really a two-man job, with one each side of the coach it was fairly straightforward, but there were however, occasions when the driver had to struggle with it on his own. Driver Len Worrall recalled the time when he was caught in a rain storm on Dartmoor and all his passengers were nuns and small children. He was unable to manipulate the roof over the sticks on his own, so simply pulled the roof canvas over the passengers heads, and they huddled underneath it until the rain stopped!

An establishment named Kingshurst, with a number of permanent elderly residents, was a regular hirer of Fleet Cars. The open coaches had caused the old folks to receive so many soakings that they threatened to take their custom elsewhere if Fleet Cars could not provide an enclosed saloon coach. In response, the Company had one coach re-bodied by Weymann in 1932 with a saloon body. The resultant vehicle was known as 'The Hearse' because it looked just like one!

Fleet Cars was licensed under the Road Traffic Act to operate seven vehicles from Paignton and fourteen from Torquay in 1932, and the authorisation to operate from Newton Abbot was added to both licences.

Each Fleet Car driver was allocated his 'own' coach, and the list of coaches and drivers for 1932, the last season in which the complete fleet was still running, was as follows:

1	L. W. Dolbear	12	L. Lewis
2	L. P. Hallett	13	E. Know
3	W. C. Cole	14	W. Palfrey
4	A. T. Hall	15	R. Hudson
5	F. Hayman	16	S. Bickford
6	L. J. Worrall	17	C. Northway
7	S. Steed	18	C. Luxton
8	J. Aston	19	W. A. Hannaford
9	R. Beer	20	W. G. H. Hodge
10	E. Jones	21	E. Cowling
11	C. Dyer		Relief Drivers were R. Scagell and A. Head
12	L. Lewis		
13	E. Knowles		

Car number 19 was something of a 'black sheep', prone to breaking down, and driver Bill Hannaford developed a flair as a booking clerk during its spells off the road.

Fleet Cars depot at Orient Road, Paignton closed on 1st March 1932 and the coaches were, for a while, garaged at the new Devon General depot at Newton Road, Torquay, where they occupied the corner nearest the road at the Lawes Bridge end.

Following Devon General's purchase of Grey Cars Ltd., from the Timpson family in 1932, the former arch-rivals, Fleet Cars and Grey Cars, found themselves both under the same ownership as subsidiary companies. Mr. Mudge, the Fleet Cars manager, was appointed Traffic Manager of Grey Cars and Fleet Cars. The Managing Director, Mr. Cownie, died on 4th December 1932 and his place on the Board was taken by Mr. F. E. Stanley.

For the 1933 season both fleets worked from the Torwood Street garage of Grey Cars and the older Fleet Cars were not all licensed, those that were, only being used on jobs such as Sunday School outings and private hire. The older Grey Cars Lancias, being charabancs, were hardly used at all and no more than five were licensed. Most of the Fleet Cars drivers were given AEC 'Mercurys' to drive but these were less powerful than the 'Rangers' which the Grey Cars men kept for themselves. It was not to be until 1936 that most of the ex-Fleet Cars men got their hands on a new coach.

The assets of Fleet Cars Ltd., were transferred to the Devon General Omnibus & Touring Co. Ltd., as from 1st November 1933, along with those of its former competitor Grey Cars Ltd. The five 'all weather' Lancias became Nos. 334 to 338 in the Devon General fleet, but kept their old livery and only ran for one more season. The sixteen older Lancias, dating from 1925/6, were never used again and were sold early in 1934. Mr. W. Denis Thomas resigned his Directorship on 28th February 1934, after which the company was wound up.

Twenty-four new AEC 'Regent' double-deckers with oil engine (nowadays called diesels) and bodied by Short Bros. replaced the Torquay trams in January 1934. 201 (OD 7488) is seen on Torquay sea front bound for Paignton.   *(K. J. Brown collection)*

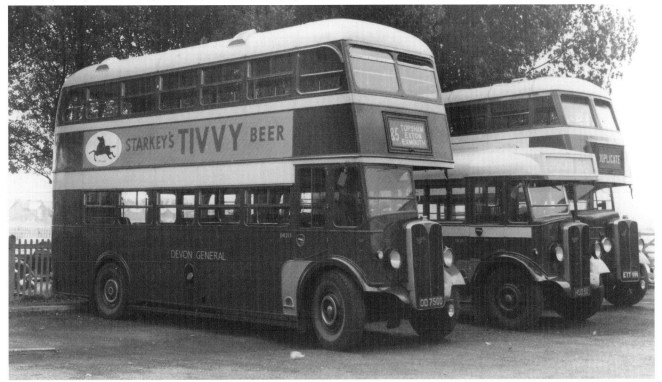

AEC Regent DR213, Regal SR511 and Regent DR238 languish on a dull spring day in the yard at Exmouth depot.

(K. J. Brown collection)

1934   Devon General put its twenty-four new AEC 'Regents' to work in Torquay, mainly on the former tram routes. The Torquay to Paignton route was the first to close, on 7th January, and the first bus next day on route 12A, as it became, was 201, in the charge of driver G. T. Crispin, who had been training tram drivers to drive buses. He had never worked on the trams, but a lot of tramway men did come over to the buses though some of the older men took the opportunity to retire. Among the latter was Mr. Charles Pugh, who had driven the first tram, back in 1907, as well as the last. Interviewed by the local press many years later, at the age of 92, still sporting his tram drivers' handlebar moustache, he commented - "Buses? I hate them! "

The reason for converting the Paignton route first was to facilitate road widening in Torbay Road (Torquay sea front), which the Council needed to complete in time for the summer season and not to exceed the grant-earning period of the works. The remaining tram routes closed on 31st January and were replaced by the following bus routes:

28A,   Shiphay Lane-Torre Station-Strand-Beacon Quay
54,   Shiphay Lane-Torre Station-Upton-St. Marychurch Town Hall
55A,   Circular Route via Wellswood
55B,   Circular Route via Ellacombe

These were identical to the tram routes, except that from Torre Station to Shiphay Lane (top) was a new extension, with an intermediate stop at Shiphay Bridge,. The opportunity was taken to introduce a one-way system so that traffic was no longer able to proceed from the Strand direct into Fleet Street, but had to proceed via Vaughan Parade, Vaughan Road, Cary Parade, and Abbey Place. To suit these requirements, buses from Paignton and Brixham (routes 12 and 12A) were then terminated at Marine Road (just opposite the Pavilion theatre) instead of at Cary Parade, which after that was only used as a terminus on two days each year when the Regatta Fair occupied the Strand.

The routes remained unchanged for many years, the last one to run in its original form being the 55A.

Another major route on which the 'Regents' were put to work was the 28, Torquay (Strand)-Kingskerswell-Newton Abbot. On their first day on this service, each one carried a fitter and a spare can of diesel fuel! Certain journeys connected at Newton Abbot with buses bound for Chudleigh (route 1) or Teignmouth (route 2). These workings on the 28 carried the destination 28 1/Chudleigh, 2/Teignmouth, though the '1/2' was soon painted-out and the rest remained on the blinds as a masterpiece of ambiguity for a long time after.

Some fares on the Torquay services were reduced in July 1934, and Sunday services were strengthened.

Pursuant to the Companies Act of 1929, a special resolution at an Extraordinary General Meeting held on 26th February passed new Articles of Association in substitution of previous articles, and these were set out in a document comprising 140 sections.

From 1st July, the Company was admitted to membership of the British Electrical Federation Ltd., which provided services including secretarial, accounting, registry of shareholders, bulk buying of stores, tyres and fuel, insurance, rating, statistical, and advertising. Scale charges or percentage commission were payable. The British Electrical Federation nominated Mr. F. B. Low as Secretary and Mr. H. W. Davis as Accountant to the Company.

Mr. D. S. McBright resigned his Directorship on 1st May, and Mr. H.A. Short, Road Transport Liaison Officer of the Southern Railway, was appointed to take his place. Hr. H. A. Nisbett, who had once been the Torquay Tramways manager, resigned his Directorship on 31st December and was succeeded by the appointment next day of Mr. P. M. Rossdale, a Director of British Electric Traction Ltd. The Chief Engineer, Mr. H E. Waghorn, resigned with effect from 31st March, and the post was not immediately filled; Mr. F. W Kerr was, from 1st November, appointed Mechanical Superintendent.

Various surplus properties were disposed of during 1934:

A small garage at Bridge Road, Torquay (ex-Timpsons and Grey Cars) was sold to W. E. Reed; a house 'Grasmere' at the junction of Lymington Road and Parkfield Road was sold to the Borough of Torquay who demolished it and the ex-Babingtons house and garage at the rear of 34/36, West Street, Ashburton were sold. Orient Road garage at Paignton was sold by auction on 25th July to R. G and C. C. Rees. In addition, Devon General and the liquidators of the Torquay Tramways Co. Ltd., jointly negotiated for the sale of the St. Marychurch premises, consisting of bus and tram depots with office block. Various leased properties were also surrendered:

9, Vaughan Parade, Torquay (ex-Grey Cars, previously Timpsons) to the Borough of Torquay
3, Torbay Road, Paignton to W. H. Hawke
14, East Street, Newton Abbot to A. C. Bulpin

Reflecting the move of the Company's offices from Exeter to Torquay, the timetable booklet from 1st January 1934 carried a picture of Torbay and Thatcher Rock on its cover, instead of Exeter Cathedral which had been depicted since 1925.

A new service 2A commenced on 1st January, Exeter to Mamhead via Kenton (Tuesdays and Saturdays) and from 1st May, service 43 (Exeter-Seaton-Lyme Regis) ceased with all its journeys being covered by the 46. Service 27A (Cullompton-Clyst Hydon-Exeter on Fridays) was then renumbered 43.

A few services were acquired from small operators in East Devon during 1934. On 27th April, the goodwill of the Sidmouth-Exeter, and Sidmouth-Sidford-Sidbury services of the Sidmouth Motor Co. & Dagworthy Ltd., Western Garage, Sidmouth was acquired; these had originally run in competition with Devon General's own services, but since 1923 had been the subject of a mutual running agreement. The Sidmouth Motor Co. had been founded in 1920 by Mr. Griffin, while W. Dagworthy had been a carriage proprietor since 1912. Dagworthy bought a Dennis bus in 1919 which he used on a service to Sidmouth Station (qv), and both from 1921 obtained a number of small vehicles, mainly Fiats, and ran services to Exeter and to Sidbury as well as being taxi proprietors. They joined forces on 24th November 1927 and in 1932 started the 'toast rack' bus services to Peak Hill and to Salcombe Hill, using converted Austin taxis. They continued in business with these services and with tours from Sidmouth until 1956.

On 15th July, the goodwill of R. P. Summers, 16, Mill Street, Ottery St. Mary was purchased, and his route from Exeter to Ottery via Metcombe and Aylesbeare was amended by Devon General to become service 38, Sidmouth-Metcombe-Aylesbeare-Exeter (Fridays only). Summers' other route was unaltered and became 39, Ottery St. Mary-Marsh Green-Rockbeare-Exeter (daily), which paralleled Devon General route 4. Summers was licensed to terminate his services in Paul Street Bus Station at Exeter, and Devon General of course took this facility over, but did not take on his licence to run tours from Ottery St. Mary. Three Counties Motors of Wincanton had applied unsuccessfully for this licence, but later withdrew it after opposition. It then lapsed. Devon General did not take over any vehicles from either of the above firms.

After a prolonged licensing battle with F. Baker of Bradninch, a new service 42 was introduced, running between Exeter, Pinhoe and Poltimore on Fridays and Saturdays only.
At Brixham, after another court battle, this time with J. Geddes (Burton Cars), Devon General started a town service from 9th July. This became route 37 (for a short time 12B) and ran from Gillard Road (for St. Mary's Bay) to Fishcombe via Ranscombe Road, Quay and railway station every half hour, which could be accomplished by one bus.

Torquay local services 32, 33, and 34 no longer provided a Chelston, Strand and Barton circular service; from 8th July, 32 became Strand to Barton (via Westhill and Hele Village or via Havelock Arms) and 33 became Strand to Chelston. 34 (Chelston - Barton) ceased and 35 ran from Castle Circus via St. Marychurch and Havelock Arms alternately to Watcombe (Potteries) or to Barton (Lummaton Cross), with a few of the Watcome Potteries buses being extended a quarter of a mile along Teignmouth Road to a crossroads, optimistically termed 'Watcombe Beach'. Short workings from Strand to Hele Village via Westhill were timetabled as 31A.

From 8th October, 33 was re-routed in Chelston, and ran via Old Mill Road, Mallock Road, Sherwell Hill, Ashfield Road, and St. Matthews Road to terminate at Herbert Road (Cockington Vicarage) instead of running via Old Mill Road, Rosery Road, Walnut Road and terminating at St. Matthews Church. Herbert Road was the nearest point accessible by bus to the picturesque Cockington Village.

The former route 42 (Okehampton-Princetown) was discontinued as such, at the end of the season, and the 'scheduled tours' or 'express services' that had been timetabled as 37 to 41 and 50 reappeared for the 1935 season as 56 to 61 respectively. Hence service numbers 37 to 42 became vacant. New routes numbered 37, 38, 39 and 42 have already been mentioned; the Exmouth-Sidmouth via Colaton Raleigh workings of route 10 were given the number 40, while the Sidmouth- Sidbury-Honiton extension of the 10 became 41. Fares could be booked through from 40 to 41 and vice versa, but the 41 gradually lost status. Service 10 remained, as Exmouth-Budleigh Salterton-East Budleigh-Otterton. The 10 served East Budleigh and Otterton villages, while the 40 stayed on the main road. Service 22 (Exeter-Ottery St. Mary-Sidmouth) was complemented by two new services, 22A, Axminster-Ottery St. Mary-Sidmouth, and 22B, Ottery St. Mary-Tipton St. John-Sidmouth. In fact all workings on the 22 and 22A interworked with the 4, with a change of vehicle at Ottery St. Mary. The summer-only Exmouth-Orcombe Point service was given number 24A, and finally the Paignton Station-Maidenway Road section of route 18 was given its own service number 18A from 8th October.

Up until 1934 Devon General had always used tickets of the 'Bell Punch' type, the conductors wearing a leather sash carrying the bell-punch machine and the tickets carried in the hand in a long wooden rack. In 1934, Ticket Issuing Machines (TIMs) were introduced on Torquay local services, the first series of thirty being purchased at the end of May. These embodied a dial, on which the fare was set, and there were facilities to print date, route number, machine number, stage boarded, and ticket serial number. These details were, by turning the handle of the machine, printed on to a plain paper roll, at first in red, after a few years changed to blue, and finally to purple. The machines continued in use until fare increases of the 1950s rendered them obsolete. Bell punch tickets continued to be used for the time being on country services, and these were in a variety of colours, overprinted with the fare value, but were not of the 'geographical' type. The serial numbers were prefixed with 'T' for Torquay or 'E' for Exeter. The racks were quite bulky, for instance no less than 23 types of ticket were carried by conductors on the Torquay to Brixham service.

Prohibition Notices were common on the vehicles of the period, but one somewhat unusual one which appeared on Devon General buses was that 'No Wireless Batteries containing acid may be carried on this vehicle', and the conductors did enforce this.

The only new buses to be delivered in 1934, apart from the balance of the 'Regents', were six Leyland 'Lion' LT5As (71-76), three with bodies by Brush and three by Short Bros. They were put into traffic at Torquay on service 30, Paignton-Babbacombe.

The thirty-two 'Lancias' from Fleet Cars and Grey Cars that had not been re-used were sold early in the year, and at the end of the season there was quite a clear-out of stock. Sales comprised the twelve 1928/9 Leyland 'Lion' PLSC buses (110-117, 124-127), the six contemporary Leyland 'Lioness' limited-stop vehicles (118-123), the five 'Super-Lancias' from Fleet Cars (334-338), and the three surviving 'Lancias', Comfy Cars (104) and Heather Tours (108-109). During the year, two Morris cars and a BSA motor cycle were purchased, a Triumph and two other motor cycles being sold off.
199 buses and coaches were in stock at the end of the year.

1934 had been the first full season of direct operation by Devon General of the former Fleet Cars and Grey Cars tours. Thirty-eight coaches were in service at the height of the season, the best being the ten ex-Grey Cars AEC 'Rangers' still in the hands of ex-Grey Cars drivers. All the coach fleet ran in Grey Cars livery except for the five ex-Fleet Cars 'Super Lancias', which remained in service until September. The Company published an illustrated guide-book describing all tours, with advertising by the café proprietors at the places visited. These booklets were produced at intervals right up to 1971 when Grey Cars tours as such, ceased.

Premises at 137, Reddenhill Road, Babbacombe were rented from Mrs. P. M. Simpson for use as a tours booking office and parcels office. This was a single-storey building on a corner plot, faced with black imitation marble panels, and was lettered up as 'Devon General' rather than 'Grey Cars'. Like the other main booking offices, it had a large coloured relief map of Devon and Cornwall in the window. This office replaced the former rented office nearby at 22, Portland Road which had been relinquished in December 1933.

The Tours offered were:
Special Extended Tours:
1   Three-day tour to Bude, Boscastle, Newquay, Lands End, Penzance, The Lizard, Falmouth
and Truro (314 miles, stopping overnight at Newquay and Falmouth). This replaced the
previous two-day tour.
2   Cheddar Gorge, Glastonbury and Wells (188 miles)
3   Lynton, Watersmeet, Minehead, Tiverton and Exe Valley (174 miles)

Whole Day Tours:
4   Falmouth and Fowey (201 miles)
5   Newquay via Bodmin Moor (176 miles)
6   Bournemouth (210 miles - allowing 2½ hours stay)
7   Clovelly and Westward Ho! (152 miles)
8   Clovelly and Bude (165 miles)
9   Lynton and Lynmouth (162 miles)
10   Bude, Boscastle and Tintagel (155 miles)
11   Ilfracombe and the Bray Valley (160 miles)
12   Minehead and Exmoor (145 miles)
13   Weymouth and Lyme Regis (169 miles)
14   Looe and Polperro (128 miles)

15	Lydford Gorge via Tavistock and Okehampton (90 miles)
16	Princetown and Plymouth (85 miles)
17	Belstone Tor (85 miles)
18	Princetown and Dartmeet (65 miles)
19	Salcombe, Slapton Sands and Dartmouth (65 miles)
20	Fingle Gorge via Dartmoor and Chagford (60 miles)
21	Exmouth and Budleigh Salterton (70 miles)

Afternoon Runs:

22	Widecombe and Becky Falls (40 miles)
23	Widecombe and Buckland Woods (40 miles)
24	Slapton Sands and Dartmouth (50 miles)
25	Steps Bridge (45 miles)
26	Buckland Beacon (42 miles)
27	Becky Falls and Haytor (39 miles)
28	River Dart (32 miles) -a joint tour by coach and steamer, tides permitting
29	Exeter via Haldon and Teignmouth (48 miles)
30	Mamhead Woods (38 miles)
31	Haytor Rocks (33 miles)
32	Lustleigh Cleave via Chudleigh Rocks (39 miles)
33	Buckfast Abbey (34 miles)
34	Mystery Tour (40 miles)
35	Coombe Cellars via Milber Downs (24 miles)

Morning Runs: (most also ran as evening runs)

36	Coombe Cellars (22 miles)
37	Berry Head (20 miles)
38	Berry Pomeroy Castle (20 miles)
39	Torquay Sightseeing Tour via Lincombe Drive, Babbacombe and Cockington
40	Kents Cavern
41	Stoke Gabriel (14 miles)
42	Dittisham Ferry (14 miles)

1935

Devon General had, by a 1929 Agreement, been empowered to operate the former GWR routes which had been transferred to Western National as their services 121 to 123 from a date to be determined. Western National suspended operation of these services from 1st October 1934, and from 1st May 1935 their former 121, Moretonhampstead Station-Chagford, appeared in the Devon General timetable as 19A. The licences for the other two services, WN 122 Bovey Tracey-Haytor-Widecombe and 123 Bovey Tracey-Manaton were transferred to J. Potter & Sons (Tor Bus) as from 1st January 1935 though it appears that they did not actually commence operation until later that month. The summer-only 'Express Services' from Exeter, also known as Scheduled Tours, reappeared under different route numbers for the 1935 season, these being:

56, (ex-37) Exeter-Bude (Tu)	59, (ex- 40) Exeter-Cheddar (Th)
57, (ex-38) Exeter-Clovelly (W)	60, (ex- 41) Exeter-Doone Valley (F)
58, (ex-39) Exeter-Lynton (M)	61, (ex-50) Exeter-Ilfracombe (MWFSa)

The return tickets were valid for 15 days except on the Doone Valley run which was a circular. The services made one return trip on the days indicated, between 12th July and 12th September. It will be seen that 56 to 60 could (in theory) be worked by one vehicle, but the Exmoor trip was limited to 20-seaters (Leyland Cubs 100-102).

A new service 62 was introduced from 1st May between Ottery St. Mary and Payhembury in East Devon. It made two return trips on Tuesdays and Thursdays only. From the same date, the Sidmouth-Sidbury extension of service 9 was designated 9A and alternate journeys on the 18 were extended from Stoke Gabriel to Aish. The 18A was extended from Paignton Station to Roundham (for Goodrington).

On 24th June, terms were agreed with A. C. Aggett of Church House Cottage, Marldon, for the purchase of his Paignton-Marldon-Compton Castle service, together with his one 20-seat Ford bus. The service was operated by Devon General from 1st August becoming route 63, and the bus became No: 104 in the Devon General fleet. The Marldon service had, from

December 1923 to late 1929, been run by the Torbay Proprietary Co. Ltd., of Oldway, Paignton (controlled by the Singer family of sewing machine fame), with a 14-seat Ford lorry-bus. The service was then operated by C. B. Foxworthy until December 1931 when Mr. Aggett took it on. He found difficulty in maintaining the service with just one bus, and shortly before he sold out to Devon General had been fined for using an unlicensed saloon car to convey fare paying passengers on a day when his bus was off the road.

The 12th July timetable brought a few more changes: service 8 became Exeter-Pinhoe-Broadclyst (double-decker worked), and a new express service, 11A, ran summer-only (not Saturdays) between Torquay and Buckfast Abbey, via Newton Abbot and Ashburton. A new 11B was created by linking selected journeys on 2 and 11 to give an Exeter-Newton Abbot-Buckfastleigh service (change at Newton Abbot). This ceased on 12th September.

In Torquay, the Lummaton Cross workings of 35 were extended to Barton (Prince of Orange), and a new 34 was introduced on 1st August from Torquay Station to Warren Road, Strand, Beacon Quay, where it reversed, and then went on to Princes Road West via Braddons Hill. It frequently carried only one passenger, and not surprisingly ceased operation before the end of the year.

A new market-day service at Tiverton was introduced from 13th September, despite objections from E. Clatworthy who operated in the area. It was service 3A, and made seven return trips each Tuesday and Saturday between Tiverton, Chettiscombe and Chevithorne.

In July, The General Manager was authorised once again to negotiate the purchase of the goodwill of the services operated by Milton Services (Crediton) Ltd. This business had originated in 1921 with a carriers service run by Wm. Milton of Crediton, which developed into a bus service between Crediton and Exeter. Following his death, his executors Messrs. A. R. Garnish and F. Milton ran the business, in which Messrs. W. J, G. J, and P. G. Greenslade acquired a 97.5% holding, and in December 1931 formed the limited company, expanding it to provide the following bus routes:

1, Exeter-Newton St. Cyres-Crediton
2, Exeter-Upton Pyne-Shobrooke-Crediton
3, Exeter-Ide-Dunchideock-Haldon Belvedere
4, Exeter-Whitestone-Heath Cross
5, Exeter-Shillingford-Clapham

Devon General secured an Agreement on 9th December to purchase the goodwill, and in 1936 assimilated the routes into its timetable as follows:

64,	Exeter-Ide-Dunchideock (-Haldon Belvedere in summer)	Daily
65,	Exeter-Whitestone-Heath Cross	TFSa
66,	Exeter-Shillingford-Kennford-Kenn	Daily
67,	Exeter-Upton Pyne	FSa
68,	Exeter-Raddons Cross	FSa
69,	Shobrooke-Crediton	FSa

Milton's Exeter-Newton St Cyres-Crediton workings were incorporated into Devon General route 7 (worked by double-deckers). No vehicles were acquired. Greenslades retained their tours licences and continued to licence coaches in Milton's name.

Devon General made application to operate a service from Three Beaches to Collaton St. Mary via Paignton, but Western National objected on the grounds that it would compete with their Paignton-Totnes service, which was their road under a 1929 agreement between the two companies. Much interim development at Paignton had rendered this agreement inappropriate, and a fresh territorial agreement was thrashed out over the next couple of years.

One trip a day on service 45, Torquay-Plymouth, had, since 1932 (or earlier) run via Avonwick instead of South Brent (two on some Saturdays but none on Sundays ran this way). These journeys were designated 45A, and from 13th September 1935 were further diverted via Ugborough. Some journeys on the 45 ran through South Brent village, others merely called at the London Hotel on the main road. This was a joint service with Western National (their 128/A/B).

A temporary diversion was made in the centre of Torquay due to road works, from 14th January to 13th April. Union Street was made one-way into town and outward bound vehicles proceeded via Abbey Road. This arrangement made its appearance again in 1965 on a permanent basis as part of the Torquay one-way system.

New vehicles added to the fleet in 1935 were two AEC 'Ranger' coaches (334-5) in Grey Cars livery and fleet-name, with 26-seat Harrington bodies, of 1931 design. These were intended for use on the three-day tour to Cornwall. Front and rear nearside doors were fitted, though only the front ones were normally used; a canvas hood could be wound right back over the rear of the vehicle to fold at waist level. Seating was soon reduced to 20 to give greater comfort and these two coaches were assigned to the two senior drivers, Hodge and Hannaford.

Two more AEC 'Regent' diesel-engined double-deckers (224-5) with 52-seat bodies by Short Bros. were delivered, these being identical to the 1933/4 batch, apart from the pattern of the seating material. They were put to work at Torquay, the three petrol-engined 'Regents' of 1932 having been transferred to Exeter and Crediton.

A busy scene in Newton Road depot, Torquay. The nearest vehicle is 85 (AUO 80) a 1935 'Camel' and one of a batch of twenty Leyland 'Lions'.
(DGO&TC)

In addition, no less than eighteen petrol-engined Leyland 'Lion' LT5As with distinctive bodies by Short Bros., seating 36, arrived. They sported a large 'hump' at the rear which housed an interior luggage rack. Invariably known as the 'Camels', they spent their early life on routes 2, 4, and 13, filling the gap in the fleet left by the withdrawal of the old PLSC 'Lions' late in 1934. The new 'Lions' were numbered 77-94.

Finally, one Leyland 'Cub' (103) was delivered, which had a 20-seat Mumford body with a large front destination box, exterior roof rack and ladder, and rear emergency door. It entered service in July at Brixham, where trouble was being experienced with full-size buses negotiating the narrow Fore Street en route to their terminus at The Quay.

The 12 terminus was moved back to Bolton Cross as from the 13th September timetable, the local service 37 being diverted at the town end of King Street to run up Fore Street to Bolton Cross, turning at Market Street and returning back down Fore Street to pick up its route again. The 'Cub' worked this service, with the driver collecting the fares, and opening the folding doors manually from a lever by his seat. To accommodate the extra mileage, the service became every 40 minutes instead of half-hourly.

A garage in New Road, Brixham was rented from R. M. Bell on a seven-year lease from 21st March, five buses being based there. Ten Leyland 'Tiger' TS2 and TS3 'Sun Saloon' coaches dating from 1930 (160-169) used on limited stop services were sold late in 1935 to Western and Southern National for use on the Royal Blue services newly acquired from Elliott Bros. of Bournemouth. They were re-bodied in 1936 and remained in use until 1953.

Other withdrawals in 1935 were the last five Lancia coaches (329-333) and ten of the AEC 'Mercury' Grey Cars (306-308, 310, 313-318). These all ran for the full summer season and were sold in September to Dawson (Dealer) of Croydon. Two 1930 Leyland 'Lion' LT2' Sun Saloons (176-177) were also sold, and a 1929 Leyland 'Titan' TD1 double-decker (140) was scrapped late in the year.
195 buses and coaches were in stock at the year end.

Miscellaneous acquisitions were two Morris vans and a motor cycle to replace earlier vehicles, one of which was the parcels van that had been converted from a Lancia charabanc in 1927.

New uniform trousers and jackets were introduced for drivers and conductors in June; these were of dark blue serge with red piping. Previously, dust coats or greatcoats had been worn over their own clothing. Brown dustcoats or dust jackets continued in summer use, along with white tops for the caps. Black shoes and tie with white shirt were still obligatory. A new badge was introduced about this time, formed of a yellow scroll inscribed 'Devon General' in red, and surmounted by a winged wheel. This only lasted for a short time until replaced by the familiar 'DG' emblem in the form of a crown design.

From 1st August, drivers' and conductors' pay was increased, generally by ½d an hour, and variations in conditions relating to Bank Holidays etc., were approved. Sundays and Good Friday were paid at ordinary rate whereas the other bank holidays were to be paid at time and a quarter. Christmas Day would be at double time. The annual holiday entitlement was seven days, for which 48 hours pay was awarded, this being the standard working week at the time.

The Company continued to modernise its ticket issuing by the purchase of ten more 'TIM' machines for use at Torquay, and a new type of machine was introduced, this being the 'Insert Setright'. The initial order was for 28, being followed later in the year by a further order for 50 for use at Exeter. The principle of this system was that a basic set of pre-numbered printed card tickets was carried in a small rack by the conductor. Tickets were single, return, exchange, and workmens, as well as a ½d value ticket, and on insertion of a ticket into the 'Setright' machine, it would print the fare in shillings and pence, the date, month and a stage number. This provided flexibility for longer routes that the 'TIM' machines did not possess, because they were restricted to the amounts which could be dialled. The 'Insert Setright' tickets were coloured as follows:

Singles	White,
Returns	Yellow,
Calendar Month Return	Pink,
Workmen's	Green,
Exchange	Salmon,
½d. value	Mauve with overprinted red ½d. (The balance of the fare being recorded by the

'Setright' in the normal way). The back of the ticket often carried an advertisement for Paignton Zoo, complete with beckoning monkey! Revisions and extensions of the penny fare stages within Torquay, took effect from 12th July.

Mention has been made of the three-day tour to Cornwall; this included first-class hotel accommodation at Newquay and Falmouth plus all meals, and all for £5.5s.0d. A two-day tour to Penzance and Lands End was also offered, but the £1.10s.0d. fare did not include hotel or meals. The Company would book passengers in at the Queens Hotel, Penzance unless they wished to make their own arrangements. Tour No:6 to Bournemouth was deleted from the programme, and tour No:30 was re-routed to Fingle Gorge and Teign Valley instead of to Mamhead Woods, which had not proved to be of sufficient attraction.

Further properties were disposed of during 1935. St. Marychurch depot, the adjoining tram depot and offices were sold jointly by Devon General and the liquidators of Torquay Tramways Co. Ltd., to the Borough of Torquay, the sale being completed on 13th March and the proceeds apportioned between the two vendors. The bus depot became a garage for the Council's fleet of lorries and dustcarts, and the tram depot was partitioned off as workshops. Included in the sale were the Babbacombe Cliff Railway and the six 'Tramway Houses', 42-52, St. Margaret's Avenue.
The Cliff Railway had been maintained by Devon General engineering staff since the closure of the tramways.

The lease of the Devon General office at 10A, Torquay Road, Paignton was surrendered to the landlord, Miss. T. Somerville.

A new post of Traffic Manager was created in May, and Mr. R. T. Hill, previously Traffic Superintendent, was promoted to fill it. Mr. J. Dawson was appointed Engineer on 1st November and Mr. H. F. Wyatt became Assistant Traffic Manager.

A fatal accident, in which two buses were involved, occurred in Torquay on 11th December. A Leyland 'Lion' on route 30, driven by G. Setters, was waiting at the junction of St. Marychurch Road with Bronshill Road, when the horse of a horse-drawn Co-op van, which had bolted down St. Marychurch Road, struck the rear of the bus with a glancing impact. It then collided with the cab side of a 'Regent' on route 55B which was crossing from Hatfield Road into Shirburn Road (driver J. Down). The animal broke its neck and died instantly, and the van driver, Sidney Field, was seriously injured and sadly died later, in hospital.

Difficulty with overcrowding, particularly at midday when workers were in the habit of going home for a quick lunch, was causing problems mainly on the 55B from Torquay (Strand) to Ellacombe. This coupled with the disorderly conduct of some of those trying to board, queue rails and short-working buses were called for, but it was not until the war years that boarding became more orderly.

1936

In January, the Company agreed to recognise the National Union of Railwaymen, to which many of the staff belonged, and the General Manager was authorised to negotiate rates of pay and conditions with them which, if possible, were to last for a period of two years. On this basis, it was agreed in September (inter alia) that time and a quarter would be paid for Sunday work, and that the maximum rate per hour would be increased to 1/3½d. for drivers and 1/1½d. for conductors. Rates and grades for maintenance staff were the subject of an agreement made on 27th February 1937. In June 1934, militant busmen had formed the branch, which now achieved 100% membership.

From February 1936, the now familiar cast-iron 'Bus Stop' signs, on black and white striped poles were erected in Torquay, but there was an argument between Devon General and the Council as to who was going to pay for them. Eventually, the parties agreed to pay half each. Many of these signs survived into the 1970s, and were even then, not replaced because they were worn out, but rather were sacrificed to further the corporate image of the National Bus Company.

On 7th February 1936 the purchase of the Teignmouth Motor Car Company from Messrs. H. Fraser and G. Rossiter was agreed. The Company had been operating since 1910, and at the time of acquisition by Devon General their services were:

(1)   Teignmouth (GPO) to Haldon Tea House, Aerodrome and Golf Club via (a) Triangle, Hollands Bridge, Brimley, Livingstone, Haldon Avenue, New Road, top of Exeter Road, Cemetery, or (b) Exeter Road.
(2)   Teignmouth (Coombe Vale) to GPO via (a) Landscore Road, bottom of Hermosa Road, Reed Vale, Deerpark Avenue, or (b) Bitton Street.
(3)   Teignmouth (GPO)-Dawlish (The Lawn) via Haldon Moor and Coast Road.
(4)   Teignmouth (GPO)-Haldon Moor, Golf Links and Aerodrome.

Devon General retained the first two services which became 70, Teignmouth Triangle-Haldon Aerodrome, and 71, Teignmouth Triangle-Coombe Vale. No separate services were maintained for the other two, though Dawlish was of course, served by Devon General route 2 anyway, and the final service mentioned was little different from the 70.

Two Commers and a Karrier were purchased from the Teignmouth Company, but were resold immediately by Devon General, which then stationed two buses of its own at Teignmouth, in premises at Courtenay Hotel Garage (off The Triangle), rented from R. J. Clarke. There had been an unusual prelude to the acquisition of the Teignmouth Motor Car Co. One of the joint proprietors, Mr. Rossiter, was called before the committee of the Haldon Golf Club to account for his actions in proposing to sell his bus service to Devon General! The golf club was served by the route to Haldon Aerodrome, and in 1927-9 had run their own bus (a 14-seater Ford UO 1075) between Teignmouth and the club, needless to say at a substantial cost. They had come to rely very heavily on Mr. Rossiter to get members to the club, and his assurances that Devon General would provide a service as good as (if not better than) his own, did little to appease some of the committee members. There were a lot of harsh words, and some resignations.

The purchase was approved in July, and completed on 30th September, of the tours licence of H. J. Lee (t/a East Devon Motor Co.) of Ottery St. Mary. He had started a garage business in 1919 and from 1920 operated one charabanc, his first vehicle being bought from Heath of Ottery St. Mary. Devon General did not acquire any vehicles from him and rarely operated any tours from Ottery St. Mary, the last being in 1939.

From 1st January, routes 1 (Exeter via Chudleigh) and 15 (Totnes) on which alternate journeys had run through to Torquay, were curtailed at Newton Abbot, connection to Torquay being via services 28, 16 and 17. From 6th July Torquay local service

31 became wholly double-deck worked, and was cut back to run from Lawes Bridge via Hele Village and Westhill to the Strand only. Westhill then ceased to be served by alternate journeys of the 32. 33 (Chelston-Strand) was extended to serve Hesketh Crescent and Meadfoot Beach. 31A (short workings to Hele Village) ceased as a separate table, being run as required within the 31 service. The 31 negotiated some very steep hills, of which Westhill Road (previously known as Blacks Hill) was particularly fearsome. (The author well remembers standing at Westhill Cross as a small boy watching the 'Regents' coming up slowly in either direction, in bottom gear. It soon occurred to him that OD 7487 was No:200, OD 7488 was 201, and so on, and that they were distinguishable from a distance by their adverts; that was perhaps when interest in all things Devon General really began!).

The timetables of the day contained a number of idiosyncrasies in the form of timetabled routes which did not actually exist, either in part or in whole; some examples were the 14A, Newton Abbot-Princetown, created by tabling selected journeys on the 16 and 23 and requiring a change at Moretonhampstead; 19A, Moretonhampstead to Chagford, also tabled as short workings under the 19; 21 was headed Cullompton-Seaton, though a change was necessary at Honiton on to the 48, which itself also appeared under the 4 table; 21A, Cullompton-Sidmouth was another such route, the tabled service being achieved by way of the 21 to Honiton and then the 41; and the 22/22A/22B which have already been mentioned. Perhaps the most unlikely service was 27, Uffculme to Totnes! Once a through service, this by now ran between Uffculme and Exeter, interworked with Exeter to Newton Abbot via the 1, and Newton Abbot to Totnes via the 15.

Service 52 Exmouth-Sidmouth-Seaton-Lyme Regis was a bit of a work of art, involving interworking with the 40 and 46. Alternate journeys between Exmouth and Sidmouth were provided by the 40 and the 52, though all appeared in each table. The 40 continued to Honiton as 41, and from these journeys passengers for Seaton and Lyme Regis were obliged to change at Sidmouth on to a 46. The 52 that did commence at Exmouth only ran as far as Seaton and not to Lyme Regis. Using these permutations, an hourly service from Exmouth to Seaton was achieved, with a two-hourly service to Lyme Regis. The village of Beer was served by the 52 but not by the 46. These connectional 'services' would have been of considerable use to holiday-makers by showing in simple form, a variety of connecting facilities that would otherwise have required considerable research among separate timetables.

Virtually all single-deck buses and coaches ordered for delivery in 1936/7 had bodies by Harrington Coachworks of Hove, and very handsome vehicles they were. The trend continued in 1938 and 1939, though by then, AEC chassis were favoured rather than Leyland, which had formed such a large part of the fleet in the early 1930s. First, in February, came ten Leyland 'Tiger' TS7 petrol-engined 'Sun Saloons' for express services (110-119). They had a sliding door, high-backed seats with brown patterned upholstery, five half-drop windows per side with glass louvres above, an emergency door at the front on the offside, a canvas-topped opening panel in the roof, and the same destination layout that had been introduced with the 'Camels' in 1935, i.e. one box for route number, alongside one for destination at the front, and a shallower box for ultimate destination at the rear. The cream waistband swept right around the saloon windows to run above them, and at the rear swept down to a 'tail'. Destination boards were carried in brackets under the middle three windows on each side, but were soon done away with as was the rear destination blind. They entered service in March and April on routes 9, 45, 46, 49 and 53. Four were based at Torquay, three at Exeter and three at Sidmouth, and this allocation stayed unchanged until 1939.

Also delivered in February were two more buses with the 'Camel' type body (95 and 96) though unlike the 1935 batch, they were on Leyland 'Lion' LT7 chassis (petrol engine) and had bodywork by Weymann, the only visible difference to the earlier ones being the pattern of the upholstery. They entered service in May and worked their entire life from Tiverton on service 3.

They were followed by four new diesel-engined double-deckers, Leyland 'Titan' TD4 (226-229). As supplied, they had a body built by Beadle very similar to the Short Bros. body on 'Regents' 200-225, but with 56-seats and a somewhat superior internal finish. Their original gearbox was unsuitable for local conditions, and was replaced in September by a box with a different gear ratio. Even so, they were never as satisfactory on hilly routes as the 'Regents'. They entered service from Torquay depot in June on the circular route 55A/B, releasing some of the 'Regents' for double-decking of service 31, and for transfer to Exeter and Crediton, where they in turn replaced older 'Titans' and 'Regents' on services 7 and 8.

Also brought into service in June and July were ten normal-control petrol-engined coaches (336-345) for the Grey Cars at Torquay. They were of the Leyland 'Tigress' type, a normal-control version of the 'Tiger' TS7, and had a Harrington 26-seat body with a sliding door at the front, and a canvas roof which retracted right down into the back locker, along with the back window panel. This was actuated by winding a handle in a socket above the driver, and they were very hard to wind back up. These coaches were in the Grey Cars livery of light grey with dark grey window surrounds and maroon wings, but carried the Devon General fleet-name on the back locker panel. They were very powerful, and were ideal for the Dartmoor hills, but were low geared and consequently very heavy on fuel. Their absolute top speed on the flat was just 43 mph. As delivered, a pair of seats was situated at the front nearside in front of the door. The General Manager decided that this arrangement did not give enough room and the double seats were replaced by a single seat in line with the door which hinged forward when the door was open. This seat was however liable to tilt forward and deposit its passenger on the floor if the driver braked suddenly. An extra seat was created in the middle of the back row, all the rest being in pairs, and this explains why the 'Tigresses' had a seat numbered 24A, but not one numbered 2. They replaced the ten AEC 'Mercurys' sold at the end of the 1935 season, and were allocated to former Fleet Cars drivers.

Meanwhile, Devon General had decided that 48 new diesel-engined single-deckers were to be ordered to replace Leyland the 'Lion' LT1 and LT2 vehicles, the exact type to be decided upon by the Managing Director Mr. Garcke, in consultation with the General Manager Mr. Porte. The type chosen for this, the largest single order ever placed by the Company, was the Leyland 'Lion' LT7 with 4-cylinder CI engine, and with Harrington 36-seat bodies. Numbered 250-297, delivery commenced in October 1936 and continued well into 1937, the buses being delivered in a fairly haphazard order. The first two went into traffic in November, and seven more in December, and it was soon apparent that they were underpowered for the duties required of them. Changing gear was quite an art - when changing up, the revs had to be allowed to noisily die away almost to nothing before engaging a higher gear. The engine ran with a unique note that is well remembered but cannot adequately be described, except that the 'Lions' growled whereas the 'Tigers' simply 'sang'! Their bodies were of the same basic design as the 'Tigers' which were obtained earlier in the year, but lacked refinements such as sun-roof, sliding door and high-backed seats. They had an additional destination box at roof level halfway along the nearside, and had six half-drop windows per side, as against five on the 'Tigers'. The seats over the wheel arches faced inwards, giving a total capacity of 36. Despite their shortcomings, they were put into traffic on some of the principal services, including routes 5, 12, 13 and Torquay local services 32, 33 and 35.

Finally, in December, another 'Tiger' TS7 'Sun Saloon' was received which was identical to the earlier batch (110-119), and was one of two on order (120 and 121), the second coming in January 1937. Both went into service from Torquay, more often than not, on the Plymouth route.

Vehicles withdrawn during 1936 were twenty-four Leyland 'Lion' LT1 and LT2s (128-131, 146-159 and 170-175), the remaining Leyland 'Titan' TD1s (138, 139, 141), and two Leyland 'Tiger' TS2s (144 and 145).

Miscellaneous disposals were: one Triumph and two BSA motor cycles, one Morris van, one Morris car and one Austin Seven car. Replacements were two Morris Commercial vans, one Morris '16' and three Morris '8' cars. Motor cycles for the use of inspectors were being phased out in favour of small cars. 202 buses and coaches were in stock at the end of the year.

It had, since the earliest days of the Company, been the practice to keep a vehicle overnight at places where a late journey in, and an early journey out, was required, and the position at the beginning of 1936 was that garage accommodation was rented at the following places:

Okehampton	(free use of Southern National ex-DMT premises)
Ottery St. Mary	(F. J. Luxton & Sons)
Tiverton	(Eastmond & Son)
Cullompton	(Whitton & Sons)
Axminster	(Packham & Company)
Crediton	(Searle & Trewin)
Brixham	(R. M. Bell)

The Board in September gave authority for the acquisition of a site, and the construction of a garage for twelve vehicles at Tiverton. At the same meeting, they authorised provision for the storage of fuel oil throughout the system. Land at Exmouth Station yard (which adjoined the bus depot) was rented from the Southern Railway for parking, from July 1936.

DEVON GENERAL

Shelter styles 3 - The large metal-framed green painted shelter at Torquay (Marine Square) was built in 1936 to accommodate queues for the busy route to Paignton and was later used as the stop for Newton Abbot. Its use ceased after redevelopment of the whole area at which time all the bus stops were relocated. *(Wilson Gould)*

During the year, bus shelters were erected at Marine Square, Torquay and at Dawlish Green, costs being shared between the Company and the local authorities, also eventually at Windy Corner, Churston, after local disagreement as to its location.

The latest position regarding picking-up and setting-down of passengers within the Exeter city limits was made clear by the Traffic Commissioners in October - no passenger was to be picked-up or set-down, other than at Paul Street.

Further new ticket machines were purchased during the year - 12 'TIMs' and 54 Insert 'Setrights', which virtually eliminated the Bell Punch type, which were then retained only for emergency use.

A new Chief Inspector appointed from 1st February was Mr. S. B. Stevenson, who succeeded Mr. G. F. Duthie having been appointed Area Traffic Superintendent for Western National at Taunton. Mr. Ben Stedham, a Torquay businessman who had been a Director since 1922, died on 20th September. Mr. H. A. Short resigned from the Board on 11th November, and the Southern Railway nominated Mr. J. C. Chambers (their road transport liaison officer) to take his place. Mr. H. W. Davis resigned as Company accountant on 31st March and was replaced by Mr. H. G. W. Teverson.

During 1936, a Standing Joint Committee was set up with the Great Western and Southern Railways, consisting of two Devon General representatives and one from each railway. They considered measures by which bus and railway services could be co-ordinated and developed in their joint interests and those of the travelling public, by the running of buses from railway stations, the issue of through tickets, interavailability of tickets, development of tourist traffic, advertising and publicity. It also made recommendations as to proposed services and fares, and to co-ordinate opposition in the Traffic Commissioners Courts, so as to avoid competing with each other, as much as possible.

1937   The Company started the year with a change of General Manager. Mr. R. G. Porte, who had been on leave of absence since 1st December 1936, resigned with effect from 28th February. Mr. F. B. Low was then appointed General Manager as well as continuing his duties as Company Secretary. He was based in London, and Mr. W. H. Geere, who had been Assistant Manager, became Local Manager. He had been in the industry since 1906, and with the Company since 1922. He continued to serve them for many more years, but never did achieve the post of General Manager.

Mr. J. Dawson resigned as Engineer having accepted a post with Western National, and in his place Mr. H. C. Manley was appointed as Mechanical Superintendent. Mr. M. W. Hedelius was appointed Chief Clerk from 7th June, and Mr. J. C. T. Hanson was appointed Assistant Company Secretary in place of Mr. H. Goodes. Col. G. S. Szlumper, a Director since 1929, resigned from the Board on 10th November following his promotion to General Manager of the Southern Railway, who nominated Mr. John Blumenfeld Elliot (also a Director of the Southern National Omnibus Co. Ltd.,) to fill the vacancy. Mr. P. M. Rossdale resigned his Directorship on 14th April, being replaced on the Board by Mr. Bruce G. White, who was also a Director of the Birmingham & Midland Motor Omnibus Co. Ltd., ('Midland Red').

1937 was Coronation year and all employees not required to work on Coronation Day were given one day's pay, and those working on that day were given one day's holiday, with pay.

Crews at Exeter, Exmouth and Sidmouth went on strike on the morning of 5th July, on the grounds that summer duties were too onerous. The strike was unofficial, and after meeting with the area officials of the NUR, the men returned to work on the evening of the same day. Certain guarantees were given by the Company as a temporary measure. 170 employees had withdrawn their labour. The Company adopted a new policy with regard to Union membership of clerical staff and Inspectors. No objection would be made to clerical staff membership of the NUR provided that a conflict of loyalties was not created, and this was accepted by the NUR, although a few staff did then withdraw their membership. Inspectors' membership of the Union would not be tolerated by the Company, and any Inspector joining the Union would be given the opportunity of leaving, or being reduced in status - provided that suitable vacancies were available.

Trouble was brewing at Torquay, where the Corporation gave notice of their intention to oppose the renewal of Devon General's road service licences on the grounds of (a) congestion in Union Street & Fleet Street, and (b) excessive fares which were somewhat higher than the Company charged in other parts of its territory. They varied between 1.04d. and 1.68d. per mile, partly due to retention of the tramway fare structure (as had been agreed by the Corporation at the time of conversion to bus operation).

The Corporation submitted proposals for alternative routes for 50% of the services and suggested fare reductions which the Company would not entertain. In view of the prospect of the issue being contested before the Traffic Commissioners, Counsel Mr. A. G. Thesiger was retained by the Company. Two meetings were then held between the parties, but although Devon General was prepared to meet 70% of the proposals, this was not acceptable. The Chairman of the Traffic Commissioners visited Torquay and indicated that he considered that a certain amount of deviation should be tried experimentally.

Thus it came about that from 22nd July, services 2, 11, 16 and 17, which ran from the centre of Torquay to points beyond Newton Abbot, were re-routed between Torquay Strand and the start of Newton Road, to run via Torbay Road, (the sea front), Belgrave Road, and South Street. Vehicles on these routes carried a 'B' at the nearside, signifying Belgrave Road, and they became known as the B routes. The move was not at all popular with the Company or with the main street traders, and the routes reverted to normal from 15th November, subject to the discontinuation of some of the stops in Union Street and Fleet Street. Following a public sitting at Torquay on 28th and 29th September, the Traffic Commissioner published his decision on 17th December. The lengthy document concluded by saying that he intended to make it a condition of the road service licences that, as from 1st March 1938, fares on local services within the Borough of Torquay should be based on a level of 1.1d. per mile, subject to a minimum fare of 1d.

A notable innovation was the 'Coastal Cruise' which ran during the summers of 1937-9 from Torquay Station to the Strand and Meadfoot, thence in a one-way circular via Marine Drive, Kents Cavern, Wellswood, Lincombe Drive, Strand and back to Torquay Station. Two small Bedfords (360-361) were bought to work this service, introduced on 23rd June as route 34. These little buses had bodies by Birch, with unglazed side windows, and were painted in a special livery of duck-egg blue and cream, with chromium-plated lettering and mouldings and the lettering 'Coastal Cruise' across the front. A leaflet with a dark blue cover depicting seagulls, gave details, a timetable and a map. The regular drivers on the service were J. Jones and A. Hayes. The Council's approval for this service had been subject to the use of 'toast rack' type vehicles, and there was initial concern that the buses were not strictly of this type.

A new Paignton local service was 18B, Hyde Road-Winsu Avenue-Preston Shelter-Sea Front (Lower Polsham Road), regularly worked by a Leyland 'Lion' of the 'Camel' variety.

From 1st March, service 66 was renumbered 66A, and a new 66B was introduced, Exeter-Shillingford-Haldon Camp (SaSuO).

Since the early 1920s, competition had been experienced between Ipplepen and Newton Abbot from G.W., W. G., R. E. and A. J. Harris, garage proprietors of Ipplepen, who ran a Wednesday-only market day service from Denbury and Ipplepen to Newton Abbot. Their stage licence was bought out by Devon General on 31st May, though Harris continued with tours and private hire work. No replacement service was put on, Ipplepen being served hourly by the 15 and Denbury several times a day by the 36D.

Negotiations were in progress with Western and Southern National regarding revised territorial agreements, and an exchange of routes was made with Western National effective from the 5th July timetable, whereby Devon General route 18, Paignton-Stoke Gabriel-Aish passed to Western National, and in its place, Paignton-Galmpton-Greenway (WN 124) became Devon General service 18. Greenway was little more than a quay from which a passenger ferry plied to Dittisham on the opposite bank of the River Dart. The route had originally been a GWR bus service, introduced in 1926. It was restricted to small vehicles, and Devon General initially allocated Leyland 'Cub' 101 to work it.

Plans for the proposed new depot at Tiverton were approved by Tiverton Council. It was to be a garage with a capacity for six vehicles, built on GWR land in Old Road (opposite the junction with Lodge Road) and with a 99-year lease which was taken out on the site from 30th September 1937. The original approval had been for a garage to hold twelve vehicles, and indeed this was required a few years later.

At Exeter, alterations were made to the lower level of Blackboy Road garage, whilst at Torquay, approval was given to lease the bottom floor of Torwood Street garage to W. Mumford & Sons Ltd., of Plymouth, who were coachbuilders and motor agents, provided that their activities did not compete with Devon General in any way. Mumford's however did not take up the lease, and Grey Cars continued to use both floors.

At Moretonhampstead, the office in Ford Street was given up.

The rest of the 48 Leyland 'Lion' LT7s (250-297 series) entered service in the early months of 1937 on services 1, 2, 4, 6, 10, 16, 21, 26, 27, 40 and the Sandford workings on 7, indirectly replacing the remaining LT2 'Lions' dating from 1930/1931 (1-24) which were sold to a dealer. Four more Leyland 'Titan' TD4s (230-233) were delivered early in the year, having Beadle bodywork similar to those of the 1936 batch. They worked from Torquay depot for most of their life, at first on services 31 and 55A/B.

For 1937/8, the Company resolved to order 7 single-deck buses, 10 'Sun Saloons', 3 double-deck buses, 8 coaches and 2 station buses. These were intended to be one-for-one replacements for the 1931 Leyland 'Lion' LT3s, the AEC 'Regal' saloons from the same year, the AEC 'Regent' lowbridge double-deckers of 1932, the last of the ex-Grey Cars AEC 'Mercury' coaches and the two Morris Commercial station buses of 1930. However, owing to proposals to put double-deckers on the Paignton-Brixham route, the double-deck order was increased to five, no single-deck order was made for the time being, and the 'Sun Saloon' order was reduced to four. The coaches were ordered as planned, and approval was given for the sale of the 'Mercury' coaches at the end of the season.

Later in the year, thirteen AEC 'Regal' and twenty-five Dennis single-deck buses were ordered, with an option to cancel twenty-two of the latter if the first three proved unsuitable or unsatisfactory in service. The first two double-deckers were delivered in the summer, so promptly, that they must have been diverted from elsewhere. Certainly South Wales Transport was receiving very similar buses at the time. They were AEC 'Regents' with 7.7-litre engines (as against the more usual 8.8) and carried fleet numbers 234 and 235. They had all-metal bodies by Weymann of a design new to Devon General, which introduced a new destination box layout (one rectangular box at the front and one over the platform) which remained standard for new double-deckers until 1952. The pair went into service on the 12A from Torquay to Paignton.

Before the end of the year, the four new 'Sun Saloons' were delivered. They were AEC 'Regals' (401-404) with Harrington bodywork, similar to those on the 'Tigers' 110-121. They did not go into traffic until May 1938, but before the end of 1937, four of the 1931 'Regals' were sold (181,183,185 and 186) as were the three petrol-engined 'Regents' (190-192) together with the eight remaining 'Mercury' coaches (301-305, 309, 311 and 312). At the end of the year, 215 buses and coaches were in stock.

Miscellaneous purchases during the year had included eight sets of Clayton Dewandre heating equipment for fitting to buses used on express services, another nine 'Insert Setright' ticket machines, and one Morris '8' car. Four BSA motor cycles were sold, and inspectors henceforth used cars or service buses.

The 1937 tours booklet was entitled 'Devon General Motor Coach Tours by the Grey Cars', whereas previously the title had been 'Motor Coach Tours by the Grey Cars (proprietors Devon General). A few alterations took place in the selection of tours offered, with a new tour, No:6 going to Weston-super-Mare and Wookey Hole, tour No:12 went to Bigbury instead of to Minehead and Exmoor, and tour No:20 was altered to also visit Fingle Gorge and Exeter.

The two-day tour to Penzance and Lands End only ran once during the 1937 season while the three-day tour did not run at all and was later deleted from the programme. The most popular 'extended-day' tour was to Looe and Polperro, which ran no less than 117 times during 1937. The two senior drivers each did 26 'extendeds' during the year; most of the others averaging 15, except for the eight most junior drivers who had the last of the AEC 'Mercurys', and these did only two each. During 1937, 333 extended tours were run, and a total of 48,201 passengers were carried on the tours. A tours booking office was rented from Mrs. G. J. Joule from 31st July, this being situated next to the Kistor Hotel in Belgrave Road, Torquay. The booking office at Paignton moved from number 20, to nearby numbers 26/28, Torbay Road.

1938

Following considerable negotiation, Agreements were made on 20th January 1938 (deemed to commence 1st November 1937) between Devon General and the Western and Southern National Omnibus Companies. These defined the areas within which services should be provided and excursions, tours and private hire operated. The Agreement was for ten years, thence from year to year, which could be terminated at six months' notice. A map defined the area in which Devon General should operate, and various clauses defined 'common roads' on which both companies could operate 'related services', and laid out agreed exceptions. Devon General's area was bounded by Kingswear, Totnes, Buckfastleigh, Ashburton, Widecombe, Warren House Inn, Okehampton, North Tawton, Morchard Road, Witheridge, Bampton, Tiverton, Cullompton, Honiton, Ottery St. Mary and Sidmouth.

The most important Western National incursion into the Devon General area was Totnes to Paignton, via the main road and Berry Pomeroy. WN also had rights to operate to Stoke Gabriel and rights to certain local services within Paignton. The main road from Totnes to Buckfastleigh was Western National territory whereas Honiton to Sidmouth was designated a 'common road'. National services specifically allowed to operate into the Devon General area, but only at the existing frequency, were:

WN 106C,	Totnes-Newton Abbot (this was cut back from 1st April 1938 to run between Totnes and Broadhempston only),	
162,	Totnes-Dartington Hall, and	
SN 146,	Bideford-Exeter, between Morchard Road and Exeter.	

The following were 'related services' to be operated at times and fares to be agreed, mileage to be equated and receipts divided between the companies proportionately:

53,	(WN 217)	Exeter-Minehead
45,	(WN128/A/B)	Torquay-Plymouth
47,	(SN 42)	Exeter-Weymouth
49,	(WN 129)	Exeter-Plymouth

Devon General, when called on by Western National to do so, was to surrender the portion of route 27 between Cullompton and Uffculme to them, but this did not occur until 1949. The Agreement empowered Devon General to operate the following services outside their area, subject to there being no increase in the existing frequencies-

3,	between Tiverton and Sampford Peverell
3A,	between Tiverton and Chevithorne
4,	between Honiton and Axminster
9A,	between Sidmouth and Sidbury
21,	between Kentisbeare and Broadhembury
23,	between Warren House Inn and Princetown
27,	between Cullompton and Uffculme
41,	between Sidmouth and Honiton
46,	between Sidmouth, Seaton and Lyme Regis
48,	between Honiton and Seaton
52,	between Sidmouth, Beer and Lyme Regis
56,	between Okehampton and Bude
57,	between Morchard Road and Clovelly

58,   between Witheridge and Lynton
59,   between Cullompton and Cheddar
60,   between Tiverton, Exmoor and Witheridge
61,   between Morchard Road and Ilfracombe

Devon General sold the Sidmouth-Seaton-Lyme Regis portion of route 52 to Southern National for a nominal consideration once the Agreement had been completed on 21st February. Certain other services which were in the timetable but were actually only journeys which could be created using two other routes, were also covered by the Agreement.

The Newton Abbot-Ipplepen-Torbryan-Broadhempston service, previously worked by Western National as part of their 106C, became Devon General service 15A as from 1st April. An imbalance of mileage on the joint Torquay-Plymouth service resulted in Western National providing vehicles for the entire service for the months of May and September 1938, and incidentally, also January 1939.

All Devon General services were suspended from the morning of 31st January until 10th February, the employees having gone on strike over the dismissal of Inspector S. T. Gillard, ostensibly on the grounds of redundancy. Terms were agreed between the Company and the NUR for settlement of the dispute, and Inspector Gillard was reinstated. During the stoppage, independent operators provided services as follows:

Newton Abbot-Buckfastleigh   C. A. Gayton, Ashburton
Exeter-Chagford   A. E. Thomas, Chagford
Exeter-Crediton   Discombe & Way, Crediton
Exmouth-Courtlands Cross   Miller & Son and/or Abbot of Exmouth

A fatal accident took place at Newton Road depot, Torquay on 16th February when Mr. E. A. Cowling, timekeeper/charge-hand and Manager's chauffeur (and who had previously been a Fleet Cars and Grey Cars driver) lost his life when he was struck by a reversing coach.

The stage services of Miller & Son, Exmouth were acquired in May. They ran from Exmouth Station to Orcombe Point (jointly with Devon General and Abbot) and to Phillips Avenue. Devon General incorporated the Orcombe Point service with their own 24A, and extended the other service, which from 7th June became route 73, Ashleigh Road-Exmouth Station-Phillips Avenue-Courtlands Cross. No vehicles were taken over from Millers, who continued to operate tours until 1953 when they were bought out by Greenslades Tours Ltd.

The Directors of Devon General considered making an offer for the purchase of Greenslades Tours Ltd., (of Exeter), but decided that in view of the low receipts per mile, it was impossible that any profit could be earned from the business and resolved to take no further action. (The resolution only referred to stage services)

The new depot in Old Road, Tiverton was completed during 1938 and was also known as Lodge Road. The garage held six buses as built, and replaced the garage in Chapel Street that had been rented from Eastmond & Son since 1924. The contractors were H. Pincott & Sons of Tiverton, who were required to complete within thirteen weeks from commencement of works on 25th February. The garage measured 65' x 35'.

From 1st August, the Southern Railway took over cartage at Budleigh Salterton which had previously been contracted to Devon General, and bought the 30cwt Morris van (DV 5836) which the Company had used there.

South Devon was hit by serious floods following a thunderstorm on 4th August, and some services were necessarily diverted. AEC 'Regent' No:200 on service 12A, was marooned in several feet of water on Torquay sea front, and it was some hours before its crew could be persuaded to 'abandon ship'. The tramlines were still in place there, and the flood waters dislodged the wooden setts, leaving the rails standing well clear of the foundations of the road. The rails had to be removed and the road resurfaced (in concrete) before traffic could be returned to normal. A Leyland 'Lion' LT5 'Sun Saloon' was also marooned a few yards away in Kings Drive whilst on service 72 and in Newton Abbot, the town centre and Kingsteignton Road were badly affected too.

South Devon was hit by serious flooding on 4th August 1938, and AEC 'Regent' 200 (OD 7487) was marooned on Torquay sea front. It never really lost the smell of the floodwater until it was re-bodied in 1949. *(Torbay Library Services)*

Mr. F. B. Low resigned as General Manager from 1st September, and Mr. R. G. James was appointed from that date. Mr. W. H. Geere became Assistant General Manager and Mr. L. J. Crook was appointed Assistant Traffic Manager in place of Mr. H. F. Wyatt who had resigned at the end of June.

A new agreement with the NUR became effective from 17th September, to last until 15th March 1941. Broadly, an extra 1d. per hour was paid, with an increase to eight days paid holiday during the year. There were also increased benefits for 'spread-over' duties.

Two alterations took place to the Torquay tours programme during 1938 in as much as tours 7 and 8 were combined to be Bude, Clovelly, and Westward Ho! Tour 36 went to Staverton and Totnes instead of to Coombe Cellars via Milber Downs and a number of other tours had their routes altered without affecting their destinations.

A new summer-only service (to which reference has already been made) started in Torquay on 6th June. This was the 72, Torquay Station-St. Marychurch Town Hall, via Lawes Bridge, Hele Village and Westhill. It provided a useful link between residential areas, stations and beaches and was regularly worked by Leyland 'Lion' No:45. From 4th July, service 31 ran up Barton Hill Road to Barton (Prince of Orange) and back, after leaving Hele Village on its way to Lawes Bridge, and similarly on the return journey. Workings of service 35 which had been extended to terminate at Barton (Jacks Lane) rather than Prince of Orange, were designated 35A.

The 'Coastal Cruise' service 34 no longer traversed Lincombe Drive, but returned from Wellswood via Ilsham Road and Meadfoot Sea Road.

Separate timetables were allocated to the following services which had previously been treated as short workings of 12 and 63 respectively:

12B,   Torquay (Strand)-Paignton (Sea Front)-Goodrington (Tanners Road)
12C,   Paignton-Preston Down Avenue

Service 63 to Marldon was re-routed via Maidenway Road instead of Preston Down Road, and the narrow section between Preston Down Avenue and Five Lanes was no longer traversed, so normal-sized buses could be used on the 63. Leyland 'Cub' No:100 thus became spare, and one of the older Leyland 'Lions' was used on this service.

A new service advertised from 12th September but actually started a little later due to cable-laying was the 16A, Moretonhampstead-North Bovey (WFSaO). North Bovey is a picturesque village with thatched cottages grouped around the village green, and the route was a steady climb up a narrow lane with high hedges and few passing places.

On the debit side, service 62 Ottery St. Mary-Payhembury (MSaO) ceased operation at the end of October, and Paignton local route 18B was cut back from Paignton Sea Front (Lower Polsham Road) to Preston shelter, which was a relic of the tram days in Torquay Road. The route of the 18B was later modified to include Langdon Road.

The Company returned to AEC for their requirements, and over the years 1938 to 1940, bought 75 'Regals', all generally similar with both Harrington or Weymann bodies. A few, including 406 (DUO 318) were converted to ambulances for the Royal Navy and did not return to bus use.
(East Pennine Transport Group)

TCR353 (ETT 992) is one of eight AEC 'Rangers' bought in 1938 for touring. During the early part of the war they were used for transporting workmen and after the war, resumed tours in the Grey Cars livery. Driver Ted Jones and his regular coach await passengers at the Pickwick Inn near Bigbury. (L.F.Folkard)

New in 1938 were three AEC 'Regent' double-deckers with all-metal Weymann bodywork. DR237 (ETT 998) is seen near Kennford, crossing the A38 on 28th November 1953, near to the former Wobbly Wheel garage. (D.J.Frost)

The four new AEC 'Regal' 'Sun Saloons' (401-404) that had been delivered the previous December went into service in May, and provided general relief to the 'express services' fleet of Leyland 'Tigers' (110-121) as well as enabling suitable vehicles to be used on the Weymouth service 47 and the summer-only Ilfracombe service 61.

Eight new petrol-engined AEC 'Ranger' touring coaches (346-353) were delivered in time for the season. Only the first one was in the traditional grey livery, the rest being turned out in all-over saxe blue. This livery was also applied to 'Tigresses' 336 and 337. The 'Rangers' had a 26-seat Harrington body with a sliding door and a canvas roof that wound back and folded below the level of the back row of seats. The front pair of seats on the nearside were forward of the entrance. They were not only powerful but also fast runners, and the absolute maximum speed recorded by one, was 58mph. They had deeper radiators than previous AECs in the fleet, though some later received the shorter variety in exchange. All the coaches were regularly manned by the same driver for the season, and following the delivery of 346-353, the Torquay coach fleet was manned as follows;

1931 AEC 'Rangers'

319 - H. Northway	324 - C. Ford
320 - R. Luke	325 - S. Bickford
321 - R. Gardner	326 - J. Travis
322 - P. Orsman	327 - P. Ead
323 - W. Gayton	328 - J. Jones

1935 AEC 'Rangers'

334 - P. Rowland	335 - E. Knowles

1936 'Leyland 'Tigresses'

336 - R. Scagell	341 - L. Lewis
337 - L. Worrall	342 - C. Dyer
338 - A. T. Hall	343 - J. Aston
339 - L. W. Dolbear	344 - W. Cole
340 - E. Jones	345 - F. Hayman

1938 AEC 'Rangers'

346 - W. Hannaford	350 - W. G. H. Hodge
347 - C. Luxton	351 - C. Northway
348 - W. Palfrey	352 - R. Down
349 - L. P. Hallett	353 - C. Weekes

Further new vehicles were three AEC 'Regents' (236-238) with body by Weymann. They were very similar to the two delivered in 1937 except that the new trio had the 8.8 litre engine and seated 54. They went into service in July from Torquay depot. Thirteen new AEC 'Regals' (405-417) had Harrington 35-seat body very similar to those on the, LT7 'Lions', including the destination box halfway down on the nearside. They entered service in July on routes 2 and 12, four being based at Kingsteignton, three at Exeter and six at Torquay. 413 was fitted with a Clayton automatic lubricating system.

DEVON GENERAL

The Exeter area destination blind, as fitted to the new 'Regals' carried the following names, which were hardly arranged in a logical order. Two names separated by / indicates a display on two lines.

KENNFORD	HONITON
RADDONS CROSS	MINEHEAD
HONITON CLYST	LITTLEHAM
ROCKBEAR X RDS	BROADCLYST / CULLOMPTON
EXETER	CULLOMPTON / UFFCULME
TORQUAY	PINHOE/ BROADCLYST
PRIVATE	SEATON
TOPSHAM	NEWTON ABBOT
WOODBURY	MORETONHAMPSTEAD
CREDITON	CHAGFORD
BUDLEIGH SALTERTON	OKEHAMPTON
EAST BUDLEIGH	POLTIMORE
EXMOUTH	OTTERY ST. MARY
BUDLEIGH SALTERTON / OTTERTON	SANDFORD
NEWTON POPPLEFORD / SIDMOUTH	WHITESTONE / HEATH CROSS
SIDBURY	TIVERTON
SIDMOUTH	DEPOT

Three Dennis 'Lancet' II buses (298-300) with Harrington 35-seat body entered service in July, two from Torquay depot for routes 13 and 33, and one from Kingsteignton for route 1. The bodywork was very similar to that of 405-417, but was adapted for the Dennis chassis, and the interior decor incorporated green upholstery and green panelling. Their 4-cylinder engine did not perform well on the Devon hills and was difficult to start in cold weather, and there were other inconveniences such as their tank filler being on the opposite side to the rest of the fleet. The Company exercised its option, and not unsurprisingly, did not take the remaining 22 that had been provisionally ordered. Before the end of the year, all three had been transferred to Brixham for service 12 to Torquay.

Finally, there were two new Bedford station buses (450 and 451) with 14-seat bodywork by Birch, to replace the Morris Commercials at Sidmouth and Budleigh Salterton. They entered service in August, and were renumbered M418/9 early in 1939. Unlike earlier station buses, they had no roof-rack or rear ladder, but there was a luggage space behind the back seats, and a wide rear door with no wing windows.

Only a few buses were disposed of in 1938: the Ford (104) ex-Aggett and the two Morris Commercials (178-9) went in November. At the same time, the old B-type tower wagon was withdrawn; it had latterly not seen much use except as a carnival float. Leyland 'Lion' LT3 No:27 was approved for conversion to a breakdown vehicle, but no substantial work could have been involved as it was once again licensed for passenger service in the summer of 1939. Six 'Regals' (180/2/4/7-9) ran until 25th September and were licensed to Greenslades Tours Ltd., from the following month; they were however still included in the Devon General total stock of 241 at the end of the year.

Miscellaneous purchases during 1938 had included one staff car and another ten 'Setright' ticket machines, this time of the 'long range' variety, of which a further ten were purchased in 1939.

1939 Timetable No:88, published on 1st April, showed many changes in both appearance and format, while the route structure was rationalised so as to eliminate most of the services with 'A' and 'B' suffixes, and also to eliminate a few timetabled services which in fact were covered in their entirety by other routes or combinations of services. The timetable cover featured a picture of Leyland 'Tiger' BDV 10 still in the traditional red and black with a background of palm trees. Services which no longer appeared in the book were:

12C,	Paignton-Preston Down Avenue (incorporated into 63)
14A,	Newton Abbot-Princetown (covered by 16 and 23)
17,	Torquay-Bovey Tracey (short working of 16)
19A,	Moretonhampstead-Chagford (short working of 16 and 19)
21/ 21A,	merged as 21, Cullompton-Honiton only (Sidmouth and Seaton, extensions covered by 41 and new 52, respectively)
22/A/B,	merged as 22 Sidmouth-Ottery St. Mary only (remainder of former 22/22A covered by 4)
24,	Exmouth-Lympstone (short working of 5)
25,	Budleigh Salterton (covered by 10 and 40)

29A,	Moretonhampstead-Okehampton via Chagford and South Zeal (covered by 6 and 16)
39,	Exeter-Ottery St. Mary via Rockbeare and Marsh Green (incorporated into 4)
45A,	Torquay-Plymouth via Avonwick (incorporated into 45)
52,	Exmouth-Sidmouth-Seaton-Lyme Regis (covered by 40, 46 and 48)
66A/B,	merged as 66, Exeter-Shillingford-Kennford-Kenn

The Exmouth-Budleigh Salterton section of service 5 was discontinued, being covered by 10 and 40. The Exeter-Newton Abbot-Totnes portions of service 27 were eliminated, being covered by 1 and 15. The Exeter-River Dart service, previously 51, appeared in the timetable without route number. The former 'limited stop' services from Exeter that had been routes 56 to 61 appeared in a green-tinted paper supplement and were described as 'Service Tours'.

Although the Sidmouth-Beer-Seaton service had, by agreement, passed to Southern National early in 1938, Devon General resumed a few workings on Tuesdays and Thursdays between Sidmouth, Seaton and Lyme Regis, and these appeared in the timetable from 1st April 1939 as service 48. The former 48, (Exeter-) Honiton-Seaton became 52. Service 46 at that time still ran from Torquay to Exeter (Express) and then on to Seaton and Lyme Regis via Sidmouth. Services that were given their own distinguishing route numbers were:

17,	Roundham-Paignton Station-Maidenway Road Circular	Previously 18A
24,	Newton Abbot-Decoy	Previously 36B
25,	Newton Abbot-Highweek	Previously 36C
34,	Torquay (Castle Circus)-St. Marychurch-Barton (Jacks Lane)	Previously 35A
36,	Newton Abbot-Kingsteignton-Sandygate	Previously 36A
39,	Newton Abbot-Ogwell-Denbury	Previously 36D
50,	Newton Abbot-Ipplepen-Broadhempston	Previously 15A
51,	Torquay (Strand)-Torbay Hospital	Previously 51A
56,	Paignton (Hyde Road)-Langdon Road-Preston Shelter	Previously 18B
57,	Torquay (Pavilion)-Preston and Paignton Sea Front-Goodrington	Previously 12B
58,	Exeter-Clyst St. Mary-Exton-Exmouth	Previously part 5A
59,	Exmouth-Littleham	Previously part 5A
60,	Torquay-Buckfast Abbey	Previously 11A
61,	Tiverton-Chettiscombe-Chevithorne	Previously 3A
62,	Exeter-Mamhead	Previously 2A
74,	Exmouth Station-Orcombe Point	Previously 24A
75,	Honiton-Talaton	Previously 4A
76,	Crediton-Sandford	Previously part 7
77,	Sidmouth-Sidford-Sidbury	Previously 9A
78,	Newton Abbot-Chagford-Drewsteignton	Previously 29B
79,	Moretonhampstead-North Bovey	Previously 16A
80,	Torquay Station-Marine Drive Circular	Previously 34

Service 81, while not shown on the buses or in the timetable, became the duty number for buses to the newly-built Torquay Girls Grammar School in Shiphay Lane. It should also be stressed that no services were either lost or created by the above amendments to the timetable. All route numbers from 1 to 81 were now allocated, with 12A, 28A and 55A/B being the only ones with alpha suffixes - these were all double-deck routes having the numbers on the blinds.

Most of the single-deck fleet had separate route number blinds, two alternate ones being fitted for either Torquay or Exeter areas. No numbers with suffixes could be displayed on these. Deliveries in 1939 had two-track route-number boxes each with a 0 to 9 blind. Route numbers provided on the Torquay area blind were: 1, 2, 11-18, 24, 25, 28, 30-37, 39, 44 - 46, 50, 51, 54 - 57, 60, 63, 70 - 72, 80, and on the Exeter area blind: 1-10, 16, 19 - 23, 26, 27, 29, 38, 40 - 43, 46 - 49, 52, 53, 58, 59, 61, 62, 64 - 69, 73 - 79.

The Company made application to the Traffic Commissioners for permission to run a new service - Tuesdays and Saturdays only, between Tiverton and Uplowman. Clatworthy's of Tiverton already provided an allegedly rather expensive service, and objected to the application. The result of the application was never published due to the intervention of the war, but Devon General never ran the service.

A leaflet published at Torquay listed express services to Sidmouth and Lyme Regis (daily by route 46) and to Ilfracombe (MWFSaO), Bude (TuO), Clovelly (WO), Lynton (MO), Cheddar (ThO) and Doone Valley (FO). Period return tickets were available and valid for 15 days. The leaflet did not make it clear that it was necessary to change at Exeter for the Ilfracombe, Clovelly, Lynton, Cheddar and Doone Valley services, or that a marathon journey on route 16 was necessary, changing out in the wilds of Whiddon Down, in order to participate in the Bude service. The present-day Trades Description Act would have had a field day. The leaflet which also gave details of services operated in and from Torquay, was an attractive production with a photograph of one of the new 'Regals' on the front. It was printed on the reverse of a colourful map which the Company had produced in 1935 but had evidently vastly over-ordered, so much so, that copies were still available in 1984!

A one-way system came into operation in St. Marychurch, Torquay from 27th May which meant that buses on routes 34, 35 54, 55B and 72 approaching St. Marychurch via St. Marychurch Road then had to leave via Manor Road. Previously Manor Road had been used in both directions.

Sabotage was suspected on 7th July when the brake pedals on several buses at Torquay depot were found to have been tampered with. A watch was kept but there was no repetition of the occurrence.

New deliveries and repaints in 1939 introduced a new style of fleet-name, DEVON GENERAL, smaller than before, in Gill Sans type lettering, and not underlined. Fleet numbers had, since 1934, been carried in red numerals on the waistband, but in March 1939 the instruction was given to prefix the numbers with letters to denote the type of vehicle. The numbers were then applied in gold transfers, just below the waistband, about one-third the size of the letters of the fleet-names and in the same style. At the same time, the white fleet numbers on the chassis dumb-irons were done away with.

Bedfords 450/451were renumbered M418/9, otherwise the actual fleet numbers remained the same. Leyland 'Lions' 25-44, 'Tigers' 132-137 and 'Cubs' 100-102, though still in stock, were not included in the scheme. 133 survived to be later allocated XL133, but when repainted in wartime grey, was liveried out as SL133. Leyland 'Lions' 45-76 were listed as 'SK' rather than 'SL' as would have been logical; the reason for this is not clear, but in any event it is unlikely that any vehicles in this range ever carried prefixes to their numbers. The full list of letters used during the currency of the prefixes from 1939 to 1962 is:

SR	Saloon AEC (Regal/Reliance)	TCC	Touring Coach Commer
SD	Saloon Dennis	TC	Touring Coach, various miscellaneous
SL	Saloon Leyland	XR	Express AEC
SB	Saloon Bedford	XL	Express Leyland
SC	Saloon Commer	M	Leyland 'Cub' or Bedford Bus (one-man)
SN	Saloon Albion	DR	Double-decker AEC (DRD with platform door)
TCR	Touring Coach AEC	DL	Double-decker Leyland
TCL	Touring Coach Leyland	DG	Double-decker Guy
TCB	Touring Coach Bedford	DD	Double-decker Daimler

Twenty-seven buses were advertised for sale by auction at Torwood Street depot on 19th April. They comprised nineteen 1931/32 Leyland 'Lions' (numbers 25, 26, 28-44), five 1929 Leyland 'Tigers' (132, 134-137) and three 1932 Leyland 'Cubs' (100-102) together with a quantity of spares. The Auctioneers were the London (Elephant & Castle) Depository Ltd., and buyers are recorded as coming from Sheffield, London, Taunton and Bude. The prices were knocked down for an average hammer price of just £49 per vehicle.

Modernisation of the fleet continued apace in 1939, with thirty-four new diesel-engined saloon buses replacing a like number of petrol-engined vehicles. They came in three batches: six AEC 'Regal' 'Sun Saloons' (XR 420-425) went into service in April and May from Sidmouth and Exeter depots, on routes 9, 46, 49 and 53, and displaced 1936 'Tigers'. Their 32-seat Harrington body had a sliding door, heaters, opening canvas centre-roof section, and high backed seats upholstered in maroon. They were generally similar to XR401- 404 of 1937, but had a less rounded dashboard arrangement. The front indicator display incorporated a two-track route number box, and the radiator carried a 'DG' triangular shaped badge instead of the 'AEC' emblem. These latter features appeared on all the 'Regals' new in 1939 and 1940.

A further batch of 'Regals' (SR426-451) did not have opening roof or heaters but were otherwise very similar to XR420-425. The 35 seats were somewhat closer together and there were five on the back row, but the standard of upholstery was the same as on the express buses. The passenger door was folding instead of sliding, and the waistband did not taper down to a 'tail' at the rear. They entered service over a period between April and July, some taking over from Leyland 'Lions' on Torquay area services 12, 13, 30, 33, 35 and 63. Others went to Exeter, Exmouth, Kingsteignton, Tiverton and Moretonhampstead depots, the type being particularly associated with routes 2, 3, 4, 5, 6, 11, 15, 16 and 19. Their reliability made them ideal for stationing at remote depots, where some remained for practically all their working life, such as SR430 at Moretonhampstead and SR451 at Axminster.

Two Leyland 'Cub' 20-seat buses were obtained in 1939, for use on restricted routes. One worked the Brixham town service 37, and M453 (DDV 453) is shown here at its Gillard Road terminus, along with driver (later Inspector) Tom Richards.
(DG Staff News)

Finally, two normal-control diesel-engined Leyland 'Cubs' (M 452/3) were delivered, and entered service in May, these being suitable for one-man operation. Four such vehicles had been authorised, but the General Manager decided that traffic requirements warranted only two. They had Weymann 20-seat body, front entrance with folding door, four half-drop windows per side, and an emergency door with two wing windows in the back. A single-line destination box was fitted front and rear. M453 worked at Brixham on the town service 37, and M452 from Exeter on the service tours. 1935 'Cub' M103, displaced from the Brixham town service, was transferred to the Paignton-Greenway service (18). All the 1939 deliveries had registration numbers that coincided with the fleet numbers, and this practice became normal (with a few exceptions) until the National Bus Company era in 1975 when Devon General vehicles were numbered within the Western National scheme.

Approval was given by the Board during 1939 for the re-bodying of the ten AEC 'Ranger' coaches dating from 1931(319-328), but due to the outbreak of war, this was never carried out. An order for 26 new 'Regal' buses nevertheless went ahead. Three Morris cars were purchased, one Rover and three old Morris cars were sold.

INVOICE   SA N⁰ 6674

Dr. to

The Devon General Omnibus and Touring Co. Ltd.

87 NEWTON ROAD

N.B. Robertson, Esq.,   TORQUAY
c/o Devon General Omnibus & Touring Co. Ltd.,
87 Newton Road,   Telephone: TORQUAY 63226
TORQUAY.

DATE   13th August,

The total number of licensed vehicles allocated to the various depots during the winter of 1938/9 and the summer of 1939 was as follows:

Depot	winter 1938/9	summer 1939
Torquay (Newton Road)	64	94
Torquay (Torwood Street)	2	30
Kingsteignton	19	23
Brixham	5	6
Teignmouth	2	5
Moretonhampstead	5	7
Exeter	25	36
Sidmouth	13	15
Exmouth	10	14
Tiverton	5	5
Crediton	2	2
Budleigh Salterton	1	1
Axminster	1	1
Cullompton	2	2
Okehampton	1	1
Totals	157	242

The Company had been in negotiation since 1938 with Torquay Corporation regarding the use of a site 135' x 80' at Vaughan Parade, Torquay for use as a bus station once the buildings already there, had been demolished. Vaughan Parade was a terrace of ten very old three-storey properties, one of which was rented to the Company, and the rear of the terrace formed the frontage of Palk Street. Early in 1939, the Council announced its intention to demolish the properties that autumn, and discussions between the two parties were resumed. The Company was, by then, thinking in terms of a site of twice the area originally envisaged, and the Council deferred negotiations as other parties were also interested. Messrs. Truman, Hanbury & Buxton submitted plans for a Public House and Restaurant on part of the site, which occupied a prime harbour-side position, and just when it seemed that the matter was about to be finalised, war was declared and demolition of the terrace was postponed. Devon General remained as tenants in occupation of number 3, and stayed there until 1986, when schemes for redevelopment of the area were still being considered. It is ironic that their principal coaching rivals in the area at that time, Wallace Arnold, took occupation of number 3 following their vacation, and that demolition of the terrace was no longer one of the redevelopment options.

The first diesel engine single-deckers in the fleet were no less than forty-eight of these Leyland 'Lion' LT7s which turned out to be under-powered for much of the work expected of them. New in 1936/37, the Company was stuck with them and all but one survived the war, with some lasting until 1950. The photo depicts 264 (CTA 75)   *(K.Brown collection)*

Section 8. The War Years, (1939 - 1945)

1939   War was declared on 3rd September, and within a week Devon General had made ten of the 1938 'Regals' (405-414) available for use as ambulances. The windows were painted over dark blue and the seats were removed. Longitudinal stretcher racks were fitted, and provision was made to load stretchers through the luggage doors at the rear. Five buses were soon reconverted. Two normally stayed in reserve at Kingsteignton depot, and the rest were at Devonport in the charge of Devon General men seconded to the Royal Navy. One of them was driver P. J. Rowland, who recalled making fast runs to Bristol with wounded sailors. The five buses were officially on loan until 1941, when they were sold to the RN. One bus was re-purchased by Devon General after the War, and the fate of the other four is not known. They are not however thought to have been air-raid casualties.

About 100 members of the staff joined the armed forces in the first few days of the war, and in view of the reduction in services, another 200 were paid off on 23rd September. In all, 355 joined HM Forces, and there were Devon General 'reunions' in North Africa and on the Anzio beaches!

Instead of operating an autumn timetable, the winter timetable was put into operation from 5th September, and service 51 (Torbay Hospital) was temporarily suspended because of restrictions on the use of the access road. In view of the petrol and fuel-oil rationing scheme which took effect from 23rd September, services were drastically reduced from 25th September to about one half of the normal basic winter operation. A number of little-used or non-essential routes were suspended for the duration of hostilities, and some never did run again, these being:

32,	Torquay (Strand)-Castle Circus-Barton, via Teignmouth Road
57,	Torquay (Strand)-Preston Sea Front-Goodrington
60,	Torquay-Buckfast Abbey
61,	Tiverton-Chettiscombe-Chevithorne
62,	Exeter - Mamhead
69,	Crediton - Shobrooke
72,	Torquay Station-Hele Village-St. Marychurch
73,	Exmouth (Ashley Road)-Station-Courtlands Cross
80,	Torquay Station-Marine Drive Circular
--	Sidmouth Town and Station service
--	Service Tours from Exeter

Routes that were suspended altogether but later revived (albeit several years after the war in some cases) were:

14,	Newton Abbot-Haytor-Widecombe
18,	Paignton-Greenway
20,	Exeter-Bovey Tracey-Haytor-Widecombe
23,	Exeter-Princetown
37,	Brixham Town Service (Fishcombe-Quay-Gillard Road)
38,	Exeter-Metcombe-Sidmouth
42,	Exeter-Pinhoe-Poltimore
52,	Honiton-Seaton
56,	Paignton (Hyde Road)-Langdon Road-Preston Shelter
67,	Exeter-Upton Pyne
74,	Exmouth Station-Orcombe Point
78,	Newton Abbot-Chagford-Drewsteignton
79,	Moretonhampstead-North Bovey

Seventeen other routes were suspended from 25th September but were reinstated from 16th October (70 and 71 from 13th November) and the Company was able to re-engage twenty-five staff following an additional allocation of fuel. They were: 21, 24, 25, 34, 41, 43, 44, 48, 50, 63, 64, 65, 68, 70, 71, 75 and 76. On reinstatement, 70 was curtailed at New Road instead of Haldon Aerodrome, and 64 terminated at Dunchideock instead of Haldon Belvedere. 21 was split into two sections, Cullompton-Kentisbeare (FSaO) and Honiton-Broadhembury (SaO). 66 terminated at Kennford instead of Kenn. Service 43 was diverted to run from Honiton instead of Cullompton, and 68 was extended from Raddons Cross to Shobrooke. 29 was extended from Chagford to Moretonhampstead and ran daily. Services 2, 11 and 16 on which some buses had previously worked through to Torquay, were all terminated at Newton Abbot. Alternate buses on the 2 and 11 had previously worked to Torquay, while the 16 had been peculiar in that most outward journeys ran from Torquay, but most inward journeys terminated at Newton Abbot. The express service 46 was curtailed to run Torquay-Exeter only, and route 26 was cut back to run Budleigh Salterton-Woodbury only. The cut-backs of 2, 11, 16 and 46 became permanent.

The diversions of Torquay-Plymouth route 45 via South Brent Village or via Avonwick and Ugborough also ceased permanently. Other curtailments of a minor nature included 28A which terminated at the Strand instead of Beacon Quay, 31 at Barton (Prince of Orange) instead of Lawes Bridge and 33 at Hesketh Crescent instead of at Meadfoot Beach. 28A never returned to its pre-war terminus, which had been a throw-back to tram days to avoid trams having to reverse on the Strand. 33, 64 and 70 reverted to their pre-war termini after the war, except that 70 ran to Haldon Golf Club rather than to the aerodrome, which had by then been closed. 31 henceforward ran between Lawes Bridge and Hele Cross, solely on depot journeys. 12 ran between Paignton, Brixham and Kingswear only, with single-deckers, Torquay to Paignton being covered by the double-deck 12A.

The loss of a lot of un-remunerative rural mileage did serve to cushion the impact of fuel price rises imposed by the Petroleum Board during the war years, and when there were fare alterations there were decreases as well as increases, with the minimum fare remaining the same.

The prohibition on Devon General vehicles picking up and setting down within the City of Exeter was relaxed from October to assist generally in the emergency and because the City Transport Department was unable to provide bus services on a Sunday. The intention was that this dispensation was to be withdrawn at the end of the war, but it turned out to be the thin end of the wedge towards an integrated transport system for the city; a further step was made from 14th January 1940, when Devon General used ECT stops on Sundays.

From 25th September to 16th October, only 91 buses were in service - 68 single-decks and 23 double-decks. This was in dramatic contrast to the services that had been running only a month before, with 242 vehicles, the peak service being the 12 and 12A with a bus every three minutes to Paignton and every six minutes to Brixham.

The depots at Teignmouth and Brixham were closed from 25th September, but soon afterwards one or two buses were being kept overnight at each place again. All tours were suspended from the end of the 1939 season. By the end of September, no less than 151 vehicles were de-licensed, including all but a few of the petrol-engined buses. Storage presented a few problems, and they were distributed as follows:

Torquay (Torwood Street)	80	Kingsteignton	4
Torquay (Newton Road)	33	Tiverton	2
Exeter	16	Exmouth	5
Moretonhampstead	6	Sidmouth	5

Late in the year, Leyland 'Lion' No: 45 was sold to Torquay Corporation Waterworks Dept. for transporting workers to the Fernworthy Dam project, near Chagford. From 24th November, all drivers, conductors and garage staff were paid a war bonus of 4/- per week.

The office block at Torquay (Newton Road) was extended at both ends during the winter of 1939/40, the work being completed early in the new year.

Land at the rear of Sidmouth depot was purchased in November 1939, amounting to about half an acre as the Company was finding that accommodation at some of the depots was inadequate, and this provided much-needed parking space. Further land was purchased at the rear of Kingsteignton depot.

AEC 'Regal' SR439 (DDV 439) in its wartime guise of all-over grey and masked-off headlights. The fleet-name at the time remained on a background of the original red.
(London Bus Preservation Group)

Little visible alteration took place to the fleet for a few months; first noticeable changes were the masking of headlights and the painting of white edges to the front mudguards. Interior lighting was reduced, and on single-deckers the side and rear destinations were discontinued. The rear boxes were painted over, and most of those on the sides were fitted with a neat advertisement panel extolling the virtues of the Devon General parcels service. The use of 'via' boards carried in brackets below the lower-deck windows was also discontinued. From 2nd October, double-deckers were permitted on service 5 to Exmouth, and DR216 was transferred to Exeter to work it.

Mr. J. C. Chambers resigned from the Board on 8th November owing to his absence on war service, and Mr. C. W. G. Elliff was nominated in his place by the Southern Railway. He was also a Director of the East Kent Road Car Co. Ltd.

The contract for the conveyance of mail at Budleigh Salterton was terminated by the Company from 31st December, and at the same time the town and station service ceased. Wartime conditions decreed that buses through the town should use Station Road and Upper Stoneborough Lane in both directions, and this diversion away from Marine Parade and Fore Street became permanent.

1940

Wartime blackout regulations which required street and vehicle lighting to be reduced, came into force from mid-January, causing the speed limit also to be reduced to 20mph during hours of darkness, thus creating longer evening journey times.

The last of the Exmouth independent bus operators, W. J. Abbott (Exmouth) Ltd., who traded as Blue Omnibus, was bought out on 24th April, their Exmouth-Withycombe-St. Johns service becoming Devon General route 82. Also included in the purchase was Abbott's share of the Orcombe Point service (74) which was in suspension because of the war. Abbott's had, until 1935, used two Shelvoke & Drewry 'Freighters' named 'Pride of Orcombe' and 'Pride of Withycombe' on their services; this was a type with very small wheels, which found favour in several seaside resorts as a bus chassis, though more usually found under dustcarts! W. J. Abbott Ltd., had been founded in 1934 and incorporated businesses previously carried on by Abbott, Harris and Sellers. A Lympstone to Exmouth school contract was also included in the sale of the business to Devon General, but no vehicles were involved.

Timetable No: 94, published on 24th April, was the last one in which fare-tables appeared, thereafter these were published in a separate booklet.

Service 75, Honiton-Talaton, was suspended from 9th June, and the remaining portion of 26, Woodbury to Budleigh Salterton, from 15th September. Both were resumed after the war. A Sidmouth local service was operated for the period 1st July to 30th September only, as route 83, Sidmouth (Triangle)-Station, via the Post Office and Winslade Road, being worked by one of the Bedford station buses M418 and 419. The Leyland 'Cub' M103, that had originally worked at Brixham, was also sent to Sidmouth at about this time.

The Brixham local service 37 was reinstated from 15th September, but only ran from Market Street via Bolton Street, Rea Barn Road and Higher Ranscombe Road to Great Rea Road (Lytes Road), using a 'Regal' from the Kingswear service. Route 63 resumed its original course out of Paignton, via Preston Down Road instead of Maidenway Road, and in Torquay, service 54 was re-routed via Castle Circus instead of via Upton Road. The 33 was cut back from Chelston (Herbert Road) to Chelston (St. Matthews Church).

A limited tours programme was allowed to operate from 22nd March for a short time until reserve petrol stocks had been used up.

The two-level garage at Torwood Street, Torquay was requisitioned by the Royal Air Force. The upper floor was used as a training and recreation centre, a cinema being set up for instruction as well as entertainment. A number of Link Trainers were installed comprising a number of small replica aircraft designed to give ground-based instruction for 'blind' flying. There was also a boxing ring, in which some famous names appeared, such as Tommy Farr, Len Harvey, and Freddie Mills and there was one exhibition appearance by the then world champion heavy-weight, Joe Louis.
The lower floor was used by Torbay Air Raid Precautions Committee as a gas decontamination centre. The building was not handed back to Devon General until 1946, and in its place the Company took a lease on the Court Cars garage in Belgrave Road from Court Garages (Torquay) Ltd., and after alterations to the doorway, used it from 24th June for garaging and storing some of the coach fleet.

At Exeter, from 24th June, the upper level of Blackboy Road was rented to Air Service Training Ltd., buses being parked on rented land in Silver Lane, at the rear of the depot. One rented plot was formerly the garden of a house named 'Cleveland' in Belmont Road.

The Ministry of Labour declared Torbay an 'exporting area' which meant that no workers could be brought into the area, but local workers could be directed to other parts of the country, and indeed many were, including a few Devon General staff. This was to result in later problems caused by long hours and loss of rest days. Many employees were called up for military service, and a large number of conductresses were taken on, the first eight starting work on 8th August. They received the same rate of pay as their male colleagues. A number of romances sprung up, and one of the most remarkable partnerships was that of driver (later Inspector) Wyndham 'Ginger' Rogers of Torquay depot, who after the war married conductress Rene Kelly. Between them they served the Company for 90 years. Mrs. Rogers retired at the end of 1983 and was the Company's last conductress, the final months of her service being on the 120 between Newton Abbot, Torquay and Brixham, which by that time was the only route using a conductor.
Some of the older coach drivers drove buses during the war, and others were found employment in the workshops or on the vans. One lady driver was taken on in 1940, Mrs. Ruth Bate of Exeter depot.

Mr. F. E. Stanley, a Director since 1924, died on 9th July and was replaced on the Board from 10th October by Mr. P. R. Blake who was also a Director of the South Wales Transport Co. Ltd.

Originally a luxury coach for limited stop services, the last of the old Leyland 'Tiger' TS2s was converted to run on producer-gas in February 1943 and used as a staff bus. Driver Percy Rowland balefully surveys the gas trailer on SL133 (UO 9779). This bus returned to passenger service with petrol engine after the war, and was sold in 1947 for further service. (Torquay Times)

In June, Devon General formed its own Home Guard Unit (2135 Transport Company) for protection of the Company's premises, with the General Manager as its Commanding Officer. One of their duties was to go through buses returning to the depot at night to look for saboteurs; at first this was carried out with fixed bayonets, but the procedure was modified after a bayonet went through the roof of a bus! A Lewis gun was mounted on the roof of the offices at Newton Road, Torquay, but the story goes that it was only fired once, and that was at one of our own aircraft! Those days were not all humorous, however, and some local Home Guardsmen (not from the Devon General Company) lost their life when a gun exploded during practice at Corbyn Head, Torquay, while others perished in the bombing of the Palace Hotel, Torquay, which was in use as an RAF hospital. Other members of staff were enrolled into a motor-coach unit for the provision of military services if needed.

First Aid and rescue parties were formed from among the engineering staff, doing sterling work during and after a number of air raids. At both Torquay and Exeter depots gas decontamination squads were formed, being equipped and trained to deal with any civilian vehicles that might need attention in the event of a gas attack. During the evacuation of London in June, Devon General buses carried 13,000 evacuees, meeting their trains from London at local stations.

Another twenty-six new AEC 'Regals' entered service in the early part of 1940; they were of three types: SR456 was Harrington bodied with a canvas sunshine roof panel, very similar to XR420-425 but with three more seats and a folding, instead of sliding, door. It had been ordered for exhibition at the 1939 Commercial Motor Show. SR457-479 were outwardly identical vehicles with 35-seat bodywork by Weymann. Their interior finish was however in blue and fawn trim instead of maroon, and they had a swing door at the top of the steps. Some were to be found on the Torquay local services, and on a fine summer's day would run with their roof open, even in wartime. Route 2 (Exeter-Newton Abbot, via the coast road) was another of their regular stamping grounds. XR454-455 were for express services, and apart from seating three less, were identical to SR457-479. XR454 worked the 47 (Exeter-Weymouth) and XR455 the 46 (Torquay-Exeter) in their earlier days. XR454-455 and SR457-479 were delivered in the red and cream livery, but SR456 was all red. They soon all received grey roof as a wartime measure.

A few vehicles were repainted all red (including SL288 and SR427-429) but during 1940 the whole fleet was given a grey roof, and in most cases, grey waistband as well. A few still retained the large, underlined fleet-name at the time.

Early in the year, twenty-five stored petrol-engined Leyland 'Lion' LT5s (46-70) were sold to Valliant Direct Services of Ealing. A further forty-eight stored, petrol-engined vehicles were requisitioned by the military in July, consisting of six Leyland 'Lion' LT5As of 1934 (71-76), twenty LT5A and LT7 'Lions' of 1935/6 (77-96), twelve Leyland 'Tiger' TS7 'Sun Saloons' of 1936/7 (110-121) and ten AEC 'Ranger' coaches dating from 1931 (319-328). In December, two of the 1937 Leyland 'Lion' LT7s (SL 287-288) were also taken to make up a round fifty vehicles. The Military authorities eventually paid for them, but at slightly less than the Company's valuation.

A number of LT7 'Lions' were used as required for troop movements locally, but most of this large batch formed the mainstay of services from Kingsteignton, Exmouth, Sidmouth and Tiverton depots during the war years.

The Company was at this time desperately short of double-deckers - it only possessed 39 in all, and in November, relief arrived in the form of five Leyland 'Titan' TD5s with lowbridge bodies, belonging to the East Kent Road Car Co. Ltd., but in the livery of Southdown Motor Services Ltd., to whom they had already been on loan. They were hired at a cost of £3 per day per bus. Soon repainted red and grey with Devon General fleet-name and numbered DL301-305, they worked from Torquay depot and were normally used on the Torquay-Paignton-Brixham service 12, on which double-deckers had been permitted from 15th September. It was then possible to allocate two more double-deckers to work on the Exeter-Exmouth service 5.

At the end of 1940, the fleet comprised 197 buses and coaches, which included five in use by the Royal Navy as ambulances.

During the year, a new Morris van replaced one scrapped after an accident. The Company's head office at 88, Kingsway, London WC2 was evacuated on 14th September following air raid damage, and the accounting and secretarial work that had been performed there on the Company's behalf, was transferred to Torquay, where Mr. W. H. Geere was appointed Acting Accountant. Board meetings were then held in the Great Western Royal Hotel at Paddington Station.

Further much-needed land was purchased at Kingsteignton, alongside the depot. Discussions regarding the proposed bus station at Vaughan Parade, Torquay had been grinding on, but came to a final halt. A new proposal, approved in principle, was for the acquisition of land at Brixham for the ultimate construction of a bus station and garage.

1941

The Company was alive to the dangers of air raids, and dispersed as many buses as possible away from the principal depots overnight during 1941 and 1942. Eighteen buses were parked at Pocombe Quarry near Exeter, and twenty on brickworks and tipping land at Hele Road, Lawes Bridge, Torquay. Some buses were parked in suburban roads overnight, two such being Cricketfield Road and Summerfield Road, Torquay. Six double-deckers parked in the latter road every night, and the 'night emergency' bus often accompanied them. This was either Leyland 'Lion' No:27 or Leyland 'Tiger' No:133, the regular driver (J. Michelmore) being required to take it home. His hobby was doing jobs with cement, and the inside of the bus bore witness to what it had been carrying on occasion!

These parked buses never suffered any vandalism, though it was fair game for the local children, (author included) to jump on for a ride as the buses were turning, and then to 'play' with bells and destination blinds which were always left showing something unlikely, such as 'Exton' or 'Rockbeare Cross Roads'. Parking grounds were also formed adjoining Torquay, Kingsteignton, Exeter and Sidmouth depots.

Further land at Sidmouth had been purchased in February and at Torquay in March, while in October a pair of houses next to Torquay depot was purchased - 'Oakville' and 'Marietta', later 85 and 83 Newton Road, which were let to Company staff. Next to these lay the Devon Laundry, and land beyond this was acquired by Devon General to form an emergency access road to land at the side of the depot and behind the laundry, which had been brought into use for parking buses. This road was at first very rough and dusty, and became known from that time on as the 'Burma Road'.

Covered queue rails were installed at Castle Circus, Torquay for the 30 service. The cover was a very rudimentary wood and canvas affair. Queue rails were installed at thirteen other stops in Torquay later in the year to counter disorder. The Company appealed to housewives and shoppers to travel before 4.00pm so as to leave room for workers travelling home.

Negotiations regarding a proposed bus station at Brixham came to a halt after the vendor of one of the properties concerned withdrew his offer of sale as he had been obliged to re-occupy it following the destruction of his Plymouth house in an air raid.

Grey Cars excursions and tours officially ceased from 7th May, and the lease on the ex-Fleet Cars booking office at 3, Fleet Street was relinquished. It had also served as a parcels and lost property office as well as crew rooms, and these functions were transferred to 4, Vaughan Parade, which was leased for use as a mess-room, canteen, duty-room and paying-in office from the Borough of Torquay from 1st October.

New ticket machines were purchased, fifteen TIM 'Major' and twenty Setright 'Quick Issue' type. The latter issued tickets from a roll smaller and narrower than the TIMs but stiffer, and were pre-printed with 'Devon General' and conditions. Date, fare, stage boarded, etc., were selected from dials on the machine and printed on the ticket and were at first used on route 28, Torquay to Newton Abbot, by conductors from both Torquay and Kingsteignton depots. They were sometimes known as 'Trambus' machines, and were numbered D00 to D19.

A feature of the war years was National Savings weeks, the Company contributing loans towards the target set, at up to one million pounds. There were 'War Weapons', 'Warships', 'Wings for Victory' and 'Salute the Soldier' weeks during 1941-1944, and Regent DR211 ran in service covered in posters appropriate to the events in 1941-1943 and DL233 in 1944. The associated processions through the streets caused a certain amount of disruption to services.

A new local service in Sidmouth was introduced on 9th March: Sidmouth (Triangle)-Fortescue- Sidford (Post Office), and the 83, Sidmouth (Triangle)-Station was re-instated from 2nd June. The Exmouth-Exeter services were recast, and a new route 85 was created - Exeter-Topsham-Exton-Exmouth. This in effect joined up the short workings of the 58 between Exmouth and Exton with the short workings of the 5 between Exeter and Topsham. There were thus three services from Exeter to Exmouth, - the 5 via Topsham and Woodbury, the 58 via Clyst St. Mary (which was re-routed to run via Woodbury instead of Exton), and the 85. The 5 and 85 were approved for double-decker working, a lot of traffic being generated by the military camp at Lympstone.

From 7th October, workmen's services were introduced from Cullompton and Bampton to Tiverton (Heathcoat's Factory). These were financed partly by Heathcoat's and partly by low-tariff fares. Two Leyland 'Cubs' (M452/3) were transferred to Tiverton for these services, which never appeared in the public timetable but were presumably the 'missing' 86/86A. After the war, Heathcoat's bought its own Bedford bus.

From 15th October, the Brixham-Kingswear section of route 12 was run as a separate service, 12B, though '12' still appeared on the destination blinds. The garage at Brixham, rented from Bell's, was given up on expiry of the lease, and land at Mount Pleasant Quarry was rented for overnight parking of the bus on the Kingswear service, which was regularly worked by one of SR415, 405, 407 or 417 for a number of years. The same bus also worked the local service 37, but this was again suspended from 19th October, and the vehicle was then used as a relief on the 12 between Brixham and Paignton, where overcrowding remained a problem.

For a time, after the 12B was separated from the 12, the Kingswear bus continued to depart from outside the Police Station at Bolton Cross, although this involved an awkward reversing movement. Between journeys it would park in a convenient space adjacent to the Baptist Church in Market Street. It would then come out into Bolton Cross, reverse into Glenmore Road, and manoeuvre into position outside the Police Station. Later the departure point was moved to the Burton Cars stop which had always been in Market Street, but the timetables continued to show Bolton Cross! 12B arrivals from Kingswear were always in Market Street.

Also, from 15th October, the Crediton terminus was cut back from The Green to Hayward's School although a few morning and evening journeys continued to run to The Green, but for an extra 1d. fare, much to the disgust of regular travellers!

Late in 1941, the terminus of Teignmouth local service 70 was cut back from New Road to Haldon Avenue (top), and that at Shaldon (used for short workings on the 13) from The Green to Bridge End (at the junction of Bridge Road and Fore Street). The latter avoided having to traverse the narrow section of Fore Street in Shaldon.

Not many rolling stock changes took place during 1941. Five 'Regals' (406, 411-414) converted to Naval ambulances in 1939 were sold out of stock, but could still occasionally be seen parked at Kingsteignton and one sometimes came to Newton Road for mechanical attention.

One Leyland 'Lion' 'Sun Saloon', No:45 of 1932, was repurchased by Devon General from Torquay Corporation Waterworks Dept., but was soon resold to A. E. Thomas of Chagford. Leyland 'Lion' No:27 was disposed of in the autumn.

The remaining twenty touring coaches were used on workmen's services, including a daily convoy of 'Tigresses' from

Torquay to Plymouth, conveying men engaged on clearing the rubble of the March blitz which destroyed the city centre. Another convoy of 'Rangers' from Sidmouth carried men engaged in the construction of Dunkeswell aerodrome in East Devon. One of the latter vehicles also operated a school contract between Wolford Cross and Dunkeswell School.

The two 1935 'Rangers' (TCR334-335) had their seating increased to 29 in 1940, the existing 20 seats being replaced by green upholstered seats from the 'Dennis' buses SD298-300. The latter in turn, received seats that had come from the 'Regals' that had gone to the Royal Navy as ambulances.

Five Leyland 'Tigresses' (TCL336-340) were hired to the Bristol Tramways & Carriage Co. Ltd., as from 13th October for a charge of £1 per coach per day.

Five new AEC/Weymann double-deckers had been ordered in 1940, but the Ministry of Transport cancelled the Company's licence to acquire them. The order to the manufacturers however was not cancelled, but was increased to twenty, so that priority could be obtained when construction was possible.

One second-hand staff car was purchased during the year, this being a Morris 10, new in 1939.

On the Directorate, Mr. B. G. White was granted leave of absence for war work. Mr. R. W. Birch (also a Director of Birch Bros. Ltd.) was appointed to the Board on 19th November.

In Exeter, the Corporation had extended their Alphington Road service from Waterloo Road to Marsh Barton Lane in September. It had run there on market days (only) since 1939. Devon General saw this as a threat to their Alphington traffic, such as it was, on routes 1, 2 and 66. Their objections were withdrawn following an agreement with Exeter City Transport for a fares adjustment.

Devon General staff were granted a pay award by Arbitration, effective from 5th April. Most received an extra 2¾d. an hour, but less was paid below the age of 21. The Company agreed in March to make 'Safe Driving' awards to drivers who had completed ten years accident-free driving. An ex-gratia payment of five guineas was made to each, and at the start of the scheme, 47 drivers qualified. In post-war years, the annual 'Safe Driving Awards' got to be quite a social occasion with medals being presented by the Chairman of the Directors.

The fleet at the end of 1941 consisted of the following 191 vehicles:
M103, XL133, DR200-25, DL226-33, DR234-8, SL250-86/9-97, SD298-300, DL301-5, TCR334-5, TCL336-45, TCR346-53, M360-1, XR401-4, SR405/7-10/5-7, M418-9, XR420-5, SR426-51, M452-3, XR454-5, SR456-79.

Routes in operation were the following:

1	Exeter-Chudleigh-Newton Abbot	(Daily)
2	Exeter-Dawlish-Teignmouth-Newton Abbot	(Daily)
3	Exeter-Silverton-Tiverton-Sampford Peverell	(Daily)
4	Exeter-Ottery St. Mary-Honiton-Axminster	(Daily)
5	Exeter-Topsham-Woodbury-Exmouth	(Daily)
6	Exeter-Crockernwell-Okehampton	(Daily)
7	Exeter-Newton St. Cyres-Crediton	(Daily)
8	Exeter-Pinhoe-Broadclyst	(Daily)
9	Exeter-Newton Poppleford-Sidmouth	(Daily)
10	Exmouth-Budleigh Salterton-Otterton	(Daily)
11	Newton Abbot-Ashburton-Buckfastleigh	(Daily)
12	Torquay-Paignton-Brixham	(Daily)
12A	Torquay-Paignton	(Daily)
12B	Brixham-Kingswear	(Daily)
13	Torquay-Maidencombe-Shaldon-Teignmouth	(Daily)
15	Newton Abbot-Ipplepen-Totnes	(Daily)
16	Newton Abbot-Bovey Tracey-Moretonhampstead-Okehampton	(Daily)
17	Roundham-Paignton Station-Maidenway Road (Circular)	(Daily)
19	Exeter-Dunsford-Moretonhampstead-Chagford	(Daily)
21	Cullompton-Kentisbeare	(FSaO)
21	Honiton-Broadhembury	(SaO)

22	Ottery St. Mary-Tipton St. John-Sidmouth	(Daily)
24	Newton Abbot-Decoy	(Weekdays)
25	Newton Abbot-Highweek	(Weekdays)
27	Exeter-Broadclyst-Cullompton-Uffculme	(Daily)
28	Torquay-Kingskerswell-Newton Abbot	(Daily)
28A	Torquay (Strand)-Torre Station-Shiphay Lane	(Daily)
29	Exeter-Drewsteignton-Chagford-Moretonhampstead	(Weekdays)
30	Paignton Station-Torquay Station-Castle Circus-Babbacombe	(Daily)
31	Torquay (Strand)-Westhill-Hele Village-Barton-Lawes Bridge	(Daily)
33	Chelston-Strand-Hesketh Crescent	(Daily)
34	Castle Circus-St. Marychurch-Havelock Arms-Barton	(Daily)
35	Castle Circus-St. Marychurch-Havelock Arms-Watcombe Potteries	(Daily)
36	Newton Abbot-Kingsteignton-Sandygate	(Daily)
39	Newton Abbot-Ogwell-Denbury	(Daily)
40	Exmouth-Budleigh Salterton-Sidmouth	(Daily)
41	Sidmouth-Sidbury-Honiton	(FSaO)
43	Honiton-Plymtree-Exeter	(FO)
44	Newton Abbot-Hennock	(WSaO)
45	Torquay-Plymouth	(Daily)
46	Torquay-Newton Abbot-Exeter (Express)	(Daily)
47	Exeter-Weymouth	(Daily)
48	Sidmouth-Seaton-Lyme Regis	(TuThO)
49	Exeter-Chudleigh-Plymouth	(Daily)
50	Newton Abbot-Torbryan-Broadhempson	(WSaO)
53	Exeter-Tiverton-Bampton-Dulverton-Minehead	(TuSaO)
54	St. Marychurch-Torre Station-Shiphay Lane	(Weekdays)
55A	Torquay (Strand)-Wellswood-St. Marychurch	(Daily)
55B	Torquay (Strand)-Ellacombe-St. Marychurch	(Daily)
58	Exeter-Clyst St.Mary-Exton-Exmouth	(Daily)
59	Exmouth Station-Littleham Village	(Daily)
63	Paignton Station-Marldon-Compton Castle	(Weekdays)
64	Exeter-Ide-Dunchideock	(Weekdays)
65	Exeter-Whitestone-Heath Cross	(FO)
66	Exeter-Shillingford-Kennford	(Weekdays)
68	Exeter-Raddons Cross-Shobrooke	(SaO)
70	Teignmouth (Triangle)-Haldon Avenue	(Weekdays)
71	Teignmouth (Triangle)-Coombe Vale	(Weekdays)
76	Crediton-Sandford	(TuFSaO)
77	Sidmouth-Sidford-Sidbury	(Daily)
81	Paignton-Shiphay (Torquay Girls Grammar School)	(M-F, School term)
82	Exmouth Station-Withycombe-St. Johns	(Daily)
83	Sidmouth (Triangle)-S.R. Station	(Weekdays)
84	Sidmouth (Triangle)-Fortescue-Sidford	(Weekdays)
85	Exeter-Topsham-Exton-Exmouth	(Daily)

It was only in 1941 that the timetable ceased showing services 1, 2, 11, 15 and 16 as starting from Torquay; in fact 1 and 15 had terminated at Newton Abbot since January 1935 and 2, 11 and 16 had been similarly cut back in September 1939. In the intervening period, the timetable had given Torquay arrival and departure times with a footnote that it was necessary to change at Newton Abbot.

1942

The lower portion of Blackboy Road garage at Exeter was requisitioned by the Ministry of Aircraft Production from 11th May to 8th October, together with the adjoining parking land in Silver Lane, and was occupied by Air Service Training Ltd. Devon General objections were overruled by the Regional Transport Commission. Arrangements were made with Exeter Corporation for the use of part of their garage during this period, and further outstation garages were leased: at Crockernwell (on route 6 to Okehampton), at Uffculme (the far end of route 27 and one of the eastern extremities of the system), at Kenton (on route 2 between Exeter and Dawlish) and at Ottery St. Mary (served by routes 4 from Exeter and 22 from Sidmouth).

A commercial garage 'Woolbrook Motors', with flat over and lock-ups adjoining, was purchased; this lay next door to the Company's own garage at Sidmouth. Land at Marsh Barton, just outside Exeter, was purchased from Mr. E. A. Newbery with the long-term objective of construction of a new depot and workshops on the 5½ acre site. This never materialised and the land was sold to Exeter City Council in 1949.

A lock-up shop was rented at Exmouth from the Southern Railway on a short term basis as a rest room for conductresses.

The goodwill of the business of the late Capt. Hutt of Torquay was purchased for a nominal sum to protect the Company's interests after the war; he had been the founder of Fleet Cars, and until the war had operated a fleet of small open touring cars known as PC Tours. Devon General had often sent him prospective customers when their own tours had been fully booked.

A further war wage award was made on 22nd March; in general, staff were paid an extra 1d. an hour.

Exeter suffered badly with air raids during 1942, and though the Company's property escaped damage, fourteen employees lost their home in the raid of 4th May. Raids on Teignmouth and Torquay extracted a further toll. Several passengers who had just alighted from a Chelston bus in Tor Hill Road, Torquay were killed during an air raid on 6th September, and a Devon General cleaner died as a result of injuries received while at work.

Mr. H. T. Barnett, who had been Chairman of the Company since 1922, resigned on 23rd September but remained a Director. Mr. Sidney Garcke was then elected Chairman.

A new local service was introduced in Torquay on 26th April; this was the 32, Hesketh Crescent-Strand-Chelston (Haywain). Like the 33, it was restricted to single-deckers because of low bridges in Mill Lane and Old Mill Road. Service was daily at first but weekdays only from October.

Teignmouth local service 70 was extended from 8th May to form a terminal loop via Haldon Avenue, Higher Woodway Road, New Road and back via Buckeridge Road.

During the year, trees were trimmed with a view to double-deck operation of services 45 (Torquay-Plymouth) and 30 (Paignton-Babbacombe).

From 1st October, the workings of 45 via Avonwick/Ugborough and through South Brent village ceased, all journeys proceeding via the main road and South Brent (London Inn).

Many single-deck buses were repainted all-over grey; in a lot of cases the fleet-name remained on a red strip. Not many of the pre-war double-deckers received this livery, only a few of the 1934 'Regents' that were based at Exeter at the time.

Two more double-deckers arrived on loan in January; these were elderly petrol-engined AEC 'Regents' of the London Transport (ex-Tilling) 'ST' type, with outside staircase, and were used almost exclusively on route 12A between Torquay and Paignton. They retained their London Transport livery and fleet numbers (ST 932/950) throughout their stay, and did not receive numbers in the Devon General series, although 306/7 were left blank. They were hired for £25 each a month.

A notable new vehicle entered service in October - this was DL239, a Leyland 'Titan' TD7 with Weymann body. It was a 'one-off' as far as Devon General was concerned, being one of a series 'unfrozen' by the Ministry of War Transport and taken against the twenty double-deckers on order. It entered service in all-grey livery on route 28A and remained based at Torquay depot all its life. Others of this type went to Newport Corporation

Seven of the 1936 Leyland 'Tiger' TS7 'Sun Saloons' that had been requisitioned by the military in July 1940 were repurchased during 1942. These were XL110/1/3-6/8, but work was required on them before they could go back into traffic. The Company resolved that the other five should be repurchased when available, together with eighteen Leyland 'Lion' LT5As and two Leyland 'Lion' LT7s. Not all these came back into the fold however.

An Enniss Sentinel 'Victory' producer gas unit and trailer was purchased for use with the General Manager's car, Morris '16' AOD 732.

1943

The beginning of the year threw up one or two quirks in the territorial agreements with Western and Southern National. Service 53(WN 217) was covering some journeys between Minehead and Wheddon Cross previously worked by WN route 296, which in turn was ex-Heards 'Red Deer'. The income from these journeys was not relevant to the joint service. From 16th January, through working between Exeter and Minehead was suspended, and passengers were obliged to change at Tiverton, from which point WN worked to Minehead. Through running was resumed after the war, in summer 1948.

Royal Blue services ceased in October 1942, but certain stage services were put on in substitution, one of which was service 402/402A Bournemouth-Dorchester-Bridport-Exeter. This made two journeys a day and was interworked with the Exeter-Weymouth service (DG 47, SN 42) but avoided Lyme Regis. In practice Royal Blue vehicles were normally used, but the inter-relation with the joint service to Weymouth resulted in Southern National working a considerably higher mileage than Devon General on the joint service. To redress matters, Devon General XR420 worked on the Exeter to Bournemouth service for a considerable period until the mileage had been balanced. Southern National had requested a vehicle in grey livery, preferably with both fleet-names exhibited, and the names of places served painted on the window louvres! All they got was the grey livery. Mileage balancing was a phenomenon which cropped up regularly henceforth, and some very complicated issues arose; for instance the insurance position when one Company's crew was driving the other company's bus. Another permutation arose after the Exeter Joint Services Agreement was instituted; Devon General using an Exeter Corporation bus for mileage balancing on the Weymouth service, perhaps with a Southern National crew!

Early in 1943, the Ministry of War Transport issued a directive to Devon General to order nineteen Producer Gas trailer units from the Bristol Tramways and Carriage Company Ltd. Four further units were ordered later.

Road improvements were made at Sandygate (at the end of the Newton Abbot/Kingsteignton built up area) so that buses with gas trailers could turn without having to reverse. Service 28, Torquay-Newton Abbot had, in 1940, become interworked with 36, Newton Abbot-Kingsteignton-Sandygate and no reversing was necessary anywhere. Routes for gas operation had to be reasonably level with termini which did not require reversals, and the 'gas buses' were among the first double-deckers to be used on the lengthy 45, Torquay to Plymouth. They also saw service on 12, Torquay-Brixham where quite a lengthy circuit was necessary to turn. They turned in Brixham via Bolton Street Doctors Lane, Burton Street and Bolton Street.

The last of the old petrol-engined Leyland 'Tiger' TS2s of 1929, by then in all-grey livery and renumbered SL133, was early in March, the prototype conversion by the Company for producer gas operation. It towed a small black trailer with a vertical combustion chamber; this burned anthracite and produced carbon monoxide fumes which passed through a purifier, before being piped to the engine, and re-ignited. SL133 was used as a staff bus, but is not known to have run in public service in this form. The Company possessed another twenty-two trailer units, but only another six buses (DR203/6/9/10/9/38) - all AEC 'Regents' were converted.

The first one into public service, later in March, was DR210 on route 28A, and it is recalled that a vigorous change-down would produce backfiring, and flames would come from the air intake pipe of the trailer! All except DR238 were from the 1934 series.

The trailers were left outside Torquay depot in the forecourt at the Newton Abbot end, and the buses parked inside without them. This operation lasted for just over a year, the double-deckers reverting to diesel power while the 'Tiger' lay out of use, first at Sidmouth and then back at Newton Road until after the war. For many years after, buses that had worked on gas could be distinguished by a circular patch on their back panel.

Western National used producer gas in the Plymouth area at the time, and one of their Bristol K5Gs (usually 316) with gas trailer regularly ran to Torquay on the 128 service, passengers sometimes having to walk up Totnes Hill.

An interesting experiment also took place in March, when the Torquay parcels van FTA 503 was converted to run on town gas, which was carried in a bag on the roof. It ran 6,671 miles in this form, but by the end of the year the bag was patched and leaking and had become porous. Consumption of gas at best was 12.12 cubic feet to the mile, but had deteriorated to 14.77 cu.ft/mile. It was reconverted to petrol in February 1944.

Some routes, though heavily trafficked, were restricted to single-deck operation, and in an attempt to increase vehicle capacity, a few AEC 'Regals' were given perimeter seating, with seats longitudinally down each side, thus giving a larger standing capacity. Only five were converted (SR405/8/15-7), and they saw service on routes 3,(Exeter-Tiverton) and 11,(Newton Abbot-Buckfastleigh) and maybe others, but all were reconverted to normal seating in 1945.

The fleet was augmented by new double-deckers built to 'utility' standards, three different types being delivered. Firstly, in May, came DG240, a six-cylinder Guy 'Arab' with Park Royal body having thinly-upholstered seats of the pattern used on DL239. Next, in June, came DD241-242, two Daimler CWG5s with Duple bodies, also having thinly upholstered seats. The final and largest batch were seventeen Guy 'Arabs', DG308-317 and DG243-249, these having five-cylinder Gardner engine and Weymann bodywork with wooden slatted seats. All the utility buses had very few opening side windows, partly compensated for by having opening toplights to the front top deck windows. Roof domes front and rear were very angular, and not shaped into the graceful curves of pre-war coachwork.

All but the last four (DG246-249) went into service during 1943 and were in all-grey livery. They were allocated to Torquay and Kingsteignton depots and mainly worked routes 28, (Torquay-Newton Abbot), 36, (Newton Abbot-Kingsteignton-Sandygate) and 12, (Torquay-Paignton-Brixham). Their delivery enabled the borrowed buses to be returned, DL301-305 to East Kent and ST932/50 to London Transport. At the same time, some more of the pre-war double-deckers were transferred to Exeter and East Devon, and double-deckers appeared for the first time on the Tiverton-Halberton-Sampford Peverell section of route 3.

Leyland 'Titan' TD4s DL226 and DL227 both had a spell on this working, and seem to have been very breakdown and accident prone. 'Regent' DR237 replaced them in 1944 and stayed at Tiverton for a number of years as that depot's only double-decker. Exmouth depot gained one or two 'Regents' for the services to Exeter; low bridges were the main reason why more double-deckers could not be employed in East Devon at that time, though routes 7 and 8, as well as short workings on the 4 and 5, had been double-deck operated for many years prior to the war. In the Torquay area, the busy route 30, (Paignton Station-Torquay Station-Babbacombe) was converted to double-deck 'Regents' displaced from the 12 and 28 being used in preference to Leylands or Guys.

Sidmouth local services 83 and 84, as well as Teignmouth local service 71, were suspended from 7th March because of a fuel shortage.

Several more of the vehicles that had been requisitioned by the military in 1940 were repurchased by Devon General in 1943; these consisted of two Leyland 'Tiger' TS7 'Sun Saloons' (XL112/121) and eleven Leyland 'Lion' LT5A ('Camels') SL78-80, 82, 84-86, 88, 90, 91, 93. After body attention, the 'Sun Saloons' and three of the 'Camels' went back in to service in 1943 in grey livery, the other eight of the latter not being ready for service until 1945. It was the sight of SL90 in grey, making a rare appearance on route 35, (Watcombe) that reawakened your scribe's interest in buses. Also 'demobbed' in 1943 was SL287, a Leyland 'Lion' LT7, but sister vehicle SL288 did not return from war service.

The roadway giving access to the site that the Company had acquired at Marsh Barton, Exeter, was lowered where it passed under the Teign Valley branch of the GWR so as to enable double-deck vehicles to reach it, and hard core was laid down to form a dispersal parking ground.

A further war wage increase was awarded from 4th July, amounting to one and a third pennies an hour for employees over 21 years of age.

The original destination blinds fitted to the 1934 'Regents' had various additions spliced in over the years, the most recent being for service 30 on its double-decking. The blind on DR207, a Torquay vehicle at this time, comprised the following destinations and was more of less standard for this type of box, which was to be found on DR200-225 and DL226-233. Vehicles in the Exeter area also had displays relevant to the Exmouth to Exeter and Tiverton to Sampford Peverell services.

In the list of destinations given below, a '/ ' indicates a two-line display and a second '/' shows a three-line display. The service number was in full size characters at the extreme left.

4	HONITON CLYST/ROCKBEARE X ROADS		54	ST.MARYCHURCH/BABBACOMBE
5	COUNTESS WEAR/TOPSHAM		54	SHIPHAY VIA/TORRE STATION
7	NEWTON ST.CYRES/CREDITON		28A	SHIPHAY VIA/TORRE STATION
7	CREDITON		28A	STRAND /BEACON QUAY
7	SANDFORD			CASTLE CIRCUS
8	PINHOE/BROADCLYST		12A	PAIGNTON
	EXETER			PRIVATE
30	CASTLECIRCUS/TORQUAYSTATION/PAIGNTON			STRAND
30	TORQUAYSTATION/CASTLECIRCUS/BABBACOMBE			TORQUAY
30	BABBACOMBE		31	WESTHILL
30	CASTLE CIRCUS		31	WESTHILL/HELE VILLAGE
	DEPOT			WESTHILL/HELE VILLAGE/LAWES BRIDGE
28	TORRE STATION			WESTHILL/HELE VILLAGE/BARTON
28	TORRE STATION/NEWTON ABBOT			BARTON
55A	CIRCULAR ROUTE/VIA WELLSWOOD			LAWES BRIDGE
55B	CIRCULAR ROUTE VIA ELLACOMBE		28½	CHUDLEIGH/TEIGNMOUTH

1944

The remaining four Guys were delivered early in 1944, the last three (DG247-249) making a welcome return to red and ivory livery, though still with grey roof. Repainted vehicles started to receive this livery from March onwards, XR455 and SR463 being early examples.

The delivery of the Guys had enabled more pre-war double-deckers to be transferred to Exeter and beyond, including DR234/5 which went to Crediton for route 7, and remained there for the rest of their days. The Crediton services reverted to their former terminus at the Green from 1st February, but intermediate stops in the town were revised. About a dozen double-deckers were by then in the Exeter area, and the Tiverton-Halberton-Sampford Peverell section of route 3, which was double-deck worked normally by DR237, was given a distinguishing route number, 87.

The Daimlers DD241/2, which cannot be recalled on any other routes but 28 and 45, were non-standard and unpopular, and just after being repainted red and ivory, a deal was done with Rhondda Transport Co. Ltd. and they were exchanged for two five-cylinder Guy 'Arabs'. These duly arrived, one in grey and one in Rhondda livery, still carrying their fleet numbers 176 and 177, and the unfamiliar registrations ETX 832 and 833. They were repainted red and ivory and numbered DG318/9, joining their brethren on the 28 route. They had thinly upholstered seats but were otherwise very similar to DG308-317, except that their radiator did not project so far.

The Grey Cars were no longer required on workmen's and military services, and some of the six 1938 'Rangers' at Sidmouth saw occasional use on local stage services before being stored there. The other four 'Rangers' were stored at Moretonhampstead. Of the 'Tigresseses', three were stored at Torquay (Newton Road), one at Sidmouth and six at Court Garages in Belgrave Road, Torquay, along with the two 'Coastal Cruise' buses. Leyland 'Cub' M103 was another vehicle to be stored at Sidmouth, and this one never ran again as a bus.

All the foregoing, as well as many of the bus fleet, were overdue for rehabilitation, but the Leyland 'Titans' were probably in the worst condition. DL226-229 were taken out of service late in 1944 having got into a very rough state, and were sent to Northern Coachbuilders for re-bodying. On one of DL227's last runs with original body, it seemed likely that body and chassis were going to part company en route!

'Tigers' XL111/2/4/6 were given body overhauls by Tiverton Coachbuilders; XL112 received low-backed seats that had come out of one of the 'Regals' that had gone to the Royal Navy, and all lost the glass louvres to their half-drop windows.

Newton Abbot UDC informed the Company that the Market Square was unlikely to be available as a bus station after the war and suggested that the Company should make arrangements to provide its own bus station. Devon General requested the Council to earmark a suitable town centre site while they continued to use the Market Square on a year to year basis; however, the Council's reaction to this request appears to have been to serve a Notice to Quit expiring on 25th March 1945. The Company held over after this date, and it was ten years later before they moved to their own bus station, though they had to pay dearly for their use and occupation of the Market Square in the meantime.

Two Devon General drivers, J. J. George and W. G. Willis of Kingsteignton depot, were elected to the Newton Abbot UDC after the war and each served for one year as Chairman of the Council, their responsible and commonsense approach to local affairs earning them much respect.

The Traffic Manager, Mr. R. T. Hill, had joined HM Forces and during his absence Mr. L. J. Crook was appointed Acting Traffic Manager. A new appointment during the war years was that of General Superintendent, and this position was held by Mr. J. Petrie, who was employed on a year to year basis. He resigned on 29th February due to ill health. Mr. Petrie had been Assistant General Manager of Northern General Transport Co. Ltd., from 1926 for about ten years, and prior to that had bus management experience in Madrid and Hong Kong. He retired to Spain but returned to England during the war years. His Devon General duties entailed much travelling, and had included making the arrangements for the wartime overnight dispersal of vehicles (qv).

A strike was narrowly averted during August, due to tension over long hours and loss of rest days. The management agreed to look at the schedules with a view to giving platform staff fewer hours to work.

In November, the Ministry of War Transport decided to abandon the Producer Gas scheme and authority was given for disposal of all the equipment except for the producer-unit of the staff car. The trailer units were sold for next to nothing.

From 10th August, the ARP Committee only occupied a small part of the ground floor of Torwood Street garage, the rest then being in the occupation of the Ministry of Works.

The dispersal yard at Newton Road was extended by hardcore surfacing of the land acquired in August 1943.

Mr. B. G. White, who had been given leave of absence from his Directorship, received a knighthood in November 1944 in recognition of his work on the 'Mulberry Harbours', the prefabricated ports used in the invasion of Normandy.

1945

There were heavy snowfalls at the end of January and early in February, so much so that all services were withdrawn on the first evening, but several vehicles were stranded away from home, and crews had to 'put up' for the night.

Four of the suspended services were re-instated in the early part of the year, 71 at Teignmouth from 13th March, 83 and 84 at Sidmouth from 27th March, and 37 at Brixham from 4th June. 84 terminated at Sidford (Stevens Cross) and 37 just ran from Market Street to Lytes Road.

Drivers and Conductors at Torquay depot staged a one-day strike on Easter Monday, 2nd April, so no services operated from Torquay that day, but other depots were not affected.

The Bodyshop Superintendent at Torquay, Mr. W. H. Giles had resigned at the end of 1944, and he was succeeded by Mr. F. A. Harrison, who had earlier worked for Brush Coachworks at Loughborough and for City of Oxford Motor Services Ltd. He was immediately faced with a fleet badly in need of attention as well as a depleted workforce, some of whom he had to train in body-building skills. He kept meticulous records which give full details of all works carried out and fortunately these records have been made readily available. Meanwhile, Mr. Giles had set up his own company, Devon Coachbuilders Ltd., at premises in Petitor Road, Torquay, and they built a few bodies for local coach operators.

The four 1936 Leyland 'Titan' TD4s (DL226-229) returned from Northern Coachbuilders early in 1945 with very ugly and austere bodies, which retained the original seats that had been re-upholstered. They re-appeared in service over a period from February to May. The last one, DL227 celebrated the end of the war by receiving a cream roof (in place of the grey) when repainted at Newton Road, as did SL256 and XR401.

Various experimental liveries were tried in May and June. SL79, 82, 84, 85 and 93 were red with ivory waistband and grey roof, SL258 was all red apart from ivory window surrounds, SL259 and 264 were red with ivory waistband and roof, SL265 was as SL264 but the ivory of the roof was continued down over the rear dome to waistband level. The livery applied to SL259 and 264 was adopted as standard but it seems strange that the attractive pre-war livery did not re-appear. Double-deck vehicles were repainted with the waistband above the lower deck windows instead of below them. There was also a somewhat narrower band below the top deck windows.

The first Devon General buses to appear with brand new bodies after World War II were eight Leyland 'Titan' double-deckers of 1936/7 whose original Beadle bodies had got into such a poor state, they would not have lasted much longer. DL227 (BDV 14) is one that was re-bodied by Northern Coachbuilders in 1945 and is seen at the Strand in Torquay. It was withdrawn in 1956.
(Omnibus Society/J.R.Cull collection)

A major rehabilitation programme was put in hand, with many of the Leyland 'Lion' LT7s and AEC 'Regals' receiving major body overhauls, mostly by outside coachbuilders such as Longwell Green (Bristol), Tiverton Coachbuilders, and later Portsmouth Aviation. The capacity of the bodyshop at Newton Road was limited to three vehicles, or four at a squeeze, hence the need to contract-out much of the work. This programme continued over the next few year with a view to making the wartime Guys less unpleasant to travel in, 184 sets of half-drop windows were ordered for fitting to them.

he vehicles which received major body overhauls during the year, although they were not visibly altered except for the removal of the side destination boxes where previously fitted, were as follows:

By Tiverton Coachbuilders:	SL79, 82/4-6, 93, 280/92
By Mumford:	SL266/78
Devon General:	SL253/70/90, TCL337/9-342
Longwell Green:	SL255/6/8/9/61/2/4/5/71/4/5/7/83/5/6/9/91/3/4, XR401/4, SR410.

From May, the outside contractors also repainted the vehicles they had rebuilt, whereas previously they had been painted at Newton Road. The paint-shop there had a capacity of 3-4 vehicles, which could normally be turned out in a week in the pristine finish for which the Company was well known, under the watchful eyes of the Paint-shop Foreman, Mr. A. W. Nias.

Wartime additions to the fleet included Guy 'Arabs' with Weymann bodywork, which included wooden slatted seats, These were, however, replaced with upholstery after the war. DG310 (JTA 310) is one which did not get re-bodied and is seen in Marine Square, Torquay en-route for Paignton in February 1953. (L.F.Folkard)

Due to the large number of passengers using the buses during the period of the post-war fuel shortage, people were finding difficulty in getting on buses to take them to work. A 'priority travel' scheme was therefore introduced by the Company in Torquay from 18th June, and shortly after, in Paignton and Newton Abbot. Firms were able to nominate employees to whom priority travel cards would be issued, which when produced would entitle the holder to board the bus before other waiting passengers. In practice, most stops were marked so that two queues formed and 'priorities only' became a familiar cry from the conductors. There had been pressure from the local councils for such a scheme since 1942.

A limited programme of tours was re-introduced from Torquay in June, when two of the Leyland 'Tigresses' (TCL339 and 341) were prepared for service at Newton Road, and repainted saxe-blue.
Both carried Devon General fleet-name, but a third, later (TCL340) revived the 'Grey Cars' fleet-name that had been dropped since 1936. It was not logical to have a blue 'Grey Car'. The next coach to be treated was TCL337 which appeared in a modified version of the old Grey Cars livery, light grey with maroon wings and cream relief. These four were the only coaches to run in 1945, and were driven on a rota by the pre-war drivers who were still available. There was a heavy demand for the tours, and it was not unusual for booking office staff to arrive for work to find a queue of seventy people outside the office.

A serious accident occurred on 13th July, when SL257, a Leyland 'Lion' LT7 in grey livery, left the road approaching Ashburton while working on route 11 and hit a stone barn at the foot of Linhay Hill. One passenger lost her life, and driver J. French, two conductresses and two passengers were injured. The bus was badly damaged, the cab being smashed, the radiator pushed back into the engine, the chassis twisted, the steering wheel bent, all seats twisted out of position and a lot of glass was broken. The vehicle was brought back to Torquay depot, where not unsurprisingly, it was scrapped early in the following year.

Towards the end of 1945, six new Guy 'Arab' buses were put into service, these being DG320-325 with 6-cylinder engine and bodywork by Park Royal, being similar to DG240 of 1943 but built to relaxed utility specification. They had a curved roof-dome, front and rear, interior lights covered by decorative circular glass shades, and most noticeable of all, comfortable upholstered seats. They entered service in Torquay in the new red and ivory livery, and enabled more AEC 'Regent' double-deckers to be sent up to Exeter taking the total there to fifteen.

Devon General attempted, in July, to obtain the agreement of Exeter City Council to the marking of fixed stopping places within the city, but the Council reminded the Company of the 1936 prohibition and the 1939 relaxation, stating that any stops other than Paul Street were granted only from a courtesy point of view, and by agreement with the city police. Following the applications made by both Devon General and Exeter Corporation to the Traffic Commissioners late in the year, no agreement could be reached between the two parties, but it was resolved that rather than resist each others applications, the possibility would be explored of entering into an Agreement for the co-ordination of services within a radius of seven miles of the city, in the same way that Plymouth Corporation and Western National were by then, already working.

The upper level of the Blackboy Road garage, Exeter, was returned to the Company on 1st October after its wartime use by the Air Service Training Ltd. At Sidmouth, the former Woolbrook Service Station with flat and lock-ups became surplus to requirement, and authority was given for its disposal.

A parcels and enquiry office at 7, Torbay Road, Paignton was vacated on 24th June.

In connection with a National Savings Week campaign, SD299 was decorated on 17th October by George Dyment (the Company's contract sign-writer), in pale cream livery with silver bells, inscribed 'Thanksgiving Week' and 'Give thanks by saving' in blue gothic-style lettering.

1945 finished with another serious accident, when on 7th December SR462 ran off the road near Starcross while overtaking a lorry, and hit the parapet of a bridge over a culvert. Part of the parapet was knocked into a field, the front wheel of the bus being broken off. The bus came to rest on the remains of the parapet. Two passengers were injured. SR462 was extricated with some difficulty, returned to Torquay depot where it was repaired and returned to active service in the spring of 1946.

Lord Mildmay of Flete resigned from the Board on 31st January and Sir Bruce White on 21st March. The number of Directors was thus reduced to eight. Mr. E. A. Bond resigned as Secretary on 30th November, and Mr. F. B. Low once again took on this position.

The Leyland 'Tigress' coaches were added to the touring fleet in 1936 at which time the Grey Cars name was dropped. After the war, the popular fleet-name was revived as seen on TCL344 (AOD 607) with roof open at Looe in 1948 alongside one of the more modern Bedford OB coaches.

(L.F.Folkard)

Section 9. Post-war boom (1946 - 1955)

1946   A number of changes took place both on the Board of Directors and in the senior management; Mr. Sidney Garcke resigned as Chairman and as a Director on 29th March, his successor as Chairman being Mr. J. S. Wills (a Director of British Electric Traction Co. Ltd.,) who himself had succeeded Mr. P. R. Blake on the Board of Devon General from 31st January. Mr. J. W. Womar (also a Director of Sheffield United Tours Ltd.,) came straight in as Managing Director. On 25th April, Mr. H. T. Barnett and Mr. R. W. Birch both resigned; the former had served for 24 years on the Board, being in the Chair for all but four of them. Mr. C. W. F. Hope (who became the Earl of Hopetoun) and Mr. P. Yorke were elected to fill vacancies; they were also Directors of Western Welsh Omnibus Co. Ltd., and Hebble Motor Services Ltd., respectively. Mr. R. T. Hill resumed his position as Traffic Manager following his demobilisation from HM Forces at the end of 1945, and Mr. L. J. Crook was promoted to Assistant Traffic Manager. Mr. N. W. F. Folkard was promoted to Tours Superintendent from 1st April, and Mr. P. C. Wickens was appointed Assistant Engineer from 1st July.

The touring side of the business was re-established under its new superintendent during the year, with Torwood Street garage being released by the Royal Air Force etc. and reinstated for use by coaches. All the coach fleet was overhauled and repainted with the Grey Cars name in a slightly modified version of the old and well-remembered livery, in time for the summer season. Nineteen worked from Torquay with a regular driver to each coach, but the other one, Leyland 'Tigress' TCL342, was sent to Exeter, from whence tours under the Grey Cars name had not previously operated. So successful was the venture, that two Leyland 'Tiger' TS7 'Sun-Saloons' (XL110/5) were hurriedly repainted into Grey Cars livery, renumbered TCL110/5, and also sent to Exeter.

The pre-war offices at 3, Vaughan Parade, 137, Reddenhill Road, and Belgrave Road in Torquay plus 26/28, Torbay Road in Paignton all came back into use, and picking-up and setting-down was also undertaken at sub-post office agencies in Chelston and Barton, on the outskirts of Torquay.

The roster of regular drivers for the nineteen Grey Cars based at Torquay during 1946/7 was as follows:

TCR334 - W. Bray	TCL344 - E. Knowles
TCR335 - W. Hannaford	TCL345 - G. Crispin
TCL336 - R. Scagell	TCR346 - C. Weekes
TCL337 - H. Roberts	TCR347 - L. Hallett
TCL338 - R. Down	TCR348 - W. Cole
TCL339 - R. Gardner	TCR349 - L. Worrall
TCL340 - P. Ead	TCR350 - W. G. H. Hodge
TCL341 - J. Maidment	TCR351 - A. T. Hall
TCL343 - P. Rowland	TCR352 - L. Dolbear
	TCR353 - E. Jones

Relief drivers were Messrs. P. Cole and G. Stear

During July, their Royal Highnesses Princess Elizabeth (later to become Queen Elizabeth II) and Princess Margaret visited South Devon, and were conveyed by Devon General vehicles. Grey Car TCR350 and new AEC 'Regal' bus SR480 were used, being driven by the senior coach driver, W. G. H ('Scatter') Hodge. After this, the 'royal' driver would take great pleasure in pointing out to his passengers the very seats in which the Princesses sat, and the story still got told even after he had been given a new coach!

Twenty-eight AEC 'Regal' saloons were on order, and one was added to cover the loss of SL257 (q.v.). They were delivered between July and December, numbered SR480 to 508, and were of a completely different design from the 1940 'Regals', having rather austere and angular Weymann bodywork. To obtain earlier delivery, they had been built on shells of a design produced for London Transport. The roof and destination box protruded over the front of the vehicle, and there was no rear destination box at all. The suspension was harder, and the tubular-framed seats were upholstered in blue-patterned moquette with brown leather trim but were less comfortable than previously. Interior lower panels were painted blue, with light oak varnished window pillars and surrounds, although windows remained of the half-drop variety. The ivory waistband was much broader than specified, but this was narrowed at their first repaint. The first few went into service on Torquay and Paignton local routes, the remainder being spread all over the system. There were some strange initial problems with these buses which included brake squeal and passengers receiving electric shocks from parts of the bodywork!

The last of the 1929 Leyland 'Tigers', SL133, which had lain out of use for a couple of years, was put back into running order, surprisingly repainted wartime grey again, and returned to service in the Torquay area, running extras on route 30, Paignton to Babbacombe. Four Leyland 'Titan' TD4s (DL230-233) were sent to Strachan's for re-bodying, and in marked contrast to the four of this type re-bodied the previous year, were given stylish and comfortable bodies.
Major body overhauls of three Leyland 'Lion' LT7s and eleven AEC 'Regals' were completed during the year, but some of

the LT7s whose repairs had been deferred, never did get done, four being sold (SL254/68/79/84) and one (SL257) scrapped, following its accident.

The two former 'Coastal Cruise' buses (M360 and 361) now found themselves out of work, for the Marine Drive at Torquay had been declared unsafe for large vehicles following landslips at the Kilmorie end. This was to prove a continuing problem, and to this day, vehicles over 3 tons (unladen) are not allowed on the Marine Drive. After spending most of the war years in store at Court Garages in Belgrave Road, the two buses were rebuilt for use on country services, being fitted with side windows (they were unglazed before) and a folding door.

One Leyland 'Lion' LT5A (SL89) and one Leyland 'Tiger' TS7 (XL117) were repurchased from the military late in the year; the former, not in bad condition, was resold at a good price, but the latter, which was in a thoroughly deplorable and rat-infested state was rebuilt and returned to service in 1947. Vehicles which received major body overhauls during 1946 were:

Devon Coachbuilders, Torquay (completed by Devon General):	TCR334/5
Tiverton Coachbuilders:	SL260/273
Devon General:	SL282, M360/1, TCL336/8, TCR348
Longwell Green:	TCL343-5, TCR346/7/9-53, XR402/3, SR405/7-9/15-7, XR420/1.

XR402 had been the only vehicle allocated to the 'depot' at Kenton; this was no longer used after the bus went for rebuilding, and the lease was surrendered in the following year.

A 30cwt van was purchased to replace the 1935 van used by the Torquay Engineering Dept, a Lister garage sweeping truck for Newton Road depot was obtained, and authority was given for the purchase of an AEC 'Matador' lorry for use as a breakdown vehicle. Approval was also given for the conversion of Leyland 'Cub' M103, long disused, to a general utility vehicle to carry staff, passengers and goods. This conversion was not completed until 1948 and it was then used purely as a stores van, though retaining a few seats.

At Newton Abbot, a further five year lease on the 'bus station' in Market Square was negotiated, retrospective from 25th March 1945. A rest room for staff was rented in Mortuary Lane, of all places.

The commercial garage, flat, and lock-ups next door to the Woolbrook depot at Sidmouth were sold at the end of January to Messrs. C. H. Horwell and C. A. Carnell.

The ticket machine stock in 1946 comprised:
40 x TIM standard of 1934, and 11 of 1937. 15 x TIM Major of 1941, 55 standard Insert Setrights of 1935, 54 of 1936, 2 of 1937, 10 x Long-Range Setrights of 1938, 10 of 1939, 20 x Quick Issue Setrights of 1941. Another 40 x TIM and 25 Improved Long-Range Setrights were on order

DR201 was seriously damaged when it overturned near Woodbury on 26th August 1946 after a bee distracted the driver and he lost control. It was recovered by a passing detachment of Royal Engineers and driven most of the way back to Torquay!

(L.F.Folkard collection)

The Company's third major accident in twelve months took place on 26th August. DR201, one of the 1933 AEC 'Regents', was being driven from Exmouth to Exeter on route 5 by driver F. Brice of Exmouth depot when a bee got into his cab, causing him to lose control of the bus, which hit the verge and overturned down a grass bank and into a field near Woodbury. It was recovered by a passing detachment of the Army with the aid of their AEC 'Matador' lorry; the unit had just returned from North Africa where they had been engaged on the recovery of tanks in the desert, so this exercise caused them few problems. DR201 was badly damaged, the upper deck being virtually crushed, but nevertheless it was driven to Torquay by Running Shift foreman Jim O'Connell, reaching Kingskerswell before finally succumbing due to loss of oil. The Company was still very short of double-deckers, and the decision was taken to repair DR201. It was rebuilt in the Newton Road work-shops, receiving a new top deck, and returned to service in 1947.

A few of the services suspended at the outbreak of war recommenced operation from 10th February 1946, these being:

18,	Brixham-Churston-Galmpton-Greenway (Weekdays)
51,	Torquay (Strand)-Torbay Hospital (WSaSuO)
78,	Drewsteignton-Sandypark-Chagford-Moretonhampstead-Newton Abbot (WO)

A few services were extended, or re-extended to pre-war termini:

33,	re-extended to Chelston (Herbert Road) - actually by 3rd June 1945
36,	extended from Newton Abbot (Market Square) to Newton Abbot (GWR Station)
37,	extended to operate as Fishcombe-Brixham Quay-Fore Street-Market Street (reverse)-Bolton Street-Rea Barn Road-Great Rea Road (Lytes Road).

One of the Leyland 'Cubs' M452/3 returned to Brixham to work the 37, and during service breaks made three trips on the 18 to Greenway.

Other alterations of a fairly minor nature took place as follows:

21,	resumed Cullompton-Honiton journeys on Saturdays only - on Fridays it only ran Cullompton-Broadhembury. By the end of 1946 it was running every weekday Cullompton-Honiton, via Payhembury on TuFSaO, and via Broadhembury on MWThO.
28A,	had become weekdays only in 1942 but reverted to daily in the Summer of 1946.
41,	operated on Saturdays only
43,	operated on Tuesdays and Fridays only, Tuesdays via Talaton and Fridays via Clyst Hydon
48,	operated on Mondays, Wednesdays and Thursdays by Devon General, and on Tuesdays, Fridays and Saturdays by Southern National.
50/53,	worked each weekday
55A,	arrived, and 55B departed from Torquay (Pavilion) instead of Strand
85,	did not run on Sundays, and 58 on Sundays only, ran via Exton instead of Woodbury. By the summer of 1946, 85 ran again on Sundays and all journeys on 58 were via Woodbury.
68,	operated on Tuesdays and Saturday
76,	worked each weekday

In the June 1946 timetable, certain journeys on the 32 and 33 were extended from Hesketh Crescent to Meadfoot Beach, reviving pre-war practice, while two more suspended routes were reopened:

42,	Exeter-Pinhoe-Poltimore	(Weekdays)
79,	Moretonhampstead-North Bovey	(Weekdays)

The 3rd November timetable acknowledged the existence of Burton Cars of Brixham by including their workings in the 12B table between Brixham and Kingswear. It also reintroduced services 56 and 57, though with different routes from pre-war:

56,	Paignton (Regent car park)-Preston Shelter-Shorton Valley	(Weekdays)
57,	Torquay (Marine Parade)-Preston Shelter-Shorton Valley	(Weekdays)

In practice, the same bus worked both routes, going from Torquay to Paignton and vice versa via Shorton Valley. The only routes that were double-deck operated (or mainly so) were 5, 7, 8, 12/12A, 28/28A, 30, 31, 36, 45, 51, 54, 55A/55B, 85 and 87. By November, they were also working on 49 (Exeter-Plymouth).

Most routes were allotted specific vehicles, and a list of the allocation in November 1946 follows. Vehicles not listed were either delicensed or else traffic spares, and the latter worked the routes not listed, as well as providing replacement or extra vehicles for the main routes. It will be seen that very few Leyland buses had any regular duties at the time.

1	SR467/90/91	29	SR435/448
2	SR431/44/66/86-88	30	DR211/2/22/3. XR404, SR419
3	SR409/76/89	31	DR200/2/7/8/20
4	SR434/9/51	32/33	SR456/7/72/5/9
5/85	DR205/10/5/7	34/35	SR446/9/64/74
6	SR408/26/37	36	DG315/316
7	DR234/5	39	SR468
8	DR213	45	DG324/325
9	XR424, SR427/441	46	SR442/462
10/40	SR494/5	47	SR463/477
11	SR483/485/493	48	SR432
12/12A	DL226-229, DG308-310,314	49	DR218
12B	SR407	51	DG323
13	SR416/482/498	54	DR203
15	SR429/443	55A/B	DR219/21/24, DG320-322
16	SR438/460	56/57	SR461
17	SR480/481	58	SR471
18/37	M453	59	SL252
19	SR430/465	63	SR445
22	XR420	70/71	SR428
27	SR433/469/470/478	82	XR454
28	DL239, DG243/4/7/8, 311/317	83	M419
28A	DG249	87	DR237

The 1938/40 AEC 'Regals' were all either rebuilt or re-bodied after the war, such as SR477 (DOD 477) posed outside the depot at Newton Road, Torquay during 1947.

(K.J.Brown collection)

Another serious accident occurred on 19th October when SR487, working on route 2 near Bishopsteignton, was in collision with a lorry carrying German prisoners of war, among whom there were several casualties. The bus sustained front-end damage, and the chassis frames had to be straightened at the front-end and a replacement front axle, engine and gearbox fitted.

1947

From 28th January until mid-February, heavy falls of snow, which later froze, caused suspension and interruption of services, and with passengers only making essential journeys, receipts were dismally low. The staff however reacted excellently, the drivers in particular bearing the brunt of the arctic conditions, while long spells of night work were put in to recover vehicles.

Whistles were issued to conductors from 31st January, particularly for use when reversing. The whistle code was one short blast for stop, two for start, three for full-up, and four for emergency stop - in fact the same as the bell code.

Interavailability of road and rail tickets was extended from 3rd March to include journeys from Exeter to Chudleigh, Chudleigh Knighton, Christow and Ide on the GWR Teign Valley line, and to Exminster, Starcross, Dawlish and Teignmouth on the main line to the west.

The Wilts & Dorset Omnibus Co. was operating between Dorchester and Weymouth, and it was agreed that their return tickets would be accepted on Devon General vehicles on service 47 between these points.

Special single fares were advertised for passengers carried on depot workings between Moretonhampstead Square and Garage (1d.) and between Cullompton (Higher Bull Ring) and East Culm Buildings (2d.).

Torquay depot workings all conveyed passengers at the normal service 28 (or 31) fares, showing 'Lawes Bridge' as their destination.

The National Insurance Act 1946, called for increased contributions to pension schemes, and the Trustees of the Devon General scheme therefore canvassed contributors to see whether they wished the scheme to continue with higher contributions. By a large majority, the scheme continued.

A new Staff News Magazine was published monthly from January; at first it comprised a single folded sheet without illustrations, but gradually increased in size and scope over the years.

From 2nd January, the Company meetings were once again held at 88, Kingsway, London WC2. More changes in the Directorate took place, and the Company obtained permission to cease listing the Directors' names on their letter headings. The Earl of Hopetoun resigned on 3rd July, and Mr. T. R. Williams, who was also a Director of the East Kent Road Car Co. Ltd., was appointed in his place. On 4th December, Mr. J. S. Wills resigned, and Mr. W. T. James was appointed to the Board and elected Chairman. He was also a Director of Aldershot & District Motor Services Ltd. The Directors toured the Company's installations on 29th to 31st July. AEC 'Regal' 'Sun-Saloon' XR454 was made available for their use, having been re-trimmed and repainted, and looked very smart. Its rear destination box had a blind re-fitted, and this carried but one destination - 'Private'. The tour became an annual event thereafter.

Further changes took place in the Company's senior management. Mr. R. T. Hill resigned as Traffic Manager on 22nd February, having obtained a post with the Tanganyika Government and Mr. L. J. Crook was promoted to Traffic Manager as from 1st April. Mr. E. C. Hill was appointed Assistant Traffic Manager from 14th July. Following his appointment as Area Engineer with Wallace Arnold Tours Ltd., Mr. H. C. Manley resigned as Chief Engineer on 30th June, and Mr. G. S. Sedgwick was appointed Chief Engineer in his place on 1st November. The Chief Clerk, Mr. M. W. Hedelius resigned as from 31st July, and his place was taken by Mr. F. J. Selway. Chief Inspector S. B. Stevenson had left at the end of 1946 to take up a post with the Western Welsh Omnibus Company as Area Superintendent at Barry.

The question of a bus depot and station at Brixham was revived, and the purchase of some land at the rear of Fore Street known locally as Gulleys Yard, was approved. Devon General also had their sights on the provision of a bus station in the Central car park at Paignton which was owned by the Great Western Railway, and following a meeting between the parties, the GWR was left to pursue the matter with Paignton Urban District Council.

Extensions to Sidmouth and Kingsteignton depots were planned, but the Ministry of Works refused to grant the necessary licences.

Greenslades Tours Ltd., offered their Witheridge and Tiverton area stage services to Devon General, together with two vehicles, and this purchase was approved in principle. Western and Southern National raised no objection, and the Agreement was completed on 26th November subject to only one vehicle being acquired, and to the approval of applications to the Licensing Authority for transfer of the Road Service Licences. This was obtained in time for Devon General to take over operation of the services from 1st January 1948.

After many months of hard work behind the scenes, Exeter Corporation and Devon General evolved a scheme for the co-ordination of services, and an Agreement was entered into on 14th January 1947. The signatories were Messrs C. J. Newman (Town Clerk of Exeter), J. S. Wills and J. W. Womar, (Directors of Devon General) and F. B. Low (Company Secretary). The area concerned was centred on Exeter, and bounded by Exmouth, Starcross, Haldon Racecourse, Christow, Tedburn St. Mary, Sandford, Thorverton, Hele, Rockbeare and Woodbury. A Joint Committee was established comprising five members from the Council and five from the Company, to deal with:

a) the routes and timetable of any alterations or extensions
b) commencement or discontinuance of services
c) type of vehicles to be used
d) tickets, fares and fare stages
e) services or journeys to be operated by each party
f) interavailability of tickets
g) any other relevant matters

Each party to collect and bring into account on a quarterly basis, the revenue due within the co-ordinated area, having regard to hiring of vehicles, proportion of fares from services partly within the area, and proportion of charges for carrying of luggage. The Agreement which ran to 25 pages, no less, provided inter-alia for Devon General buses to work on city services, and for Exeter Corporation buses to work on country services within the designated area, to produce more or less equal mileage and for pooling of receipts. The services operated by the Corporation wholly within the co-ordinated area immediately prior to the appointed day were:

A,   Whipton (The Mede)-Marsh Barton Lane (Licence H1286)
B,   Sweetbriar Lane (Chard Road)-Exwick (H6636)
C,   Paul Street-Burnt House Lane (H1287)
D,   St. David's Station-Sylvan Road (H1288)
F,   Cowley Bridge-Hill Barton Road (H1292)
G,   St. David's Station-St. Leonards (H1289)
O,   Cross Park (Heavitree)-Redhills (H1284)
S,   Cross Park (Heavitree)-Broadway (H1284)

The services operated by Devon General within or partly within the co-ordinated area immediately prior to the appointed day were 1, 2, 3, 4, 5, 6, 7, 8, 9, 19, 19A, 27, 29, 42, 43, 46, 47, 49, 53, 58, 64, 65, 66, 68, 76 and 85. 19A, Exeter-Leigh Cross-Christow was introduced because the Great Western Railway was unwilling to add to their train service or even to restore a working that had been suspended at the outbreak of war. 19A made three return trips a day, and although listed in the Joint Services documentation, did not commence until after 2nd March.

The first stage of the agreement was introduced in May, and provided for interavailability of tickets and for Devon General to pick up and set down short distance passengers within the city. Prior to this, their power to pick up or set down at all within the city limits other than at Paul Street, had been brought into question, as this had only been granted as an emergency measure in the early days of the war. Nevertheless, the practice had continued (though only picking-up or setting-down passengers from beyond the boundary) the full fare to or from Paul Street being charged. There were many teething problems, some of which were not easily resolved. Until 15th May, there was resistance from the crews to the new arrangements. Four more services that had been previously suspended, re-commenced:

26,   Exeter-Woodbury-Budleigh Salterton (Weekdays) from 28th July
67,   Exeter-Upton Pyne (FSaO) from 31st January
73,   Exmouth (DG Garage)-Albion Hill (via Exeter Road, Park Road, and Marpool Hill) from
        12th October - this was only a portion of the 73 that had operated in 1938/9
74,   Exmouth (DG Garage)-Orcombe Point (summer only), from 13th July.
70,   Teignmouth local service, had three journeys a day extended to Haldon Golf Club.
66,   Exeter-Shillingford-Kennford was re-extended to its pre-war terminus at Kenn from 31st January

Following an application made on 15th November, services 4, 9 and 47 were completely re-routed within Exeter. They had previously left Paul Street via North Street, South Street, Magdalene Street and Magdalene Road, and had entered the city from the Heavitree direction via the same route. Their new route to and from Paul Street was via Queen Street, New North Road, Paris Street, and Heavitree Road, to regain their previous route in Fore Street, Heavitree.

Exeter Corporation services A and F became linked between Hill Barton and Whipton by an extension along Hill Barton Road, that portion of which was part of the A38 Exeter bypass. This created service A/F, Cowley Bridge-New North Road-Heavitree Road-Hill Barton-Whipton-Pinhoe Road-High Street-Alphington (Marsh Barton Lane) and vice versa.

In connection with this revision, and in order to remove anomalies in the fares between the two operators, Devon General fares between Paul Street and Gallows Corner (near the Lower Hill/ Barton Road turn-off) on routes 4 and 9 were reduced from 3d. to 2½d., and the same reduction was applied to routes 8 and 27 between Paul Street and Whipton (Warwick Way). The latter two services were re-routed from Paul Street via Queen Street and New North Road to Sidwell Street.

From 24th November, Exeter Corporation took over operation of route 58, Exeter-Clyst St. Mary-Exmouth, and from then on, normally used double-deckers.

Service C was extended along Burnt House Lane to Rifford Road from 22nd December.

At the other end of the system, three routes were renumbered; the two legs of the Circular Route at Torquay, 55A and 55B, were renumbered 55 and 50 respectively, and the existing 50, Newton Abbot-Broadhempston, was renumbered 88.

A number of bus stop posts of a new concrete type was supplied by London Transport for experimental purposes, which were sited in both Exeter and Torquay. One, outside Newton Road depot at Torquay, even had the familiar London Transport 'bulls-eye' sign still on display. The concrete posts were later produced in quantity by the Teign Valley Concrete Co. Ltd., of Trusham.

Eight AEC 'Regent' IIIs with pre-selector gearbox were bodied by Weymann in 1947 on chassis originally destined for London Transport where they would have been designated 'RT'. DR327 was pictured on a crowded Torquay Strand in August 1952.
(Alan B. Cross)

A stockpile of new 'Regent' III chassis destined for London Transport had been built-up at the AEC works at Southall, and with the agreement of all concerned, eight were allocated to Devon General. Once bodied, they were given the fleet numbers DR326-333. In appearance they were quite unlike the pre-war 'Regents', having a 9.6-litre engine mounted very low (as on the London Transport 'RT') and this gave the driver excellent visibility. For the first time, passengers could see more than just the head of some of the shorter drivers! All of course had pre-selector gearbox, which took some drivers by surprise, but these eight were probably the smoothest-running of any of the Company's vertical-engined double-deckers. They were given all-metal bodywork by Weymann, of a very pleasing design, with flared 'skirts' and wind-down half-drop windows.

They went into service from Torquay depot, being particularly associated at first with the circular route 55A/B, which became 55/50 as mentioned above. This body style remained basically the same for all deliveries until 1952, though there were no more of the 'RT' type. Also, the back indicator boxes on DR326-333 were not perpetuated. The new 'Regent' III had flexible joints between the bottom of the side pillars and the ends of the body bearers, designed to relieve stresses that were prone to fracture the latter. This was only partially successful, for they suffered a lot from fractured bearers in their later days. The starters on this type were liable to lock-up, and instructions were issued that they could be freed by removing the cover over the flywheel housing (using a locker key), and rotating the flywheel with the foot, which normally freed the starter. This invariably happened if the vehicle was left with the gear engaged when stopping. The practice of stopping engines by placing in gear and engaging the clutch was widespread, and was ordered to be discontinued. The correct method was to pull back the top of the accelerator pedal (except on some AEC 'Regents' which had a separate control).

Difficulty with the Guy buses was often experienced by drivers. Their gearbox was back to front and eventually had a replacement gear-knob fitted which was red in colour and indicated the pattern of the gearbox.

A Leyland 'Titan' PD1 (CVA 430) with Alexander 56-seat body ran for a short while as a demonstrator, and an AEC 'Matador' lorry was purchased from the Royal Air Force for conversion to a recovery vehicle, soon being fitted with a crane. It always operated on trade plates. Orders for a new parcels van and two staff cars could not at this time, be fulfilled.

At the beginning of the year, twelve more of the 1936/7 Leyland 'Lion' LT7s (SL251/52/ 56/63/69/72/75/76/81/87/95/97) were sold, reputedly for service in Czechoslovakia. Five more, (SL250/77/91/94/96) were sold for further service in Somerset. Also sold, for re-bodying as a coach, was the old 1929 'Tiger' SL133, for which a very good price was obtained. One of the 1938 'Regals' that had been converted to a Royal Navy ambulance, SR412, was repurchased, overhauled by Devon General, and put back into service. Three more of the 1937 'Tigers' were rebuilt for use as Grey Cars, TCL113 by Mumford of Lydney, TCL117 by Tiverton Coachbuilders and TCL118 by the Mumford-associated firm HTP Motors of Truro. These brought the Exeter touring fleet up to six (one of which worked from Exmouth), and their long-serving drivers, locally known as the 'big six', were Messrs S. Turner, T. Bartlett, S. Weekes, H. J. Gardner, T. Rhodda, and F. Rendell who was the Exmouth driver. Tours operation at the Exeter end was administered by a Mr. Kerslake.

AEC 'Regent' double-decker DR201, which had overturned in August 1946, was rebuilt at Newton Road and returned to service at Torquay. The Company was so proud of the job that for a time, only certain drivers were allowed to drive it!

AEC 'Regent' DR201 was rebuilt in the Company's own workshops in 1947, which almost amounted to a re-bodying. The Bodyshop Foreman was so proud of their efforts that the bus was cosseted thereafter. It is shown in its new form passing Torquay coach station.
(L.F.Folkard)

Also rebuilt during 1947 were nine more AEC 'Regals', of which XR422/4 were dealt with by Longwell Green Coachworks of Bristol, SR429/38 by Portsmouth Aviation, and XR425, SR446/66/74/77 by Devon General. SR477 was given green interior plastic panelling, and its sunshine roof was removed and panelled over. SR446 had been used by learner drivers at Torquay and had got into a very bad state. After being rebuilt it was somewhat surprisingly returned to the same duties, and was soon just as bad again.

New tubular-framed seats with blue vinyl upholstery replaced the wooden slatted seats in the seventeen Guy 'Arab' buses of 1943/4, and these vehicles were also fitted with ten half-drop windows.

The Sidmouth 'station buses' M418 and 419 were re-seated to carry 20 passengers, green seats being used that had come out of the Dennis buses of 1938.

On 19th February 1947, another double-decker over-turned, this time near the 'Three Horseshoes', between Exeter and Crediton on service 7. This was DR234 which, not being too badly damaged, was repaired and returned to service.

Finally, ten 'Speed' Setright ticket machines carrying numbers D001 to D010 were purchased during 1947, three being loaned straight away to Exeter City Transport for a period of three months from March.

1948

Mr. R. G. James, who had been General Manager since 1st September 1938, resigned with effect from 31st January to become General Manager of the East Kent Road Car Co. Ltd. In his place, Mr. A. J. White was appointed from 1st February; he had previously been General Manager of East Midlands Motor Services Ltd., at Chesterfield. Sir James Milne, who is probably best known for having been the General Manager of the Great Western Railway (and having 'Castle' class locomotive 7001 named after him) resigned as a Director of Devon General on 1st April. In his place, Mr. K. W. C. Grand was elected; he was Chief Regional Officer of British Railways Western Region and had been Superintendent of the line on the Great Western, in addition to being a Director of the Western Welsh Omnibus Co. Ltd. At the same time, Mr. J. Elliott resigned from the Directorate, and Mr. J. C. Chambers was elected in his place, this being his second term of office as a Director, a position which he also held with Maidstone & District Traction Ltd.
Mr. F. B. Low resigned as Company Secretary on 7th October, and Mr. Ivan M. Smith was appointed to this position. Mr. Smith was also Secretary of other BET group companies.

At this time, the total number of staff employed was: Torquay-602, Exeter-272, Kingsteignton-179, Exmouth-94, Sidmouth-73, Tiverton-48, Moretonhampstead-19, which totalled 1287. This rose to 1361 in the summer.

Drivers and conductors were awarded a pay increase of 7/6d a week, and Sunday work was paid at time and a half.

The Company's ambitions for a bus station and depot at Brixham were frustrated when Brixham Council refused to accept the plans and the option to purchase the properties concerned, lapsed on 31st March.

Change of ownership of the Company's office at Newton Abbot led to their being served with a Notice to Quit. The new owners offered a new lease but on unacceptable terms, so the General Manager was authorised to negotiate a lease of premises owned by the National Farmers Union, and others. Eventually a lease was taken on part of 16, Sherborne Road (opposite the Market Square) from a Mr. W. J. Morris.

Devon General commenced operation of their newly-acquired services in the Witheridge and Tiverton areas on 1st January. The area served was to the north-east of Devon General territory, and to the south of Southern National's North Devon area, being bounded approximately by Crediton, Tiverton, and South Molton. The Witheridge Motor Transport Co. Ltd., had been formed in 1920 to operate bus services in the area in succession to old-established carriers Thomas & Tidball, and later C. & W. Maire, which in any case was bought out by the Greenslade brothers in 1933, and who then founded Greenslades Tours Ltd., but continued to run the services under the name of Witheridge Transport. In 1938, they also acquired the services that had been run by H. L. Gunn of Rackenford.
This was a sparsely-populated area, and many of the routes were just operated on market days.
Ten routes taken over by Devon General were numbered as follows:

91,	South Molton-Witheridge-Tiverton (Weekdays) -one Friday journey on to Exeter.
92,	Tiverton-Calverleigh-Rackenford (Weekdays)
93,	Witheridge-Puddington-Pennymoor-Tiverton (Tuesdays)
94,	Witheridge-Rackenford-Oakford-Tiverton (Tuesdays)
95,	Witheridge-Rackenford-South Molton (Thursdays)

96,	Witheridge-Morchard Bishop-Exeter (Weekdays)
97,	Witheridge-Cheriton Fitzpaine-Tiverton (Tuesdays and Saturdays)
98,	Witheridge-Cheriton Fitzpaine-Crediton-Exeter (Fridays and Saturdays)
99,	Tiverton-Stoodleigh (Tuesdays)
100,	S. Molton-Bishops Nympton (Weekdays) -One Tuesday journey extended to Ash Mill

Also transferred, were licences for excursions & tours from Witheridge and South Molton. Four drivers from Greenslades at Witheridge transferred to Devon General, and four conductors were taken on, as well as a depot clerk. Six Bell-Punch ticket machines were used at Witheridge from 1st January until mid-February while the conductors were trained on the 'Setright'. The machines were borrowed from Exeter Corporation, and were the last Bell-Punch machines to be used by Devon General. Five buses were based at Witheridge - for the first few weeks of 1948, at the garage in Fore Street that had been retained by Greenslades. However, it was found that its use was not covered by Agreement, so the buses were moved over to The Square, where an office was rented from W. J. Gold. Four of these buses were the Bedfords of 1937/8, and the fifth was an ex-Greenslades Bedford EFJ 548 which had been repainted into Devon General livery and numbered M610. This remained in the Witheridge area until July 1948, though the other Bedfords were soon replaced by AEC 'Regals'. It is related that shortly after Devon General commenced working these routes, M610 stopped to pick-up passengers at the roadside, when one of them would not get on, saying "I'll wait for our little yellow bus".

Devon General introduced two new services of its own in the Tiverton area from 1st January:

| 101, | Tiverton (Heathcoat's Factory)-Tiverton (Elmore) (Mondays to Fridays) |
| 102, | Tiverton (Fore Street)-East Butterleigh Cross (Tuesdays) |

Through running of service 53 between Exeter and Minehead, which had been suspended in 1943, was re-introduced from 1st July 1948, with a change of vehicle at Tiverton no longer necessary.

The only new coaches available after the war were the ubiquitous 29 seater Bedford OBs with Duple coachwork and Devon General purchased ten of them for Grey Cars in 1947 for 1948 delivery. This is TCB604. (J.W.Wilkins)

Most of the Bedford OB Grey Cars were down-seated and cascaded to bus work and looked quite smart in bus livery as shown on SB602 and 603 in Paignton bus station. They were eventually replaced by the Albion Nimbus 31 seaters in 1958. (J.W.Wilkins)

Delivery of the large number of vehicles on order was considerably delayed, due in part to a strike at Duple Coachbuilders. The first to arrive were ten Bedford OB coaches (TCB600-609) with the standard Duple body of the time which had a sliding roof panel but did not have the transparent panels of the later 'Vista' type body. They introduced a modified version of the Grey Cars livery, having maroon waistband and wings, grey body and cream roof.

The standard post-war single-deck type was the AEC 'Regal' with Weymann body of which 69 were obtained new between 1946 and 1948. A typical example is SR515, seen outside the depot in Old Road, Tiverton in February 1953. (D.J.Frost)

Forty AEC 'Regals' (SR509-548) had Weymann 35-seat bus bodywork, very similar to SR480-508 but with a rear route number box set in the roof dome. Delivery of this batch was spread over eleven months, the chassis for eighteen of them being stored at Torwood Street garage in the early part of the year, so that priority could be given to the bodying of the eighteen AEC 'Regent' IIIs also then on order. The later deliveries of the 'Regals' had sliding vents instead of half-drop windows.

The eighteen AEC 'Regent' III double-deckers (DR549-566) had a 9.6litre engine and pre-selector gearbox, but differed from their predecessors DR326-333 in having their engine mounted higher (making them more accessible for maintenance) consequently having a smaller window for the driver and a taller radiator. Destination boxes were fitted at the front and side, but not at the rear and windows were of the sliding vent type. The drivers who delivered these drove back the chassis that had been stored at Torwood Street. Most of the 'Regents' worked from Torquay when new, but soon moved away and were a favourite type for the introduction of double-deckers on former single-deck routes.

TCR633 (LTA 633) was one of twenty-four AEC 'Regal' III Duple coaches which replaced most of the pre-war Grey Cars fleet in 1948/50. The picture taken for publicity purposes, is at Oldway Mansion, Paignton   *(DGO&TC)*

Finally there were twelve AEC 'Regal' III half-cab coaches (TCR611-622) all in full Grey Cars livery, only the first four however arriving in time for the 1948 season. They had Duple 32-seat coachwork of the firm's then standard design but with upswept back under the boot area to give clearance when using the River Dart ferry crossing to or from Dartmouth. A number of Devon General's own modifications that had originally been specified were not incorporated due to an order still in force prohibiting the building of 'luxury' coaches. The older drivers hated them because they were enclosed and separated from their passengers, which inhibited 'telling the tale' thus reducing their tips at the end of the tour! The first four did not even have a public address system, although the rest did. Having said that, they were good reliable coaches, fast, comfortable and powerful and even very light on maintenance. All went into service from Torwood Street depot, and TCR615-622 were always based there. The delivery of these new coaches enabled two of the Bedford coaches to be transferred to Exeter.

The standard destination blind fitted to single-deck vehicles in the Torquay area (also covering Kingsteignton and Moretonhampstead depots) contained, in order, the following destinations:

OAKHAMPTON	DEPOT	PRESTON DOWN
WHIDDON	DECOY	AVENUE
DOWN	HIGHWEEK	COMPTON
SOUTH ZEAL	DENBURY	CASTLE
CHAGFORD	HENNOCK	PRIVATE
MORETONHAMPSTEAD	DAWLISH	DUPLICATE
NORTH BOVEY`	TEIGNMOUTH	MEADFOOT BEACH
BOVEY TRACEY	NEW ROAD	HESKETH CRESCENT
DREWSTEIGNTON	COOMBE VALE	STRAND
CHUDLEIGH	SHALDON	LAWES BRIDGE
BUCKFASTLEIGH	MAIDENCOMBE	CHELSTON
ASHBURTON	TORQUAY	HAYWAIN
TOTNES	PLYMOUTH	CHELSTON
IPPLEPEN	KINGSWEAR	HERBERT ROAD
BROADHEMPSTON	BRIXHAM	WESTHILL
IDEFORD	PAIGNTON	CASTLE CIRCUS
ARCH	GREENWAY	BARTON
KINGSKERSWELL	ROUNDHAM	WATCOMBE
NEWTON ABBOT	MAIDENWAY ROAD	HELE VILLAGE
EXETER		

Due to the limited supply of new chassis for the home market, Ministry of Transport authority was obtained to re-body fifteen of the 1939/40 AEC 'Regal' saloons so these were given new Weymann bodywork similar to those on the new 'Regal' buses delivered at this period. The old bodies were scrapped at Torquay (SR426/7/36/44/45/50/7, SR460/1/4/7/71/72/75/79). Because of the large number of pre-war 'Regal' buses out of service for rebuilding or re-bodying, it was not possible as had been intended, to withdraw the Leyland 'Lions' from the fleet, and very few vehicles were disposed of during this year. Seven Leyland 'Tiger' TS7 'Sun Saloons' of 1936/7 (TCL110, XL111/2/4, TCL115, XL116/121) were sold to Ribble Motor Services in Lancashire for further service, and one Leyland 'Lion' of each of the two remaining types (SL78 and 286) was withdrawn for spares. The two AEC 'Ranger' Grey Cars coaches of 1935 (TCR334 and 335) and the ten Leyland 'Tigress' coaches (TCL336-345) did not run again after the end of the 1948 season.

Vehicles which received major body overhaul during the year were as follows:

By Devon General	DR208/9/11/7/21/24
Portsmouth Aviation	DR203/5/10/19, SR428/30/32-35/7/39-43/47-49/51/58
Longwell Green	XR423, SR459/462/465/468

Some detail alterations resulted: SR458 had its sunshine roof removed and panelled over, the 1934/5 'Regent' buses lost their waistband moulding beneath the lower deck windows, and DR203/5/10/17/19 had their half-drop windows replaced by sliding vent type. These as well as DR224 had new destination boxes front and side to similar dimensions as the post-war standard. All lost their front half-drop windows on the top deck. Fleet number plates were fitted experimentally to DR217 and 221, but these did not find favour and were soon replaced. DR217 had been the last to run in the wartime drab grey livery.

The oldest of the three Leyland 'Cub' buses, M103 was converted to a stores van but retained its bus fleet number.

AEC 'Regal' SR503 was badly damaged at the front end as a result of an accident in the spring which caused the cab and front bulkhead to be scrapped. The rest of the body was then left up on chocks in the yard at Newton Road whilst the chassis had been sent away for straightening. The body was later repaired when the two were re-united.

The Ministry of Transport vehicle examiner found that the 1943/44 Guy 'Arab' double-deckers were actually wider than permitted by regulations then in force, and that there was ¾" too little headroom in the lower saloon. Narrower mudguards were thus fitted which reduced the overall width to 7'6", and the lower saloon was given a recessed floor which provided the requisite headroom.

Late in the year, thirteen of the 1933-5 'Regents' were taken out of service to be re-bodied by Brush Coachworks (DR200/2/4/6/7/12/3/4/6/7/12/13/14/16/20/2/3/5). Their old bodies were tipped off the chassis and burned in the yard adjoining Torquay depot which took place during foggy weather, and a story circulated at the time that one of the new buses had been scrapped and burnt by mistake!

A new service appeared in the summer timetable dated 11th July 1948 which was 90, Newton Abbot-Ideford on a Wednesday and Saturday. Non-timetabled service 89 covered workings between Paignton and Fenton School at Churston. Other service alterations were:

3 re-extended from Tiverton to Sampford Peverell to cover withdrawal of double-deck service 87 (Tivrton-Halberton-Sampford Peverell).
18 ran from Greenway to Paignton (Regent car park instead of to Brixham) thus reverting to its pre-war route. It no longer inter-worked with the 37, the bus involved making five round trips from Paignton to Greenway plus four to Marldon as a 63. The former Greenslades M610 was transferred from Witheridge to cover these workings.
35 was extended from Watcombe Potteries to Watcombe Roundabout via Pavor Road and Fore Street, Barton as the roads had been widened when the new housing estate had been completed.

In Brixham, service 37 was split into three sections, with the Market Street to Lytes Road becoming 37A, Market Street to the Quay and Fishcombe was 37B whilst the 37C covered Market Street to Quay and on to Berry Head Road. All however were worked by one bus, to begin with a Leyland 'Cub' which made fifteen journeys on 37A, fifteen on 37B and eleven as a 37C. The A and B were the two ends of the previous 37, while the C from Fishcombe turned into King Street and along Berry Head Road to reverse at Shoalstone car park. It returned via King Street, left into Fore Street and into Market Street for a journey to Lytes Road as a 37A.

Pre-war 38 was re-introduced but running on Fridays only and between Exeter and Metcombe. The Exeter Express service 46 was extended from Torquay to terminate at Paignton, in the Regent car park.

Exmouth local service 73 was also extended from Albion Hill to Turner Avenue, and some journeys on 82 were terminated at Lovelace Crescent instead of St. John's.

Lastly, Sunday services were introduced at Newton Abbot, these being 24 to Decoy, 25 to Highweek and on the 88 to Broadhempston. There was also a Sunday service between Exeter and Budleigh Salterton on service 26.

The next timetable which was dated 31st October saw some more changes. A new service on Mondays to Fridays was 103 from Dawlish (Green) to Ashcombe (Church) which was operated with a small bus.

In Torquay, the 28A was extended a short distance from the top of Shiphay Lane up to Dairy Hill via Shiphay Avenue to serve the many new houses built there.

Some teething troubles were being experienced with the new AEC 'Regal' and 'Regent' III brake squeal, brake fade and the emission of black smoke being the most tiresome. These were all cured once the brake drums and shoes had been modified and the fuel injection adjusted. Some drivers were reluctant to report vehicles with smoky exhausts, there being a theory that they ran better that way!

Monthly figures were published for each depot showing miles run per involuntary stop, average miles per gallon of fuel oil, and average miles per gallon of lubricating oil, and it is interesting to note that Kingsteignton depot, which always had the reputation of being allocated the oldest and roughest vehicles in the fleet, consistently turned in the best figures on all three counts!

Fuelling and fuel storage was becoming a problem. The Chief Constable of Exeter made a complaint regarding congestion caused in Blackboy Road by vehicles waiting to be fuelled during the nightly run-in of buses. As a result, a 5,000 gallon tank at the lower floor of the depot was brought into use, and all vehicles parking there or in the yard at the back were fuelled from it. War damage and general repairs were carried out at this depot, and the Council repaired the surface of Silver Lane, alongside the depot, which gave rear access. Rust had eaten through two of the underground fuel storage tanks at Torquay, and they were taken out of use. Three new over-ground tanks were erected, which with the two remaining underground ones gave a total storage capacity of 21,000 gallons.

Although the Grey Cars tours were having a very successful season, no expansion of activities was possible because of a

12½% reduction in the amount of fuel allowed; this led to the unsatisfactory situation of intending passengers being turned away while coaches lay out of use.

Nationally the use of electricity was restricted, and instructions were given that all users had to reduce their consumption by 20% between the hours of 8.00am and 12noon, and again in the afternoons between 4.00pm and 5.30pm.

The sixteen remaining 'Setright' ticket machines that had been purchased in 1941 were sold, and replaced by twenty 'Setright' machines of a newer type, which over the next several years gradually replaced the 'TIM' and 'Insert Setright' machines. Trials were carried out with 'Ultimate' machines, which provided different colour tickets for a range of fares, the machine carrying a row of ticket rolls each with a dispensing lever. As these were limited to five values, they were not really suitable for most Devon General services.

There were still many issues to be resolved with regard to the Exeter Joint Services agreement, notably the carriage of parcels, and few visible changes took place there during the year as far as Devon General was concerned. Exeter Corporation had at last taken delivery of eighteen Leyland buses that had been on order for a long time, and with the rapid expansion of the city's housing estates, was able to open a few new routes, all operated by itsown fleet at this stage:

K,   Bedford Circus-Pennsylvania, commenced 19th January
C/W,   South Street-Countess Wear, commenced 1st February
J,   Bedford Circus-Crossmead, commenced 25thApril, and from 8th August was extended to run
        South Lawn Terrace-Crossmead
M,   Paul Street-St. Johns Road (via Barrack Road), commenced 25th July.

It was also agreed that Exeter Corporation should augment the Devon General service on route 64, Exeter-Ide-Dunchideock, and that they would share the cost of operating Paul Street bus station, which was handling 110,000 vehicle departures per annum, or just over 300 per day. Proposals were submitted to Devon General by the Corporation for the linking of routes O/S and C, between Burnt House Lane (Rifford Road) and Cross Park, via Rifford Road, the whole area being a large new housing estate, and this link took effect from 15th November.

Interavailability of British Railways tickets was still advertised, but seemingly was a little-used facility, mainly because railway cheap day returns were not valid for a return journey by bus; indeed only fifteen rail tickets were presented on the Exeter-Exmouth bus services during July and August.

A number of route adjustments were made with Western and Southern National, as a result of which Devon General lost its new-found presence in South Molton, these changes being effective from 3rd July. The South Molton excursions & tours licence was transferred to Southern National, route 91 became Witheridge-Cruwys Morchard-Tiverton (Daily), and Witheridge to South Molton became served by Southern National route 159 which ran in connection. Route 95 became 'joint with Southern National' but it only ran one journey a week, and had disappeared from the Devon General timetable by 1950. Route 94 became jointly operated with Western National (WN 225) as Tiverton-Knowstone-Rackenford. Route 100 passed to Southern National, and days of operation of some of the 'market day' routes were altered:

92   to Tuesdays, Fridays and Saturdays
99   to Tuesdays and Fridays
102   to Tuesdays and Saturdays.

These alterations did away with one complete duty, and a new local service was introduced in Tiverton which utilised the vehicle displaced:

106,   Tiverton (Cotteylands)-Norwood Road (Weekdays)

Devon General did not have destinations for routes 91 to 102 on its existing blinds, and a new area blind for Tiverton and Witheridge was produced. It carried the following destinations, in order. Note: " / " indicates a two line display:

PRIVATE
DUPLICATE
MINEHEAD
TIVERTON
SAMPFORD PEVERELL
EXETER
CRUWYS MORCHARD/TIVERTON
CRUWYS MORCHARD/WITHERIDGE
LOXBEARE CROSS/RACKENFORD
TEMPLETON
LOXBEARE CROSS/TIVERTON
PENNYMOOR/TIVERTON
WAY VILLAGE
PENNYMOOR/WITHERIDGE
KNOWSTONE/TIVERTON
KNOWSTONE/WITHERIDGE
OAKFORD
RACKENFORD/SOUTH MOLTON
RACKENFORD/WITHERIDGE
MORCHARD BISHOP/EXETER

MORCHARD BISHOP/WITHERIDGE
CHERITON FITZPAINE/TIVERTON
CHERITON FITZPAINE/WITHERIDGE
PUDDINGTON/EXETER
MUDFORD GATE/WITHERIDGE
STOODLEIGH/TIVERTON
ELMORE
OLD ROAD
FORE STREET
HEATHCOATS FACTORY
EAST BUTTERLEIGH/CROSS
NORWOOD ROAD
COTTEYLANDS
DAWLISH
TEIGNMOUTH
NEWTON ABBOT
TORQUAY
EXMOUTH
SIDMOUTH
EXCURSION & TOUR

1949

Grey Cars tours were now being operated from Tiverton and Witheridge, the Exeter area fleet having been augmented by four more Bedford coaches. The Tiverton car at this time was Leyland 'Tiger' TCL117. The rented office at Witheridge was used for booking tours, but for the time being the office at Tiverton depot had to suffice for bookings from that town until more central premises could be obtained. Advertised pick-up points in the area included such remote places as Morchard Bishop, Worlington, Meshaw, Thelbridge, and Black Dog!

Two new routes were introduced in South Devon before the summer starting from 10th April, 104, Newton Abbot-Coffinswell-Daccombe was a 'country' route, worked by small capacity Bedfords, and only ran on Wednesdays and Saturdays. The village of Daccombe was actually only a comparatively short distance from the Barton terminus of Torquay local services 31 and 34, easy walking distance but up a steep, narrow and twisting hill, completely impossible for buses.
105 was a new Paignton local service, introduced from 29th May, Paignton (Regent car park)-Barton Avenue. It ran up some very steep hills to the edge of a new housing estate, and was to be extended a number of times over the ensuing years.

The summer timetable, dated 17th July, contained a number of other changes, some of which had been implemented between timetables prior to that date; four more of the routes which had been suspended in 1939 were re-introduced:

14,	Newton Abbot-Haytor-Widecombe (summer only)	from 3rd July
23,	Exeter-Moretonhampstead-Princetown (summer only)	from 3rd July
52,	Exeter-Honiton-Seaton (daily in summer, WSaSuO in winter)	from 10th April
75,	Honiton-Buckerell-Feniton-Talaton (WSaO)	from 10th April

The remaining services suspended in 1939 (20, 60, 61, 62, 69, 72 and 80 and the Budleigh Salterton station service) ceased to be listed in the timetable after 17th July.

18	was extended from Paignton to terminate at Preston Shelter (summer only), making six trips to Greenway, four to Preston, and four to Marldon (as 63).
21	was curtailed to run on WSaO, all journeys serving both Broadhembury and Payhembury
27	was also curtailed to run between Exeter and Cullompton only, the section on to Uffculme being served by Western National routes 262 and 282 only, from 29th May. Nevertheless, Devon General continued to base a vehicle at Uffculme until 1954
64	was re-extended from Dunchideock to Haldon Belvedere from 3rd July, (summer only), and in East Devon, the 38 had its one journey a week extended from Metcombe to Sidmouth.

Following the re-introduction of service 75, the 43 was altered to run from Cullompton instead of Honiton on Mondays, Wednesdays and Fridays, while on Saturdays, it just worked between Exeter and Clyst Hydon.

A new Paignton local service (summer only) from 17th July was 107, Preston Shelter-Churston Station, via Paignton Seafront and Roundham. This did not appear in the public timetable.

Route 29 was diverted at Cheriton Cross to run into Cheriton Bishop and back again, while two Saturdays-only short workings on the 6 from Okehampton to South Zeal were extended to South Tawton.

The 71 at Teignmouth was extended from Coombe Vale via Fourth Avenue and Mill Lane to terminate at Mill Lane (Hutchings Way).
Route 35 at Torquay had, by 16th October, been extended from Watcombe Roundabout via West Pafford Avenue to terminate at Mincent Hill.

On the Exeter joint Services, route M, introduced the previous year, had not proved a success, and was withdrawn early in 1949.

A car park alongside the bus station at Paul Street (but at a slightly lower level) was brought into use during 1949 as an additional bus terminus - this extra space had been badly needed. From 13th June, Devon General took over some of the workings on city services B and G, and the termini were added to the destination screens on selected vehicles: St. Leonards G, St. David's Station, Exwick B, and Sweetbrier Lane B. From the same date, Exeter City vehicles operated certain journeys on the 5, 7, 8 and 85 and also assisted with summer extras to Exmouth.

A busy scene in Fleet Street, Torquay in the early 1950s, with three AEC 'Regents' visible. The street is now pedestrianised and one side has been redeveloped, and known as Fleet Walk. Buses are however once again allowed to mingle with shoppers, albeit at a low speed!
(Herald Express Newspapers)

Brush re-bodied thirteen 1934/5 AEC 'Regent' double-deckers in 1949, and in this form they worked all over the system until withdrawn and sold in 1957. DR204 (OD 7491) was photographed outside Newton Road depot, Torquay. (DGO&TC)

Some AEC 'Regent' IIIs with pre-selector gearbox were transferred to Exeter for the first time, and another innovation on the B and G was the introduction of the 'Ultimate' ticket system. These machines proved fast and effective at a time when the Corporation was still using the 'Bell Punch' system. On 14th November, Corporation buses took over further workings on the 5/85 and also single-deck routes 66 and 76, their single-deck fleet being hitherto rather under-utilised. Their bus No.66 often worked on route 66. Devon General handed back operation of the B and G, and instead took over some of the workings of O/S/C.

The thirteen re-bodied AEC 'Regents' of 1933/5 returned from Brush in June, and very smart they were. A new feature was a buzzer situated behind the mirror on the stairs, which was supposed to act as a warning when the bell was rung, in an effort to cut down platform accidents and this also appeared on subsequent new vehicles. They also revived a feature last seen on the 1938 single- deckers which was the addition of a chromium-plated bumper on the offside corner panel. With a view to avoiding duplication at peak periods, they were used largely to replace single-deckers on some of the busiest routes, trees having been trimmed where required. They took over operation of service 11, Newton Abbot to Buckfastleigh on 10th July, DR225 making the first trip, also short workings on the 16 between Newton Abbot and Bovey Tracey (Coombe Cross). A little later they went on to the 1 from Newton Abbot to Exeter via Chudleigh, the 4 from Exeter to Axminster and the 27 from Exeter to Cullompton.

New vehicles delivered during the year were twenty-six more AEC 'Regent' IIIs (DR567-592), with Weymann body almost the same as the 1948 batch but with half-drop windows instead of sliding vents. A further difference was that the 1949 deliveries, including the re-bodied ones, had their interior finish (waist rails, cant rails and window pillars) in a very dark plum lacquer, whereas the standard finish had been in light oak. The plum colour looked rather sombre, and whilst this style was retained, no others were turned out like it. DR578/80-4/7-92 although delivered in August and September 1949, did not enter service until March 1950.

Eight more AEC 'Regal' III half-cab Grey Cars went into service in 1949, though delivered in the previous year, and four more of this type (TCR624-627) arrived late in 1949 but were not used until 1950.

The 1948/9 version of the AEC 'Regent' III from Weymann, of which 44 were added to the fleet. Some went to Exeter for city services in 1950 following the Joint Services Agreement of 1947. DR579 is however seen in Torwood Street, Torquay, bound for Hesketh Crescent. (S.E.Letts)

Rather surprisingly (as they had not been rostered for any of the more important routes for years), the entire service on route 3, Exeter-Tiverton-Sampford Peverell was worked by Leyland 'Lion' LT7s for a few weeks in June; this was to be virtually their swan song, as ten (SL253/60/1/71/4/8/80/2/9/93) were withdrawn in November, along with the remaining ten Leyland 'Lion' LT5As (SL79/80/2-4/6/8/90/1/3). They were stripped at Newton Road and most were removed during 1950, though two saw use as carnival floats - SL278 in 1949 as 'The Stork Club' and later as 'HMS Spinach' of Popeye's Navy, and the chassis of SL280 in 1950 as 'Transport in the Stone Age' - a theme which had been used previously and really gave the staff scope to go all out!

The ten Leyland 'Tigress' Grey Cars were scrapped at Newton Road during the winter of 1949/50 along with the two 1935 'Rangers', ironically by their former regular drivers.

The two AEC 'Regents' of 1937 (DR234/5) were also withdrawn, their metal-framed bodies having become very noisy with rattles due to rivet-holes wearing oval.

The only vehicles to receive major body overhauls were 'Regal' SR431 and Guy DG240 at Torquay, plus 'Regal' SR470 at Longwell Green Coachworks.

In an experiment to increase ventilation on their upper decks, 1948 'Regent' IIIs DR552/5/7/62/4 received 'Widney' type hopper ventilators to their front windows. No more were altered, but the modification was a feature of subsequent new deliveries.

During the year, two staff cars were purchased and one sold, and a prototype underfloor-engined Leyland 'Olympic' demonstrator was tried on the Chelston routes in Torquay.

A pre-fabricated concrete queue shelter was designed by the Company and produced by the Teign Valley Concrete Co. Ltd., of Trusham. Among the first to be erected were those at Lymington Road, Castle Circus, St. Annes Road, Hatfield Cross and Chatto Road (all in Torquay), and at Newton Abbot railway station. Shelters already existed, in most cases maintained by the local Authority, at Brimley (near Bovey Tracey), Newton St. Cyres, Newton Abbot (Market Square), Milber (Newton Abbot), Churston (Windy Corner) and Preston. In and around Torquay there were already shelters at Lawes Bridge, Old Mill Road, Strand, Marine Square and the wartime canvas-covered structure at Castle Circus for service 30. There were in various other places, shelters that could be used by waiting passengers but were not necessarily built for that purpose, for instance at Teignmouth (Triangle) and St. Marychurch (Town Hall). There was also a number or shelters erected by or for Western National on routes jointly operated with that company. The concrete shelters multiplied in the next few years, and apart from the reinforced glass panels, were reasonably durable. Some still exist, even in places where there is now no bus service!

Various improvements took place at Torquay depot - a new tyre store and workshop was built behind the Social Club, and a new canteen was erected adjoining the south-west corner of the garage. New fuel pumps were installed at Torwood Street, Kingsteignton, Exeter, Sidmouth, Exmouth and Moretonhampstead depots, the old ones at the latter, still being hand-operated.

The garage at Ottery St. Mary, rented from the East Devon Motor Co. Ltd., was vacated on 30th June, and vehicles then had to park in the station yard.

The Company's land at Marsh Barton Lane, near Exeter, together with a large area of surrounding land was zoned as a light industrial site by Exeter City Council under powers provided by the 'Town & Country Planning Act', and there was a proposal to lay a railway line through it. Following veiled hints of a compulsory purchase order, Devon General voluntarily sold their land to the City Council, which offered in exchange, a long lease on a site fronting Alphington Road, at the corner of Marsh Barton Lane. The Company retained the option on this site for several years, but discussions proceeded regarding the possibility of a site nearer the city centre.

Changes on the Board were the resignation of Mr. Peter Yorke on 4th February, being replaced by Mr. P. G. Stone Clark, and the resignation of Mr. J. C. Chambers on 3rd November. Mr. W. H. F. Mepsted was appointed on 18th December, and Mr. Yorke later rejoined the Board. The Exeter Area Traffic Superintendent, Mr. D. J. Chalker resigned from 31st July, and Mr. J. H. Richardson was appointed to this position as from December.

The procedure for vehicle overhaul and maintenance at this period was briefly as follows:

Servicing and light maintenance was carried out at the garages at Exeter, Kingsteignton, Exmouth, Sidmouth, Tiverton and Moretonhampstead, as well as at Torquay. This included inspections, greasing and oil checks on rear axles and gearbox every 1,000 miles, engine oil changed at 5,000 miles, and injectors changed at 7,500 miles. Re-fuelling, lubrication, wheel changes and cleaning were carried out overnight.
Vehicles were docked at Torquay every 30,000 miles, which amounted to a complete inspection and minor engine overhaul. Pistons were drawn according to fuel consumption and re-ringed where necessary and reconditioned cylinder heads were fitted, fuel pumps removed and checked for calibration. All accident damage was repaired, paintwork touched-up, and body-holding bolts checked. On completion, the vehicle was road tested and the bodywork thoroughly cleaned.
With increased reliability of post-war vehicles, the docking interval was gradually increased to 75,000 miles, and consideration was even given to docking on an 'involuntary stop' basis only! Complete chassis overhaul was carried out at 150,000 miles comprising the replacement of all assembled parts by reconditioned units and a thorough examination of the chassis frame (the body not being removed for this operation). A complete body overhaul and repaint was carried out every two years.

A 'Kardex' system was utilised for all vehicle and component records, incorporating a coloured marker for identification of vehicles on which experiments were carried out and the depot to which they were allocated. All these fascinating records were under the meticulous control of Mr. W. H. (Bill) Childs.

New standard destination blinds were designed for the re-bodied 'Regents', and these were also fitted to the post-war 'Regent' IIIs which had the same type of box. There were Exeter, Torquay and Newton Abbot variations. Service 87 was included (though this had not run as such since 1948 when it again became part of the 3) and a few routes were included on the blind in anticipation of double-deck operation. One such was the 19, but on which double-deck operation was never implemented!

1950   Further integration with Exeter Corporation on the joint services took place from 27th March, with Corporation vehicles working most scheduled journeys on the 5, 7, 8, 42, 58, 66, 76 and 85. By the summer timetable, they were working 64, 65 and 68 also, having taken delivery of six new Daimler single-deckers (71-76) with Weymann bodies identical to those on SR509-548. Devon General took over virtually the entire operation of city routes O/S/C which was a complicated schedule, running either from Redhills (O), or Broadway (S) in the west of the city, via the city centre to Rifford Road, out via Heavitree and back via Topsham Road or vice versa to terminate at South Street. Just to make matters more involved, some journeys on the Rifford Road leg terminated at Paul Street (C) in the city centre. Staff and buses from Exmouth and Crediton were involved, and running was arranged so that they worked into Exeter in the morning as 5/85 or 7, took up their duties on O/S/C, made a return journey on 5/85 or 7 to change crews, took up working for the rest of the day as O/S/C, and finally returned home for the night as the last 5/85 or 7. Exeter Corporation buses from the 5/85 and 7 covered the resultant gaps in the O/S/C service. New AEC 'Regent' IIIs DR578/80-4/7-92, which had been in store since being delivered in 1949, went into service on these routes.

The 'Ultimate' ticket machines were limited to five pre-printed values of ticket, and were suitable only for city service. To avoid changes in machine when crews changed from city to country service, or vice versa, they were replaced from 27th March by 'Speed Setright' machines which had already been tried on some country routes. All staff at Exmouth, Exeter and Crediton were instructed in their use, and the Corporation staff were trained for their acceptance and cancellation of 'Setright' tickets.

Elsewhere, several new services were introduced:

108,	Newton Abbot-Huxnor Cross (WSaO) from 12th July 1950	
109,	Torquay (Marine Square)-Warren Road from 12th March 1950	
110,	Newton Abbot (Buckland Rd)-Broadlands Estate (Greenway Rd) (weekdays) from 22nd May.	
111,	Torquay (Pavilion)-Hoxton Road-Windsor Road (daily from 2nd July)	

Three routes running on just one day a week from Crediton, first appeared in the 24th September timetable:

68,	Crediton-Shobrooke-Raddons Cross (ThO)
69,	Crediton-Sandford-Kennerleigh-Black Dog (ThO)
113,	Crediton-New Buildings-Morchard Bishop (TuO)

110	ran between two housing estates, via the town centre.
108,	was a country route, worked by small Bedford buses
111	a double-deck route (but worked by single-decks for winter 1950/1) served an area of terraced houses lying between the 50 and 30 routes.
112 and 112A were contract services that never appeared in the published time-tables.	

More extensions to existing routes took place in Torquay from 2nd July:

28A, Shiphay-Strand was extended up Babbacombe Road to Wellswood, thence via Middle Warberry Road to terminate at Lower Warberry Road (Police Box). This was an area where the elite used to live, but by 1950 most of the big old houses had been divided into flats or flat-lets. There were no direct roads to the town centre that were suitable for buses.
35 was terminated at Willow Avenue instead of Mincent Hill; this was a little way short of the previous terminus, but instead of turning in Mincent Hill on a service road that was really too narrow to take a bus, it turned into Willow Avenue where it was facing the right direction for its journey back into town. Some journeys of the 35 went to a completely different terminus. Instead of turning right at Watcombe roundabout into the estate, they turned left up Halsteads Road, which ran through the new Coombe Pafford estate, and terminated at Lummaton Cross, which was also passed by the 34 on its way to Jacks Lane, Barton.
54 at Shiphay had its terminus extended by one stop to Dairy Hill, to which point the 28A had been extended in the previous year.
107, the summer-only service, by now in the timetable, was extended from Churston Station to Galmpton (Post Office).
From 22nd February, a winter service was introduced on the 14, which had been intended as a summer-only route. The winter service however only ran from Newton Abbot to Haytor (not on to Widecombe) and only ran on Wednesdays and Saturdays.

Days of operation of some other routes were extended in the summer - 64 and 65 ran daily, and Devon General buses ran on route 48 daily albeit jointly with Southern National. These services reverted to the previous arrangements for the winter. 83, Sidmouth Triangle-Station, ceased as such at the end of the summer, being replaced by a diversion of the 22, which was re-routed to leave Sidmouth via Winslade Road, Station and Bulverton Road.

Double-deckers were put on to the 15, (Newton Abbot-Totnes) from 2nd July, two of the 6-cylinder Guys normally being used.

Additions to the fleet in 1950 comprised the balance of twelve AEC 'Regal' III half-cab Grey Cars (TCR623-634) with Duple 32-seat body, the last four being fitted with heaters for winter use. They were very similar to TCR611-622 of 1948/9, and like them, had an upswept back to clear the ferry ramps at Torpoint and Dartmouth. Four of the earlier batch, TCR611-614, worked from Exeter for the 1950 season, and some of this type were always based there for the remainder of their time in the fleet.

Five more AEC 'Regal' IIIs (SR593-597) had Weymann 35-seat bus bodies similar to those on SR509-548, but the newer type of engine and improved suspension gave a smoother ride. The new five were initially used on the longer routes out of Exeter such as the 46 to Torquay and the 23 to Princetown. Three more 1940 'Regals' (SR463/73/78) were also given new Weymann bodies of this type.

The remaining fourteen Leyland 'Lion' LT7s (SL255/8/9/62/4-7/70/3/83/5/90/2) were withdrawn, not having worked since 1949, and the eight AEC 'Ranger' Grey Cars of 1938 (TCR346-353) followed suit at the end of the season. The three Dennis 'Lancets' (SD298-300), always odd men out, were also withdrawn, as were the two Leyland 'Cubs' (M452/3) and the ex-Greenslades Bedford bus M610. None of these was disposed of until the spring of 1951, when all were sold to a dealer in Birmingham. A new Austin A70 staff car was bought and the Morris 16 was sold. Two new Morris vans were purchased.

The programme of major body overhaul was virtually completed with the rebuilding of 'Regal' SR476 and Guys DG310/6 at Torquay. The latter received new roof dome, front and rear, as well as a rear corner number-plate (previously painted on the window). No more Guys were modified as the decision was taken to re-body the rest of the 1943 series.

The Company was anxious to put double-deckers on to the busy routes 2, 3 and 9 in order to reduce duplicate working of single-decks and permission was obtained for double-deckers to work in Sidmouth, which cleared the way for their introduction in 1951. However, there were problems with the 3, where the road level under West Exe railway bridge at Tiverton had been built-up too high for normal height double-deckers to pass under. Five Leyland 'Royal Tiger' 43-seat underfloor-engined single-deckers were ordered for this route in view of the apparent unwillingness of Devon County Council to lower the roadway. Leyland Motors, on learning of the problem, offered the Company early delivery on six lowbridge-bodied Leyland 'Titan' PD2 double-deckers at a very favourable price, and these were therefore ordered for route 3.

Route 2 was dependent on the demolition of a bridge at Powderham before double-deckers could be used, and here too there were some initial difficulties.

Two 8-feet wide double-deckers were received on loan during the year - these being AEC 'Regent' III, OFC 403 from City of Oxford Motor Services Ltd., (in their livery) and a new Leyland 'Titan' PD2/3 in grey undercoat which was registered locally as MTA 747. The Oxford vehicle stayed for several weeks and was used on services in the Torquay area. The Leyland did not stay long and eventually passed into the ownership of an independent operator in Scotland.
Devon General ordered 34 eight-feet wide 'Regent' IIIs for delivery in 1951/2, as well as the six from Leyland, already mentioned.

Extensions to Tiverton depot were approved to enable the garage to accommodate an additional 10 vehicles with the purpose of doing away with the necessity of leaving five buses at Witheridge overnight. Tenders were accepted from the Fairfield Engineering Co. Ltd., of Glasgow for the steelwork, and from R. E. Narracott & Sons Ltd., of Torquay, for the building work.

Planned extensions to Sidmouth depot were cancelled in view of economies in operations anticipated on introduction of double-deckers.

Leyland Motors made Devon General an offer they couldn't refuse, for six PD2 'Titan' lowbridge double-deckers which could be used on the Exeter-Tiverton service 3 where the route passed under the low Exe railway bridge. The six buses arrived but in the meantime the roadway had been lowered so they were not needed. They were used mainly in the Exeter area although one was often to be found on the Brixham-Kingswear 12B service. DL642 is seen at Castle Circus, Torquay in June 1953. *(L..F.Folkard)*

Some employees had by this time completed 40 years service with Devon General and associated companies, and it was resolved henceforth that each employee completing 40 years would be presented with a suitable gift. A 'Long Service Award' evening was thereafter held annually, usually at a Torquay hotel, when the presentations were made by the Chairman of the Directors. The first recipients were:

Messrs. W. H. Geere (1906), A. Bishop (1907), W. G. H. Hodge, F. J. Dore (1908), T. Shobbrook, and G. Bellamy (1910). The social evening was always a good opportunity to hear the 'old stagers' regale their reminiscences, some of which have found their way into these pages. One such true story concerned a peak-hour extra on the 28 at Torquay Strand. Visitors always seem to have difficulty pronouncing ' Kingskerswell' correctly (Kings-kers-well), usually managing to come out with something like 'Kinkers-well'. The locals call it 'Kerswell' anyway. An extra bus was put on from the Strand to Kingskerswell, and the Strand Inspector announced 'Kingskerswell bus-Kerswell only". Nobody moved, so with great presence of mind, he then called 'anyone for 'Kinkers-well' whereupon several holidaymakers came forward and boarded!

1951

The principal route alteration of the year was the re-casting of the Chelston services in Torquay following the double-deck conversion of route 33 from 1st July. The 32 remained single-decker operated, and just ran from Chelston (Haywain) to the Strand, via Mill Lane. Low bridges prevented double-deckers working this way (though on a number of occasions they had a good try!) and route 33 was completely altered to become two routes, but without distinguishing numbers. All journeys commenced at Hesketh Crescent (with a few extended to Meadfoot Beach) and ran thence via Torquay Strand, Union Street, Tor Hill Road and Lucius Street. Here the single-deck 32 (and the former 33) turned off into Belgrave Road. The new 33 went straight ahead, via Falkland Road, Abbey Gates, Walnut Road, and over the railway. Those bound for Herbert Road went straight ahead, via Walnut Road and St. Matthews Road.
The other leg of the 33, which went to The Reeves Road, came over the railway at Walnut Road then turned right into Rousdon Road, thence via Ashfield Road, Sherwell Hill, Boundary Road and Burridge Road to terminate at The Reeves Road (top). Inward-bound 33 ran between Walnut Road and Falkland Road via Rathmore Road to give a better route across the awkward five-way junction at Abbey Gates. No double-deckers at the time had 'Chelston' on their destination blinds, so a few were painted-up and spliced into existing blinds on some of the 1947/8 AEC 'Regent' IIIs. These were somewhat ambiguous, the same display being used for either destination in Chelston, and read:

CHELSTON
33 (Herbert Road)
For
Cockington
(Reeves Road)

Other service alterations comprised the re-introduction from 1st July of route 20, Exeter-Chudleigh-Bovey Tracey-Haytor-Widecombe (summer only). It had been suspended from outbreak of war in 1939. Route 107 re-appeared for the summer, but was re-routed to run Preston-Paignton-Goodrington-Broadsands Park Road (viaduct) and from that point, a footpath ran to the popular Broadsands Beach. Route 18 was no longer extended to Preston in summer, and terminated at Paignton (Central car park). Route 111 in Torquay was extended from 1st July a short distance from Windsor Road (top of Ellacombe Church Road) to form a terminal loop via Reddenhill Road, Warbro Road, and Windermere Road.

From 3rd December, route 110 in Newton Abbot was extended from Buckland Road through the housing estate to terminate at Moorland View, and operated daily.

Journeys on route 48 that were worked by Southern National became shown in the timetable as SN route 45.

Four more main routes were converted to double-deck from 25th March (Easter). Route 9 was diverted to avoid a low railway bridge, and thus entered Sidmouth via Bulverton Road, Station and Alexandria Road instead of via Woolbrook.

The old stone bridge on the Earl of Devon's estate at Powderham was blown up by the Royal Engineers on 18th March enabling route 2 to be double-decker worked throughout.

Sidmouth services 22 (to Ottery St. Mary) and 77 (to Sidbury) also became double-deck worked, but permission to operate them in the Sidmouth area, it was found, did not extend to the Sidmouth- Exmouth route 40.

An order for six additional lowbridge Leyland PD2s that had been authorised was never placed.

From October, route 6 was partially double-deck operated. Vehicles for the above services were made available by the delivery of fourteen new AEC 'Regent' IIIs, (DR646-659) with 8-feet wide Weymann body, the first of this width in the fleet. These were allocated to Torquay for services 12, 30 and 31 and a number of AEC 'Regent' IIIs of 1947-9 were transferred to Kingsteignton, Exeter, and Sidmouth for the 2, 9, 22 and 77 services.

The low bridge at West Exe (13' 11" headroom), just outside Tiverton, had always inhibited double-deck operation of route 3 to Exeter. The six lowbridge-bodied Leyland 'Titan' PD2s (DL640-645) that had been ordered to work it, took over from 1st June, five being allocated to Tiverton depot and one to Exeter. (They could also work on Tiverton local services 101 and 106).

Extension to Tiverton depot commenced in 1951 but it was to prove a long drawn-out job.

The other batch of new vehicles obtained in 1951 was a series of five 30' long Leyland 'Royal Tiger' single-deckers (SL635-639) with underfloor engine, full front, power door, and Willowbrook 43-seat bodywork, and these really made the half-cab 'Regals' look very dated. Furthermore, they were very smooth running, fast and comfortable. Their speed was deceptive, and at least one driver was prosecuted for exceeding the speed limit in their early days. Although ordered with the intention of service on route 3, DL640-645 went on to that route instead, and the 'Royal Tigers' when new, worked on 46, Paignton-Torquay-Exeter (Express) and 13, Torquay-Teignmouth, with two based at Torquay, two at Teignmouth, and one at Exeter. The 'Royal Tigers' were turned out in a new version of the livery: this was all red below the waistband, (which comprised a polished metal strip), and all ivory above, except for a red curved-ended 'flash' which ran the length of the vehicle above the windows on each side. The mudguards, which had previously been black, became maroon on all vehicles about the same time (this variation having first been tried in 1949). This livery was applied to all subsequent single-deckers until replaced by the NBC livery from 1972 onwards, though the polished waistband did not appear on any more new vehicles from 1965, and some of the small Albion 'Nimbus' buses, together with the later 'Reliances' and Bristol 'LHSs', did not have the red 'flash' above the windows.

The first under-floor engine buses for Devon General were six Leyland 'Royal Tiger' saloons delivered in 1951. Their style of bodywork set the pattern for future years, and here SL639 (MTT 639) crosses Avenue Road in Torquay en-route for Chelston on a section of route now no longer served by bus. (L.F.Folkard collection)

The Leyland (lowbridge) PD2s also sported a modified livery, though in their case it was not applied to anything else, at least until the lowbridge Bristol VRs arrived. There was only one waistband, and the ivory roof was continued down over the back of the vehicle to top-deck waist level, but this latter feature was never repeated. The Leylands had a white steering wheel to distinguish them as lowbridge vehicles.

A new standard double-deck blind was fitted to DL640-645 when new, and transferred to Guys and other vehicles which later replaced them. The following displays were provided:

	OLD ROAD	2	DAWLISH
	EXETER	2	TEIGNMOUTH
	TIVERTON	2	NEWTON / ABBOT
	EXETER / VIA SILVERTON		EXMOUTH
	EXETER / VIA MAIN ROAD		BUDLEIGH / SALTERTON
	TIVERTON / VIA SILVERTON		SIDMOUTH
	TIVERTON / VIA MAIN ROAD		WITHERIDGE
	SAMPFORD PEVERELL	4	OTTERY / ST MARY
101	ELMORE		CROCKERNWELL
	FORE / STREET		TEDBURN / ST MARY
106	HEATHCOATS / FACTORY		SOUTH / ZEAL
106	NORWOOD / ROAD		OKEHAMPTON
106	COTTEYLANDS		

A ' / ' indicates two-line display, with route number placed centrally.

Seventeen of the nineteen wartime 5-cylinder Gardner-engined Guy 'Arabs' were given new bodies by Charles H. Roe of Crossgates, Leeds, being completed in May/June. At the same time, their chassis were modernised with lower-mounted radiators and they were given the now much sought-after 'Indian Chief' radiator cap. They returned to service initially from Torquay and Kingsteignton depots. DG243-249, 308/9/11-5/7 retained the seats that had been fitted in 1947, but DG318/9 were given new, and their old seats were put into DL239 and DG240.

One of the 1934 'Regents', DR218, which had escaped the 1948 programme, was given a major body overhaul at Torquay, receiving new front and side destination display but retaining half-drop windows. The solitary Leyland 'Titan' TD7, DL239, was similarly treated.

No buses were withdrawn during 1951 and one van was bought and two sold, including the Leyland 'Cub' converted from

Most of the wartime Guy 'Arab' buses were re-bodied in 1951 and some were regularly to be found on the Exeter-Tiverton service 3 for which they were fitted with platform doors in 1953. DG313 is seen in Fore Street, Tiverton passing a 'Regal' on the Minehead service.

(S.E.Letts)

a bus. One staff car was added to the fleet. The 327 buses and coaches comprising the fleet at 1st June 1951 were:

TCL113/7/8, DR200-225, DL226-233, DR236-238, DL239, DG240/3-9, DG308-325, DR326-333, M360-361, XR401-404, SR405/7-10/2/5-7, M418-419, XR420-425, SR426-451, XR454-455, SR456-548, DR549-592, SR593-597, TCB600-609, TCR611-634, SL635-639, DL640-645, DR646-659.

The Company's regulations regarding children's travel were amended at the beginning of January. Henceforward only the first child under three years of age with any one passenger could travel free, any others being charged half fare.

D. C. Venner successfully applied to the Traffic Commissioners for an Excursion & Tours licence from Witheridge to which Devon General formally objected, but the hearing was told that only 27 tours had been operated in 1948, seven in 1949, and four in 1950! It was therefore granted.

A pay award was made to staff of an additional 7/- to 11/- per week, with improvements in holiday benefits, and a general increase in fares took place on 29th July, which was to prove to be the start of an ever-growing spiral.
A series of strikes took place at various depots on Saturdays in October as a protest over the autumn schedules.

The Company purchased the land at Silver Lane, Exeter at the rear of Blackboy Road depot that had previously been rented for parking, and an Agreement was finally secured on 15th May for a parcels service within the area of the Exeter Joint Services.

Mr. J. W. Womar, Managing Director, resigned his seat on the Board on 18th September, Mr. P. G. Stone Clark became Managing Director, and Mr. P. Yorke was elected to the Board. Mr. W. J. Coad became Company Secretary.

The standard Torquay area double-deck blind, as fitted to the re-bodied Guys, included the following displays:

12	BRIXHAM
12	PAIGNTON
12	PAIGNTON / BRIXHAM

12	WATERSIDE
12	WINDY / CORNER
12	BROADSANDS
28	KINGSKERSWELL
28	LAWES / BRIDGE
	TORQUAY
28	KINGSKERSWELL / NEWTON ABBOT
28a	STRAND / SHIHAY / (DAIRY HILL)
28a	STRAND / ST MATTHIAS CHURCH / LOWER WARBERRY RD
30	BABBACOMBE
30	CASTLE CIRCUS / TORQUAY STATION / PAIGNTON
30	TORQUAY STATION / CASTLE CIRCUS / BABBACOMBE
30	TORQUAY / STATION
	CASTLE / CIRCUS
31	WESTHILL / HELE VILLAGE / BARTON / (PRINCE OF ORANGE)
31	WESTHILL / HELE VILLAGE / BARTON / (JACKS LANE)
31	CASTLE CIRCUS / WESTHILL
31	WESTHILL / HELE CROSS
	STRAND
	DEPOT
	PRIVATE
	DUPLICATE
45	PLYMOUTH / (THROUGH SERVICE)
45	TOTNES
45	PAIGNTON / TORQUAY / (THROUGH SERVICE)
46	TORQUAY / PAIGNTON / EXPRESS SERVICE
46	TORQUAY / EXPRESS SERVICE
46	EXETER / EXPRESS SERVICE
50	ELLACOMBE / ST. MARYCHURCH
50	ELLACOMBE / STRAND
	PLAINMOOR
51	TORBAY / HOSPITAL
54	CASTLE CIRCUS / SHIPHAY / (DAIRY HILL)
54	CASTLE CIRCUS / ST. MARYCHURCH
55	WELLSWOOD / TORQUAY PAVILION
55	WELLSWOOD / BABBACOMBE / ST MARYCHURCH
	SHIPHAY / GRAMMAR / SCHOOL
111	PAVILION
111	HOXTON ROAD / WINDSOR ROAD (TOP)

Routes operated as at 1st July 1951 were as follows (all ran daily unless otherwise stated):

1,	Exeter-Chudleigh-Newton Abbot
2,	Exeter-Dawlish-Teignmouth-Newton Abbot
3,	Exeter-Tiverton-Sampford Peverell
4,	Exeter-Ottery St. Mary-Honiton-Axminster
5,	Exeter-Topsham-Woodbury-Exmouth
6,	Exeter-Crockernwell-Okehampton
7,	Exeter-Newton St. Cyres-Crediton (Green)
8,	Exeter-Pinhoe-Broadclyst
9,	Exeter-Newton Poppleford-Sidmouth
10,	Exmouth-Budleigh Salterton-Otterton
11,	Newton Abbot-Ashburton-Buckfastleigh
12,	Torquay-Paignton-Brixham
12A,	Torquay-Paignton
12B,	Brixham-Kingswear (Jointly with Burton Cars)
13,	Torquay-Shaldon-Teignmouth
14,	Newton Abbot-Haytor-Widecombe (In winter, Newton Abbot-Haytor only)

15,	Newton Abbot-Ipplepen-Totnes
16,	Newton Abbot-Bovey Tracey-Moretonhampstead-Chagford-Okehampton
17,	Roundham-Paignton-Maidenway Road
18,	Paignton-Churston-Galmpton-Greenway
19,	Exeter-Dunsford-Moretonhampstead-Chagford
19A,	Exeter-Leigh Cross-Christow
20,	Exeter-Chudleigh-Bovey Tracey-Haytor-Widecombe (summer only)
21,	Cullompton-Broadhembury-Payhembury-Honiton (WSaO)
22,	Sidmouth-Tipton St. John-Ottery St. Mary
23,	Exeter-Moretonhampstead-Princetown (summer only)
24,	Newton Abbot-Decoy
25,	Newton Abbot-Highweek-Mile End
26,	Exeter-Woodbury-Budleigh Salterton
27,	Exeter-Broadclyst-Cullompton
28,	Torquay-Kingskerswell-Newton Abbot
28A,	Torquay (Lower Warberry Road)-Strand-Shiphay (Dairy Hill)
29,	Exeter-Drewsteignton-Moretonhampstead (weekdays)
30,	Paignton-Torquay Station-Babbacombe
31,	Torquay (Strand)-Westhill-Hele Village-Barton (depot runs only to or from Lawes Bridge)
32,	Torquay (Strand)-Chelston (Haywain)
33,	Meadfoot Beach-Hesketh Crescent-Torquay (Strand)-Chelston (Herbert Rd or Reeves Rd)
34,	Torquay (Castle Circus) -St. Marychurch-Havelock Arms-Barton (Jacks Lane)
35,	Torquay (Castle Circus) -St. Marychurch-Watcombe (Willow Avenue) or Lummaton Cross
36,	Newton Abbot-Kingsteignton-Sandygate
37A,	Brixham (Quay)-Lytes Road
37B,	Brixham (Quay)-Fishcombe
37C,	Brixham (Market Street)-Berry Head
38,	Exeter-Metcombe-Sidmouth (FO)
39,	Newton Abbot-Ogwell-Denbury
40,	Exmouth-Budleigh Salterton-Colaton Raleigh-Sidmouth
41,	Sidmouth-Sidbury-Honiton (SaO)
42,	Exeter-Pinhoe-Poltimore (weekdays)
43,	Cullompton-Plymtree-Clyst Hydon-Exeter (TWFSaO)
44,	Newton Abbot-Hennock (WSaO)
45,	Torquay-Paignton-Totnes-Plymouth (Joint with WN128)
46,	Paignton-Torquay-Exeter (Express)
47,	Exeter-Honiton-Axminster-Bridport-Weymouth (Joint with SN 42)
48,	Sidmouth-Seaton-Lyme Regis (Joint with SN45)
49,	Exeter-Chudleigh-Plymouth (Joint with WN 129)
50,	Torquay (Pavilion)-Ellacombe-St. Marychurch
51,	Torquay (Strand)-Torbay Hospital (WSaSuO)
52,	Exeter-Honiton-Seaton (WSaO in winter)
53,	Exeter-Tiverton-Dulverton-Minehead (Joint with WN 217)
54,	Shiphay (Dairy Hill)-Torre Station-St. Marychurch (weekdays)
55,	Torquay (Strand)-Wellswood-St. Marychurch
56,	Paignton-Preston-Shorton Valley (weekdays)
57,	Torquay (Marine Square)-Preston-Shorton Valley (weekdays)
58,	Exeter-Clyst St. Mary-Woodbury-Exmouth
59,	Exmouth-Littleham Village
63,	Paignton-Marldon-Compton Castle
64,	Exeter-Ide-Dunchideock (Haldon Belvedere in summer)
65,	Exeter-Whitestone-Heath Cross
66,	Exeter-Shillingford-Kennford-Kenn (weekdays)
67,	Exeter-Upton Pyne (FSaO)
68,	Exeter-Raddons Cross-Shobroke (TuSaO- two Thursday journeys Crediton- Raddons Cross)
69,	Crediton-Sandford-Kennerleigh-Black Dog (ThO)
70,	Teignmouth (Triangle)-New Road-Haldon Golf Club
71,	Teignmouth (Triangle)-Coombe Vale-Mill Lane (Hutchings Way)
73,	Exmouth (DG Garage)-Turners Avenue (weekdays)
74,	Exmouth (DG Garage)-Orcombe Point (summer only)

75,	Honiton-Buckerell-Feniton-Talaton (WSaO) also Honiton-Gittisham (SaO)
76,	Crediton-Sandford (weekdays)
77,	Sidmouth-Sidford-Sidbury
78,	Drewsteignton-Chagford-Moretonhampstead-Newton Abbot (WO)
79,	Moretonhampstead-North Bovey (weekdays)
81,	Paignton-Shiphay (Girls Grammar School) M-F term time only
82,	Exmouth-Withycombe-St. John's or Lovelace Crescent
84,	Sidmouth (Triangle)-Fortescue-Sidford (most workings provided by route 48)
85,	Exeter-Topsham-Exton-Exmouth
88,	Newton Abbot-Torbryan-Broadhempston
89,	Paignton-Churston (Fenton School) M-F term time only
90,	Newton Abbot-Ideford Village (WSaO)
91,	Witheridge-Cruwys Morchard-Tiverton
92,	Tiverton-Calverleigh-Rackenford (TuFSaO), Tiverton-Templeton (TuO)
93,	Witheridge-Puddington-Pennymoor-Tiverton (TuO), one journey Tiverton-Way Village
94,	Witheridge-Oakford-Tiverton (TuO - joint with WN 225), Tiverton-Oakford (SaO)
96,	Witheridge-Morchard Bishop-Exeter
97,	Witheridge-Cheriton Fitzpaine-Tiverton (FO)
98,	Witheridge-Cheriton Fitzpaine-Crediton-Exeter (FSaO)
99,	Tiverton-Stoodleigh (TuFO)
101,	Tiverton (Heathcoats Factory)-Elmore (M-F)
102,	Tiverton-East Butterleigh Cross (TuSaO)
103,	Dawlish (Green)-Ashcombe (Church) (WSaO)
104,	Newton Abbot-Coffinswell-Daccombe (WSaO)
105,	Paignton-Barton Avenue (weekdays)
106,	Tiverton (Cotteylands)-Norwood Road
107,	Preston-Paignton-Broadsands Park Road (weekdays-summer only)
108,	Newton Abbot-Huxnor Cross (WSaO)
109,	Torquay (Marine Square)-Warren Road (weekdays)
110,	Newton Abbot (Buckland Estate)-Broadlands (weekdays)
111,	Torquay (Pavilion)-Windsor Road
113,	Crediton-New Buildings-Morchard Bishop (TuO)

The fleet of Albion and Commer vehicles purchased with the services of Mrs. Hart of Budleigh Salterton in 1952. None ever ran for Devon General.   *(L.F.Folkard)*

1952

This was a busy year for Devon General, and an interesting time for the enthusiast. Vehicles and stage services were taken over from two independent operators during the year, firstly, on 17th March, an agreement was reached with Mrs. W. A. Hart, of 3, Clinton Terrace, Budleigh Salterton, that Devon General would purchase five of her vehicles and take over operation of Hart's service from Exmouth to Ladram Bay, via Budleigh Salterton and Otterton. Devon General incorporated this service in route 10 from 1st June, with one extra 'Regal' running to Ladram Bay in summer and terminating at Otterton in winter. A Budleigh Salterton-Exmouth Grammar School contract was also taken over, but Mrs. Hart retained the licenses to operate a Budleigh Salterton local circular service, Station Road-Knowle-Raleigh Road-High Street-Station Road (which she had started in 1949), as well as excursions and tours from Budleigh.

The five vehicles acquired comprised two Commer Centaurs, one Commer Centurion and two Albion Victors. Devon General did not use any of these, and after several months in store in the yard at Torquay depot, they were written off as unserviceable at the end of 1952 and sold for scrap the following year. Mr. P. Hart had commenced operating in 1927 (plans for a bakery business having fallen through) and his wife carried on the business after his death in 1937. The Exmouth service ran throughout the war years, and in one of the enemy hit-and-run raids, the body of one of the Commers was almost destroyed, yet it was still possible to drive the remains of the vehicle back home. Mrs. Hart finally retired from the business on 21st March 1959 when the excursions and tours licence, together with six vehicles (which they did not use), were sold to Greenslades Tours Ltd., while the licence for the local service was surrendered, and subsequently granted to Nightingale's Coaches of Budleigh Salterton. From 1957-9, Mrs. Hart had traded in partnership with her daughter, Mrs. K. Bantham. Hart's vehicles carried a dark maroon livery with yellow waistband, edged in black.

The other operator whose stage services were purchased, was Balls Bus Services Ltd., of 65, Queen Street, Newton Abbot. Agreement was reached on 21st October that Devon General would take over operation of their two stage services from 2nd November, these being Newton Abbot (65, Queen Street)-Combeinteignhead-Shaldon (Green) and Newton Abbot (65, Queen Street)- Combeinteignhead-Stokeinteignhead-Maidencombe. Both services were extended by Devon General to terminate at Newton Abbot (Market Square) and they were given route numbers 116 and 117 respectively.

One bus, a wartime Bedford, came with the deal, but Devon General never used it, and it was stored in the yard at Torquay (Newton Road) depot until 1953 when it was sold. Henry and Barton Balls had been in business since 1905, at first as ironmongers but later becoming involved in the motor trade. During 1919 a service to Combeinteignhead was started, at first using motor cars and running on market days only. A charabanc was obtained in 1921, soon followed by others, and 'Newtonian' tours and private hire were operated as well as the market day bus service which was extended to serve Stokeinteignhead and Shaldon. It became daily from 1927, also taking in Maidencombe. The business was sold to Messrs. A. H. Stabb and E. J. Lucy in 1946, who, in 1949 formed two companies, Balls Bus Services Ltd., and Balls Ltd., the latter continuing to operate tours and contracts until 1954 under the name of Balls Tours Ltd., when these too were bought out by Devon General. Livery since about 1946 had been dark blue, with cream roof, wings, and flash, with the fleet-name in script-style diagonally across the back of the vehicle. Mr. Horace Wells had driven their service bus from 1929 right up until 1952, retiring when it was sold to Devon General.

The return of the seventeen re-bodied Guys in 1951 had provided another source for the substitution of double-deckers on more routes. The busy 35 to Willow Avenue (Torquay) received them on 2nd March and the 34 likewise, but this was altered to run via Fore Street (Barton) and Halsteads Road instead of the lower part of Happaway Road, thus replacing the 35 workings that had run to Lummaton Cross. The 34 was, for a short time, extended to Barton Hall, which had become a holiday camp, but only appeared in the timetable once; after that, un-timetabled buses carrying either 31 or 34 route number ran direct from Barton Hall to the town.

Also on 2nd March, double-deckers took over the Newton Abbot service 110, Buckland Estate-Broadlands.

From 6th July, normal-height double-deckers replaced the lowbridge Leyland PD2s on route 3, Exeter-Tiverton-Sampford Peverell, made possible because West Exe bridge had been raised by British Railways, the job being done overnight! (So much for the County Council's reluctance to lower the roadway). The lowbridge PD2s were re-deployed on routes 4, 9, 47, 48 and 52. As far as the 9 was concerned, normal height double deckers were permitted anyway, but some variants of the 4 had been limited to single-deck.

Other services to be double-decked were the 105 from 1st June, the 71 in Teignmouth from 16th June (for several years DR200 was rostered to work this route), the 6 (throughout) and the 39 and 46 from 6th July. The latter (Paignton-Torquay-Exeter Express) soon became double-deck 'as required', for instance for football or shopping traffic.

About the same time, 42 and 66 were double-decked, at least on an occasional basis, these usually being worked by Exeter Corporation vehicles. Within the city of Exeter, some Devon General vehicles were, from November, working routes D/G (very appropriately!). A new service H, Stoke Hill-St. David's Station (to Bedford Circus only - evenings and Sundays) was at first worked by the Corporation, but later underwent many changes. One Devon General bus periodically worked on route J for mileage balancing purposes, and for the same reason, Exeter Corporation vehicles sometimes worked the 47 to Weymouth and the 49 to Plymouth.

Also new in 1936/7 were twelve petrol-engine Leyland 'Tiger' TS7 single-deckers primarily for use on the express services. After military service, most returned to bus use but some were unexpectedly turned out as Grey Cars from 1946 to augment the touring fleet at Exeter. (Haynes of Dulwich)

BDV 8 started out as XL117 and is a Leyland Tiger TS7 with Harrington 32 seat coachwork built in 1936. Originally in bus livery it was rebuilt by Mumfords to a coach in 1947 and became TCL117 as shown above. (J. W. Wilkins)

Timetable No:124, effective from 6th July, introduced a new-look cover. The red and cream cover, incorporating a picture of BDV 10 (sold in 1940!), was done away with, and in its place, came a full-colour diagrammatic map of the system, with the necessary headings superimposed, with a picture of an AEC 'Regent' III on the front, and a Leyland 'Royal Tiger' on the back. For the first time too, details of Exeter City services were included, as well as the Licensing Authority's 'H' road service licence numbers shown against each table in the book. Principal service amendments were:

105	extended from Barton Avenue to Foxhole Estate (Ramshill Road)
21	no longer served Payhembury, all journeys going via Broadhembury
75	diverted between Talaton and Sidmouth Junction via Payhembury.

28A extended from Shiphay (Dairy Hill) to Torridge Avenue (Avon Road) via Marldon Road and Dart Avenue. The leg of the 28A between Strand and Lower Warberry Road ceased operation, and was instead added to the

111, which became Windermere Road-Strand-Lower Warberry Road.

A new service, 114 ran the short distance from Newton Abbot (Market Square) to Knowles. Hill, but was withdrawn again from 21st September, Knowles Hill instead being served by a diversion of the 25 route to Highweek. Also from 21st September a new 115 was introduced - Newton Abbot (Market Square)-Wolborough Hill (Penshurst Road). This ran Monday to Friday during school term only. 56 and 57 were linked to give a through service 56, Torquay (Strand)-Preston-Shorton Valley-Paignton, from 21st September.

For operational purposes, routes 28 and 31 were also linked, which meant that Kingsteignton crews were working the local service in Torquay to Hele Village and Barton. Whilst they were still learning the route, black boards were postioned at each corner, bearing a large '31' and an arrow! This only lasted from spring 1952 to summer 1953.

Short workings between Lympstone and Exmouth on service 5 were diverted via Hulham Road. Some vehicles at Exmouth were found to have incorrect destinations on their blinds, which were sent back to Torquay for alteration. Some included 'Moorfields Estate' (which simply did not exist) and some showed 'Witycombe' instead of Withycombe. The Company, on its literature and blinds referred to Turner Avenue as 'Turners Avenue' - this conversion of road names to the possessive is a common South Devon habit which is easily acquired! From 25th November, buses on service 82 ran into Exmouth via Waverly Road instead of Park Road.

The Royal Show was held at Stover Park (near Newton Abbot) for four days in early July, and a special bus service was put on from Newton Abbot station, with service 16 being diverted off the main Newton Abbot to Bovey road while the show was on. To cover for vehicles on the show service and to assist generally for the summer, six AEC 'Regents' (registered HFC 951-956) were borrowed from City of Oxford Motor Services Ltd. They worked from Kingsteignton and Exeter depots, and saw service on routes 1 and 2 (Newton Abbot-Exeter), 16 (Newton Abbot-Bovey Tracey), 27 (Exeter-Cullompton), and 36 (Newton Abbot-Kingsteignton-Sandygate). They all returned to Oxford at the end of the summer.

Additions to the fleet were nineteen more 8-feet wide AEC 'Regent' IIIs (DR660-678) with Weymann body, similar to those purchased in 1951. They went into service from Torquay depot, mostly on routes 12, 28 and 31, releasing narrow bodied 'Regents' for the route conversions already detailed, and displacing the pre-war 'Titans' from regular working on the 12. The Company by then had a vast surplus of AEC 'Regal' single-deckers in good condition, and a number were sold off to other BET companies - thirteen to Rhondda Transport (XR401/4, SR412/28/33/4/7/48/9/56/62/8/76, four to Mexborough & Swinton (SR441/2/7/51) for feeder services to their trolleybuses, and fifteen to Thomas Bros. of Port Talbot (SR429-32/5/8-40/3/58/9/65/6/74/7). The vehicles for Port Talbot and Mexborough were repainted in their new livery before leaving Torquay, and looked very smart.

Two members of the loan arrangment from City of Oxford Motor Services were AEC/Weymann Regent HFC 951 (H138) and Park Royal HFC 954 (H135), both seen on layover in Exeter's Paul Street bus staion on 7th August 1952 *(Alan B. Cross)*

Continued on page 169

DR203 (OD 7490) was a 1934 AEC 'Regent' originally built with a Short body, later converted to run on producer-gas, rebuilt by Portsmouth Aviation in 1948 and finally converted to open-top by Longwell Green, Bristol in 1955. It is pictured passing Corbyn Head on Torquay sea-front in the summer of 1959. (L.F.Folkard)

In pristine condition though carrying an inappropriate destination display is fully restored AEC 'Regent' III Weymann DR661, turning at Orcombe Point in Exmouth. (L.F.Folkard)

In 1954, the last of the AEC 'Regal' IV coaches was received from Park Royal (TCR692-697) and the doyen of the class TCR692 is seen leaving Torwood Street garage in July 1958 with driver 'Scatter' Hodge at the wheel. (L.F.Folkard)

A very rare colour picture of a 1946 AEC 'Regent' II, one of six that were acquired from Leicester Corporation in an exchange deal for six Devon General 'Regal' saloons. This is DR700 (DJF 326) photographed especially to show the advertisement for 'Madge Mellors' (from whom the picture was kindly acquired.) (NBR Collection)

The photograph shows the Editor in 1994 alongside the AEC 'Regent' III 585 (KOD 585) which he almost single-handedly restored for the Devon General 75th Anniversary celebrations in 1994, inside Newton Road depot. (DGS collection)

Displaying the result of an argument with a car, AEC 'Regent' III Weymann DR663 is at the top of the Burma Road at Newton Road depot and will shortly be taken into the body shop for repairs. This is February 1965. (N.Bruce-Robertson)

Affectionately referred to as the 'fire engines', AEC 'Regent' III Weymann DRD735 is one of 12 such vehicles and stands in Newton Abbot depot having just been refuelled. The queue barriers can be seen that were installed when the site was used as the temporary bus station.
(N.Bruce-Robertson)

AEC 'Regent' V, DRD786 with Metro-Cammell body and fitted with platform doors for use on country services. Note the Grey Cars advert which was a common local feature when available sites prevailed.
(DGS collection)

Colour photographs of the Commer Beadle TS3 saloons are not too common, but the lines of SC791 are shown here to good effect whilst it is parked-up at Exeter bus station in the summer of 1964. *(N.Bruce-Robertson)*

AEC 'Reliance' Weymann SR803 was more often than not, to be found operating between Exeter, Tiverton and Sampford Peverell on the 3. It is seen here at rest at the back of Blackboy Road depot in company with AEC 'Regent' III DR734 and an unidentified 'Regent' V, in the summer of 1964. *(N.Bruce-Robertson)*

A pleasing view of AEC 'Regent' V, DR819 on lay-over in Paris Street bus station during the crew break. As many did, it is displaying a nice Grey Cars advert on the nearside.
(DGS collection)

Showing its very un-imaginative design by Willowbrook, Albion Nimbus 843 dating from 1958 was caught on lay-over at Exeter bus station on 2nd October 1970.
(B. Parnell)

Very noisy but very comfortable with their leather seats, were the chassis-less Commer TS3 Grey Cars with Beadle 'Rochester' coachwork. They normally operated out of the Exeter area and TCC846 and 847 and another are awaiting disposal at Newton Road in 1965. (N.Bruce-Robertson)

When new, the Willowbrook 'Viking' coaches were rather drab with little styling. After the arrival of the 'Viscount' model, the opportunity was taken to add flashes to match them and this enhanced their appearance ten-fold as shown by TCR851 and another, parked-up in Vaughan Parade, Torquay on an evening private hire in January 1965. (N Bruce-Robertson)

Showing well the immaculate way the paint shop turned out the vehicles, MCW Leyland 'Atlantean' DL882 was driven out of the paint shop on a Friday afternoon in January 1965, prior to going back into service on the Saturday. (N.Bruce-Robertson)

This photograph is of another bus that I drove out of the paint shop on a Friday afternoon. Roe bodied Leyland 'Atlantean' 913 also displays the colourful hand-painted DULUX advert in February 1965. It is fortunately now preserved. (N.Bruce-Robertson)

In 1961, nine convertable Metro-Cammell bodied Leyland 'Atlanteans' entered service, all named after West Country 'Sea Dogs'. 932 (Earl Howe) is at the Strand, Torquay whilst still in active service. (DGS Collection)

The last open-platform AEC 'Regent' Vs to be ordered were 6 Weymann bodied 59 seaters, delivered in 1962 for use on Exeter city services. Among other slight differences, the curved fronts to the mud-guards made these stand out from the previous batches. 945 waits at St. David's station (DGS collection)

Representing the order for seven 41-seat AEC 'Reliance' service buses from Marshall is SR955, caught sun-bathing at Blackboy Road, Exeter during that hot and sunny summer of 1964.

(N.Bruce-Robertson)

Albion Nimbus / Harrington bodied SN958 'out the back' at Newton Road depot in November 1964. This design was far more acceptable than the earlier Willowbrook version, as on 838-843.

(N.Bruce-Robertson)

A typical Grey Cars coach of the sixties is TCR968, an Exeter allocated AEC Willowbrook 'Reliance', seen here in the summer of 1964 at the back of Blackboy Road depot. (N.Bruce-Robertson)

AEC 'Regent' V 984 was one of the first batch of front entrance AEC double-deckers for the Company, and here it is, no doubt after its last repaint into traditional livery and looking very smart too, whilst on lay-over at Exeter bus station. (DGS collection)

Another AEC 'Regent' V 975 stands alongside the washing plant at Newton Road depot. The curved metal-roofed building on the right was the tyre workshop and store, as photographed in February 1965. (N.Bruce-Robertson)

Just one short of the highest numbered vehicle to be delivered new to the Devon General Omnibus Company is AEC 'Reliance' SR990, (990 MDV) one of the seven Marshall examples, and the last design before the new standard BET curved windscreen model was introduced. It is under the familiar clock in Newton Abbot bus station on a sunny January day in 1965. (N.Bruce-Robertson)

Harrington AEC 'Reliance' 41 seater was an exception and spent most of its life at Exeter where it is shown at Paris Street in 1964 looking as immaculate as it ever did. (N.Bruce-Robertson)

Four of the longest-ever saloons were taken into stock in 1964, all for use in the Exeter area. 9-11 (9-11 RDV) were for service 9, Exeter-Sidmouth whereas 12 (12 RDV) had a higher ratio gearbox for the Exeter-Plymouth 129 service. 11 is in for maintenance at Blackboy Road in the summer of 1964. (N.Bruce-Robertson)

502 was one of the first batch of front-entrance 69-seat double-deckers to be received, there being eight AEC 'Regent' Vs by Willowbrook, and it is seen at Exeter having worked in from Newton Abbot via the coast road on service 2 on 13th December 1970.
(B.Parnell)

Although shown here in preservation days, AEC 'Regent' V Park Royal 69 seater 513 (CTT 513C) is in as new condition approaching Torquay sea-front on a rally day. A great credit to all those involved in its restoration.
(DGS collection)

Willowbrook bodied AEC 'Regent' V 59 seater of 1965, seen in immaculate preservation condition in Babbacombe Road, Torquay.
(L.F.Folkard)

As direct replacement for the little Albion Nimbus vehicle, these Bristol LHS /Marshall bodied 33-seat saloons were also the last single-
deckers to be delivered new to Devon General in traditional colours. 92 is at Exeter on 28th July 1973. *(B.Parnell)*

Leyland 'Atlantean' 872 having been converted for one-man operation with lowered destination box, was repainted into a modified version of traditional livery without the upper ivory band. It is seen here at Torquay Strand on the Barton 31 route. (DGS collection)

Leyland 'Atlantean' 905 (905 DTT) had been modified and rebuilt for one-man operation, had its destination equipment lowered and repainted into modified livery. It is however here being crew worked on the 28A when photographed at The Strand in Torquay.
(K.Falconer)

Newly repainted AEC 'Regent' V 976 does look smart in NBC poppy red, but as soon as the shine wore off, the livery went flat, dull and uninteresting. This picture was taken on 26th August 1974 in Exeter bus station. (B.Parnell)

Leyland 'Titan' 283 was one of fairly few Exeter Corporation vehicles to receive the full traditional Devon General livery, largely because for a long time the Exeter paintwork remained in such good condition. 283 is on its home ground in the High Street, Exeter (Photobus)

One of the livery changes inflicted by the NBC regime was the unfortunate introduction of all-white for coaches with a single coloured band which related to their past livery. The band of course was in light grey for Grey Cars, dark blue for Royal Blue and a green blue for Greenslades. The comparison is quite clear in this view of 25, a Harrington AEC 49 seater, with a 41 seater behind.

(DGS collection)

Grey Cars had the long-term loan of a Bristol RE/Plaxton from Black & White Motorways of Cheltenham, for use as the team coach for Torquay United Football Club. It was quite coincidental that its registration number RDG 309G included the letters DG. It is pictured at Newton Road.

(DGS collection)

Compare this picture of Leyland 'Atlantean' 882 in NBC leaf green, with that on page 152, where the same bus has just been repainted in true Devon General style. Here it is working an Exeter city service in Paris Street on 14th March 1980, being some 21 years old at the time! *(B.Parnell)*

Another picture for comparison, this time former Sea-Dog open-top 'Atlantean' DL927 (Sir Martin Frobisher) but by now re-named Admiral Hardy, sits at Dawlish Green en route for Newton Abbot in Devon General NBC poppy red and white, but with the early style red and blue double 'N'. *(Keith Falconer)*

With a jolly good summer load, Bristol VR/ECW open-top 934 (VDV 134S - Golden Hind) passes the end of Cockington Lane between Torquay and Paignton in the early days of Western National control. 934 was passed around the West Country depots receiving several different liveries before finally being withdrawn by Firstbus in 2006. *(Keith Falconer)*

For the Devon General 65th Anniversary in 1984, Bristol VR/ECW 1126 (XDV 606S) was immaculately repainted by Devon General Limited into traditional livery - the only curved windscreen VR to be so treated. It is pictured at the Strand, Torquay, on service and being admired by waiting passengers. *(Keith Falconer)*

One of the first Bristol VR/ECW double-deckers to be repainted into NBC corporate poppy red is 1113, (VDV 113S) seen leaving Newton Road depot on its first duty in its new guise. 1113 later passed to Midland Fox.   (Keith Falconer)

One of the Bristol VR/ECW double-deckers that passed into the ownership of the new Devon General Ltd., in their new colour scheme which included a flowing fleet-name as seen on 579 (VOD 599S).   (Keith Falconer)

Although one of the last chassis to be built by Bristol, 1804 (A680 KDV) is officially recorded as a Leyland Olympian. It was one of the first new buses to be delivered to the new Devon General Ltd., in October 1983, although in poppy red. Five years later it was repainted into the cream and red scheme. Since then however it has seen several operators and liveries but has now been rescued for preservation and restored in 2006 to the livery shown. (Keith Falconer)

From 31st March 1996, Reeve Burgess bodied Mercedes 709D was renumbered 425 by Stagecoach. Delivered to Devon General Ltd., in 1988 as number 83 in the new cream and red livery, it latterly carried an all-over advert paint scheme for Panasonic and was one of the last Mercedes to remain in service, being withdrawn in September 2000, and never having carried Stagecoach livery! (Keith Falconer)

BBC2 commissioned a short film written by M. J. Read entitled 'Waving to a train'. The initial scene was shot at Exeter St. David's Station, the first bus ride was on AEC 'Regal' saloon SR510 with actors playing all parts except the fully uniformed conductor who was played by vehicle owner John Corah. *(Photograph supplied by Keith Falconer)*

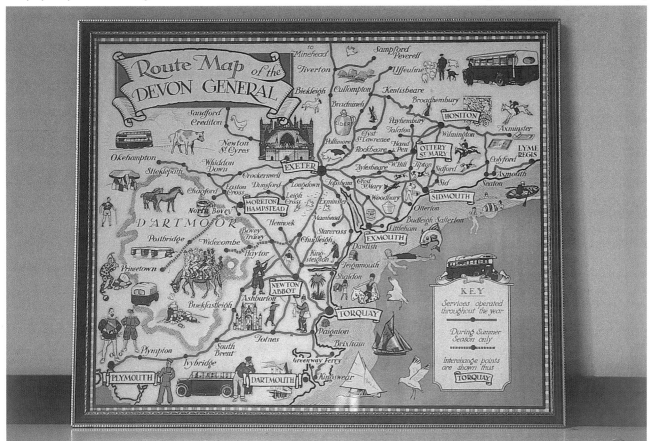

The colourful map produced by Devon General which graphically illustrated some of the Company's bus routes with their legends. Because of the spelling mistake of 'Kingsteignton' they were never issued and a large quantity survives intact. *(L.F.Folkard)*

A selection of Devon General timetable books along with some Grey Cars excursions booklets showing the wide variety of designs used over the years.

(L.F.Folkard)

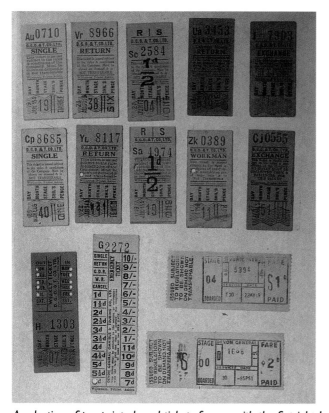
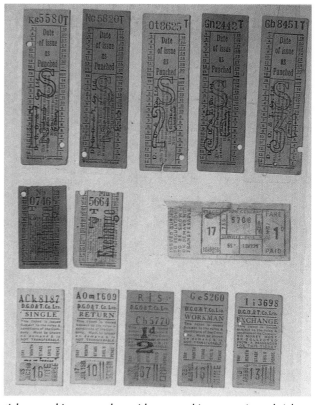

A selection of pre-printed card tickets for use with the Setright Insert ticket machines, together with some white paper issued tickets from a TIM. The pink ticket with many punch holes is a weekly ticket issued by booking offices and was the last type of ticket to be issued by an Insert machine. The very long ones at the top of the picture appear to be Emergency tickets, issued by a conductor when his ticket machine failed.

(L.F.Folkard)

Six 'Regals' of the 1946 batch (SR484/6/7/98,502/4) were exchanged with Leicester Corporation for six of their 1946 'Regents' with Park Royal body similar to those on DG320-325. The 'Regals' were painted into Leicester livery before leaving Torquay, but the 'Regents' ran for several months in Leicester's livery in Torquay before being repainted into Devon General colours. At first, they were given fleet numbers DR101-106, but these were later changed to DR698-703. Immediately before acquisition by Devon General, these six 'Regents' had been running on loan to Potteries Motor Traction Ltd., in the Stoke-on-Trent area, and Devon General's Chief Engineer and Body Superintendent journeyed to Stoke to inspect them before deciding to have them.

During this year, twenty 'Regals' were dismantled at Torquay and their bodies scrapped, though two were for a time used as tree loppers. The twenty were: XR402/3, SR405/7-10/5-7, XR420-425, SR446, XR454/5 and SR469. A lot of silver-painted chassis frames arrived in the depot yard, most bore no identification, but it was ascertained that the majority were from London Transport STLs, and had been reconditioned by ACV Sales Ltd. The 7.7-litre engine, wheels, and units from the dismantled 'Regals' were fitted to these chassis, and they were sent away to have lightweight double-deck bodies fitted during 1952/3. The first chassis, which came from Devon General's own DR234 with the units from XR403 went to Saunders Roe for bodying, the rest were sent to Weymann.

Two of the remaining Leyland 'Tiger' TS7s of 1936 (TCL113/8) were sold during 1952, and the two small Bedford station buses (M418/9) were also withdrawn. M419 had not been used since early in 1951.

The first of the Bedford Grey Cars (TCB600) was down-graded to a bus, and reduced to 20 seats to conform with route restrictions. It was repainted red with ivory flash and roof, and re-classified SB600.

The twelve AEC 'Regal' III Grey Cars of 1948 were sold to the Western Welsh Omnibus Co. Ltd., in October and November in anticipation of new deliveries.
Three staff cars were purchased and three sold. Fifty more 'Speed Setright' ticket machines were purchased, to replace more of the old 'TIMs'.

Mr. J. H. Richardson resigned with effect from 29th February as Area Traffic Superintendent at Exeter, having obtained the post of Traffic Manager with East Yorkshire Motor Services. Mr. F. A. Noble succeeded him from 1st March, and occupied the property 'Berwyn' at Tedburn St. Mary which the Company had recently purchased. He had previously been Superintendent in charge of Crosville's Wrexham depot.

At Tiverton, an office was rented in Fore Street for booking tours.

The registered office of the Company moved from 88, Kingsway, London. WC2 to Stratton House, Piccadilly, London. W1 on 17th March; the last meeting to be held at No:88 was on 12th February. The arrangement with the BET Federation Ltd., for the provision of secretarial services was terminated by the Company as from 30th September; these duties henceforth being carried out locally, and Mr. W. H. Geere, the Assistant General Manager, also became Company Secretary from 1st October.

A disconcerting trend at this time was the exodus of skilled fitters, who were obtaining higher-paid positions mainly with local quarries. Difficulty was experienced in recruiting qualified replacements.

In September, responsibility for the staff canteen at Newton Road was taken over by the Company from the Recreation Club at very short notice, the consequence of which the stewardess became one of the Engineering Department staff!

1953

The Authorised and Issued Capital of the Company was increased from £350,000 to £950,000 by capitalisation of reserves.

A general fares increase took place on 18th January, following a public hearing on 2nd January. New fare stages were introduced with the object of encouraging short distance travel. H. D. Gourd & Sons were obliged to increase their fares between Teignmouth and Newton Abbot because Devon General claimed seniority on this route; Gourds contested the MOT order, but in the end had no option but to conform.

Early in the year, double-deckers commenced running service 12B, Brixham-Kingswear. These were of the 'lowbridge' bodied Leyland PD2 type, and Burton Cars also bought one to work their share of the joint service. The use of 'lowbridge' vehicles was necessary because of the limited turning facilities at Kingswear, where the road simply ended in a ferry slipway, and buses had to turn by reversing under a low archway between the railway station and the Royal Dart Hotel. Queues of traffic for the ferry were commonplace, and often delayed the buses.

The depot extension at Tiverton, started in 1951, was at last completed. Among the trials and tribulations during the works, a 5,000-gallon fuel tank rolled away while being unloaded from a British Road Services lorry, stopping just short of the railway line and having flattened all the allotments in its path!

The charge hands' office at Torwood Street depot, Torquay, was rebuilt to form a new booking and enquiry office, with access from the street.

'Essex' type bus washers were installed at Torquay (Newton Road), Exeter and Kingsteignton depots, and a hut at Ottery St. Mary station (where two buses parked overnight) was rented from British Railways.

Changes to the Board of Directors during the year were the resignation of Mr. C. R. Dashwood from 15th September, and the consequent appointment of Mr. A. W. Tait on 6th October. Mr. E. C. Hill, Assistant Traffic Manager, was appointed Traffic Manager of the South Wales Transport Co. Ltd., at Swansea.

Eight more staff completed 40 years service with the Company, while, no less than 131 had by this time completed 25 years. The last eleven conductresses at Torquay depot were given notice in the autumn, though some were taken back in the following summer. Conductresses continued to be employed full-time at Kingsteignton depot.

Conductor G. Stone of Torquay depot lost his life on 23rd October following a fall after hitting a tree whilst changing the side destination whilst the vehicle was in motion in St. Marychurch. Another serious accident took place on 20th July when a tyre burst on DR223 whilst running fully loaded on service 31 in Lymington Road, Torquay. It swerved and crashed into a tree, but this avoided a four-foot drop into a public park; three passengers were seriously injured. The Brush bodywork withstood the impact well but underneath it was repaired using a new chassis-frame from a London Transport 'STL' thus DR223 finished its days with neither its original body nor chassis!

Route 26 between Exeter and Budleigh Salterton was altered to run via Clyst St. Mary, Woodbury Salterton and Woodbury instead of via Topsham, Clyst St. George and Woodbury.

The terminus of 45 and 49 in Plymouth moved from the Technical School to a temporary bus station on a cleared site in Union Street, from 1st February.

A new country service operated by small Bedford buses was introduced from 15th April which was 118, Newton Abbot-Ipplepen-Compton-Marldon (WSaO), and from the same date, some journeys on the 16 were diverted to serve Heathfield.

Exeter service C/W was extended from Countess Wear (hence CW) to Topsham, but it was to be many years before anybody thought to renumber it T.
The following amendments took place from 14th June:

Routes 12 and 28 were combined to operate as a through service; 12, Newton Abbot-Torquay-Paignton-Brixham. Route numbers 12A and 28 were no longer used.

Torquay crews came out on strike for four days over the schedules, and during that time, Kingsteignton crews operated between Newton Abbot and Lawes Bridge only. Some journeys on the 13 which had previously been short workings from Torquay to Maidencombe Cross, were extended to Stokeinteignhead over the route of the 117, some of which journeys were correspondingly terminated at Stoke. These journeys on the 13 were usually worked by one of the re-bodied 1934 'Regents', DR222 being a regular performer. Confusion was caused to visitors wanting to go to Teignmouth who boarded these 13s at Torquay because the Company did not seem inclined to give a distinguishing route number.

The ex-Balls service 116 was extended over the bridge from Shaldon into Teignmouth. Service 70 workings to Haldon Golf Club were re-routed in Teignmouth via Bitton Street, Hermosa Road and Yannon Drive, but reverted to the normal route from 29th June at the request of Teignmouth Council.

At Newton Abbot, the residents of Highweek had objected to the 25 being diverted via Knowles Hill, and as a result, these diversions were reduced to a few journeys on Wednesdays and Saturdays only.

A new double-deck route 59A at Exmouth ran from DG Garage to Littleham Village via Pier, Esplanade, Carlton Hill, Salterton Road, and Littleham Cross. The existing 59 ran via Pier, Cranford Avenue and Douglas Avenue.

Friday journeys on route 67 ran to Upton Pyne by way of Brampford Speke.

Route 62 re-appeared after fourteen years suspension, to run between Dawlish (Green) and Mamhead Park (Arch Drive), via Cockwood. It ran on Mondays, Wednesdays and Fridays only, during summer. The pre-war 62 had run from Exeter to Mamhead.

The 107 did not re-appear in the 1953 timetable, but instead, additional workings were included in the 12 table between Preston, Paignton and Three Beaches.

Three return trips a day on service 15 were introduced between Newton Abbot and Abbotskerswell (Butchers Arms), this being another case where no distinguishing service number was alloted, although it was a 'branch' off the main route.

Workmen's services were introduced from Heathfield (Candy's Factory) to Kingsteignton & Newton Abbot and also to Chudleigh. These did not appear in the timetable, but may well have been known by route number 119. Another such new service was Newton Abbot to Milber (Centrax Factory), which eventually got into the timetable (in 1965) as route 120.

From 23rd August, route 17 at Paignton was extended at both ends, to run from Goodrington (Cliff Gardens) to Marldon Cross (Torbay Chalet Hotel), and as part of the route was common with the 105, the two services appeared in the same table and both became double-deck operated. At first, they ran alternately via Blatchcombe Road and via Maidenway Road, but following local protests, all workings on the 17 were routed via Maidenway Road.

Tests were carried out early in the year on various ferries and moorland bridges by a Leyland 'Royal Tiger' (30' x 7'6"), in readiness for new AEC 'Regal' IV coaches of the same dimensions.

A one-off was DR679, an AEC 'Regent' III with prototype Weymann 'Aurora' lightweight metal body which was exhibited at the 1952 Commercial Motor Show in London. It is seen here at Torquay Strand on the inner circle 115 service. DR679 is now in active preservation.
(P. Yeomans)

Twenty double-deckers were created in 1953/4 using second-hand AEC 'Regent' chassis frames on which were fitted engine and running units from surplus 'Regals' whose registrations they retained. New light-weight bodies were constructed, the first being DR705 (ETT 995) seen outside the old bus and tram depot at Westhill Avenue, Torquay having worked a football special service to a Torquay United match.
(D.J.Frost)

The first new vehicle to be delivered for service in 1953 was DR679 which had been exhibited at the 1952 Commercial Motor Show at Earls Court in London. It did not have a conventional exposed radiator, but instead sported a 'grille' which became the style for subsequent AEC 'Regent' IIIs. The body however was a one-off design, which became known as the Weymann 'Aurora'. Developments moved on rapidly and production models were produced as the lightweight 'Orion' type. DR679 also had a synchromesh gearbox, and this became standard on all future 'Regents' of the 646-678 batch during the year.

The first of the lightweight double-deckers using the engine and units of withdrawn 'Regals' (known as the light sixes) was next to appear. Although ordered in November 1951 it was DR681 which was initially registered NUO 681, but before going into service was re-registered ETT 995 and given a new fleet number of DR705. It had the engine and units from XR403 and the chassis frames from DR234 and carried a very light weight Saunders Roe body. It entered service on 1st March on the Torquay circular routes 50/55, being monitored for running costs against DR679. Not surprisingly, DR705 produced the better results by far, having a 7.7-litre engine whilst DR679 was the heavier body with 9.6-litre engine.

Later in the year, another fourteen 'light-sixes' arrived from Weymann (DR704/6-718) and they took over most of the service on the 12 being shared between Torquay and Kingsteignton depots. Consequently, some of the 1951 'Regent' IIIs which were displaced, were transferred to Sidmouth for use on the 9 to Exeter.

One Guy was transferred to Witheridge to work route 96, Witheridge-Morchard Bishop-Exeter in June, and another followed in October for service 91 (Tiverton-Witheridge). The two regular Witheridge vehicles had been the ex-Rhondda pair, DG318 and 319.

The rest of the 'light sixes' as they became known, had bodies built by Weymann as depicted by DR711 (DUO 327) at Willow Avenue, Torquay to which point buses now no longer run. (L.F.Folkard)

The other new vehicles to be delivered during 1953 were twelve AEC 'Regal' IV coaches for Grey Cars tours from Torquay (TCR680-691). These had underfloor 9.6-litre engine, and Willowbrook 30' x 7'6" coachwork, with the driver back in amongst his passengers (as opposed to the previous batch of half-cabs), with seating for 41, both of which pleased the drivers. For coaches, their bodies had somewhat austere lines, as they had been designed eventually to be cascaded to buses, but in the event, this never came about. They were comfortable vehicles, with new style upholstery in grey and maroon, going into service in June and July, all being allocated in order of seniority to regular drivers.

1953 allocation of Grey Cars to drivers:

TCR	623	E. Lawrence		TCR	680	W. G. H. Hodge
	624	Exeter Car			681	A. T. Hall
	625	W. Hawke			682	L. P. Hallett
	626	F. Wollacott			683	E. Jones
	627	Exeter Car			684	L. Worrall
	628	S. Quick			685	P. J. Rowland
	629	J. Short			686	R. Scagell
	630	Exeter Car			687	G. T. Crispin
	631	Exeter Car			688	H. Roberts
	632	L. Harry			689	W. Bray
	633	A. Holland			690	P. Cole
	634	J. J. Lowe			691	G. Stear
TCB	602	J. Prewett				
	604	J. George		Relief		W. A. Hannaford
	605	R. Rundle		Relief		R. Easterbrook
	606	Exeter Car				
	608	Exeter Car				
	609	Exeter Car				

Leyland 'Tiger Cub' demonstrator OTC 738 on trial in service over a few Torquay routes in the summer of 1953, one of which was the 46, Torquay-Exeter express service. It obviously did not impress or prove itself, as no order followed. It was photographed at Castle Circus, outside the Library.
(L.F.Folkard)

A Leyland 'Tiger Cub' demonstrator (OTC 738) ran on loan during June and again in July and August. It had a Saunders Roe 44-seat body and was painted all-red. It was tried on services 13, 32 and 46, but due to poor mechanical condition it did not give of its best.

The last of the 1936 Leyland 'Tiger' TS7s (TCL117) ran only in August during 1953 and was then withdrawn; four more of the Bedford 'Grey Cars' were converted for use as country buses (SB601-3/7), and AEC 'Regal' III coaches were sent to Exeter to replace them.

There remained a surplus of single-deck buses, and four AEC 'Regals' were loaned to South Wales Transport Co. Ltd., for use in the Swansea area during July and August. One of these, SR494, was the subject of a 'standee' experiment by Devon General. It had its seating reduced to 28 and later to 27, all seats on one side being single, and the floor bearers were strengthened because of the additional weight of standing passengers. It only saw one month's service in this form, being nominally allocated to Brixham. Four more of this type (SR480, 500/1/8) were sold in April to Thomas Bros. of Port Talbot to join the other ex-DG 'Regals' there, and SR481 was sold to the Millbrook Steamboat & Trading Co. Ltd., of Millbrook, Cornwall for use on stage services on the far side of Plymouth Sound which ran in connection with their Cremyll ferry.

A Yugoslav trade delegation looking for good second-hand AEC vehicles had been introduced to Devon General by ACV Sales Ltd., and after inspecting the buses available, they selected fifteen (SR470/82/3/8-97/9 and 503) which included the 'standee' bus. The difficulties of translation from Serbo-Croat to Devonian having been overcome by the use of French, the delegation made it quite clear that if SR494 was not included, together with the conversion drawings, there would be no deal. Unfortunately they were not so particular regarding the transit arrangements, for by the time the bank transfer had been made it was the middle of winter, and during their journey across Europe on open railway wagons, many suffered cracked cylinder block, nobody having thought to have them drained before loading. Some, at least, later ran in Belgrade.

Other buses withdrawn from service during 1953 had been the two former 'Coastal Cruise' buses M360/1 and DR215 - the first of the redoubtable 1934 'Regents' to go - which was downgraded to a tree-cutter by having its top removed.

Eight of the re-bodied Guys, DG311-5/7-9, returned to Roe in the early part of the year, to be fitted with a platform door and heaters.

1954   Further capitalisation of reserves enabled the authorised and issued capital to be increased from £950,000 to £1,150,000.

Mr. V. Radford replaced Mr. A. W. Tait on the Board from 1st April.

Two coach operators were bought out during 1954; the first, in April, was A. E. Townsend, of Babbacombe, Torquay, followed by Balls Tours Ltd., of Newton Abbot (whose stage services had been purchased by Devon General in 1952). Both held excursion & tours licences, and ran extended tours to other parts of the country, a field into which Devon General had not previously ventured.

Arthur Townsend, who had previously owned a model 'T' Ford lorry in 1927 (jointly with C. Farmer) purchased an Austin 20 tourer. Farmer died shortly afterwards, and Townsend bought out his garage business. Early in 1931 he purchased the business and charabanc of A. Wilson, who traded as 'Ideal Coaches' from 147, Reddenhill Road, Babbacombe, Torquay, where there was a booking office and a small lock-up garage. The fleet was re-equipped with new coaches and a livery of 'French' grey and maroon was adopted with 'Townsend's Coaches' in Gothic-style lettering. Townsends used a garage at the rear of 19, Petitor Road, St. Marychurch, Torquay, and its lease was included in the sale of the business to Devon General, who relinquished it in June 1954, and garaged the coaches at Torwood Street.

Seven coaches were purchased from Townsend's (four Dennis 'Lancet' IIIs, one Tilling Stevens, and two Bedford SBs) and another Bedford that had been on order was delivered direct to Devon General in May although in Townsend livery. They were given fleet numbers TC736-743. One of the AEC 'Regal' IV Grey Cars, TCR682, was repainted into Townsend's livery, which with their fleet-name was retained until 1958. Three of the drivers who transferred with the business, Messrs F. Perrett, A. S. Moon, and E. Crouch had each been with Townsend for over 20 years, and continued with Devon General until their retirement, except for Stan Moon who eventually became a private chauffeur. The 'Extended Tours' operated by Townsend, and from 1954 offered by Devon General, were:

8	days to Derbyshire Dales, North and Mid Wales, (21 guineas)
12	days to Scotland & Northern Highlands (37 guineas)
3	days to Lands End and Cornish Coast (£3.19s.6d)
8	days to the English Lakes & Blackpool (21 guineas),
7	days to the Isle of Wight, South Coast and London (20 guineas).

The purchase of Balls Tours Ltd., of Newton Abbot was agreed on 6th June and added five more vehicles to the fleet - two Bedford OB buses and three Commer coaches, which were given fleet numbers (SB744, SB746, SC745, TC747-748) the two latter being repainted into Grey Cars livery, and based at Kingsteignton depot for use on school contracts. These included one to Hennock from Newton Abbot, which stipulated the use of coaches, and for the next three summers, were used on tours during the school holidays, working from Exeter, Torquay, or Tiverton as required. No great attempt was made by Devon General to establish a tours base in Newton Abbot, though there was a booking office at 16, Sherborne Road (by the Market Square) where coaches picked up. The three other vehicles were de-licensed, but late in the year SB744 was repainted into Devon General bus livery and went back into service from 1st January 1955.

Negotiations were in hand for the acquisition by Devon General of the stage services of H. D. Gourd & Sons of Bishopsteignton, and this deal was completed as from the first day of 1955, SB744 being destined to work their service. The other two ex-Balls vehicles were never used by Devon General.

For several years, Newton Abbot Council had not welcomed Devon General's presence in the Market Square, and so high was the rent sought in consideration of a new lease, that the Company started looking for an alternative site for a bus station.

Several unusual looking coaches were acquired in 1954 with the business of Balls Tours of Newton Abbot, and among them was Commer 'Avenger' MOD 44 which became TC748 in the Devon General/Grey Cars fleet. It was normally used on school contracts around Newton Abbot but went on tours in the summer. It is leaving Torwood Street garage, Torquay in September 1954.
(L.F.Folkard)

In Paignton, a bus station was established on land at the Regent car park, and a property 17, Dartmouth Road was purchased so as to be able to provide land for an entrance to the site, with exit being via Station Square. Western National local routes used the station on a shared basis with Devon General services 17, 18, 30, 46, 56, 63 and 105, but not for the time being, the 12 or 45. The site was leased from British Railways from 25th March.

Kingsteignton depot was improved by the provision of two new pits (from which ground water had to be continuously pumped), with a new entrance to the garage from the parking ground alongside. A new toilet block was erected on land at the rear.

At Torquay depot, a hydraulic lifting ramp was installed outside the garage, at the south end.

Alterations were carried out at the premises that had been leased at 28A, Fore Street, Tiverton to form a Tours booking office, parcels office, conductors paying-in room, mess-room, and toilets, and it opened on 22nd December. Two 'out-station' depots were closed and the rented premises given up at Crediton at the end of July, (their three duties being transferred to Exeter), and Uffculme, (which had not been served by a Devon General route for five years), had its one duty transferred to Tiverton at the end of November.

During March, a depot identification disc was fitted to the rear of all buses in the fleet, each depot being denoted by a different coloured disc. On single-deckers, it was carried on the corner of the rear route number box (or thereabouts), and on double-deckers it was carried on the waistband. The discs were of alloy, and fitted on to rubber studs. Various rumours as to their purpose were rife among the travelling public, the most commonly held beliefs being that they were either bells for use when the vehicle was reversing, or else they were television interference suppressors! The different colours for the various depots were:

Torquay-Green • Exeter-Blue • Kingsteignton-Yellow • Exmouth-Red • Sidmouth-Black • Moretonhampstead-Brown • Tiverton-Red/Green.
Brixham - Green/Yellow, was added in 1957 as but the system fell into disuse from 1962 although the discs remained in place. Another addition to the rear of all vehicles comprised rear reflectors which were fitted to the whole fleet by the end of September to conform to new regulations.

Double-deckers were introduced from 1st January on routes 10 and 40 following the lowering of the roadway at Kersbrook Bridge, near Budleigh Salterton; the trusty 1948/9 'Regents' were used.

Double-deckers were introduced from 1st May on route 13 between Torquay and Teignmouth and from 13th June this route was extended to Dawlish in summer only, being advertised as the 'Coastal Special', 8-foot wide 'Regent' IIIs being used.

Principal service alterations in the summer timetable were:

Route 5 linked with 7 and 74 to give a through service, Crediton-Exeter-Exmouth-Orcombe Point. The linking of the 5 and 7 was permanent, all journeys becoming 5. After 15th September, the service was Crediton-Exmouth only, and route 74 as such, ran between Exmouth and Orcombe Point for another week. A new route 57, Exeter (Paul Street)-Digby Hospital ran on WSaO and was joint with Exeter Corporation which introduced its own hospital service M, Exeter (Paul Street)-Princess Elizabeth Orthopaedic Hospital, which ran FSuO. Route 19A, (Exeter-Christow) also served Bridford on certain journeys, different timetables being operated according to the day of the week.

At Tiverton, the 101 was extended from Elmore, or ran alternately to Cowley Moor where a new housing estate had been built. It then ran each weekday.

A new route 2A was introduced from 11th July, summer only, which ran from Exeter (Paul Street) daily to Dawlish Warren via Rifford Road, Countess Wear and Kenton. The housing estates at the first two named were a good catchment area for a day at the seaside, and on a good day, as many as four buses would operate on certain timetabled journeys - 1934 'Regents' being normally used.

From 12th July, services 13 and 31 were routed out of Torquay via Abbey Road instead of Union Street, and this diversion was the forerunner of the town centre one-way system which was to come later.

The 15th September timetable brought further changes. Route 62, Dawlish-Mamhead ceased for good, and the 85 from Exmouth to Exeter was extended to Crediton.
The 50 and 55 at Torquay were timetabled as one-way circulars for the autumn/winter of 1954/5 only, which operationally they always had been, and the 111 was extended from Windermere Road to Quinta Road (Cedar Road). The 33 service at Torquay underwent more changes during the year; from 13th June, the Reeves Road journeys ceased to use Sherwell Hill, and instead proceeded via Sherwell Lane, Sherwell Valley Road, Sherwell Rise South and Burridge Road to terminate at Boundary Road. This only lasted for three months, as from 19th September this leg of the 33 terminated at Chelston (Haywain), which is situated in Sherwell Valley Road, and the single-deck 32 was correspondingly extended from there to Boundary Road over the former 33 route. None of the roads in the area had been built with buses in mind, and it abounds in steep hills and tight turns; piecemeal residential development meant that there were no through roads, and public transport requirements for the area were constantly changing.

Much the same could be said about Brixham, where from 19th September the 37A was diverted via Edinburgh Road and Sellick Avenue on its route from Lytes Road to Market Street.

New vehicles during 1954 were six more AEC 'Regal' IV Grey Cars (TCR692-697) similar to those obtained in 1953, but with Park Royal body. There were also five more AEC 'Light Six' rebuilds with Weymann 'Orion' body (DR719-723) and these joined the earlier ones on route 12. Twelve AEC 'Regent' IIIs (DR724-735) also had the Weymann 'Orion' lightweight body, but these were 8' wide and had a platform door. These were put to work on routes 2 and 9, and were soon nicknamed the 'Fire Engines' due to their appearance with their covered-in front.

Another AEC 'Regal' was sold during 1954 to the Millbrook Steamboat & Trading Co. Ltd., (SR444), three Bedford OB coaches were sold to Greenslades Tours Ltd., (TCB605/6/8) and further conversions of this type (to bus) left only one, TCB609, in the Grey Cars fleet.

A spectacular accident, fortunately without serious results, occurred on 4th February when DR648, on the 6.45am Sidmouth-Exeter route 9 with driver W. Damerell of Sidmouth depot, collided with a lorry at Aylesbeare Common, and plunged off the road, over a bank and into a copse. It remained upright, coming to rest in deep leaf-mould which later froze. The bus though not extensively damaged, was extricated with some difficulty. It was carrying nearly thirty passengers, but they all fortunately escaped injury. By this time, fibre-glass panels were being used to replace corner panels damaged in accidents.

Seven Guys, DG309/11-3/7-9 were given luggage racks in their lower-deck and their seating was reduced by two, to fifty-four.

The Exeter Corporation Transport Department was going through an unhappy time as they were operating at a loss, and there had been no new vehicles since 1950. Their long serving manager, Mr. B. Y. Smith-Saville had retired in 1951 through ill-health, and his successor, Mr. G. Armstrong, had not stayed long in Exeter. From August 1954, the Assistant Manager Mr. E. T. Salter, who had been heavily involved in setting-up the joint services agreement in 1946/7, acted as Manager on a temporary basis. The City Council was prepared to consider a surrender of its licence and to transfer the undertaking to Devon General through a Parliamentary Bill, but the Company did not feel able to guarantee protection of jobs or of superannuation rights, and the negotiations broke down. There had been strong local feeling against disposal of the undertaking.

Several demonstration vehicles were tried by the Company during this year and ran in actual service. A Guy 'LUF' with Saro 44-seat body (LJW 336), an AEC 'Regent' III with Park Royal 60-seat body (7194 H), an AEC 'Reliance' with Park Royal 44-seat body (50 AMC), and a Commer TS3 coach with Beadle bodywork (RKR 120).

A scheme for a new bus station at the Esplanade, Teignmouth, was agreed between Teignmouth Council and Devon General, but such was the strength of local feeling against bus shelters on the Esplanade, that it did not proceed, and The Triangle continued as the town's principal bus stop and terminus.

A proposal was made to run double-deckers on route 19, Exeter-Moretonhampstead-Chagford, for which a trial run had already been made and Licensing Authority approval received. However, as already recorded, it was not implemented due to local concern as to the state of the roads. Destinations for this route had already been included on the blinds of the newest double-decker vehicles.

Heavy rain and gales at the end of November brought flooding to the Exe Valley, Tiverton being badly affected. Buses ran axle-deep through flood-water in the Loman Green area.

Replacement of the Company's ticket machine stock was continuing, and by 1954, Speed 'Setright' machines numbered up to D195 were in use. Finally, it should be mentioned that the 'Priority Travel' scheme was discontinued from 27th March.

Destination blind display of AEC 'Regent' IIIs, DR724-735, as delivered, were as follows. There was also a three-track route number display within the same frame:

PRIVATE
CHUDLEIGH
NEWTON ABBOT / VIA CHUDLEIGH
EXETER / VIA CHUDLEIGH
NEWTON ABBOT / VIA DAWLISH / & TEIGNMOUTH
EXETER / VIA TEIGNMOUTH / & DAWLISH
STARCROSS
DAWLISH
TEIGNMOUTH
ALPHINGTON
SAMPFORD PEVERELL / VIA SILVERTON / & TIVERTON
TIVERTON
EXETER
HONITON / VIA OTTERY ST. MARY
OTTERY ST. MARY
AXMINSTER / VIA OTTERY ST. MARY / & HONITON
SOUTHWOOD / CROSS
EXETER / AIRPORT
EXMOUTH / VIA WOODBURY
EXETER / VIA WOODBURY
OKEHAMPTON
CROCKERNWELL
TEDBURN ST. MARY
SOUTH TAWTON
SOUTH ZEAL
CREDITON
BROADCLYST
POLTIMORE
DIGBY / HOSPITAL
SIDMOUTH
SIDBURY

CHAGFORD / VIA MORETONHAMPSTEAD
EXETER / VIA MORETONHAMPSTEAD
MORETONHAMPSTEAD
LEIGH CROSS
LONGDOWN
DUNSFORD
CULLOMPTON / VIA BRADNINCH
CULLOMPTON / VIA HELE CROSS
EXETER / VIA HELE CROSS
EXETER / VIA BRADNINCH
SANDYGATE
NEWTON ABBOT
TORQUAY
TORQUAY / PAIGNTON / (EXPRESS SERVICE)
TORQUAY / EXETER / (EXPRESS SERVICE)
EXETER
EXETER / VIA BUCKFASTLEIGH / & ASHBURTON
PLYMOUTH / VIA ASHBURTON / & BUCKFASTLEIGH
EXMOUTH / ORCOMBE POINT / VIA EXTON
EXMOUTH / ORCOMBE POINT / VIA WOODBURY
EXETER / CREDITON / VIA EXTON
EXETER / CREDITON / VIA WOODBURY
EXMOUTH / VIA CLYST ST. MARY
EXETER / VIA CLYST ST. MARY
HEATH CROSS
KENN / KENNFORD / VIA SHILLINGFORD
EXMOUTH / VIA EXTON
EXETER / VIA EXTON
TOPSHAM
FAIRMILE

1955   Exeter Corporation appointed a new Transport Manager, Mr. W. Astin, who was previously Manager at Chester. He sold a number of surplus vehicles for further service, and instituted a programme for fleet renewal of, in general, five vehicles a year. His experience at Chester with Guy chassis and Massey bodies was reflected in the orders placed by Exeter, several of which favoured these manufacturers.

Some alterations to the Exeter city services took place as from 27th February. Route H ceased operation, and the D was extended from Sylvan Road to Stoke Hill to replace it. The C and the G also ceased, and the O/S was extended from South Street, the S to St. David's Station via Queen Street and St. David's Hill, and the O looping back on itself via High Street, Bedford Street and St. Leonards Road to terminate at St. Leonards, which covered the former G entirely. With these changes, Devon General buses only worked on city services O/S and D and Exmouth depot ceased to participate in them. From 6th November Exeter Corporation took over operation of route 26 to Budleigh Salterton, and Devon General ran on city route J.

Devon General had been made aware of the success enjoyed by certain other coastal resort operators by re-introducing open-top double-deckers, and decided to inaugurate its own open-top services.

One was to run along Exmouth sea front to Orcombe Point - the existing route 74 - and the other was an entirely new route, 12A from St. Marychurch, Town Hall, via Babbacombe Downs, Wellswood, Torquay sea front, Preston and Paignton sea fronts, Roundham, Goodrington, and terminating at Broadsands Park Road (railway viaduct). To gain access to Preston sea front meant passing under a railway bridge in Seaway Road that was too low for normal double-deck operation, and there were long negotiations before the necessary licence could be obtained. This was afterwards referred to as the 'battle of the heads'! Operation was conditional on a dead stop immediately before passing under the bridge, with the conductor warning the top deck passengers to remain in their seats, and standing at the top of the stairs to ensure that they did so. The service did not operate via Preston sea front after dark, so as to miss the bridge altogether.

The buses ran in normal service on the 12 from 19th June until 12A could commence on 17th July. Six of the 1934/5 'Regents' (DR203/5/10/8/9/24) had their top removed and were rebuilt by Longwell Green to work the services. Five of the buses worked from Torquay and one (DR218) from Exmouth and they were painted in a new livery of ivory with red bands and maroon wings, DR218 retaining half-drop windows.

Devon General completed the purchase and commenced working the stage services of H. D. Gourd & Sons of Bishopsteignton on 2nd January. The services were Bishopsteignton-Teignmouth and Bishopsteignton-Newton Abbot, but Devon General combined them as one route, 2B, Newton Abbot-Bishopsteignton-Teignmouth. One Bedford coach was included in the purchase, but Devon General never used it, preferring a more modern Bedford bus that had been inherited from Balls Ltd., the previous October. H. D. Gourd had been in business as a carrier since 1896 and ran a horse bus service to Teignmouth, later obtaining a second horse bus. Before, the first world war, he purchased a 1906 Daimler chassis and mounted the open-sided body from the second horse bus on it, but, during the war, the service was maintained by his wife, driving the original horse bus.

His sons joined him in the business in 1921 and in 1934 they bought-out S. G. Taylor, another local carrier. Apart from buses and coaches, they also operated lorries and cattle trucks, the fleet being mainly second-hand, and their yard at Radway Garage in Bishopsteignton, was a veritable Aladdin's cave! Mr. Gourd (senior) had by that time, passed on, and his son Douglas looked after the bus and coach side of the business while the other two sons managed the lorries. The firm continued to operate tours and private hire after the stage services had been sold. Doug Gourd was the star driver and became a well known local character whose accomplishments included the playing of tunes on a watering can! He eventually threw in his lot to Dawlish Coaches but continued to drive for them up to the age of 78, always wearing his traditional white-topped uniform cap.

On 19th June, a temporary bus station was opened in Kingsteignton Road, Newton Abbot, which was built on the site of Marlborough Villa, an old house that the Company had purchased earlier in the year for demolition. The site was cleared and surfaced and a prefabricated office was provided, with enquiry counter, conductors room, inspectors room, and staff toilets. The Market Square was given up as a bus terminus, but the premises at 16, Sherborne Road were retained for the time being. The ultimate aim was to build a depot and servicing area on the site of the temporary bus station, with a permanent bus station to be provided on an adjacent site. Outward journeys in the direction of the railway station ran via Kingsteignton Road and The Avenue before turning into Queen Street.

Another temporary bus station was opened in July, at Brixham, on a site in Bank Lane, prior to the construction of a permanent bus station and depot.

A new 'depot' for one bus, (in the railway station yard at Tiverton Junction), came into use from October. The alterations to the rented offices at Tiverton had been completed in January, and the Witheridge office was given up at the end of the summer. Parcel agencies in the Tiverton and Witheridge area included Black Dog, Puddington, Rackenford, Sampford Peverell, and Withleigh.

A general fares increase took effect on 27th March, and following a wage award on 20th November, further fare 'adjustments' were applied for.

Route 16 became double-deck operated throughout from 1st October using Guys, some of which became based at Moretonhampstead and Okehampton. The section of this route between Bovey Tracey and Moretonhampstead was a very difficult road, narrow, hilly and twisting.

Another route to be double-decked at the end of the year was Teignmouth local service 70.

From 19th June, the joint services with Western National all became known solely by their Western National numbers, thus 45, 49, 53 and 94 disappeared from the timetable as such, becoming 128, 129, 217, and 225. The joint service 47, which had also been Southern National 42, remained 47, the National re-numbering their route in this case. The 217 (formerly 53) reverted to a daily through working from Exeter to Minehead for the summer only, in 1955 and 1956.

Other service alterations were the linking of routes 1/15, 2/11, and 3/85 for the summer only, to form through services. Two hours in a Guy from Sampford Peverell to Exmouth on the 3/85 must have been quite a ride and an occasion is recalled when a cyclist overtook one of the Guys going up a hill in the Exe Valley!

The Buckfastleigh terminus of the 2/11 became Woodholme car park, vehicles reaching it via the bypass and West End. Previously buses had run through the village and terminated at West End.

In Brixham, alternate journeys on the 37A (in summer only), ran to Wall Park Road (Halfway House) instead of turning off Higher Ranscombe Road to terminate at Great Rea Road / Lytes Road. From 1st June, 37B and 37C were combined as 37B, Berry Head-Quay-Fishcombe for the summer only, being split again from 1st October, because Fore Street became closed to traffic from 1st June to 30th September. Two buses were now required to work the Brixham local services.

The Abbotskerswell journeys of service 15 were, from 19th June, extended through country lanes to the hamlet of Stoneyhill, while at Dawlish, some journeys on the 103 were operated as a local service, Port Road-Town Centre-Coronation Avenue.

The saga of the Chelston routes 32 and 33 continued. From 19th June, the Herbert Road journeys of 33 were continued to The Reeves Road, via Thorne Park Road and Nut Bush Lane until 16th September, when they were diverted via Herbert Road and Boundary Road. The single-deck 32 was once again terminated at Chelston (Haywain) from 19th June, but from 10th October was extended along Sherwell Valley Road to terminate at Weeksland Road. A completely different route 32 (double-deck) ran to the Haywain via Walnut Road and Ashfield Road, introduced from 19th June, in place of the Haywain part of the 33, and was from 30th October, extended from the Haywain via Queensway and Raleigh Avenue, to the top of the latter road, which was a very stiff climb. Having two different 32s (one restricted to single-deckers) was confusing for public and staff, and as if to emphasise the situation, one night in March 1956, DR573 returned to the depot via the single-deck 32 route, losing its roof under Old Mill Road railway bridge in the process. It was to be another five years however, before the route numbers were to be distinguished.

A new local service at Torquay from 30th October was 121, Strand-Wellswood-Illsham Valley (for Meadfoot Beach), which after one winter's trial operation, became summer only. Another Torquay local service, the 51 to Torbay Hospital, became daily following the relaxation of visiting restrictions.

Newton Abbot local service 25 was, from 30th October, incorporated into the 110 to give a through service from Buckland Estate (Moorland View) to Broadlands Estate, Highweek, and Mile End - the journeys to Knowles Hill previously timetabled as 25 now appeared under 110. Some journeys on the 11 operated via Broadlands Avenue but soon reverted to the main Ashburton Road, leaving 110 serving Broadlands.

From 18th September, some journeys on 22, Sidmouth-Ottery St. Mary were routed via Fluxton instead of Wiggaton, and from the same date, some workings on Tiverton Local route 101 were further extended from Cowley Moor to Wilcombe Estate.

The driver of DR573 took a short cut back to Torquay depot, unfortunately under the low bridge in Mill Lane! The bus was repaired and returned to service during 1956, and the bridge remained in place to claim further victims! (L.F.Folkard)

Only two new vehicles went into service during 1955; these were AEC 'Reliance' coaches with 8' wide Weymann 'Fanfare' body, and were for use on the extended tours to Scotland and the English Lakes, etc., their wider body prohibiting use on most of the West Country moorland tours, but they appeared on occasions on other suitable local excursions. Numbered TCR749 and 750, they were in a modified livery of grey with cream window surrounds and maroon skirting. Regular drivers were F. Perrett and A. S. Moon, both formerly with Townsend's.

Six of the 1951 AEC 'Regent' IIIs (DR646-651) were fitted with a platform door, and put to work on routes 128 (Torquay-Plymouth) and 2 (Exeter-Newton Abbot via the coast). They moved around the system and also saw service on routes 1, 3, 4, 10, 12, 40 and 46.

Another life was lost on 12th June as a result of the practice of altering the rear side destination box whilst on the move. Conductress Mrs. A. Parken who was but 5'0" tall, over-balanced at Kingsteignton and fell off a 'Regent' III whilst the platform doors were open, there being no central handrail.

Towards the end of the year, twenty AEC 'Regal' saloons, including all the remaining examples of the 1939, 1940 and 1946 batches were sold to Enterprise Services of Jamaica, a company which had been bought by the British Electric Traction Ltd. (BET). They were modified and repainted in Devon General livery in the Torquay workshops for use in their new home, along with 'Enterprise' fleet-name. The twenty were SR426/7/36/45/50/7/60/1/3/4/7/71/2/3/5/8/9,505-507. They were all fitted with a roof-rack and rear ladder, heavy duty springs and a pair of formidable horns. They were shipped in January 1956, but apparently proved unsuitable for the work expected of them, and only had a short life in their new surroundings. Destination blind displays were manufactured and fitted to the 'Regals' and displayed the following names:

KINGSTON	MANDEVILLE / EXPRESS
BEECHERS TOWN	MILK RIVER
BATH	MONTEGO BAY
CHRISTIANA	OCHO RIOS
CEDAR VALLEY	OCHO RIOS / (MILFORD)
CLAREMONT	PORT MARIA
GLENGOFFE	PORT ANTONIO
GRANGE HILL	PRATVILLE
KELLITTS	RETREAT
LORRIMERS	ROCKY POINT / (PORTLAND COTTAGE)
MANDEVILLE	REACH
MORANT BAY	WILLIAMS FIELD
MAY PEN	

During December, the first ten of an order for twenty AEC 'Regent' V double-deckers was delivered, but none entered service until the new year. One of this type, a demonstrator (88 CMV) had been on loan during 1955, and a notable vehicle demonstrated on route 12 during March was STF 90, a Leyland PDR1 double-decker, having a rear engine, with 61-seat, rear entrance, full-fronted body by Saunders Roe. It looked more a trolleybus than anything previously seen and was the prototype from which the celebrated 'Atlantean' evolved. Both of these demonstrators were in a green and cream livery.

Two AEC 'Reliance' Weymann Fanfare coaches were bought in 1955 to work the expanding programme of holiday tours to Scotland and the Lakes that had been recently acquired with the Townsend's business. TCR750 is seen outside the Vaughan Parade, Torquay booking office. (L.F.Folkard)

Not often photographed, two of the recovery vehicles together, parked inside Newton Road garage. RV2 is a Longwell Green conversion based on a shortened AEC 'Regal' chassis and parts, whereas RV1 is an ex-Royal Air Force AEC 'Matador' (L.F.Folkard)

With the frame of XR424 and units left over from the light-six conversions, Devon General built up a shortened chassis to make up a second recovery vehicle. It was sent to Longwell Green for bodywork, and the same firm carried out a major overhaul on two of the 1945 Guy double-deckers (DG324 and 325).

Two new staff cars were purchased.

Section 10. Economies and new procedures (1956 - 1961)

1956   A general fares increase took place on 18th March, and following a wage award on 4th November, a further application was made. Due to the oil shortage caused by the Suez crisis, a surcharge was added to certain fares from 22nd December; this 'temporary' increase was made permanent to cover the November wage increase.

The site of a brewery at Brixham was purchased, and the old malt house was demolished to make way for a new bus station and depot situated between Middle Street and Bank Lane. A second pre-cast concrete building was added at the temporary Newton Abbot bus station which contained a staff canteen and public toilets.

On the Board of Directors, Mr. V. Radford resigned on 27th September, and British Railways' nominee Mr. J. Gillespie was appointed.

The stage services of another independent operator were acquired on 1st June; these were from the Sidmouth Motor Co. & Dagworthy Ltd., which worked two local routes with a variety of small vehicles, including some with open-sided 'toastrack' bodies, as well as orthodox coaches. The licences and all vehicles were initially sold to Greenslades Tours Ltd., of Exeter, which only took one coach into its fleet and resold the rest. The two services were immediately transferred to Devon General as 122, Sidmouth (Bedford Lawn)-Salcombe Regis and 123, Sidmouth (Bedford Lawn)-Peak Hill. From 16th September, they were merged as 122, Salcombe Regis-Sidmouth-Peak Hill, being curtailed from 28th October to operate as Sidmouth-Salcombe Regis (TuFO) via Fortescue and Sidford.

Devon General worked the service with a Bedford OB bus; it was a very hilly route requiring small vehicles, and the Company had nothing that was ideally suited to it. SB603/4 and SB744 had their seating reduced to 24 to work it.

Three routes out of Sidmouth were withdrawn from 28th October: the 38, which ran to Exeter via Metcombe (FO) was replaced by an additional working under route 4, Exeter-Tipton St. John, via Aylesbeare and Metcombe. The 84, Sidmouth-Fortescue-Sidford (Stevens Cross) was covered by the 48 and 122 services, and withdrawn without replacement was the Saturdays-only 41, Sidmouth-Sidbury-Honiton. The two Saturdays-only return trips between Honiton and Gittisham on route 75 were discontinued, the village instead being served by one diverted Honiton-Talaton journey of the same service.

Route 118, a country service from Newton Abbot to Marldon via Ipplepen was withdrawn from 24th June, but a new 124 appeared briefly; this ran from Bishopsteignton to Haldon Moor on Sundays only, but ceased from 16th September. 115, Newton Abbot-Wolborough Hill ceased operation on 31st July, and most workings on the 36 from Sandygate were terminated at Newton Abbot bus station, only a few peak-hour journeys going on to the railway station.

Route 14, Newton Abbot-Haytor-Widecombe was withdrawn altogether from 28th October, this service was also provided by J. Potter & Sons ('Tor Bus') via a different route, and this appeared in the Devon General timetable from 30th June the following year. Devon General route 20 continued to serve Widecombe from Exeter for two more summers, and as part of an agreement with Tor Bus, all journeys on the 16 were diverted to serve Heathfield. The three or four journeys a day which Devon General had previously operated via Heathfield, had been a contentious point in negotiations with Tor Bus, and from 24th June, Devon General actually had a restriction placed on its licence, prohibiting the picking-up of passengers for Newton Abbot at Heathfield and vice versa. Following the agreement, tickets of both companies were inter-available over the common sections of route.

Effective from 28th October, route 79, Moretonhampstead-North Bovey, was reduced to Wednesdays and Saturdays only; the Company had wanted to cease its operation altogether, but after local discussion agreed to a reduced service at enhanced fares.

From the same date, route 70 at Teignmouth no longer served Haldon Golf Club in winter.

The Brixham local services 37A and 37B ran as in the previous summer, from 1st June to 30th September, but from 28th October, 37A/B and C were combined as one service 37, Brixham (Bus Station)-Lytes Road-Berry Head Road-Quay-Fishcombe (daily). The extension from Wall Park Road was via a link road built by the US Army in 1943/4 to provide a second access to the invasion embarkation point by the breakwater. This road joined Victoria Road and the bus proceeded thence via Berry Head Road and King Street to The Quay and Fishcombe. In this form the route remained stable until 1968.

At Torquay, the summer extension of 32/33 from Hesketh Crescent to Meadfoot Beach no longer operated, the beach now being served by the 121 which approached from the opposite direction (via Wellswood).

The 217, from 28th October, only ran through from Exeter to Minehead on Saturdays - at all other times, a change at

Tiverton was necessary, and this arrangement became permanent.

Exeter route D to Stoke Hill, which had previously run via Prince Charles Road, had some journeys routed via Mincinglake Road instead.

No less than forty-two new vehicles were placed in service during this year. Thirty of them were the latest type of AEC 'Regent', the Mark V which had the 7.7-litre engine and new frontal styling. Their lightweight Metro-Cammell body was very similar to those on the previous 'Regent' buses (DR724-735) but a new destination display was introduced with a wide 'final' destination display under which a 'via' box was situated alongside a three-track number box. The same was carried on the rear. Ten of them, (DR770-779) were for use on Exeter city services O and S and all had open-back platform.

The other twenty (DR760-769 and DR780-789) came later, and had an electrically operated platform door for country services 3, 4, 46, 47, 128 and 129. Those on the 3 were soon diverted away and used extensively on the 2, 10 and 40, being replaced on the 3 with the Guys. Also this year came the chassis-less Commer Beadle TS3 vehicles with revolutionary two-stroke three-cylinder engine.

In 1956, six Commer-Beadle chassis-less coaches were bought having two-stroke engine. They were divided between the Townsend's and Grey Cars fleet and were similar in appearance to the 1953/4 AEC 'Regal' IVs. The Commers were noisy and unpopular but lasted until 1964 when all went to dealers instead of the usual route via Greenslades. All saw further service elsewhere.
(East Pennine Transport Group)

Twelve of these were obtained, four were coaches in Townsend's livery (TCC751-754), two in Grey Cars livery (TCC755-756) and six saloon buses suitable for one-man operation (SC757-759 and SC790-792). They were economical vehicles when running but did not prove particularly reliable as well as being very noisy.

Initially they were used as traffic spares at Torquay and Exeter but changed depots frequently, mostly ending up at Newton Abbot. The coaches with bodywork similar to TCR680-697 circulated variously between Torquay, Exeter, Exmouth, Tiverton and Kingsteignton depots.

The introduction of all these new vehicles brought about the Company's first mass withdrawal of double-deckers, and a lot of old 'favourites' came off the road. Six of the 1934 AEC 'Regents' (DR201/8/9/11/17/21), the eight Leyland 'Titan' TD4s of 1936/7 (DL226-233), the three AEC 'Regents' of 1938 (DR236-238), the solitary Leyland 'Titan' TD7 (DL239) and three of the original wartime Guy buses (DG240, 310 and 316). Three of the vehicles that had come from Balls Ltd., (SB744/6 and SC745) and the one from Gourds were also withdrawn.

Four 1945 Guys (DG320-323) received a major body overhaul at Longwell Green Coachworks and DR560/1/3/4/74 were fitted with straight-drop rear panels in place of the flared ones originally fitted, but none of the others were treated this way except DR678 in 1957.

The new recovery vehicle referred to earlier was given the fleet number RV2 and allocated to Exeter depot where it remained. Two more staff cars were purchased.

Detergent oils were first used this year, and these increased average engine life from 50,000 to 150,000 miles necessitating another review of overhaul procedures.

Commer-Beadle also supplied six TS3 service buses in 1956 and SC758 (ROD 758) presents its rear three-quarter view whilst in Paignton bus station.

(DGS collection)

D.G. 120A

THE DEVON GENERAL OMNIBUS AND TOURING CO. LTD.

To ....

From ....

Subject ....

Your Ref ....

Our Ref ....

Date ....

Many new AEC 'Regent' V lightweight double-deckers with Metro-Cammell 'Orion' bodywork entered service in 1956 numbering no less than thirty in total. Ten had open platform for Exeter city services, whereas, the others had a platform door for country workings. DR786 was pictured in Bridport on the Exeter to Weymouth through service. (S.E.Letts)

Two of the numerous Weymann built AEC Reliances SR799 of 1956 and (behind) SR824 of 1958. It is a wet summer Saturday with a visiting coach parked at the top of the yard which has a good selection of what would be termed 'classic' cars today. (N.Bruce-Robertson)

1957   Mr. A. J. White resigned as General Manager in March, having obtained the equivalent post with Maidstone & District. Appointed in his place from 30th May was Mr. T. L. C. Strange, a Lancastrian, born in 1909, who had been General Manager of Rhondda Transport from 1952, and previously with Western Welsh and Ribble Motor services. Mr. Strange arrived after the end of the post-war boom, when a drop in patronage was already evident and profits no longer flowed automatically. New ideas were needed in order to keep the Company's operations viable, and one-man operation of vehicles wherever practicable became the favoured means of achieving economies, but much patient negotiation was necessary with staff and trade unions.

Mr. P. G. Stone Clark, a Director since 1949 and Managing Director since 1951, retired from the Board on 6th June and a Mr. W. M. Dravers was appointed and immediately elected Managing Director.

Devon General bought out another Torquay coach operator just before the start of the season, this being Falkland Garages Ltd., which ran four brown and cream liveried Bedford coaches from premises in Lime Avenue, trading under the name of Falkland Coaches. The firm had been founded in 1920 by Mr. W. Minshull. After his death in 1928, the business was carried on by his wife until 1935 when she sold it to Mr. R. I. Colley. In 1937, a limited company, Falkland Garages Ltd., was formed, but it remained under the control of Mr. Colley, who came over to Grey Cars in 1957. A booking office in Belgrave Road came with the deal, but not the garage, which was relinquished. The four coaches (later numbered TCB820-823) ran in Falkland livery for the 1957 season, at the end of which TCB820 was sold with the other three being repainted into Grey Cars livery.

Further properties were purchased at Newton Abbot in connection with the establishment of a permanent bus station and garage, and land for parking was rented at Marsh Road. The office at 16, Sherborne Road was given up on expiry of the lease. Also given up early in the year was the parking ground at Crockernwell where one bus for route 6 spent the night.

Land was purchased at Paignton for construction of a permanent bus station in the Regent car park, where land for parking was meantime rented from British Railways.

The bus station and depot at Brixham was completed and brought into use on 3rd November having the usual offices, and equipment for re-fuelling, greasing and running repairs. Eight buses were kept there overnight and during the daytime the garage was used as the bus station, also shared by Burton Cars for their workings on route 12B to Kingswear. The temporary bus station in Bank Lane was therefore relinquished, as was the parking ground at Mount Pleasant quarry. Brixham depot was then allocated its own discs, these being half green and half yellow.

From 1st March, three routes were created to serve the new Standard Telephones & Cables Ltd., factory in Brixham Road, Paignton:

123, Brixham-STC Factory
124, Paignton (Bus Station)-Foxhole Estate-STC Factory
125, Lawes Bridge (DG Depot)-STC Factory.

124 was soon altered to commence its journey at Lawes Bridge, and 125 was renumbered 122 from 27th October, but none of these services appeared in the public timetable until 1965.

Some workings of route 18 were diverted to serve the STC factory (out and back from Windy Corner) and these did appear in the timetable from 30th June.

Service alterations from this same date again linked routes 2 and 11 for the summer. 109 was renumbered 57, 104 was renumbered 107, and 57 became 109, so that these three routes became:

57, Torquay (Marine Square)-Warren Road
107, Newton Abbot-Coffinswell-Daccombe
109, Exeter (Paul Street)-Digby Hospital.
Exeter city service B (operated by the Corporation) was extended from Sweetbrier Lane to Thornpark Rise.

All services were suspended from 20th to 29th July because of an official strike over pay. As a result of a national wage settlement, fares were again increased, from 15th September.

From 11th August, new service 104 ran from Paignton (Bus Station) via Marldon Road to Foxhole Estate (Fernicombe Road), and was double-decker worked from the start. In consequence, the frequency of the 17 was reduced, and all 105 buses were routed via Blatchcombe Road. This hilly area of Paignton was difficult to operate and later would result in special buses being ordered. One journey on service 108 was extended on Saturdays from Huxnor Cross through a narrow country lane to Marldon (Church House Inn).

Daily Peak Hill-Sidmouth-Salcombe Regis workings resumed between March and October, and these ran as service 122 as well as the Tuesday and Friday journeys to Sidford (Stevens Cross). The route was renumbered 125 from 27th October.

An unofficial survey of the Exeter Joint Services revealed that 19 Devon General vehicles were allocated to work services O/S and D, while City of Exeter vehicles were deployed on Devon General services as follows:

Routes 5/85 - 11 vehicles,
8/27 - 4 buses,
58 - 2 buses
and one on each of services 42, 65, 67, 66, 68, 26 and 64.
As 67 and 68 only operated on certain days of the week, there were thus 23 buses normally involved. Ordinary service requirements on the city routes which the Corporation worked with its own vehicles were:

A/F - 9	C/W - 3	K -1
B - 4	J - 2	M - 1

Devon General received twenty-seven new vehicles in 1957, thirteen were AEC 'Regent' V rear-platform double-deckers (DR807-819) with Metro-Cammell body similar to those bought in 1956, and these were put to work on Exeter city services O and S.

The other fourteen were AEC 'Reliance' 41-seat single-deckers (SR793-806) with Weymann body of which the last six had transparent sun-hatches in the roof. These were all equipped for one-man operation which had been tried experimentally on route 46 in May, but they were not at first operated as such. Two were tried at Moretonhampstead on service 19 and one at Exmouth on the 82. This arrangement was not long lasting and the vehicles were spread between Torquay, Brixham, Exeter and Tiverton depots with rostered duties on services 32, 37, 46, 56 and 57 as well as general traffic spares.

All these new buses entered service in June or July causing withdrawals of thirteen AEC 'Regent' buses dating from 1934/5. These were buses that had been re-bodied by Brush, DR200/2/4/6/7/12/13/14/16/20/22/23 and 225, and fourteen of the AEC 'Regal' saloons of 1948 (SR509-520/2/3). Sold at the end of the season were the last two former Balls' coaches (TC747 and 748) and the four ex-Townsend's Dennis coaches (TC736-739).

Two new staff cars were bought and three were sold, and demonstration buses on loan during the year were NSG 298, an Albion 'Nimbus' designed for routes where a small but powerful vehicle was required, and (60 MMD) an AEC 'Bridgemaster' which was a low-height double-decker of longer length, but still being a half-cab rear entrance bus.

AEC 'Regent' buses which had a platform door were re-classified 'DRD' instead of just 'DR' but only received their new suffix as they were repainted.

1957 was also the last year in which the 'Insert Setright' ticket machines were used on buses although they continued to be used at enquiry offices for the issue of weekly tickets.

Allocation of coaches to drivers, for the 1957 season was:

Grey Cars		TCR687	- R. Scagell	**Townsend's**	
		TCR688	- H. Roberts		
-TCR623	- P. Ead	TCR689	- W. Bray	TC736	- ? Stone
TCR624	- R. Rundle	TCR690	- P. Cole	TC737	- P. H. Tillbrook
TCR625	- P. Edmunds	TCR691	- G. Stear	TC738	- L. Hawkings
TCR626	- E. Burbidge	TCR692	- W. G. H. Hodge	TCC751	- E. Crouch
TCR627-630	- Exeter Cars	TCR693	- A. Holland	TCC752	- H. Sutcliff
TCR631	- L. Harry	TCR694	- P. Hallett	TCC753	- R. Blackler
TCR632-634	- Exeter Cars	TCR695	- E. Jones	TCC754	- W. Steer
TCR680	- E. Lawrence	TCR696	- L. Worrall		
TCR681	- Exeter Car	TCR697	- P. Rowland	**Falkland's**	
TCR682	- H. Hine (Townsend's fleet)	TC740	- W. Hannaford		
TCR683	- F. Wollacott	TCR749	- F. Perrett	TCB820	- W. King
TCR684	- J. J. Lowe	TCR750	- A. S. Moon	TCB821	- ? Smith
TCR685	- W. Hawke	TCC755	- Exeter Car	TCB822	- M. Loader
TCR686	- R. Easterbrook	TCC756	- G. T. Crispin	TCB823	- W. Weymouth

From 1st January 1958, Grey Cars, Townsend's and Falkland's were amalgamated with full inter-changeability of staff and vehicles. Drivers Moon, Perrett, Crouch, Hine and Sutcliffe of Townsend's, and drivers Weymouth and Smith of Falkland were transferred to Devon General staff.

1958 The Chairman's report to the 1958 Annual General Meeting gave some interesting facts and figures. Passengers carried during 1957 had been five million less than in 1956, which had been partly due to the strike, but was mainly because of changing social patterns and the increase in private car ownership. This trend had been apparent since 1952. 72% of the routes and 40% of the mileage were being operated at a loss. The twenty-seven new vehicles which entered service in 1957 plus the six new Commer-Beadle coaches that had been delivered during that year cost a total of £155,000. There was a total of 233 employees, 19% of whom had completed 25 years service with the Company. Figures were presented showing how each £1 of income was spent:

Wages	10s.0d.
Dividends	1s.0d.
Provision for renewals	2s.3d.
Publicity	3d.
Administration	4d.
Taxes	3s.3d.
Fuel	1s.0d.
Other materials	1s.7d.
Rates, rents & insurance	4d.
	£1. 0s.0d.

Early in the year, site work started in connection with the new bus station in Kingsteignton Road, Newton Abbot, and a number of properties, including a blacksmith's forge and a wine merchant's store, were demolished. Vehicles were parking on the cleared site by August.

Mr. T. R. Williams, a Director since 1947, resigned on 27th November, and his place on the Board was taken by Mr. R. J. Ellery, a nominee of National Electric Construction Co. Ltd.

Two drivers each completed 50 years service in April - W. G. H. Hodge, who had started on the Torquay trams in 1908 as a boy conductor, and F. Dore, who had been a conductor on the Torquay & District steam buses before transferring to the trams. The two men were actually very similar in appearance, but there the resemblance ended. 'Scatter' Hodge was a flamboyant character who got his nickname through once driving a tram from Torquay to Preston and back before the inspector knew he had gone! He loved 'telling the tale', and drove Royalty in July 1946. He would normally include 'a thrill for the ladies' in his tours, which consisted of tearing down a narrow leafy lane and over a hump-back bridge at Liverton being a favourite place for this! Fred Dore was a much quieter man, quite happy to ply to and fro on route 30 or around the 50/55 circular with a double-decker. He retired in October, and 'Scatter' Hodge did likewise, a month later.

New vehicles obtained during the year were fourteen AEC 'Reliance' buses, (SR824-837) all suitable for one-man operation. These had Weymann bodywork similar to SR793-800 of 1957, and they replaced another fourteen of the 1947/8 half-cab 'Regals' (SR521/5/7-9/31/2/5/8/40/1/4-6) largely at Tiverton, and were the last single-deckers delivered with an offside cab entrance.

Another Albion 'Nimbus' demonstrator, 330 CTD was on loan early in the year, and six buses of this type for restricted routes were delivered with Willowbrook 31-seat body (SN838-843) of which SN839 was exhibited at the Commercial Motor Show and later ran on loan to Aldershot & District. They replaced the remaining Bedford OB buses (formerly coaches) in the fleet (SB600-604, 607 and TCB609).

Six Commer TS3s, with two-stroke engine and really handsome Beadle 'Rochester' coachwork, (TCC844-849) had been delivered late in 1957 to replace the coaches then sold, but they did not enter service until April 1958.

Finally, there were ten AEC 'Reliance' coaches with Willowbrook 'Viking' coachwork (TCR850-859) but these had low-back seats which proved unpopular with passengers on long journeys. They went into service in June and replaced the AEC 'Regal' half-cab Duple Grey Cars (TCR623-634), most of which had not been used since the end of the 1957 season. All were sold to Greenslades at Exeter which had also become a BET associated company in 1953. All these new coaches were in the modified Grey Cars livery which had first appeared in 1955 on TCR749/750 and the rest of the coach fleet was gradually repainted in the same style which did not however suit some of the coach designs. The remaining ex-Falkland coaches had only just been repainted into the previous style with a cream roof but all of these (TC740, TCB741-743, TCB821-823) were sold in any case in October. The entire fleet was now diesel-engined.

Other events of the year were a national wage award in October, a new booking office replaced the old Falkland office in Belgrave Road, Torquay, and the Isle of Skye was added to the holiday tour programme (12 days for 34 guineas).

Two new vans replaced old ones, three new staff cars were purchased, two old ones were sold and one was written off! The latter was the Chief Engineer's car which had overturned following a collision on Haldon Moor - he was unhurt and cleared of any blame.

Less fortunate however, was cleaner J. R. Wright of Kingsteignton depot who lost his life on 27th March when he was knocked down by a reversing bus.

An important development took place with the introduction of 'one man' buses on a number of routes, including some that had previously been double-decker operated. The 22, (Sidmouth-Ottery St. Mary) was converted in March and was diverted into and out of Sidmouth via Woolbrook at about the same time.

The routes serving Witheridge were entirely one-man operated from July, and by the 19th October timetable, routes 3, 20, 22, 29, 48, 69, 76, 91, 92, 93, 96, 97, 98 and 225 were shown as being so operated. AEC 'Reliance' and Albion 'Nimbus' buses were used for the first conversions, and the programme continued, not on a geographical basis, but rather as local staff agreements could be negotiated.

The new Bretonside bus station in Plymouth opened in March, and this became the terminus for services 128 and 129.

From 9th June, a new route 20 provided a replacement for the British Railways Teign Valley branch line on its closure. It ran on weekdays only, Exeter-Leigh Cross-Trusham-Newton Abbot, but few journeys ran over the whole route.

The former 20, Exeter-Widecombe, ran under service number 14 from 6th July to 7th September on Wednesdays and Sundays only, (and on the occasion of Widecombe Fair), after which it ceased permanently.

Route 23, Exeter-Princetown, was also withdrawn permanently from 30th August. Other service alterations during the year included: 108 extended from Marldon (Church House) to Five Lanes from 16th March, but cut back to Huxnor Cross again from 19th October; 54 was extended from Shiphay (Dairy Hill) to Torridge Avenue over the same route as the 28A from 30th March; 17 was extended from Marldon (Torbay Chalet Hotel) to Marldon (Belfield Avenue) from 6th July. From 15th September, route 18 operated weekdays only; this service had ceased its diversion to the Standard Telephone Company's factory from 16th February.

Services 2 and 11 were not linked for the summer as they had been the previous two seasons.

From 29th September, all Sidmouth-Fortescue-Sidford journeys were run under service number 48 instead of 125. The only other journeys the 48 then made were Sidmouth-Seaton-Lyme Regis on a Wednesday. Route 76 was extended from Sandford to New Buildings on Tuesdays and Saturdays, thus permanently replacing 113, 69 became Crediton-Sandford-Kennerleigh, and ran on Saturdays only after 6th July, no longer serving the Cinema in Crediton.

The express service 46 was, as usual, extended to Paignton for the summer, but from 19th October was cut back permanently to terminate in Lymington Road, Torquay.

Some journeys on route 3 were, from the same date, diverted to serve the village of Thorverton which was just off the main road.

From 30th March, the Budleigh Salterton short workings on route 10 were diverted via the Littleham Estate in Exmouth. A new route 60 was operated during the summer only between Littleham Village and Sandy Bay Holiday Camp, daily on a locally-published timetable; services 59 and 59A provided connections into Exmouth, and a tours booking office was established at Sandy Bay.

On the Exeter city services, route D was extended from Stoke Hill to Beacon Heath via Calthorpe Road and Beacon Lane from 14th October. It still ran through Stoke Hill Estate alternately via Prince Charles Road or Mincinglake Road.

1959   The policy of conversion to one-man working wherever possible, continued with routes 44, 46, 90, 103, 107, 108, 125 and 217 all becoming single-manned during the year, all but 46 and 217 using Albion 'Nimbus' vehicles.

The Traffic Commissioners attached two unusual conditions to the licence for route 107, (Newton Abbot-Coffinswell-Daccombe) "the service to be operated by Albion 'Nimbus' vehicles, and the driver to sound his horn at all dangerous corners!"

Two journeys on route 19A on Tuesdays and Saturdays were diverted to terminate at Doddiscombsleigh (Nobody Inn) instead of Christow from 10th January, and another general fares increase took effect from 1st February.

Following closure of the British Railways branch line to Moretonhampstead, all journeys on the 16 ran via Lustleigh Station, from Kelly Cross, as from 1st March.

Timetable No:142, dated 19th April, was never generally issued due to a dispute in the printing trade, while No:143, effective from 5th July, was published late for the same reason.

The rapidly-growing University complex at Exeter by this time merited a bus service, and joint service U was introduced between Bedford Street and the University, worked by Corporation vehicles.

Another service for specialised needs was a coach link from Exeter Airport to Torquay and Paignton, which commenced operation on 6th September.

Route 46, the 'Exeter Express', was, from 5th July extended from Castle Circus (Lymington Road) through Torquay town centre via Union Street, Fleet Street, Strand and Torwood Street to terminate in the upper floor of the Grey Cars garage.

Routes 22 and 78 exchanged numbers from 5th July, as did 24 and 109, so that the resultant services became:

22,   Drewsteignton-Chagford-Newton Abbot (WSaO)
24,   Exeter (Paul Street)-Digby Hospital (WSaO - joint service)
78,   Sidmouth-Tipton St. John-Ottery St. Mary (daily)
109,   Newton Abbot-Decoy (daily)

A new open-top service 12C was introduced from 19th July, using vehicles which would otherwise have worked on 12A, which was reduced correspondingly. 12C ran from St. Marychurch (Town Hall), via Torquay, Paignton (Bus Station), Goodrington and Churston to Kingswear, from whence passengers could take the ferry to Dartmouth. The section of route between Churston and Hillhead was a steady climb on a little-used main road, giving fine views back over Torbay, and the sound of the 1934 'Regents' could really be savoured at their best hereabouts.

Route 48, after its numerous constrictions, was finally withdrawn altogether from 6th October. Its Sidmouth-Fortescue-Sidford journeys again becoming a part of service 125.

A minor alteration took place to route 99, which as from 6th October no longer ran as a circular route, and instead operated via Washfield in both directions. A loop was, however, still made around the terminal area of Stoodleigh (Post Office), Ash Cross and Stoodleigh Estate.

A number of changes took place on the Board of Directors; Mr. K. W. C. Grand resigned on 6th May, and Mr. H. G. Bowles, Assistant General Manager of British Railways (Western Region) took his place. Mr. W. T. James, who was Chairman, resigned on 26th November; his place on the Board being taken by Lord Buckhurst (one of the few peers of the realm to hold a PSV licence), and Mr. W. M. Dravers, previously Managing Director, became Chairman. The Directors had, from 1947, made an annual tour of the Devon General system, staying either at the Livermead House Hotel, Torquay (which was then BET owned), or at the Manor House Hotel, near Moretonhampstead, which was railway owned. A specially prepared Grey Cars coach took them on their visits, for which interesting souvenir hard-cover booklets were produced. One of the newest coaches was used with a few seats being removed for the provision of tables and storage of essential (liquid) supplies! The driver for this duty was usually either E. Jones or L. Worrall, both of whom were provided with a grey chauffeur's uniform, complete with cap.

New coaches obtained in 1959 comprised six more AEC 'Reliance' Grey Cars with Willowbrook 'Viking' coachwork, identical to the batch purchased in 1958 apart from having normal high-backed seats. They were numbered TCR889-894 and entered service in May.

TCR893 was one of the 1959 Willowbrook Viking coaches but seen here after re-styling in an effort to modernise them and to match the later Viscounts. It is pictured at the top of the Burma Road. (N.Bruce-Robertson)

Seventeen of the new and revolutionary Leyland 'Atlantean' double-deckers arrived and went into service on the 12 in June and July. Numbered DL872-888, they had 78 seats with rear engine (mounted across the back of the vehicle) and front passenger entrance with platform door under the control of the driver. Bodywork was by Metro-Cammell, and all went to Torquay, Brixham and Kingsteignton depots. From the start of the winter timetable, they also appeared on service 28A (Shiphay), which also covered evening journeys on the 32/33 between The Strand and Hesketh Crescent.

The displaced double-deckers were transferred around accordingly, and the remaining Guys, disused since November 1958, were withdrawn (DG243-249, 308/9/11-15/17-21/23-25) together with DG322 which had latterly been in use as a tree-lopper, having had its top removed since 1957.

Twelve more AEC 'Reliance' saloons (SR860-871), delivered in March, replaced the last of the 1948 AEC 'Regals' (SR524/6/30/3/4/6/7/9/42/3/7/8). These had Willowbrook bodywork, slightly more angular than the previous Weymann examples and with a new and very much larger front destination display. They were allocated to Exeter, Sidmouth, and Kingsteignton depots. Two new vans and three staff cars were bought during the year to replace older vehicles.

A new day-tour was introduced from Torquay to Lands End, and a new booking office was built at 147, Reddenhill Road, (Babbacombe) Torquay (on the former Townsend's site) with a concrete stand for two coaches alongside. The office at 137, Reddenhill Road which Devon General had rented for many years was then given up, and the premises became a ladies' hairdresser.

A cafeteria was leased out at 17, Dartmouth Road (adjoining Paignton bus station) which was a property that the Company had owned since 1954.

Southern National sold the former DMT garage and works at Okehampton, the building being acquired by Watkins & Rosevear Ltd., makers of agricultural machinery. Devon General continued, for the time being, to park a bus overnight at the premises, but shortly after, moved it to the Market Street car park.

864, a 1959 Willowbrook built AEC Reliance, newly repainted, sits alongside the washer unit at Newton Road. Note the excessively tall number blinds. (N.Bruce-Robertson)

Parcel vans operated out of Exeter and Torquay, for onward delivery of items sent by country bus. In the villages, agents would handle the parcels traffic on and off the buses. (L.F.Folkard collection).

Newton Abbot bus station when fairly new, as the concrete is still clean. It is 10.41am probably on a Sunday morning as 'Atlantean' 882 sets off for Brixham leaving behind a 'Regal', a 'Reliance' and a 'light-six' double-decker. (Herald Express Newspapers)

Kingsteignton depot in March 1959 with some of the twelve new Willowbrook AEC 'Reliance' buses after only a few days in service. (D.J.Frost)

1960   The new bus station at Newton Abbot opened on 10th January. It had one long covered platform, with snack bar, offices, and toilets. The entrance and exit were in Kingsteignton Road, and a double line of buses could park on the forecourt which was surveyed by a high mounted clock.

The first bus to depart from the new bus station was the 9.18am to Brixham on the 12, with driver Dudley Harvey and conductor Thomas Passmore. It left unceremoniously, and watched by a lone bus spotter. The first bus to arrive was driven by Gordon Hole. Inspector E. S. (Teddy) Rawle was in charge of the new station.

The adjacent site of the temporary bus station was then cleared, apart from the canteen building, and a small two-bay servicing depot, with washing and fuelling facilities was built, together with walled parking for about six buses on this triangular site at the corner of Kingsteignton Road and Cricketfield Road. This addition was completed in September, and Kingsteignton depot closed at the end of the month, its allocation being transferred to Newton Abbot.

Some shelters from the temporary bus station were re-erected at various points around the town. The Kingsteignton garage (which still stands) and adjacent parking land were sold to British Road Services Ltd., on 28th November, but as there was still insufficient parking space at the new premises, some buses continued to park on a rented site in Marsh Road.

At the same time, work was progressing on a new permanent bus station at Paignton, on the existing site (formerly known as Regent car park), this becoming a somewhat larger building than at Newton Abbot. Due to the low-lying ground and high water-table, piling was not possible and Dutch technology was sought which involved the laying down of large fibre 'mats' prior to construction.

A property in Paignton, at 59, Torbay Road, was purchased by the Company and this was a shop divided into two units, part of which became a tours booking office, replacing the leased premises at 26/28, Torbay Road from 1st April. The other part of the premises was let to the 'Olde Fashioned Humbug Shoppe'.

Blackboy Road depot at Exeter was acknowledged to be unsuitable for the larger vehicles now being operated as part of it was not high enough to accommodate double-deckers, access was difficult, there was no adequate forecourt and it was not central enough. Over 100 'dead' miles a day were being worked and as no major improvements had been carried out since the 1920s, the Company had thoughts and plans for a new depot much nearer the city centre, but it was to be another thirteen years before they came to fruition.

The summer of 1960 was a very wet one, and trouble was experienced with flooding, particularly in Torquay, Tiverton and Exmouth. The worst July for 20 years was blamed for a drop of a quarter of a million passengers compared with the previous July. Devon General could however still cater for those who wanted to enjoy the 'summer' elsewhere and the long-distance holiday tours programme advertised was:

English Lakes & Yorkshire Dales,
Isle of Wight, South Coast and London,
Derbyshire Dales, North and Mid-Wales,
English Lakes & Blackpool,
Scottish Highlands and the Trossachs,
Isle of Skye,
Highlands and Western Isles (Mull, Tobermory and Iona),
Lands End & Cornish Coast.

A notable retirement on 30th April was that of Mr. W. H. Geere, Assistant General Manager and Company Secretary, who had served the industry for 54 years having begun working for the National Electric Construction Co. Ltd., in London in 1906. He came to Devon General in 1922.

A reduction in the platform staff working week from 44 hours to 42 hours, along with a wage award, together added £75,000 of additional costs for the year, or 10% on to the Company's wage bill. Accordingly fares were increased from 10th July.

There had been a certain amount of staffing problems with the 'new' Leyland 'Atlantean' - crews had at first refused to carry standing passengers, but this was resolved on 18th December. During the year, the 'Atlanteans' were down-seated by two, to 76, so that luggage racks could be fitted on the lower deck, at the front on the offside, under the stairs.

On the Board of Directors, there were several comings and goings; Mr. C. W. G. Elliff resigned on 29th February, and Mr. F. W. H. Mepstead on 31st March. Mr. D. McKenna and Mr. C. Williams, both officials of British Railways (Southern Region), were appointed in their place. On 30th November, Lord Buckhurst resigned and his place was taken by Mr. F. K. Pointon.

The Board then comprised Mr. W. M. Dravers (Chairman), Messrs. H. G. Bowles, R. J. Ellery, J. Gillespie, F. K. Pointon, C. Williams, P. Yorke, and D. McKenna.

Principal route alterations during the year involved the short workings of service 92 to Templeton which ceased from 4th January and Rackenford journeys were diverted to serve Templeton on Tuesdays only. From the same date, some journeys on the 101 were re-routed to serve Tiverton Secondary Modern School instead of Heathcoats Factory.

A new Exeter Joint Services route G was introduced from 17th April, Crossmead to Beacon Heath via Old Tiverton Road and this was worked by Devon General vehicles.

At Newton Abbot, service 109 was extended to run Decoy (Fountain)-Newton Abbot-Buckland Estate (Moorland View), and incorporated the Wednesday and Saturday journeys to Knowles Hill, previously run as 110 (which continued otherwise unaltered).

In the summer timetable, effective from 3rd July, routes 2/11 were again linked until 10th September, but this was the last summer that this took place. Route 5 was no longer extended from Exmouth (DG Garage) to Orcombe Point for the summer, and the service was run as route 74 using open-topper DR218. A new route 83 was introduced between Exmouth and Littlemead Lane Estate.

Due to summer traffic congestion, route 12 was operated in two sections, Torquay-Newton Abbot and Torquay-Paignton-Brixham. This was a reversion to the former situation, when the route numbers were 28 and 12, but no attempt was made to revive the number 28. This practice became regular working each summer from then on.

Two daily journeys on 18 were diverted to serve Broadsands Park Road at times of the year when the open-top service was not operating, and terminal problems at Kingswear were relieved by the construction of a turning circle about 200 yards short of the ferry. It was a major civil engineering project, jutting out high above the railway land, and supported by massive concrete pillars and beams. By virtue of its shape, it soon became known as the 'Banjo'. There was then no need for low-bridge double-deckers to work the 12B from Brixham and in summer, the open-top 12C from Torquay also terminated at the Banjo. AEC 'Reliance' saloons worked the 12B from July, and the service became OMB in October, reverting to crew operation in the summer when double-deckers were often necessary.

The de-greasing ramp in use, complete with operator in his oil-skins as 'Atlantean' 901 is prepared for its MoT at Newton Road, Torquay. A filthy job at the best of times!

(N. Bruce-Robertson)

In January 1965, Tottenham Hotspur played Torquay United at Plainmoor, and a fleet of buses conveyed away-supporters from the railway station and awaited their return after the match for which they are seen parked-up in St. Marychurch Road with 904 leading at least fourteen other buses. (D.Frost)

New vehicles in 1960 were twenty-three more Leyland 'Atlantean' double-deckers (DL895-917). These had 75-seat all-metal bodywork by Chas. H. Roe of Crossgates, Leeds (although originally ordered from Park Royal), and these were not quite so well proportioned as the Metro-Cammell buses on the 1959 series.

They proved in time to be not so structurally sound either, as they leaked badly right from the start and strengthening kits were provided by Park Royal for the floors of both decks. Within a few years they were badly affected by rust, and all eventually had to be taken out of service for complete rebuilding, or in some cases, premature withdrawal.

A few had advertisement panels on the offside, illuminated by fluorescent tubes, as did other new vehicles over the next few years, but these turned out to be an unnecessary fitting. They would run down the battery if left on while the engine was not running, and allowed the ingress of rain water to the bodywork. Unlit advertisements could be read perfectly well in town lighting, whilst in the country 'the cows were not interested in advertisements' (a quote attributed to the General Manager).

These 'Atlanteans' worked from Torquay, Newton Abbot, and Brixham depots mainly on the 12, but also on the 28A, 30, 31, 50 and 55 services. Two were put to work on the 128 (Torquay - Plymouth) from October. In all, they replaced the twenty-six 1947/8 AEC 'Regent' IIIs (DR326-333, DR549-566) which saw further service with other operators, some going to Western Welsh for use on a contract serving the Milford Haven oil terminal. Also withdrawn in 1960 were the six ex-Leicester Corporation 'Regents' (DR698-703) that had been acquired on an exchange of vehicles in 1952.

On loan for six days in October was AEC 'Reliance' demonstrator WJU 407 with Willowbrook 41-seat coach body, which was tried on Grey Cars tours. Two Morris vans were purchased to replace older vehicles.

Convertible Leyland 'Atlantean' DL932 'Earl Howe' in winter condition at Hatfield Cross, Torquay during the winter of 1961/2. As a result of considerable accident damage suffered in the bad winter weather, these vehicles were mothballed after every summer thereafter, and they could be found covered in polythene sheets on the upper floor of Torwood Street garage, only seeing the light of day for repainting etc. *(L.F.Folkard)*

1961

Two new batches of Leyland 'Atlanteans' were delivered during March and April. The first seven (DL918-924) were similar to the previous year's delivery having Roe body with outside illuminated advertisement panels, but all interior lighting was by fluorescent tubes. The front nearside platform window incorporated a ventilator, but this was soon replaced by a plain glass window due to leaks. DL921 was fitted with a turbo-charger unit soon after delivery, and entered service on route 105 (Paignton-Foxhole) on 1st April along with DL875 which had already been thus rebuilt. DL881 and DL924 also later received turbo-chargers.

The next batch comprised nine 'Atlanteans' with 75-seat bodywork by Metro-Cammell. They were fitted with a detachable roof so that they could work the open-top services during the summer, and normal services during the winter. They arrived in the well recognised open-top style of reversed livery. The roof unit was a precision job, so that any roof would fit any vehicle.

Each roof was secured by twenty fixing bolts, with a multi-point electric plug at the front. Two lifting brackets were mounted on each side of the roof. A specially made lifting frame, once a part of the frame of the former bus washer, was installed in the depot roof at Newton Road and it was a half-hour task to fit or remove a roof using this apparatus. Once removed they were carried and stored, three at a time, on racks constructed on the chassis of the three withdrawn AEC 'Regent' ex-Leicester double-deckers (DR701-703). The new open-toppers were designed with the help of Crosville Motor Services which already had experience of removable tops. They were numbered DL925-933 (925 GTA etc) being named after famous West Country 'Sea Dogs', as follows:

DL925	Admiral Blake
DL926	Sir Francis Drake
DL927	Sir Martin Frobisher
DL928	Sir Humphrey Gilbert
DL929	Sir Richard Grenville
DL930	Sir John Hawkins
DL931	Sir Thomas Howard
DL932	Earl Howe
DL933	Sir Walter Raleigh

A naming ceremony was held in Paignton bus station on 11th May to formally launch the 'Sea Dogs' when DL928 was officially named 'Sir Humphrey Gilbert' by Commander Walter Raleigh Gilbert (of Compton Castle) and who was a direct descendant. After the ceremony, a demonstration of the roof removal was given at Newton Road depot. Commander Gilbert later supplied prints of engravings of the original 'Sea Dogs', and these were fitted inside the lower saloon of each vehicle, as appropriate, in a glass covered picture frame.

A new route 12D, St. Marychurch (Town Hall) to Brixham, via Torquay and Paignton was introduced from 1st July, and the 'Sea Dogs' could also be used on the 12B, Brixham-Kingswear in summer as well as on the existing 12A and 12C open-top services. Interestingly and surprisingly, the duties of individual buses were alternated to satisfy requests from parents whose children wanted to ride on each one! Exmouth however lost out as no new open-top was allocated there.

The extensive improvements at Paignton bus station were completed early in the year, one long covered platform with offices, toilets and sales kiosks being provided. One of the early events to be held there was the open-top naming ceremony, referred to above.

One of the last revenue-earning duties for the old open-top buses (converted from the 1934 'Regents') was a trip to Epsom Racecourse for the 1961 Derby, where five (DR203/5/18/19/24) acted as hospitality grandstands for pre-booked parties from London. After the race, drivers R. Beer, L. Harry, W. Waddle, E. Burbidge and F. Knapman gave the buses a final fling with a fast run back down the A303. The sixth bus, DR210, had been sold in March for further service with Thomas Bros. of Port Talbot, and was eventually acquired for preservation in the West of England.

The next new vehicles to appear in 1961 were nine 41-seat AEC 'Reliance' Grey Cars (TCR934-942) with Willowbrook 'Viscount' coachwork. These were more stylish than their 'Viking' predecessors with transparent roof-lights, an inward sloping rear window (often likened to the Ford Anglia car of the times) and carried a maroon band and flash to relieve the expanse of grey panelling. The first seven were of 7'6" width for local excursions whereas the last two (TCR941/2) were to the 8'0" width and just 37 seats for use on the longer holiday tours. These latter two eventually replaced the two Weymann 'Fanfare' coaches (TCR749 and 750).

The others replaced the oldest of the AEC 'Regal' IV coaches (TCR680-688 of 1953) all of which were transferred to Greenslades Tours Ltd., at Exeter. Fourteen AEC 'Regent' III double-deckers of 1949 were disposed of during the year, these being DR567-77/9/85/6.

A new holiday tour to Northern Scotland, Braemar and Loch Maree was introduced for the 1961 season.

Improvements to the depots included the provision of a 'Widney' bus washer at Newton Abbot depot, a 'Februat' portable (coach) washer for Torwood Street (Torquay) depot, and a variant of the same make but suitable for double-deckers at Exmouth depot.

At Newton Road depot, behind the Devon Laundry, a two-bay fuelling tower was constructed with overhead tanks, along with an adjacent bus washer. A concrete road surface was laid through this area with a direct connection on to the main road. From September, buses were able to enter this road which was on a gentle slope, and be re-fuelled, drive through the wash and proceed, still dripping, into the garage via the side doorway for parking.

The garage doorway at the south end was for outward vehicles only, and that at the north end was not at that time in regular use for vehicle movements. This new procedure overcame the problem of buses waiting in Newton Road to be able to enter the garage for fuelling, and at the same time released space on the garage floor which had previously been kept clear for vehicles using the 1952 roof-mounted washing frame.

Further one-man bus operation took place with routes 2B, 6, 18, 19, 19A, 21, 75 and 79 being converted from 1st January, as did 16 between Okehampton and Chagford (where a change of vehicle was necessary). Newton Abbot area services 14, 15, 88, 116 and 117 also became single-manned from 1st October.

The other local services were also re-organised from that date, the routes to Decoy and Highweek (Mile End) once again became separate services operated from Newton Abbot bus station. Decoy became route 14, and Highweek regained its old number of 25. Route 36 was linked to the Buckland Estate services, and disappeared as a service number for the time being. The Buckland routes were thus:

109,   Buckland Estate-Queensway-Newton Abbot-Kingsteignton-Sandygate
110,   Buckland Estate-Oakland Road-Newton Abbot-Kingsteignton-Sandygate

Service 2B in Bishopsteignton was extended from Ring of Bells to Radway and back, from 1st January (reviving a diversion that had ceased from 2nd October 1960) and from 1st October was further extended to Teign Close.

Routes 83 at Exmouth and 125 at Sidmouth became summer-only operations, whilst at Paignton, local services 17, 104 and 105, by now worked by 'Atlanteans', were re-routed via Well Street and Church Street instead of via Cecil Road and Torquay Road, to avoid summer congestion in the last-named, but the cure proved worse than the disease and they reverted to the normal route later in the year!

At Torquay, the single-deck 32 was extended further up Sherwell Valley Road to terminate at Hawkins Avenue. Further alterations took place to the Chelston routes from 26th November. The 33, instead of running via Boundary Road to terminate at The Reeves Road, was diverted along the newly widened Nut Bush Lane to terminate at Highland Road. The single-deck 32 to Hawkins Avenue was renumbered 32A, and a new (also single-deck) route 32B was introduced which branched off the 32A at the end of Sherwell Lane to run up to the top of The Reeves Road which is a very steep hill. The double-deck 32 to Raleigh Avenue was unaltered this time. Certain journeys on the 33 were once again extended from Hesketh Crescent to Meadfoot Beach in the summer.

Another Torquay local service, 111, was curtailed to run Strand-Lower Warberry Road only, while three new routes were introduced from 26th November, all being double-deck operated:

114,   Inner Circle via Strand, Ellacombe, Quinta Road, Wellswood, and back to the Strand (daily)
115,   which was simply a reverse of 114.
118,   Strand-Shiphay (Collaton Road) via Teignmouth Road, Hele Village, Lawes Bridge and
        Cadewell Lane (weekdays).

The 114 and 115 covered the withdrawn portion of the 111, and 118 provided an alternative service to Hele, and to new housing developments at Shiphay and Cadewell.

Service 129 (Exeter-Plymouth) from 2nd July was re-routed to run via Bovey Tracey, and some journeys on route 16 ran via the Hawkmoor Chest Hospital instead of dropping visitors at the gate on the main road.

Exeter joint service 65 was diverted on its way out of Exeter, via a new estate at Barley Mount.

Directors continued to come and go; Mr. C. Williams resigned on 8th August on his retirement from British Railways, and Mr. F. P. B. Taylor was appointed in his place. The Tiverton depot superintendent, Mr. F. T. George, was promoted to Area Traffic Superintendent, Torquay, in place of the late Mr. G. Young, who had only been promoted to the post less than two years previously on the retirement of Mr. J. Mitchell. The new Superintendent at Tiverton was Mr. D. N. Flower.

An unofficial strike of 250 maintenance workers took place between 9th June and 10th July, arising out of a dispute over the withdrawal of a ½d. per hour 'scarcity bonus'. Cleaning and re-fuelling was carried out by supervisory staff, including the General Manager, and there was no major disruption of services. An official strike, over the same issue, this time supported by drivers and conductors, took place between 5th and 14th August.

A nasty accident occurred on 28th September, when the driver and passenger in an Austin A40 car lost their life in a head-on collision with AEC 'Regent' double-decker DRD728 on route 2 near Bishopsteignton.

List of Routes as at 2nd July 1961 (Timetable No:149)
All routes are daily unless otherwise stated.

1,   Exeter-Chudleigh-Newton Abbot
2,   Exeter-Dawlish-Teignmouth-Newton Abbot
2A,   Exeter-Dawlish Warren (summer only)
2B,   Newton Abbot-Bishopsteignton-Teignmouth OMB
3,   Exeter-Tiverton-Sampford Peverell OMB
4,   Exeter-Ottery St. Mary-Honiton-Axminster
5,   Crediton-Exeter-Woodbury-Exmouth
6,   Exeter-Crockernwell-Okehampton   OMB
8,   Exeter-Pinhoe-Broadclyst
9,   Exeter-Newton Poppleford-Sidmouth
10,   Exmouth-Budleigh Salterton-Otterton (-Ladram Bay in summer only)
11,   Newton Abbot-Ashburton-Buckfastleigh
12,   Newton Abbot-Torquay-Paignton-Brixham (run in two sections during summer)

12A,	St. Marychurch-Torquay-Paignton Sea Front-Broadsands (summer only open top service)
12B,	Brixham-Kingswear
12C,	St. Marychurch-Torquay-Paignton Bus Station-Kingswear (summer only open top service)
12D,	St. Marychurch-Torquay-Paignton Sea Front-Brixham (summer only open top service)
13,	Torquay-Maidencombe-Teignmouth (-Dawlish in summer only)
15,	Newton Abbot-Ipplepen-Totnes
16,	Newton Abbot-Bovey Tracey-Moretonhampstead-Chagford-Okehampton (partly OMB)
17,	Goodrington (Cliff Gardens)-Paignton-Marldon
18,	Paignton-Churston-Greenway OMB
19,	Exeter-Moretonhampstead-Chagford OMB
19A,	Exeter-Leigh Cross-Christow OMB
20,	Newton Abbot-Trusham-Leigh Cross-Exeter (Weekdays) OMB
21,	Cullompton-Broadhembury-Honiton (WSaO) OMB
22,	Drewsteignton-Chagford-Moretonhampstead-Newton Abbot (WO) OMB
24,	Exeter-Digby Hospital (WSaO)
26,	Exeter-Woodbury-Budleigh Salterton
27,	Exeter-Broadclyst-Cullompton
28A,	Shiphay-Torre Station-Strand
29,	Exeter-Drewsteignton-Moretonhampstead (Weekdays) OMB
30,	Paignton-Torquay Station-Babbacombe
31,	Strand-Westhill-Hele Village-Barton
32,	Chelston (Weeksland Road)-Strand
32,	Chelston-Raleigh Avenue-Strand-Hesketh Crescent
33,	Chelston (The Reeves Road)-Strand-Hesketh Crescent (-Meadfoot Beach in summer)
34,	Castle Circus-St. Marychurch-Havelock Arms-Barton (Jacks Lane)
35,	Castle Circus-St. Marychurch-Havelock Arms-Watcombe (Willow Avenue)
36,	Newton Abbot Station-Kingsteignton-Sandygate
37,	Brixham (Bus Station)-Lytes Road-Berry Head-Fishcombe
39,	Newton Abbot-Ogwell-Denbury
40,	Exmouth-Budleigh Salterton-Sidmouth
42,	Exeter-Pinhoe-Poltimore
43,	Cullompton-Plymtree-Clyst Hydon-Exeter (TuWFSaO)
44,	Newton Abbot-Hennock (WSaO) OMB
46,	Torquay-Newton Abbot-Exeter OMB
47,	Exeter-Axminster-Weymouth
50,	Strand-Ellacombe-St. Marychurch
51,	Strand-Torbay Hospital
52,	Exeter-Honiton-Seaton
54,	St. Marychurch-Castle Circus-Shiphay (Weekdays)
55,	Strand-Wellswood-St. Marychurch
56,	Torquay (Strand)-Shorton Valley-Paignton (Weekdays)
57,	Torquay (Strand)-Warren Road (Weekdays)
58,	Exeter-Clyst St. Mary-Exmouth
59,	Exmouth-Cranford Avenue-Littleham Village
59A,	Exmouth-Littleham Village
60,	Littleham Village-Sandy Bay (summer only)
63,	Paignton-Marldon-Compton Castle
64,	Exeter-Ide-Dunchideock (-Haldon Belvedere in summer)
65,	Exeter-Whitestone-Heath Cross
66,	Exeter-Shillingford-Kennford-Kenn (Weekdays)
67,	Exeter-Upton Pyne-Brampford Speke (FSaO)
68,	Exeter-Raddons Cross-Shobrooke-Crediton
69,	Crediton-Sandford-Kennerleigh (SaO) OMB
70,	Teignmouth (Triangle)-New Road-Haldon Golf Club
71,	Teignmouth (Triangle)-Mill Lane
73,	Exmouth (DG Garage)-Turners Avenue (Weekdays)
74,	Exmouth (DG Garage)-Orcombe Point (summer only)
75,	Honiton-Gittisham-Buckerell-Talaton (WSaO) OMB
76,	Crediton-Sandford-New Buildings (Weekdays) OMB
77,	Sidmouth-Sidford-Sidbury
78,	Sidmouth-Ottery St. Mary OMB

79,	Moretonhampstead-North Bovey (WSaO) OMB
81,	Paignton-Shiphay (girls Grammar School) (M-F term time only)
82,	Exmouth-Withycombe-St. Johns (Weekdays)
83,	Exmouth-Littlemead Lane Estate (summer only)
85,	Crediton-Exeter-Exton-Exmouth
88,	Newton Abbot-Torbryan-Broadhempston OMB
89,	Paignton-Churston (Fenton School) (M-F term time only)
90,	Newton Abbot-Ideford Village (WSaO) OMB
91,	Witheridge-Tiverton OMB
92,	Tiverton-Calverleigh-Rackenford (TuFSaO) OMB
93,	Witheridge-Puddington-Pennymoor-Tiverton (TuO) OMB
96,	Witheridge-Morchard Bishop-Exeter OMB
97,	Tiverton-Cheriton Fitzpaine-Poughill (TuO) OMB
98,	Exeter-Crediton-Cheriton Fitzpaine-Witheridge (FSaO) OMB
99,	Tiverton-Stoodleigh (TuFO)
101,	Tiverton (Sec. Mod. Sch./Heathcoats Factory)-Wilcombe Est./Elmore-Cowley Moor (Weekdays)
102,	Tiverton-East Butterleigh Cross (TuSaO)
103,	Port Road-Dawlish-Ashcombe (MFO) OMB
104,	Paignton-Marldon Road-Fernicombe Road
105,	Paignton-Blatchcombe Road-Ramshill Road
106,	Tiverton (Cotteylands)-Norwood Road (Weekdays)
107,	Newton Abbot-Coffinswell-Daccombe (WSaO) OMB
108,	Newton Abbot-Huxnor Cross (WSaO) OMB
109,	Buckland Estate-Newton Abbot-Decoy
110,	Buckland Estate-Newton Abbot-Highweek (Mile End)
111,	Torquay (Quinta Road)-Strand-Lower Warberry Road
116,	Newton Abbot-Combeinteignhead-Shaldon-Teignmouth
117,	Newton Abbot-Combeinteignhead-Stokeinteignhead-Maidencombe
120,	Newton Abbot-Milber (Centrax Factory) - works service
121,	Torquay (Strand)-Wellswood-Meadfoot Beach (Illsham Road) - summer only
122,	Lawes Bridge (DG depot)-STC Factory - works service
123,	Brixham (Bus Station)-STC Factory - works service
124,	Lawes Bridge (DG depot)-Foxhole Estate-STC Factory - works service
125,	Sidmouth (Peak Hill)-Salcombe Regis (Church) - summer only
128,	Torquay-Totnes-Plymouth
129,	Exeter-Chudleigh-Plymouth
217,	Exeter-Tiverton-Dulverton-Minehead OMB
225,	Tiverton-Oakford-Rackenford (TuSaO) OMB

City of Exeter routes (Exeter Joint Transport):

A/F,	Marsh Barton Road-Hill Barton-Cowley Bridge
B,	Exwick-Thornpark Rise
C/W	Paul Street-Countess Wear-Topsham
D,	St. David's Station-Beacon Heath
G,	Crossmead-Beacon Heath
J,	South Lawn Terrace-Crossmead
K,	Bedford Street-Pennsylvania
O/S,	Redhills/Broadway-High Street-Rifford Road-St. Leonards/St. David's Station
M,	Paul Street-Orthopaedic Hospital (WFSaO)
U,	Bedford Street-University (M-F, term time only)

Section 11. Winds of change, (1962 - 1968)

1962 The Road Transport Bill published in 1962 was to have far reaching effects on the Company and its structure. As things stood, the ordinary shares of the Company were held by the National Electric Construction Co. Ltd., (36%), the British Transport Commission, as successors to the shares acquired by the railways in 1929 (36%), with the remaining 28% held by other investors. Four Directors were nominated by BET and four by the BTC and the partnership formed thirty years previously, had done much to co-ordinate road and rail transport in the Company's area. The new Bill sought to destroy this partnership by transferring the shares representing railway capital, not, as might have been expected, to the British Railways Board, but to a new Transport Holding Company, which was to have no connection with the railways at all. Boardroom contact with the railways was not yet lost however, which was just as well in view of the impending rail closures in the area.

Mr. D. McKenna resigned from the Board, and Mr. R. L. P. Cobb was appointed, both being British Railways nominees.

A general fares increase was effective from 17th June, necessary because of a wage settlement in May 1961, together with improved conditions of service and an increase in fuel tax. Following an appeal by Devon County Council and other Local Authorities, the Minister of Transport gave a decision favourable to the applicant, to a certain extent, and as a result, some fares were reduced as from 31st March 1963.

A further contraction of Devon General's territory occurred from 15th April with route 47 no longer being worked as a through service from Exeter to Weymouth. A Devon General vehicle then only worked as far as Axminster, where passengers were obliged to change on to a Southern National bus. At the same time, routes 4, 47 and 52 became one-man worked. Further changes took place from 7th October, when 52, (Exeter-Seaton) ceased altogether, a Seaton connection being advertised at Axminster via Western National service 213 which came from Taunton. From the same date, 47 ceased to run direct between Exeter and Honiton, being diverted via Ottery St. Mary.

Summer-only Exmouth local service 83 became one-man operated, and 59 was re-routed to run from Exmouth (DG Garage) to Littleham Village via Pier, Pavilion, Maer Road and Salterton Road from 10th June.

All summer Saturday journeys on service 217 to Minehead were extended to terminate at Butlin's Camp.

A new limited-stop service, curiously numbered 700, ran on Sundays only, 8th July to 2nd September, from Kingsteignton (Sandygate) via Newton Abbot, Torquay Ring Road and Paignton to Goodrington, primarily for the benefit of beach-goers. Paignton local service 104 was extended a short distance at Foxhole to terminate at Fernicombe Road (Belfield Road). The short 57 from Torquay (Strand) to Warren Road ceased from 10th September, but re-appeared for the next few seasons as a summer-only service. Some limited-stop journeys were re-introduced on 128 (Torquay-Plymouth) cutting the journey time by 25 minutes.

A notable retirement on 20th January was that of driver H. Hallett of Axminster, after 36 years service, all of it having worked on route 4.

The 1962 season saw the linking of the English Lakes holiday tour with Scotland (Ayrshire and the Burns country) instead of with Blackpool. Lands End and the Cornish Coast no longer featured as a holiday tour, as it was now run as a day tour.

Plans for a new bus station in Exeter were prepared by the City Council and work commenced in August 1962. A site in Paris Street had been chosen because of its proximity to the High Street and the inner bypass but due to the slope of the site, the building was to be on two levels, the upper being the bus station, and the lower as the coach station. Design and construction was carried out under the direction of the City Architect, Mr. H. B. Rowe, while the City Engineer, Mr. J. Brierley, directed the work in connection with bus and coach hard-standing, perimeters, and planting. Main contractor was Staverton Contractors Ltd., reinforced concrete and foundation work was by Helical Bar & Engineering Ltd., and Messrs. Ruddock & Meighan were contractors for the hard-standing.

Between February and June, the styling and livery of the rather plain Willowbrook 'Viking' bodywork on TCR850-859 and TCR889-894 was altered to match the newer 'Viscount' bodies. They were given maroon lower panels and flash, and the 'Grey Cars' emblem was moved further forward. At the same time, the prefix to the fleet number was dropped. Over the next couple of years, the prefix was removed from the numbers of all buses as well, but only as they came in for repaint. The first bus to be so treated was DR815 on its repaint in June, following a lengthy rebuild as a result of major accident damage sustained at Exeter.

Four batches of new vehicles were delivered in the early part of the year; first came three Albion 'Nimbus' buses (SN957-

959) built by Harrington with 31 seats and having but three large windows on each side. SN957 went into service in March at Sidmouth, and the other two followed in May to Newton Abbot. Next came nine more AEC Willowbrook 'Reliance' 'Viscount' Grey Car coaches (TCR960-968). They were the same as the previous year's deliveries but had improved public address equipment.

Seven AEC 'Reliance' buses (SR950-956) with 41-seat Marshall bodywork (being very similar to the Willowbrook-bodied SR860-871 of 1959), were delivered and these introduced deeper side panels and without lifeguard rails. They went into service in April and May from Newton Abbot, Exeter, Ottery St. Mary and Axminster for service 4.

Finally, seven AEC 'Regent' V double-deckers were delivered, (943-949) these having 59-seat Weymann body very similar to DR807-819, and all for use on Exeter city services. They retained rear-entrance open platform at the insistence of Exeter City Council, but were of improved specification with heaters, fluorescent lighting, and illuminated offside advert panels. They entered service in May. Three new staff cars were bought to replace older cars.

Vehicles withdrawn were the remaining twelve 1949 AEC 'Regent' III double-deckers, (DR578/80-4/7-92), together with the last five AEC 'Regal' half-cab saloons (SR593-597), and the last nine AEC 'Regal' IV Grey Cars (TCR689-697), the latter being sold to Greenslades Tours Ltd., as was then the established practice.

Because of recurring mechanical trouble, Leyland designed various modifications which were made to the 'Atlanteans', notably with regard to the gear-change mechanism and clutch. DL905 was fitted with a fluid fly-wheel, followed by the remainder of the 'Atlanteans' and all were rebuilt with fixed windscreens replacing the original opening screens, all of which leaked badly in heavy wet weather.

City of Oxford Motor Services was experiencing a severe shortage of skilled fitting staff, and to alleviate their problems, four of their AEC 'Regent' III Weymann double-deckers were sent to Torquay for mechanical overhaul between October and December. For the record, these were UWL 939 on 30th October, UWL 938 on 12th November, UWL 937 on 27th November, and UWL 935 on 12th December. The vehicles came laden with all the necessary spares.

The year ended with severe disruption of services due to snow from 29th December onwards, and these conditions persisted through January and into February of the new year.

1963

Not many changes took place to services in 1963, despite poor results in 1962. Route 700 re-appeared for the summer, and ran daily from 2nd June, extended to Broadsands. The Torquay- Torbay Hospital service 51 was withdrawn from 14th April but reinstated from 29th September.

Following improvements to the roads serving Dawlish Warren, route 103 (which only ran on Mondays and Fridays) was extended from Dawlish to Dawlish Warren except in summer, when the 2 from Exeter and a new seasonal extension of the 13 from Torquay served the Warren as from 2nd June. Route 103 terminated at Port Road during that period.

One journey on each summer Saturday on route 217 ran limited-stop between Plymouth and Minehead (Butlin's Camp), via Exeter and Tiverton, and from 14th April, one journey on 47 (Exeter-Axminster) was diverted via Whimple instead of Rockbeare. A new works service, 126, ran between St. Marychurch and the STC Factory as from 4th August.

British Railways closed the Churston-Brixham branch line on 11th May, and apart from a short-lived supplementary service on summer Saturdays between Churston Station and Brixham, passengers to and from Brixham had to wait on the main road for a 12. Needless to say, they soon preferred to make their entire journey by road, and a lot more than local traffic was lost by the railway.

Another major rail closure took place on 5th October, when the Exe Valley branch line from Exeter to Tiverton and Dulverton succumbed. Although reasonably well patronised, there appeared to be no attempt to run the trains more economically, a fairly frequent service of two-coach steam trains being the order of things until the last day when diesel locos with more coaches were put on to convey the people who had come to ride the trains for the last time. The line was largely paralleled by routes 3 and 217, but some villages at the Exeter end were not well served by bus. More journeys on route 3 were therefore diverted via Thorverton, and route 67 was operated each weekday to Brampford Speke, returning via Upton Pyne. Some journeys on the 3 ran limited-stop to shorten journey time.

A new city service M ran as from 1st October, between (Exeter) High Street and Higher Barley Mount, where the sound of the AEC 'Regent' V as it climbed the hill to the terminus had to be heard to be believed. The Barley Mount Estate had previously been served by a diversion of the 65, which reverted to its former route, the previous service M having finished that summer.

In organisational changes, arising from the 1962 Transport Act, Messrs. R. L. Cobb and F. P. B. Taylor resigned from the Board of Directors, and were replaced by Mr. L. Mapleston (Secretary of the Transport Holding Company) and Mr. F. D. Pattison (Divisional Manager, Plymouth, of BR Western Region).

A Daimler 'Fleetline' demonstrator (4559 VC) was on loan from 17th June to 5th July and was operated on services 104 and 105 (Paignton-Foxhole Estate) which were normally operated by 'Atlantean' with a turbocharger.

Devon General often had a Demonstrator vehicle from all sorts of manufacturers etc., and orders did not necessarily follow! One such, was Daimler 'Fleetline' 4559 VC which was used in June 1963 on the hilly 104/105 Foxhole Estate route where it is seen here.
(L.F.Folkard)

The first new vehicles of 1963 were seven more 41-seat AEC 'Reliance' saloons (985-991) with Marshall bodywork similar to those that had been delivered in 1962 and went into service at Newton Abbot and Torquay. Next came sixteen AEC 'Regent' V double-deckers (969-984) with 59-seat Metro-Cammell body, having front entrance, fixed windscreen, and illuminated offside advertisement. The indicator display at the front only, used lower-case lettering for the 'via' blind, which was to the nearside, with the three-track route number box to the offside and the extreme destination over the top. At the back, only a three-track route number box was provided.

These went into service at Torquay, Newton Abbot, and Moretonhampstead depots - the first and last time that the latter depot received any double-deckers from new. None went to Exeter, as there was still the embargo on front-entrance double-deckers working city services. These new buses enabled the withdrawal of the five Leyland 'Royal Tiger' buses of 1951 (SL635-639) and the twenty AEC 'Light Six' double-deckers, DR704-723 that had been re-built in 1953/4 using parts of pre-war 'Regals'.

1963 was proving to be a bad year for accidents; on 24th May, two young Exmouth men were killed when their car was in collision with a bus at Exminster, and on 15th June a police cadet from Coventry lost his life when his car collided with a bus at Churston.

AEC 'Reliance' Grey Car TCR859 was involved in a serious accident on 3rd August when it overturned at Shepton Mallet whilst on a private hire for Willeys Foundry of Exeter. The coach was badly distorted, yet on inspection by the Ministry of Transport examiner, the coach, which it had been feared might be a write-off, was found to be mechanically perfect. The accident happened in the height of the summer season, when all available vehicles were desperately required, and as the workshops did not have too much work in hand, Mr. F. Harrison, the Bodyshop Superintendent was convinced that provided spares were available and with some overtime working, his men could get 859 back on the road in a fortnight.

The Assistant Engineer, Mr. G. Truran was dispatched to Willowbrook at Loughborough in one of the vans, and he collected the necessary pillars and roof members. On his way back, he slept in the van in the Buckinghamshire countryside near to where the Great Train Robbery was taking place! He knew nothing of this at the time and was not stopped or questioned. All the damaged pillars in 859 were straightened or renewed, roof rebuilt, windows and panelling replaced and the coach was repainted and back in service on 16th August. The body staff rightly regarded this as their best-ever achievement.

Driver A. Pugh of Newton Abbot depot with Commer-Beadle bus SC757 was involved in a head-on collision on 1st October with Royal Blue coach 2206 (which was running empty) at Jews Bridge, near Chudleigh. One (bus) passenger lost her life as a result, and both drivers, the conductor of SC757, and two passengers were seriously injured, with another twenty less seriously hurt. The passengers were all workers at Candy's factory at Heathfield, and SC757 was on a contract service taking them home. The bus was scrapped during November as it was so badly damaged.

The Tor Bus service between Newton Abbot, Haytor and Widecombe, which had been run by the Potter family for over 40 years, ceased operating at the end of August because a continuing recession in passengers rendered the service no longer viable.

This was before the days of County Council subsidies, and brought home the fact that two thirds of the Devon General routes were run with receipts below the average operating costs. The 12 and a few other services literally carried the rest. To alleviate this situation, a general fares increase was implemented on 4th August.

Late in the year, eight new AEC 'Reliance' Grey Cars (1-8) with 41-seat Harrington 'Cavalier' bodywork were delivered for service in the following new year. At 31'5" they were slightly longer than all previous coaches, but retained the 7'6" width, so necessary to negotiate the moorland bridges. AEC had been given the contract to supply all new coach chassis on the understanding that 7'6" vehicles were to be supplied at no extra cost if required. 1-8 introduced a simplified 'GREY CARS' fleet-name in white letters edged in maroon on the boot door, but still carried the traditional style fleet-name emblem on the side panels. The rear styling was applied to all subsequent new Grey Cars, later with the addition of the word 'Devon' below the fleet-name, and upon repaint was also carried by examples of the 1959, 1961 and 1962 batches.

A new fleet-numbering system was implemented, the plan being to number coaches and single-deck buses in a common series from one upwards, while double-deckers would be numbered from five-hundred and one onwards.

Following the sale of Silver Star Motor Services of Porton, to Wilts & Dorset, their three 'Atlantean' buses were offered to Devon General by the Bristol Omnibus Co. Ltd., who had acquired them. In view of problems at that time being experienced with this type of vehicle, the offer was declined so Bristol decided to keep them. They received Bristol fleet numbers 7997-7999, and one is now preserved in original Silver Star livery.

Three new staff cars were bought during the year to replace old cars, and another demonstrator bus was tried which was a Dodge (2498 PK) with a 42-seat MCW body.

During the year, a further seven City of Oxford buses were overhauled at Torquay depot - AEC 'Reliance' WJO 738 arriving on 29th March, 'Regent' V 952 AJO on 23rd April, 951 AJO on 21st May, 'Regent' III UWL 929 on 17th October, 'Regent' V 948 AFC on 12th November, 195 BFC on 29th November and 189 AWL on 22nd December.

1964
Three more batches of new vehicles were delivered in the early part of the year, firstly eight heavy-weight AEC 'Regent' V double-deckers with 30' long, 69-seat front-entrance body by Willowbrook. These had the AV590 engine which was the equivalent of the 9.6-litre engine fitted to the 'Regent' III, and the gearbox was very similar also. Numbered 501-508, they entered service in April on the Torquay circular routes 50 and 55.

The 'Atlanteans' which had been working these routes were then transferred to the Chelston services 32 and 33. The Company had reverted to AEC double-deckers because of the mechanical problems still being experienced with 'Atlanteans'. Vehicle purchasing policy was determined by individual companies but subject to final approval by BET Head Office at Stratton House.

The eight new Grey Cars (1-8) that had been in store since the previous November also went on the road in April, and No:1 with driver L. Worrall, was a natural choice for the Directors tour at the end of the month. Five more AEC 'Reliance' saloons (13-17) with 41-seat Willowbrook body and suitable for one-man operation, were arguably the most handsome of the post-war single-deckers. They had innovative wrap-around front and rear windscreen, and with 9-12, were the last ones to have the stainless alloy waistband between the two colours. Two (13 and 14) went into service in April on the Chelston routes 32A and 32B, and two (15/16) went to Exeter to work the Express 46. The last one, 17, was allocated to Newton Abbot and was usually to be found on service 15 to and from Totnes. 15 and 16 however started something new by having yellow numerals and destination displays for express workings and blue characters for the remainder.

Further AEC 'Reliance' saloons were delivered in 1961 but this time to the new modern BET standard design not previously seen in Devon. Five of them in this order were numbered 13 - 17. The first two started their service life on the 32A/B Chelston routes where 14 is seen at The Strand in Torquay with the 1931 built wooden shelter still in existence. (DGS collection)

Four long-wheelbase AEC 'Reliance' saloons (9-12) were then delivered; these had a Marshall built body with no less than 53 seats, were 36' long but 8'2½" wide, and powered by the larger 590 engine. A wider entrance than had been customary on single-deckers was fitted, and they went into service in June. Numbers 9-11 replaced double-deckers on route 9 (Exeter-Sidmouth) and 12 did likewise on the joint route 129 (Exeter-Plymouth). The latter bus had a six-speed gearbox and went 'like the wind', but the box was later replaced with a conventional four-speed unit following complaints from drivers who had received fines for speeding!

Buses had a planned life of twelve years with the Company, and coaches eight (to be increased to ten if necessary), and the new vehicles resulted in the withdrawal of the 'Fanfare' coaches 749/750, Commer-Beadle coaches 751-756, Leyland 'Titan' lowbridge double-deckers 640-645, and the first of the 8' wide AEC 'Regent' IIIs 646-659. The coaches all ran for new owners, but not all of the double-deckers saw further use. Three new Austin 'Mini' staff cars were purchased.

By the end of 1963, the stock of 'Speed Setright' ticket machines had increased to 390, and nine more new machines in 1964 brought their numbers up to D399, this being the final numbered machine in the 'D' series.

A new range of Grey Cars tours was introduced, known as Diamond Tours, which operated in spring and autumn using inexpensive hotels. Destinations were:

North Wales and the Lake District
North Wales and Blackpool
Folkestone
London
Isle of Wight.

These proved popular and continued to run each year.

OFFICIAL OPENING

of the

New Bus and Coach Station

Paris Street, Exeter

by

The Right Worshipful The Mayor of Exeter

(ALDERMAN P. A. SPOERER)

on

Thursday, 16th July, 1964

at 11 a.m.

The Devon General Omnibus & Touring Co. Ltd.

Western National Omnibus Co. Ltd.

Southern National Omnibus Co. Ltd.

Greenslades Tours Ltd.

The cover of the specially printed brochure to commemorate the opening of the new bus station.   (DGO&TC)

Exeter Bus Station in its early days showing AEC 'Reliance' 9 on the right with 986 just leaving on the 46 Express for Torquay. 802 is at the platform displaying service 96 on the back, Regent 'V' 976 is on service 2, then there is an ECT Daimler saloon and a Western National Bristol LS. Next is a Corporation Leyland Titan, a Willowbrook low-back seat Grey Car and behind that an off service city bus. The railings are in place but still to be installed.   (L.F.Folkard collection)

The new bus and coach station in Paris Street, Exeter opened on 5th July, and all routes that had hitherto used Paul Street (except city route CW) then terminated at Paris Street. It was owned by Exeter Corporation and leased to Devon General.

One long platform was provided, with a cantilever roof over eighteen bus stands, with additional lay-over space in the open. Entry was via Cheeke Street and exit was directly on to Paris Street. Two lines of buses could park parallel to the platform along the wall and adjacent to Bampfylde Street, and two bays were provided for parcel vans.

The coach station was alongside the bus station but at a lower level, and included a very large parking ground where city buses would park at night. The administration block between the two stations included a cafeteria, shop, booking hall, lost property office, parcels office, inspectors office, staff canteen, toilets and cash office. The station was officially opened on 16th July by the Lord Mayor of Exeter, Ald. P.A. Spoerer, accompanied by civic dignitaries and representatives of the Directors and management of Devon General, Greenslades Tours Ltd., Western National and Southern National. The assembly later wined and dined at the Imperial Hotel.

The Exmouth local services were re-organised from 27th September to give a through service from Littleham to Withycombe, becoming: 59 St. Johns-DG Garage or Withycombe to Littleham via Cranford Avenue and 59A, Withycombe-Littleham via Rolle Street and Salterton Road. 82 and 83 ceased, the former being absorbed in the 59/59A and the latter because the Littlemead Estate became served all year round by diversions of the 5 and 85 services. One-man operation at Exmouth then ceased for the time being, the 83 having been thus worked.

The summer-only service 700, which in its two seasons so far, had not produced very satisfactory revenue, was altered to run from Newton Abbot to Brixham via the Torbay ring road, thus missing the centre of Torquay, and then via Paignton and Goodrington (limited stop). In this form it was more successful

From 3rd May, journeys on 109 through the Buckland Estate at Newton Abbot were routed alternately via Queensway or Sandringham Road.

Some journeys on route 9, Exeter-Sidmouth, became limited-stop from July.

A new service 23, Newton Abbot-Haytor-Widecombe (WFSO) commenced on 5th June. This was taken over at the request of the Traffic Commissioners, from the Dartmoor Bus Service of Haccombe, which since 2nd September 1963 had operated an ambitious timetable, but a sporadic and unreliable service after Tor Bus had ceased trading. Snells of Newton Abbot had also operated the service for one week and then withdrew.

Another new route, 36, commenced on 27th September from Torquay (Castle Circus) to Watcombe Park (Moor Lane), following the existing 34 and 35 as far as Watcombe Potteries, then via Teignmouth Road and Moor Lane. It was double-decker operated, the first bus being 'Regent V' 971.

Towards the end of the year, two demonstrator buses were tried on the Torquay Circular routes 50 and 55 to measure their performance against that of the long-wheelbase 'Regents'. From 1st September to 9th October, there was 888 DUK, a Guy 'Arab' with 72-seat Strachan body in silver livery, and from 16th to 27th November, Leyland 'Atlantean' SGD 669 with Alexander body in yellow and white, originally operated by Glasgow Corporation before being purchased by Leyland as a demonstrator. It had recently returned from Paris. It was not a lot different from the 'Atlanteans' already operated by Devon General, (except in design) but the engine had been especially tuned to give a higher performance, and the steering wheel had been repositioned.

1963s unhappy chapter of accidents continued into 1964; on 23rd January the driver of a car travelling at 70/75mph collided head on with a stationary bus on route 19 near Dunsford in the Teign Valley, and on 18th March, conductor I. Bridgman was knocked down and killed by a reversing bus at Coombe Cross, Bovey Tracey - his attention apparently having been diverted by a passing car.

Frequent changes in railway management was reflected in the Devon General Directorate; Mr. F. D. Pattison resigned from the Board and his place was taken by Mr. C. Hankins.

The overhaul programme on behalf of City of Oxford Motor Services continued, with another seven of their vehicles being dealt with in the early part of the year: 'Regent' V, 956 AJO arriving on 18th January, 'Reliance' WJO 739 on 9th February, WJO 736 on 23rd February; WJO 737 on 9th March, 'Regent' V, 188 AWL on 21st March, and finally 'Regent' V, 962 AJO on 19th April.

1965
There was a one day strike on 6th February by staff at all depots, except Tiverton, Sidmouth, Ottery St. Mary, Moretonhampstead and Okehampton, over alleged delay in settling a wage claim. Working crews from these outposts received a frosty welcome at Exeter bus station.

Timetable No:158, dated 2nd May, appeared in a new format. The pages were A5 size, and the cover was in orange and white with a very diagrammatic map and prominently titled 'Road-Rail timetable'. 24-hour times were used throughout and there was a good folded map inside the back cover which showed railways as well as bus routes. The tables were without vertical lines, and there were diagrammatic maps of the town centres of Torquay, Newton Abbot and Exeter. That of Torquay was particularly useful because it showed the one-way system to be introduced on 23rd May. (Basically, buses from the Newton Abbot direction entered Torquay via South Street, Tor Hill Road, and the lower part of Union Street. Outward bound buses ran via Abbey Road, Higher Union Street, and Beenland Gardens. A small part of South Street and the lower part of Tor Hill Road was used by buses in both directions. A narrow back-street named Pimlico was used as a slip-road to enable buses routed via Ellacombe to reach Market Street without traversing the one-way system, though those on the 30 from Babbacombe to Paignton were not so lucky, having to make a long detour via Union Street and Abbey Road to get from Castle Circus to Lucius Street. Buses to Chelston could no longer serve Castle Circus in the outward direction. Two buses were driven around the one-way system before the start of services on 23rd May by Inspector J. Langmead and driver J. Alsop to ensure that all the islands were negotiable.

Though Sunday services were curtailed on seventeen routes, not many other changes took place to the remaining routes. At Tiverton, service 101 to Cowley Moor was re-routed through the Lansdown Estate, and buses bound for Heathcoats Factory were routed via Paul Street and Church Street to reduce congestion in West Exe North.

A new day-tour to St. Mawes and St. Just was run from Torquay, and in anticipation of the Severn Bridge opening for traffic, licences were sought for tours to Cardiff and Barry Island.

From 30th May, a new service numbered 800 ran one return trip on the evenings of Wednesday, Saturday and Sunday from Teignmouth to Paignton via Kingsteignton, Newton Abbot and Kingskerswell for the benefit of Bingo patrons.

Applications for fares increases in Torquay and Paignton were, on 2nd June, deferred by the Traffic Commissioners, but changes in Exeter fares were approved because of the move of the bus station.
A number of route changes were brought in with the 26th September timetable, services 1, 39 and 66 being reconstituted to run as follows:

1,   Chudleigh-Newton Abbot-Denbury (one-man operated)
66,   Exeter-Kennford-Chudleigh (operated by City of Exeter Transport Dept)

The new schedules for the 66 were not implemented until 11th October because of a dispute by Exeter CT crews who objected to the late finish resulting from the final run to Chudleigh. Route 20 was diverted to serve Chudleigh Knighton. One journey a day on service 12 between Torquay and Newton Abbot became limited-stop (M-F peak hours) and used the number 12X with yellow service numbers, where fitted.

On Sundays, the Brixham local service 37, between bus station and Wall Park Road only, became operated jointly with the Burton bus service.

A new short working of the 18 was introduced, Paignton Bus Station-Broadsands Road (Brunel Road), four journeys being made each weekday to cater for a new housing development.

A few workings on the 4 were diverted to serve Whimple station, the Hand & Pen timing point on the main road being some distance away; the 4 between Exeter and Ottery St. Mary also became jointly operated with Exeter CTD.

One-man buses were put on to Torquay local services 54, 56, and 63, while the 51 to Torbay Hospital was reduced to two trips a week, these being on Wednesdays. Routes serving local factories appeared in the timetable for the first time, having previously run unpublicised since 1953 (120), 1957 (122-124) and 1963 (126). They were:

120,   Newton Abbot (bus station)-Milber (Centrax Factory) weekdays
122,   Lawes Bridge (DG depot)-White Rock (Gibson Gardens) for STC factory (M-F)
123,   Brixham (bus station)-Standard Telephone Co's Factory (M-F)
124,   Lawes Bridge (DG depot)-Torquay (Pavilion)-Paignton (Foxhole Estate)-STC factory (M-F)
126,   St. Marychurch-Lawes Bridge-Shiphay-Marldon-Kings Ash-STC factory (M-F)

A new service from 31st October was 500, Preston Down Road (Templar Road)-Paignton (bus station)-Waterside-Standard Telephone Company's Factory (limited stop). This was an hourly service with one-man buses whereas the other services to the STC factory ran only at shift times.

Bus crews were occasionally called on to exercise their initiative in circumstances not covered by the rule-book; for instance on 16th November driver Larkworthy and conductor Williams on the Rifford Road route in Exeter took their bus and all its passengers to the Royal Devon & Exeter Hospital after a passenger had started to bleed profusely.

Later that month, conductor/driver Cecil Marchant found a pig standing at the bus stop in Churston and there seemingly being nobody in charge of it, he took it on his bus to Paignton Police Station!

The year 1965 saw the arrival of another five BET type saloons, this time built by Park Royal. The long route 4 from Exeter to Axminster was the regular run for most of them, and here, 19 (CTT 19C) is seen at the new bus station at Paris Street, Exeter which was opened in July 1964
(DGS collection)

Three batches of new vehicles entered service on 1st May, these being the first in the fleet to carry the year suffix on the registration (CTT 18C etc.). AEC 'Reliance' single-deckers 18-23 were very similar to 13-17, delivered in 1964, the only visible difference being that the new series did not have the polished metal waist strip. Most of them went into service on route 4, being out-stationed at Ottery St. Mary and Axminster.

AEC 'Regent' V double-deckers 509-514 had 69-seats with AV590 engine and Park Royal bodywork. 515-520 were shorter Willowbrook-bodied 59-seat buses with AV470 engine. All were front-entrance as were all subsequent double-deckers delivered new to the Company. The long vehicles were put to work on the Torquay circular routes 50 and 55, releasing the previous year's delivery for service elsewhere, notably on routes 2 and 9. The shorter vehicles took over the duties of some of the older 'Regents', 515 at Exeter, 516 at Cullompton on the 27, 517/8 at Exmouth, 519 at Sidmouth and 520 at Torquay.

Withdrawn and sold were the twenty 'Regent' IIIs of 1952/3 (660-679).

The imposing exit from Newton Road depot is clearly shown as AEC Weymann 'Regent' III, DR670 prepares to hit the road with the party of visiting Omnibus Society members, closely followed by Regent 'V' Weymann 983. (N.Bruce-Robertson)

An enthusiasts' tour on 21st March around the Torbay area in 670 was one of their last duties, and since then, few significant types have disappeared from the fleet without a similar mark of appreciation.

During November, a Leyland 'Atlantean' demonstrator with Park Royal body and blue and white livery (KTD 551C) with 11.1-litre 0680 engine was operated on the hilly Paignton local routes 17, 104 and 105 to determine the most suitable gear ratio for the six vehicles of that type already ordered for delivery in 1966, specifically for service on those routes.

The Grey Cars booking office at 59, Torbay Road, Paignton, closed at the end of the summer, having become unnecessary since booking facilities became available at the bus station.

Fifteen new 'Speed Setright' ticket machines purchased during the year were the final delivery of the 'Mk I' machine, and started a new number series, E001 to 015.

1966

A new tour was added to the spring and autumn 'Diamond Tours' programme which was to Cromer, Buxton and the Derbyshire Dales. The Holiday Tours to the Trossachs and Skye by this time included Edinburgh in their itineraries.

Following a fares increase on 20th March, a few changes in the bus routes took place. The section of the 17 between Goodrington (Cliff Gardens) and Paignton bus station was instead served by short workings of the 18, and from 1st April, as a result of the introduction of a new one-way system in Paignton, traversed Seaway Road, Eugene Road and Paris Road instead of part of Torquay Road, in the inward direction.

A new Monday to Friday (school term) service 14S was operating in Newton Abbot by 8th May between Aller Park, Decoy & All Saints Primary Schools.

The 25th September timetable gave service number 59B to the Exmouth-St. Johns workings previously included under the 59, and the same timetable showed joint services 42 and 64-68 as one-man operated, though in fact they had to await delivery of suitable new buses to the City of Exeter fleet, which came in the shape of five Leyland 'Leopards' (1-5) having Massey body with front entrance and centre exit. The summer extension of 64 to Haldon Belvedere had finished permanently from 27th August.

Service 16 became operated throughout by one-man single-deckers from 8th May, as a result of which Moretonhampstead depot lost its two double-deckers, and the last couple of conductors were found duties based at Newton Abbot. The Coombe Cross short working terminus of the 16 at Bovey Tracey was altered to Coombe Close to facilitate reversing, likewise that at Denbury on the 1 was extended to Down Lane, and the 63 at Marldon to Peters Crescent.

All workings on 5/85 were diverted to call at Exeter St. David's Station, thus providing a link between the bus station and the two main railway stations.

The final order for short AEC 'Regent' V buses was built by Metro-Cammell with 59 seat front-entrance bodywork and more powerful 9.6-litre engine for use on the hilly routes in Torquay. 525 (EOD 525D) is seen turning at Dart Avenue, Torquay. 524 of this batch is preserved.
(the late G.H. Truran/Omnibus Society)

New vehicles delivered during the year were eight AEC 'Reliance' Grey Cars with Harrington 'Grenadier' 49-seat coachwork. Numbered 24-31, they were built to the then maximum permitted size of 36'0" long by 8'2½" wide. They had the 590 engine with 6-speed gearbox incorporating an overdrive and entered service between March and May.

Five more AEC 'Regent' V double-deckers (521-525) arrived which had the short MCW 59-seat front-entrance body and also with the more powerful 590 engine, as fitted to the longer 'Regent' Vs. These were for use on the steeply-graded Torquay local services, where earlier 'Regent' Vs having the AV470 engine had not proved entirely satisfactory. 521-525 entered service in July on the 111, 114, 115, and 118 group of services.

Lettering on the blinds of the new buses was also in blue; this was designed to show up better at night, but unfortunately they did not show up so well by day!

Six more Leyland 'Atlanteans' (526-531) were delivered which were especially designed for use on the hilly 104 and 105 routes in Paignton, on which they entered service in June. Their bodywork was 75-seat by Willowbrook, and they had the 11.1-litre Leyland O680 engine. The turbocharger was removed from the vehicles previously so fitted for these routes, having proved costly in terms of engine replacement.

Six new 'Atlanteans' with up-rated engine were delivered in 1966 specifically for use on the 104 and 105 routes in Paignton where the heavy passenger loading and steep hills required increased power. They were quite different in appearance from all previous models and lasted until 1984 when all were broken up. 528 when new is just entering Paignton bus station in June 1966. (DGS collection)

Vehicles sold in 1966 were the twelve AEC 'Regent' IIIs of 1954 (724-735) as well as no less than nineteen Grey Cars comprising the six Commer-Beadle TS3s (844-849), five of the 1958 'Reliances' (850-854) and another six 1958/9 'Reliances' (857-859/890-892). All were sold in December to Greenslades Tours Ltd., of Exeter, except for the Commers. Grey Cars 893/894 became the property of Court Garages (Torquay) Ltd.

Three new Morris vans replaced those purchased in 1958/9, and the Devon General parcels service made the national headlines when, for a few days, bottles of mothers' milk were rushed from Paignton to the premature baby unit at Exeter Hospital via service 46 and parcels van V21 with driver P.Ward, although this was a regular occurrence from Newton Abbot where mothers' milk was sent by service 2 to Exeter hospitals. Consignments of blood had, on occasion, been transported by similar means.

On 1st October, Devon General acquired the whole of the share capital of Court Garages (Torquay) Ltd., and Bute Court Garages Ltd. The former operated excursions and tours under the name of Court Coaches, with five Bedford SB petrol-engine coaches, on licences from Torquay covering 77 destinations.
The business had started in 1928 and was the last surviving local E & T operator in Torquay. Tours started from Belgrave Road, where a garage and booking office was rented from Bute Court Garages Ltd., which also provided the vehicle maintenance. There was also a rented booking office in Vaughan Road, which had previously been a joint venture with Falkland Coaches Ltd., under the style of 'Devon Tours & Cruises', and Devon General had shared in it since 1957 after they bought out Falkland Coaches. An earlier firm trading as Court Cars, under the ownership of F. E. Hall, had sold out to A. Timpson & Son Ltd., in 1929, who at that time, had just established themselves in the area. Bute Court Garages Ltd., was a garage business with twelve self-drive hire cars, one of which operated as a taxi in winter. The Belgrave Road site consisted of two adjoining garages, an office and a flat. Devon General had rented garage space there in 1940-1945 for storage of coaches.

Two Grey Cars AEC Willowbrook 'Reliances' were transferred to Court Coaches to replace their petrol-engine Bedfords. Former TCR893 is seen just after the repainting into cream and orange.   *(N. Bruce-Robertson)*

In September 1966, two AEC 'Reliance' Grey Cars, 893 and 894 were painted in the cream and orange Court Coaches livery and were transferred to Court Garages (Torquay) Ltd., from 1st October, despite there being no diesel fuel at Belgrave Road. Devon General provided garaging, fuelling, cleaning and maintenance on a recharge basis, vehicles being garaged at Torwood Street, or at Newton Road in winter. Mr. K. J. Brown was promoted from bus inspector to manage Court Garages (Torquay) Ltd., and Bute Court Garages.

Excursions continued to be operated under separate Company names, but any excess bookings on Court Coaches were passed to Grey Cars and vice versa. The registered office of the two Court companies became 87, Newton Road, Torquay, and the Directors were Mr. W. M. Dravers (Chairman), who held a similar position on the Devon General Board; Mr. T. L. C. Strange, the General Manager of Devon General, and Mr. S. J. B. Skyrme, who had been appointed a Director of Devon General from 1st May in succession to Mr. F. K. Pointon. Company Secretary, in common with Devon General was Mr. D. H. Passmore. Another new Director on the Devon General Board, but un-connected with Court Garages, was Mr. J. J. Donovan, the local British Rail Manager who succeeded Mr. V. Hankins. The Directors intended to expand the Court Garages business to include van hire, but unfortunately BET entered into an agreement with Swan Car Hire nationwide, which effectively quashed this proposal.

1967   New bus services subsidised by British Rail were introduced from 6th March following the closure of their Sidmouth Junction-Sidmouth and Exmouth branch lines, together with the stations at Sidmouth Junction, Ottery St. Mary, Tipton St. John, Sidmouth, Newton Poppleford, East Budleigh, Budleigh Salterton and Littleham. Honiton became the railhead for East Devon, and the new (one-man operated) rail replacement bus services were as follows:

130,   Exmouth Station-Tipton St. John (Weekdays)
131,   Honiton Station-Sidmouth, via Ottery St. Mary & Tipton St John (Weekdays)
132,   Whimple Station-Honiton Station (Weekdays)
133,   Whimple Station-Ottery St. Mary (Weekdays)
134,   Sidmouth-Honiton Station, via Sidford & Sidbury (Saturdays)

AEC Reliance/Marshall 42 sits inside Torwood Street garage which was at this time, the terminus of the 46 from Exeter. It is seen when fairly new in 1967. On the far left is the stairway leading down to the lower floor. (N.Bruce-Robertson)

132 and 133 incorporated a few journeys operated since 1965 as service 4. 130 and 131 interconnected at Tipton St. John, where one day the General Manager arrived to find the buses still there seven minutes after departure time, with the crews having a good chat. After a verbal blasting from Mr. Strange, departure was made post haste! Railway booking offices were established in Devon General offices at Exeter, Tiverton, Newton Abbot, and Torquay (Belgrave Road) in addition to those already in being at Babbacombe and Brixham.

In the Grey Cars 'Diamond Tours' programme, a new tour to Scotland, 'Oban and Central Highlands' was introduced. A new holiday tour entitled 'Bridge of Allan and Central Highlands' was also advertised. The former tours booking office at 59, Torbay Road, Paignton was sold during 1967 as it had not been used as such since 1965.

In Torquay, a new route 80S ran from 21st February (Mondays to Fridays), from Chelston (Hawkins Avenue) to Audley Park and Cuthbert Mayne Schools (term time only). From 10th April, new route 82 serving the Broadpark Estate ran from Mead Road via Torquay Station and Lucius Street to the Strand, returning via Torbay Road instead of Lucius Street. It was worked by a one-man bus (usually 'Nimbus' 838) with a 6d. flat fare. Other route changes which took place with the 7th May timetable were:

10,   no longer extended from Otterton to Ladram Bay, 28th August 1966 had been its last day of operation on Hart's former service.
25,   was diverted to Highweek (Applegarth Estate) instead of Mile End.
31,   was extended from Barton (Prince of Orange) to Jacks Lane.
34,   was extended from that point via Barton Hill Road, Barchington Avenue, and Swedwell Road to Moor Lane, returning as 36.
36   was extended in the opposite direction from Moor Lane to return as 34.
43   became one-man, (though some journeys had been thus since 1961).

From 24th September, the Teignmouth local services 70 and 71 were combined as 70, Mill Lane-Triangle-New Road (Exeter Road). The extension to Haldon Golf Club ceased permanently from the same day.

On the Exeter city services, alternate journeys on route D ran to Beacon Heath (Central Avenue) instead of Stoke Hill, route O was extended a short distance from Broadway to Hatherleigh Road, and S was extended from Redhills to Higher Barley Mount, a very severe climb!

With further expansion of the Buckland and Chichester estates at Newton Abbot, a new service 108 was introduced, Sandygate-Kingsteignton-Newton Abbot (bus station)-Drake Road-Buckland Estate, (the 109 ran through Buckland Estate via Queensway with 108 now providing the service via Sandringham Road). The three routes 108/109/110 each ran on an hourly headway providing a combined 20-minute service to the estate. The existing 108 to Huxnor Cross was renumbered 113, these changes taking place on 24th September. Another new route in the area was the 119, Newton Abbot (bus station) to Newtake Estate (Twickenham Road) via the railway station, Penn Inn, and Newtake Rise. Starting on 11th December, it made twelve return journeys each weekday. The 'Bingo bus', service 800, was extended from Teignmouth to Dawlish.

New vehicles delivered in 1967 were five AEC 'Reliance' 41-seat buses with lightweight Marshall bodywork of BET standard design but with Devon General modifications. Fleet numbered 40-44, they were very similar in appearance to 18-23 of 1965, but their dimensions were 30' 6" x 8' 0", and they had the new AH 505 engine, which was an up-rated successor to the AV470.

1967 saw the delivery of eight new Grey Cars, this time with 49-seat Duple Northern coach bodies. The opportunity was taken to update the livery style as depicted by 39 (HOD 39E) outside Newton Abbot railway station. (D.J.Frost)

These were followed by eight new Grey Cars (32-39) which were AEC 'Reliances' with Duple 'Commander' coachwork, overall dimensions being 36' x 8'2½" - so not for the moorland tours! Like 24-31, they had the 9.6-litre AEC 590 engine and 6-speed gearbox incorporating overdrive, while sliding vent windows were fitted at a time when most operators were going for fixed glass and forced ventilation.

The remaining five Commer-Beadle buses (758/9 and 790-792) were sold, as were the remaining three AEC 'Reliance' Grey Cars with Willowbrook 'Viking' bodies (855, 856 and 891).

AEC 'Reliance' bus 869 was scrapped in July as it had lost the whole of its offside in a collision with a Renwicks Fuel lorry near Honiton Clyst on 23rd December 1966, in which bus driver K. Wright of Exeter depot unfortunately lost a leg. The Company was able to keep him on for a time as a parcels clerk.

At this time there were problems at Exmouth, where there were complaints about the state of the buses used there, alleging (probably correctly) that they were throw-outs from Exeter and Torquay. One particular 'black sheep' was named in the local press as 767, which emitted clouds of black exhaust. Following the complaints, 767 was taken away, only to reappear a couple of weeks later with the exhaust worse then ever!

The 6.19am service from Littleham Cross to Exmouth Station, which was an additional service put on after the closure of the railway between these points, was found to have been used by only one passenger during June and two during July! This journey was then discontinued, the Company's chairman making pointed reference to Local Authorities who had been in the habit of pressing for unnecessary bus services to replace withdrawn railway services. The public had been deserting bus services just as they had deserted the railway, and a campaign was started by the Company to involve Local Authorities in the subsidising of services and the provision of cheap travel for pensioners. Several towns did initiate concessionary fare schemes, usually in the form of the issue to pensioners, of transport tokens of a set value per annum. These schemes varied from one area to another.

Getting back to Exmouth, a long-running dispute with certain residents of Littleham Estate over proposals to divert service 10 came before a meeting of the Traffic Commissioners held in Exmouth on 20th December. The Company wished to re-route buses on the hourly Budleigh Salterton service so as to avoid Midway, which was a road in which indiscriminate parking was rife and where a large number of children used to play. The residents objected to a proposal to re-route the outward buses via a service road and to return via the main Salterton Road. Three lay-bys on the service road were to replace existing stops at Drakes Avenue, Brickworks and Capel Lane. The Company won the day, but the residents' representative, Mr. J. Beresford (the only non-professional witness at the hearing) was congratulated by the Chairman on his conduct of their case. The re-routeing took place from 21st January 1968.

Exeter too had its share of problems. A one-way system in High Street and Sidwell Street came into operation on 17th October, but buses were allowed to travel against the flow. From 24th October, Exeter Corporation crews put a ban on overtime, and would not carry standing passengers, and this lasted for a couple of months. Services operated by Devon General crews were not affected, as they were members of the NUR and the Corporation crews were taking their lead from the T & GWU.

The Exeter City Transport undertaking was running at a loss, and after a lot of discussion, fares on the city services were increased by nearly 50% from 26th November in the middle ranges, though some fares (to Alphington, Pinhoe, and Topsham) went down, and about one third remained unchanged. There had already been a general fares increase from 2nd July, the same day on which a wage settlement became effective. The point was made that sixteen million less passengers had been carried during 1957-66 than during 1947 to 1956.

The closure of Exe Bridge and the introduction of a one-way system in Tiverton from 30th May affected services as follows:
3, 97, 101 and 106 were diverted at the western end of Exe Bridge via Leat Street, Kennedy Way (the new northern bridge), Bolham Road, Newport Street, William Street and Barrington Street, to Station Road (3 and 97) or Chapel Street (101 and 106). Return via Gold Street, Fore Street and St. Peter Street to Bolham Road, etc.
91, 92, 93 and 99 were diverted at the junction of Longdrag Hill with Rackenford Road via Kennedy Way, etc, as above.
102 from Fore Street terminus via St. Peter Street, Newport Street, William Street and Barrington Street to Station Road, to return direct via Gold Street.
225 from Loman Green via Gold Street, Fore Street, St. Peter Street to Bolham Road, return via Newport Street, William Street, Barrington Street.
217 from western end of Exe Bridge via Leat Street and Kennedy Way, then double run to centre via Bolham Road.

The new bus station at Phoenix Lane (just off Fore Street) in Tiverton opened on 23rd July, and from 10th October, a parcels agency was started there on behalf of British Rail, for a trial period of 24 weeks. Parcels of up to 3cwt were accepted for onward transit to BR and inward parcels were held for collection at Phoenix Lane. In the first three weeks, only one parcel was handled. The previous office at 28A, Fore Street, Tiverton was relinquished, and this 'listed building' was eventually demolished having been gutted by fire in December 1968. The freehold of the depot in Old Road, Tiverton was purchased by the Company on 1st March 1968.

Late in the year, congestion in Fore Street, St. Marychurch, Torquay, which had long been a problem, was blamed on the buses by the traders (never mind the lorries delivering to their shops!). Devon General had by then started to use 'Atlanteans' on the routes traversing Fore Street (34/35/36), but following a request from the local Road Safety Committee, these routes reverted to operation by short, front entrance 'Regent' V double-deckers, though one 'Atlantean', usually 906, was included in the roster to 'show the flag'. Plans existed for a new road to bypass Fore Street, which was to become a pedestrian precinct, but it was to be several more years before this came about.

The single-track railway between Paignton and Kingswear had come under consideration for closure, and from 26th November an experimental bus service between these points operated every Sunday evening, two return trips being made - it was not a success however and was discontinued. Co-operation with the railways had been taken a step further on 28th September when the road/rail ticket interavailability was extended to allow holders of cheap-day returns to make their return journey by either means without payment of a supplementary charge.

During the latter part of 1967, three buses were fitted with load meters, which recorded the comings and goings of passengers. Micro-switches under each seat were actuated by passengers sitting down or getting up. Single-deckers thus equipped were tried on route 500, and 'Regent' V 509 was also fitted. Another experiment was the use of a Ford demonstration bus on the Torquay-Chelston services for two weeks from 5th October.

The Ford/Yeates demonstrator SVW 275D that was tried on the 32B service which terminated at the top of the steep Reeves Road in Chelston, Torquay, where it is seen prior to the reversal for the return trip to the Strand. (N.Bruce-Robertson)

Twenty-five new ticket machines (serial numbers E016-040) introduced the Mk II 'Speed Setright', these were little different outwardly to the Mk I, except for the conical fare dials and more modern style 'Setright' badge on the front plate. Both these and the Mk Is registered fares from 0/0d. to 19/11½d., fare stages 00 to 99, the day and month of issue, the machine serial number, and seven ticket classes: DOG / EXCH / CHILD / CM RTN / WKM RTN / CD RTN / SINGLE.

An unlikely new 'competitor' emerged in East Devon on 23rd October, when the GPO introduced a mail bus service between Honiton and Luppitt, via Combe Valley, Wolford and Dunkeswell, and this ran twice a day. Several such services were introduced throughout the country, perhaps the best known being in Scotland.

Several inches of snow fell on 8th December, and widespread disruption of services was caused. Some country services could not be operated, including 92 and 99 out of Tiverton, where snow was over a foot deep.

The first year's trading of the subsidiary Company, Court Garages (Torquay) Ltd., showed a modest profit of £2836. The five petrol-engine coaches had been sold, including some direct to Eire and Jersey, and three new diesel-engine Bedford Duple coaches brought the fleet back to five.

On the Devon General Board, Mr. C. L. Rowbury (a Transport Holding Co. nominee) was appointed from 12th July in succession to Mr. J. J. Donovan of British Rail, but it was towards the end of the year that the really big news broke - British Electric Traction, which controlled Devon General and many other bus companies, had reached agreement to sell their bus interests to the Transport Holding Company; they would thus be effectively 'Nationalised'. This in a predominantly Conservative area caused grave misgivings, except perhaps in Exmouth where one of the local cynics wrote to the paper to express the belief that they could not possibly get a worse service than they already had!

One of the Duple Bedford diesel-engine coaches that were bought for Court Coaches, itself soon to be repainted into the NBC all-white with light grey band Grey Cars livery. It is seen at Newton Road. (N.Bruce-Robertson)

1968

1968 was a year of many changes, the most far-reaching of which was the acquisition of Devon General by the Transport Holding Company. An agreement made in November 1967 became unconditional on 6th March 1968, and under its terms, the Transport Holding Company acquired, with effect from 1st March 1968, that part of the equity capital held by the British Electric Traction group, totalling 463,731 ordinary £1 Stock units, thus increasing its holding to 74% of the ordinary stock of the Company. As a result of an offer made to the remaining ordinary stockholders, the Transport Holding Company increased its holding to 98% of the ordinary stock and 95% of the preference stock, and sought to acquire the remainder under the provisions of s.209 of the Companies Act 1948. A Transport Bill was laid before Parliament which provided for the setting-up of a National Bus Company which would absorb the bus and coach interests of the Transport Holding Company in England and Wales, and empower the Minister of Transport to establish Passenger Transport Authorities (PTA) replacing existing municipal operators, initially in Greater Manchester, Merseyside, Tyneside, and the West Midlands but subsequently in other areas of the country as defined.

These moves brought in their wake a number of changes to the Board; Mr. J. T. Robinson was appointed a Director on 21st June and became chairman on 21st November, when Mr. W. M. Dravers resigned. Mr. Dravers had been an energetic chairman during his nine years in office, and apart from his official duties had attended many social functions such as safe-driving awards and long-service presentations. Mr. Robinson was Executive Director of the Tilling Association and Chairman of the Bristol Omnibus Co. Ltd., the Western and Southern National Omnibus Companies, and Greenslades Tours Ltd. Another new Director was Mr. B. Griffiths, also an Executive Director of the Tilling Association and Chairman or Director of their companies in South Wales. Mr. S. J. B. Skyrme and Mr. H. G. Bowles resigned from the Board, and the last Board meeting to be held at Stratton House, Piccadilly, took place on 20th November.

Leaving aside company politics within the bus industry, Devon General still had a service to run, and quite a number of changes took place that were unconnected with the power game being enacted at higher levels.

Early in January, slight alterations were made to some of the bus routes into and out of Exeter bus station, making use of bus lanes which had been used by the Corporation buses since 16th October 1967. Two services were taken over from Western National:

223, Tiverton-Brushford Cross via Bampton and Morebath, from 1st January,

300,   Tiverton-Halberton-Tiverton Junction (previously WN 287) from 6th May.

Both were weekday-only services making but one trip a day; the 223 - a short working of a Western National service, being very early in the morning. Other Western National services also covered most journeys between Tiverton and Tiverton Junction.

Service 56 was, from 5th February re-routed in Paignton to serve Albany Road and Occombe Valley Road, with only four journeys a day continuing to Torquay and the rest terminating at Preston (Butland Avenue). A fifth journey was extended to Torquay from 12th May for the benefit of shoppers.

From 1st April, the Brixham local service 37 was extended from Fishcombe to Valletort Park via Northfields Lane and Lichfield Drive, returning via Smardon Avenue. The existing out and back section of route along Great Rea Road with a reversal at Lytes Road was discontinued.

Timetable No:164, effective from 12th May, was to last for twelve months, with supplementary leaflets being published as required, and this was to be the future trend.

In the Torquay area, the Chelston routes, which had remained static for a few years, were altered by the linking of the termini of 32 and 33 to form a Chelston circular service. The 33 was extended from Highland Road along a widened portion of Nut Bush Lane, turning into Drake Avenue (a new road) and into a widened portion of Upper Cockington Lane - quite a steep hill - thence via Hawkins Avenue, which was a new road that connected with the top end of Sherwell Valley Road and went on to link up with the 32 terminus at Raleigh Avenue. The 33 then returned to town over the 32 route and vice versa. The single-deck 32A was extended a short distance from Sherwell Valley Road along Hawkins Avenue to terminate at Upper Cockington Lane.

The Exeter city services were completely re-cast from 12th May as follows:

A,   Marsh Barton-Hill Barton via High Street and Whipton
A/F,   as above, but extended to St. David's Station via Heavitree Road and Queen Street.
B,   Central Avenue-Hatherleigh Road via Prince Charles Road, Blackall Road, Queen Street and
       Cowick Street.
C,   Cowley Bridge-Crossmead via New North Road and Cowick Street.
D,   St David's Station-Whipton Barton Road via Queen Street and Pinhoe Road
G,   Thornpark Rise-Exwick via Pinhoe Road, High Street and Redhills
J,   South Lawn Terrace-Crossmead via Sidwell Street and Cowick Street
K,   Pennsylvania-Higher Barley Mount via Sidwell Street and Cowick Street
M,   Prince Charles Road-Higher Barley Mount via High Street and Cowick Street
O,   Central Avenue-Hatherleigh Road via Sidwell Street and Cowick Street
R,   Rifford Road Circular (in both directions) via Topsham Road, South Street, High Street, Paris
       Street, Heavitree Road and Rifford Road
S,   St. Leonards-High Meadows via Paris Street, High Street, Cowick Street
T,   Paul Street-Topsham via South Street and Topsham Road
U,   University-Paris Street bus station via Union Road and Sidwell Street.

This re-organisation was done with the aim of 'modernising' the services and making them more direct. Work started in Exeter during 1968 on the first of two new bridges to replace the existing bridge over the River Exe.

A new service 41, Honiton Station to Exmouth, via Sidmouth Junction, Ottery St. Mary and West Hill made one return trip on summer Sundays from 9th June to 18th August for the benefit of residents wishing to go to the seaside for the day. From the 12th May timetable, Exmouth local service 59/A was extended in Withycombe from Bradham Lane top to Churchill Road via Brixington Lane. 59/A/B was also re-routed via Withycombe Road and Grange Terrace instead of Waverly Road and Gipsy Lane. 73 was diverted via Withycombe Road instead of Park Road in both directions.

Following its unfortunate passage under the Old Mill railway bridge in Torquay, MCW Leyland 'Atlantean' 875 was rebuilt with a top supplied by Willowbrook. This view in the Burma Road, shows its changed appearance prior to re-entering service. Below is the rear view.

(N.Bruce-Robertson)

Services 57 and 121 at Torquay, which only ran in the summer months and worked by the same bus, were converted to one-man operation from 7th July, but the Company was unable to obtain agreement with the NUR over the single-manning of local services 111, 114, 115 and 118 which it had envisaged converting at the end of the summer. The Company then threatened to withdraw these services altogether. The General Manager, Mr. T. L. C. Strange, held an unprecedented meeting with a committee of employees, and though the problem was not immediately solved, the air was cleared and eventual agreement was reached in the following year.

Late in the year, service 800, the Bingo bus, once more started and finished at Teignmouth, the extension to Dawlish being discontinued.

The new Exe Bridge at Tiverton opened on 31st October, and services 3, 97, 101, 106 and 217 then reverted to their pre-May 1967 routes other than now having to circuit the town centre one-way system. Further alterations took place from 16th December in as much as 99 and local 102 became one-man operated, a new local service 100 was introduced, services 101 and 106 were re-organised with the resultant routes being:

100,	Broomhill-Phoenix Lane-Tidcombe
101,	Cowley Moor-Phoenix Lane-Cotteylands
106,	Wilcombe-Phoenix Lane-Norwood Road

All were one-man operated, and ran on weekdays only, the use of conductors at Tiverton then ceased. Changes to routes incorporated in the above services included:

106 to Norwood Road -	buses divert at Belmont Road along Longmeadow, turning at Oak Crescent
106 to Wilcombe Estate -	ran from the station on a circle via Old Road, Halsbury Road, Mackenzie Way, Blackmore Road, Lazenby Road, Harrowby Close, and The Avenue
101 to Cotteylands -	diverted after crossing Exe Bridge to run via West Exe South, Howden Road, Orchard Way, Broad Lane, King Street, rejoining the former route in Wellbrook Street
100 from Broomhill -	from junction of Southfield Way and Charter Close, ran via Southfield Way, Broomhill and Bakers Hill to join 101 at Wellbrook Street. After the town centre, 100 proceeded via Station Road, Canal Hill, Tidcombe Lane and Glebelands Road to turn at St. Lawrence Close.

The long-awaited Paignton one-way system came into operation on 1st April; this had been devised by the former Paignton Urban District Council but the newly-formed Torbay County Borough had formulated an alternative plan which came into operation a few months later. Basically the system involved a clockwise circuit of Hyde Road, Victoria Street, and Torquay Road, with only buses allowed to turn from Victoria Street into Torquay Road. After a few months, the Torbay scheme was substituted; Victoria Street was closed to through traffic, and the circuit went via Station Square and Gerston Road instead. Buses going into the bus station from the Torquay direction had to negotiate Gerston Road twice, once to get to the entrance and again having left the exit; the residents had to put up with all this extra traffic for another 26 years.

Teignmouth too had designed a town centre one-way system, under which buses would no longer use the stops at the Triangle. Some shopkeepers objected to passengers queuing outside their shops (previously they had waited on the Triangle) and there was a move by some of the local councillors to make the buses terminate in the railway station forecourt, and there was also a proposal to have a maintenance depot in French Street. Talks were held, but neither scheme proceeded. As events turned out, town and station were soon to be separated by a dual carriageway inner bypass road, however, buses out-stationed at Teignmouth did alter their nightly parking place to the former goods yard on the up side of Teignmouth station, but much later.

The Grey Cars excursion fares were increased in the summer by up to 1/-. Specimen fares became:

Princetown & Dartmeet	12/6
Clovelly	18/6
Becky Falls & Haytor	7/6
Torquay sightseeing	6/-

The worst floods in any summer since 1952 hit the West Country on 10/11th July with East Devon being particularly badly hit. Many small bridges were washed away, including an important one on the main A30 at Fenny Bridges.

On 31st March, the Exeter area superintendent, Mr. F. A. Noble, retired; he had held this position since 1952 (previously being with Crosville Motor Services), and was succeeded by Mr. I. G. Morton.

On 31st August, driver F. Rendell of Exmouth depot retired having driven there for 45 years, and since 1947 had driven Grey Cars in the summer when one was allocated to Exmouth. 1968 was appropriately the last season in which a Grey Car was based there.

At Axminster there was a crisis in September, when both the drivers stationed there, resigned due to ill health. The Company had to consider withdrawal of the last journey into Axminster at night and the first one out in the morning until Devon County Council made accommodation available for a new driver.

It was announced in September that road improvements were to be carried out between Sampford Peverell and Holcombe Rogus (near the Somerset border), so that the bus service 3 could be extended to the latter village.

During March, thirteen new AEC 'Reliances' of three different types were delivered, and all went into service from 1st April. Ten (45-54) were on the long-wheelbase 6U3ZR chassis, had 36' x 8'2½" (11 x 2.5 metre) lightweight body by Willowbrook, to BET specification and again with DG modifications. They had two emergency doors, one each side at the rear, and there were large luggage racks but nevertheless still plenty of leg room. There were two transparent panels in the roof. Power unit was the 691 engine of 11.3-litre capacity coupled to a six-speed ZF gearbox.

The first three (45-47) were designated for use on route 46 (Torquay-Exeter) and although they were built with 49 seats, all were reduced to 41, only to revert to 49 again in July. This was because the single-manning agreement for that service had only covered 41-seat vehicles.

The last seven (48-54) were 51-seat and went from new to Exeter, Exmouth and Sidmouth depots, where they spent practically all of their working life. There were considerable initial local misgivings as to their suitability in the Exmouth area, especially on services 10 and 40 where they replaced double-deckers. Further alarm was caused by the Company's intention to single-man the 10 and 40 from 22nd September 1968 and the Exmouth local services from 1st January 1969, but it was somewhat later than these dates before agreement was reached with the Union, so meantime they ran with conductors, even on the Saturday-only 134 which had hitherto been one-man.

The other three new 'Reliances' (55-57) were of the shorter, 41-seat variety with Marshall body, AH505 engine and 5-speed gearbox. These were 32'8" x 8'2½" (10 x 2.5 metre) and were of generally similar outline to 40-44 of 1967, but had one less window per side. They went new to Newton Abbot depot and remained there, apart from their final few months. It should be mentioned that these three (and 58-81 which followed) were built to meet certain criteria as to dimensions, to enable the Company to qualify for the Bus Grant which the Government had made available to meet 50% of the cost of new vehicles. These buses were built longer than necessary, with overhang fore and aft, simply to qualify for the grant!

The first four long 'Reliances' (9-12 of 1964) were converted for one-man operation and in the process, the cab was made larger and passenger seating reduced to 51.

Towards the end of the year, delivery commenced of a batch of ten Leyland 'Atlanteans' (532-541) with 0680 11.1-litre engine, MCW (Cammell-Laird division of Beaumaris, Anglesey) bodywork, with shells built by the parent company at Elmdon, Birmingham. They had a lower entrance step than previous 'Atlanteans', and the staircase was of a modified design without the sharp turn. 534-535 went into service on 1st November on the Chelston services 32 and 33, while 532-533 went into service at Exeter on the Rifford Road service R.

There had been a long-standing objection to the use of front-entrance buses on the city services, but this had at last been overcome, though the kerb at the turn into Holloway Street had to be moved back two feet to accommodate the 'Atlanteans'. During the next couple of months, 536-539 also went into traffic at Exeter, being joined gradually by other 'Atlanteans' transferred from the Torquay end of the system. 538 was one of the very last of this type to run for Devon General, being in use until January 1984 on the Rifford Road service.

The delivery of 541 was considerably delayed, and it was not put into service until March 1969. This one and 540 spent much of their time on the Torquay to Teignmouth service.

Withdrawals during the year were twenty-four of the 1956 AEC 'Regent' Vs (760-783) with MCW lightweight body, which by then had become quite battered. Four staff cars and a van were sold, being replaced by new vehicles, and the two Court Coaches 'Reliances' were sold at the end of the season.

During 1968, ten Willowbrook AEC Reliances entered service, the first three (45-47) having 49 semi-coach seats for use on the Torquay-Exeter Express. The others had 51 bus seats. It was not thought at the time, that one day 45-47 would be repainted into a reversed livery. 46 is shown here when brand new. See also photo on page 237   (N.Bruce-Robertson)

Final delivery of new buses to the Devon General Omnibus & Touring Company Ltd., were two batches of AEC 'Reliances' in December 1970 although they did not enter service until 1971 by which time Western National officially owned them. This 1976 picture of number 77 (TUO 77J) with Torquay harbour in the background, shows the NBC version of the Devon General poppy red and white livery in which most of these finished their days in 1980.   (L.F.Folkard)

Section 12. National Bus Company and the end of an era (1969-1970)

1969 Under s.28 of the Transport Act 1968, the National Bus Company became the successors to the Transport Holding Company's bus interests. From 1st January 1969, Devon General thus became a subsidiary of the National Bus Company, as did Court Garages (Torquay) Ltd., Bute Court Garages Ltd., and the neighbouring companies of Greenslades Tours (Exeter) Ltd., Western National Omnibus Co. Ltd., and Southern National Omnibus Co. Ltd. The Chairman of Devon General gave assurances that the fleet-names would be retained, and that the buses would not be painted green!

Exeter City Council was unhappy with the Joint Services Agreement, and considered proposals to either re-negotiate it, to invite the National Bus Company to manage the undertaking, or to sell the undertaking to the National Bus Company. The Council at its meeting on 9th July resolved to negotiate for the sale of the undertaking, provided that there would be no detriment to the existing staff conditions. During the early years of the Joint Services Agreement, it had worked in Exeter's favour, but in recent years, with the city services buoyant and the country services in decline, losses were being incurred - £25,922 for the financial year 1968/9. The Council at its meeting on 4th November resolved to sell the undertaking to the National Bus Company for £190,000 (subject to valuation).

Several management changes took place in Devon General during the year; Mr. T. L. C. Strange, General Manager, retired on 31st January after twelve years in office and 42 years in the industry. He was the Company's longest-serving General Manager, and his place was taken by Mr. L. J. Crook, who had been with the Company since 1938 and as Traffic Manager since 1947. The new Traffic Manager was Mr. B. L. Rootham from the Bristol Omnibus Co. Ltd. Mr. G. S. Sedgwick, Chief Engineer since 1947, retired at the end of September following his recovery from a serious illness. Mr. G. K. Metcalfe was appointed Area Engineer-Devon General and Greenslades, with Mr. B. T. Hancock, of Western and Southern National, as acting Chief Engineer. The Company Secretary, Mr. D. W. Passmore also resigned to assist in the setting up of London Country Bus Services Ltd., his staff car and the computer from Devon General going with him for use in his new role as Secretary of the new Company. Mr. R. Wigmore, from Western National, became Secretary of Devon General, Court Garages (Torquay) Ltd., and Bute Court Garage Ltd. The Tours Superintendent, Mr. N. W. Folkard, retired at the end of the year after 42 years service and Mr. K. J. Brown, who had managed Court Garages, was promoted to take his place.

The Board of Directors in 1969 comprised Mr. J. T. E. Robinson (Chairman), Mr. B. Griffiths (Vice Chairman), Messrs. R. J. Ellery, J. Gillespie, L. Mapleston, C. L. Rowbury and P. Yorke. Mr. Rowbury who was a British Rail official left during the year to take up a post in Scotland, and Mr. J. Palette (BR Divisional Manager at Bristol) replaced him on the Board. Before the end of the year, Mr. H. L. Ellis, Director and Manager of Southern and Western National, was appointed to the Board. It was resolved by the Board of the subsidiary Company of Bute Court Garages Ltd., (Messrs. Robinson, Griffiths and Ellis) that due to low profits, restrictions in capital expenditure and the prospect of a substantial increase in rent, that :-

(a) the management and administration effort in running the business could be put to better use in
    the main activity of running buses and coaches
(b) the hire car fleet should not be renewed
(c) the business should be sold as a going concern, or the lease surrendered and the assets sold.

Having failed to find a purchaser for the business, the Company offered the landlord a surrender of the lease, but his terms were not acceptable and so trading continued for the time being.

There was heavy snow in South Devon on 20th February, and a rapid thaw brought floods to Torquay sea front. One bus on the 128 from Plymouth arrived at Torquay some seven hours late!

In July and August two tropical storms in the space of eleven days brought floods to Torquay town centre and many shops were flooded on each occasion. The shopkeepers blamed the buses for driving too fast through the water and creating 'bow waves', to which the Company responded that once in the water, there was no way of knowing how deep it was, and no warning signs had been erected.

A general fares increase, the first for two years, was proposed, with increases geared to the decimalisation of coinage due to take place in 1971. At the same time, anomalies in child fares in Exeter were cleared up; students over 16 years of age were no longer permitted to travel at child rate, which they had been hitherto if wearing cap or scarf. 23-year old university students had been in the habit of taking advantage of this concession. Devon General fares for children within the city were increased by ½d. to bring them into line with those charged by Exeter Corporation.

In February, the Corporation placed five new dual-door Leyland 'Panther' single-deckers (6-10) in service, and with their assistance, routes 8, 26, 27 and 58 became one-man operated. The 26 in Budleigh Salterton was curtailed at Cricketfield Lane from 5th January. The Exeter-Plymouth service 129 was also converted to one-man at about the same time. The portion of the 47 that was worked by Southern National (Axminster-Weymouth) was renumbered 447. Routes 9 and 77 became one-man operated from 11th May, as did the summer-only 2A from its re-commencement in June.

In Torquay, service 82 was extended from Mead Road to Broad Park Estate (Broadley Drive / Brendons Avenue) from 3rd March and following long negotiations, local services 111, 114, 115 and 118 all became one-man operated from 22nd September. The 118 was re-routed, leaving its original route at the end of Lymington Road, then proceeding via Pennys Hill, Cricketfield Road, Barton Road (none of which had ever had a bus service) to Hele Cross, then via its existing route to Collaton Road (terminus), returning via Cross Park Avenue and Higher Cadewell Lane to rejoin its outward route in Cadewell Lane. The 111 terminus was altered to Middle Warberry Road (Bien Venue).

From 21st September, Teignmouth local service 70 was extended from Exeter Road to loop around Maudlin Drive, and service 71 was re-introduced. 71 ran to Maudlin Drive via New Road and Exeter Road, and 70 to Exeter Road and New Road via Maudlin Drive. The last named road has a very steep section from which excellent panoramic views over Teignmouth and Shaldon can be obtained.

Most journeys on the 43 were re-routed to leave Exeter via Heavitree Road and Honiton Clyst, thence via Broadclyst, rejoining its normal route at Dog Village. Some Sunday journeys on the 6 were extended to Market Place in Okehampton so as to connect with Jennings service to Bude.

On the vehicle side, four new Leyland 'Atlanteans' (542-545) with Willowbrook bodywork were all ready for delivery, painted and lettered, when the NBC diverted them to Yorkshire Traction, which ran them in full Devon General livery until their first repaint.

Sixteen new AEC 'Reliance' buses (58-73) were delivered to Devon General, going into service in March and April, mostly from Tiverton on route 3, but Exeter, Okehampton, Torquay and Newton Abbot also had some. They were 32'8" long and 8'2½" wide (10 x 2.5 metres), having 41-seat bodywork by Marshall, and AH 505 engine with five-speed gearbox. They did not have the red band above the windows, everything above the waistband being ivory. Some were at first painted cherry red, a lighter colour than the normal Devon General livery, and not all at first carried fleet-names. The intention was to display adverts below the windows, on slotted boards, but in practice the adverts were simply affixed to the panels in the usual way. Adverts were also applied in this position to some of the older vehicles in the fleet, even including one or two of the 1958 'Reliances'.

Two more diesel-engined Bedford SB5 coaches were delivered for the Court Coaches fleet, which replaced the two ex-Grey Cars 'Reliances' 893 and 894. Also sold were two Grey Cars 'Reliances' (934 and 935), two AEC 'Regent' V double-deckers dating from 1956 (788 and 789) together with ten of the 1957 batch of 'Reliance' saloons (794-797, 800, 802-806). Two new staff cars and a van were purchased.

Western National 1057, one of their first Bristol VRs with Gardner engine, ran on loan from 19th May to 6th June on routes 31 and 104/105, and as a result, nine VRs were ordered. Many more were to follow later, and this type eventually became the most numerous of double-deckers in the area.

Grey Cars tours were no longer advertised from Tiverton for the 1969 season, but the Company secured a contract for conveying the Torquay United football team to their away matches for the 1969/1970 season, and a new Plaxton bodied Daimler 'Roadliner' coach, RDG 309G was hired for this purpose from Black & White Motorways of Cheltenham. The regular driver on this contract was G. Foskett, who in 1987 was the principal of a group of drivers who bought out the Torbay area tours operations of Devon General, and re-introduced the Grey Cars name. The hired coach was painted in a modified Grey Cars livery of all white with a broad pale grey band, the fleet-names being in large plain white letters.

Four new Leyland 'Atlanteans' (542-545) with Willowbrook bodywork were all ready for delivery, painted and lettered, when the NBC diverted them to Yorkshire Traction, which ran them in full Devon General livery until their first repaint. This is 544 (OTT 544G) which was later re-registered RHE 449G. (DGS)

This was to become the Grey Cars variant of a new corporate livery introduced by National Travel (South West), and became standard. It was, quite naturally, considered most unattractive after the style in which Grey Cars had previously and traditionally been turned out. Car 34 was the first of the existing fleet to receive this livery in December 1969, and other Grey Cars of the 1964, 1966 and 1967 batches also received it in 1970 and 1971 as well as new deliveries. The Court Coaches were similarly treated.

Devon General could still boast an impressive number of long-serving staff; one had served over 50 years, two with over 45 years, 38 with over 40 years, not to mention no less than 138 with 25 years service to their credit.

Another fifty 'Speed Setright' Mk II ticket machines were purchased in 1969, numbered E041 to E090.

The 1969 summer allocation of Grey Cars to drivers was:

1 -	G. T. Crispin		36 -	? Biggs
2 -	Exeter Car (later to W. Weymouth)		37 -	Exeter Car
3 -	W. Weymouth (later spare car)		38 -	B. Goodman (later R. Tout)
4 -	H. Hine		39 -	J. McDonald
5 -	Exeter Car		937 -	C. Wiggins
6 -	Exeter Car		938 -	A. J. C. Durham
7 -	H. Sutcliffe		939-	Exeter Car (later Goodman)
8 -	F. H. Cahill		940 -	Exeter Car (later de-licensed)
24 -	E. Crouch		941 -	spare
25 -	S. Davies		942 -	spare
26 -	R. Tout (later de-licensed)		960 -	L. S. Redfern
27 -	E. Leech		961 -	W. Hext
28 -	D. Ware		962 -	Exeter Car
29 -	K. Falconer		963 -	M. R. Barrow
30 -	E. Singleton		964 -	R. C. Coulton
31 -	D. Briggs		965 -	S. Quick
32 -	K. Grimshaw		966 -	R. Johns
33 -	E. Burbidge		967 -	Exeter Car
34 -	W. Waddle		968 -	R. C. Felthouse
35 -	Exeter Car			

1970

The wind of change in the bus industry had turned into a hurricane, and it was destined to be the last year of existence for the Devon General Omnibus & Touring Co. Ltd. From 1st February, the head office was transferred from 87, Newton Road, Torquay, to National House, Queen Street, Exeter. Mr. L. J. Crook retired as General Manager on 28th February, and Mr. B. L. Rootham took his place, but only until 1st September, when he returned to the Bristol Omnibus Co. Ltd., as Traffic Manager. No General Manager as such was appointed in his place, but a new post of Commercial Manager was created and Mr. J. S. K. Clarke was appointed to fill it. He was a comparative newcomer to the local scene. A long-serving Devon General man, Mr. H. G. Palk (Assistant Traffic Manager since 1st January 1969) was appointed Traffic Manager.

Closer links were established with Greenslades Tours Ltd., following their acquisition by the National Bus Company on 1st January 1969, and Mr. E. Hartnell, who had been Traffic Manager of Greenslades, was appointed to a new post as Publicity Manager for Devon General, Western National and Greenslades. Mr. J. Bayliss was appointed Exeter Area Traffic Superintendent (the post previously held by Mr. Clarke), and Mr. C. J. A. Madge, who for many years had been running shift foreman at Torquay depot, was appointed Assistant Area Engineer. From 1st September, Mr. H. L. Ellis became Managing Director of the Devon General Omnibus & Touring Co. Ltd., and of Greenslades Tours Ltd. Mr. E. W. Butcher, Director and General Manager of the Bristol Omnibus Co. Ltd., was appointed a Director of Devon General and of Greenslades.

From the summer of 1970, Greenslades Tours Ltd., assumed responsibility for all Holiday Tours previously run by Grey Cars, and also took over operation of the Grey Cars tours from Exeter. They were already well established at Teignmouth, Dawlish, Exeter, Exmouth, Budleigh Salterton and Sidmouth, and this just left Devon General (through Grey Cars and Court Coaches) with tours from Torquay, Paignton and Newton Abbot.

Grey Cars had, to an increasing extent over the previous few years, supplied vehicles for the Associated Motorways services to London and the South Coast as well as on occasion, to the North of England. This may have been because their newer coaches were too wide to be used on the local Dartmoor tours. The express services were built up under the National Bus Company and later marketed under the well known National Express brand name.

Apart from taking over the assets of the Transport Holding Company, the National Bus Company also negotiated the purchase of some municipal transport undertakings, one of these being Exeter Corporation, and after agreement had been reached between the parties, the purchase was completed on 31st March 1970. The NBC vested the former Exeter Corporation transport undertaking as part of the Devon General Omnibus & Touring Co. Ltd., from 1st April, and they thus operated the city services direct instead of through the cumbersome Joint Services Agreement.

The Mayor of Exeter (Ald. W. J. Hallett) arranged a reception for long-serving busmen by way of a 'thank you' for services rendered, but several chose to stay away, believing that they had nothing to celebrate. Mr. W. Astin, who had been General Manager and Engineer of Exeter CTD carried on for a short while in an advisory capacity, and retired before the end of the year. Mr. R. T. Williams, who had been Rolling Stock Superintendent, was appointed Exeter Area Mechanical Superintendent.

The 230 Transport Department staff came over to Devon General, and the fleet was renumbered by the addition of 200 to their existing numbers. The vehicles had been so well kept that it was a long time before any of them required repainting, and quite a number never did carry Devon General red.

They continued to use the depot at Heavitree Road and in all, 65 vehicles were taken over, but four Leyland PD2 double-deckers were sold soon after, in May. Seven dual-door one-man Leyland 'Panther' saloons that had previously been ordered by the Corporation were delivered in August in green and cream but with Devon General style fleet numbers 211-217 although carried the EXETER fleet-name and city crest. They replaced the last of the city fleet of Leyland 'Titan' PD2 double-deckers of 1947/48 as well as six of their 1956/57 Guy double-deckers. Sold at the same time was a 'Titan' that had been used as the tree-lopper.

208 was a former Exeter Corporation Leyland 'Panther' with Marshall dual door body, an arrangement peculiar to the Corporation.
(L.F.Folkard collection)

New vehicles delivered to Devon General proper at the end of the year were eight AEC 'Reliance' saloons (74-81) with AH505 engine and Willowbrook 43-seat bodywork, 32'8" in length (10 metres), together with six 'Reliance' saloons (82-87) but these had the AH691 engine and 51-seat bus body, again by Willowbrook but this time 36'0" long (11 metres). All these were to the new maximum width of 8'2½" and carried their fleet-name well forward so as to allow for advertisement panels to be fixed later. None actually entered service until February 1971.

Also regarded as part of the Company's stock at the end of the year were five Bristol RE chassis, destined to be fitted with Plaxton 'Panorama Elite' 47-seat coach bodies for Grey Cars and allocated fleet-numbers 450-454. One coach that had been ordered by Greenslades went from new to the Grey Cars fleet in May 1970, this being an AEC 'Reliance' with 49-seat Plaxton body, and given the number 499.

Another AEC 'Matador' lorry was purchased during 1970, and converted to a recovery vehicle to replace the aged RV2 (which was constructed by Devon General from spare 'Regal' parts in 1955/56). The faithful old-timer was given a farewell party by the staff at Exeter before it left!

Eleven AEC 'Reliance' Grey Cars of 1961/2 were also sold during the year, ten going to Greenslades (937-942 and 960-963) and one to Western National (936). One AEC 'Regent' (667) that had been used for tree-lopping since 1964 was sold, and a van was transferred from Western National.

Commencing in 1970, a process which continued for the next few years, was the removal of one double-seat from the front nearside of all one-man AEC 'Reliance' saloons, in order to provide more room for parcels and luggage.

Four passengers were injured when on 14th April, AEC 'Reliance' 860 overturned between Clyst St. Lawrence and Westwood while working service 43. Driver A. Goffey of Cullompton depot escaped unhurt.

The rail replacement services in East Devon had not been well used, and application was made, and granted, for drastic reductions. Services 130, 132 and 133 all ceased operation, but a new variation of the 4 was introduced from 10th May, Ottery St. Mary-Exeter via Sidmouth Junction Station (Feniton) and Whimple, station and village.

Another service to finish was the 51 (Torbay Hospital), which was replaced by a diversion of the 118 through the Hospital grounds. Services 24, 123 and 126 became one-man operated.

In conjunction with associated companies, a 'Travel Anywhere' ticket, offering seven days unlimited travel in Devon, Cornwall and Somerset was introduced at the modest price of £2-5s-0d.

Two more employees notched up 50 years of service with Devon General and its predecessors - Drivers S. C. Emmett and W. A. H. Delafield, of Torquay depot, both of whom had previously been tram drivers.

After several months of speculation, it came as no great surprise when it was announced that, as from 1st January 1971, the operations of the Devon General Omnibus & Touring Co. Ltd., were to be taken over by the Western National Omnibus Co. Ltd., and all assets and liabilities at 31st December 1970 were to be transferred. The fleet-name and Devon General livery were to be retained, (so it was publicly stated) but for operational purposes, Devon General would simply be an area of Western National, with their registered office at National House, Queen Street, Exeter.

To prepare for the introduction of decimal coinage in February 1971, Western National converted seven Bristol 'LS' single-decker buses to decimal training units, and Devon General had the use of one of these (TU5). It was equipped with ciné and slide projectors, sound tapes, and visual aids.
Fifty fully-decimalised ticket machines numbered, E091 to E140 were purchased in readiness, and earlier machines were converted to decimal with kits supplied by 'Setright'. The 'new-pence' fares on the new and converted machines ranged from 0.00d. to 1.99½d. Not all pre-decimal machines were converted. In April 1970, 84 'Speed Setright' machines were inherited from the Exeter Corporation Transport Department; machines 010 to 071 were of the Mk.I type (delivered in three batches between 1952 and 1963), while 072 to 093 were decimalised Mk.II models delivered in 1969. The ticket class details were different from Devon General models, being D or L / SINGLE / MNY.RTN / C.D.RTN / WKM.RTN / EXCH / CHILD: the Mk.II machines substituted DOG for D or L.

The final event of note in 1970 occurred in December, when 'Atlantean' 933 'Sir Walter Raleigh' ran in Exeter, decorated and in open-top form. It was operated during weekday evenings on the run-up to Christmas on a 'Christmas Nightrider' service to see the lights, with which Exeter's main shopping streets were highly decorated. This was repeated in 1971 and 1972.

Services in operation at the end of the separate existence of the Devon General Omnibus & Touring Co. Ltd., on 31st December 1970 were as follows: (all daily unless otherwise shown - * is OMB ser vice)

1,	Chudleigh-Newton Abbot-Denbury*
2,	Exeter-Dawlish-Teignmouth-Newton Abbot
2A	Exeter-Beacon Heath-Bus Station-Rifford Road-Dawlish Warren (summer only) *
2B,	Newton Abbot-Bishopsteignton-Teignmouth*
3,	Exeter-Silverton-Tiverton-Sampford Peverell *
4,	Exeter-Ottery St. Mary-Honiton-Axminster*
5,	Crediton-Exeter-Topsham-Woodbury-Exmouth*
6,	Exeter-Crockernwell-Okehampton*
8,	Exeter-Pinhoe-Broadclyst*
9,	Exeter-Newton Poppleford-Sidmouth*
10,	Exmouth-Otterton Village
11,	Newton Abbot-Ashburton-Buckfastleigh

12,	Newton Abbot-Torquay-Paignton-Brixham
12A,	Babbacombe-Torquay-Paignton-Broadsands (summer only - open top service)
12B,	Brixham-Kingswear (one-man in winter)
12C,	Babbacombe-Torquay-Paignton-Kingswear (summer only - open top service)
12D,	Babbacombe-Torquay-Paignton-Brixham (summer only - open top service)
13,	Torquay-Maidencombe-Shaldon-Teignmouth (extended to Dawlish Warren in summer)
13,	Torquay-Maidencombe-Stokeinteignhead
14,	Newton Abbot-Decoy*
14S,	Newton Abbot-Decoy and All Saints Primary Schools (M-F school term time only)
15,	Newton Abbot-Ipplepen-Totnes*
16,	Newton Abbot-Bovey Tracey-Moretonhampstead-Chagford-Okehampton*
17,	Paignton-Maidenway Road-Marldon Cross (Belfield Avenue)
18,	Paignton-Roundham-Galmpton-Greenway* (weekdays)
19,	Exeter-Dunsford-Moretonhampstead-Chagford*
19A,	Exeter-Leigh Cross-Christow* (weekdays)
20,	Exeter-Leigh Cross-Christow-Chudleigh-Newton Abbot * (weekdays)
21,	Cullompton-Broadhembury-Honiton* (WSaO)
22,	Drewsteignton-Chagford-Moretonhampstead-Newton Abbot* (WO)
23,	Newton Abbot-Haytor-Widecombe* (WFSaO)
24,	Exeter-Digby Hospital* (WSaO)
25,	Newton Abbot-Highweek (Applegarth Estate)
26,	Exeter-Woodbury-Budleigh Salterton*
27,	Exeter-Broadclyst-Hele Cross-Cullompton*
28A,	Torquay (Strand)-Shiphay (Torridge Avenue)
29,	Exeter-Drewsteignton-Chagford-Moretonhampstead* (weekdays)
30,	Babbacombe-Castle Circus-Torquay Station-Paignton
31,	Torquay (Strand)- Westhill-Hele Village-Barton (Jacks Lane) depot journeys run to and from Lawes Bridge
32,	Torquay (Hesketh Crescent)-Strand-Chelston Circular via Raleigh Avenue & Nut Bush Lane.
32A,	Torquay (Strand)-Sherwell Valley- Chelston (Upper Cockington Lane)
32B,	Torquay (Strand)-Chelston (The Reeves Road)
33,	Torquay (Hesketh Crescent)-Strand-Chelston Circular via Nut Bush Lane & Raleigh Avenue
34,	Torquay (Castle Circus)-St. Marychurch-Barton-Watcombe Park (Moor Lane)
35,	Torquay (Castle Circus)-St. Marychurch-Watcombe Estate (Willow Avenue)
36,	Torquay (Castle Circus)-St. Marychurch-Watcombe Park (Moor Lane)
37,	Brixham (Bus Station)-Valletort Park (one-man on winter Sundays)
40,	Exmouth-Budleigh Salterton-Newton Poppleford-Sidmouth
41,	Honiton Station- Ottery St. Mary-Exmouth (summer Sundays only) *
42,	Exeter-Pinhoe-Poltimore*
43,	Cullompton-Plymtree-Clyst Hydon-Exeter * (TWFSaO)
44,	Newton Abbot-Hennock * (WSaO)
46,	Exeter-Torquay* (limited stop)
47,	Exeter-Ottery St. Mary-Honiton-Axminster* (connection to Weymouth)
50,	Torquay (Strand)-Ellacombe-St. Marychurch
54,	Shiphay (Torridge Avenue)-Castle Circus-St. Marychurch (weekdays)
55,	Torquay (Strand)-Wellswood-St. Marychurch
56,	Torquay (Strand)-Shorton Valley-Paignton *
57,	Torquay (Strand)-Warren Road (summer only) *
58,	Exeter-Clyst St. Mary-Woodbury-Exmouth *
59,	Withycombe-Exmouth-Cranford Avenue-Littleham Village
59A,	Withycombe-Exmouth-Salterton Road-Littleham Village
59B,	Exmouth-Withycombe-St. Johns
60,	Littleharn Village-Sandy Bay (summer only)
63,	Paignton-Marldon-Compton Castle*
64,	Exeter-Ide-Dunchideock* (weekdays)
65,	Exeter-Whitestone-Heath Cross* (weekdays)
66,	Exeter-Shillingford-Kennford-Chudleigh* (weekdays)
67,	Exeter-Upton Pyne-Brampford Speke* (weekdays)
68,	Exeter-Raddon Cross-Shobrooke-Crediton* (TuThSaO)
69,	Crediton-Sandford-Kennerleigh* (SaO)
70,	Teignmouth (Mill Lane)-Triangle-New Road-Maudlin Drive

71,	Teignmouth (Mill Lane)-Triangle- Maudlin Drive-New Road
73,	Exmouth-Turner Avenue (weekdays)
74,	Exmouth-Orcombe Point (summer only)
75,	Honiton-Buckerell-Feniton-Talaton* (WSaO)
76,	Crediton-Sandford-New Buildings* (weekdays)
77,	Sidmouth-Sidford-Sidbury*
78,	Sidmouth-Ottery St .Mary*
79,	Moretonhampstead-North Bovey* (WSaO)
80S,	Chelston (Hawkins Avenue)-Audley Park & Cuthbert Mayne Schools (M-F School term time)
81,	Paignton-Shiphay-(Girls Grammar School) (M-F School term time)
82,	Broadpark Estate-Castle Circus-Torquay (Strand)-Broadpark Estate* (weekdays)
85,	Crediton-Exeter-Topsham-Exton-Exmouth*
88,	Newton Abbot-Ipplepen-Broadhempston* (weekdays)
89,	Paignton-Fenton School (M-F School term)
90,	Newton Abbot-Ideford Village* (WSaO)
91,	Witheridge-Tiverton* (via Withleigh & Mudford Gate)
92,	Tiverton-Calverleigh-Rackenford* (TuFSaO)
93,	Witheridge-Puddington-Pennymoor-Tiverton* (TuO)
96,	Exeter-Crediton-Morchard Bishop-Witheridge* (weekdays)
97,	Tiverton-Poughill* (TuO)
98,	Exeter-Crediton-Cheriton Fitzpaine-Witheridge* (FSaO)
99,	Tiverton-Stoodleigh* (TuFO)
100,	Tiverton (Tidcombe)-Broomhill* (weekdays)
101,	Tiverton (Cotteylands)-Cowley Moor* (weekdays)
102,	Tiverton-East Butterleigh Cross* (TuSaO)
103,	Dawlish/Port Road-Ashcombe* (summer TuFO)
104,	Paignton-Marldon Road-Foxhole Estate (Fernicombe Road)
105,	Paignton-Blatchcombe Road-Foxhole Estate (Ramshill Road)
106,	Tiverton (Wilcombe Estate)-Norwood Road* (weekdays)
107,	Newton Abbot-Coffinswell-Daccombe* (WSaO)
108,	Buckland Estate-Drakes Road-Newton Abbot-Kingsteignton-Sandygate
109,	Buckland Estate-Queensway-Newton Abbot-Kingsteignton-Sandygate
110,	Buckland Estate-Oakland Road-Newton Abbot-Kingsteignton-Sandygate
111,	Torquay-(Strand)-Middle Warberry Road*
113,	Newton Abbot-Kingskerswell-Huxnor Cross* (WSaO)
114,	Torquay Inner Circle* (via Ellacombe, Quinta Road, Wellswood, Strand)
115,	Torquay Inner Circle* (via Wellswood, Quinta Road, Ellacombe, Strand)
116,	Newton Abbot-Combeinteignhead-Shaldon-Teignmouth* (weekdays)
117,	Newton Abbot-Combeinteignhead-Stokeinteignhead-Maidencombe Cross* (weekdays)
118,	Torquay (Strand)-Barton Road-Torbay Hospital-Collaton Road*
119,	Newton Abbot-Newtake Estate-Twickenham Road* (weekdays)
120,	Newton Abbot-Milber (Centrax Factory) (weekdays)
121,	Torquay (Strand)-Wellswood-Meadfoot Beach* (summer only)
122,	Lawes Bridge-Torquay-Paignton-Broadsands-STC Factory-White Rock (Gibson Gardens)* (M-FO)
123.	Brixham (Bus Station)-STC Factory* (weekdays)
124,	Lawes Bridge-Torquay-Preston-Foxhole Estate-STC Factory (M-FO)
125,	Peak Hill-Sidmouth-Salcombe Regis* (summer only)
126,	St. Marychurch-Shiphay-Marldon-STC Factory (M-FO)
128,	Torquay-Paignton-Totnes-Plymouth (joint with WNOC)
129,	Exeter-Chudleigh-Bovey Tracey-Ashburton-Plymouth* (joint with WNOC)
131,	Sidmouth-Tipton St. John-Ottery St. Mary-Honiton (Station)* (weekdays)
134,	Sidmouth-Sidbury-Honiton (summer SaO)
217,	Exeter-Tiverton-Dulverton-Minehead* (bus station)
	(Plymouth-Exeter-Minehead (Butlin's Camp) (summer SaO)
223,	Tiverton-Brushford Cross* (weekdays-one daily short working on this WN service)
225,	Tiverton-Oakford-Rackenford* (TuO) (joint with WNOC)
300,	Tiverton (bus station)-Tiverton Junction Station* (weekdays)
500,	Preston Down Road (Templar Road)-Paignton (bus station)-STC Factory* (limited stop)
700,	Newton Abbot-Torbay Ring Road-Paignton-Brixham (summer only)
800,	Teignmouth-Kingsteignton-Newton Abbot-Shiphay-Paignton (Odeon) (WSaSuO)

Exeter City services:

A ,   Marsh Barton-Whipton-Hill Barton
B,   Hatherleigh Road-Broadway-Blackall Road-Beacon Heath
C,   Crossmead-High Street-Cowley Bridge
D,   St. David's Station-Central Station-High Street-Whipton Barton
F,   Hill Barton-Heavitree-Central Station-St. David's Station
G,   Thorn Park Rise-Exwick
J,   South Lawn Terrace-High Street-Crossmead
K,   Higher Barley Mount-Redhills-High Street-Pennsylvania
M,   Higher Barley Mount-Redhills-High Street-Mincinglake Road-Stoke Hill
O,   Hatherleigh Road-Broadway-Old Tiverton Road-Beacon Heath
R,   Rifford Road-Topsham Road-High Street-Heavitree Road-Rifford Road (circular)
S,   St. Leonards-High Street-Bowhay Lane-High Meadows
T,   Paul Street-Countess Wear-Topsham
U,   Bedford Street-University (M-F term time only)

In addition, the following non-timetabled services were licensed to run as required:

Exmouth (Rolle College)-Exeter (St. David's Station)
Chudleigh-Chudleigh Knighton-Heathfield (Candy's Works)
Newton Abbot-Kingskerswell-Torquay (Plainmoor) for Torquay United football matches
Brixham-Torquay (Plainmoor) for Torquay United football matches
Exeter-Haldon Racecourse
Exeter (Broadway/Redhills)- Whipton
Countess Wear-Exeter City football ground
Thornpark Rise-Exeter St. David's Station
Topsham-Countess Wear-Vincent Thompson School

The fleet at 31st December 1970 comprised the following vehicles, all of which passed into Western National ownership:

1-8	(1-8 RDV)	AEC 'Reliance'	(1963)	Harrington	C41F	Grey Cars
9-12	(9-12 RDV)	AEC 'Reliance'	(1964)	Marshall	B51F	*
13-17	(13-17 RDV)	AEC 'Reliance'	(1964)	Willowbrook	B41F	*
18-23	(CTT 18-23C)	AEC 'Reliance'	(1965)	Park Royal	B41F	*
24-31	(EOD 24-31D)	AEC 'Reliance'	(1966)	Harrington	C49F	Grey Cars
32-39	(HOD 32-39E)	AEC 'Reliance'	(1967)	Duple Northern	C49F	Grey Cars
40-44	(HOD 40-44E)	AEC 'Reliance'	(1967)	Marshall	B41F	*
45-47	(LUO 45-47F)	AEC 'Reliance'	(1968)	Willowbrook	B49F	*
48-54	(LUO 48-54F)	AEC 'Reliance'	(1968)	Willowbrook	B51F	*
55-57	(LUO 55-57F)	AEC 'Reliance'	(1968)	Marshall	B41F	*
58-73	(OTA 58-73G)	AEC 'Reliance'	(1969)	Marshall	B41F	*
74-81	(TUO 74-81J)	AEC 'Reliance'	(1970)	Willowbrook	B43F	*
82-87	TUO 82-87J	AEC 'Reliance'	(1970)	Willowbrook	B51F	*
201-205	(GFJ 601-605D)	Leyland 'Leopard'	(1966)	Massey	B41D	Ex-ECT
206-210	(MFJ 386-390G)	Leyland 'Panther'	(1969)	Marshall	B47D	Ex-ECT
211-217	(TDV 211-217J)	Leyland 'Panther'	(1970)	Marshall	B47D	**
251,253	(UFJ 291,293)	Guy 'Arab' IV	(1957)	Massey	H30/26R	Ex-ECT
256,259	(UFJ 296,299)	Guy 'Arab' IV	(1957)	Park Royal	H31/26R	Ex-ECT
260-264	(VFJ 995-999)	Leyland 'Titan' PD2/40	(1958)	Weymann	H31/26R	Ex-ECT
265-269	(XFJ 750-754)	Guy 'Arab' IV	(1959)	Weymann	H31/26R	Ex-ECT
270-274	(970-974 AFJ)	Guy 'Arab' IV	(1960)	Massey	H31/26R	Ex-ECT
275-279	(475-479 CFJ)	Leyland 'Titan' PD2A/30	(1961)	Massey	H31/26R	Ex-ECT
280-284	(480-484 EFJ)	Leyland 'Titan' PD2A/30	(1962)	Massey	H31/26R	Ex-ECT
285-289	(85-89 GFJ)	Leyland 'Titan' PD2A/30	(1963)	Massey	H31/26R	Ex-ECT
290-294	(AFJ 90-94B)	Leyland 'Titan' PD2A/30	(1964)	Massey	H31/26R	Ex-ECT
295-299	(DFJ 895-899C)	Leyland 'Titan' PD2A/30	(1965)	Massey	H37/28R	Ex-ECT
450-454	(UUO 450-454J)	Bristol RELH6L		Plaxton	C47F	GC ***
493-495	(JTA 763-765E)	Bedford SB5	(1967)	Duple	C41F	CC
496-497	(CXF 256-257G)	Bedford SB5	(1969)	Duple	C41F	CC

499	(RFJ 828H)	AEC 'Reliance'	(1970)	Plaxton	C49F	GC
501-508	(501-508 RUO)	AEC 'Regent' V	(1964)	Willowbrook	H39/30F	
509-514	(CTT 509-514C)	AEC 'Regent' V	(1965)	Park Royal	H40/29F	
515-520	(CTT 515-520C)	AEC 'Regent' V	(1965)	Willowbrook	H33/26F	
521-525	(EOD 521-525D)	AEC 'Regent' V	(1966)	Metro-Cammell	H34/25F	
526-531	(EOD 526-531D)	Leyland 'Atlantean'	(1966)	Duple (L'borough)	H44/31F	
532-541	(NDV 532-541G)	Leyland 'Atlantean'	(1968/9)	M.C.W. (Anglesey)	H43/32F	
784-787	(TTT 784-787)	AEC 'Regent' V	(1956)	Metro-Cammell	H33/26RD	
793/8/9	(VDV 793) etc	AEC 'Reliance'	(1957)	Weymann	B41F	
801	(VDV 801)	AEC 'Reliance'	(1957)	Weymann	B41F	
807-819	(VDV 807-819)	AEC 'Regent' V	(1957)	Metro-Cammell	H33/26	
824-837	(XTA 824-837)	AEC 'Reliance'	(1958)	Weymann	B41F	
838-843	(XTA 838-843)	Albion 'Nimbus'	(1958)	Willowbrook	B31F	
860-868	(860-868 ATA)	AEC 'Reliance'	(1959)	Willowbrook	B41F	
870-871	(870-871 ATA)	AEC 'Reliance'	(1959)	Willowbrook	B41F	
872-888	(872-888 ATA)	Leyland 'Atlantean'	(1959)	Metro-Cammell	H44/32F	
895-917	(895-917 DTT)	Leyland 'Atlantean'	(1960)	Roe	H44/31F	
918-924	(918-924 GTA)	Leyland 'Atlantean'	(1961)	Roe	H44/31F	
925-933	(925-933 GTA)	Leyland 'Atlantean'	(1961)	Metro-Cammell	H44/31F	****
943-949	(943-949 HTT)	AEC 'Regent' V	(1962)	Weymann	H33/26R	
950-956	(950-956 HTT)	AEC 'Reliance'	(1962)	Marshall	B41F	
957-959	(957-959 HTT)	Albion 'Nimbus'	(1962)	Harrington	B31F	
964-968	(964-968 HTT)	AEC 'Reliance'	(1962)	Willowbrook	C41F	GC
969-984	(969-984 MDV)	AEC 'Regent' V	(1963)	Metro-Cammell	H33/26F	
985-991	(985-991 MDV)	AEC 'Reliance'	(1963)	Marshall	B41F	

Other rolling stock transferred included two AEC 'Matador' recovery vehicles, eight vans and eight staff cars. Note - where an asterisk* appears above in the fleet details, a programme was in hand to reduce the seating of these buses by two, in order to provide additional luggage space.

** Denotes ordered by ECT   *** Denotes on order   **** Denotes convertible open top   CC is Court Coaches
GC is Grey Cars

An unusual vehicle to be found in the Devon General fleet is this Bristol FSF 60 seater built by Eastern Coach Works of Lowestoft which came from Western National with the fleet number 1013. It was new to the Bristol Omnibus Company in 1960 as their 6009 and is seen here in Dawlish in January 1978.

(GWE Starcross)

Section 13. Western National (1971-1982)

1971

It is not proposed to give a detailed history of the events from 1971, for the story mainly belongs in the annals of the Western National Omnibus Co. Ltd. However, there follows an outline of the many changes which took place which concerned the area of the former Devon General Omnibus & Touring Co. Ltd.

Western National lost no time in closing Exeter (Blackboy Road) garage, which for many years had been deemed unsuitable for present day operations. Its allocation was from 27th March transferred to the former Corporation garage at Heavitree Road, though many vehicles were obliged to continue to park in the coach station overnight.

The subsidiary business of Court Garages (Torquay) Ltd., was wound up, and in February, the five coaches were repainted white and grey and given Grey Cars fleet-name. They were only in these colours for a few months, because from 2nd May all Grey Cars coach operations and fleet was transferred to Greenslades Tours Ltd.

A unified numbering scheme for the Western National, Devon General and Greenslades fleets was produced on 13th May and renumbering of the former Grey Cars into the 300 and 400 series commenced in June. Accordingly, Western National vehicles with numbers in the 400 series became 1200s, but no Devon General buses were renumbered.

The associated car hire business of Bute Court Garages Ltd., still carried on, and although a prospective purchaser was found, there were difficulties over the lease, and when these were eventually resolved, the purchaser was no longer interested.

The timetable published for the twelve months commencing 9th May 1971 was in exactly the same form as previously, and gave no indication of the changes which had already taken place or were about to do so; for instance, Grey Cars tours were still being advertised. A number of bus services had alternative routes and short workings, and in several instances these were given distinguishing numbers, usually with a lettered suffix.

One-man operation of some double-deck services was introduced, the first being the 11 (Newton Abbot-Buckfastleigh). This was a very gradual process however and was not completed until 1984.

During 1971, most of the 'Atlanteans' of the 872-888 and 526-541 series were modified for one-man operation, with the rest following soon afterwards. It was a more gradual process with the other 'Atlanteans', some of which were in need of major rebuild, indeed some never did get converted. The work entailed the installation of ticket machine and till, periscope mirror for the driver to see the upper deck, lowering of the front destination display so that it could be changed by the driver, removal of the rear route number box (where fitted), and the provision of reversing lights and warning horn. Most of 872-888 and 895-924 lost their top front opening ventilator windows.

Moretonhampstead depot closed from 13th September, likewise Tiverton garage closed its doors from 6th October. A number of country services ceased in each case. Both garages were sold, Tiverton becoming a depot for lorries and plant of Tiverton (later Mid Devon) District Council, and Moretonhampstead became a motor engineering workshop, both buildings surviving intact today. Buses were then kept nearby in the open, the small bus station at Phoenix Lane being used at Tiverton and a public car park at Moretonhampstead.

Nine Bristol 'VRs' (542-550) with Eastern Coachworks 70-seat body entered service in August and September, (see outside back cover) pure Western National, but at first in traditional Devon General livery. They led rather a nomadic existence, working all over the Devon General area at one time or another, as well as latterly in Cornwall. Later in the year, another seven Leyland 'Panthers' were delivered for the Exeter area, though in traditional Devon General livery.

Sold during 1971 were AEC 'Regent' Vs 784-787 and 807-819, most of which had become very run down, as well as AEC 'Reliance' 798 and Albion 'Nimbus' buses 838/839; Exeter Guys 251/259 and 265-269 were also withdrawn; 267 had been repainted in Devon General livery as recently as February 1971 and was the first ex-Corporation vehicle to have been so treated.

A promotion to encourage the use of service 46, the Torquay-Exeter express, produced a new livery for the three buses concerned, 'Reliances' 45-47 were repainted in a reversed livery, ivory with maroon window surrounds, lettering, and relief. Passengers were exhorted to take the 46-mile round trip to Exeter on service 46 with bus number 46 for 46p. The trio ran in these colours for the next three years.

Delivered in 1968 were three 49-seat AEC Willowbrook 'Reliances' (45-47) in Devon General livery, but all were repainted into a reversed scheme for use on the 46, Exeter-Torquay Express service. Fleet number 46 passes Milber as a train of Mark 1 carriages from Plymouth heads in the same direction. (DGS collection)

1972

Keeping abreast of developments within Exeter, the City services were once again re-organised from 9th January, still remaining faithful to their traditional lettered routes (which indeed they do to the present day).

The annual timetable was published on 7th May, and quite a number of service changes took place, though only a very small number of routes were no longer operated.

Six small new single-deck buses were delivered early in the year; they were Bristol 'LH6L' type, with 33-seat Marshall body, and were the last to be delivered in traditional Devon General livery replacing the remaining Albion 'Nimbus' buses 840-843 and 957-959. Also withdrawn during the year were AEC 'Reliances' 793, 799 and 801, AEC 'Regent' V 949 and ex-Exeter Guys 270-274.

Repaints from October 1972 were in the NBC poppy red (lighter and duller than Devon General red), double-deckers being given a red roof and just one white waistband, whereas single-deckers were at first given a not unattractive livery of red with white window surrounds. Devon General fleet-name and NBC logo were carried in large white letters on the side panels towards the front on double-decks, and on the front side roof panel on single-decks. Wheels (not tyres!) were grey. The last buses to be repainted in traditional Devon General style had been short AEC 'Regent' Vs 515-520 and 'Panthers' 214/6. The only former Exeter Corporation buses to have been given traditional Devon General livery were 201-210, 267/276/278/280-286.

Following the adoption of the NBC corporate livery, advertisements started appearing in hitherto unused places on both repainted and un-repainted vehicles, for instance below the windscreen on both single- and double-decks, above the front destination of double-decks, and on the side panels of single-decks, below the windows. All-over advertising first appeared in April, when 'Atlantean' 533 was repainted yellow and covered internally with carpet pieces as an advertisement for 'Richard King' carpets. This was only the first of many advertising buses, usually on two-year contracts.

Mr. D. Dyment was appointed Commercial Advertising Superintendent, and he prepared advertising buses at Newton Road in the ensuing years for the whole of the West of England, brand new buses sometimes being used as the vehicles selected had to be mechanically reliable.

Most double-deckers in the old livery had their Devon General fleet-name transfers painted out and replaced by NBC style lettering. Single-deckers in old livery retained old style fleet-name because the new style would have to go on the roof panels which in many cases were ivory and would have offered no background to the white letters.

Ten Bristol 'SUL4A' buses with Eastern Coachworks 36-seat body were transferred by Western National into the Devon General area fleet, working mainly from Exeter and Newton Abbot. Dating from 1960-1962, they were no great acquisition, their cramped seating and contra gear selection made them unpopular with passengers and drivers alike.

There had for several years been Union objection to one-man operation of single-deckers with more than 41 seats, but these were finally overcome. Modifications carried out to vehicles included removal of the rear route number box, and the change-over of the front display so that the route number was always on the off side and the destination on the nearside. Reversing lights and warning horn were also fitted.

An alarming incident took place on 12th April, when a bus on the Torquay to Exeter service seized-up while descending Telegraph Hill. The gearbox flew up through the floor of the bus and hit the roof, showering the 20 passengers with oil and metal fragments. Nobody was hurt, but the Company had to foot the bill for cleaning the passengers clothing!

1973   A serious accident occurred on 12th January, when AEC 'Regent' 504 ran off the road and overturned into a field at Coombe Cross, Tipton St. John after driver/fitter R. Reed of Sidmouth depot had died at the wheel. It was carrying 62 school-children on their way to Kings School at Ottery St. Mary, though luckily none was seriously hurt, the worst injury being a broken leg. They had to smash their way out of the bus as it came to rest with a tree blocking the emergency door. 504 was repaired and returned to service, after which it could be distinguished from the rest of the series by a different internal finish.

Early in the year, the convertible open-top 'Sea Dog Atlanteans' were repainted in a distinguishing NBC livery of red lower panels, top-deck window surrounds and roof, with everything else white.

The first buses to be delivered new to Devon General in NBC livery were five Bristol/ECW RELLs. They had Exeter's dual door arrangement and mainly worked east from the City.
(the late G.H. Truran/Omnibus Society)

New vehicles allocated by Western National to the area fleet during the year were fourteen more Bristol 'VRs' with Eastern Coachworks 77-seat body, slightly longer than their predecessors, having a more stylish front with wrap-around windscreen. Most initially worked from Torquay, but Exeter and Exmouth also received a few. There were five new Bristol 'RE' 48-seat single-deckers, having ECW body with both front and centre doors; these spent much of their time working from Tiverton.

Three more venerable oddments were also transferred by Western National into the area; a 30-seat Bristol 'SUS' which had already seen service with British European Airways at their Penzance helicopter port and with Greenslades Tours as a feeder bus for their long-distance tours; a 37-seat Bristol 'SUL' with dual-purpose body for contract work, and a 15-year old Bristol 'MW' that had started life as a Royal Blue coach and came already converted for dual-purpose use on a works contract.

Withdrawals consisted of AEC 'Reliances' 824-837 and former City of Exeter 'Titans' 275 and 277.

Principal changes in the 6th May timetable were the re-organisation of the Exmouth local services and for the summer of 1973 and 1974, the Torquay to Newton Abbot section of the busy 12, prone to delays in heavy traffic, was run as a separate service numbered 22.

The subsidiary Company Bute Court Garages Ltd., was wound up during the year, its eight hire cars and one van being sold and the lease of the premises being taken over by Torquay Motors.

1974

The livery that had been applied to single-deck vehicles was not in accordance with the NBC corporate identity manual, and at headquarters insistence, vehicles from early in 1974 were turned out in all-red, apart from a single white waistband which stopped short at the doorway. From the front aspect thus, vehicles appeared entirely red. The full list of those which had received the incorrect styling was 17, 40-44, 49, 54, 59, 68, 70-72, 85, 201-205, 211-213, 215 and 217.

New vehicles allocated to the area fleet were eight Bristol 'LH' 43-seat single-deckers with ECW body, and four Bristol 'REs' with 47-seat Plaxton coach body in dual-purpose livery of red below waistband and white above. These were for the longer 'prestige 'routes such as Torquay-Plymouth and Torquay-Exeter, though it was not unknown for one to turn up on a filling-in duty to Watcombe Estate! The Bristol 'LH' was the replacement for the AEC 'Reliance', though a very uncomfortable substitute.

Withdrawn during the year were the last of the rear-platform AEC 'Regent' Vs (943-948) which had spent most of their life on Exeter city services, and also 'Reliances' 860-866, 870, 951 and 953-956, of which 951 and 955 had only just been repainted in NBC livery! Guy 256 was repainted in City of Exeter green and cream, and attended a few local events and rallies. Late in the year it was put to work on the Watcombe routes in Torquay, where it and its sister 253 became a familiar sight. One or two ex-Exeter double-deckers were drafted into Torquay and Newton Abbot each summer to assist with the holiday traffic.

In December, six Leyland 'Nationals' with front and centre doors were delivered, but none entered service until the new year.

1975

A new depot was built for Western National in Belgrave Road, Exeter which adjoined the bus and coach station, being on the site of a former Co-op distribution depot. Buses parked within a walled compound, with a single entrance and exit into Belgrave Road. The bus washing plant lay parallel to this road, while covered servicing bays and the administration block lay at a slightly higher level, facing in the opposite direction. There was only limited parking space, and much of the Exeter allocation continued to park in the bus and coach stations. The new depot was opened on 20th March by the then Minister of Transport, Mr. F. Mulley. As a direct consequence, Heavitree Road depot was closed on the same day, and was soon cleared out and demolished. Flats were eventually built on the site after several years of desolation.

The narrow Fore Street, St. Marychurch, Torquay was bypassed by a new extension of St. Marychurch Road early in the year, and the services to Watcombe were then able to make a fast detour around this bottleneck. New Leyland 'Nationals' were allocated to these services and the Torquay Inner Circle route, although their centre exit doors were not normally used.

Some curtailment and re-arrangement of services took place in the winter of 1974/5 particularly at Exmouth, and single-manning was introduced on some of the routes worked by the long single-deckers having 49 seats and more.

Complete renumbering of routes in the area took place from 4th May, to give a unified scheme for Western National, Devon General and Plymouth Joint Services. Former Devon General routes were renumbered within the series 100-119 (Paignton and Brixham), 120-161 (Torquay), 173-198 (Newton Abbot and Teignmouth), 330-383 (Exeter and East Devon), though the Exeter city services retained their letters.

Devon County Council published timetables for all independent services in the county; these were numbered in the 600s, and were incorporated in the Devon General area timetable.

New vehicles allocated by Western National to their Devon General area were eight more Bristol 'LH' buses, four more Bristol 'RE' dual-purpose coaches, along with two Bristol 'VR' double-deckers, the latter two not entering service until

1976. Transferred from other areas was one Bristol 'LDL' already converted to open-top and named 'Admiral Boscawen' and seven dual-purpose conversions of Bristol 'MWs' that began their life as Royal Blue coaches. Two Leyland 'Leopards' with 51-seat Marshall bus body came from Gosport & Fareham (Southdown until 1972). All the foregoing received the appropriate variation of NBC poppy red livery. Leyland 'Atlantean' 926 'Sir Francis Drake' was transferred to Western National at Falmouth, while withdrawn and sold were 969-984, the short, front entrance 'Regent' Vs of 1963, and Marshall-bodied 'Reliances' 985-991 of the same vintage. Of these, 969, 974, 976, 979 and 988 had received NBC poppy red livery. Meanwhile, rear-platform double-deckers continued to soldier-on in Exeter.

Bristol 'LHS' number 92 was seriously damaged on 5th June when it went out of control on Jockey Hill, Crediton, whilst on a morning journey from Sandford. It crashed into Palm Cottage, the home of a Mrs. D. Parr, and demolished her conservatory. Driver K. Greenwood of Exeter and one passenger were seriously injured, and another fifteen passengers received hospital treatment. 92 never ran again in the Devon General area, eventually returning to service at Truro, and later at Bridport.

1976

The new annual timetable published on 2nd May covered the whole of Devon and was produced in collaboration with the County Council. It contained quite a number of changes and a sign of the times was that several country routes had been passed over to private firms with lower overheads. Among villages to lose their services from the major Company were Coffinswell, Daccombe, Widecombe, Ideford and Hennock.

In 1976, two of the 1964 front-entrance AEC 'Regent' V 69 seaters were converted to open top primarily for the service between Torquay and Dawlish Warren. 507 was then repainted into an unusual style and named 'Prince Regent'. It awaits its crew outside Newton Road depot.
(Herald Express Newspapers)

Two AEC 'Regent' Vs, 507 and 508 were converted to open-top in March and given the names 'Prince Regent' and 'Regency Princess'. They were intended for a new limited-stop service between Torquay and Dawlish Warren, but in fact saw little use on this service which was normally worked by 'Sea Dog Atlanteans'.

New vehicles for the Devon General area this year were two more Leyland 'Nationals' (with front door only) and seven more Bristol 'VRs'. Second-hand vehicles were four Leyland 'Leopards' from Southdown and two short front-entrance Bristol 'Lodekkas' of the 'FSF' type which came from Western National but originated with Bristol Omnibus Company. These two went on to the Exeter to Newton Abbot via the coast services, all were repainted in NBC red livery, but none lasted in the area for very long.

Withdrawals from the area fleet were the Bristol 'SUSs' and 'SULs' that came from Western National in 1972, plus one Bristol 'MW'. AEC 'Reliances' 867, 868, 871, 950 and 952, all by then in NBC red, were also withdrawn. 'Reliances' 12-17 were transferred to Cornwall early in the year, followed by two Bristol 'VRs' in June and 'Reliances' 18-23 in September. Some of these were repainted green with Western National fleet-name. 16 had been repainted red in February in another variation of the corporate livery, with the white band continuing around the front of the vehicle at a lower level, this style later becoming standard.

Towards the end of the year, all un-rebuilt Roe-bodied 'Atlanteans' were taken off the road and put into store at Torquay. Over the next few years, some were completely rebuilt and returned to service, but some never ran again. By the end of 1976, no buses remained in service in Devon in the old traditional Devon General colours, although a few saloons lingered on in Cornwall.

1977   The annual timetable was published on 22nd May, and contained few major changes; noteworthy was the withdrawal of services to the villages of Puddington and Pennymoor, which were taken over by a private operator, and the introduction of a new local service in Brixham, serving the Summercombe Estate, for which Western National acquired two Ford/Alexander 'midi-buses'.

New vehicles for the area in 1977 were eight Bristol 'LHs' with Plaxton dual-purpose body but used mainly on stage services such as the lengthy Newton Abbot to Okehampton route. Six more standard Bristol 'LHs' with Eastern Coach Works bus bodywork followed, and then five more Leyland 'Nationals' for the Exeter to Tiverton services. Late in the year came nine ECW built Bristol 'VRs' with convertible open-top. Five entered service at Torquay in November with their tops on, and the rest came on the road in the new year. They were numbered 934-942 (following on from the 'Sea Dog Atlanteans') and were in the white and red livery introduced in 1973 being named after famous warships:

934 Golden Hind,	937 Victory,	940 Invincible,
935 Triumph,	938 Warspite,	941 Illustrious,
936 Revenge,	939 Renown,	942 Hermes.

Western National obtained a large number of second-hand 'Atlantean' buses from Maidstone & District, Hants & Dorset and other companies for service in Cornwall, but one of these found its way straight into the Devon General area fleet for use in Exeter. 'Sea Dog Atlantean' 925 'Admiral Blake' was transferred to Cornwall, and the Devon area received Bristol 'LDL' converted open-top 'Sir Humphrey Davy' in exchange. Most of the second-hand Leyland 'Leopards' were transferred away. A Ford 'Transit' minibus came into the area in connection with a 'Community Bus' experiment in the Exe Valley, and another much-travelled Transit, Western National No:1 was also used in the Devon General area for a time.

Two Bristol 'VR' double-deckers were painted silver and blue and lettered appropriately to commemorate the Queen's Silver Jubilee. They circulated around the West of England and generated numerous short-term transfers to the Devon General area in the same way that the advertising buses were doing.

'Reliances' 18-23 returned to the Devon General area from Cornwall in February and one of these, 21, was the very last bus to run in the old Devon General colours, by then very battered and scruffy. It ran in Torquay for a few days before being re-panelled and repainted into NBC red, only for the whole batch to be sold during July and August! Also withdrawn were AEC 'Regent' Vs, 509, 515 and 516, plus 'Reliance' 52 which was scrapped at Plymouth following an accident at Halfway House on the Exeter-Sidmouth service. Six of the Bristol 'MW' dual-purpose 'imports' were returned to Western National for disposal, and finally, late in the year, 'Reliance' 12, always reckoned to be a 'flyer', returned from Cornwall.

1978   Greenslades Tours operations from Torquay, Teignmouth, Totnes, Newton Abbot and Plymouth were transferred to Western National from 16th April, and Torwood Street garage at Torquay closed on the same day. The booking office remained open for the time being, but the Torquay based vehicles were transferred to the Devon General area fleet at Newton Road depot. None of the coaches transferred to Greenslades from Grey Cars in 1971 remained in the fleet by that time. Taken over from Greenslades were one Bedford 'VAS' 29-seater, six narrow Plaxton bodied Bristol 'LHs' for moorland tours, and five Bedford Duple 'YRT' 53-seaters. All were in white NBC coach livery.

Thus it was that Devon General once again operated local tours from Torquay and also supplied coaches for National

Express services. Some drivers who had transferred to Greenslades with Grey Cars in 1971 came back to Torquay and drove buses in the winter, whereas others opted to stay with Greenslades, by then under the control of the NBC coaching arm, National Travel (South West) Ltd., even though this meant travelling to and from Exeter every day for duty.

From the 21st May timetable, many changes took place to the routes serving Tiverton and Cullompton; services running up the Exe Valley were terminated at Tiverton, with points beyond such as Sampford Peverell and Holcombe Rogus being served by extensions of routes running via Cullompton, which were to loop back into Tiverton. Services to Stoodleigh and to Rackenford were withdrawn, being replaced by the 'Exe Valley Market Bus', the first minibus being supplied by the Department of the Environment and maintained by Western National, which also trained the volunteer drivers.

At Torquay, existing services were extended and linked to form a Strand-Lower Chelston-Shiphay-Hele-Strand circular, worked by Leyland 'National' buses, as two low bridges limited the route to single-deck.

A new city circular was provided in Exeter, primarily to serve the Royal Devon & Exeter Hospital, and the two midi-buses from Brixham were transferred to work it along with two shortened Fords from Midland Red. Exmouth local services were extended from Withycombe to serve new housing at Bystock.

One of the very successful number of all-over advertising buses turned out in the 1970s. Bristol VR number 1117 was in a black and gold livery for John Hill.
(L.F.Folkard)

New vehicles supplied to the Devon General area during the year were all further deliveries of existing types: four Bristol Plaxton 'LH' dual-purpose coaches, seven Bristol/ECW 'LH' buses, and twelve Bristol/ECW 'VR' double-deckers. Two of the VRs were delivered painted all-black; this was a base for all-over adverts for 'John Hill' the house of 1,000 lights. The lettering was applied in gold, and looked very smart. Two other 'VRs' were similarly treated for Western National and one for Hants & Dorset, and at one point, four of them were in Devon General territory at the same time.

Another eight Leyland 'Nationals' were put into service mainly at Torquay and Brixham. One was for the summer 'Park and Ride' scheme at Brixham, where cars parked in a field at Churston, about two miles away. This facility continued in subsequent summers. A former Royal Blue coach replaced the last Bristol 'MW' on contract work, the newcomer being a Bristol/Duple 'RE'.

A large number of former Devon General buses were transferred to other areas: 'Sea-Dog Atlantean' 927 (Sir Martin

Frobisher) was transferred to Weymouth, where it was renamed 'Admiral Hardy'. AEC 'Reliances' 40-44 were repainted NBC corporate (leaf) green with Western National fleet-name and transferred to Somerset and Dorset, as was 'Reliance' 12 which had already seen service in Cornwall. These transfers took place in June, while in October, 9-11 were transferred to Somerset & Dorset (just having been repainted red!) and 55-63 to Cornwall, of which some at least later became green. Probably the most unusual transfer was 'Atlantean' 900 to Helston. It was repainted in a simple chocolate and cream livery to commemorate the 75th anniversary of the first Great Western Railway bus service, which ran from Helston to The Lizard. It worked the rest of its days in these colours, but actually was not a very good choice for the Lizard service. The Roe-bodied 'Atlantean' was among the highest buses in the fleet, and much damage was done to the roof and even windows, by low trees along the route.

Withdrawals from the area fleet were ex-City of Exeter Leyland 'PD2s' 276, 278, 295-299 and AEC 'Regent' Vs 517-522, 524 and 525, as well as open-top 507 and 508, the two Bristol 'LDL' open-tops ex-Cornwall, and the two Bristol 'FSFs'. The open-top buses were sold for further use. The use of a 'Sea Dog Atlantean' in open top form gradually became rarer, and some were converted to one-person operation. The 'Warship' class, unlike the 'Sea Dogs' did not have interchangeable tops, and so each top carried its fleet number in small figures.

A new type of ticket-issuing machine was fitted to vehicles in the Torquay area - this was the 'Almex', of Swedish design, which dispensed small flimsy tickets, entirely printed by the machine. The Company name appeared as Western National, and these tickets were never issued carrying the Devon General name.

1979

The annual timetable commencing 20th May was another bumper edition, produced in conjunction with Devon County Council, giving details of all bus services within the county, and also ferries, railway services to and within Devon (including the preserved lines), the cliff railways at Lynton and Babbacombe, express coach services provided by National Express, Scottish Omnibuses, Western SMT, Wallace Arnold and Yelloways (to and from Devon), and even the Seaton Tramway. Air services from Exeter and Plymouth were also included, as well as an insert bus map. There were town maps of the principal centres, and all this for only 30p.

The parcels service had not been mentioned for some years, but was still in operation at this time, minimum charge for weight not exceeding 4lbs was 25p, and maximum weight, by then reduced to 42lb, was 65p for any distance within the network served by Devon General and Western National. Newsprint went for considerably less. All this information was included.

'One-person' services (there were by this time some lady drivers) were no longer shown as such in the timetable, the only crew-operated services by this time being some of the Exeter city routes, the Buckland group at Newton Abbot, the Newton Abbot-Torquay-Brixham 12, some of the Torquay local services in summer, and (not for much longer) Exeter to Newton Abbot via the Coast.

During the spring and summer, the National Bus Company carried out a countrywide Market Analysis Project (MAP) to survey bus usage. Two surveyors rode on each bus sampled, one counting the number of persons boarding and alighting and also stop-watching the time the bus passed certain stops. The other surveyor handed out and collected 'on-bus' survey forms from passengers. The project leader for the south-west was Mr. R. C. Anderson F.C.I.T.

New vehicles during 1979 were seven narrow Bristol/Plaxton 'LHs' with dual-purpose body. These replaced the similar vehicles that had come from Greenslades Tours, which in turn were transferred to other areas for use as buses.

Withdrawn vehicles were 'Reliances' 40-44 which finished their days away from the Devon General area, plus former Exeter City 'Leopards' 201-205 and 'Titans' 260, 279-284. The last short 'Regent' V, 523, was also withdrawn.

Two of the 'Sea Dog Atlantean' buses, 931 and 933, lost their name and had their top re-fitted permanently. They were repainted in a new livery with lower-deck all red, upper-deck front, side, and rear panels - all white, with top-deck window surrounds and roof being red. They carried all-round adverts on the white areas for a local window firm, which was so pleased with the results that they later contracted for all-over advertising buses. The new livery was known as 'Unibus'.

Complete overhaul and conversion to 'driver-only' of the stored 'Atlanteans' continued, and in October, 920 and 921 were overhauled, painted green, and sent to Cornwall with Western National fleet-name. Then came the announcement, not entirely unexpected, that Devon General NBC 'poppy' red livery was to be discontinued (apart from open-top buses) and that all future repaints would be in NBC leaf green, and lettered as Western National. The Devon General area would in future be known as the Torbay & Exeter area. However, repaints from December again carried the Devon General name, albeit on green buses. A half-hearted attempt was made to fit Western National-style fleet-number plates to buses which still carried transfer numbers.

1980

This was the year of the holocaust for former Devon General vehicles. By the end of the year, only Leyland 'Atlanteans' remained in service out of the vehicles which had passed to Western National ownership on 1st January 1971. Thirty-one new Bristol 'VRs' were allocated to the Torbay & Exeter area, plus three Leyland 'Nationals' of an improved design. Three small Bristol 'LHS' ECW buses were funded by Devon County Council on condition that they remained in Devon. Thirteen new Leyland 'Leopard' coaches were allocated to the area, initially for National Express services.

From the end of February, the Exeter-Newton Abbot (via the coast) services went over to driver-only, with Bristol 'VRs' replacing the ten remaining AEC 'Regent' Vs, whose last runs were patronised by a large number of enthusiasts. This then really was the end of an era, for AEC double-deckers had been in the fleet since 1919. Some 'Regents' remained licensed for a few more months, but had no regular duties after that. The very last one to run in revenue service was 513, being withdrawn from Exeter on 31st October. Their AEC compatriots, the 'Reliances', were all taken out of service with what seemed indecent haste; 64-67 and 82-87 briefly served first in other Western National areas, and some were even loaned to South Wales Transport Co. Ltd. After July, only four were running in the Devon General area, and all of these were taken out of service at Exeter on 30th November.

The remaining City of Exeter vehicles fared no better; 'Panthers' 206-210 were sold to dealers, 217 was converted to a mobile exhibition vehicle, and 221 was scrapped after an accident. 211 and 216 were also involved in minor accidents and although repairs were started, they were never finished. By September only three 'Panthers' were in service, and only one (213) had received NBC green livery. All were out of traffic by the end of the year and disposed of in 1981. All the remaining City of Exeter double-deckers were withdrawn during the year comprising Guys 253 and 256, and Leyland 'Titans' 285-294. The last of these open-platform buses ran on services A, F and D on 30th August.

A number of 'Atlanteans' which had lain out of use at Torquay since the end of 1976 awaiting possible rebuilding, were in fact then scrapped - the last one to be rebuilt was 909, turned out in May in green 'Unibus' livery. 895 was started but never completed, and the call never came for 902, 903, 910, 914, 917 and 922 so they were all scrapped. 'Sea Dog' 932 lost its name and was repainted in red 'Unibus' livery but surprisingly, never had its front end altered, the prime reason for it being selected for later preservation.

A large concentration yard for withdrawn vehicles was set up on a site at the east end of Exeter Airport, and over 100 buses were parked there before being disposed of. Torquay and Sidmouth depot yards, and the site of the former power station at Newton Abbot were also used for the storage of withdrawn vehicles pending disposal. The buses were kept in hand because there had been concerns regarding possible delays in new deliveries.

Quite apart from the new vehicles already mentioned, numerous transfers from other areas of Western National took place during the year, and some of the vehicles sent in did not stay very long. Noteworthy was the transfer of four ageing Bristol 'FLFs' to Sidmouth, which took over some school duties from Seaton on closure of that Western National depot.

British Rail redeveloped their Exmouth station area, a single dead-end track being all that remained. The imposing station building was demolished and replaced by a much smaller structure. An extension of Imperial Road along former railway land provided a relief road to part of the town centre. At the same time, Exmouth bus depot was demolished and replaced by a small bus station and servicing depot within a walled compound.

On 4th October, 'Atlantean' 879 was stolen from the bus park at Newton Abbot and driven at high speed up the A380 and M5, causing damage to several vehicles in its wake. It was eventually stopped near Cullompton by six police cars and the culprit apprehended. 879, which had not long been back in service after a head-on collision in Exeter High Street, was once again repaired for a few more months service.

The timetable dated 18th May was the last one to be published in the excellent comprehensive all-county format, and produced few significant changes as far as the Torbay & Exeter area was concerned. However, the day of reckoning was approaching, and in the light of the marketing analysis project (MAP) recommendations, together with a continuing decline in traffic receipts, drastic cuts in services were made from 30th November. Many country services and little-used town services were withdrawn without replacement, evening and Sunday services ceased on all but the most important routes and a number of town and city services were re-organised. A completely new timetable was published for the Exeter area from 30th November. Torquay area changes were dealt with by means of a bulky amendment leaflet, but for 1981/2/3, separate timetables were produced for Torbay area and Exeter area.

Paignton local services were logically integrated with those operated from Western National Totnes depot (which ironically closed soon after) as routes 100 to 104, and these became the subject of frequent changes. The villages of Compton and Galmpton had their services from Paignton withdrawn. In Torquay, three meandering 'circular' routes served the more populated areas on Sundays and evenings in the winter to replace services withdrawn entirely; Newton Abbot area saw comparatively few changes, but many long-established services in East Devon ceased.

Others were drastically re-organised, with villages such as Brampford Speke, Raddon Cross, Shobrooke, Morchard Bishop, Thelbridge, Black Dog, Witheridge, Withleigh, Cruwys Morchard, Nomansland, Sandford, New Buildings, Poltimore, Ide, Dunchideock, Kentisbeare, Broadhembury, Awliscombe, Plymtree, Clyst Hydon, Talaton and Gittisham, all losing their services altogether. All the foregoing service cuts and alterations had the effect of making about 20% of the drivers redundant.

1981 Another twenty-one Bristol 'VR' double-deckers went into service from new, and among buses transferred into the area were five Leyland 'Atlanteans' with Alexander low-height bodies. These had been new in 1971 to Western Welsh, but since 1972 had run for Western National based at Callington until that depot closed in 1980. They were transferred to Newton Abbot, where they stayed for the rest of their service. Most of the transfers to the Torquay and Exeter area were however more Bristol 'VR' double-deckers and Bristol 'RE' saloons.

More of the 'Atlantean' type withdrawn early in the year were 873, 875-879, 884-888, 898, 899, 900, 901, 905, 906, 908, 911, 912, 916, 923 and 924, most of which were sold for scrap, even though some had only been rebuilt in the past two or three years. Four more, 896, 904, 919 and 933 came off service at the end of 1981 and were sold in the new year, 933 seeing further service on London open-top sightseeing tours.

Accidents will happen! 'Atlantean' 541 was well loaded with school-children when its driver attempted to take it under Sharon House railway bridge in Torquay, only ever on the single-deck route from Chelston. It was in June 1981 and remarkably no one was badly hurt. 541 was repaired using a roof robbed from one of the convertible 'Atlanteans'. (Herald Express Newspapers)

On 23rd June, 'Atlantean' 541 was driven under the very low bridge in Old Mill Road, Torquay with a full load of schoolchildren. Fortunately they were alerted to the danger and there were no casualties. 541 received a replacement top-deck that had come off 933, and was back in service in July.

A sad departure from Torquay depot on 4th September was that of the Company's last AEC bus, 'Reliance' 76, which had lain there since withdrawal at the end of 1980. Its engine was 'suspect', so the last spare AEC505 engine on the premises was fitted. A second-hand gear stick had to be obtained from the Midlands, and 76 was then ready to leave for the last time. This was not quite the end of the story however, for she was last heard of as having been converted to a mobile fish and chip van in Kent! Sic Transit Gloria.

Advertisements appeared on the top-deck sides of the open-top buses for the first time in 1981, the Company's in-house features being advertised, such as National Holidays or concession tickets. The open-top services however were not immune to rationalisation, as the Kingswear service became routed via Brixham, and the service to Brixham (only) was withdrawn.

Evening and Sunday buses reappeared for the summer on some services, and the three Torquay evening and Sunday circular services ceased for the summer, but just two of them where re-introduced in the autumn.

Another of the services that ceased at the end of November 1980 was revived; this was the Sidmouth to Honiton rail link, which was renewed by the expedient of extending on to Honiton, some journeys on the Sidmouth-Sidford service.

In May 1981, the Exeter-based operations of National Travel (South West) were transferred to the Torbay & Exeter area of Western National, together with their 1961-built garage at Willeys Avenue. The Greenslades fleet-name was retained however.

1982

The Western National depot at Totnes closed in January, and its workings on the Paignton local services and between Paignton and Totnes were taken over by Torquay depot, which received some of the buses from Totnes.

Services in the whole of the Exeter-Newton Abbot-Totnes-Buckfastleigh-Plymouth 'corridor' were drastically re-organised, through the introduction of a range of 'South Devon Express' services worked by Leyland 'Leopard' coaches. These displayed a distinguishing livery of white with 'speed lines' at the front end. Some of these services were quite short-lived, with only the Torquay-Plymouth and Exeter-Plymouth services standing the test of time.

Summer services to Dartmoor were tried again from Torquay and Newton Abbot to Widecombe and beyond, with some journeys worked in part by local operators Beard's or Wood Bros. This concept was considerably developed a few years later.

The pattern of the services to Okehampton from Exeter and from Newton Abbot were also altered considerably, that from Newton Abbot being terminated at Chagford where for a time, connection was made with a service from Exeter.

Only one open-top service ran in the summer, this being from Babbacombe to Brixham via Torquay and Paignton, though it no longer went under the low bridge in Seaway Road so missed Paignton sea front altogether. Thus, open-top services to Paignton Zoo, Kingswear and Dawlish Warren all ceased.

A rail strike in July caused large numbers of extra coaches and double-deck buses to be used on inter-city services. Some double-deckers from South Devon ran as far as Birmingham.

The remaining 1959 'Atlantean' buses 872, 874, 880-883 were taken out of service during the year, as were Roe-bodied 897, 918 and 921 along with open-top buses 926 and 927. The latter two had been used in Cornwall and Dorset, and were sold for further use. Bristol 'VR Warship' open-tops were sent to replace them. Late in the year, 'Atlantean' 537 was sold direct into preservation. The only original Devon General vehicles then remaining in the fleet, all 'Atlanteans', were 526-536, 538-541, 909, 915, 928-930 and 932.

Also transferred out of the area were fourteen Bristol 'LH' buses, four Bristol 'RE' coaches, and two Leyland 'National' saloons. Bristol 'RE' bus 225 was modified to carry 27 disabled persons. Double-deckers received to replace the 'Atlanteans' were eleven Bristol 'VRs' which were second-hand from City of Oxford, West Riding and United Auto.

Towards the end of the year came the announcement that, in accordance with National Bus Company policy, Western National Omnibus Co. Ltd., was to be re-organised and split into four separate operating companies:

Western National Ltd.,	- to serve Cornwall, Plymouth district and South Hams,
Southern National Ltd.,	- to serve Somerset and Dorset,
Devon General Ltd.,	- to serve South and East Devon,
North Devon Ltd.,	- to serve North Devon.

Maintenance was to be carried out by a Company to be known as Herald Engineering Ltd., which would also set out to attract business from the private sector. Thus, at the eleventh hour, with only a few vehicles left of the former Devon General Omnibus & Touring Co. Ltd., fleet, and most vehicles in the area now in green livery, Devon General was re-born, together with the remnants of the Greenslades Tours operation. With all the recent route closures and alterations to services, it might have been thought that some stability had come to the network, but in the light of subsequent events, this turned out not to be the case, but that is another fascinating story.

Section 14. Depots and bus stations

1. TORQUAY (NEWTON ROAD)

A freehold site for a new garage and works was purchased in April 1930 from Mr. Ben Stedham, one of the Directors. It was situated in Newton Road, Torquay, opposite the Great Western Railway line, and between Old Woods Hill and Hele Road, about two miles from Torquay Strand. The purchase price was £4466.00.

Tenders were invited for the construction of garage, workshops and offices; the contract for the steelwork was awarded to the Lambhill Ironworks of Glasgow, and a local firm, P. W. Wilkins & Son Ltd., secured the building contract. Construction took place during 1931/2, the total cost being £27,808. By September 1931, the garage was complete enough for the Company to be able to transfer its Torquay bus allocation from Westhill Avenue (St. Marychurch) and that depot closed on 24th September. The Fleet Cars depot at Orient Road, Paignton closed on 1st March 1932, and the 21 Fleet Cars for a time also garaged at Newton Road, using the corner at the Lawes Bridge end, before moving to the Grey Cars garage at Torwood Street.

A recreation room and canteen were built alongside the garage at the Torquay end in 1932/3, and during October 1933, the Company's offices moved from Blackboy Road, Exeter into the new premises at the front of the depot in Torquay. The workshops at Torquay were brought into full operation during that year, and with a garage capacity of 85 vehicles, the Company was now ready to receive the fleet of 24 diesel-engined double-decker buses which were to replace the Torquay trams in January 1934.

By 1939, it was apparent that the office accommodation was inadequate, and the block was extended at both ends up to the two front entrances to the garage. The work was done during the winter of 1939/40 by R. E. Narracott & Sons Ltd., of Torquay. The extensions blended perfectly with the original building.

The total area of the buildings was then 7,085 sq. yards, of which the garage, which had no internal roof supports at all, accounted for 4,420 sq. yards.

64 vehicles operated from Torquay in the winter of 1938/9, and by the summer of 1939, the allocation had risen to 98.

Additional plots of land on the Torquay side of the depot (lying behind the Devon Laundry) were purchased in March 1941, December 1942 and August 1943. A parking ground was established on this land, most of which was given a hardcore surface. A new entrance from Newton Road to this land was formed; access was via an un-surfaced road formed between house numbers 67 and 69 Newton Road. This was very rough and dusty and soon became known as the 'Burma Road'. In October 1941, two houses 'Marietta' and 'Oakville' (83 and 85 Newton Road) were purchased for key staff. These lay between the garage and the laundry. The Devon General premises themselves became numbered 87 Newton Road, and appropriate brass numerals were affixed to the main entrance door to the offices. Just before the war, two flag-staffs had been erected outside the building.

Ancillary buildings added during the war years included engineers' offices inside the garage, and a uniform store (which was at first in an air raid shelter in the yard). In 1949, a new canteen was built by the south-west corner of the depot, and a tyre store was formed at the rear of the social club.

The development of the site, which then comprised 20,722 sq. yards, or over four acres, was then practically complete.

Fuel storage for 15,000 gallons was provided in four underground tanks, but by 1948 it was found that two had rusted through, and so three new over-ground tanks were erected, one by each entrance to the garage, which brought the storage capacity up to 21,000 gallons.

In 1952, an 'Essex' bus washing machine was installed. This was in effect, a frame that was lowered down over a bus, first to wash it, and secondly to wipe it with rotating brushes. It was suspended from the garage roof, and took up quite a lot of parking space. There were also several instances of buses being driven in and out before the machine was clear of them!

The garage itself was built with two double-width entrance doors facing out on to Newton Road, with another set at each side of the garage at the ends. Those at the south (Torquay) end were regularly used for access to the yard at the side, but those at the north end were never used, for that end of the garage saw no further adjacent development, and eventually a road (Woodland Road) was formed past it to give access to the Woodlands Trading Estate which was built on the site of the Old Woods Brickworks which used to occupy the land. The garage floor was uninterrupted by supporting pillars, and was cleaned by a mechanical truck.

Seven T-headed inspection pits were provided, three for use by central workshops for docking and overhaul, and four for use by the garage staff for running repairs. The pit area was modernised in 1959/60.

The various shops were separated from the garage by a continuous row of sliding steel doors of double-deck height which ran across the whole width of the garage. The de-greasing shop adjoined the overhaul pits. It was equipped with an ICI Trichlorethylene plant and streamline filter, and had an area of 384 sq. feet. The Unit Bench, Machine shop, and Engine shop were not physically divided from each other; their total area was 3,689 sq. feet. The Unit Bench dealt with the overhaul and repair of chassis units with the exception of the engine. The main units dealt with were gearbox, differential, front axle, steering box, and brake components.

The Machine shop dealt with reclaimation of chassis components, re-sleeving and boring of cylinders, line boring of bearings and re-seating of cylinder heads, etc. The machinery included two lathes, radial drill, shaping machine, main-bearing line boring machine, connecting-rod boring machine, Paddon cylinder boring machine, Snow surface grinder and a power press. The Engine shop rebuilt ten engines a month.

The Blacksmith's Shop, with an area of 258 sq. feet dealt with road spring repairs and general smithing, but latterly spring repairs were contracted out and very little general smithing was done here. The Tinsmith's shop with 409 sq. feet repaired radiators, exhaust pipes, etc., and overhauled ticket machines.

The Electrician shop, actually three separate shops of 287, 103 and 172 sq. feet, overhauled and repaired electrical components and charged batteries.

The Welding shop, with 198 sq. feet, housed acetylene and electric welding equipment, and also had a gas-fired furnace for pre-heating.

The Fuel Injection shop, also 198 sq. feet, serviced and overhauled fuel pumps and injectors. The latter were changed every 5,000 miles at home depots. The shop was rebuilt in 1959 and a Hartridge fuel pump testing machine was installed.

The Stores ran the full length of the garage, behind the shops, and had an area of 8,698 sq. feet. The 'Stormor' system of metal storage bins was employed. Some items were supplied to other depots on an impress basis at weekly intervals.

The Engineering Records office, the Chief Engineer's office (on two floors) and the Body Superintendent's office are self explanatory.

The Body shop at 3,884 sq. feet gave both routine maintenance and complete body overhauls, together with accident repairs. Until the 1950s it was geared to composite framed, alloy panelled bodies, but the coming of metal framed bodies and fibre-glass panels led to a revision of techniques and new equipment. Traditionally, the principal machines were a band saw, circular saw, planer, spindle moulder and mortising machine. All framing and panel work could normally be done here, and some very extensive rebuilds which really amounted to re-bodying were carried out here. The only parts bought in were proprietory items such as window frames, ventilators, handrail assemblies, etc. plus an occasional domed panel where the original was beyond beating out. Later, snap-rivetting and fibre-glass moulding and repairs became the order of the day with roof domes still being bought in. The Body shop had a capacity of three vehicles, or four at a squeeze. A major rebuilding job could take a couple of months, and often did.

Within the Body shop was the Trimmers shop for maintenance of upholstery and re-trimming, and the ticket machine section (repairs and maintenance of TIM and 'Setright' machines). Originally the Trimmers shop, later became the Tyre shop, when it was not used directly by Devon General. Tyres were supplied and fitted under contract by one of the major tyre firms, and their men operated in this shop, which had an area of 950 sq. feet. It was later taken in to the Paint Shop, giving them extra capacity of one more vehicle.

The Paint shop with an area of 2,639 sq. feet turned out three fully repainted vehicles each week. All were hand-painted, after having had all dents and scratches filled and smoothed. After priming (on new panels), two coats of undercoat were normally applied, followed by one of gloss, after which the transfers were applied, the vehicle finally being given a coat of clear varnish.

Next on the tour around the depot, come the most un-glamourous of the various shops and offices; the boiler house which later became the uniform store, the mess room, later the fibre-glass shop and the Mens lavatory with areas of 290, 500 and 370 sq. feet respectively.

By the south entrance were situated the transformer house, the Ladies' lavatory and the oil and grease store, with respective areas of 140, 103 and 132 square feet, and the Running Shift office.

A hydraulic ramp and steam-cleaning plant were installed adjacent to the outside wall of the boiler house in 1954, when a reorganization of the workshops was carried out.

During 1961 a washing plant and two-bay fuelling point with three overhead fuel tanks were built on the Company's land at the rear of the Devon Laundry, and the former 'Burma Road', which was then surfaced in concrete, became the entrance for all vehicles coming in to the depot. Having fuelled and passed through the washer, they entered the depot through the side door opposite the social club. The south door was from then on, used for outward vehicles only, and the north door was rarely used again for vehicle movements. The mechanism for raising and lowering the old bus washer inside the garage found a new use; lifting the tops off the 'Sea Dog' Atlanteans and their successors, and lowering them on to the mobile storage racks.

After the opening of the new fueller/washer, the original uniform store was rather in the way of vehicle movements, and it was not many years later before it was demolished.

Much of the yard at the side of the depot was by then surfaced, and used to a growing extent for the parking of drivers' private cars. A lot of buses, particularly delicensed ones, were stored here and until the end of Devon General's separate existence in 1971, this was the concentration yard for all vehicles prior to sale. A few were cut-up here, though any signs of untoward activity of this nature would bring forth protests from nearby residents whose premises backed onto this area.

After Western National took over in 1971, the depot gradually lost its importance, though improvements were carried out to the pits in winter 1971/2 when they were enclosed by a new flank wall and sliding doors. A suspended ceiling was installed, and an air heater and exhaust extractor made working conditions more bearable and acceptable.

Much of the maintenance work, both chassis and body, was then sent to Laira Bridge (Plymouth) or further afield. Most of the clerical functions were transferred to National House, Exeter, and when the new Exeter depot and offices opened in 1975, they took more work away from Torquay.

A subsidiary Company, Herald Engineering Ltd., was formed by Western National to service the vehicles of its subsidiary companies and others, and all the workshop staff at Newton Road became employed by them. However, late in 1983 they ceased operations, and maintenance work at Torquay was carried out direct by the newly-formed Devon General Ltd.

In July 1985, it was announced that 'Asda' had expressed interest in acquiring the garage site for the construction of a superstore, but Devon General Ltd., was not at that time prepared to consider selling it. However, planning permission was sought by the Company (initially refused) for a new depot on the land which it owned at the rear of 61-73 Newton Road. The Company, during 1986, agreed in principle to sell the premises subject to the necessary planning permissions being obtained.
Alterations to the offices in March 1986 to accommodate the Bayline minibus administration seemed to indicate that no imminent disposal of the premises was likely and much of the under-utilised office space was brought back into use with the whole place being smartened up. The house 'Oakville' 85 Newton Road (next door to the depot) became mess accommodation for the minibus crews, while the front of the depot and offices displayed the new-style fleet-name a few days after the Company was privatised on 19th August 1986.

Interest in the sale of the depot was revived early in 1988; though local planners did not favour the site for a superstore. This did not deter developers from expressing their interest in acquiring the site especially as local planning decisions at the time were being seemingly almost invariably overturned on appeal. Devon General was now keen to sell, and announced plans to vacate the site.

On 20th March, the Bayline minibus unit moved to a new headquarters at Paignton bus station, where a small servicing bay had been built. The remaining minibuses for the 12 service and the few remaining 'big buses' were sent to Newton Abbot on 17th April, leaving only the workshops functioning at Newton Road, with a handful of staff in the offices, part of which had already been let out. A few buses were kept on the premises awaiting repair, and a few new minibuses were stored there. The workshops were rapidly run down, and the depot and offices closed from 2nd August 1988. The remaining equipment, machinery, office furniture, two former 'Regent' chassis used for the storage of removable top-decks, 300 ticket machines and all sorts of odds and ends were sold by public auction, on site, on 6th September by Messrs. Husseys of Exeter. Van C656 FFJ was still in the paint shop in several pieces, and the auction went on around it!

The last bus to be painted at Newton Road had been 1178, and one of the last to leave the premises was the accident-damaged 1230, which was towed away on 6th August.

Grey Cars continued to use their office, store and parking space until the end of September, and the canteen, social club and toilets remained open for a little longer, with a few minibuses parking outside during drivers' breaks. The depot remained empty and 'for sale' throughout 1989. Asda was interested in the site but was unable to obtain planning permission for a large superstore. The depot was eventually sold in 1990 to Great Mills plc, and that October, the roof was taken off and the two adjacent houses were demolished.

In February 1991 the depot, offices and social club were demolished. The site was soon occupied by itinerant caravan dwellers, but Devon General Ltd., which retained ownership of part of the land constructed a new minibus depot on it which opened in April 1992.

The outside stone wall along the front of the depot remains, but the vehicle entrance and exit are now filled in by almost-matching stone wall, but to a lower height, and so can easily be identified. The site is currently a Focus DIY store.

1. TORQUAY (WESTHILL AVENUE)

This depot, also known as Plainmoor or St. Marychurch, was built to house the buses of the Torquay Tramways Co. Ltd., during 1921 on a 60' x 300' site owned by Torquay Corporation, and adjoining the tram depot. It was constructed of steel-girder framing with corrugated iron cladding and was still under construction on 3rd June 1921, when a petrol storage tank exploded, destroying one bus and a brand new charabanc, as well as severely damaging the tram depot.

Under the terms of an Agreement dated 16th November 1922 (but retrospectively effective from 1st June 1922), the depot was sold to the Devon General Omnibus & Touring Co. Ltd., following the Company's acquisition of the motor bus undertaking of the Tramways Company.

The Tramways bus fleet at its maximum extent had been 36 vehicles (6 double-deck, 17 single-deck and 13 charabancs) but the newest twelve were delivered only a few days before Company reorganisation, and some went virtually from new to Devon General depots. At the end of 1922, some 24 vehicles were based at Torquay, there being 24 licensed drivers and 21 conductors.

Following the acquisition of Fleet Cars Ltd., in December 1924, Devon General's charabanc operations in the area were carried on under the name of Fleet Cars; this side of the business expanded, and in May 1925, a separate depot at Preston, Paignton, was purchased for Fleet Cars, some of the Devon General drivers transferring.

Fleet Cars vehicles however returned to Westhill Avenue for major overhauls. A few Devon General charabancs remained at Torquay as traffic spares, summer services, and private hire, but most were transferred away.

The depot allocation built up again as local bus services were established in the area, and a driver who joined the Company in 1928 recalled that there were nineteen drivers there at the time. That was the year in which limited stop services were introduced and proved very successful; additional new and larger vehicles being purchased, and it could be foreseen that, a few years hence, accommodation would have to be found for the successors to the trams, whether bus or trolleybus being at that time, uncertain.

The tramway offices were not included in the lease to Devon General, and wooden sheds and railway carriage bodies served as their depot offices and stores, the body from bus 42 being later added as a crew room.

In 1928, the tramway offices were extended for the use of Devon General, the work being carried out by P. W. Wilkins & Co. Ltd. A 30-cwt floor crane was installed at the depot in November 1928.

In April 1930, a large site at Newton Road was purchased for the construction of a new garage, workshops and offices, which were to be the Company's operational headquarters, and by September 1931, it's construction was far enough advanced for the Company to be able to vacate the Westhill Avenue premises. By then, about 60 traffic staff (inspectors, drivers and conductors) were based there.

The trams finished in January 1934, and apart from twelve sold to Plymouth, all were broken up at the depot. Torquay Tramways Co. Ltd., went into voluntary liquidation on 19th April 1934, and agreement was reached on 13th July between the liquidators, Devon General and Torquay Corporation, that the latter would purchase the bus and tram depots and offices, the Tramway Company's six houses and its Babbacombe Cliff Railway, all for the sum of £10,000. The transaction was completed on 13th March 1935.

The former bus garage became a depot for the Council's fleet of 36 or so refuse vehicles, lorries, tower wagons and gully emptiers, while the tram depot was partitioned-off for use as workshops. The premises changed little in the next half-century, but in 1992 planning permission was obtained for social housing on the site.

The depot and offices were demolished during 1993, and a development of houses and flats was built, and named 'Tramways'. A length of track and some setts are displayed at the entrance, together with a plaque commemorating the tramways.

1. TORQUAY (COURT GARAGES)

When Torwood Street depot was requisitioned for war purposes in 1940, Devon General rented covered accommodation at Court Garages, Belgrave Road (corner of Chestnut Avenue) for garaging and storing some of the coach fleet, and after alterations to the doorway, took possession on 24th June. It was vacated early in 1946, by which time the stored vehicles had been brought out for re-conditioning, and Torwood Street garage once again became available. Court Coaches meantime had re-commenced tours from Belgrave Road.

The premises once again came under Devon General tenancy in September 1966, when they bought out the Court Garages companies, but continued trading there under the old names until 1971(coaches) and 1973(hire cars). The lease of the premises was then taken on by Torquay Motors, who specialised in performance cars. They did not stay very long however, and a tyre and exhaust centre is now firmly established at the time of writing.

1. TORQUAY (TORWOOD STREET)

This garage, a short distance from Torquay Strand, was purchased freehold in November 1933 from Grey Cars Ltd. It had been built in 1930 for A. Timpson & Son Ltd., who at that time controlled Grey Cars. It will be recalled that Devon General gained control of Grey Cars Ltd., in March 1932.

The area of the site was 2,424 sq. yards but the floor area of the building, which is on two floors, is 4,848 sq yards. The main entrance was (and still is) in Torwood Street which this leads into the top floor, while the entrance to the bottom floor was in Torwood Gardens Road, at the rear. The official total capacity was 110 vehicles.

The bottom floor incorporated two inspection pits, mess-room, fuelling facilities and printing office for publicity material. Movements on the lower floor were restricted by a large number of upright pillars, but movements on the top floor were unhindered. The top floor also incorporated a booking office and waiting room, drivers room and toilets. There was a flight of steps to the bottom floor at either end of the garage.

The touring fleet of Devon General perpetuated the name of Grey Cars, except for the 1936-45 period, and tours started and finished from the top floor, which was originally intended for use only by private cars. The bottom floor was used for parking and maintenance, and there was no public access.

On outbreak of war in September 1939, 80 vehicles were put into store at Torwood Street, but during 1940 the whole garage was requisitioned; the top floor was used by the Royal Air Force for training purposes, containing Link trainers (which simulated 'blind' flying), a cinema, gymnasium and boxing ring. The lower floor was used by Torbay Air Raid Precautions Committee as a gas decontamination centre.

The whole place was returned to Devon General in 1946, by which time the touring fleet was once again resplendent in Grey Cars livery. Nineteen coaches were in operation as against thirty pre-war.
The doorway of the top floor was heightened in 1947 to allow double-deckers to enter, and this floor was used as a layover point in summer and for storage of delicensed vehicles in winter. Twenty new AEC 'Regal' chassis were stored there in the early part of 1948, until such time as Weymann could accept them for bodying.

A completely new concrete top floor was laid in 1951 and during the work, one new section with workmen on it, fell down to the floor below, fortunately without any personal injury. A new booking office was formed in 1953, and in the same year, much larger coaches were obtained. Even larger coaches with 49 seats were bought in 1966/7, and these became increasingly difficult to manoeuvre on the lower floor, which became used more for parking drivers' cars.

Garage foreman from 1947 to 1959 was Mr. W. Tarr, who then moved to a similar post at Newton Road. He had been with the Company since 1925. For most of the post-war years, charge-hand/driver at Torwood Street was Mr. W. Hannaford. He manned the booking office except in the afternoons, when he took a coach out, usually on the Slapton Sands run. Driver L. A. Worrall took over from Mr. Hannaford when he retired in 1969.

Devon General's touring and coach interests were transferred by the NBC to Greenslades Tours Ltd., of Exeter, as from 1st May 1971, and with them went the entire Grey Cars fleet and Torwood Street garage. During the period of Greenslades' occupation, ownership of the garage became vested in National Travel (South West) Ltd., (the coaching arm of the NBC) passing in 1977 to the Western National Omnibus Co. Ltd.

The garage was finally vacated on 16th April 1978, when the former Greenslades operations in Torquay became operated by Western National under the name of Devon General. The booking office remained open a little longer, closing on 31st March 1980.

The premises were then sold, and reopened in July 1981 as a DIY store by Marley Homecare Ltd., who in turn vacated in 1987. Late in 1990, the building was sold for use as a ten-pin bowling centre, in which form it survives, the exterior being little altered.

2. PAIGNTON (ROUNDHAM GARAGE)
In April 1923, Devon General rented part of Roundham Garage, Roundham Road (near Paignton Harbour) from Messrs. Noble, Langbridge & Tucker, who operated 'Comfy Cars'. Devon General was at that time running two buses on the Paignton-Brixham service, augmented in good weather by two charabancs.

From the summer of 1925, the Brixham-Paignton service was extended to Torquay, and it was about that time that the Paignton allocation was transferred to premises at Churston, rented from Prout's Garage.

2. PAIGNTON (ORIENT ROAD, PRESTON)
On 1st December 1924 Devon General had bought out the touring firm of Fleet Cars Ltd., but no garage had been acquired with the business. Following an inspection by the Managing Director, the Primrose Garage in Orient Road was purchased by Devon General in May 1925 from the Midland Bank Ltd. It had previously housed the charabancs of A. K. Gully's Primrose Cars, but this firm had got into financial difficulties and ceased trading. The garage was situated just off Torquay Road, the entrance being opposite the side wall of the tram depot, and was used to accommodate the Fleet Cars vehicles.

On 1st January 1926, Devon General bought out Comfy Cars, running them for two seasons under their old name, and extended the garage to house the augmented fleet which had grown to a total of 21 coaches with one open touring car. When Devon General ceased to use Prout's Garage at Churston in 1930, the five buses from there became based at Orient Road, under the supervision of Inspector R. Bowden.

Following construction of the new depot at Newton Road, Torquay, Orient Road garage closed (on 1st March 1932), and was sold by auction on 25th July 1934 to Messrs. R. G and C. C. Rees. Houses were built on the site soon after.

2. PAIGNTON (CHURSTON)
Premises were rented at Prout's Garage, in virtually open country, between Churston and Brixham, from about 1925, with up to five buses being based there. Crews had to cycle out from Paignton or Brixham, or catch the train to Churston GWR station close by, to take up their duties. This arrangement however, ceased in 1930, and the buses then became based at Orient Road in Preston.

2. PAIGNTON (BUS STATION)
Prior to 1946, Devon General services terminating in Paignton town centre had used bus stops around the end of Hyde Road, known variously as Park Corner, Dendy Road, Coysh's Shop or GWR Station.

The 56 from its re-introduction in 1946 terminated at Regent car park (opposite the GWR Station and behind the Regent Cinema), being joined in 1948 by services 17, 18, 46 and 63 together with the new 105 from 1949, when the site became known as Central car park. It was at that time still a public car park. It was in 1954 that Devon General rented a site there, with the ultimate aim of
establishing a permanent bus station.

The site had an area of 3,741 sq. yards, and a property at 17, Dartmouth Road was purchased so as to provide an exit from the bus station into that road. Part of the house was let-out as a cafeteria with a flat above. Service 30 used the site from 1954, and 128 from 1956. Devon General purchased the site in 1957, but up until then, the only bus station furniture was a set of free-standing bus stop signs mounted on old bus wheels which provided a suitably weighty base.

Plans were drawn up for a permanent bus station, and construction commenced in 1959, though this was a long-drawn-out job and was not completed until 1961. Difficulty had been experienced in providing firm foundations, due to the high water-table in the area, and Dutch advice was sought. Eventually, a fibre 'mat' was put down on which the buildings were then constructed.

The bus station had one long covered platform with seventeen queue stands (lettered A to Q). Facilities provided were public toilets, a staff mess-room, inspectors' office, left luggage, parcels and enquiry offices, a built-in sales kiosk, and later, two additional 'prefabricated' kiosks (one in 1964 and one in 1965) as well as a 'photo-me' machine. Trading rights were let out.

Meantime, buses on route 12 were serving the site (from 1957) and Western National moved their terminus for the Totnes and local service from outside the railway station, plus the Stoke Gabriel service that they had acquired from 'The Dart' (C. B. Foxworthy) which had previously terminated in Victoria car park. A Grey Cars booking office within the bus station replaced that at 59, Torbay Road in 1965.

Originally, buses entered the bus station from the Station Square direction; however, from 1968, they all entered the bus station from Dartmouth Road and left via Station Square and Gerston Road. Two circuits of the latter road were necessary for buses from Torquay bound for Brixham, and the residents had to put up with this for another 26 years until Great Western Way was built, which linked Paignton Station Square with Dartmouth Road direct (in the outward direction).

The lower-lettered stands (furthest from the railway station) were at first used by Western National services, but from 1st January 1971 the two companies became integrated under Western National ownership and the local services underwent many changes. The stands were re-organised and renumbered 1 to 19, with 15 to 19 being used by National Express services. There was room for layover parking opposite the platform, beyond which the old buildings of Station Lane were gradually demolished for redevelopment, car parking, or road improvements.

The Regent Cinema, at the corner of the bus station, was demolished early in 1986 and redeveloped as shops and flats. In February 1986, re-fuelling facilities were installed for the minibuses on the Bayline services introduced on the 23rd of that month. A large rectangular fuel tank was provided at ground level opposite the main concourse, and minibuses were parked overnight within the bus station.

The bus stands reverted to lettered designations A to P (except I), with A to E being used by the Bayline services, which loaded parallel to the platform instead of obliquely as previously. A bus washing plant was ordered, but delivered late, and it was not brought into use until May.

From 20th March 1988, the Bayline Minibus unit was transferred from Torquay to Paignton, together with an additional 36 vehicles, and a small servicing bay was built. Further re-organisation in April 1992 on the opening of the new depot at Regent Close, Torquay resulted in the loss of some vehicles and duties, but at the same time there were additions consequent upon the closure of Brixham depot. 25 vehicles were based at Paignton for the summer of 1995, but responsibility for their maintenance was transferred to Torquay, and from winter 1995/6 they garaged there also.

Following the sale of Devon General Ltd., to Stagecoach, the servicing bay was used as a paint shop and the fuel tank was removed. Until July 1996, specific vehicles continued to be allocated to Paignton services until new destination displays were obtained which covered all the Torbay routes.
Nowadays, the former cafeteria is let out as an office, the kiosks have gone, and left luggage/parcels are no longer handled. The enquiry office also deals with bookings for National Express services and for tours operated by the present proprietors of Grey Cars, as well of course for sales of the various multi-journey bus tickets available.

3. BRIXHAM (NEW ROAD)
Garage accommodation was rented at Bell's Garage in New Road from 1935 on a seven year lease. Five or six buses were based there, one of which was a Leyland 'Cub' for the local service 37, the others being Leyland 'Lions' of varying types, for the 12 service. The petrol-engined 'Lions' were supplemented by the diesel-engined LT7 variety in 1937, 264-6 being based there for a time, and in 1938 for a while by the Dennis 'Lancets' 298-300.

In 1939, the depot received a complete allocation of new vehicles, one Leyland 'Cub' and five AEC 'Regal' saloons, but was closed on the outbreak of war and relinquished when the lease expired in 1942.

3. BRIXHAM (MOUNT PLEASANT ROAD)
The Kingswear portion of route 12 was worked independently by one 'Regal' after the main service became double-decked in 1940, and this bus (plus a 'Cub' for the local service, when running) was based in an open yard at Jones' quarry in Mount Pleasant Road. A third bus was added in 1955 after normal-size vehicles began working on the local service.

The yard was given up when the new bus station and depot opened on 3rd November 1957.

3. BRIXHAM (BUS STATION)
A bus station had been planned for Brixham since before the war, and a temporary station was established on a site in Bank Lane in July 1955.

A permanent bus station and depot was built on the site of an old malt house, lying between Bank Lane and Middle Street, work commencing in October 1956. The Architect was Mr. W. E. Gott, OBE, and the general contractors were R. E. Narracott & Sons Ltd. The new depot, which served as a bus station by day, was built of Staffordshire brick and had full-width folding doors at each end. It could hold eight buses, two for the local service, one for Kingswear and five for the Newton Abbot route.

Alongside was a snack bar, enquiry office, crew room and toilets. No maintenance was carried out, just fuelling and cleaning. The depot was officially opened on 30th October 1957 by Mr. S. W. Nelson, CBE, chairman of the Western Traffic Area Commissioners, and DR764 on route 12 was ceremonially driven in, with driver S. Quick and conductor F. Pauley.

Service use commenced on 3rd November and the depot disc code was green and yellow. The area of the freehold site was 672 sq. yards, and the station catered for 1,414 scheduled departures a week during summer and 975 during winter, plus duplicates during the peak period. Inspector-in-charge was Mr. T. J. Richards, who had been with the Company since 1930. A first floor office extension was added in 1965.

The bus station was also used by Burton Cars which shared operation of the service to Kingswear, and later ran local services of their own. Devon General bought out this firm in August 1988, but continued to run some vehicles   under the 'Burton' name until January 1993.

From March 1980, Brixham became an 'out-station' of Torquay depot, and had no specific vehicle allocation of its own. However, with the growth of minibus operation, it regained its own allocation, which stood at fifteen vehicles at the end of 1989.

The bus station closed on 26th April 1992, and its allocation and duties were transferred to Paignton and Torquay. The building was demolished late in 1994 and the site is earmarked for a 'town square' feature.

Kingsteignton depot on 19th June 1960, shortly before closure. Some of the ornamental balls on the gable wall found their way on to employees' gate-posts!

(D.J.Frost)

4. KINGSTEIGNTON

Devon General, in its earliest years on the Exeter-Torquay routes, kept one bus overnight in the yard of the Bradley Hotel at Newton Abbot, but by February 1921 were using a garage at Kingsteignton rented from Lord Clifford of Chudleigh, and in April 1923 purchased the garage, together with an adjoining house and land, for £7,061. It lay on the north side of Newton Road about one mile away from Newton Abbot, and had formerly been part of Oakford Farm. The roads to Teignmouth and to Exeter diverged just past the depot, at a point known as Kingsteignton Fountain.

The ground floor of the depot house was converted to a waiting room, and the first floor flat was occupied by a member of staff. Inspector A. Bishop was transferred from Torquay Tramways in 1922 to superintend the depot, a duty later shared by Inspector E. S. Rawle.

When new local services around Newton Abbot started in 1930, the accommodation at Kingsteignton depot became insufficient, so in the same year, an extension was built at the side of the original garage, running behind the house. The garage building was thus L-shaped, with an area of 893 sq. yards, with a capacity for 16 vehicles. Mr. W. S. Hall was depot superintendent in the 1930s, and the staff numbered about 80.

By the winter of 1938/9, 19 buses were allocated to Kingsteignton, and this increased to 23 in the summer of 1939, some of these having to park on open land alongside the depot. Additional land was purchased in 1941, and more in 1946, bringing the overall site to 4,697 sq. yards.

Part of the land alongside was rented to the military during the war years, and two of the Royal Navy ambulances converted from Devon General 'Regals' could sometimes be found there. There was no vehicular access to the land at the rear and most of it was never developed by the Company although the land at the side had been hardcore surfaced in 1941.

Alterations to the garage made in 1954 were; the installation of two new pits adjoining the office, a garage entrance from the parking ground and a toilet block at the back. As the building was on low-lying ground, pumps had to be provided to keep the pits clear of water.
Coloured disc codes were carried by the buses from March 1954 and yellow denoted Kingsteignton. The depot superintendent by this time was Mr. F. A. Avery.

By 1957, 44 vehicles were allocated to Kingsteignton, and some had to be parked on land at Newton Abbot Racecourse, half a mile away on the opposite side of the main road, and vehicles also parked on land in Kingsteignton Road, Newton Abbot that had been acquired for the site of a new bus station.

A temporary bus station had been opened in June 1955, and when the new permanent bus station opened in January 1960, a two-bay servicing depot, with limited parking, was built on the site of the temporary station which was completed in September 1960. Kingsteignton depot then closed, its allocation of 34 vehicles being transferred to Newton Abbot.

Kingsteignton depot was sold on 28th November 1960 to British Road Services for use as a lorry depot, and it later became an agricultural implement depot. It remains intact though modern showrooms and fascias have been added. Some of the stone balls which used to adorn the front gable have found their way on to the gateposts of the houses of former staff!

5. NEWTON ABBOT

It was not until 1960 that Devon General opened a depot in Newton Abbot itself, but the town had always been an important point on the Company's map.

In the very early days of 1919/20, one bus was garaged overnight in the yard of the Bradley Hotel (now the Jolly Farmer). Services called at a stop in Queen Street, near the junction with Wolborough Street (known as the Drum Clock), and later moved just around the corner into Kingsteignton Road.

From December 1921, the Torquay Tramways Company rented a garage for four vehicles at the Sawmills in The Avenue. This only lasted for a few months, until they became operated by Devon General and based at Kingsteignton.

After negotiations with Newton Abbot UDC and four other bus operators in November 1923, the Council erected a loading island and glass-roofed shelter in the Market Square for use as a bus stand, and Devon General took a lease on it in 1924. The area of the site was 1,313 sq. yards. An office was rented in Market Square from March 1930, and a staff mess room in Bearnes Lane, from 1931.

A tours office at 14, East Street was rented from A. C. Bulpin following the acquisition of his touring business by Grey Cars Ltd., in 1929, passing to Devon General in November 1933, but was relinquished in December 1934.

The office in Market Square was given up in 1948, and instead, premises were rented at nearby 16, Sherborne Road for use as a parcels and booking office.

From 1946, an employees rest room was rented at Mortuary Lane (!) from the Council, who by this time no longer looked so favourably on Devon General's occupation of Market Square. By 1954, increased usage and vastly increased rents caused the Company to seek an alternative site for its terminus.

Early in 1955, Devon General bought a large old house, Marlborough Villa, in Kingsteignton Road, about 200 yards from the Market Square, and demolished it. On the site was built a temporary bus station with an area of 1,058 sq yards. It comprised eight pre-cast concrete queue shelters, an office block containing enquiry office, conductors room, inspectors office and toilets. Use of the station commenced on 19th June 1955, and at the same time, the premises at Market Square and Mortuary Lane were relinquished, although the office at 16, Sherborne Road was retained until 1957. A second pre-cast concrete building was added to the bus station in 1956, built over the Mill Leat on steel supports with a concrete platform. It housed a staff canteen and public lavatories. Station Inspector was the long-serving Inspector E. S. Rawle.

The whole area was destined to become a servicing bay to replace Kingsteignton depot when a permanent bus station was built later. Further properties were purchased for demolition in 1957, and land at Marsh Road was rented for parking. Construction then commenced of a new permanent bus station in Kingsteignton Road, just to the town side of the temporary one which opened on 10th January 1960. It had one long covered arrival and departure platform with a number of queuing points which buses approached diagonally, reversing out. They entered the station from the Kingsteignton end, and left from the Newton Abbot end.

The total area of the site was 2,436 sq. yards. Behind the platform lay the triangular-shaped station building, with snack bar, kiosk, canteen/rest room, inspectors office, cleaners room, cash room, enquiry/parcels offices, staff and public toilets. It lay parallel to Kingsteignton Road, where a large square clock was mounted on a tall column.

The other two sides of the triangle were formed by Marsh Road and the backs of houses in Elm Road. A double line of buses could park between the two entrances, opposite the platform, without interfering with arrivals and departures. Inspector E. S. Rawle was station inspector until his retirement in 1963, when Inspector E. J. Morgan took charge.

A small fuelling, washing and servicing depot with two pits was built next door on the site of the temporary bus station (the canteen building being retained) and this opened, in September 1960, when Kingsteignton depot was closed and its allocation transferred. Depot superintendent was Mr. F. A. Avery.

Right from the start, there was never enough parking space at the bus station and depot, and buses have been variously parked at the racecourse, at the site of the demolished generating station (1981/2) and at the public car park in Cricketfield Road, where, after public protest, the number of buses was limited to ten.

The parking ground on the site of the generating station was used in the early part of 1981 as a concentration yard for withdrawn vehicles, mostly Atlanteans, including some that had come up from Cornwall. Some of Devon General's better ones had gone to Cornwall as short-term replacements. Use of the car park in Cricketfield Road ceased in September 1985, but fresh permission was obtained in December 1986 for overnight parking of up to thirty minibuses there. This arrangement ceased in May 1987, but by April 1988, with the transfer of Torquay's remaining allocation to Newton Abbot, a compound for parking was rented at the racecourse, which from time to time had accommodated buses ever since the 1950s.

Planning permission was granted for a major town centre redevelopment scheme embracing the site of the bus station, and in a surprisingly rapid sequence of events, the bus station closed on the night of Saturday 29th June 1991 with demolition taking place the following week.

The depot remained in use, and buses also parked at the racecourse until 26th April 1992 when the allocation was transferred to the new depot at Torquay (Regent Close).

Demolition of Newton Abbot depot (garage/workshop) commenced on 3rd August, and a series of bus stops in Courtenay Street and an awkwardly-placed one in Sherborne Road replaced the bus station. The site was soon redeveloped with a block of offices including a Jobcentre, all of which were built in a very short space of time. The depot site became a car park for the staff of the offices.

6. ASHBURTON

Ashburton was first served by Devon General in 1920 when a short-lived two-day a week service ran from Newton Abbot to Buckfastleigh. Torquay Tramways bus service from Torquay via Newton Abbot was introduced in the following year, and merged with Devon General as route 11 in 1922. From June 1925, service 15 from Torquay via Totnes was terminated at Ashburton, and two vehicles were then kept there overnight.

In February 1927 land was purchased at Dropping Wells, Ashburton, and it was planned to build a garage for four buses there. A booking and parcels office with inspectors' flat above was rented in West Street from Mr. James Fogden in February 1927.

On 20th May 1927, Devon General agreed to buy out their principal competitor in the area, E. O. Babington (Blue Saloon Motor Bus Service). Included in the transaction was a house and garage for four buses at the rear of 34/36 West Street, and Devon General took this over as their depot from 25th May. That summer, Ashburton was served by a new route from Exeter to Buckfastleigh, where connection was made with DMT service to Plymouth.

One inspector, five drivers and five conductors were based at Ashburton at that time, but with the cessation of the Torquay via Totnes service in September 1927, and the creation in 1928 of a joint Exeter-Plymouth through service, Ashburton lost much of its importance as far as Devon General was concerned.

The depot was closed, and the crews transferred to Kingsteignton. The land at Dropping Wells was sold in 1929 to Babington who built a filling station on the site. The house and garage in West Street were sold in 1934 and amazingly, remained little altered sixty years later! Some residual land still remained in the Company's ownership, and occasionally, disused buses were parked there 'out of the way' - especially at such times as the annual Directors' visits!

7. TEIGNMOUTH

Teignmouth was served by Devon General route 2 since the earliest days of the Company, but it was not until 1936, when the services of the Teignmouth Motor Car Co. were bought out, that two buses were kept there to work on the local services 70 and 71, and also route 13 to Torquay. They were stabled in premises at Courtenay Garage, off The Triangle, rented from Mr. R. S. Clarke, and later at County Motors in Bitton Park Road, rented from Messrs. T. G and D. M. Eaton. An extra vehicle was added each summer.

For the summer of 1939, five single-deck vehicles were based at Teignmouth, but the depot was closed between 25th September and 13th November 1939, and for the rest of the war years, the allocation was two, one each for the 13 and local service. This was increased after the war by a second vehicle for each service, those for the local service being supplied by Kingsteignton and those for the 13 by Torquay.

By 1951, five saloons were garaged in a recently-vacated Greenslades depot at the junction of Bitton Street and Exeter Road. The advent of double-deckers however necessitated a return to County Garage, where buses parked in the open at the rear of the premises off First Avenue. Route 71 was double-decked in 1952, 13 in 1954, and 70 at the end of 1955.

In 1968, there was a move to try and establish a bus station in the forecourt of the railway station, but the Company was not in favour. However, subsequently, buses were parked overnight in the former goods yard on the 'up' side of Teignmouth station, entry being via Lower Brimley Road.

From 26th October 1986 the local services became operated by minibuses, and vehicles were no longer kept at Teignmouth overnight. For the previous two years or so, buses had parked on the railway station forecourt rather than in the old goods yard due to vandalism at the latter. In charge of operations at Teignmouth during the post-war Devon General years was Inspector H. B. Wilbourne.

8. MORETONHAMPSTEAD

Devon General first came to Moretonhampstead in 1924, when the Devon Motor Transport Co. Ltd., relinquished their services in the area from 8th June, following the territorial agreement between the two companies. The DMT lease on the White Hart garage in Station Road, where one bus was kept, ran until 29th September and Devon General had the use of it until then. After that, one or two buses were garaged at Chagford (Stevens Garage, also referred to as Cranfords). Crews had to cycle out from Moretonhampstead every day; the first driver and conductor were Sid Payne and Ernie Coles, who were transferred from Tiverton, to be joined by driver Frank Brend and conductor Lester Crump.

Services were expanded in May 1928, when five vehicles were kept in a rented garage and yard at Colwill Mews, Court Street, Moretonhampstead. Operations were under the supervision of Inspectors Rawle, Westlake, and Tucker, with 22 staff being employed there.

In May 1931 a freehold site on the opposite side of Court Street was purchased, and a garage for 15 vehicles was erected by Messrs. Hugh Mills & Co. Ltd., of Newton Abbot. The area of the site was 818 sq. yards, and the floor area of the garage was 616 sq. yards. A small office was provided just inside the entrance, and there was a mess room and toilets at the rear of the garage. The depot superintendent for most of its existence was Mr. B. Saffin, appointed in November 1931. He normally worked an early and a late shift. On his retirement in January 1971 he was succeeded by Mr. D. Place, who had been a conductor and later a driver at the depot from 1955.

The garage was never used to its full capacity, the pre-war allocation being seven buses in summer and five in winter, Leyland 'Lions' predominating. Until the mid-1930s, no Sunday services were worked.

On outbreak of war in 1939, all services were drastically reduced, and Moreton received an allocation of almost-new AEC 'Regals', some of which (notably SR430) spent virtually their entire life working from there. In September 1939, six Leyland 'Lions' were stored in the garage, but they soon went back into service at other depots.

During the war years, part of the depot was used by the military, and in 1944/5, four AEC 'Ranger' Grey Cars coaches were stored there following use as workmen's buses. It was not until 1949 that power-operated fuel pumps were installed; up until then the pumps had been manually operated.

Double-deckers became based at Moretonhampstead from 1955, the designers of the depot in 1931 having had the foresight to build the garage tall enough. From 8th May 1966, it became 'conductorless' with all services by then being worked by one-man single-deckers. The last three conductors transferred to Newton Abbot.

For 11 weeks up to 8th May 1971, the local Fire Service shared the garage while the fire station was under reconstruction, but following the take-over of Devon General by Western National, service cuts were made and Moretonhampstead depot closed from 13th September 1971, though use of the garage continued for a short while.

Four vehicles continued to be kept in the public car park at Station Road and later at Court Street, where a bus interchange point was established almost opposite the closed garage. Eight drivers continued to be employed for the time being, but with continuing reductions in services, the allocation in 1982 was reduced to three vehicles, two in September 1987, and just one in September 1989.

Operation of the remaining service was transferred to Bayline Ltd., from May 1992, and to Keith Williams Travel Ltd., from 7th May 1994. Other small operators became familiar   in the area, but the bulk of the former Devon General services continued, with County Council subsidy, albeit in the hands of Western National or South Western.

The former bus garage was sold by Western National for use as a motor engineering workshop, and it survives to this day, little unaltered, the present owners being Court Street Motors Ltd.

9. EXETER (BLACKBOY ROAD)
Land in Blackboy Road was acquired on 29th September 1920 for the erection of a garage, workshop and offices, the site being purchased for £2,300 from the Exeter Industrial & Co-operative Society.

The new garage was formally opened on 1st July 1921, with workshop and office extension completed on 1st February 1923. A further office extension was made in 1926, the contractors for the latter being Messrs. Soper & Ayres. The area of the buildings was 1,823 sq. yards, and the garage had a capacity of 32 vehicles.

It was in two sections; the top garage fronting Blackboy Road had an area of 863 sq. yards, and the lower garage, which housed the workshops, was slightly smaller at 777 sq. yards. The remaining floor area can be accounted for by the ancillary buildings. Access to the lower garage was via Silver Lane, which ran down the side of the garage, city side.

The garage was ½ mile from the original bus stand in New North Road, and one mile from the Paul Street bus station, established in 1930. Heavy overhauls were carried out at Blackboy Road during the winter months, with vehicles being serviced overnight in the summer. On account of the shortage of vehicles, many bodies were interchanged during 1921-3 to keep services running with the appropriate type of vehicle.

The foreman at Blackboy Road, and later Chief Engineer, was Mr. H. Carter, and subsequent Chief Engineers in the 1920s were Mr. Hunter and Mr. Gore.

Boys were taken on as apprentices up until 1922 when Torquay Tramways bought out Devon General, and it was not until 1959 that apprenticeships resumed (by then at Torquay).

Blackboy Road was, from 1921 until October 1933, the Company's administrative headquarters, the management and offices then moving to the new premises built at Newton Road, Torquay. The General Manager, Mr. D. Campbell, retired through ill-health just before the move, and his successor Mr. R. G. Porte arrived just in time to superintend the operation, which was carried out in a single weekend.

An Area Traffic Superintendent and an Area Engineering Superintendent remained at Exeter together with their respective staffs. Docking and body overhauls and painting were carried out at Torquay after 1933, but Exeter continued to give light overhauls and routine maintenance to its own vehicles and also those based at Exmouth, Moretonhampstead and Tiverton. Sidmouth vehicles also came to Exeter for this type of work after 1947, until which time they had looked after their own.

Exeter kept vehicles overnight at Axminster, Okehampton, Ottery St. Mary, Cullompton and Crediton, with Uffculme, Kenton and Crockernwell being added to the list during the war. Tiverton and Witheridge also became 'out-stations' of Exeter after Tiverton depot closed in 1971. (The term 'out-station' incidentally was a word coined by Western National, and was never heard in the old Devon General days. They were all 'depots' in those times, even if they just housed one vehicle in a rented yard)

By the early 1930s, various unsatisfactory aspects of Blackboy Road depot had become apparent; double-deckers could only use one half of the upper garage, there was no 'reception' area and vehicles awaiting fuelling had to queue in Blackboy Road; access to the lower garage was awkward, and with more and larger vehicles, the garage was not large enough.

Various sites for alternative depots were considered, including Haven Road and a portion of the Southern Railway goods yard lying between Queen Street and St. David's Hill, but none was proceeded with, and it was not until the second world war that anything positive was done.

Land at the rear of the depot with access from Silver Lane, was rented in 1940 for parking, from Mr. H. Bradbeer and two others, and was eventually purchased in 1951/2 for £2,700. It was, up to that time, very rough and only in latter times was it properly surfaced.

The Air Ministry requisitioned the upper garage from 1940 until 1945 when it was rented to their subsidiary Air Service Training Ltd. The lower garage was, from 11th May to 8th October 1942, rented to the Ministry of Aircraft Production. During those months in 1942, Devon General rented accommodation at the Exeter Corporation garage in Heavitree Road, and the Corporation also helped them out in 1944 for a time when buses could not enter the lower garage (all that was in their possession at the time) due to the re-surfacing road works in Silver Lane.
Alternative land for parking was purchased at Marsh Barton in 1942, on the outskirts of the city, and at one time it was the intention to build a depot there. A hard-core park was formed, and access under the GWR Teign Valley line was improved by lowering the roadway to take double-deckers.

However, the plans for a depot there were dropped as it was rather far from the city centre, and Exeter Corporation was anxious to acquire the land in any case. Under thinly-veiled hints of a compulsory purchase, Devon General sold the land to them in 1949, but did not take up the Council's offer of a long lease on an alternative site in Alphington Road.

During the war, alternative fuelling facilities had been provided at Paul Street, but after Devon General regained possession of the whole of Blackboy Road, there arose a further problem with buses queuing in the main road, this time due to the installation of an 'Essex' bus washer in 1952.

The Company was becoming ever more concerned by the large number of 'dead' miles run per day between Blackboy Road depot and Paul Street bus station. However, a lot of buses could normally be found at the latter point laying over, particularly after additional parking at Paul Street had been made available. The fuelling situation had been alleviated by the provision of a 5,000-gallon tank on the lower floor of Blackboy Road in 1948.

The long-term aim of a bus station and depot in the centre of Exeter came a step nearer in 1964, when the new bus and coach station in Paris Street was opened. This lay nearly opposite the Corporation bus depot in Heavitree Road. Devon General was then able to park some vehicles in the bus station at night.

Exeter Corporation sold its bus undertaking to the National Bus Company from 1st April 1970, and it was placed under the control of Devon General. A few DG single-deckers then became based at Heavitree Road, and a few ex-Corporation double-deckers at Blackboy Road. This was only a short-term arrangement, as under the NBC, Blackboy Road depot closed on 27th March 1971. Its allocation was nominally transferred to Heavitree Road, but a large number of vehicles were kept overnight in the bus and coach stations.

Blackboy Road depot was demolished, and its site redeveloped as 'Belmont Court' flats.

9. EXETER (HEAVITREE ROAD)

Exeter Corporation sold its bus undertaking to the National Bus Company with effect from 1st April 1970, and it was placed under the control of Devon General. Heavitree Road depot (also referred to as Paris Street) had been built in 1905 to house the Exeter Corporation Electric tram fleet, entrance being from Heavitree Road (where it joined Paris Street) via a triangular junction, the only point on the tram system where cars could be turned.

When Exeter Corporation commenced operating their own buses in 1929, a side extension was built to the depot, and in 1931 when tram services ceased, most of the pits were filled in though the track remained in place.

During the middle 1930s, the bus fleet expanded considerably, and a further extension was built. A series of five entrances was made into Athelstan Road, which ran along the back of the depot. The extension and the adjoining swimming baths were built on the site of the former Gold's garage, which had rented premises to Devon General in 1919-21 to house their original fleet before Blackboy Road depot was built.

Thus Devon General returned to the site in April 1970. A few Devon General single-deckers were allocated to Heavitree Road and a few ex-Exeter double-deckers to Blackboy Road, otherwise both fleets kept to their own territory for the time being.

However, on 27th March 1971 Blackboy Road depot was closed and all Exeter vehicles were then nominally based at Heavitree Road. As it only had a capacity of about sixty vehicles, the remaining forty or so parked overnight in the bus and coach stations, just across the road. Heavitree Road was the Company's oldest depot and not really suitable for current operating conditions.

History repeated itself when a site for a new depot in Belgrave Road was purchased from the Co-operative Wholesale Society, for which it had been a milk distribution depot. Buses parked on the site until construction commenced. Belgrave Road depot opened on 20th March 1975 and Heavitree Road closed from the same day, soon being cleared out and demolished.

The last things to come out were the old tram rails, which the Seaton Tramway had hoped to buy but unfortunately the demolition contractors had cut them into four-foot lengths, making them unsuitable for further use. Flats have been built on the site of Heavitree Road depot.

9. EXETER (PAUL STREET)

Following acute congestion problems around the Company's terminus stop in New North Road near the Theatre Royal, a site for a bus station was leased from Exeter City Council in Paul Street, after demolition of some derelict buildings. An existing building was adapted to provide lavatories, booking and parcels office, cloakroom and left-luggage office.

The bus station was in effect a large open tarmac yard, with a single entrance/exit into Paul Street. There were no loading islands, and facilities for passengers were minimal. Buses came in and out and reversed among waiting passengers, but no serious mishaps were recorded.

Very few alterations were made during the Company's occupation, which initially was on a 14-year lease from 25th December 1930, and was progressively extended until 1964. A male staff rest room was adapted from 1st November 1939; the entrance into Paul Street was widened to 60 feet in 1936 and four extra rooms were provided on the first floor of the administration block between 1st October 1939 and 24th December 1946.

Two extra rooms in nearby Nelders Yard were rented from 1st November 1941. Two stores, numbers 8/9, Nelders Yard were rented from 17th June 1946 for use as male lavatories.

In 1949, much-needed extra terminal space was created by the leasing of the 'No:2' car park, next door to the bus station in Paul Street, but at a lower level. This again was purely an open tarmac yard.

DEVON GENERAL
a NATIONAL bus company
Devon General

One of a series of pictures taken at Paul Street bus station in Exeter in the mid 1950s, conveying well the general atmosphere of this busy place. It closed in 1964 when the new bus station at Paris Street opened. Among buses visible are two of the wartime Guys which were re-bodied by Roe in 1951, and two Regent IIIs new in 1964, with Weymann light-weight bodies. (Courtenay Press)

In the post-war years, portable bus-stop terminal notices were affixed to old bus wheels laid flat and although these were readily portable, they were heavy enough not to be easily pushed over.

Exeter City buses regularly used Paul Street from 1947 under the Joint Services agreement, and an occasional Western or Southern National worked in from Plymouth, Barnstaple, Minehead or Weymouth. Up until 1934, Mr. R. P. Summers had terminated his Ottery St. Mary services in Paul Street bus station, but as far as is known none of the other independents working into Exeter shared the facilities with Devon General.

Exeter Corporation served notice on Devon General to vacate the Paul Street premises on 29th September 1959, but the Company successfully negotiated an extension until new premises could be found.

The City Council made available a site in Paris Street for a new bus and coach station, and prepared the plans. Work commenced in August 1962 and by July 1964 it was ready for occupation.

Devon General moved out of Paul Street on 5th July 1964, and the site was then used for car parking. An approach ramp to the multi-storey car park built on the opposite side of Paul Street absorbed most of the 'No.2' park, with a new shopping development being built on the site of the bus station. The back wall however was part of the old City wall, and much of this visible in old photographs survives, and can still be seen today as a good point of reference.

9. EXETER (PARIS STREET)
With the continued growth of Exeter, it had been realised for some years that the limit of the capacity of Paul Street bus station and the nearby coach park had been reached, and conditions for both operators and public were becoming very unsatisfactory.

An inner bypass to the city was also considered a necessity and in 1949 it was decided that this would run to the south of High Street. On traffic management grounds, it was also decided that a new and more convenient bus and coach station could also be situated on the south side of High Street in close proximity to the inner bypass road in order to obviate the main bulk of traffic from the south having to cross High Street, and for these reasons, a site in Paris Street was chosen.

Plans for the new station were prepared by Exeter City Council and the project commenced in August 1962. The site sloped considerably from north to south, and this was exploited in the planning of the station, in which the upper level became the bus station and the lower, the coach station. The main entrance terrace leading off Paris Street was placed midway between the levels and also lead to a public cafeteria.

The design and construction of the buildings was carried out under the direction of the City Architect Mr. H. B. Rowe, while the work in connection with hard standings, perimeters and landscaping was under the direction of the City Engineer Mr. J. Brierley. Staverton Contractors Ltd., carried out the main building work. Helical Bar & Engineering Ltd., executed the reinforced concrete frame and foundations, Ruddock & Meighan were the contractors for the hard-standing and perimeter work and all the shrubs and garden features were planted by the City's Parks Department.

The bus station was leased to Devon General which started to use it on 5th July 1964, with the official opening ceremony on 16th July by the Lord Mayor of Exeter, Ald. P. A. Spoerer, accompanied by civic dignitaries and representatives of the Directors and management of Devon General, Western and Southern National and Greenslades Tours, all of whom dined afterwards at the Imperial Hotel.

The bus station was used by all Exeter Joint Services except the city (lettered) services, as well as by Grey Cars tours, the Southern National service from Bideford and the Joint Services from Plymouth and Minehead.

There were eighteen bus departure bays, into which buses drove head-on and reversed out, each bay being indicated by a lettered sign. A stand indicator was provided on the platform to show from which bay each service departed. The equivalent of two bays was provided opposite the parcels office for the use by Devon General or traders' vans. There was lay-over parking space for two rows of buses alongside the boundary wall, which ran parallel to Bampfylde Street.

The passenger concourse covered an area of 4,000 sq. feet, with seating accommodation, timetable posters, automatic vending machines and telephone kiosks provided. An enquiry office and waiting room also incorporated a tours booking office, and offices were also provided for parcels & left luggage, inspectors, duty-clerks, cashing-up room with wall safe and lockers, as well as a staff canteen and kitchen.

The coach station, on the lower level, adjoined the bus station and provided connecting facilities for long-distance coach services. The coach park was designed to hold 72 coaches, but in practice was used for overnight parking of a substantial number of buses. In hindsight, the facilities of the coach station for passengers proved to be inadequate by comparison with those of the adjoining bus station, with no loading islands for coaches, and the passenger shelters were rather bleak by present-day standards.

The administration block included an inspectors' room, chart room, waiting room and toilets. The cafeteria only opened at 'shop' hours, although vending machines were provided.

Buses and coaches had separate entrance and exit, vehicles entering from Cheeke Street and departing into Paris Street. The shortcomings of the coach station were acknowledged during 1984 by the movement of coach departures to the top (bus) section of the station. The complex was updated and an inspectors' office was built on the concourse and public address equipment installed.

10. CREDITON

Crediton has been served by Devon General since December 1920, at first in competition with Devon Motor Transport Co. Ltd., who withdrew from the area as a result of a 1924 agreement. A bus had been kept overnight at Crediton since 1928 at least, and from 12th August 1931, one and later two double-deckers were kept in a garage in Mill Street, rented from Messrs. Searle & Trewin. Exeter to Crediton was one of the few routes in the area that could be worked by double-deckers, and the garage was high enough to accommodate them. A third bus, a single-decker, was added to the allocation to work the service to Sandford in 1950, and one bus then parked in the open.

From 1950 under the Exeter Joint Services Agreement, Exeter Corporation buses operated most scheduled workings on the Crediton-Exeter route, which was then extended to run through to Exmouth. Devon General still kept two double-deckers at Crediton, but used them on Exeter city services, returning to Crediton at night and to change crews.

This method of working was unnecessarily complicated, and at the end of July 1954, Crediton depot was closed and all its turns worked from Exeter.

11. CROCKERNWELL
Crockernwell lies between Exeter and Okehampton, and when buses were dispersed from Exeter in 1942, a garage for one bus was rented from Mr. E. C. Edwards. For several years this was SR426 and it worked on route 6. By 1950, land only was rented, at first from Mr. M. B. Linds and later from Mr. B. Laws. From November 1952, the allocated bus was a double-decker, but the lease of the parking land was terminated early in 1957.

12. OKEHAMPTON
The stabling of buses at Okehampton commenced in July 1923, and Devon General rented garage accommodation for two vehicles from Horn's, a local dairy, though this was reduced to one in 1928 when the depot at Moretonhampstead opened. By 1936, the bus was stabled at the former DMT Company's garage and works, then in the ownership of Southern National. They sold the premises in 1959 to Messrs. Watkins & Rosevear, who traded in tractors and agricultural implements. For a time the Devon General bus continued to park there, but by 1963 a space in the public car park at Market Street was rented. This arrangement ceased from 30th August 1997.

13. KENTON
From 1942, when vehicles were dispersed from Blackboy Road garage in Exeter, covered accommodation for one bus was rented at Kenton from a Mr. Davey. The lease of the premises was terminated in 1947.

14. OTTERY ST. MARY
Ottery was first served by Devon General in August 1921, and one or two vehicles were based there from June 1927 onwards. Garage accommodation was rented from F. J. Luxton & Sons, but this was relinquished in the winter of 1937/8 and the buses were based instead at Sidmouth. Devon General returned to Ottery in 1942, this time in premises of the East Devon Motor Company.

From 1st July 1949, the two buses parked in the yard of the railway station, where a small office was also rented. Use of the station yard continued for a short while after the railway closed in 1967, following which buses parked at the rear of the Plume of Feathers Inn.

15. AXMINSTER
Devon General served Axminster from 1922 onwards, and one bus was kept overnight at the end of the long route 4 from Exeter, except for the 1924-7 period, when the service was curtailed at Honiton three days a week.

Overnight parking at Axminster resumed in June 1927, and from May 1929, garage accommodation was rented from Packham & Co., and later from Mr. S. J. Wakley of Station Garage in Western Road. Driver H. Hallett served there throughout this period and until his retirement in 1962. One bus continued to stay the night at Axminster until 23rd December 1984.

16. CULLOMPTON
Devon General opened its route to Cullompton in 1921, and by the following year was keeping a bus there overnight. With more routes in the area, a second bus was kept from 1927. A lock-up garage was rented from 29th September 1931 from Whitton & Sons, who operated a haulage business in Station Road. In 1948, the Road Haulage Executive became the Company's landlords, having taken over Whitton's lorries, though they resumed the transport business at a later date. The buses parked in the open after route 27 was double-decked in 1949. From 1960 the buses parked in the railway station yard, and after its closure, moved to the rear of the Culm Garage.

17. UFFCULME
Garage accommodation for one vehicle was rented from Messrs. Trenchard & Redwood (later from Mr. W. H. Redwood solely) from 1942 until 30th November 1954. Interestingly, the route to Uffculme was not served by Devon General after 1949, and for the following five years the bus worked on the Exeter to Tiverton service.

18. TIVERTON (CHAPEL STREET)
This garage for three buses was rented from Mr. F. G. Eastmond from 22nd March 1924 until 1938. It had been the garage for Croscols Ltd., which Devon General bought out in 1924, and prior to that, Mr. Eastmond (who became a Director of Croscols) had operated buses and charabancs on his own account. Devon General had kept one or two buses at Tiverton overnight from October 1922 until the acquisition of Croscols Ltd.

18. TIVERTON (LODGE ROAD)
Built on a 1,568 sq. yard site adjoining the railway station, which was rented from the Great Western Railway on 99-year lease dating from 30th September 1937, the garage was erected during 1938 at a cost of £1,795, the floor area being 279 sq. yards.

The depot could hold six buses, and was half a mile away from the town centre. It later became known as Old Road, the junction of the two roads being right outside. A small extension was built in 1942/3, but a much larger one was added in 1951-3. Work commenced on 27th August 1951, but the steelwork was not in position until February 1953, completion eventually being on 18th July 1953 at a cost of £10,281.

The floor area was then 906 sq. yards, with the increased capacity for eighteen vehicles. However, there were never that many based there. One unnerving incident that happened during construction was when a 5,000-gallon fuel tank rolled away while being unloaded from a British Road Services lorry. It stopped short of the railway line but flattened a few allotments in its path!

Steelwork for the extension had been by the Fairfield Engineering Co. Ltd., of Glasgow and the building construction by R. E. Narracott & Sons Ltd., of Torquay.

Devon General held an excursion & tours licence from Tiverton, and between 1932 and 1939 used a Leyland 'Cub' on these duties in conjunction with the 'service tours' from Exeter. From 1949 a Grey Car was sent to Tiverton to work tours from there each summer until the end of the 1968 season, after which tours were no longer advertised.

The freehold of the land on which the depot was situated was purchased in 1967, but on 6th October 1971, after Devon General had been absorbed into the Western National empire, Tiverton depot was closed. It remained empty until sold to Mid Devon District Council, which now use it as a highways depot, the building being little altered. A few buses continued to be out-stationed at Tiverton, and parked at the new bus station in Phoenix Lane.

18. TIVERTON (PHOENIX LANE)
Phoenix Lane bus station was formed on the site of some demolished property, and slopes away from Fore Street to lead to a public car park. The bus station and office opened in 1967 and replaced a rented office at 28a, Fore Street, which was destroyed by fire soon after the move. Two bus shelters were provided on the north side of the road with a reserved bus lay-by on the south side for Devon General and associated services.

In December 1968 the local services were re-organised, and all became one-man operated. A new Exe bridge had been opened and a town centre one-way system introduced, making service changes necessary.

Following closure of the depot on 6th October 1971, a few buses parked overnight at Phoenix Lane, though by 1988 this was down to one. A new office was erected in 1980 alongside the original one, which was then removed and its site cleared. The new building was a one-storey prefabricated low-maintenance unit by Lesser Building Systems Ltd., and contained waiting room, enquiry office, paying-in room, staff room, toilets and stores.

Further redevelopment took place in the vicinity, and by 2002 a multi-storey car park had been built opposite the bus station, and Phoenix Lane itself extended to form a junction with the new western bypass road which had been formed largely on the site of the old railway track.

18. TIVERTON JUNCTION
One bus was stabled on the forecourt on the down side of Tiverton Junction station (which was actually at Willand) from October 1955 and until the end of 1957. It worked on route 3 (Exeter-Tiverton-Sampford Peverell).

19. WITHERIDGE
Operations in this area were taken over from Greenslades Tours Ltd., on 1st January 1948. Devon General continued to use Greenslades former garage in Fore Street for a few days until it was discovered that its use was not covered by agreement. Vehicles then parked overnight in The Square, where an office was rented from Mr. W. J. Gold (given up in autumn 1955). Witheridge ceased to be served by Devon General from 29th November 1980.

20. SIDMOUTH (MILL STREET)
Devon General buses had commenced running to Sidmouth in July 1921, and in the following year, garage accommodation was rented from Martin's Lavender Garage, in Mill Street (by the junction with Russell Street). Five drivers were based there. The site became insufficient for traffic needs, so accommodation was rented at Newton Poppleford.

A new site was purchased at Lower Woolbrook, 1½ miles from Sidmouth town centre, in 1929, and a new garage for ten vehicles was built there, opening in 1930. The rented premises continued as garages in private ownership, that at Mill Street only being demolished in 1990.

Sidmouth (Woolbrook) depot, opened in 1930 and sold for redevelopment in 1996. (L.F.Folkard)

20. SIDMOUTH (WOOLBROOK)

Built on a site purchased in May 1929, the garage was completed in 1930, and had ten vehicles. Steelwork was by Walker Bros. of Walsall and building construction by the G. A. Northcote Company of Sidmouth. The floor area was 778 sq. yards, and the depot fronted on to Woolbrook Road, about 1½ miles from the centre of Sidmouth.

The vehicle allocation by the summer of 1939 had risen to 15, and additional land at the rear of the depot was purchased in November 1939, followed by more in February 1941, giving a total site area of 3,166 sq. yards. The land at the rear was hardcore-surfaced during 1941.

During the war, Sidmouth depot became host to a number of AEC 'Ranger' coaches that were used on a workmen's service to Dunkeswell aerodrome, and they were also occasionally used on local services.

Woolbrook Service Station, next door to the Company's depot, was bought in 1942 together with a flat above, and some lock-up garages but they were sold again in 1946. The land behind the depot was used for storage, and some interesting vehicles were there for a time, including SL133, the last of the 1929 Leyland 'Tigers' which had been converted to run on producer gas. Leyland 'Cub' M103 and some of the coaches were also stored at Sidmouth.

Plans for the extension of Sidmouth garage were never carried out due to a reduced allocation consequent upon the conversion to double-deckers on most services in 1951/2. Under the 1954 scheme, Sidmouth vehicles were denoted by a black disc.

In 1973, the mess-room and stores at the rear of the garage were demolished to give direct access to the yard through a new door at the back of the garage, taking in the site of the former allotments. Ex-Exeter Corporation Leyland 'Titan' 275 served as a mess-room while this work was going on. The area was used in the 1980s as a concentration yard for withdrawn vehicles.

After being on the market for some years, the depot was vacated on 20th July 1996, though the allocation, for a long time, had been only three or four buses, with the garage used for storage of sundry vehicles. It was finally demolished to provide access to a supermarket which was built on land at the rear. A few buses then parked at the premises of Messrs. Potburys which brought immediate protests from local residents in the area complaining about the noise of buses starting up first thing in the morning!

21. EXMOUTH (NEW STREET)
Devon General's first garage in Exmouth was opened in 1921, and held five vehicles. It was close to the Company's office at 15, Exeter Road, just around the corner in fact, but the accommodation soon became inadequate and vehicles parked and were washed, in the street. By 1929/30, vehicles were parked in Exmouth SR station yard and in 1930, land was leased from the Southern Railway for construction of a new garage in Imperial Road, next door to the station.

The New Street garage was closed on 24th September 1931 and was sold to Mr. G. Picketts (Wet Fish Merchants) on 2nd December 1931. The office became a fruit-shop belonging to the same firm. The garage later became a second-hand furniture store and the office became a DIY shop.

21. EXMOUTH (IMPERIAL ROAD)
The new garage opened in September 1931 and had a capacity of 11 vehicles. Steelwork was by J. Partridge & Co. Ltd., and building construction by Messrs. Abels. The site was leased from the Southern Railway for 42 years, the area of the buildings being 687 sq. yards, and of the whole site 783 sq. yards. There was a rear door into the goods yard, where parking land was leased from 1936. Also provided was a general office, waiting room, superintendent's office, rest room and stores. Once the new Exmouth garage had opened, buses were no longer kept at East Budleigh.

The railway station area was redeveloped in 1980, the old station building was demolished, and a single platform without even a run-around loop had to suffice for the rail traffic. The bus depot was also demolished, and replaced by a bus station with seven stands and a small servicing depot within a walled compound. The rest of the former station and goods yard area was used to form a car park, and a new road to Exeter which bypassed some of the town centre. The new road to the car park and the rear of the depot yard is named The Royal Avenue.

22. EAST BUDLEIGH
One, and later two, buses parked overnight in the yard of the Rolle Arms between 1921 and 1931, crews having to cycle out from Exmouth.

23. BUDLEIGH SALTERTON
Following the Southern Railway's acquisition of an interest in Devon General, a DG van and a station bus were based at the railway station from 1930. Both had previously been supplied by private contractors. The goods delivery service reverted to the Southern Railway in 1938, the station bus service ran until late in 1939 and the associated contract for the carriage of mail between station and post office was terminated at the end of that year.

Following the curtailment of several bus workings at Budleigh Salterton in December 1988, one bus was kept there each night for a time.

24. NEWTON POPPLEFORD
A garage in Station Road was rented from Mr. W. Potter, who had demolished an existing carpenter's shop, installed petrol pumps, and raised the garage roof so as to enable six buses to be stabled there. The premises were vacated when Woolbrook depot opened in 1930, but the garage continued in business under the title of Oak Tree Garage.

Section 15. Fleet details (1919-1972)

All vehicles known to have been owned or operated by the Devon General Omnibus & Touring Co. Ltd., are listed, though details are incomplete in the case of some early vehicles. Abbreviations used under 'body type' are made up as follows:

B	Single-decker bus	H	Double-decker (highbridge)
C	Coach	L	Double-decker (lowbridge)
Ch	Charabanc	OT	Open-top double-decker
ChB	Charabus	CO	Open-top convertible double-decker

Next follows the number of seats, with top-deck first in the case of double-deckers, with finally a letter to denote the entrance position, as follows:

F	Front	R	Rear ('os' after the 'R' denotes open staircase)
C	Centre	D	Dual

Some older vehicles do not fit too readily into the above scheme, for instance some had some seats alongside the driver, and many of the charabancs, which at first had a door to each row of seats on the nearside, were rebuilt to front entrance and centre gangway, around 1928. Not all body changes in the early years are on record, so there are one or two gaps.
Some details, notably seating capacities and dates of withdrawal, differ from previously published records, and those given in the pages that follow are based on information from Company and motor taxation records that in some cases, have not previously been made available. It should be borne in mind that vehicles often remained on the Company's books for several months after being withdrawn from service.
Vehicles are listed one per line up to 1933, but after this date when registrations were generally consecutive, they are presented in batches.

Vehicles obtained by the original Devon General Omnibus & Touring Co. Ltd. 1919-1922

Date first Licensed	Fleet No	Registration Number	Chassis Make	Chassis Number	Body builder	Body type	Date Withdrawn
11.6.19	1	T 6942	AEC 'YC'	11423	Hora	OT18/22Ros	1930
11.6.19	2	T 6944	AEC 'YC'	10459	Hora	OT18/22Ros	1928
11.6.19	3	T 6946	AEC 'YC'	11311	Hora	OT18/22Ros	1932

Note: These were named 'Sir Francis Drake', 'Sir Walter Raleigh' and 'Sir John Hawkins'
1 later ran with Hora body from (or identical to) numbers 4 or 5 and in 1928 was re-licensed as a Daimler 'Y' with Ch32 body.
2 had been re-bodied as a charabanc by 1927 and renumbered.
3 was rebuilt and re-bodied in 1926 as OT26/24Ros, and renumbered 72

12.1.20	4	T 7750	AEC 'YC'	15087	Hora	B35R	1922
12.1.20	5	T 7752	AEC 'YC'	15086	Hora	B35R	1930
9.4.20	6	T 8328	AEC 'YD'	15296	Dowell	Ch28	1932
9.4.20	7	T 8330	AEC 'YD'	15297	Dowell	Ch28	1931
23.3.20	8?	T 8232	AEC 'YC'	10179?	Lorry/bus		1922
23.3.20	9?	T 8234	AEC 'YC'	12817	Lorry/bus		1931
20.7.20	10?	T 9234	Federal	13079	Lorry/Charabanc	1922	
??.12.20	11	LF 8399	AEC 'B'	B1629	LGOC	OT18/16Ros	1922

Note: 4 probably sold as a lorry-bus
5 re-licensed as a Daimler 'Y' by 1928, carrying Ch30 body, renumbered 4
6 re-built and re-bodied in 1926 as OT26/24Ros, renumbered 71
7 re-built and re-bodied in 1927 by Hall Lewis as ChB32F and renumbered 87
TA 8232 ex-London General via AEC Ltd., re-registered from LU 8066
TA 8234 ex-London General via AEC Ltd., re-registered from LU 8153, carried bus body by 1926, and in 1927 was rebuilt and re-bodied by Hall Lewis as ChB32F and renumbered 89
11 was re-registered locally as TA 820 on 24.3.21 and rebuilt as B20R

14.5.21	12	FJ 1696	AEC 'YC'		B32R		1931
14.5.21	14	FJ 1697	AEC 'YC'	8872		B32R	1927

Date	Fleet No.		Registration	Make	Chassis No.	Body	Seating	Year
14.5.21	15		FJ 1698	AEC 'YC'	11588		B32R	1927
20.7.21			FJ 1780	Daimler 'Y'	4122		B32	1927
20.7.21			FJ 1781	Daimler 'Y'	6428		B32	1930
20.7.21	17		FJ 1782	Daimler 'Y'	7312		B32F	1931
29.7.21			FJ 1794	Daimler 'Y'	4241		Ch32	1931
29.7.21			FJ 1795	Daimler 'Y'	4185		Ch32	1931
29.7.21			FJ 1796	Daimler 'Y'	3377		Ch32	c1929

Note: FJ 1696/8 licensed as charabancs by 1926

FJ 1696 re-licensed as a Daimler 'Y' by 1927 when rebuilt and re-bodied by Hall Lewis as ChB32F, and renumbered 86

FJ 1781 re-bodied by Thompson as ChB32F in 1926 and renumbered 40?

Vehicles new to Torquay Tramways Co. Ltd., 1920-22 and transferred to the Devon General Omnibus & Touring Co. Ltd., from 1st June 1922

The Tramways fleet number (where known) is in the second column. Devon General originally kept the Tramways number in most cases but later renumbered (more than once in some cases). The bracketed numbers are among those later given by Devon General.

Date	Tram No.	(DG No.)	Registration	Make	Chassis No.	Body	Seating	Year
6.5.20	1	(60)	T 8188	AEC 'YC'	14896	Brush	B26F	1929
6.5.20	2	(61)	T 8190	AEC 'YC'	14894	Brush	B26F	1929
??.5.20	9	(63)	T 8194	AEC 'YC'	14899	Brush	B26F	1929
??.5.20	4?	(64)	T 8196	AEC 'YC'	14893	Brush	B26F	1929
??.5.20	5?	(65)	T 8198	AEC 'YC'	14892	Brush	B26F	1931
??.5.20	6?	(66)	T 8200	AEC 'YC'	14897	Brush	B26F	1929
??.5.20	7?	(67)	T 8202	AEC 'YC'	14898	Brush	B26F	1931
??.5.20	8	(68)	T 8204	AEC 'YC'	14901	Brush	B26F	1929
12.4.21	10?		TA 1008	Daimler 'Y'	6008	Roberts	Ch30	1927
12.4.21	11?		TA 1009	Daimler 'Y'	6580?	Roberts	Ch30	1930
12.4.21	12?		TA 1010	Daimler 'Y'	6631	Roberts	Ch30	1930
12.4.21	13?		TA 1004	AEC 'K'	20505	LGOC	OT24/22 Ros	1926
12.4.21	14?		TA 1005	AEC 'K'	20506	LGOC	OT24/22 Ros	1926
12.4.21	15?		TA 1006	AEC 'K'	20507	LGOC	OT24/22 Ros	1926
29.4.21	16		TA 1168	AEC 'K'	20508	LGOC	OT24/22 Ros	1926
29.4.21	17?		TA 1169	AEC 'K'	20509	LGOC	OT24/22 Ros	1926
29.4.21	18?		TA 1170	AEC 'K'	20510	LGOC	OT24/22 Ros	1926
29.4.21	23	(85)	T 8192	Daimler 'Y'	6613	?	Ch30	1930
1.7.21			TA 1676	Daimler 'Y'	6329	Roberts?	Ch30	1929
1.7.21		(2)	TA 1677	Daimler 'Y'	5601	Roberts?	Ch30	1930
1.7.21		(1)	TA 1678	Daimler 'Y'	7002	Roberts?	Ch30	1929
1.7.21	24	(5)	TA 1679	Daimler 'Y'	6516?	Roberts?	Ch30	1931
30.7.21		(84)	TA 1934	Daimler 'Y'	6166	Roberts?	Ch30	1931
9.3.22	3	(62)	TA 3094	AEC 'YC'	14895	S & B	B32F	1930
31.5.22	28	(6)	TA 3797	Daimler 'Y'	6300		Ch28	1930
31.5.22	25		TA 3802	Daimler 'Y'	5999		Ch28	1931
31.5.22	26	(3)	TA 3803	Daimler 'Y'	6984		Ch28	1930
3.6.22	27		TA 3848	Daimler 'Y'	6324		Ch28	1931
31.5.22		(19)	TA 3794	Daimler 'Y'	5881	S & B	B32F	1930
31.5.22		(20)	TA 3795	Daimler 'Y'	5891	S & B	B32F	1929
31.5.22	29	(21)	TA 3796	Daimler 'Y'	6500	S & B	B32F	1930
31.5.22		(23?)	TA 3798	Daimler 'Y'	4382	S & B	B32F	1930
31.5.22	33	(24?)	TA 3799	Daimler 'Y'	4327	S & B	B32F	1930
31.5.22	36	(25?)	TA 3800	Daimler 'Y'	6561	S & B	B32F	1930
31.5.22		(26?)	TA 3801	Daimler 'Y'	6529	S & B	B32F	1929
3.6.22		(22?)	TA 3849	Daimler 'Y'	6541	S & B	B32F	1930

Note: AEC buses shown as B26F were originally B32F.

TA 3094 originally seated 39

T 8202 was latterly a charabanc numbered 12

T 8198 also became a charabanc numbered 18

TA 3094 was a replacement for the original No:3 (T 8192) which was destroyed in the depot explosion on 3 June 1921. The same chassis was re-used, but the original registration had meantime been transferred to new charabanc No:23.

Seating of charabancs 10-12 was later reduced to 29

Daimlers TA 1934 and T 8192 were rebuilt and re-bodied by Hall Lewis in 1927 as ChB32F, and re numbered 84 and 85.

Seating of charabancs TA 1677/8 was finally 32, and TA 1679 was 29

One of the AEC 'K' type was latterly numbered 49

The second batch of 1921 charabancs was numbered 19-24, but the order within the series is unknown. Likewise the 1922 buses were in the series 29-36.

S & B is Strachan and Brown

Vehicles obtained by the Devon General Omnibus & Touring Co. Ltd., in 1922-23

3.10.22	27	TA 4625	Daimler 'Y'	4357	S & B	B32F	1930
20.10.22	28	TA 4701	Daimler 'Y'		S & B	B32F	1930
7.10.22		TA 4645	Daimler 'CB'		S & B	B20F	1927
1.11.22		TA 4754	Daimler 'CB'		S & B	B20F	1927
New 1916		MX 9272	Daimler 'Y'	3353		B26	c1928
29.1.23	29	TA 5222	Daimler 'Y'	6580?	S & B	B32F	1930
29.1.23	30	TA 5223	Daimler 'Y'		S & B	B32F	1929
28.2.23	31	TA 5440	Daimler 'Y'	6580?	S & B	B32F	1930
28.2.23	32	TA 5441	Daimler 'Y'	6516	S & B	B32F	1929
12.5.23	16?	TA 6339	Daimler 'Y'	4262	Second-hand	Ch28	1930
20.7.23		TA 7157	Daimler 'Y'	3987		B32	1928
27.7.23	88	TA 7256	Daimler 'Y'		Hall Lewis	ChB32F	1931

Note: The fleet numbers quoted are those latterly carried (not originally).

TA 5441 was originally numbered 58.

TA 4625, 4701, 5440 and 5441 were originally licensed to seat 40 by means of collapsible seats across the gangway, but this practice was not allowed after about 1926. The seating was then reduced to 32.

TA 7256 received its Hall Lewis charabus body in 1927.

All were on reconditioned chassis ex-Army via Roberts (Dealer).

Vehicles acquired from Croscols Ltd., 8A Fore Street, Tiverton, in March 1924

28.7.20	T 9364	Napier 25/30hp 3213N		Ch19	1924
?.2.21	FM 1941	Daimler		B26R	1927
?.2.21	FM 1942	Daimler		B26R	1927
22.7.21	TA 1870	Fiat		Ch14	1927
1.12.22	TA 4851	Daimler 'CB'	1918	B20F	1927
28.2.23	TA 5391	Daimler 'CB'	2469	B20f	1927

Note: T 9364 was new to Eastmond, Tiverton, and was never used by Devon General.

FM 1941/2 were first licensed to Captain Youlton of Cheshire. (Messrs Eastmond and Youlton became directors of Croscols Ltd.) Both vehicles also quoted as 35-seat which probably included the collapsible ones.

Vehicles obtained by Devon General during 1924

4.4.24	33	TA 9408	Daimler 'Y'	6208	S & B	B32F	1930
4.4.24	34	TA 9409	Daimler 'Y'	4202	S & B	B32F	1930
12.4.24		TA 9540	Daimler 'Y'	7198?	Thompson?	ChB32F	1929
4.6.24	35	TT 193	Daimler 'Y'	7031	S & B	B32F	1930
4.6.24	36	TT 194	Daimler 'Y'	6137	S & B	B32F	1930
1.7.24		TT 485	Daimler 'Y'	4070		Ch28	1929
1.7.24		TT 486				Ch28	1930
10.1.25		TT 2236	Daimler 'Y'	5740	Thompson	ChB32F	1928

Note: All the above chassis were reconditioned ex-Army, via Lowe (Dealer).

TA 9408/9 and TT 193/4 were originally licensed to seat 40 but reduced to 32 in about 1926.

Fleet numbers quoted above are not the originals but those carried latterly.

Vehicles transferred from Fleet Cars Ltd., to Devon General in 1925

?.?.19	76?	DB 1567	Dennis			Ch28	c1927
?.?.19	77?	DB 1569	Dennis			Ch28	c1927
?.?.19	78?	DB 1723	Dennis			Ch28	c1927
?.?.19	79?	DB 1724	Dennis			Ch28	c1927
14.5.23	80	TA 6347	Lancia 'Tetraiota' 189			Ch18	1931

Note: Fleet numbers quoted above are the originals. The four Dennis vehicles were grouped 76-79 but the order is uncertain.
80 was later renumbered 101 - it is believed.

Vehicles delivered new to Devon General in 1925

30.5.25	50	TT 4077	Dennis 40hp	40340	Hall Lewis	B26F	1931
30.5.25	51	TT 4078	Dennis 40hp	40342	Hall Lewis	B26F	1931
30.5.25	52	TT 4079	Dennis 40hp	40352	Hall Lewis	B26F	1931
30.5.25	53	TT 4080	Dennis 40hp	40354	Hall Lewis	B26F	1931
1.7.25	54	TT 4563	Dennis 45hp	45093	Hall Lewis	B32F	1931
1.7.25	55	TT 4564	Dennis 45hp	45095	Hall Lewis	B32F	1930
1.7.25	56	TT 4565	Dennis 45hp	45061	Hall Lewis	B32F	1931
1.7.25	57	TT 4566	Dennis 45hp	45060	Hall Lewis	B32F	1930
1.7.25	58	TT 4567	Dennis 45hp	45050	Hall Lewis	B32F	1931
1.7.25	59	TT 4568	Dennis 45hp	45052	Hall Lewis	B32F	1931

Note: 54-59 as first licensed, seated 28

Vehicle transferred from Fleet Cars Ltd., Torquay, during 1926

2.5.23	100?	TA 6433	Lancia 'Tetraiota' 37		Ch18	1931

Note: This vehicle was new to Langbridge & Tucker (Comfy Cars) Paignton, and had passed to Fleet Cars on 1st January 1926.

Chassis acquired from Whitton, Cullompton during 1926

23.3.23	41?	TA 5708	AEC 'YC'	8303	Thompson?	ChB28F	1930

Note: Body fitted in 1926 (TA 5708 first registered as a Daimler)

Vehicles delivered new to Devon General during 1926

31.7.26	73	TT 9268	AEC '506'	506033?	Hall Lewis	B32F	1933
31.7.26	74	TT 9269	AEC '506'	506028	Hall Lewis	B32F	1933
31.7.26	75	TT 9270	AEC '506'	506035?	Hall Lewis	B32F	1933
31.7.26	76	TT 9271	AEC '506'	506029	Hall Lewis	B32F	1933
20.8.26	77	TT 9480	AEC '506'	506027	Hall Lewis	B32F	1932
23.8.26	78	TT 9494	AEC '506'	506034	Hall Lewis	B32F	1932

Note: These six vehicles were part-exchanged for the six AEC 'K' type in 1926.

Vehicles acquired from the Torquay-Chelston Car Co. Ltd., on 3rd January 1927

10.3.22	98	TA 3098	Leyland 'G7'	12373	Leyland	B31R	1927
14.5.26	99	TT 8164	Leyland 'Lion'	45154	Leyland	B31F	1933

Vehicles delivered new to Devon General, January 1927

In part exchange for four Daimler 'CB's.

14.1.27	79	UO 845	AEC '506'	506121	Hall Lewis	B32F	1933
14.1.27	80	UO 846	AEC '506'	506122	Hall Lewis	B32F	1933
21.1.27	81	UO 927	AEC '506'	506123	Hall Lewis	B32F	1933
21.1.27	82	UO 928	AEC '506'	506124	Hall Lewis	B32F	1933
28.1.27	83	UO 980	AEC '506'	506143	Hall Lewis	B32F	1932

Note: 79-83 were originally 28 seaters.

Vehicles transferred from Fleet Cars Ltd., during 1927

2.5.23	102?	TA 6434	Lancia 'Z1'	4097		Ch14	1927
7.4.24	103	TA 9441	Lancia 'Tetraiota'	163		Ch18	1931
9.4.25	104	TT 3356	Lancia 'Pentaiota'	625		Ch20	1934

Note: These vehicles had been new to Comfy Cars, Paignton, and had been acquired by Fleet Cars on 1.1.26

Vehicles acquired from E. O. Babington (Blue Cars) Ashburton Motor Works, East Street, Ashburton on 20th May 1927

?.4.20		EB 2187?	Fiat 15/20hp		Dowell	Ch14	c1927
?.4.20		EB 2188?	Fiat 15/20hp		Dowell	Ch20	c1927
			Maxwell 30cwt			B14	c1927
28.2.23		TA 5449	Maxwell 30cwt	E21890		B14	c1927
30.7.23		TA 7282	Berliet 35cwt	10583		B20F	c1927
21.8.23	105	TA 7490	Lancia 'Tetraiota'	203		B20F	1931
18.11.24	106	TT 1761	Lancia 'Pentaiota'	539		B20F	1931
2.11.26	107	UO 97	Berliet	30762		B20F	c1928
6.7.26		TT 8954	Berliet	30754		B20F	c1930
4.11.25	69	TT 6254	Albion 24hp	4129G		B24F	1933
	70	TT 6255	Albion 24hp	4129K		B24F	1933

Note: TA 5449, TA 7282 and the other Maxwell had been acquired by Babington from Turner (Speedwell),
Kingsteignton   in September 1925.

Vehicles delivered new to Devon General, October 1927 to January 1928
in part exchange for eight AEC 'YC' and Daimler 'Y' buses

7.10.27	90	UO 4164	ADC '506'	506275	Hall Lewis	B32F	1933
7.10.27	91	UO 4165	ADC '506'	506274	Hall Lewis	B32F	1933
10.10.27	92	UO 4189	ADC '506'	506273	Hall Lewis	B32F	1933
13.10.27	93	UO 4227	ADC '506'	506276	Hall Lewis	B32F	1933
17.12.27	94	UO 4675	ADC '506'	506284	Hall Lewis	B32F	1933
17.12.27	95	UO 4676	ADC '506'	506283	Hall Lewis	B32F	1933
13.1.28	96	UO 4960	ADC '506'	506281	Hall Lewis	B32F	1933
13.1.28	97	UO 4961	ADC '506'	506282	Hall Lewis	B32F	1933

Vehicles transferred during 1928 from Fleet Cars Ltd.
Acquired by them in May 1928 from G.G.Gullick, t/a Heather Tours, Paignton

4.6.27	108	UO 2811	Lancia	3813		Ch18	1934
?.4.27	109	ML 4014	Lancia	342		Ch18	1934

Note: ML 4014 had been first registered by the Curtis Automobile Co. Ltd., of London NW10, the British
concessionaires   for Lancia

Vehicles delivered new to Devon General during June to August 1928

?.6.28	110	UO 6853	Leyland 'Lion'	46673	Hall Lewis	B32D	1934
?.6.28	111	UO 6854	Leyland 'Lion'	46670	Hall Lewis	B32D	1934
?.6.28	112	UO 6855	Leyland 'Lion'	46671	Hall Lewis	B32D	1934
?.7.28	113	UO 7303	Leyland 'Lion'	46747	Hall Lewis	B32D	1934
?.7.28	114	UO 7304	Leyland 'Lion'	46745	Hall Lewis	B32D	1934
?.7.28	115	UO 7470	Leyland 'Lion'	46748	Hall Lewis	B32D	1934
?.7.28	116	UO 7469	Leyland 'Lion'	46746	Hall Lewis	B32D	1934
?.7.28	117	UO 7471	Leyland 'Lion'	46749	Hall Lewis	B32D	1934
?.8.28	118	UO 7851	Leyland 'Lioness'	47423	Hall Lewis	C26F	1934
?.8.28	119	UO 7852	Leyland 'Lioness'	47424	Hall Lewis	C26F	1934
?.8.28	120	UO 7910	Leyland 'Lioness'	47425	Hall Lewis	C26F	1934
?.8.28	121	UO 7911	Leyland 'Lioness'	47426	Hall Lewis	C26F	1934
?.8.28	122	UO 7950	Leyland 'Lioness'	47427	Hall Lewis	C26F	1934
?.8.28	123	UO 7951	Leyland 'Lioness'	47428	Hall Lewis	C26F	1934

Note: Vehicles 110-117 were classified Leyland 'Lion' PLSC3, whereas 118-123 were Leyland 'Lioness' PLC.

Vehicles acquired from the Great Western Railway in 1929

Originally owned by Ashcroft & Kent, Paignton, and acquired together with the goodwill of their Torquay to Paignton service.

?.?.28	142	UO 5995	Leyland 'Lion'	46333	Metcalfe	B31F	1933
?.7.28	143	UO 7430	Leyland 'Lion'	47132	Arlington	B32	1933

Note: Both of these vehicles were Leyland 'Lion' PLSC

Vehicles delivered new to Devon General during 1929

?.3.29	124	UO 9690	Leyland 'Lion'	47514	Hall Lewis	B32D	1934
?.3.29	125	UO 9691	Leyland 'Lion'	47513	Hall Lewis	B32D	1934
?.3.29	126	UO 9692	Leyland 'Lion'	47512	Hall Lewis	B32D	1934
?.3.29	127	UO 9813	Leyland 'Lion'	47511	Hall Lewis	B32D	1934
?.6.29	128	DV 925	Leyland 'Lion'	50130	Hall Lewis	B31D	1936
?.6.29	129	DV 926	Leyland 'Lion'	50129	Hall Lewis	B31D	1936
?.6.29	130	DV 1044	Leyland 'Lion'	50131	Hall Lewis	B31D	1936
?.7.29	131	DV 1616	Leyland 'Lion'	50132	Hall Lewis	B31D	1936
?.3.29	132	UO 9759	Leyland 'Tiger'	60463	Hall Lewis	C26F	1939
?.3.29	133	UO 9779	Leyland 'Tiger'	60461	Hall Lewis	C26F	1947
?.3.29	134	UO 9780	Leyland 'Tiger'	60462	Hall Lewis	C26F	1939
?.5.29	135	DV 116	Leyland 'Tiger'	60464	Hall Lewis	C26F	1939
?.4.29	136	DV 160	Leyland 'Tiger'	60465	Hall Lewis	C26F	1939
?.5.29	137	DV 226	Leyland 'Tiger'	60466	Hall Lewis	C26F	1939
?.5.29	138	DV 225	Leyland 'Titan'	70538	Hall Lewis	L24/24R	1936
?.?.29	139	DV 2149	Leyland 'Titan'	70537	Hall Lewis	L24/24R	1936
?.?.29	140	DV 2304	Leyland 'Titan'	70536	Hall Lewis	L24/24R	1935
?.?.29	141	DV 2356	Leyland 'Titan'	70539	Hall Lewis	L24/24R	1936
?.?.29	144	DV 2326	Leyland 'Tiger'	60347	Hall Lewis	C30F	1936
?.?.29	145	DV 2355	Leyland 'Tiger'	60346	Hall Lewis	C30F	1936

Note: 124-127 were Leyland 'Lion' PLSC3
        128-131 were Leyland 'Lion' LT1
        132-137 and 144/5 were Leyland 'Tiger' TS2   , 132-137 were latterly B30F.
        138-141 were Leyland 'Titan' TD1
        None of the above were alloted prefixes to their fleet numbers under the 1939 scheme, but 133 became listed as XL133, and on repainting into wartime grey, carried the number SL133.

Vehicles delivered new to Devon General during 1930

March	146	DV 3898	Leyland 'Lion'	50722	Hall Lewis	B32F	1936
March	147	DV 3899	Leyland 'Lion'	50723	Hall Lewis	B32F	1936
March	148	DV 3900	Leyland 'Lion'	50717	Hall Lewis	B32F	1936
March	149	DV 3901	Leyland 'Lion'	50727	Hall Lewis	B32F	1936
April	150	DV 3902	Leyland 'Lion'	50725	Hall Lewis	B32F	1936
March	151	DV 3903	Leyland 'Lion'	50718	Hall Lewis	B32F	1936
April	152	DV 4114	Leyland 'Lion'	50716	Hall Lewis	B31D	1936
?.4.30	153	DV 4115	Leyland 'Lion'	50721	Hall Lewis	B31D	1936
?.4.30	154	DV 4116	Leyland 'Lion'	50720	Hall Lewis	B31D	1936
?.4.30	155	DV 4117	Leyland 'Lion'	50728	Hall Lewis	B31D	1936
?.4.30	156	DV 4118	Leyland 'Lion'	50724	Hall Lewis	B31D	1936
?.4.30	157	DV 4119	Leyland 'Lion'	50729	Hall Lewis	B31D	1936
?.4.30	158	DV 4120	Leyland 'Lion'	50719	Hall Lewis	B31D	1936
?.4.30	159	DV 4121	Leyland 'Lion'	50726	Hall Lewis	B31D	1936
?.4.30	160	DV 4890	Leyland 'Tiger'	60821	Hall Lewis	C31F	1935
?.4.30	161	DV 4891	Leyland 'Tiger'	60820	Hall Lewis	C31F	1935
?.4.30	162	DV 4889	Leyland 'Tiger'	60819	Hall Lewis	C31F	1935
?.4.30	163	DV 4925	Leyland 'Tiger'	60823	Hall Lewis	C30F	1935
?.5.30	164	DV 5475	Leyland 'Tiger'	60822	Hall Lewis	C30F	1935
?.5.30	165	DV 5476	Leyland 'Tiger'	60818	Hall Lewis	C30F	1935
?.5.30	166	DV 5477	Leyland 'Tiger'	61220	Hall Lewis	C30F	1935
?.5.30	167	DV 5478	Leyland 'Tiger'	61223	Hall Lewis	C30F	1935
?.5.30	168	DV 5479	Leyland 'Tiger'	61221	Hall Lewis	C30F	1935
?.5.30	169	DV 5480	Leyland 'Tiger'	61222	Hall Lewis	C30F	1935

?.5.30	170	DV 5481	Leyland 'Lion'	51092	Hall Lewis	B31D	1936
?.5.30	171	DV 5482	Leyland 'Lion'	51088	Hall Lewis	B31D	1936
?.5.30	172	DV 5483	Leyland 'Lion'	51093	Hall Lewis	B31D	1936
?.5.30	173	DV 5484	Leyland 'Lion'	51089	Hall Lewis	B31D	1936
?.6.30	174	DV 5766	Leyland 'Lion'	51090	Hall Lewis	B31D	1936
?.6.30	175	DV 5765	Leyland 'Lion'	51091	Hall Lewis	B31D	1936
?.6.30	176	DV 5767	Leyland 'Lion'	50916	Hall Lewis	C32F	1935
?.6.30	177	DV 5835	Leyland 'Lion'	50917	Hall Lewis	C30F	1935
?.7.30	178	DV 5834	Morris Comm.	6620	Park Royal	B12F	1938
?.9.30	179	DV 6853	Morris Comm.	7914	Park Royal	B12F	1938

Note: Following the bankruptcy of Hall Lewis, most Leyland buses were completed by Park Royal.
146-159 were Leyland 'Lion' LT1
160-165 were Leyland 'Tiger' TS2
166-169 were Leyland 'Tiger' TS3
170-177 were Leyland 'Lion' LT2

Vehicles delivered new to Devon General during 1930 - 1931

1930	1	DV 7307	Leyland 'Lion'	51260	Park Royal	B31D	1937
1930	2	DV 7308	Leyland 'Lion'	51261?	Park Royal	B31D	1937
1931	3	DV 7424	Leyland 'Lion'	51262	Park Royal	B31D	1937
1931	4	DV 7425	Leyland 'Lion'	51264?	Park Royal	B31D	1937
1931	5	DV 7426	Leyland 'Lion'	51265	Park Royal	B31D	1937
1931	6	DV 7428	Leyland 'Lion'	51268	Park Royal	B31D	1937
1931	7	DV 7429	Leyland 'Lion'	51263	Park Royal	B31D	1937
1931	8	DV 7430	Leyland 'Lion'	51267	Park Royal	B31D	1937
1931	9	DV 7710	Leyland 'Lion'	51266	Park Royal	B31D	1937
1931	10	DV 7712	Leyland 'Lion'	51269	Park Royal	B31D	1937
1931	11	DV 7713	Leyland 'Lion'	51270	Park Royal	B31D	1937
1931	12	DV 7714	Leyland 'Lion'	51271	Park Royal	B31D	1937
1931	13	DV 7715	Leyland 'Lion'	51274	Park Royal	B31D	1937
1931	14	DV 7709	Leyland 'Lion'	51272	Park Royal	B31D	1937
1931	15	DV 7890	Leyland 'Lion'	51273	Park Royal	B31D	1937
1931	16	DV 8082	Leyland 'Lion'	51275	Park Royal	B31D	1937
1931	17	DV 8083	Leyland 'Lion'	51277	Park Royal	B31D	1937
1931	18	DV 8084	Leyland 'Lion'	51276	Park Royal	B31D	1937
1931	19	DV 8504	Leyland 'Lion'	51278	Park Royal	B31D	1937
1931	20	DV 8505	Leyland 'Lion'	51279	Park Royal	B31D	1937
1931	21	DV 8506	Leyland 'Lion'	51435	Park Royal	B31D	1937
1931	22	DV 8507	Leyland 'Lion'	51436	Park Royal	B31D	1937
1931	23	DV 8508	Leyland 'Lion'	51437	Park Royal	B31D	1937
1931	24	DV 8509	Leyland 'Lion'	51438	Park Royal	B31D	1937

Note: All were Leyland 'Lion' LT2 and were described as having 30 seats when authorised for sale.
Numbers 1 and 2 entered service in 1930.
Numbers 3-13 were taken into stock in 1930 although some were still being bodied. These and
14-20 entered service early in 1931.
21-24 comprised a supplementary order placed late in 1930 to replace the last eight Dennis buses of 1925
which were deemed unworthy of further expenditure.

Vehicles delivered new to Devon General during 1931.

1931	180	DV 9216	AEC 'Regal'	662681	Park Royal	C26F	1939
1931	181	DV 9217	AEC 'Regal'	662679	Park Royal	C26F	1937
1931	182	DV 9218	AEC 'Regal'	662680	Park Royal	C26F	1939
1931	183	DV 9219	AEC 'Regal'	662678	Park Royal	C26F	1937
1931	184	DV 9220	AEC 'Regal'	662676	Park Royal	C26F	1939
1931	185	DV 9333	AEC 'Regal'	662804	Park Royal	C26F	1937
1931	186	DV 9334	AEC 'Regal'	662807	Park Royal	C26F	1937
1931	187	DV 9335	AEC 'Regal'	662806	Park Royal	C26F	1939
1931	188	DV 9336	AEC 'Regal'	662805	Park Royal	C26F	1939

1931	189	DV 9337	AEC 'Regal'	662677	Park Royal	C26F	1939
1931	25	DV 9338	Leyland 'Lion'	51608	Park Royal	B31F	1939
1931	26	DV 9339	Leyland 'Lion'	51609	Park Royal	B31F	1939
1931	27	DV 9572	Leyland 'Lion'	51607	Park Royal	B31F	1941
1931	28	DV 9655	Leyland 'Lion'	51610	Park Royal	B31F	1939
1931	29	DV 9721	Leyland 'Lion'	51612	Park Royal	B31F	1939
1931	30	DV 9722	Leyland 'Lion'	51613	Park Royal	B31F	1939
1931	31	OD 832	Leyland 'Lion'	101	Park Royal	B31F	1939

Note: 180-189 had body numbers 3090-3099

25-30 were Leyland 'Lion' LT3 and had body numbers 3106-3111 and were in part exchange for the Hall Lewis bodied AEC 'YC' and Daimler 'Y' (84-89)

31 was a Leyland 'Lion' LT5 and had body number 3189 and was the prototype LT5 'Lion' as exhibited at the 1931 Commercial Motor Show in London.

The seating of 180, 182, 184, and 187 - 189 was latterly B32F

Vehicles delivered new to Devon General during 1932

1932	32	OD 1827	Leyland 'Lion' LT5	371	Weymann	B31F	1939
1932	33	OD 1828	Leyland 'Lion' LT5	374	Weymann	B31F	1939
1932	34	OD 1829	Leyland 'Lion' LT5	372	Weymann	B31F	1939
1932	35	OD 1830	Leyland 'Lion' LT5	377	Weymann	B31F	1939
1932	36	OD 1831	Leyland 'Lion' LT5	373	Weymann	B31F	1939
1932	37	OD 2294	Leyland 'Lion' LT5	573	Weymann	B31F	1939
1932	38	OD 1832	Leyland 'Lion' LT5	379	Weymann	B31F	1939
1932	39	OD 1833	Leyland 'Lion' LT5	380	Weymann	B31F	1939
1932	40	OD 1834	Leyland 'Lion' LT5	572	Weymann	B31F	1939
1932	41	OD 1835	Leyland 'Lion' LT5	574	Weymann	B31F	1939
1932	42	OD 1836	Leyland 'Lion' LT5	376	Weymann	B31F	1939
1932	43	OD 2293	Leyland 'Lion' LT5	378	Weymann	B31F	1939
1932	44	OD 2292	Leyland 'Lion' LT5	375	Weymann	B31F	1939
1932	190	OD 2260	AEC 'Regent'	6611808	Brush	L26/26R	1937
1932	191	OD 2259	AEC 'Regent'	6611806	Brush	L26/26R	1937
1932	192	OD 2261	AEC 'Regent'	6611807	Brush	L26/26R	1937
1932	45	OD 2291	Leyland 'Lion' LT5	551	Weymann	B30F	*1939
1932	46	OD 2290	Leyland 'Lion' LT5	552	Weymann	B30F	1940
1932	47	OD 2540	Leyland 'Lion' LT5	546	Weymann	B30F	1940
1932	48	OD 2541	Leyland 'Lion' LT5	548	Weymann	B30F	1940
1932	49	OD 2542	Leyland 'Lion' LT5	549	Weymann	B30F	1940
1932	50	OD 2543	Leyland 'Lion' LT5	550	Weymann	B30F	1940
1932	51	OD 2544	Leyland 'Lion' LT5	545	Weymann	B30F	1940
1932	52	OD 2545	Leyland 'Lion' LT5	547	Weymann	B30F	1940
1932	100	OD 2836	Leyland 'Cub' KP3	620	Weymann	C20F	1939
1932	101	OD 2837	Leyland 'Cub' KP3	622	Weymann	C20F	1939
1932	102	OD 2838	Leyland 'Cub' KP3	621	Weymann	C20F	1939

Note: 45-52 were 'Sun Saloons' and allotted numbers SK45-52 in the 1939 scheme, but as far as is known, none ever carried the prefix. *45 was re-purchased and sold again in 1941.

Vehicles delivered new to Devon General during 1933

1933	53	OD 5854	Leyland 'Lion'	2589	Weymann	B31F	1940
1933	54	OD 5855	Leyland 'Lion'	2590	Weymann	B31F	1940
1933	55	OD 5856	Leyland 'Lion'	2591	Weymann	B31F	1940
1933	56	OD 5857	Leyland 'Lion'	2592	Weymann	B31F	1940
1933	57	OD 5858	Leyland 'Lion'	2593	Weymann	B31F	1940
1933	58	OD 5859	Leyland 'Lion'	2595	Weymann	B31F	1940
1933	59	OD 5860	Leyland 'Lion'	2594	Weymann	B31F	1940
1933	60	OD 5861	Leyland 'Lion'	2596	Weymann	B31F	1940
1933	61	OD 5862	Leyland 'Lion'	2602	Weymann	B31F	1940
1933	62	OD 6148	Leyland 'Lion'	2604	Weymann	B31F	1940
1933	63	OD 5863	Leyland 'Lion'	2597	Weymann	B31F	1940
1933	64	OD 5864	Leyland 'Lion'	2598	Weymann	B31F	1940
1933	65	OD 5865	Leyland 'Lion'	2599	Weymann	B31F	1940

1933	66	OD 5866	Leyland 'Lion'	2600	Weymann	B31F	1940
1933	67	OD 5867	Leyland 'Lion'	2601	Weymann	B31F	1940
1933	68	OD 5868	Leyland 'Lion'	2605	Weymann	B31F	1940
1933	69	OD 5869	Leyland 'Lion'	2606	Weymann	B31F	1940
1933	70	OD 6149	Leyland 'Lion'	2603	Weymann	B31F	1940

Note: 53-70 were Leyland 'Lion' LT5 and allotted numbers SK53-70 under the 1939 scheme but as far as is known, none ever carried the prefix. Their body numbers were W937-954 but not in order.

63-70 were 'Sun Saloons'.

Vehicles acquired from Grey Cars Ltd., on 1st November 1933

Grey Cars fleet-numbers in brackets.

1930	(1)	301	GC 4841	AEC 'Mercury'	640009	Harrington	C23F	1937
1930	(2)	302	GC 4842	AEC 'Mercury'	640004	Harrington	C23F	1937
1930	(3)	303	GC 4843	AEC 'Mercury'	640013	Harrington	C23F	1937
1930	(4)	304	GC 4844	AEC 'Mercury'	640008	Harrington	C23F	1937
1930	(5)	305	GC 4845	AEC 'Mercury'	640006	Harrington	C23F	1937
1930	(6)	306	GC 4846	AEC 'Mercury'	640011	Harrington	C23F	1935
1930	(7)	307	GC 4847	AEC 'Mercury'	640012	Harrington	C23F	1935
1930	(8)	308	GC 4848	AEC 'Mercury'	640007	Harrington	C23F	1935
1930	(9)	309	GC 4849	AEC 'Mercury'	640005	Harrington	C23F	1937
1930	(10)	310	GC 4850	AEC 'Mercury'	640010	Harrington	C23F	1937
1931	(11)	311	GN 7316	AEC 'Mercury'	640063	Harrington	C22F	1937
1931	(12)	312	GN 7317	AEC 'Mercury'	640069	Harrington	C22F	1937
1931	(13)	313	GN 7318	AEC 'Mercury'	640071	Harrington	C22F	1935
1931	(14)	314	GN 7319	AEC 'Mercury'	640070	Harrington	C22F	1935
1931	(15)	315	GN 7320	AEC 'Mercury'	640068	Harrington	C22F	1935
1931	(16)	316	GN 7321	AEC 'Mercury'	640072	Harrington	C22F	1935
1931	(17)	317	GN 7322	AEC 'Mercury'	640073	Harrington	C22F	1935
1931	(18)	318	GN 7323	AEC 'Mercury'	640064	Harrington	C22F	1935
1931	(21)	319	GN 7302	AEC 'Ranger'	665014	Harrington	C26F	1940
1931	(22)	320	GN 7303	AEC 'Ranger'	665017	Harrington	C26F	1940
1931	(23)	321	GN 7304	AEC 'Ranger'	665018	Harrington	C26F	1940
1931	(24)	322	GN 7305	AEC 'Ranger'	665013	Harrington	C26F	1940
1931	(25)	323	GN 7306	AEC 'Ranger'	665016	Harrington	C26F	1940
1931	(26)	324	GN 7307	AEC 'Ranger'	665015	Harrington	C26F	1940
1931	(27)	325	GN 7308	AEC 'Ranger'	665019	Harrington	C26F	1940
1931	(28)	326	GN 7309	AEC 'Ranger'	665020	Harrington	C26F	1940
1931	(29)	327	GN 7310	AEC 'Ranger'	665021	Harrington	C26F	1940
1931	(30)	328	GN 7311	AEC 'Ranger'	665022	Harrington	C26F	1940
1923	(41)		DV 1521	Lancia 'Tetraiota'	131		C20	1934
1926	(49)		TT 8217	Lancia 'Super Penta'	1223		Ch20	1934
1926	(50)		TT 8218	Lancia 'Super Penta'	1229		Ch20	1934
1926	(51)		TT 8816	Lancia 'Super Penta'	1230		Ch20	1934
1927	(52)		UO 2694	Lancia 'Super Penta'	1472		Ch20	1934
1927	(53)		DY 4573	Lancia 'Super Penta'			C22	1934
1927	(54)		DY 4574	Lancia 'Super Penta'			C22	1934
1927	(55)		DY 4575	Lancia 'Super Penta'			C22	1934
1928	(56)		UO 6715	Lancia 'Super Penta'	2446		C25F	1934
1928	(57)	329	UO 7253	Lancia 'Super Penta'	2437		C26F	1935
1928	(58)	330	UO 7254	Lancia 'Super Penta'	2447		C26F	1935
1928	(59)	331	UO 7255	Lancia 'Super Penta'	2448		C26F	1935
1928	(60)	332	UO 7256	Lancia 'Super Penta'	2449		C26F	1935
1928	(61)	333	UO 7257	Lancia 'Super Penta'	2450		C26F	1935

Note: All retained Grey Cars fleet-name and livery.

41-56 never ran in service for Devon General (41-52 being charabancs).

53-61 were 'all weather' coaches with retractable roof.

18, the chassis number is alternatively quoted as 640128.

1-12, 21-23, 53-55 were new to A. Timpson & Sons,

6-10 were transferred to Grey Cars in 1930, all the remainder in 1932.

41 and 42 were originally registered TA 6901 and TA 7231 (and as Ch20) but were re-bodied and re-registered in 1929.

52 was ex-Hampton Motor Company of Torquay, in 1929

319 - 328 were allotted numbers TCR319 - 328 under the 1939 scheme and were to have been re-bodied, but they were instead sold in 1940, never having carried the prefix (as far as is known).

Vehicles acquired ex-Fleet Cars Ltd., 1st November 1933 (Fleet Cars numbers in brackets)

---	(1)	1922	TA 3753	Lancia 'Tetraiota'	64	Weymann C337	C20F	1934
---	(2)	1925	TT 3165	Lancia 'Pentaiota'	727	?	C18F	1934
---	(3)	1925	TT 3162	Lancia 'Pentaiota'	711	?	C18F	1934
---	(4)	1925	TT 3621	Lancia 'Pentaiota'	756	?	C18F	1934
---	(5)	1926	TT 8647	Lancia 'Pentaiota'	1046	?	C20F	1934
---	(6)	1925	TT 3841	Lancia 'Pentaiota'	782	?	C18F	1934
---	(7)	1925	TT 4894	Lancia 'Pentaiota'	887	?	C20F	1934
---	(8)	1925	TT 3840	Lancia 'Pentaiota'	786	?	C18F	1934
---	(9)	1925	TT 3620	Lancia 'Pentaiota'	755	?	C18F	1934
---	(10)	1925	TT 3163	Lancia 'Pentaiota'	725	?	C18F	1934
---	(11)	1925	TT 4668	Lancia 'Pentaiota'	863	?	C18F	1934
---	(12)	1925	TT 4895	Lancia 'Pentaiota'	878	?	C20F	1934
---	(13)	1925	TT 3328	Lancia 'Pentaiota'	754	?	C18F	1934
---	(14)	1925	TT 4667	Lancia 'Pentaiota'	865	?	C18F	1934
---	(15)	1925	TT 3164	Lancia 'Pentaiota'	726	?	C18F	1934
---	(16)	1925	TT 4105	Lancia 'Pentaiota'	784	?	C18F	1934
334	(17)	1927	UO 2724	Lancia 'Pentaiota' S	1487	?	C20F	1934
335	(18)	1927	UO 2722	Lancia 'Pentaiota' S	1485	?	C20F	b1934
336	(19)	1927	UO 2720	Lancia 'Pentaiota' S	1483	?	C20F	1934
337	(20)	1927	UO 2721	Lancia 'Pentaiota' S	1484	?	C20F	1934
338	(21)	1927	UO 2723	Lancia 'Pentaiota' S	1486	?	C20F	1934

Note: Number 1 had a saloon body built in 1932 - it was new to Comfy Cars, Paignton, as a charabanc, and passed to Fleet Cars Ltd., on 1.1.1926. 2-16 were centre-gangway coaches with a removable canvas roof and removable celluloid side screen. 17-21 were 'all-weather' coaches with full-height sides and a retractable canvas roof. Only the 'Super Lancias' (S) ever ran for Devon General, albeit still in Fleet Cars livery, lasting until the end of the 1934 season. The other sixteen were sold early in 1934.

Vehicles delivered new to Devon General, entering service in 1934

200 - 223	OD 7487-7510	AEC 'Regent'		Short Bros.	H28/24R

Chassis numbers: 06612437/40/35/39/38/36/41/42/44/43/45-58

Note: 200 to 208 were delivered late in 1933
Fleet numbers became DR200-224 under the 1939 scheme
DR200, 202, 204, 206, 207, 212-214, 216, 220, 222 and 223 were re-bodied by Brush in 1949 and became H30/26R.
DR203, 205, 210, 218 and 219 were rebuilt as open-top 31/24-seat in 1955
DR203, 206, 209, 210 and 219 were converted to run on producer gas during 1943/44

Dates of withdrawal:
1953	DR215	
1956	DR201, 208, 209, 211, 217 and 221	
1957	DR200, 202, 204, 206, 207, 212 - 214, 216, 220, 222 and 223	[DR213 Preserved]
1961	DR203, 205, 210, 218 and 219	[DR210 Preserved]

71 - 73	OD 9484-9486	Leyland 'Lion' LT5A		Short Bros.	B31F
74 - 76	OD 9487-9489	Leyland 'Lion' LT5A		Brush	B31F

Chassis numbers: 4467/68/71/66/69/70

Note: Fleet numbers allotted under the 1939 scheme were SK71-76, but as far as is known, none ever carried the prefix. Seating was altered to 32 in 1938.

Date of withdrawal:
All in 1940

Vehicles delivered new to Devon General and entering service in 1935

77 - 94   AUO 72-89   Leyland 'Lion' LT5A   Short Bros.   B36F
Chassis numbers: 5712/5/6/8/7/4/9/20/13/22/1/3/4/6/7/8/9/5

Note: Fleet numbers allotted under the 1939 scheme were SL77-94. Not all may have ever carried the prefix. All were
           withdrawn and sold in 1940 but some were subsequently re-purchased.

Dates of withdrawal:
      1946   89
      1947   SL78
      1948   SL79, 80, 82, 84, 85, 86, 88, 90, 91 and 93

224 - 225   AUO 90-91   AEC 'Regent'   Short Bros.   H28/24R
Chassis numbers: 06612939/40

Note: Fleet numbers became DR224 and DR225 under the 1939 scheme
           DR225 was re-bodied by Brush in 1949 and became H30/26R
           DR224 was rebuilt in 1955 as open-top, seating 31/24

Dates of withdrawal:
      1958   DR225
      1961   DR224

334 - 335   AUO 199/198   AEC 'Ranger'   Harrington   C26F   Grey Cars
Chassis numbers: 665053/4

Note: Seating reduced to 20 in 1935 and increased to 29 in 1940
           Fleet numbers became TCR334 and TCR335 under the 1939 scheme, and during 1946 the two vehicles ran with
           fleet numbers incorrectly exchanged.

Date of withdrawal:
      1949   TCR334 and TCR335

103   AUO 512   Leyland 'Cub' KP2   Mumford   B20F
Chassis number: 3954

Note: Fleet number became M103 under the 1939 scheme.

Date of withdrawal:
      1948   M103 and converted to a van

Vehicles acquired on 24th June 1935 from A. C. Aggett, Marldon

104   JY 3912   Ford   Mumford   B20F (new 1934)
Chassis number: BB 5310820

Date of withdrawal:
      1938   104

Vehicles acquired on 7th February 1936 from the Teignmouth Motor Car Company

---	DV 5335	Commer 'Invader' 6TK	Willowbrook	B20F (new 1930)
---	DV 5336	Commer 'Invader' 6TK	Willowbrook	C20 (new 1930)
---	UO 2380	Karrier	Unknown	C20 (new 1927)

Chassis numbers: 28052, 28111, H1054.

Note: None ever ran for Devon General.
           UO 2380 was new to Miller of Exmouth

Date of withdrawal:
      1935   DV 5335, DV 5336 and UO 2380

Vehicles delivered new to Devon General during 1936

336 - 345   AOD 599 - 608   Leyland 'Tigress'   . . .   Harrington   C26F
Chassis numbers: 9318-27

Note: Originally in light grey and maroon livery, but did not carry Grey Cars fleet-name until 1945.
          Renumbered TCL336-345 under the 1939 scheme.

Date of withdrawal:
      1949   TCL336-TCL345

110 - 119   BDV 1 - 10   Leyland 'Tiger' TS7   Harrington   B32F (Sun Saloons)
120 - 121   CTA 109 - 110 Leyland 'Tiger' TS7   Harrington   B32F (Sun Saloons)
Chassis numbers: 8929-38, 12213/4

Note: 120 did not enter service until 1st January 1937
          Fleet numbers became XL110 - XL121 under the 1939 scheme, but XL110, 113, 115, 117
          and 118 were latterly repainted as Grey Cars and renumbered TCL110, 113, 115, 117 and
          118. All were sold in 1940 but most were later re-purchased.

Date of withdrawal:
      1948   TCL110, 115, XL111, 112, 114, 116 and 121
      1952   TCL113, 118,
      1954   TCL117

95 - 96   BDV 11 - 12   Leyland 'Lion' LT7   Weymann   B36F
Chassis numbers: 8939/40   Body numbers: C5000/1

Note: Allocated fleet numbers SL95 and SL96 under the1939 scheme.

Date of withdrawal:
      1939   SL95 and SL96

226 - 229   BDV 13 - 16   Leyland 'Titan' TD4   Beadle   H30/26R
Chassis numbers: 9155-9158   Body numbers: 462/4/3/5

Note: Renumbered DL226 - DL229 under the 1939 scheme. Re-bodied by Northern Counties to
          H30/26R in 1945.

Date of withdrawal:
      1956   DL226 - DL229

Vehicles delivered new to Devon General in winter 1936/37

250 - 297   CTA 61 - 108   Leyland 'Lion' LT7   Harrington   B36F
Chassis numbers: 11851-98

Note: Renumbered SL250-297 under the 1939 scheme.
          Only 250-257 and 263 entered service in 1936
          SL287 sold in 1940 and later re-purchased

Date of withdrawal:
      1940   SL288
      1945   SL257
      1946   SL254, 268, 279, 284
      1947   SL250-252, 256, 263, 269, 272, 275-277, 281, 287, 291, 294-297
      1948   SL286

1949   SL253, 260, 261, 271, 274, 278, 282, 289, 293
1950   SL255, 258, 259, 262, 265, 266, 270, 273, 283, 285, 290, 292,. 264,.267,.280

Vehicles delivered new to Devon General in 1937

230 - 233   CTA 111 - 114   Leyland 'Titan' TD4   Beadle   H30/26R
Chassis numbers: 12215-8   Body numbers: 560-563

Note: Renumbered DL230-233 under the 1939 scheme.
Re-bodied by Strachan in 1946 to become H30/26R.

Date of withdrawal:
1956   DL230 - DL233

360 - 361   CTT 660 - 661   Bedford WTB   Birch   B24F
Chassis numbers: 111538/48

Note: These vehicles were originally in a duck-egg blue and cream livery for the 'Coastal Cruise' service, and had unglazed side windows. They were converted to normal buses in 1946 and renumbered M360 and M361 under the 1939 scheme.

Date of withdrawal:
1953   M360 and M361

234 - 235   DTT 47 - 48   AEC 'Regent'   Weymann   H30/26R
Chassis numbers: 06615343/4   Body numbers: M1128/7

Note: Renumbered DR2324 and DR235 under the 1939 scheme. They were fitted with the 7.7-litre engine instead of the more usual 8.8-litre unit, and had all-metal bodywork

Date of withdrawal:
1949   DR234 and DR235

Vehicles delivered new to Devon General in 1938

401 -404   ETT 993 - 996   AEC 'Regal'   Harrington   B32F
Chassis numbers: 06622446-9

Note: These were 'Sun Saloons' for the express services, and were actually delivered in December 1937, although did not enter service until May 1938. They were renumbered XR401-404 under the 1939 scheme. The seating was latterly increased by one to 33.

Date of withdrawal:
1952   XR401 to XR404

346 - 353   ETT 985 - 992   AEC 'Ranger'   Harrington   C26F
Chassis numbers: 665093-100

Note: 346 was delivered new in a light grey and maroon livery with the others being in saxe-blue. They were renumbered TCR346-353 under the 1939 scheme, and all received Grey Cars livery in 1946. The seating was altered to 27 in 1949.

Date of withdrawal:
1950   TCR346 - TCR353

236 - 238   ETT 997 - 999   AEC 'Regent'   Weymann   H28/26R
Chassis numbers: 06615436-8   Body numbers: M1453-55

Note: They were renumbered DR236 - DR238 under the 1939 scheme. DR238 was converted to run on producer-gas in 1943/44.

Date of withdrawal:
        1956   DR236 - DR238

405 - 417   DUO 317 - 329 AEC 'Regal'   Harrington   B35F
Chassis numbers: 06623025-37

Note: Allocated numbers SR405-417 under the 1939 scheme. 405-414 were converted to ambulances in 1939, of which
         406, 411-414 were purchased by the Royal navy in 1941, whilst the rest were returned for use and conversion back
         to a bus. SR405, 408, 415-417 received 'perimeter' seating for 30 in 1943, but re-converted to conventional 35 in
         1945. SR412 was re-purchased in 1947.

Date of withdrawal:
        1951   SR405, 407- 410, 412, 415 - 417

298 - 300   DUO 330 - 332 Dennis 'Lancet' II   Harrington   B35F
Chassis numbers: 175557/60/64

Note: All were renumbered SD298-SD300 under the 1939 scheme

Date of withdrawal:
        1950   SD298 - SD300

450 - 451   EUO 192 - 193 Bedford WLG   Birch   B14F
Chassis numbers: 0158716, 0159116

Note: These were both station buses for use at Budleigh Salterton and Sidmouth and were renumbered M418 and M419
         under the 1939 scheme. They were converted to 20 seats in 1947 for use on conventional country services.

Date of withdrawal:
        1952   M418 and M419 (450 and 451)

Vehicles delivered new to Devon General in 1939

XR420 - 425   DDV 420 - 425 AEC 'Regal'   Harrington   B32F
Chassis numbers: 06623300-5

Note: These six buses were 'Sun Saloons' for express services and had their seating capacity increased to 33 latterly

Date of withdrawal:
        1953   XR420 - 425

SR426 - 451   DDV 426 - 451 AEC 'Regal'   Harrington   B35F
Chassis numbers: 06623306-31

Note: SR426, 427, 436, 444, 445 and 450 were re-bodied in 1948 by Weymann to B35F

Date of withdrawal:
        1952   SR428-435, 437-443, 446-449 and 451
        1953   SR444
        1954   SR426, 427, 436, 445 and 450

M452 - 453   DDV 452 - 453 Leyland 'Cub' KPZ04   Weymann   B20F
Chassis numbers: 201468/9   Body numbers: C5419/20

Date of withdrawal:
        1950   M452 and M453

Vehicles delivered new to Devon General in winter 1939/40

XR454 - 455	DOD 454 - 455	AEC 'Regal'	Weymann	B32F
SR456	DOD 456	AEC 'Regal'	Harrington	B35F
SR457 - 479	DOD 457 - 479	AEC 'Regal'	Weymann	B35F

Chassis numbers: 06623459/8, 06623392, 06623435-57

Note: XR454 and 455 were 'Sun Saloons' for express services.
        SR457, 460, 461, 464, 467, 471, 472, 475 & 479 were re-bodied in 1948 by Weymann as B35F.
        SR463, 473 and 478 were re-bodied in 1950 by Weymann as B35F.
        XR454 and 455 were latterly B33F
        SR474 was later stored for preservation.

Date of withdrawal:
      1952   XR454, 455, SR456, 458, 459, 462, 465, 466, 468, 469, 474, 476 and 477
      1953   SR470
      1955   SR457, 460, 461, 463, 464, 467, 471 - 473, 475, 478 and 479.

Vehicles hired from East Kent Road Car Co. Ltd., from November 1940

DL301 - 305	AJG 31 - 35	Leyland 'Titan' TD5	Park Royal	L27/26R

Chassis numbers: 301034-8   Body numbers: 5382-6

Note: These were new in 1938 and arrived at Devon General in Southdown livery but were repainted into Devon General livery soon after entering service. They were returned to East Kent in 1943 following delivery of the 'Guys'.

Vehicles hired from London Transport from 14th January 1942

ST932	GK 1008	AEC 'Regent'	Tilling	H27/25Ros
ST950	GK 1026	AEC 'Regent'	Tilling	H27/25Ros

Chassis numbers: 661664/87

Note: Both of these buses retained London Transport livery and fleet-numbers. They had outside staircase and both were returned to London after the 'Guys' were delivered in 1943.

Vehicles delivered new to Devon General in 1942

DL239	HTA 302	Leyland 'Titan' TD7	Weymann	H30/26R

Chassis number: 307050   Body number: C7459

Note: Originally in wartime grey livery, this bus was ordered by Newport Corporation but diverted to Devon General.

Date of withdrawal:
      1955   DL239

Vehicles delivered new to Devon General in 1943

DG240	HTA 740	Guy 'Arab' I 6LW	Park Royal	30/26R

Chassis number: FD2555868   Body number: 21017

Note: Originally in wartime grey livery.

Date of withdrawal:
      1956   DG240

DD241 - 242	HTA 881 - 882	Daimler CWG5	Duple	H30/26R

Chassis numbers: 11383/8   Body numbers: 34560/76

Note: Originally in wartime grey livery. In 1944 exchanged with Rhondda Transport for 'Guys' DG318 and 319.

DG308 - 317 JTA 308 - 317 Guy 'Arab' II 5LW Weymann H30/26R
Chassis numbers: FD25955/75/87, 26047/8/50/87/88, 26103/7
Body numbers: C7899/904/907/920/919/922/926-929

Note: Originally in wartime grey livery
  DG308, 309, 311-315 and 317 were re-bodied by C.H.Roe of Leeds as H31/25R
  DG311-315 and 317 were fitted with platform doors in 1953
  DG309, 311, 312, 313 and 317 were fitted with luggage racks in 1954 which reduced the seating to H31/23.

Date of withdrawal:
  1956 DG310 and 316
  1959 DG308, 309, 311-315 and 317 [DG314 preserved]

DG243 - 245 JTA 543 - 545 Guy 'Arab' II 5LW Weymann H30/26R
Chassis numbers: FD26278/80/81 Body numbers: C7957-9

Note: Originally in wartime grey livery, and re-bodied in 1951 by C.H.Roe of Leeds as H31/25R

Date of withdrawal:
  1959 DG243 - 245

Vehicles delivered new to Devon General in 1944

DG246 - 249 JTA 546 - 549 Guy 'Arab' II 5LW Weymann H30/26R
Chassis numbers: 26401/3-5 Body numbers: C7982/3/4/92

Note: DG246 was delivered in wartime grey livery, all the others in DG livery. They were re-bodied by C.H. Roe in Leeds in 1951 as H31/25R

Date of withdrawal:
  1959 DG246-249

Vehicles received by Devon General in June 1944 in exchange for Daimlers DD241/242

DG318 - 319 ETX 832 - 833 Guy 'Arab' I 5LW Weymann H30/26R
Chassis numbers: FD25468/77 Body numbers: C7337/41

Note: Both were re-bodied by C. H. Roe of Leeds in 1951 as H31/25R and in 1953 they were fitted with platform doors and luggage racks at which time the seating was reduced to H31/23R

Date of withdrawal:
  1959 DG318 and 319

Vehicles delivered new to Devon General in 1945

DG320 -325 GTT 420 - 425 Guy 'Arab' II 6LW Park Royal H30/26R
Chassis numbers: FD27914/7/23, 28013/4/20 Body numbers: 30978-80, 30998-31000

Dates of withdrawal:
  1957 DG322
  1959 DG320, 321, 323 - 325

Vehicles delivered new to Devon General in 1946

SR480 - 507 HTT 480 - 507 AEC 'Regal' Weymann B35F
SR508 JTT 708 AEC 'Regal' Weymann B35F
Chassis numbers: 06624806-32, 06625079, 06624833 Body numbers: C9046-73, 167

Note: SR494 was converted to a standee bus with just 27 seats and capacity for 22 standing in 1952.

Date of withdrawal:
        1952   SR484, 486, 487, 498, 502 and 504
        1953   SR480-483, 485, 488-497, 499-501, 503 and 508
        1955   SR505, 506 and 507   [SR487 preserved]

Vehicles delivered new to Devon General in 1947

DR326 - 333   HTT 326 - 333   AEC 'Regent' III   Weymann   H30/26R
Chassis numbers: 0961218-24/30   Body numbers: M3053/48/55/2/1/49/54/60

Note: These buses were built on London Transport type chassis with low-mounted radiator and pre-selector gear-box.

Date of withdrawal:
        1960   DR326 - 333

Vehicle acquired from Greenslades Tours Ltd., Exeter, on 1st January 1948

M610   EFJ 548   Bedford WTB   Tiverton   B25F
Chassis number: 7890

Note: This vehicle was new in 1938 and was acquired with the Witheridge Transport services formerly operated by
        Greenslades

Date of withdrawal:
        1950   M610

Vehicles delivered new to Devon General in 1948
TCB600 - 609 JUO 600 - 609   Bedford OB   Duple   C29F
Chassis numbers: 63393, 65082, 69859, 71117, 71224, 71454, 73118, 75437, 76097, 76253
Body numbers: 47690-9

Note: All these were delivered in full Grey Cars livery, but TCB600-604 and 607 were cascaded for bus use and repainted
        in bus livery between 1952 and 1954, at which time they were re-classified and numbered SB600 etc.
        SB600 and SB601 were converted to 20-seat in 1953,
        SB603 and 604 to 24-seat in 1956.

Date of withdrawal:
        1954   TCB605, 606 and 608
        1958   TCB609, SB600, 601, 602, 603, 604, 607   [SB608 was saved for preservation but was later abandoned]

SR509 - 548   HUO 509 - 548 AEC 'Regal'   Weymann   B35F
Chassis numbers: 06625519-58
Bodynumbers:9195/88/94/89/92/91/3/0/8/7/9/6/226/04/1/3/5/2/19/6/08/6/21/13,
9200/7/27/09/20/15/25/11/24/3/10/22/14/7/8/2.

Note: Bodies numbered C9188 to 9209 had half-drop windows; the remainder were fitted with sliding vent windows.

Date of withdrawal:
        1957   SR509-520, 522 and 523
        1958   SR521, 525, 527-529, 531, 532, 535-538, 540, 541, 544-546
        1959   SR524, 526, 530, 533, 534, 536, 537, 539, 542, 543, 547 and 548   [SR510 is preserved]

DR549 - 566   JUO 549 - 566   AEC 'Regent' III   Weymann   H30/26R
Chassis numbers: 09611224-33, 9612E1234-41
Body numbers: M3273/8/68/79/85/71/69/80/75/70/76/82/83/74/77/81/72/84

Date of withdrawal:
        1960   DR549 - 566

TCR611 - 622 JOD 611 - 622 AEC 'Regal' III   Duple   C32F
Chassis numbers: 9621A332-9/326-9   Body numbers: 45336-42/7/3-6

Note: These were all in full Grey Cars livery and with upswept rear-end in order to clear ferry ramps.
        615-622 although delivered in 1948 did not go into service until 1949.

Date of withdrawal:
        1952   TCR611 - 622

Vehicles delivered new to Devon General during 1949

DR567 - 592 KOD 567 - 592 AEC 'Regent' III   Weymann   H30/26R
Chassis numbers: 9612E2477-2502   Body numbers: M3780/77/79/78/82/86/81/85/84/83/88,99/89
96/802/794/93/92/87/90/91/800/01/795/97/98

Note: DR578, 580-584, 587-592 were stored for the winter of 1949 and therefore did not enter service until 1950, and
        then on Exeter city services.

Date of withdrawal:
        1961   DR567-577, 579, 585 and 586
        1962   DR578, 580-584, 587-592   [DR585 is preserved]

Vehicles delivered new to Devon General during 1950

SR593 - 597 LUO 593 - 597 AEC 'Regal' III   Weymann   B35F
Chassis numbers: 6821A448-452   Body numbers: C9393/92/89/91/90

Date of withdrawal:
        1962   SR593 - 597   [SR595 preserved]

TCR623 - 634 LTA 623 - 634 AEC 'Regal' III   Duple   C32F
Chassis numbers: 9621A773-784   Body numbers: 55181/77-80/3/2/4/4/6/8/7

Note: Delivered in full Grey Cars livery, and with the upswept rear-end in order to clear ferry ramps.
        TCR624-627 were actually delivered late in 1949 but did not enter service until the 1950 new season.

Date of withdrawal:
        1958   TCR623-634   [TCR629 is still in use with a Classic tour company]

Vehicles delivered new to Devon General during 1951

SL635 - 639 MTT 635 - 639 Leyland 'Royal Tiger'   Willowbrook   B43F
Chassis numbers: 502625/2/3/4/6   Body numbers: 50826/7/8/30/29

Date of withdrawal:
        1963   SL635-639

DL640 - 645 MTT 640 - 645 Leyland   Leyland   L27/26R
Chassis numbers: 511256/8/9/61/57/60

Note: These were lowbridge type double-deckers having side gangway on the off-side upstairs.
        DL643 lost its DL prefix on repainting in 1962.

Date of withdrawal:
        1964   DL640 - 645   [DL640 preserved]

DR646 - 659 MTT 646 - 659 AEC 'Regent' III   Weymann   H30/26R
Chassis numbers: 9613A2586-99   Body numbers: M4477/86/81/90/78/83/82/85/84/88/87/89/80/79

Note: These were the first 8 feet wide vehicles in the fleet following the change in regulations.
DR646-651 were fitted with platform doors in 1955 and renumbered DRD 646-651 during 1957-1959.
DRD646, 649, DR653, 656 and 658 lost their prefix on repainting during 1962/3.

Date of withdrawal:
1964   DRD646-659

Vehicles delivered new to Devon General during 1952

DR660 - 678   NTT 660 - 678   AEC 'Regent' III   Weymann   H30/26R
Chassis numbers: 9613A7154-72   Body numbers: M5511/14/15/09/16/19/21/08/18/20/10/06/17/13/07/12/22/
04/05

Note: DR661, 662, 666, 669, 670 and 673 lost their DR prefix on repainting in 1962/3 but
DR670 carried the DR again for its last few days of its service in 1965.

Date of withdrawal:
1964   DR667 (for removal of top for use as a tree lopper)
1965   DR660-666, 668-678   [DR661 is preserved]

DR679   NTT 679   AEC 'Regent' III   Weymann   H30/26R
Chassis number: 9613s7173   Body number: M5523

Note: DR679 had a concealed radiator, and the new design of body was named 'Aurora', being quite different from those
fitted to DR660 etc. It was exhibited, prior to delivery, at the Commercial Motor Show in London, and remained
very much a one-off prototype.

Date of withdrawal:
1965   DR679   [now preserved]

Vehicles acquired from Leicester Corporation Transport in July 1952

DR698 - 70   DJF 324 - 328   AEC 'Regent' II   Park Royal   H30/26R
DR703   DJF 330   AEC 'Regent' II   Park Royal   H30/26R
Chassis numbers: 06617518/9/3/21/2/6   Body numbers: 31753/7/8/62/3/5   New in 1946

Note: Leicester Corporation numbers were 211 - 215 and 217. Devon General initially allocated them fleet-numbers
DR101-106, but these were soon changed to 698-703. They all ran in Leicester livery of red and cream for their
first year in Devon and were repainted into traditional livery in 1953.

Date of withdrawal:
1960   DR698-702, 703

Vehicles hired from City of Oxford Motor Services Ltd., July to August 1952

H138 - 139   HFC 951 - 952   AEC 'Regent'   Weymann   H26/26R
H133   HFC 953   AEC 'Regent'   Weymann   H26/26R
H135 - 136   HFC 954 - 955   AEC 'Regent'   Park Royal   H26/26R
H145   HFC   AEC 'Regent'   Park Royal   H26/26R
Chassis numbers: 06616589/92/3/0/1/4   Body numbers: C5421-3, 5691-3   New in 1939

Note: These buses were hired to cover vehicles used on the special service work in connection with the Royal
Agricultural Show held at Stover near Newton Abbot. They were returned to Oxford at the conclusion of the
show.

Vehicles acquired from Mrs. W. A. Hart, Budleigh Salterton on 17th March 1952

	AYC 106	Albion 'Victor' PK115	Harrington	C27C
---	DTA 499	Albion 'Victor' PK115	Tiverton	B30F
---	OD 8725 - 8726	Commer 'Centaur'	Tiverton	B20F
---	BTT 186	Commer B3	Tiverton	B20F

Chassis numbers: 25002D, 25012H, 56034, 56033, 63010

Note: AYC 106 was new in 1935, DTA 499 was new in 1936, OD 8725-6 were new in 1934 and BTT
        186 was new in 1935. None of them were allocated fleet numbers by Devon General or indeed used by the
        Company.

Vehicle acquired from Balls Bus Service Ltd, Newton Abbot on 21st October 1952

| --- | FTT 800 | Bedford OWB | Duple | B30F |

Chassis number: 21332. Body number: 38863   New in 1944

Note: This vehicle was not allocated a fleet-number by Devon General or ever used by them.

Vehicles delivered new to Devon General during 1953

| **TCR680 - 691** | NUO 680 - 691 | AEC 'Regal' IV | Willowbrook | C41F |

Chassis numbers: 9822s1624-35   Body numbers: 53094/6/5/7-53105

Note: TCR682 was in Townsend's livery between 1954 and 1958, whilst all the others were in Grey Cars colours.

Date of withdrawal:
        1961   TCR680 - 688
        1962   TCR689 - 691

| **DR705** | ETT 995 | AEC Rebuild | Saunders Roe | H30/26R |

Chassis number: 06615343   Body number: 1436

Note: DR705 was a lightweight vehicle built on the frames from DR234 and with running units from
        XR403. It was originally allocated the registration number NUO 681 with fleet number DR681 but changed before
        actual registration, to ETT 995 at which time it was given the new fleet number of DR705.

Date of withdrawal:
        1963   DR705   [now preserved]

DR704	ETT 994	AEC Rebuild	Weymann	H32/26R
DR706	DUO 317	AEC Rebuild	Weymann	H32/26R
DR707 - 710	DUO 319 - 322	AEC Rebuild	Weymann	H32/26R
DR711 - 713	DUO 327 - 329	AEC Rebuild	Weymann	H32/26R
DR714 - 715	DDV 420 - 421	AEC Rebuild	Weymann	H32/26R
DR716	DDV 446	AEC Rebuild	Weymann	H32/26R
DR717 - 718	DOD 454 - 455	AEC Rebuild	Weymann	H32/26R

Chassis numbers: 06622447/3025/7-30/5-7/3300/1/26/3459/8
Body numbers: M6191/95/201/198/92/99/97/89/94/200/190/96/93/88

Note: These were all light-weight double-deckers, more commonly known as the 'light-sixes', and were constructed from
        parts of AEC 'Regals' XR402, SR405, 407-410, 415-417, XR420, 421, SR446, XR454, 455 (whose registrations they
        took), with re-conditioned second-hand chassis frames.

Date of withdrawal:
        1963   DR704, 706 - 718

Vehicles delivered new to Devon General during 1954

| DR719 - 722 | DDV 422 - 425 | AEC Rebuild | Weymann | H32/26R |
| DR723 | DOD 469 | AEC Rebuild | Weymann | H32/26R |

Chassis numbers: 06623302-5/3447   Body numbers: M6465/4/7/8/6

Note: These were all light-weight double-deckers, more commonly known as the 'light-sixes', and were constructed from parts of AEC 'Regals' XR422-425, SR469, (whose registrations they took), with re-conditioned second-hand chassis frames.

Date of withdrawal:
  1963   DR719 - 723

DR724 - 735   PDV 724 - 735   AEC 'Regent' III   Weymann   H32/26R
Chassis numbers: 9613s8090-8101   Body numbers: M6462/54/3/9/5/60/3/1/58/2/6/7

Note: These were double-deckers of light-weight construction with platform doors and concealed radiator. DR730 had an extra seat and was classified as H33/26R. They were renumbered DRD724-735 in 1957-1959 and the prefix removed from them in 1962.

Date of withdrawal:
  1966   DR724 - 735

TCR692 - 697   PDV 692 - 697   AEC 'Regal' IV   Park Royal   C41F
Chassis numbers: 9822s1786-91   Body numbers: 37246-51

Note: All were in Grey Cars livery, and it was originally proposed to cascade them to service buses after their eight years' service as coaches, but in the event, this was never carried out.

Date of withdrawal:
  1962   TCR692 - 697

Vehicles acquired from A. E. Townsend, Torquay on 1st April 1954

TC736 - 737	JOD 638 - 639	Dennis 'Lancet' III	Dutfield	C33F
TC738 - 739	KOD 116 - 117	Dennis 'Lancet' III	Dutfield	C33F
TC740	MTA 567	Tilling Stevens	Dutfield	C33F
TC741	NTT 246	Bedford SB	Duple	C33F
TC742	OUO 587	Bedford SB	Duple	C35F
TC743	POD 908	Bedford SBG	Burlingham	C36F

Chassis numbers: 393J3, 439J3, 608J3, 620J3, 9619, 5851, 16254, 29139

Note: All retained Townsend's livery. TC740-743 were repainted into Grey Cars livery in 1958. TC741-743 were renumbered TCB741-743. TC740 had a full-fronted body.

Date of withdrawal:
  1957   TC736 - 739
  1958   TC740 - 743

Vehicles acquired from Balls Tours Ltd., Newton Abbot in September 1954

SB744	LTT 44	Bedford OB	Mulliner	B28F
SC745	KTT 44	Commer 'Commando'	Whitson	C29F
SB746	JDV 789	Bedford OB	Mulliner	B31F
TC747	LUO 444	Commer 'Avenger'	Harrington	C32F
TC748	MOD 44	Commer 'Avenger'	Heaver	C33F

Chassis numbers: 115870, 17A1113, 67110, 23A0146, 23A0564

Note: SC745 and SB746 never ran in service for Devon General
SB744 was repainted into bus livery, and
TC747 and 747 into Grey Cars livery
SB744 and TC747 were new in 1949, SC745 was new in 1948, SB746 was new in 1947,
TC748 was new in 1951.

Date of withdrawal:
   1956   SB744, SC745, SB746
   1957   TC747, 748

Vehicle acquired from H. D. Gourd & Sons, Bishopsteignton on 1st January 1955

| --- | ETG 295 | Bedford WTB | Wilmott | C20F |

Chassis number: 20016   New in 1939

Note: ETG 295 was never used by Devon General.

Date of withdrawal:
   1957   ETG 295

Vehicles delivered new to Devon General during 1955

TCR749 - 750   ROD 749 - 750   AEC 'Reliance'   Weymann 'Fanfare' C37F
Chassis numbers: MU3RV640/1   Body numbers: M7016/7

Note: These were both for Grey Cars.

Date of withdrawal:
   1964   TCR749 and 750

Vehicles delivered new to Devon General during 1956

TCC751 - 756   ROD 751 - 756   Commer TS3   Beadle   C41F
Chassis numbers: JCB647-652

Note: TCC751-754 were originally in Townsend's livery, but were repainted into Grey Cars from 1958, whereas TCC755
   and 756 were always Grey Cars.

Date of withdrawal:
   1964   TCC751 - 756

SC757 - 759   ROD 757 - 759   Commer TS3   Beadle   B40F
Chassis numbers: JCB653-655

Note: SC757 was involved in a very serious accident at Heathfield when it collided with a Royal Blue coach as a result
   of which it was scrapped in Newton Road body shop in 1963.

Date of withdrawal:
   1963   SC757
   1967   SC758 and 759

DR760 - 779   ROD 760 - 779   AEC 'Regent' V   Metro-Cammell   H33/26R
DR780 - 789   TTT 780 - 789   AEC 'Regent' V   Metro-Cammell   H33/26R
Chassis numbers: MD3RV031-50/218-227

Note: DR760, 770-776, 778 and 779 were actually delivered late in 1955.
   All had lightweight metal bodywork.
   DR760-769 and DR780-789 had platform doors and were renumbered DRD 760 etc during 1958-1960. All lost
their prefix on repainting between 1962 and 1964. DR784-787 became the property of Western National   from   1st
January 1971 but they never ran again on service.

Date of withdrawal:
   1968   DR760-783
   1969   DR788 and 789   [DRD765 and DRD781 are preserved]

SC790 - 792   TTT 790 - 792   Commer TS3   Beadle   B40F
Chassis numbers: JCB656-658

Note: SC791 lost its SC prefix on repainting in 1963.

Date of withdrawal:
        1967   SC790-792

Vehicles delivered new to Devon General during 1957

SR793 - 806   VDV 793 - 806   AEC 'Reliance'   Weymann   B41F
Chassis numbers: MU3RA1410-2/20/14/5/21/3/18/9/3/6/22/3
Body numbers: M8016/23/2/0/1/18/7/9/1/4/2/3/0/5

Note: SR801-806 had opening glass roof-panels. All lost their prefix on repainting between 1962 and 1965.

Date of withdrawal:
        1969   SR794-797, 800, 802-806
                SR793, 798, 799 and 801 passed to Western National on 1st January 1971
        1971   SR798
        1972   SR793, 799 and 801   [SR798 is in store pending preservation]

DR807 - 819   VDV 807 - 819   AEC 'Regent' V   Metro-Cammell   H33/26R

Note: All these had rear open-platform for use on Exeter city services. They lost their DR prefix on repainting during the
        period 1962 - 1963. All passed to Western National on 1st January 1971.

Date of withdrawal:
        1971   DR807 - 819   [DR817 and DR818 are preserved]

Vehicles acquired from Falkland Coaches, Torquay during June 1957

TCB820   MOD 363   Bedford SB   Duple   C33F
TCB821   NDV 44   Bedford SB   Duple   C33F
TCB822   BEN 500   Bedford SB   Yeates   C35F
TCB823   SUO 826   Bedford SB   Duple   C36F
Chassis numbers: 2181, 9600, 10157, 37378

Note: TCB822 was new to Auty, Bury in 1953.
        TCB820 was new in 1951, and retained Falkland livery
        TCB821 was new in 1952
        TCB823 was new in 1955.
        Apart from TCB820, all were repainted into Grey Cars livery.

Date of withdrawal:
        1957   TCB820
        1958   TCB821, 822 and 823.

Vehicles delivered new to Devon General during 1958

SR824 - 837   XTA 824 - 837   AEC 'Reliance'   Weymann   B41F
Chassis numbers: MU3RV 1767-80   Body numbers: M8381/0/2/3/90/89/8/93/2/85/91/86/7/4

Note: All lost their SR prefix on repainting during the period 1962 to 1964, and passed to Western National on 1st
        January 1971.

Date of withdrawal:
        1972   SR824 and 826
        1973   SR825, 827-837

SN838 - 843   XTA 838 - 843   Albion Nimbus   Willowbrook   B31F
Chassis numbers: 82050G/H/C/D/E/F   Body numbers: 58005/6/2/3/4/1

Note: These were big little buses and were purchased to replace the Bedford OB buses. All lost their SN prefix on
        repainting during the period 1962 to 1964. They passed to Western National on 1st January 1971.

Date of withdrawal:
1971   SN838 and 839
1972   SN840 - 843   [SN839 is preserved]

TCC844 - 849 XTA 844 - 849   Commer TS3   Beadle 'Rochester'   C41F
Chassis numbers: JCB 754-757/89/90

Note: All were in Grey Cars livery.

Date of withdrawal:
1966   TCC844 - 849

TCR850 - 859 XTA 850 - 859   AEC 'Reliance'   Willowbrook 'Viking'   C41F
Chassis numbers: MU3RV 2075-84   Body numbers: 58102/8/4/9/3/6/10/05/7/11

Note: All in Grey Cars livery, and lost their TCR prefix on refurbishment during 1962.

Date of withdrawal:
1966   TCR850 - 854, 857, 858 and 859
1967   TCR855 and 856   [TCR851 is awaiting preservation]

Vehicles delivered new to Devon General during 1959

SR860 - 871   860 - 871 ATA   AEC 'Reliance'   Willowbrook   B41F
Chassis numbers: 2MU3RV2127-38   Body numbers: 59291-302

Note: All lost their SR prefix on repainting during the period 1963 - 1964.
869 was withdrawn after a bad accident in 1967.
860 - 868, 870 and 871 passed to Western National on 1st January 1971.
860 - 866 were loaned to Alder Valley in July 1974 to assist with their vehicle shortage, still in full Devon
General livery at the time.
867, 868 and 871 received the NBC poppy red livery in 1974.

Date of withdrawal:
1974   860 - 866 and 870
1976   867, 868 and 871

DL872 - 888   872 - 888 ATA   Leyland 'Atlantean'   Metro-Cammell   H44/34F
Chassis numbers: 590513/615-7/592/627/68/76/7/59/89/7/8/755/4/65/6
Body numbers: H051196/1 - 17

Note: The Atlantean was fitted with a pneumo-epicyclic semi-automatic gearbox
The seating was altered to 44/32 when a luggage pen was fitted to each bus in 1959/60.
All lost their DL prefix on repainting between 1963 and 1965, and passed to Western National from 1st January
1971.
875 received a new roof by Willowbrook following a low-bridge accident in 1968.
Eight were converted to one-man operation in 1971/72, but the rest were not so modified until 1977-1980.
All received NBC poppy red livery between 1973 and 1975,
882 and 883 becoming NBC leaf green in 1980.
872, 881, 882 and 884 were transferred to Western National Cornish depots towards the end of their days.

Date of withdrawal:
1981   873, 875 - 879, 884 - 888
1982   872, 874, 880, 882 and 883
1983   881   [872 is preserved]

TCR889 - 894 889 - 894 ADV   AEC 'Reliance'   Willowbrook 'Viking'   C41F
Chassis numbers: 2MU3RV 2348-53   Body numbers: 59365-70

Note: All Grey Cars and lost their TCR prefix on refurbishment in 1962.
893 and 894 were transferred to Court Coaches and re-painted in their orange and cream livery in 1966.

Date of withdrawal:
    1966   889, 890 and 892
    1967   891
    1968   893 and 894   [890 preserved]

Vehicles delivered new to Devon General during 1960

DL895 - 917   895 - 917 DTT   Leyland 'Atlantean'   Roe   H44/31F
Chassis numbers: 592467/71/2/81/2/91/2/3, 592517/8/9/30/72/97/98/99, 592506/7/8/45/69/70, 600097
Body numbers: G05042-64

Note: DL897 - 899, 902 and 913 had illuminated offside advert panels when new.
    All lost their DL prefix during repaint between 1962 and 1963, and all passed to Western National on 1st January 1971.
    896 - 901, 904 - 909, 911 - 913, 915 and 916 were adapted and modified for one-man operation during 1971 and 1978.
    896 - 902, 904 - 909, 911 - 916 received NBC poppy red livery during the period 1973 to 1977
    895, 902, 903, 910, 914 and 917 last ran in 1976/77 and were retained until 1980 for possible rebuild but the decision was changed and they were scrapped at Newton Road, Torquay.
    900 was repainted in Great Western Railway livery of chocolate and cream and sent to Cornwall to commemorate 75 Years of railway buses.
    899, 907, 909, 913 and 915 received NBC leaf green livery in 1979/80, 907 actually carried Western National fleet-name.

Date of withdrawal:
    1981   898 - 901, 905, 906, 908, 911, 912 and 916
    1982   896, 897 and 904
    On the separation of Western National from 1st January 1983, 909 and 915 became the property of Devon General Ltd., and 907 and 913 of Western National Ltd., but all four were taken from service later in the same year.
    1983 - 907, 909, 913 and 915   [913 is preserved]

Vehicles delivered new to Devon General during 1961

DL918 - 924   918 - 924 GTA   Leyland 'Atlantean'   Roe   H44/31F
Chassis numbers: 602568/9/70/93/4/2622/3   Body numbers: G05254-60

Note: All originally were built with illuminated offside advert panels which were lit by fluorescent tubes as were the internal lights, which if all left on without the engine running, caused flat batteries and consequent problems. The advert panels were soon removed. All lost their DL prefix on repainting during 1963 and 1964. As with the rest of the fleet, all passed to Western National on 1st January 1971 and received NBC poppy red livery in the period 1972 - 1973. All were converted for one-man operation between 1972 and 1977.
    920 and 921 were treated to NBC leaf green livery in 1979 and were transferred to Cornwall depots.
    918 also received the green livery but with Devon General fleet-name.

Date of withdrawal:
    1980   922
    1981   923 and 924
    1982   918, 919 and 921
    1986   920, having been passed to North Devon Ltd., from 1st January 1983.

DL925 - 933   925 - 933 GTA   Leyland' Atlantean'   Metro-Cammell   CO44/31F
Chassis numbers: 602642-4/64-66/728-730   Body numbers: H052698/1-9

Note: These nine buses were built with removable tops for easy conversion to open-top. They were in a reversed livery
and all named after local 'Sea Dogs' (as were the original buses in 1919) as follows:
DL925   Admiral Blake
DL926   Sir Francis Drake
DL927   Sir Martin Frobisher
DL928   Sir Humphrey Gilbert
DL929   Sir Richard Grenville
DL930   Sir John Hawkins
DL931   Sir Thomas Howard
DL932   Earl Howe
DL933   Sir Walter Raleigh

DL925 was de-named by 1983, DL927 was renamed Admiral Hardy from 1978, DL931 and 933 were de-named in
1979, and DL932 was de-named in 1980. All lost their DL prefix on repainting in 1962, transferred to Western
National on 1st January 1971 and in 1972 they received a modified version of the NBC corporate poppy red livery,
having more white than red. All except 932 were converted for one-man operation between 1975 and 1981.
927 was transferred to Dorset in 1978
925 and 926 were sent to Cornwall in 1977/1975
931 and 933 received NBC poppy red Unibus livery in 1979, and 932 in 1980.
933 received NBC leaf green livery in 1981
928-930 and 932 became the property of the new Devon General Ltd., on 1st January 1983
925 and 931 became the property of the new Western National Ltd., on 1st January 1983
925 was later transferred to North Devon Ltd., (t/a Red Bus) and it was re-registered ADV 299A whilst running
for them up until 1991.

Date of withdrawal:
1982   926, 927 and 933
1983   928, 929, 930, 931 and 932
1991   925   [931 and 932 preserved]

TCR934 - 940   934 - 940 GTA   AEC 'Reliance'   Willowbrook   C41F
TCR941 - 942   941 - 942 GTA   AEC 'Reliance'   'Viscount'   C37F
Chassis numbers: 2MU3RV3090-8   Body numbers: 60669-77

Note: All Grey Cars and lost their TCR prefix on repainting during 1964 and 1965.
TCR941 & 942 were 8' wide for extended tour work whereas the rest were 7'6" for Dartmoor.

Date of withdrawal:
1969   TCR934 and 935
1970   TCR936 to 942 All passed to Greenslades Tours of Exeter   [TCR935 is preserved]

Vehicles delivered new to Devon General during 1962

943 - 949   943 - 949 HTT   AEC 'Regent' V   Weymann   H33/26R
Chassis numbers: MD3RV558-564   Body numbers: M176/7/8/3/2/4/5

Note: These buses were the last ordered with open rear platform for use on Exeter city services.
They had illuminated offside advert panels and it was not long before they too were discontinued. All were
transferred to Western National on 1st January 1971 but none ever received NBC poppy red livery.

Date of withdrawal
1972   949
1974   943 - 948

SR950 - 956   950 - 956 HTT   AEC 'Reliance'   Marshall   B41F
Chassis numbers: 2MU3RV3943-9   Body numbers: B3042/5/39/40/1/3/4

Note: All lost their SR prefix in 1965 on repaint. They were transferred to Western National on 1st January 1971.
         950-952 and 955 received NBC poppy red livery in 1974.
         950 was transferred to Cornwall for a few months in 1974/5.
         964 worked at Taunton for a few months in 1974

Date of withdrawal:
         1974   951, 953 - 956
         1976   950 and 952

SN957 - 959   957 - 959 HTT   Albion 'Nimbus'   Harrington   B31F
Chassis numbers: 82065D/E/F   Body numbers: 2585-7

Note: All lost their SN prefix on repaint in 1963/64 and were transferred to Western National on 1st January 1971. None
         stayed long enough to be repainted into NBC livery.

Date of withdrawal:
         1972   957 and 958
         1974   959

TCR960 - 968   960 - 968 HTT   AEC 'Reliance'   Willowbrook 'Viscount'   C41F
Chassis numbers: 2MU3RV3934-43   Body numbers: 61764/1/5/6/7/2/0/3/8

Note: All Grey Cars and lost their TCR prefix during 1964/5. 964-968 transferred to Western National on 1st January
         1971.

Date of withdrawal:
         1970   960 - 963 passed to Greenslades of Exeter (from Devon General)
         1971   964 - 968 passed to Greenslades of Exeter (from Western National)
         [TCR960 is preserved]

Vehicles delivered new to Devon General during 1963

969 - 984   969 - 984 MDV   AEC 'Regent' V   Metro-Cammell   H33/26F
Chassis numbers: MD3RV566-581   Body numbers: H054490/1-16

Note: These were the first front-entrance Regent Vs for the fleet. All were delivered with illuminated offside advert panels
         but these were panelled over except for 976, 978 and 983 which for some reason retained them. All were
         transferred to Western National on 1st January 1971.
         969, 974, 976 and 979 received NBC poppy red livery during 1973-75.

Date of withdrawal:
         1975   969 - 984

985 - 991   985 - 991 MDV   AEC 'Reliance'   Marshall   B41F
Chassis numbers: 2MU3RV4418-24   Body numbers: B3061/56/7/9/8/60/2

Note: All were transferred to Western National on 1st January 1971.
         988 received NBC poppy red livery in 1974
         991 was the highest number allocated to a new vehicle with Devon General, and from now on, a new system was
         introduced starting at 1 for single-deckers and 500 for double-deckers.

Date of withdrawal:
         1975   985 - 991   [991 survives awaiting preservation]

1 - 8   1 - 8 RDV   AEC 'Reliance'   Harrington 'Cavalier'   C41F
Chassis numbers: 2MU3RA4971-8   Body numbers: 2850-7

Note   All Grey Cars, and the first vehicles to come within the new fleet numbering system starting from 1. During 1970 they were treated to the all-white paint scheme with a central wide band of grey on which sat a fairly large GREY CARS in capital letters. All passed to Western National on 1st January 1971 and to Greenslades of Exeter on 2nd May 1971.

Number 1 was used by the Directors for their annual tour of inspection from 1964 onwards.

Date of withdrawal:
    1971   1 - 8 (to Greenslades of Exeter)   [1 is preserved]

Vehicles delivered new to Devon General during 1964

9 - 12   9 - 12 RDV   AEC 'Reliance'   Marshall   B53F
Chassis numbers: 2U3RA4967-9, 2U4RA4970   Body numbers: B3249-52

Note: These were the first 36' long vehicles in the fleet, and although delivered with 53 seats, were   altered to 51 in 1968 so that the driver's cab could be enlarged.

12 from new had a high-ratio axle to increase its speed for use on the Exeter-Plymouth 129 service, but was later converted to standard following speeding fines being incurred by drivers! All were transferred to Western National on 1st January 1971. The seating was further reduced in 1974 down to 49 on conversion to one-man operation. All received NBC poppy red livery during the period 1974-76.

12 became green in 1976, reverting to poppy red in 1977/78 and saw service in Cornwall.

They were transferred to the Western National's Somerset and Dorset area in 1978.

Date of withdrawal:
    1980   9 - 12   [9 is preserved]

13 - 17   13 - 17 RDV   AEC 'Reliance'   Willowbrook   B41F
Chassis numbers: 2MU3RA4962-6. Body numbers: 648/75701 - 652/75705

Note: All transferred to Western National on 1st January 1971. The seating was reduced to 39 during the period 1969 to 1973. All received NBC poppy red livery, 17 becoming leaf green in 1976 following which it was sent to Cornwall.

13, 15 and 16 were also transferred to Cornwall in 1976 but all returned to South Devon in 1977.

Date of withdrawal:
    1977   13 - 17

501 - 508   501 - 508 RUO   AEC 'Regent' V   Willowbrook   H39/30F
Chassis numbers: 2D3RA1463-70   Body numbers: 640/75467-647/75474.

Note: These were the largest AEC 'Regent' Vs the Company had ever received, although more were to come soon. All passed to Western National on 1st January 1971 and received NBC poppy red livery during 1974 and 1975.

507 and 508 were converted to open-top in 1976 and repainted into white and poppy red, taking the names of ' Prince Regent' and 'Regency Princess' respectively.

Date of withdrawal:
    1978   507 and 508
    1980   501 - 506   [503 and 507 are awaiting preservation]

Vehicles delivered new to Devon General during 1965

18 - 23   CTT 18 - 23C   AEC 'Reliance'   Park Royal   B41F
Chassis numbers: 2MU3RA5511-6. Body numbers: 51691-6

Note: These were similar to the first batch of BET single-deckers (13 - 17) but had fewer embellishments. All passed to Western National on 1st January 1971. Between 1969 and 1971 all were down-seated to 39.

18 - 21 and 23 received NBC poppy red livery between 1975 and 1977.

22 became green in 1976 and was transferred to Cornwall.

18, 19, 21 and 23 also were sent to Cornwall in 1976 but returned to Torquay in 1977 together with 22

Date of withdrawal:
    1977   18 - 23   [23 is preserved]

509 - 514   CTT 509 - 514C AEC 'Regent' V   Park Royal   H40/29F
Chassis numbers: 2D3RA1648-53 Body numbers: 51593-8

Note: All transferred to Western National on 1st January 1971 and received NBC poppy red livery during 1976.

Date of withdrawal:
    1977   509
    1978   512   [513 is preserved]

515 - 520   CTT 515 - 520C AEC 'Regent' V   Willowbrook   H33/26F
Chassis numbers: 2MD3RA610-5 Body numbers: 936/76758-941/76763 (518,516,515,519,520)

Note: All transferred to Western National on 1st January 1971 and received NBC poppy red livery in 1976.

Date of withdrawal:
    1977   515 and 516
    1978   517 - 520   [518 is preserved]
    1980   510, 511, 513, 514

Vehicles delivered new to Devon General during 1966

521 - 525   EOD 521 - 525D   AEC 'Regent' V   Metro-Cammell   H34/25F
Chassis numbers: 2D3RA1802-6 Body numbers: HO51941/1-5

Note: They were the last AEC 'Regent' V double-deckers to be ordered by Devon General.
          All transferred to Western National on 1st January 1971 and received NBC poppy red livery 1972/3.

Date of withdrawal:
    1978   521, 522, 524 and 525
    1979   523   [524 is preserved]

526 - 531   EOD 526 - 531D Leyland 'Atlantean'   Willowbrook   H44/31F
Chassis numbers: L45024/5/40/1, L60050/1
Body numbers: 1154/78172 - 1159/78177 were on buses 526, 528 - 531, 527 (in that order)

Note: All transferred to Western National on 1st January 1971 and adapted for one-man operation. All received NBC
          poppy red livery between 1972 and 1973,
          526 and 527 became leaf green with Devon General fleet-name in 1981. All were transferred to the new Devon
          General Ltd., on 1st January 1983.

Date of withdrawal:
    1983   526, 528 and 531
    1983   527, 529 and 530

24 - 31   EOD 24 - 31D   AEC 'Reliance'   Harrington 'Grenadier'   C49F
Chassis numbers: 2U3RA6023-30 Body numbers: 3207-14

Note: All Grey Cars and delivered in full Grey Cars livery. They were the largest coaches to be introduced into the fleet
          at that time, soon to be followed by more however. During 1970,
          25, 27, 30 and 31 were treated to the all-white paint scheme with a central wide band of grey on which sat a fairly
          large GREY CARS in capital letters. All passed to Western National on 1st January 1971 and to Greenslades of
          Exeter on 2nd May 1971.

Vehicles delivered new to Devon General during 1967

32 - 39   HOD 32 - 39E   AEC 'Reliance'   Duple 'Commander'   C49F
Chassis numbers: 2U3RA6454-61.
Body numbers: 1752/79682 - 1759/79689 were on coaches 39, 38, 37, 36, 35, 34, 32 and 33

Note: This was the second batch of 49 seat coaches in the fleet, and broke away from livery tradition by having a cream roof. Between 1969 and 1970 they all received the all-white paint scheme with a central wide band of grey on which sat a fairly large GREY CARS in capital letters. All passed to Western National on 1st January 1971 and to Greenslades of Exeter on 2nd May 1971. They were bodied by Duple (Northern).

40 - 44   HOD 40 - 44E   AEC 'Reliance'   Marshall   B41F
Chassis numbers: 2MU3RA6462-6 Body numbers: B3847-51

Note: 42 was delivered late in 1966 and stored until the rest arrived for introduction into service in 1967. All transferred to Western National on 1st January 1971. During the period 1971 to 1973 the seating was reduced to 39. All received NBC poppy red livery in 1973 but in 1978 were put into leaf green and transferred to Western National's Somerset & Dorset area.

Date of withdrawal:
     1979   40 - 44

Vehicles delivered new to Devon General during 1968

45 - 47   LUO 45 - 47F   AEC 'Reliance'   Willowbrook   B49F
Chassis numbers: 6U3ZR6924-6   Body numbers: CF1558/80727, CF1559/80726, CF1560/80728

Note: Although delivered with 49 seats, they were all reduced to 41 before entering service due to one-man operation restrictions, but increased after further negotiations to 49 in July 1968. All received a reversed livery as branding for the Torquay to Exeter express service 46 and were transferred to Western National on 1st January 1971. From 1974 they were down-seated again, this time to 47 and repainted into NBC poppy red livery.
45 was painted NBC leaf green with Western National fleet-name in 1979, whilst 47 was similarly treated early in 1980 but with Devon General fleet-name.

Date of withdrawal:
     1980   45 - 47   [47 is preserved]

48 - 54   LUO 48 - 54F   AEC 'Reliance'   Willowbrook   B51F
Chassis numbers: 6U3ZR 6927-33
Body numbers: CF1591/80729, to CF1597/80735 were carried by buses 49, 48, 50 - 54 (in that order)

Note: All transferred to Western National on 1st January 1971.
Seating reduced to 49 during the period 1971 to 1974, and all received NBC poppy red livery between 1973 and 1975.
48 was repainted again into leaf green with Western National fleet-name in 1979 and transferred to the Somerset & Dorset area.
50 also went into green in 1979 but with Devon General fleet-name.

Date of withdrawal:
     1977   52 (following an accident)
     1980   48, 49, 50, 51 and 54

55 - 57   LUO 55 - 57F   AEC 'Reliance'   Marshall   B41F
Chassis numbers: 6MU3R6934-6 Body numbers: B4081-3

Note: All transferred to Western National on 1st January 1971 and seating reduced to 39 between 1972 and 1975. In 1975 too, all were treated to NBC poppy red livery but were then sent to Cornwall in 1978.
56 and 57 were repainted into leaf green livery with Western National fleet-name.

Date of withdrawal:
     1980   55 - 57

532 - 541   NDV 532G   Leyland 'Atlantean'   MCW   H43/32F
Chassis numbers: 703740/1/91/2/3846/72/3/4/3951/2 Body numbers: H052675/1 -10

Note: Transferred to Western National on 1st January 1971 and adapted for one-man operation between 1971 and 1973, at the same time receiving NBC poppy red livery. During 1980/81 they were all repainted leaf green albeit with Devon General fleet-name. All but 537 were then transferred to the new Devon General Ltd., on 1st January 1983. 533 carried all-over advertising from 1972 to 1974.
537 was sold, quite uncharacteristically, directly into preservation, in 1982.

Date of withdrawal:
    1982   537 (direct into preservation)
    1983   532 - 534, 536, 539 - 541
    1984   535 and 538   [537 is preserved]

Vehicles ordered by Devon General for delivery in 1969

542 - 545   OTT 542 - 545G Leyland 'Atlantean'   Willowbrook   H44/31F
Chassis numbers: 804467/8/4232/1   Body numbers: CF1801/2/0, 1799 (in that order)

Note: These four buses were completed by Willowbrook in full Devon General livery, and immediately prior to collection, the order was cancelled and the buses diverted to Yorkshire Traction Ltd., in which fleet they became 747 - 750, being re-registered RHE 447 - 450G.

Vehicles delivered new to Devon General during 1969

58 - 73   OTA 58 - 73G   AEC 'Reliance'   Marshall   B41F
Chassis numbers: 6MU3R7052-67   Body numbers: B4263/54-6/60/2/53/64/65, B4261/57-9/68/6/7

Note: All transferred to Western National on 1st January 1971. Seating was reduced to 39 and all received NBC poppy red livery during the period 1972-76.
58 - 63 were transferred to Cornwall in 1978,
65 and 67 were transferred to Cornwall in 1979,
64 and 66 were transferred to Cornwall in 1980.
Of these, 59, 60 and 65 received NBC leaf green livery with Western National fleet-name.

Date of withdrawal:
    1980   58 - 73

Vehicle hired by Devon General from 4th September 1969

---   RDG 309G   Daimler 'Roadliner'   Plaxton 'Panorama'   C47F
Chassis number: 36303   Body number: 693360

Note: This coach was hired from Black & White Motorways Ltd., of Cheltenham and was used for conveying the Torquay United football team to their away matches for which it was fitted out with tables and bar etc. It was also repainted in the all-white paint scheme with a central wide band of grey on which sat a fairly large GREY CARS in capital letters. It was returned to Cheltenham on 18th May 1970.

Vehicles delivered new to Devon General during 1970

74 - 81   TUO 74 - 81J   AEC 'Reliance'   Willowbrook   B43F
Chassis numbers: 6MU3R7296-7303   Body numbers: CF2055-62

Note: All were transferred to Western National on 1st January 1971 which was actually before the buses went into service. The seating was reduced to 41 over a period of several years, and all received the NBC poppy red livery between 1974 and 1976.
77 was transferred to Cornwall in 1980.

Date of withdrawal:
    1980   74 - 81

82 - 87   TUO 82 - 87J   AEC 'Reliance'   Willowbrook   B51F
Chassis numbers: 6U3ZR 7310-5   Body numbers: CF 2041-6

Note: All were transferred to Western National on 1st January 1971 which was actually before the buses went into service. The seating was reduced to 49 during 1971 and 1972. All received NBC poppy red between 1973 and 1975.

82 and 83 were transferred to Somerset & Dorset area in 1980,
84 and 85 were transferred to North Devon in 1980, and
86 and 87 went to Cornwall the same year.

Date of withdrawal:
1980   82 - 87

499   RFJ 828R   AEC 'Reliance'   Plaxton   C49F
Chassis number: 6U3ZR7418   Body number: 708905

Note: This coach was part of a diverted order from Greenslades Tours Ltd., and arrived in modified Grey Cars livery. Seating could be easily altered to 33 for special work. Although it became the property of Western National from 1st January 1971, ironically it was transferred to Greenslades Tours Ltd., from 2nd May 1971, along with the total Grey Cars operation.

Vehicles transferred to the Devon General Omnibus & Touring Co. Ltd., on 1st April 1970 from the City of Exeter Transport Department
(Exeter City Transport fleet-numbers are shown in brackets)

---	(13-14)	HFJ 140 - 141	Leyland 'Titan' PD2/1	Leyland	H30/26R
245	(15)	HFJ 142	Leyland 'Titan' PD2/1	Leyland	H30/26R
---	(17-18)	HFJ 144 - 145	Leyland 'Titan' PD2/1	Leyland	H30/26R

Chassis numbers: 480631/4/2/0/5

Note: These were new in 1948. Where no fleet-number is shown in the first column this indicates that the buses did not run for Devon General.

Date of withdrawal:
1970   13, 14, 15 (245), 17 and 18 [15 and 17 preserved]

250	(50)	TFJ 808	Guy 'Arab' IV	Massey	H30/26R
251 - 254	(51-4)	UFJ 291 - 294	Guy 'Arab' IV	Massey	H30/26R
255 - 259	(55-9)	UFJ 295 - 299	Guy 'Arab' IV	Park Royal	H31/26R

Chassis numbers: FD 73287, 73679/80/6/7, 73574/80-83   Body numbers: 2250-4, 39413-7

Note: 251, 253, 256 and 259 were transferred to Western National on 1st January 1971.
None ever received traditional Devon General livery but   253 was repainted into NBC poppy red in 1978.
256 was repainted and maintained in City of Exeter livery until withdrawn.

Date of withdrawal:
1970   250, 252, 254, 255, 257 and 258
1971   251 and 259
1980   253 and 256   [250(50) and 256(56) preserved]

260 - 264 (60-4) VFJ 995 - 999   Leyland 'Titan'PD2/40   Weymann   H31/26R
Chassis numbers: 581113-7   Body numbers: M8049/6/8/50/47

Note: All transferred to Western National on 1st January 1971 and received NBC poppy red livery in 1974.

Date of withdrawal:
1976   261 - 264
1979   260   [260(60) earmarked for preservation]

265 - 269	(65-9)	XFJ 750 - 754	Guy 'Arab' IV	Weymann	H31/26R
270 - 274	(70-4)	970 - 974 AFJ	Guy 'Arab' IV	Massey	H31/26R

Chassis number: FD 74278-82/585/7-90   Body numbers: M8889/7/91/0/88, 2381/0/79/82/3

Note: All were transferred to Western National on 1st January 1971.
267 received traditional Devon General livery in 1971.

Date of withdrawal:
    1971   265 - 269
    1972   270 -274   [274(74) is preserved]

275 - 279 (75-9)	475 - 479 CFJ	Leyland PD2A/30	Massey	H31/26R
280 - 284 (80-4)	480 - 484 EFJ	Leyland PD2A/30	Massey	H31/26R
285 - 289 (85-9)	85 - 89 GFJ	Leyland PD2A/30	Massey	H31/26R
290 - 294 (90-4)	AFJ 90 - 94B	Leyland PD2A/30	Massey	H31/26R
295 - 299 (95-9)	DFJ 895 - 899C	Leyland PD2A/30	Massey	H37/28R

Chassis numbers: 610082-4/90/1, 620405/6/23-5, L00490/1/526-8, L20493/4/547-9, L41916-8, L42168/9
Body numbers: 2420/1/19/8/22, 2468/9/6/70/1, 2525/7/8/4/6, 2569/8/6/5/7, 2630/29/8/31/2

Note: 275 - 299 were tin-front Leylands with concealed radiator. All were transferred to Western National on 1st January 1971.
        276, 278, 280 - 286 received traditional Devon General livery in 1971/2.
        276, 278 - 299 were repainted between 1974 and 1976 into NBC poppy red livery.

Date of withdrawal:
    1973   275 and 277
    1978   276, 278, 295 - 299
    1979   279 - 284
    1980   285 - 294   [286(86) is preserved, 284(84) is earmarked for preservation]

201 - 205 (1-5) GFJ 601 - 605D Leyland 'Leopard'   Massey   B41D
Chassis numbers: L62213/532/3/631/44   Body numbers: 2675/6/9/8/7

Note: All transferred to Western National on 1st January 1971, and all received NBC poppy red livery in 1973.

Date of withdrawal:
    1977   201 - 205

206 - 210 (6-10) MFJ 386 - 390G Leyland 'Panther'   Marshall   B47D
Chassis numbers: 801544/5/649/50/746   Body numbers: B4146/7/5/9/8

Note: All transferred to Western National on 1st January 1971, and all were repainted in traditional Devon General livery in 1972 and NBC poppy red in 1974/5.

Date of withdrawal:
    1980   206 - 210

Vehicles ordered by City of Exeter Transport Department but delivered new to Devon General during 1970

211 - 217   TDV 211 - 217J Leyland 'Panther'   Marshall   B47D
Chassis numbers: 7001303/4/465/6/569/70/94. Body numbers: B4533/2/5/4/8/6/7

Note: All were delivered and entered service in green and cream livery together with EXETER fleet-name and city crest. They were transferred to Western National on 1st January 1971. 214 and 216 received traditional Devon General livery on their first repaint in 1972, but all were treated to NBC poppy red livery between 1972 and 1975.

Date of withdrawal:
    1980   211 - 217   [217 is preserved but as mobile exhibition vehicle]

Vehicles ordered by City of Exeter Transport Department but delivered new to Western National in 1971

218 - 224   VOD 218 - 224K Leyland 'Panther'   Marshall   B47D
Chassis numbers: 7103049-51/3213-6 Body numbers: B4822/0/1/3/6/4/5

Note: The order had been amended in time for the livery to be changed to traditional Devon General and indeed they were delivered thus. All of course received NBC poppy red on their first repaint between 1975 and 1976.

Date of withdrawal:
      1980   218 - 224

Vehicles ordered by Devon General but delivered to Western National during 1971

450 - 454   UUO 450 454J   Bristol RELH6L   Plaxton 'Panorama Elite'   C47F
Chassis numbers: RELH-4-328 to 332   Body numbers: 713879-83

Note: These coaches were on the list of assets that passed to Western National on 1st January 1971. At that time however, they were still in build and were not delivered until after the Grey Cars operations had been transferred to Greenslades Tours Ltd., on 2nd May 1971. They were diverted to Greenslades though delivered in a modified version of the Grey Cars livery.

542 - 550   VOD 542 - 550K Bristol VRT/SL6G   ECW   H39/31F
Chassis numbers: 2-202 to 2-210   Body numbers: 18907-15

Note: These 9 double-deckers were delivered in traditional Devon General livery although in a modified style as there was no ivory band below the upper deck windows. (See outside back cover)
542 - 547 received NBC poppy red livery during 1974/5
548 became an overall advert in 1975, whereas
542, 549 and 550 were treated to NBC leaf green with Western National fleet-name and
544 - 547 were similarly repainted but carried Devon General fleet-name.
With the break-up of Western National on 1st January 1983, 548 and 550 became the property of the new Western National Ltd.,
543 and 549 went to Southern National Ltd.,
544 - 547 went to Devon General Ltd., and were painted in a new maroon and cream livery
542 went to North Devon Ltd.
544 latterly reverted to NBC poppy red livery.   [550 is preserved]

Vehicles ordered by Devon General but delivered to Western National 1972

88 - 93   VOD 88 - 93K   Bristol LH6L   Marshall   B33F
Chassis numbers: LHS120-125   Body numbers: 30851-6

Note: These were the very last buses to be delivered in traditional Devon General livery.
88 - 91 and 93 received NBC poppy red livery in 1975/6
92 was repainted green with Western National fleet-name and transferred to Cornwall in 1977 following a bad accident when it was severely damaged.
88 - 90 received NBC leaf green with Devon General fleet-name in 1981/2.
With the break-up of Western National on 1st January 1983,
88 - 90 became the property of Devon General Ltd., and
91 - 93 of Southern National Ltd.
88 and 89 reverted to NBC poppy red livery in 1983.

Date of withdrawal:
      1984   88 - 90   [88 is stored pending preservation]

Court Garages (Torquay) Ltd.

The share capital of this touring Company was acquired by the Devon General Omnibus & Touring Co. Ltd., on 1st October 1966. The Court Coaches fleet at that time comprised the following five petrol-engine vehicles, all of which were taken out of service that day, and sold early in the new year:

1.4.61	690 GUO	Bedford SB3	87319	Duple	C41F
1.4.63	544 NUO	Bedford SB3	91684	Duple	C41F
1.4.64	610 STT	Bedford SB3	94136	Duple	C41F
1.4.65	CUO 149C	Bedford SB3	96944	Duple	C41F
1.3.66	FTT 432D	Bedford SB3	6817637	Duple	C41F

Two Devon General 'Grey Cars' (893/894) were repainted into Court Coaches cream and orange livery, and transferred to the ownership of Court Garages (Torquay) Ltd., which remained as a separate Company with Devon General nominated directors, as from 1st October 1966.

1.5.59	893 ADV	AEC 'Reliance'	Willowbrook	C41F
1.5.59	894 ADV	AEC 'Reliance'	Willowbrook	C41F

Three new Bedford diesel-engine coaches were purchased and added to the fleet in 1967, and two more replaced the AEC 'Reliances' which were withdrawn at the end of the 1968 season. The new fleet then comprised the following:

1.5.67	JTA 763E	Bedford SB5	7802536	Duple	C41F
1.5.67	JTA 764E	Bedford SB5	7802566	Duple	C41F
1.5.67	JTA 765E	Bedford SB5	7803235	Duple	C41F
2.4.69	CXF 256G	Bedford SB5	466343	Duple	C41F
2.4.69	CXF 257G	Bedford SB5	466109	Duple	C41F

The Company was wound-up in February 1971, and the five coaches were transferred to the ownership of Western National (which had absorbed Devon General on 1st January) and all were repainted into the all-white scheme with a central wide band of grey on which sat a fairly large GREY CARS in capital letters. They were given fleet numbers 493 - 497 respectively. In May 1971 they were transferred to Greenslades Tours Ltd., along with the rest of Grey Cars and operations.

Vehicles loaned to the Devon General Omnibus & Touring Co. Ltd., for demonstration

During Year	Loaned By:	Registration Number:	Make:	Chassis Number:	Body Builder:	Type:
1929	AEC Ltd	MT 1257	AEC '426'	426106	Unknown	Unknown
1930	Daimler Co.	DV 5055	Daimler	7340	Unknown	Unknown
1947	Leyland Mtrs	CVA 430	Leyland PD2	EX1	Alexander	H30/26R
1948	Leyland Mtrs	EOC 242	Ley. Olympic	3	MCW	B40F
1950	C.O.M.S.	OFC 403	'Regent' III	12A438	Weymann	H30/26R
1950	Leyland Mtrs	MTA 747	Leyland PD2	502439	Leyland	H30/26R
1953	Leyland Mtrs	OTC 738	Ley. Tiger Cub	515176	Saro	B44F
1954	ACV Sales	7194 H	'Regent' III	U163633	Park Royal	H32/28R
1954	ACV Sales	50 AMC	'Reliance'	U163452	Park Royal	B44F
1954	Guy Motors	LJW 336	Guy LUF	71567	Saro	B44F
1954	Beadle	RKR 120	Commer TS3	JCB317	Beadle	C35C
1955	ACV Sales	88 CMV	'Regent' V	MD3RV001	Park Royal	H33/28R
1955	Leyland Mtrs	STF 90	PDR1	530001	Saro	H37/24R
1957	Leyland Mtrs	NSG 298	Albion Nimbus	82000C	Alexander	B31F
1957	ACV Sales	60 MMD	Bridgemaster	MD3RA003	Crossley	H41/31R
1958	Leyland Mtrs	330 CTD	Albion Nimbus	82004E	Alexander	B31F
1960	ACV Sales	WJU 407	'Reliance'	2MU3RA3076	Willowbrook	C41F
1963	Daimler Co.	4559 VC	'Fleetline'	60065	N. Counties	H43/33F
1963	Dodge	2498 PK	Dodge	5306/SPEC/643	Weymann	B42F
1964	Guy Motors	888 DUK	Guy 'Arab' IV	FD75320	Strachan	H41/31F
1964	Leyland Mtrs	SGD 669	'Atlantean'	623350	Alexander	H44/34F
1965	Leyland Mtrs	KTD 551C	'Atlantean'	L23296	Park Royal	H44/31F
1966	Ford Motor	SVW 275D	Ford	Unknown	Yeates	B41F
1969	WNOC	OTA 291G	Bristol VRT	VRT/SL123	ECW	H39/31F

Note: All these ran in public service for evaluation, in most cases for no more than a few days. There were other vehicles borrowed for demonstration purposes, particularly in the pre-war years and which have gone un-recorded.

Vans, lorries and service vehicles of the Devon General Omnibus & Touring Co. Ltd.

Year Service	Fleet No:	Registration Number:	Main Type:	Duties:	Withdrawn:	Note:
1919	--	T 7518	Wolsley 25hp lorry	Parcels/Goods	1921	(A)
1920	8	T 8232	AEC 'YC' lorry-bus	Parcels/Goods/bus	1922	(A)
1920	9	T 8234	AEC 'YC' lorry-bus	Parcels/Goods/bus	1922	(AB)
1920	10	T 9234	Federal lorry/chara	Parcels/Goods/chara	1922	

1921	---	FJ 1779	Ford Van	Parcels	1929	(ZR)
1927	---	TA 1870	Fiat Van	Parcels	1929	(CR)
1927	---	TA 6434	Lancia Z1 Van	Parcels	1935	(C)
1927	---	----------	Morris Van	Parcels	1936	
1928	---	TA 3098	Leyland G7lorry	Parcels/Goods	c1931	(C)
1929	---	FJ 1782	Daimler Y lorry	Rubbish collection	c1931	(C)
1929	---	DV 1615	Morris Van	Engineering	1936	
1930	---	DV 5836	Morris 30cwt	B. Salterton Goods	1938	
1934	---	TA 1803	AEC 'B' Tower	Recovery/Tree cutter	1938	(D)
1935	V5	AMU 544	Morris 30cwt	Parcels	1940	
1935	V6	AUO 445	Morris 5cwt	Parcels/Publicity	1951	
1936	V7	AOD 211	Morris 30cw	Engineering (Torquay)	1946	
1936	V8	AOD 212	Morris 30cwt	Engineering (Exeter)	1942	
1939	V9					(N)
1940	V10	EOD 978	Morris 10cwt van	Various	1953	
1941	V11	FTA 503	Austin 5cwt van	Parcels/Publicity	1953	(E)
1946	V12	GUO 772	Morris 30cwt van	Engineering/Stores	1958	
1948	M103	AUO 512	Leyland 'Cub' KP2	Engineering/Stores	1951	(CF)
1950	V14	MTT 393	Morris 10cwt van	Parcels (Torquay)	1959	
1951	V15	MUO 296	Morris 15cwt van	Parcels (Exeter)	1959	
1951	V16	NTA 115	Morris 15/20cwt van	Engineering (Torquay)	1958	
1953	V17	OTT 621	Morris 10cwt van	Publicity (Torquay)	1960	
1953	V18	NUO 692	Morris 10cwt van	Engineering (Exeter)	1960	
1958	V19	XOD 376	Morris 30cwt lorry	Engineering (Torquay)	1967	
1958	V20	XOD 377	Morris 20cwt van	Engineering (Torquay)	1966	
1959	V21	711 BOD	Morris 20cwt van	Parcels (Torquay)	1966	
1959	V22	712 BOD	Morris 20cwt van	Parcels (Exeter)	1966	
1960	V23	709 DOD	Morris 20cwt van	Engineering (Exeter)	1967	
1960	V24	710 DOD	Morris 20cwt van	Publicity (Torquay)	1968	
1966	V25	FOD 948D	Morris 20cwt van	Engineering (Torquay)		(L)
1966	V26	GTA 641D	Morris 20cwt van	Parcels (Exeter)		(L)
1966	V27	GTA 642D	Morris 20cwt van	Parcels (Torquay)	1973	(L)
1967	V28	JDV 833E	Morris 30cwt lorry	Engineering (Torquay)	1977	(L)
1967	V29	KTA 518E	Morris 20cwt van	Engineering (Exeter)	1973	(L)
1968	V30	MUO 656F	Morris 20cwt van	Publicity (Torquay)	1978	(L)
1969	V31	ODV 294G	Austin Mini-van			(L)
1970	----	ADV 969B	Austin A60 van		1970	(SL)
1970	----	GFJ 735D	Hillman van		1970	(TL)
1947	RV1	Trade Plate	AEC 'Matador'	Recovery (Torquay)	1982	(GL)
1956	RV2	Trade Plate	AEC 'Regal'	Recovery (Exeter)	1970	(H)
1970	----	Trade Plate	AEC 'Matador'	Recovery (Exeter)	1981	(IL)
1953	DR215	OD 7502	AEC 'Regent'	Tree Lopper	1956	(J)
1957	DR204	OD 7491	AEC 'Regent'	Tree Lopper	1957	(J)
1957	DG322	GTT 422	Guy 'Arab'	Tree Lopper	1959	(J)
1963	DR720	DDV 423	AEC Rebuild	Tree Lopper	1963	(J)
1964	DR667	NTT 667	AEC 'Regent' III	Tree Lopper	1970	(J)
1970	-----	HFJ 133	Leyland PD2/1	Tree Lopper	1970	(MJ)
1946	-----	HTT 508	Lacre depot cleaning vehicle at Torquay		Unknown	(K)

Note:

(A)	Ex-War Department chassis (T 8232/4) via London General	
(B)	Bus body from c1922. Lorry body, probably to T 7750, sold in 1922.	
(C)	Conversion from a bus	
(D)	Ex-Torquay Tramways Co. Ltd., (tower wagon)	
(E)	Ran on town gas carried in a gasbag on the roof, from 3/43 to 2/44	
(F)	Destined to be V13, but always carried ex-bus number M103	
(G)	Ex-RAF Fitted with crane, storage lockers & bench by DG. Re-registered PFJ 899M by WN in 1974.	
(H)	Chassis constructed from remains of bus XR424	
(I)	Numbered RV7 and re-registered PFJ 849M by WN in 1974	

(J)	Ex-buses with top-deck removed. SR469 and 424 also saw temporary use as tree loppers in 1952, also open-top buses were used as required.
(K)	Registration was only carried for a short while as this vehicle never ran on public roads. At least two others were subsequently owned.
(L)	V25 - V31, RV1 and RV7 passed into the ownership of WN on 1st January 1971.
(M)	Ex-City of Exeter Transport Department bus No: 6
(N)	V9 allocated to conversion of bus UO 9779 which did not in the event, take place.
(R)	One became the refuelling tender at Torquay in 1927.
(S)	Ex-Western National (WN)
(T)	Ex-Greenslades Tours Ltd.
(Z)	Originally described as a 'Humber' van

(J.G. Slater)

Since the formation of the Devon General Society in 1982, over 80 issues of the in-house magazine DiGeSt have been published, along with almost a hundred editions of the bi monthly Newsletter. Many members have collected and retained a full set of each, and indeed many are still available. New members are always welcomed, and further details and an application form can be obtained from the Membership Secretary on www.devongeneral.org.uk

Appendix 1. Depot capacity and maximum allocation

Depot	Capacity	Allocation Pre-War	Allocation 1.6.50
Torquay, Newton Road	85	98	103
Torquay, Torwood Street	110	30	31
Kingsteignton	16	23	39
Brixham	2	6	2
Teignmouth	4	5	4
Moretonhampstead	15	7	5
Exeter, Blackboy Road	32	36	64
Sidmouth	10	15	17
Exmouth	11	14	17
Tiverton	5	5	10
Crediton	2	2	3
Ottery St. Mary[1]	2		
Axminster	1	1	1
Uffculme	1		1
Cullompton	3	2	2
Okehampton[2]	1	1	1
Crockernwell	1		
Witheridge[3]	5		
Totals:	**298**	**247**	**308**

Note:
1	No garage, vehicles parked in railway yard
2	Free accommodation by arrangement with Western National Omnibus Co.
3	No garage, vehicles parked in The Square.

Appendix 2. Company statistics

Year	Revenue £	Expenditure £	Profit £	Miles	Passengers	Vehicles
1922	72,308	66,134	6,174	N/A	N/A	61
1926	134,362	107,704	26,658	2,088,659	6,427,786	80
1930	238,524	170,120	68,404	4,448,775	12,382,219	144
1934	347,279	270,788	76,491	5,587,435	15,838,457	199
1937	368,002	281,749	86,253	7,365,848	26,491,023	211
1938	352,143	280,458	71,685	7,399,949	27,369,244	241
1939	361,341	283,122	78,219	6,794,126	28,820,113	241
1940	388,809	263,548	125,261	5,053,428	29,340,057	195
1941	533,103	286,249	246,854	5,975,918	37,977,131	191
1942	528,133	294,313	233,820	5,503,500	35,277,560	189
1943	553,958	293,115	260,843	5,204,231	35,673,052	224
1944	604,440	317,296	287,144	5,327,739	39,192,599	228
1945	641,793	356,812	284,981	5,698,928	42,212,433	234
1946	722,398	442,782	279,616	7,394,276	46,362,596	259
1947	767,449	493,298	274,151	8,338,595	49,090,624	249
1948	884,040	633,481	250,559	9,703,435	56,527,949	321
1949	904,743	669,035	235,708	10,228,994	59,419,573	314
1950	880,515	723,32	157,194	10,215,433	63,650,357	331
1951	942,711	792,108	150,603	9,945,104	63,163,906	327
1952	1,036,021	860,865	175,156	9,952,818	63,694,551	302
1953	1,105,389	878,374	227,015	9,968,887	62,285,365	284
1954	1,165,246	910,418	254,828	10,497,095	53,121,895	313
1955	1,219,715	976,943	242,772	10,846,516	61,866,674	316
1956	1,247,434	1,024,693	222,741	10,699,644	59,350,605	313
1957	1,277,349	1,025,733	251,616	9,756,588	54,378,198	315
1958	1,333,667	1,024,414	309,253	9,971,641	53,696,616	305

Appendix 3. Paint specification

Devon General paint colour specification from the records of Mr. Frank Harrison, Body Shop Superintendent. All refer to the products of T & R Williamson* of Ripon, York.
In the cab of vehicles painted, the date would be hand painted in 1" high white letters together with a W (for Williamsons) or P (for Parsons) etc..

Red (bus)	SP 1304	Body colour
Ivory (bus)	SP 521 (later SP 6773 as 'Ripcerol')	Roof and bands
Dark Red (both)	SP 1183	Wings and flash
Grey (Coach)	SP 1184	Body colour
Cream (coach)	SP 1185	Coach relief
Blue (bus)	R 84	Internal
Brown (bus)	G 442	Cab, boot and floor area
Cream	SP 6487	Bus ceiling
Spectrum blue	O 012	?
Opal	7 -075	?
Gull Grey	9 094	?
Chalk	9 093	?
Opal	SP 69102	?
Green	SP 652	Exeter City vehicles
From 1969		
Western White	SP 6970	National white
Blue/Green	SP 6969	Greenslades
Grey	SP 6964	Grey Cars

*Note: Other Companys also provided paint from time to time, these being:
Parsons, Nulac, Vulcan, Glossex and Dulux. Not all colours are recorded however.

Appendix 4. Other publications about Devon General

Other publications devoted to Devon General, some of which may be out of print, are:

1.   **History of Devon General**, published by Ian Allan Ltd., 1966 (More of a detailed fleet list)
2.   **Devon General - A pictorial history** by Leslie Folkard and Philip Platt. Published by Roundoak Publishing in 1994.
3.   **Devon General in Preservation**. An A5 booklet with details and colour photographs of the buses and coaches in   preservation, published by the Devon General Society in 2003.
4.   **Glory Days of Devon General**, another pictorial book by Colin Morris and published by Ian Allan in 2006.

Forthcoming publications:
5.   **My time within**. A detailed account of the 6 years (1963-1969) spent with Devon General as a traffic apprentice, starting at Newton Road, Torquay. Due to be published by the Devon General Society in 2008.

Appendix 5. Staff Disposition (as at 1st June 1950 and 1951) (for comparison)

Traffic Department:	1950	1951
Inspectors	31	31
Drivers (Male)	334	303
Driver-Conductors (Male)	196	196
Conductors (Male)	448	403
Conductresses	61	45
Parcel Boys	2	1
Total:	1,072	979

Engineering:		
Chassis Maintenance	108	110
Body Maintenance	38	36
Lighting maintenance	12	13
Cleaners & Others	115	99
Total:	273	258

Administrative & Clerical:		
Men	60	63
Youths	3	3
Women	24	28
Girls	14	12
Total:	101	106

Others:	Total:	4	3

GRAND TOTAL:	**1450**	**1346**

DR714 was one of the many AEC 'light-sixes' rebuilt from single-deckers by Weymann and seen here in the temporary bus station at Paignton in the fifties. These buses were the mainstay of the 12 route until replaced by the Atlanteans in 1959. (DGS collection)

Appendix 6. Devon General in miniature

The following models have been produced since 1986 of Devon General buses and Grey Cars coaches. DG Society Member Royston Morgan was instrumental in encouraging many of them to be produced and actively advised Corgi and EFE on the make up, livery and other details necessary to produce an authentic model. Many models can still be found at toy swap-meets and via specialist dealers as well as often on ebay. Some are now scarce and the prices will reflect this. Be advised however that some models are not authentic, marked thus*.   (E indicates an EFE model)

Scale:	Type:	Livery:	Comments:	Year:
1:50	Bedford OB	Grey Cars	TCB600. Well represented / accurate.	1986
1:50	Bedford OB	Devon General	As above but in authentic bus livery	1990
1:50	AEC Regal	Grey Cars	TCR629. Looks good but not strictly authentic as 1 too many window bays.	1990
1:76E	AEC RT*	Maroon/Cream	Limited edition Roadrunner model. Has Paignton Zoo adverts. Rare. £100-£150.	1990
1:76E	AEC Reliance	Grey Cars	1 RDV. Harrington Cavalier 41 seater	1991
1:64	AEC Regent*	Devon General	A Routemaster casting with an AEC Regent III radiator. Numbered MTT 648 With local adverts.	1991
1:76E	Leyland Atlantean	Devon General	882 ATA. MCW bodied, local adverts, Shows 12 Brixham. Very accurate.	1994
1:76E	AEC Reliance	Devon General	9 RDV. 36' Marshall shows 9 SIDMOUTH Red colour a bit suspect.	1994
1:76E	Leyland Lowbridge	Devon General	DL640 type. Good model but suspect red colour. Shows TIVERTON	1994
1:76E	AEC Regent V	Devon General	943 HTT. Good model, good colour, local adverts. Shows Crossmead J service.	1995
1:50	Leyland Atlantean	Devon General	Produced as boxed set for 75th Anniversary	1995
1:50	Guy Arab Utility	Devon General	Good model	1995
1:50	Leyland Atlantean	DG Open top	932 GTA - Earl Howe. Accurate model	1995
1:76	AEC Regent V	Devon General	DR817. Accurate model. Exeter service	1995
1:76E	Bristol VR	Maroon/Cream	Based on short-lived O/T livery 'Invincible'	1996
1:76E	AEC Reliance	Devon General	SR950. Marshall. Local adverts, shows Service 16.	1997
1:76E	Bedford OB	Grey Cars	TCB604 showing Buckfast Abbey.	1998
1:76E	Bedford OB	Devon General	SB604 in bus livery, showing EXMOUTH	1998
1:76	Leyland Atlantean	Devon General	537. MCW Manchester type. Excellent Model with great detail and adverts.	1998
1:76	Guy Arab Utility	Devon General	DG323 shows TEIGNMOUTH 2	1999
1:76E	Guy Arab Utility(2)	Devon General	DG320.Special edition, only 500 produced	2000
1:76	Mercedes Benz	Maroon/Cream	New era model. Ring/ ride service shows Budleigh Salterton	2000
1:76E	Bristol VR	Devon General	1126. Traditional commemorative livery with grey wheels	2004
1:76	Bristol VR	Devon General	Above re-issued / different adverts	2007

ST. DAVIDS STATION

SOUTHSTREET S

DEVON GENERAL

PDV
731

VDV
812